the UNDERSIDE of American History: Other Readings

THIRD EDITION

VOLUME I: to 1877

Edited by
THOMAS R. FRAZIER
The Bernard M. Baruch College of The City University of New York

Under the General Editorship of
JOHN MORTON BLUM
Yale University

HARCOURT BRACE JOVANOVICH, INC.
New York San Diego Chicago San Francisco Atlanta

To the
Stewart A. Newman family

ISBN: 0-15-592847-3

Library of Congress Catalog Card Number: 77-91913

Printed in the United States of America

Preface

The past two decades have seen a rising tide of protest from segments of American society that have felt themselves excluded from the American dream. Neither the protest nor the exclusion is new, however. From the beginning of New World settlement, the benefits reaped from development have been unequally distributed. Historians of America, for the most part, have only recently begun to deal in any satisfactory manner with the causes and consequences of this inequity. Traditional history textbooks have tended to smooth out the past to give a picture of gradual but steady change, suggesting that Americans are a single people with a clear common goal that they are progressively achieving. The protest of the 1960s, however, shattered that consensus, as the untold history—the "underside" of American life—emerged to challenge and disturb the nation.

The Underside of American History, Third Edition, presents a selection of nontraditional readings in American history and is intended to supplement existing textbooks. The first two editions dealt with a variety of groups in American society, among them American Indians, blacks, women, East Asian immigrants, poor whites, Mexican-Americans, children, and industrial workers. This third edition, in which over half of the selections are new, continues the concerns of the first two editions, adding such topics as the elderly, working-class culture, ecological disaster, migrant farm workers, and frontier violence. This collection points out that many of the problems of America today have existed since the nation's beginning, and it suggests that until some creative resolutions of the inequities of American life are found, conflict, stress, and repression will continue to characterize much of American society.

The articles in this collection are arranged in roughly chronological order: Volume I begins with the colonial period and continues through Reconstruction, and Volume II covers mainly the period between Reconstruction and the present. Each volume contains a general introduction presenting the major themes to be taken up in the readings. In addition, each selection is introduced by a brief headnote that places the selection in historical context and explains its significance. Annotated bibliographies, with books available in paperback marked by an asterisk, close each of the collection's major sections. And for the instructor's convenience, a test booklet on the two volumes is also available.

I gratefully acknowledge the advice and assistance of the following historians: Carol Ruth Berkin of Baruch College of the City University of New York, Stanley Buder of Baruch College of the City University of New York, Mary Beth Norton of Cornell University, Paula Fass of the University of California at Berkeley, Laurence Veysey of the University of California at Santa Cruz, Daniel Walkowitz of Rutgers University, and Gary Nash of the University of California at Los Angeles.

THOMAS R. FRAZIER

Contents

Introduction

This introduction is intended to provide a broad overview of the often neglected aspects of American history treated in the following selections. In these pages, the traditional emphases have been abandoned. The stress in many cases is on the failings of the system; the focus here is not on the victors but on the victims. Other selections deal with material or episodes from the past that are left out of or given short shrift in the standard histories. The result, of course, is not a comprehensive or balanced view of our history, but an attempt to redress an existing imbalance. These notes and these readings, unless they are considered within a larger context, provide a distorted view of history. They are, however, an essential part of the whole story, and they must be taken into account in any attempt to reach a valid assessment of the American past.

It is natural that the study of the history of the United States should concentrate in the beginning on the English colonization of the North American continent. It was, after all, not the French or Spanish but the English who gained a secure foothold in this part of the New World by the middle of the seventeenth century, and it was their institutions that prevailed in shaping the new society.

When the English began settling the Eastern seaboard of what was to become the United States, they found it virtually free of European colonization from Maine through Georgia, with the exception of the Dutch settlements in New Netherland, around present-day New York. They were thus freed from the necessity of adapting to any established social or religious system. Moreover, chiefly because of the distance that separated the colonies from the mother country, they were very nearly free from English control. Left to their own devices, their first problem was that of surviving in the wilderness—a feat that they were able to accomplish with the help of the Indians who were already well established in the territory. Then, typically, came the problem of turning the vast natural resources of the New World to their profit. As the early colonists concentrated on building up their strength, they began to consider their Indian neighbors a threat to their progress.

The "Indian problem" provided the first major test of English policy in the New World, and the settlers, by all accounts, fell far short of what might be desired. Their way of dealing with these aliens in their new society was simply to displace them by any means at hand. The Indians struggled with all the skill at their disposal—often with French and Spanish support—to preserve their lives, their culture, and their land, but they were no match for the technologically more advanced Europeans, and their civilization ultimately came to an end under the onslaught of Western ideas and ambitions. The Indians who survived the initial confrontations with the colonists were forced to retreat southward and westward, and their sporadic attempts at organization and resistance proved futile.

During the early decades of the nineteenth century, the Indians again mounted a significant opposition to the dominant policy toward them. One group—the Five Civilized Tribes of the southeastern United States—tried to escape alien status by assimilating to the dominant way of life. Their offer was rejected, and they not only remained foreign but were forcibly moved outside the borders of the then existing states. Another group of Indians, in the old Northwest, sought to revitalize their culture through a revival of native religion which encouraged some measure of acculturation. The Indians were continually displaced until there was no more vacant land. They were then removed to reservations on undesirable property, most of it west of the Mississippi River.

A second major threat to the progress of the English in the New World was the chronic shortage of settlers to provide a labor base for economic development in the colonies. Here, two major sources of supply were found. First, poor whites from Europe—primarily from England in the seventeenth century—were brought to the New World as indentured servants. Under the popular "headright" system of land distribution, anyone who paid for a passage to the New World received fifty acres of land. Thus investors could send over settlers, and both would presumably profit from the transaction. The investors, whether or not they also emigrated to the New World, could acquire title to large estates and claim most of the profits from their cultivation. The servants worked for a specified number of years in return for their passage and, sometimes, a percentage of the profits. When their term of service expired, they became freemen with the right to participate in colonial government and to hold land without sharing profits or paying rents to absentee landlords.

During the first hundred and fifty years of settlement, the practice of indentured servitude was a major source of new population for the New World. Moreover, during most of the seventeenth century, indentured servants were the main labor force in the colonies. Some of these servants ultimately prospered in the New World. Others, upon achieving their independence, moved into the yeoman farmer class of the developing society and established small subsistence farms. Though they thus lived in freedom, they never really shared in the nation's wealth, and many of their descendants live in poverty to this day in the foothills of the Appalachian Mountains.

By the end of the seventeenth century, a second and vastly more profitable labor supply had opened up to the colonists—African slavery. The first Africans, involuntary immigrants and, with the Indians, perpetual aliens, were brought to North America in 1619, and Africans arrived in increasing numbers in the two centuries before the trade was officially banned in 1808. By 1790, when the first federal census was taken, black people made up 19.3 percent of the total population of the United States. Over fifty thousand Afro-Americans, scattered throughout the nation, were free, yet even they were not permitted to move into the mainstream of American life. A few blacks in Eastern cities led relatively comfortable lives and attained some measure of economic security, but most lived the lives of unskilled laborers and met racial discrimination on every hand. In the North, white craftsmen protested against the employment of blacks in the skilled trades, giving rise to a pattern of black exclusion from certain crafts that has continued to the present, with ruinous economic results for the black community.

Any consideration of the oppression suffered by blacks in this country, however, must focus first on plantation slavery in the South. From the beginning, the great majority of Afro-Americans were slaves in the South, employed in various occupations ranging from skilled craftsman to common field hand. By 1860 almost half of the four million slaves in North America were engaged in cotton production, an economic fact that seems to have had the deciding voice in the controversy over the continuation of slavery in the South. Relying almost exclusively on imported African labor, nineteenth-century white Southerners developed a thriving plantation economy. In the process, they developed a devastating system of chattel slavery—perhaps the most devastating in the modern world in terms of its long-range impact. Further, by identifying slavery with color, they set into motion a pattern of color discrimination that has had endless reverberations for North American society. Over the years, the African and his descendants, along with the Indians, have been the most oppressed segments of American society.

The life of a Southern slave was almost totally circumscribed by his master. He was deprived of education, was given little opportunity for self-improvement and advancement, and, in some cases, was even denied the security of family life and religion. The slaves fought the system by developing a subculture of their own, reaching back for what they could recover from their African past, borrowing some from the whites, and adding elements drawn from their own unique experience in the Americas. More visibly, they protested their condition by rebelling and conspiring to rebel, by running away, and by refusing in innumerable ways to cooperate with the system.

Nonetheless, the superior power and efficiency of the slave system effectively limited the experiences of most of the black bondsmen. When emancipation came at the conclusion of the Civil War, few of the freedmen were trained in the skills freedom would require, and since racial prejudice persisted among even their liberators, blacks were given little opportunity during Reconstruction to move into positions of economic independence. In 1877, when the Reconstruction period ended and federal troops were removed from the South, most of the freed blacks who remained had been forced back into positions of dependence on white society. The South's recovery from the war, like her earlier rise to economic stability, was achieved at the expense of the black man, who was relegated by law and custom to a position of agricultural serfdom.

A third initial challenge faced by the English in the New World was basically governmental. How was order to be established and upheld in the vast new territory opened up by colonization? The process was by no means as orderly as some accounts of colonial history suggest. The English system of representative government was adapted for use in some of the colonies, but others were ruled indirectly from England through governors or proprietors. When colonists throughout the country began to demand a high degree of self-government, conflict between governors and settlers became commonplace, and violence was often the issue. Indeed, violent struggles against the English authorities marked most attempts to establish order within the individual colonies. In addition, in almost every colony serious struggles took place between the settlers in the coastal areas and those of the interior, who vied over the distribution of power and benefits and, not least, the system of taxation.

The issue of colonial self-government ultimately led to the struggle for independence. The leaders in this fight were for the most part members of the political elites of the colonies and descendants of the English settlers. Independence won, it was they who met in Philadelphia in 1787 to shape the American nation.

Although the political genius of a number of the Founding Fathers cannot be questioned, there were grave deficiencies in the outline they drew up for the form of the new nation. Slavery, to take a prime example, was given permanent legal status in the Constitution of 1787, and in the same document Indians were recognized as a people apart from the mass of Americans. A less obvious but perhaps more serious flaw in the legacy of the Founding Fathers was a pattern of thinking not explicitly articulated. That is, many of their ideas seemed to proceed from the assumption that the people of the United States would share the same language, religion, customs, and political and economic institutions. The strain toward homogeneity that can be seen in the thought of the earliest American political theorists has been at the root of many of the nation's difficulties for the past two hundred years. For since the first surges of nationalism in the revolutionary era, American leaders have tended to regard any challenge to the political and economic status quo as an alien threat, as something foreign to and incompatible with the American way of life.

For the first century of the new nation's life, many of the so-called alien ideas came from real aliens—either from immigrants or from domestic aliens who were barred from citizenship, the Indians and the African slaves. Later, even challenges brought by the native-born were frequently considered to be alien-inspired and were suppressed in the name of patriotism. Political power remained largely in the hands of the descendants of the Protestant English settlers, and their traditions continued to set the patterns of political, economic, and cultural life in the United States. Although foreign emigration would continue and would even be promoted, the tacit assumption was that immigrants would conform to the dominant way of life. Those who could not or would not could expect to meet serious opposition.

The first political parties in this country appeared in the 1790s, when Madison and Jefferson sought to organize opposition to Alexander Hamilton, President Washington's strongest advisor. Members of the existing government took the name of Federalists, and their opponents called themselves Republicans. Party organization at state and local levels developed rapidly, and the party system in the United States was institutionalized within a few decades. Naturally, party strife was rampant from the beginning, and one of its first products was the passage of the flagrantly repressive Alien and Sedition Acts in 1798, an expression of early nativist sentiment as well as an attempt to stifle Republican opposition. These acts were hotly protested, and by the time they went out of effect in 1801, they had stirred up the first of many furious debates between nationalists and the advocates of states' rights.

In the nineteenth century, immigration proceeded apace. After the 1840s, a massive influx of Irish and German Catholics began to threaten Protestant hegemony on the Eastern seaboard. Most of the new immigrants were unskilled and penniless, and they came too rapidly to be dispersed and in too great numbers to be assimilated. Public programs to help them get settled in homes and jobs were at first nonexistent. Many immigrants found themselves placed in prisons, juvenile homes, mental hospitals, and the like–institutions growing in number and intended to care for the socially "undesirable." Public systems of education, whatever the good intentions that lay behind them, attempted to drill the newcomers in the dominant way of life, and many immigrant groups, clinging to their traditions, resisted by setting up private school systems. Suspicion of anything foreign, fear that by sheer numbers the immigrants would dilute the dominant Anglo-Saxon strains of the American population, and virulent anti-Catholicism contributed to the rise of a nativist movement that stretched across almost a century before it finally subsided. In many cities of the Northeast, there were violent clashes between Protestants and Irish Catholics, provoked primarily by the refusal of the Catholics to accept Protestant indoctrination.

Along with religious conflicts came bitter competition for jobs in the Northeast. By mid-century the Industrial Revolution had overtaken the United States, and the machinery of production had become so efficient that for the first time in American history there was a surplus of unskilled labor. This provided factory owners, members of a rising industrialist class, with the opportunity to stretch hours and reduce wages in the search for greater profits. Wage reductions, in turn, often meant that women and children had to go to work in the mills and mines in order to bring family incomes up to survival level. The struggle of the unskilled worker and the urban factory operative, immigrant or native-born, is one of the major motifs of nineteenth- and twentieth-century American life. Workers were able to improve their conditions only when they presented organized resistance to the dominant economic policies through national trade unions, which were slow to evolve.

Up to this point in history, the dominant sector of Americans had been not only white, Protestant, and English, but also male. Indeed, few women in the Western world have had any direct power or influence over the direction of society until quite recently. In America, as elsewhere, women were schooled only in the domestic arts and social graces, were deprived of the right to vote, were denied participation in politics and public life, and were expected to find fulfillment by living in the shadow of a successful male. In the second quarter of the nineteenth century, however, caught up by the general movement for reform, American women began to challenge male dominance. A women's rights movement called attention to the society's prejudices against "the weaker sex," and women, despite stinging denunciations, began to take leading roles in the religious movements and communitarian social experiments of the day. The more radical women joined with radical male reformers in advocating complete reorganization of society and complete restructuring of religious life. Since many theories of male dominance were based on an analogy with the structure of traditional religion, in which God, the father, or Jesus, the male child, was the ruler of the church, many women felt it was especially in their interest to attack the traditional religion. Some became prophets and seers, and some went so far as to found new religious cults.

Even during this first period of awakening to women's rights, most women remained submissive, apparently content in their traditional roles. But as the leisure of the middle-class woman increased and as servants and machines took on many of her customary household duties, masses of women found themselves hard pressed to reconcile the roles society foisted on them with their own feelings and needs. At the same time, a growing factory and commercial system provided a new measure of independence for married and unmarried women alike, and the ranks of working women swelled.

By the 1850s, the size of the American nation had increased dramatically. National interest in geographical expansion soared, and the doctrine of Manifest Destiny emerged to glorify American conquests of new territory. Though one might have expected that the lonely struggle to pacify the wilderness—and the Indians—would lead to strong emphasis on individuality, the westward advance carried with it powerful pressure toward conformity with the Eastern establishment. Perhaps the insecurity of life on the Great Plains and in the Far West lay behind the extravagant attempts to impose on the various Western peoples a homogeneity similar to that which now prevailed in the East. In any case, geographical expansion became synonymous with the expansion of Anglo-Saxon culture and control.

Predictably, those who suffered most from the settlement and development of the West were the aliens. With the conclusion of the Mexican War in 1847, many thousands of persons of Spanish and mixed Spanish-Indian descent suddenly found themselves foreigners living within American territory. "Vigilante" justice all too often held sway in the remote and virtually lawless West, and the Chinese, chicanos, Indians, and other ethnic minorities were the most frequent victims of the summary justice dealt out by self-appointed citizen groups.

The years between the Mexican War and the Civil War were years of deepening sectional crisis, for with every new state admitted to the union, arguments over slavery grew more pointed and more intense. The westward advance continued as a backdrop to civil war and recovery. By the end of the Reconstruction period, the United States stretched from coast to coast, and Protestant-English influence over the whole area was secured. The dominant Americans would continue to strive vainly to convert all whites to their points of view. More successfully, they would continue to exclude all nonwhites from full participation in American life.

1 Colonial America

Savage War

FRANCIS JENNINGS

When the Europeans landed on the North American continent at the turn of the sixteenth century, the area north of the Rio Grande was inhabited by an estimated ten to twelve million people. Although it was at first assumed that these people—mistakenly called Indians by Columbus—were members of one cultural group, it was soon clear that they were divided into a large number of separate nations, with many separate and distinctive cultural traditions.

In the sixteenth century most of the exploration and conquest in the New World was carried out by the Spanish and the Portuguese. These early adventurers were able to justify their activities by citing the authority of the Pope, who had divided the newly discovered (for Europeans) hemisphere between Spain and Portugal with the Line of Demarcation of 1493. The Pope had given the Catholic countries a mandate to take possession of the land and to convert the natives to Christianity. And, indeed, the conquistadors were almost always accompanied by missionaries who sought to convince the conquered populations that Catholic Christianity was the one true religion. During the period of conquest, much of the Indian population from New Mexico through South America added Christianity as an overlay to their traditional religions.

The situation was very different in the area colonized by the English, where major settlement was not begun until the seventeenth century. The English intended not merely to explore, conquer, and exploit the land but also to settle on it, and the presence of many Indian nations along the Eastern seaboard presented a formidable obstacle to their attempts to secure political control and exclusive ownership of the land. The English were able to make use of existing hostilities among various Indian groups by allying themselves with one group against another. The English did not avidly seek to convert the Indians to Protestant Christianity. To the contrary, on numerous occasions they used the "heathenism" of the Indians as an excuse for betraying them, arguing that since heathens could not be expected to uphold treaties or agreements, such agreements were invalid from the start.

After centuries of scholarship that had as its main purpose the justification of the colonists' seizing Indian lands, we are now in the midst of a new perspective, one that treats the Indian peoples not as inferior but as different. Francis Jennings, an ethnohistorian at Cedar Crest College, has published a work that has challenged many of the myths of the early period of contact between Amerindian and Euroamerican. In the selection from this work reprinted below, he shows how the colonists tried to attach the label "savage" to the Indian style of warfare, in partial justification of their attempts to dispossess the Indians. Jennings' reevaluation of this process, however, indicates that war is indeed hell, but that any attempt to evaluate war as "civilized" or "savage" usually depends on which side one is on.

Myth contrasts civilized war with savage war by accepting the former as a rational, honorable, and often progressive activity while attributing to the latter the qualities of irrationality, ferocity, and unredeemed retrogression. Savagery implies unchecked and perpetual violence. Because war is defined as organized violence between politically distinct communities, some writers have questioned whether savage conflicts really qualify for the dignity of the name of war. By whatever name, savage conflicts are conceived to be irrational because they supposedly lack point or objective beyond the satisfaction of sadistic appetites that civilization inhibits, and savages are ferocious through the force of these appetites.

These images are byproducts of the master myth of civilization locked in battle with savagery. Civilized war is the kind *we* fight against *them* (in this case, Indians), whereas savage war is the atrocious kind that they fight against us. The contrast has been sustained by means of biased definition on the one hand and tendentious description on the other. Savage war has been dismissed as mere "vengeance" or "feud," and writers have made it seem incomparably more horrible than civilized

"Savage War." From *The Invasion of America: Indians, Colonialism, and the Cant of Conquest* by Francis Jennings (Chapel Hill, N.C.: The University of North Carolina Press, 1975), pp. 146–70. Reprinted by permission of the publisher and the Institute of Early American History and Culture.

This [selection] is based on a paper read at the Fourth Conference on Algonquian Studies, Sept. 26, 1971, at Big Moose, N.Y.; in revised form it was read again at the Seventh Annual Bloomsburg State College History Conference, "War and Peace," May 2, 1974, Bloomsburg, Pa.

war by dwelling upon the gory details of personal combat, massacre, and torture on the Indian side while focusing attention diversely on the goals and strategy of wars on the European side.

Still another circumstance has contributed to the myth. Indian governments held jurisdiction over relatively small territories, and there were a great many of them. No supreme power existed to suppress conflicts; the tribes settled their differences themselves by negotiation or struggle. With so many possible combinations of interest groups, statistical odds dictated frequent intertribal conflicts. European governments, in comparison, extended over larger territories, and thus the possible number of international wars was statistically a good deal less. Furthermore, European society may have deferred some "organized" warfare, not by abolishing violence, but by internalizing much of it. Nearly all the violence of Indian society expressed itself intertribally in the form of war, but internal violence in the European states required a vast apparatus for its suppression, the means of which were also violent: Londoners could always find sadistic entertainment at Tyburn or the Tower, and the gaolers buried more prisoners than they discharged. There were also means of violent struggle between nation-states other than declared war; Sir Francis Drake sacked Spanish towns in time of peace, and pirates were ever present on all the seas. We tend to glorify these "sea dogs" instead of putting them on the same low level as Indian raiders, but the victims in both cases went through much the same experiences. If we focus entirely on internal order, the Indian village was a peaceful place compared to the European town. If we focus instead on relations between polities, the nation-states were under tighter controls than the tribes.[1] It seems to me that a proper comparison should include both internal and external relations and should examine the total level of violence in each society, its forms and motives, and the methods used to control and direct it. From this perspective aboriginal Indian society appears to have been far less violent than seventeenth-century European society. The wasting wars so prominent among Indians in historic times were a factor of adaptation to European civilization.

Indian tribes were internally more peaceful than European nations partly because of the kin-oriented sanctions pervading Indian villages, as distinct from the greater impersonality of European social relationships, and partly because Indian custom defined and punished fewer crimes than European law. If there is merit in the argument that psychological aggressions are the cause of social violence (and, like most psychological explanations, this one permits large flights of fancy), then the aggressive feelings of Indians were vented mostly upon persons outside the protection of kin obligation—that is to say, outside the clan and tribe. The same customary sanctions were notably tolerant of many sorts of behavior that Europeans classed as crime, especially regarding deviant sexual and religious conduct. There was no crime of fornication or "unnatural vice" among Indians, nor was there any heresy as that was defined

[1] [J. H.] Kennedy, *Jesuit and Savage in New France*, [Yale Historical Publications, Miscellany (L. New Haven, Conn., 1950)], 114–15, 130.

by European law.[2] All sex relations except rare cases of rape were personal matters outside the jurisdiction of sachem and council, and religious *belief* was totally personal. Although participation in rituals was expected, the punishment for withdrawal was limited to public obloquy; in extreme cases the offender might be bewitched or poisoned by the tribal powwow, but such acts were clandestine. Indians knew nothing of the whole class of offenses called by European lawyers "crimes without victims." When one considers the floggings, jailings, hangings, torture, and burnings inflicted by European states for the multitude of crimes that did not even exist in Indian society, one becomes painfully aware that an incalculably great proportion of European violence against persons was inflicted by the very agencies whose ostensible function was to reduce violence. In due course "civil society" would seek to tranquilize its communities by emulating savage toleration of human variety, but even today this has still only begun.

Of crimes common to both societies, murder requires special notice. It was conceived of differently by Indian and European and was therefore punished by different processes. In Europe murder was an offense against the state; among Indians it was an offense against the family of the victim. European law demanded the murderer's life as atonement to the state; Indian custom made his life forfeit to his victim's family. In Europe the state apprehended the murderer; among Indians it was the family's obligation to do so. European observers tagged the Indian custom "revenge" and blathered much about the savagery revealed by it. Yet, as compared to the state's relentlessness, the tribe provided an institution carefully and precisely designed to stanch the flow of blood. The obligation of blood for blood could be commuted into a payment of valuable goods by the murderer's own kinsfolk to the relatives of his victim.[3] This custom (which had been known centuries earlier in Anglo-Saxon England as *wergild*) was a widespread stabilizer of Indian societies, forestalling the development of obligatory revenge into exterminating feuds. Although the term *feud* has been used freely by the condemners of savage society, Marian W. Smith has been unable to find the phenomena properly denoted by it. "True feud," she remarks, "in its threat of con-

[2] Fornication and adultery comprised most of colonial New England's court load. Edmund Morgan, "The Puritans and Sex," *New England Quarterly*, XV (1942), 596.

[3] [Daniel] Gookin, "Historical Collections [of the Indians in New England . . ." (1674), in Massachusetts Historical Society, *Collections*, 1st Sermon, I (Boston, 1792)], 149; Elisabeth Tooker, *An Ethnography of the Huron Indians, 1615–1649*, Smithsonian Institution, Bureau of American Ethnology, Bulletin 190 (Washington, D.C., 1964), 28; "Penn to Free Society of Traders, 1683," [Albert Cook] Meyers, ed., *Narratives of Early Pennsylvania*, [*West New Jersey, and Delaware, 1630–1707, Original Narratives of Early American History* (New York, 1912)], 236; [George S.] Snyderman, *Behind the Tree of Peace:* [*A Sociological Analysis of Iroquois Warfare*, *Pennsylvania Archaeologist*, XVIII, Nos. 3–4 (1948)], 31; David H. Corkran, *The Creek Frontier, 1540–1783*, Civilization of the American Indian Series (Norman, Okla., 1967), 26.

tinued violence between particular groups, is surprisingly rare in the New World."[4]

Europeans understood the *wergild* custom and used it themselves in their dealings with Indians, but only unilaterally. Europeans would pay blood money to avert Indian revenge for the killing of an Indian, but Indians were not permitted to buy absolution for the killing of a European. In the latter case the Europeans demanded the person of the accused Indian for trial in a European court.[5] In the event of nonapprehension of the suspected culprit, mass retribution might be visited upon his village or tribe.[6] The savagery of revenge, therefore, was simply a semantic function of its identification with an Indian; European revenge was civilized justice.

When Indians stirred abroad they were safe in their own territory and in those of tribes with whom they were at peace. The hospitality trait so prominent in all the tribes guaranteed to the traveler not only security but also shelter, sustenance, and sometimes sexual entertainment, all free of charge. Europeans traveling through Indian territory received the same treatment.[7] But travelers in seventeenth-century Europe risked life and property on every highway and in many inns, and they paid for all they got.

The violence and horrors of civil war were rare among Indians, probably because they tolerated secession, while England underwent the Puritan Revolution and France the Catholic-Huguenot agonies, to say nothing of dynastic upheavals by the score. Nor were there class wars or riots in Indian society. Nor did aboriginal Indians experience drunken orgies with their attendant tumults until rum and brandy were poured into the villages from Europe. Thereafter, however, drunken rage became a recurring menace everywhere.

When all this has been said, there still remains the problem of conflict between the tribes. The traditional conception of savage war depicts

[4] Marian W. Smith, "American Indian Warfare," New York Academy of Sciences, *Transactions*, 2d Ser., XIII (June 1951), 352.

[5] [Bruce G.] Trigger, "Champlain Judged by His Indian Policy: [A Different View of Early Canadian History,"] *Anthropologica*, N.S., XIII (1971), 96–97; *A Relation of Maryland* (1635), in Clayton Colman Hall, ed., *Narratives of Early Maryland, 1633–1684*, Original Narratives of Early American History (New York, 1910), 88–90; minutes, Jan. 27, 1672, and Lovelace to Salisbury, Jan. 27, 1672, in Victor Hugo Paltsits, ed., *Minutes of the Executive Council of the Province of New York: Administration of Francis Lovelace, 1668–1673* (Albany, N.Y., 1910), I, 156–57, II, 756–57.

[6] John Smith, *Generall Historie of Virginia*, in [Edward] Arber and [A. G.] Bradley, eds., *Travels and Works* [*of Captain John Smith, President of Virginia, and Admiral of New England, 1580–1631*, II (Edinburgh, 1910)], 538–39.

[7] [Robert] Beverley, [*The History and Present State of Virginia* (1705), ed. Louis B. Wright (Chapel Hill, N.C., 1947)], 186–89; Corkran, *Creek Frontier*, 23–25; [Lewis Henry] Morgan, [*League of the Ho-De-No-Sau-Nee, Iroquois* (Rochester, N.Y., 1851)], 327–29; [Roger] Williams, [*A Key into the Language of America: Or, An Help to the Language of the Natives in that part of America, called*

it as so unrelenting and frightful as to be incapable of proper comparison with the purposeful and disciplined process of civilized war. No less an authority than A. L. Kroeber has attributed to the east coast Indians of North America a kind of "warfare that was insane, unending, continuously attritional, from our point of view." It was nightmarish—"so integrated into the whole fabric of Eastern culture, so dominantly emphasized within it, that escape from it was well-nigh impossible. Continuance in the system became self-preservatory. The group that tried to shift its values from war to peace was almost certainly doomed to early extinction."[8] This harsh indictment would carry more weight if its rhetoric were supported by either example or reference. The only example that comes to mind in support of Kroeber is the Lenape mission of the Moravian church in the mid-eighteenth century. The Indians of that mission took their Christianity seriously, became absolute pacifists, and were unresistingly massacred. But their experience does not quite illustrate Kroeber's point, for their killers were not other Indians but backcountry Euramerican thugs, also Christian after a fashion, who were rather less ready to attack the old-fashioned pagan sort of Indian that fought back.[9]

Kroeber's implication of heavy casualties in aboriginal warfare is contradicted by seventeenth-century reports of Europeans with attitudes as diverse as those of Roger Williams and Captain John Underhill. From his observation post among the warring Narragansett and Pequot Indians, Williams saw that their fighting was "farre lesse bloudy and devouring than the cruell Warres of Europe."[10] Underhill was contemptuous of what Williams approved. He sneered at the Indian warriors who called off a battle after inflicting only a few deaths, and he reported complacently the Narragansetts' protest against his English-style war that "slays too many men."[11]

Imagined dogmas about warriors' lethal accomplishments have led sober scholars into impossible contradictions. For instance, Harold E. Driver has remarked, on the one hand, that "the greed, cupidity, deceit, and utter disregard of Indian life on the part of most of the European conquerors surpassed anything of the kind that the Indian cultures had been able to produce on their own in their thousands of years of virtual independence from the Old World." But Driver has also written, in

---

New-England . . . (1643), ed. James Hammond Trumbull, in Narragansett Club, *Publications*, I (Providence, R.I., 1866)], chap. 11; [John] Heckewelder, [*An Account of the History, Manners, and Customs of the Indian Nations, Who Once Inhabited Pennsylvania and the Neighbouring States* (1818), ed. William C. Reichel, Historical Society of Pennsylvania, *Memoirs*, XII (Philadelphia, 1871)], 148–49.

[8] [A. L.] Kroeber, [*Cultural and Natural Areas of Native North America*, University of California Publications in American Archaeology and Ethnology, XXXVIII (Berkeley and Los Angeles, 1939)], 148.

[9] Edmund De Schweinitz, *The Life and Times of David Zeisberger* (Philadelphia, 1870), chap. 35.

[10] Williams, *Key*, ed. Trumbull, Narragansett Club, *Pubs.*, I, 204.

[11] John Underhill, *Newes from America; or, A New and Experimentall Discoverie of New England* . . . (London, 1638), 26, 42–43.

conformity to savagery mythology, that "no young man ever thought of getting married or of being accepted as an adult citizen until he had slain an enemy and brought back a scalp to prove it."[12] The mathematical implications of the latter statement are wondrous. To demonstrate what it would mean in practice, let us imagine a situation in which two villages are perpetually raiding each other as they would be obliged to do in order to qualify their males for manhood and matrimony. Assuming that the age of eighteen is the threshold of manhood, we find that all of the eighteen-year-old men of one village achieve the right to marry by killing off an equal number of males in the other village. The total population of both villages would thus be reduced annually by the total number of eighteen-year-old men (at least this is so if the eighteen-year-olds from the two villages avoided killing each other). This is the minimum implication of one coup per warrior. If some braves showed more than minimum enthusiasm and skill, the whole process would be speeded up accordingly. Such a process would lead inexorably, year by year, not just to a low level of population, but to total extinction. The thing is impossible, of course, and so is the dogma on which it is predicated. Clearly there were young men in Indian society who got married before they ever killed anyone, and the mathematics imply that a lot of old Indian men also died without having killed. What really made an Indian youth a citizen of his community was an initiation ritual, and the process has been observed and reported thousands of times. William Penn reported that young Delawares were permitted to marry "after having given some Proofs of their Manhood by a good return of Skins" and that almost all of them were wed before they reached nineteen years of age.[13] Among the Delawares, therefore, a man could marry when he could demonstrate the ability to support a family. How many Euramerican parents have drilled that notion into their offspring? That the young Indian could gain prestige and status by killing and scalping is undeniable, and that many youngsters itched for such fame is as plain as the enlistment of European mercenaries for pay and plunder. But universal generalizations should be grounded in some minimum quantity of evidence and common sense.

Suppose it be argued that the disastrous demographic implications just presented are fallacious because warriors might diffuse the population loss by taking scalps from women and children. Deductively such an objection might have merit if not for the inductive evidence available. Contact-era Europeans agreed that, with few exceptions that occurred in the confusion of battle, Indians killed only men.[14] The cultural im-

[12] Harold E. Driver, *Indians of North America* (Chicago, 1961), 370, 384.

[13] "Penn to Free Society of Traders, 1683," Myers, ed., *Narratives of Early Pennsylvania,* 231.

[14] [Gabriel] Sagard, [*The Long Journey to the Country of the Hurons (1632)*, ed. George M. Wrong, trans. H. H. Langton, Champlain Society Publications, XXV (Toronto, 1939)], 140; [Adriaen] Van der Donck, *A Description of the New Netherlands* (2d ed., 1656), trans. Jeremiah Johnson, in New-York Historical Society, *Collections,* 2d Ser., I (New York, 1841)], 211; John Smith, *Map of Vir-*

perative may have been a survival trait rather than pure sentiment, because one reason for sparing these noncombatants was to assimilate them into the victorious tribe, thus to enlarge and strengthen it.[15] Some tribes were observed to begin war for the specific purpose of augmenting their female population.[16] Whatever the motive, the merciful custom was universal in regard to women and children.

Treatment of captured men was more varied. Early southern accounts indicate that all male prisoners were put to death except the chiefs.[17] By the seventeenth century torture of men was practiced fairly extensively, although some doubt exists about how widespread this trait had been at an earlier time. An ameliorating custom decreed the sparing of a large proportion of male captives, however. Again, the custom may have arisen out of the dire pressures of population decline, in this case pinpointed on particular families. Women among the victors, who had lost a husband or kinsman, held unchallengeable individual right to "adopt" a prisoner in his place, and the man so chosen became immediately assimilated into the tribe as well as the family. (In our terminology he was naturalized as well as adopted.[18]) Perhaps the most famous example of the custom is Pocahontas's rescue of John Smith, although Smith rejected assimilation at the first opportunity to escape. Not every European captive followed Smith's example. It was a constant crying scandal that Europeans who were adopted by Indians frequently preferred to remain with their Indian "families" when offered an opportunity to return to their genetic kinsmen.[19]

The adoption custom grew in importance with the intensification of war during the macrocontact era. Of all the Indians, the Iroquois, who are generally agreed to have been the most militaristic and to have suf-

---

ginia, in [Philip] Barbour, ed., [*The Jamestown Voyages under the First Charter, 1606–1609,* Hakluyt Society Publications, 2d Ser., CXXXVI–CXXXVII, II (Cambridge, 1609)], 372; Heckewelder, *Account of the Indian Nations,* ed. Reichel, in Hist. Soc. Pa., *Memoirs,* XII, 337–39; David Pietersz. de Vries, *Short Historical and Journal notes Of several Voyages made in the four parts of the World, namely, Europe, Africa, Asia, and America* (1655), trans. Henry C. Murphy, in N.-Y. Hist. Soc., *Colls.,* 2d Ser., III (New York, 1857), 116.

15 Snyderman, *Behind the Tree of Peace,* in *Pa. Archaeol.,* XVIII (1948), 13–15.

16 John Smith, *Map of Virginia,* in Barbour, ed., *Jamestown Voyages,* II, 360.

17 *Ibid.,* II, 361; [Marc] Lescarbot, [*The History of New France* (1618), trans. W. L. Grant, Introduction by H. P. Biogar, Champlain Society Publications, I, (Toronto, 1907–1914)], 88.

18 Morgan, *League of the Iroquois,* 341–344; Snyderman, *Behind the Tree of Peace,* in *Pa. Archaeol.,* XVIII (1948), 18; Heckewelder, *Account of the Indian Nations,* ed. Reichel, in Hist. Soc. Pa., *Memoirs,* XII, 217–18; [Cadwallader] Colden, [*The History of the Five Indian Nations Dependent on the Province of New-York in America* (Ithaca, N.Y., 1958 [orig. publ. 1727–1747])], Pt. I, chap. 1, 8; [Woodbury] Lowery, [*The Spanish Settlements within the Present Limits of the United States, 1513–1561,* I (New York, 1959; orig. publ. New York, 1901–1905)], 37.

19 [Philip L.] Barbour, [*Pocahontas and Her World* (Boston, 1970)], 23–25. I thank James Axtell for providing an advance copy of his article "The White Indians of Colonial America," *WMQ,* 3d Ser., XXXII (1975), 55–88. This is the first objective treatment, to my knowledge, of the European prisoners who refused repatriation.

fered the most debilitating casualties, seem to have practiced adoption more than any other tribe. At one time adoptees constituted two-thirds of the Iroquois Oneidas.[20] The Senecas adopted whole villages of Hurons after the breakup of the Huron "nation" under Iroquois attack,[21] and various Iroquois tribes struggled for possession of Susquehannocks after the latter's dispersal under attack from Maryland and Virginia.[22]

Still another Indian custom served (aboriginally) to reduce the deadliness of war. Indians refrained from the total war that involved systematic destruction of food and property—until its use by Europeans roused the Indians to reprisal.[23] In this respect, as in so many others, the English continued a tradition of long standing from their devastations in Ireland.[24] Burning villages and crops to reduce Irish tribesmen to subjection under Elizabeth I led naturally enough to using the same tactics against the tribesmen of Virginia.[25] A "relation" of 1629 tells how the Virginia colonists compelled a hostile Indian chief to seek peace, "being forc't to seek it by our continuall incursions upon him and them, by yearly cutting downe, and spoiling their corne."[26] The same practice was used everywhere in North America when Indian guerrilla tactics prevented Europeans from gaining victory by decisive battle.[27] According to Indian logic, such destruction doomed noncombatants as well as warriors to die of famine during a winter without provisions.

These remarks are not intended to suggest that Indians of precontact days were gentle pacifists whom the Europeans seduced to evil warlike ways. On the contrary, all evidence points to a genuinely endemic state of sporadic intertribal violence. Had this base not been present, Europeans could not so readily have achieved hegemony by playing off one tribe against another. But the dispersion of violence tells nothing of its intensity. What is especially at issue here is the significance of the data in comparison with the phenomena of war in European society. As the

20 Letter of Jacques Bruyas, Jan. 21, 1668, [in Reuben Gold] Thwaites, ed., [*The Jesuit Relations and Allied Documents: Travels and Explorations of the Jesuit Missionaries in New France, 1610–1791,* LI (Cleveland, Ohio, 1896–1901)], 123.

21 Letter of Jacques Fremin, n.d. ("Relation of 1669–1670"), *ibid.*, LIV, 81–83.

22 [Francis] Jennings, ["Glory, Death, and Transfiguration: The Susquehannock Indians in the Seventeenth Century," American Philosophical Society, *Proceedings,* CXII (1968)], 40.

23 Minutes, Aug. 26, 1645, [David] Pulsifer, ed., *Acts of* [*the Commissioners of the United Colonies of New England,* in Nathaniel B. Shurtleff and David Pulsifer, eds., *Records of the Colony of New Plymouth in New England,* I (Boston, 1859)], 44.

24 For the practice of Richard II in the late 14th century, see [J. F.] Lydon, [*The Lordship of Ireland in the Middle Ages* (Toronto, 1972)], 234.

25 *Encyclopaedia Britannica,* 11th ed., s.v. "Ireland (History from the Anglo-Norman Invasion)."

26 Capt. William Perse, "Relation," Aug. 1629, C.O. 1/5, Pt. 1, fol. 69, [Public Record Office].

27 E.g., the French foray against the Mohawks in 1666. [E. B.] O'Callaghan, ed., [*The Documentary History of the State of New-York,* I (Albany, N.Y., 1849–1851)], 70.

history of feudal Europe well exemplifies, endemic war does not necessarily imply, although it may be associated with, population decline. The fact is unlovely, but growth in human societies is demonstrably compatible with bellicosity, up to a critical level of mortality. We have no difficulty in perceiving this rule at work in, say, ancient Greece; yet we deny that the rule also applied to Amerindians when we attribute to them a savage kind of war that supposedly was incomparably more continuous, more widespread, more integral to cultural values, and more senseless in the long view than the dedicated vocation of backward but civilized Sparta—or of Athens, for that matter. To show the falsity of these absolute antitheses is a primary objective here. Indians could be and often were as stupid and vicious as Europeans, which is to say that they belonged to the same human species. They were never so much more devoted than Europeans to killing each other that their uniquely violent natures or cultures doomed their societies to perpetual stagnation.

To discover the nature of aboriginal Indian war requires a skeptical and analytical approach not only to European sources but to Indian sources as well. Like old tales in other cultures, Indian "traditions" were of several sorts: some preserved the memory of historical events, and others were invented to amuse or edify. Wendell S. Hadlock has shown how legends diffused rapidly, being adapted to the local settings of different tribes so that "a single occurrence in history has been told in varying ways so as to appear like many incidents."[28] Sometimes one may doubt whether the "single occurrence" ever did happen anywhere.

One genre of such legends, dealing with the "grasshopper war," has been interpreted by chroniclers in its multiple manifestations as literal fact demonstrating the terrible carnage that Indians would wreak over such trivial causes as a children's quarrel about possession of a grasshopper. That grasshopper hopped over a lot of territory. He spilled the same mythical blood by gallons from the Micmacs of Newfoundland to the Shawnees, Lenape, and Tuscaroras of western Pennsylvania. The story seems to have been in the same class as Aesop's fables. Whatever may have been its remote origins, it diffused so widely because of its didactic utility rather than its historical reality. Hadlock associated it with a table of similar stories that "are not so much an explanation of a war incident as philosophical explanations of tribal fission."[29]

To Frank G. Speck it was fiction, and Speck's interpretation implies bittersweet irony as to how the Indian myth was absorbed and transformed in the European myth of savagery: "In the 'grasshopper war' legend we have an example of the type of Algonkian moral teaching with which the ethnologist has long been familiar. Need the moralist point out that its clarified motive is to portray the consequences of grown-ups taking over the disputes of children, the curse of partisanship in disputes of a trivial nature, the abomination of giving way to emo-

[28] Wendell S. Hadlock, "War among the Northeastern Woodland Indians," *Am. Anthro.*, N.S., XLIX (1947), 217–18.

[29] Wendell S. Hadlock, "The Concept of Tribal Separation as Rationalized in Indian Folklore," *Pa. Archaeol.*, XVI (1946), 84–88.

tional impulses? The myth is a great composition for the lesson it carries extolling self-restraint and the virtues of deliberation before taking action that may lead to disastrous outcome."[30]

By the transforming power of the savagery myth, a fable denouncing war's irrationality was converted into evidence of the real existence of widespread irrational bellicosity. The Indian could not even preach against war without convicting himself of obsessive love for it. By the same logic Quakers would be the most militaristic of Euramericans.

Historical sources strongly suggest that aboriginal war among the hunting Indians of the cold north differed markedly from the wars carried on by the agricultural tribes farther south. During most of the year the hunters lived dispersed in family bands that were occupied full-time in making a living. Opportunity to organize concerted tribal wars existed briefly during the summer months when the bands congregated at tribal centers and had some leisure. Wars could then be organized, but they were sporadic, individualistic affairs.[31] A Jesuit observer condemned both the Indians' motives and scale of operations with a succinct phrase—"their war is nothing but a manhunt"—and narrated how a war party of thirty men dwindled to fifteen who returned home satisfied after they had taken the scalps of three unoffending members of a friendly tribe.[32] In Europe such waylaying would have been called brigandage rather than war.

Farming Indians operated on a larger scale and under the direction of tribal purposes and policies. Their more complex culture provided a variety of motives. Sometimes they fought to gain territory, although apparently not in the fashion of European empire building; when Indians fought for territory as such, they wanted to displace its occupants rather than to subject them. Lands thus made available might be occupied by the victors, left empty for use as hunting grounds, or kept as a protective buffer against distant enemies.[33]

Sometimes, it seems, agricultural Indians fought to achieve dominance—to make the defeated tribe confess the victor's preeminence. The symbol of such acknowledgment was the payment of tribute. Because the

[30] Frank G. Speck, "The Grasshopper War in Pennsylvania: An Indian Myth That Became History," *Pa. Archaeol.*, XII (1942), 34. See also C. E. Schaeffer, "The Grasshopper or Children's War—A Circumboreal Legend?" *ibid.*, XII (1942), 60–61; John Witthoft, "The Grasshopper War in Lenape Land," *ibid.*, XVI (1946), 91–94.

[31] Hadlock, "War among Northeastern Indians," *Am. Anthro.*, N.S., XLIX (1947), 211–14.

[32] Andre Richard, "Relation of 1661–1662," Thwaites, ed., *Jesuit Relations,* XLVII, 221–39.

[33] Occupation: Pequot displacement of Niantics. [Frederick Webb] Hodge, ed., *Handbook of* [*American Indians North of Mexico*, Smithsonian Institution, Bureau of American Ethnology, Bulletin 30, 2 vols. (Washington, D.C., 1907–1910)], s.v. "Pequot." Hunting grounds: Five Nations displacement of tribes around Lake Erie. Five Nations deed, July 19, 1701, *N.Y. Col. Docs.*, IV, 908. Buffer lands: Hadlock, "War among Northeastern Indians," *Am. Anthro.*, N.S., XLIX, (1947), 217.

tributary role has been much confused, it needs a moment of special attention. First, tribute should be distinguished from plunder. When the Niantics raided Long Island's Montauks for wampum in 1638, they were after loot.[34] When the Iroquois Five Nations—the Mohawks among them—required wampum from the Lenape of the Delaware Valley in the eighteenth century, they wanted ceremonial recognition of a confederate relationship in which the Iroquois were superior.[35] Several contrasts mark the difference. Loot was seized by a raiding party; tribute was presented by a diplomatic mission. Loot's value increased precisely in accordance with quantity; tribute's value was primarily symbolic, secondarily quantitative. The taking of loot was a one-sided transaction; the presentation of tribute was reciprocated by a counter presentation of wampum to confirm the tributary agreement.

The last difference was especially important, because tribute symbolized subordinate alliance rather than subjection and thus entailed obligation on the part of the superior tribe as well as the tributary. In essence the alliance entitled the tributary to freedom from molestation by its patron and to protection by the patron against attack by a third party. In return the tributary was expected to give ceremonial deference on all occasions, to allow free passage through its territory by members of the patron tribe, and to permit or encourage the recruitment of its own young men to join the patron's war parties. This sort of mutual obligation can be identified in the historic period, but it does not appear that all tributary relationships were the same; there seem to have been grades and degrees of obligation,[36] and the word *tribute* was also applied to payments of wampum or other valuable goods in the nature of a toll. For instance, English officials agreed to pay tribute to the Illinois tribes in 1764 for the privilege of unobstructed passage through the tribes' territory, and the Indians knew perfectly well that the English were not submitting or subjecting themselves by the payment.[37]

It may be said quite positively that a tributary tribe did not neces-

[34] [Benjamin F.] Thompson, [*The History of Long Island,* 2d ed., I (New York, 1843)], 89–90.

[35] Minutes, May 19, 1712, [in Samuel Hazard, ed., *Minutes of the Provincial Council of Pennsylvania . . . ,* II (Harrisburg, Pa., 1838–1853)], 546; draft minutes of treaty, Sept. 15, 1718, Logan Papers, XI, 7, and Sassoonan's speech, Aug. 7, 1741, Records of the Provincial Council and Other Papers, boxed manuscripts, fol. 1740–1749, both in Hist. Soc. Pa., Philadelphia.

[36] Snyderman, *Behind the Tree of Peace,* in *Pa. Archaeol.,* XVIII (1948), 33; Anthony F. C. Wallace, *King of the Delawares: Teedyuscung, 1700–1763* (Philadelphia, 1949), 195–96, and his "Political Organization," *Southwest. Jour. of Anthro.,* XIII (1957), 308–09; Beverley, *History of Virginia,* ed. Wright, 174; [Regina] Flannery, [*An Analysis of Coastal Algonquian Culture,* Catholic University of America Anthropological Series, VII (Washington, D.C., 1939)], 117–18; [Francis] Jennings, ["The Constitutional Evolution of the Covenant Chain," American Philosophical Society, *Proceedings,* CXV (1971)], 90–94.

[37] Gen. Thomas Gage to Johnson, May 28, 1764, [James Sullivan, et. al., eds., *The Papers of Sir William Johnson,* IV (Albany, N.Y., 1921–1965)], 433–34; Johnson to Gage, June 9, 1764, *ibid.,* XI, 223.

sarily give up title to its lands when it presented tribute. After the defeat of the upper Hudson Mahicans by the Mohawks in 1628, the Mahicans offered tribute as a means of purchasing peace, but they also sold land to the Dutch without Mohawk objection, and after two years of tribute payment they "got drunk and lost the pouch [of wampum]." Mohawk sachem Joseph Brant, who told the story, commented that the Mohawks did not "take it hard" when payment ceased.[38] Four decades later, when the Executive Council of New York considered purchase of land from the "Wickerscreek" (Wecquaesgeek) tribe, the council had to consider whether the Wickerscreeks could deliver good title, "now they are beaten off" by the Mohawks. The Indians replied that the Mohawks would not "have any pretence to their Land, though being at Warre they would destroy their Persons, and take away their Beavers and Goods."[39]

The "sales" by dominant tribes like the Pequots and Iroquois of their rights in tributaries' territory were in the nature of quitclaims, without prejudice to the tributaries' retained rights of habitation and enjoyment. The Pequots quit their own claims to the Connecticut Valley and permitted Englishmen to settle there, but after the English evicted a tributary chief, the Pequots attacked in reprisal. When the Iroquois were bribed by Pennsylvanians in the eighteenth century to "quit" a claim they had never made to the Delaware Valley, the swindle ruptured their confederacy.[40]

The customary situation was summarized by General Thomas Gage in the course of his systematic correspondence on Indian affairs with Sir William Johnson. Gage's confidential letter also clarifies the English motives that often led to the muddying of the formal records. "It is asserted as a general Principle that the Six Nations having conquered such and such Nations, their Territorys belong to them, and the Six Nations being the Kings Subjects which by treaty they have acknowledged themselves to be, those Lands belong to the King. I believe it is for our Interest to lay down such principles especially when we were squabbling with the French about Territory, and they played us off in the same stile of their Indian Subjects, and the right of those Indians." Gage went on to define the Indian customs as he privately understood them. "I never heard that Indians made War for the sake of Territory like Europeans, but that Revenge, and an eager pursuit of Martial reputation were the Motives which prompted one Nation to make War upon another. If we are to search for truth and examine her to the Bottom, I dont imagine we shall find that any conquered Nation ever formaly ceded their Country to their Conquerors, or that the latter ever required

38 Douglas W. Boyce, ed., "A Glimpse of Iroquois Culture History through the Eyes of Joseph Brant and John Norton," Am. Phil. Soc., *Procs.*, CXVII (1973), 290; Bruce G. Trigger, "The Mohawk-Mahican War (1624–28): The Establishment of a Pattern," *Canadian Historical Review*, LII (1971), 281.

39 Minutes, Oct. 30, 1671, Paltsits, ed., *Minutes of Council of N.Y.*, I, 105.

40 [Francis] Jennings, ["The Delaware Interregnum," *Pennsylvania Magazine of History and Biography*, LXXXIX (1965)], 174–98; [Anthony F. C.] Wallace, [*The Death and Rebirth of the Seneca* (New York, 1970)], 154.

it. I never could learn more, than that Nations have yielded, and acknowledged themselves subjected to others, and some ever have wore Badges of Subjection."[41]

Gage's remark refers to the most frequently mentioned motive for Indian war–behavior that is almost invariably termed *revenge.* Like most effective propaganda language, the term has a referent in reality, and also like most propaganda, it distorts that referent in the mere naming of it. Our English word implies an act of retaliation intended to inflict suffering upon an enemy and performed in part for the emotional satisfaction that the avenger will achieve from contemplation of that suffering. (Who has not hated the villainous Iago?) Revenge connotes ferocity–personal, unrestrained by charity or mercy or any of the nobler impulses of humanity–in short, savagery. The actual phenomenon in Indian society to which this name has been given did not conform to these connotations. As it manifested itself intratribally, we have already noticed revenge as an obligatory retaliation for murder, together with the commutation custom by which the obligation might be discharged in lieu of blood for blood.[42] *Intertribal* retaliation for wrongs done or fancied (a real and omnipresent occurrence) was also bound up in motives and restraints imposed by custom and social purpose, including commutation by payment between tribes as well as between families. As Marian W. Smith has noted, such retaliations bear "a legalistic tinge. They serve as mechanisms for righting the balance of sanctions in the society, and the reprisal is seen as justified, in view of the fact that it reestablishes the validity of customs which had been violated."[43]

Smith wrote in the formal language of the twentieth-century scholar. A seventeenth-century Lenape Indian phrased the "justified reprisal" idea–which in Europe might readily have been classed as "just war"–in simpler language when he told a Pennsylvanian, "We are minded to live at Peace: If we intend at any time to make War upon you, we will let you know of it, and the Reasons why we make War with you; and if you make us satisfaction for the Injury done us, for which the War is intended, then we will not make War on you. And if you intend at any time to make War on us, we would have you let us know of it, and the Reasons for which you make War on us, and then if we do not make satisfaction for the Injury done unto you, then you may make War on us, otherwise you ought not to do it." To one looking back from the twentieth century this sounds quaintly moralistic. In the era of total

41 Gage to Johnson, Oct. 7, 1772, *Sir William Johnson Papers*, XII, 994–95.

42 See the description by missionary Francesco Bressani (1653) who remarked, "it is the public that gives satisfaction for the crimes of the individual, whether the culprit be known or not. In fine, the crime alone is punished, and not the criminal; and this, which elsewhere would appear an injustice, is among them a most efficacious means for preventing the spread of similar disorders." Thwaites, ed., *Jesuit Relations*, XXXVIII, 273–87, quote at p. 277.

43 M. W. Smith, "American Indian Warfare," N.Y. Acad. Sciences, *Trans.*, 2d Ser., XIII (1951), 352. See also the discussion of revenge in Snyderman, *Behind the Tree of Peace*, in *Pa. Archaeol.*, XVIII (1948); A. F. C. Wallace, *Death and Rebirth of the Seneca*, 44–48; Heckewelder, *Account of the Indian Nations*, ed.

"preventive" war, what is one to make of "otherwise you ought not to do it"?[44]

Marian W. Smith identifies a "mourning-war" complex of traits correlating to the northern distribution of maize agriculture. By implication she makes it a development of the revenge trait, but her definition is brief and unenlightening: it is "an elaborate socio-religious complex relating individual 'emotion' to social reintegration through group activity and sanctioned homicide."[45] This seems more to describe what happens psychologically to a tribe after it has gone to war than to explain the reasons for its choosing to fight a particular foe at a certain time and place; further, it could as well apply to the nations of World War II as to aboriginal Indians.[46] Pursued to their logical assumptions, such psychological explanations of war, primitive or modern, take one ultimately to a neo-Calvinist faith in the innate depravity/bellicosity of man, a position both unwarranted by science and vicious in effect and, ultimately, a self-fulfilling prophecy that stultifies investigation of the empirical sources of war and thus guarantees war's perpetuation. We shall do better to stick with Smith's genuine insight into Indian war as a means of reestablishing the validity of violated customs; it raises questions that can be answered historically.

In sum, the motives for aboriginal war appear to have been few, and the casualties slight. Contact with Europeans added new motives and weapons and multiplied casualties. The trade and dominance wars of the macrocontact era were indeed beyond the sole control of aboriginal cultural and political institutions, because they were bicultural wars, the motives and promptings for which originated in colony and empire as well as in tribe. These wars were truly attritional for Indians—appallingly so—but they were the result of civilization's disruption of aboriginal society rather than the mere outgrowth of precontact Indian culture.

Most discussions of Indian war have probably concerned themselves less with the Indians' motives than with their manner of fighting. Every "frontier" history abounds with tales of grim figures skulking through the woods, striking from ambush, spreading havoc and desolation, and culminating their horrors with scalping, torture, and cannibalism. In many instances the tales are verifiable, and no attempt will be made here to palliate their horrors. But when atrocity is singled out as a quality exclusive to tribesmen (Indians or others), myth is being invoked against evidence—indeed against the sorrowful experience of our own twentieth

Reichel, in Hist. Soc. Pa., *Memoirs*, XII, 175–76; Tooker, *Ethnography of the Huron Indians*, 28; [John] Lawson, [*A New Voyage to Carolina* (1709), March of America Facsimile Series, No. 35 (Ann Arbor, Mich., 1966)], 199; Driver, *Indians of North America*, 354.

44 Thomas Budd, *Good Order Established in Pennsilvania & New-Jersey in America* (1685), March of America Facsimile Series, No. 32 (Ann Arbor, Mich., 1966), 33.

45 M. W. Smith, "American Indian Warfare," N.Y. Acad. Sciences, *Trans.*, 2d Ser., XIII (1951), 359.

46 See W. W. Newcomb, Jr., "Toward an Understanding of War," in Gertrude E. Dole and Robert L. Carneiro, eds., *Essays in the Science of Culture in Honor of Leslie A. White* (New York, 1960), 322–24, and Newcomb, "A Reexamination of the Causes of Plains Warfare," *Am. Anthro.*, LII (1950), 328–29.

century and our own "highest" civilization of all time. The Indians of the macrocontact era, and presumably their aboriginal ancestors also, undoubtedly showed plenty of ferocity when aroused; what will be argued here is that the records of European war of the same era display the same quality in ample measure also. There were no Indians in Ireland when Cromwell's armies made it a wilderness, nor were there Indians with Wallenstein and Tilly during the Thirty Years' War in central Europe. If savagery was ferocity, Europeans were at least as savage as Indians.

Many of the aspects of so-called savage war were taught to Indians by European example. As to torture, for example, a systematic examination of the documents of the early contact era, published by Nathaniel Knowles in 1940, found no references to torturing by Indians of the southeast coast region "until almost 200 years after white contact." Knowles added, "It seems even more significant that there are no expressions by the early explorers and colonizers indicating any fear of such treatment. The Europeans were only too willing in most cases to call attention to the barbarity of the Indians and thus justify their need for either salvation or extermination."[47] Among the northeastern Indians, Knowles found that deliberate torture, as distinct from simple brutality (i.e., unplanned and unorganized cruelty), had not been practiced in aboriginal times except by the Iroquois, who associated it with the practice of ritual cannibalism. These usages seem to have been derived from an ancient complex of customs connected with human sacrifice and perhaps tracing back to similar practices in Mexico. Iroquois torture secondarily served as a terrorist device to keep surrounding tribes in fear, but its usefulness for this purpose declined as some neighbors adopted the same trait in reprisal, much as the southern Indians had retaliated against such European tortures as burning at the stake.[48] After describing the torture of an Iroquois prisoner by Samuel de Champlain's allies, Marc Lescarbot remarked, "I have not read or heard tell that any other savage tribe behaves thus to its enemies. But someone will reply

[47] Nathaniel Knowles, "The Torture of Captives by the Indians of Eastern North America," Am. Phil. Soc., *Procs.*, LXXXII (1940), 202. This is a systematic study fundamental to any study of torture in North America. Knowles remarked that Ponce de Leon in 1613 had met a Florida Indian who understood the Spanish language, "thus making it apparent that the atrocious cruelty of the Spanish for some twenty years in the West Indies had become known to the inhabitants of the mainland prior to the discovery of the continent by the whites" (p. 156). Knowles cites the speculation of Lowery that the Floridians' resistance to the Spaniards indicated "they had learned somewhat of the treatment they were to expect at the hands of such conquerors." Lowery, *Spanish Settlements*, I, 144–45. In 1642 the Canadian Jesuit martyr Father Isaac Jogues wrote, "*Never till now* had the Indian [torture] scaffold beheld French or other Christian captives." [E. B. O'Callaghan and Berthold Fernow, eds., *Documents Relative to the Colonial History of the State of New York*, XIII (Albany, N.Y., 1856–1887], 581 (emphasis added).

[48] Knowles, "Torture," Am. Phil. Soc., *Procs.*, LXXXII (1940), 190–91, 213, 215; Heckewelder, *Account of the Indian Nations*, ed. Reichel, in Hist. Soc. Pa., *Memoirs*, XII, 343.

that these did but repay the Iroquois who by similar deeds have given cause for this tragedy."[49] Lescarbot stated positively that "our sea-coast Indians" did not practice torture, and his modern translator added a note of confirmation.[50] Although some Indians practiced the ritual cannibalism that Europeans had sublimated many centuries earlier into symbolic acts of "communion," other Indians abominated man-eating as much as the Europeans themselves. Algonquian speakers used a contemptuous epithet meaning "man-eaters" to refer to their Iroquois neighbors: it took the forms of Mengwe, Mingo, Maqua, and finally, in English, Mohawk.[51]

Europeans and Indians differed in the publicity given to torture. Europeans burnt heretics and executed criminals in ingeniously agonizing ways, but much European torture was inflicted secretly for the utilitarian purpose of extracting confessions from suspects. Public or private, European torture was performed by specialists appointed by governmental authority, whereas torture among Indians was a spectacle for popular participation as well as observation. It seems reasonable to infer that comparably painful practices in the two societies were sharply distinguished in European minds by what was conceived as their relative lawfulness. Torture by commission of civil authority was merely execution of the law, often highly approved as a means of preserving order, but torture by a self-governing rabble was savagery. The *Encyclopaedia Britannica* has noted that the name of torture has been historically used "especially" for those modes of inflicting pain "employed in a legal aspect by the civilized nations of antiquity and of modern Europe."[52] In such a context the remark of seventeenth-century friar Louis Hennepin becomes ironic: "We are surprised at the cruelty of tyrants and hold them in horror: but that of the Iroquois is not less horrible."[53]

Plenty of sadism was evident in both cultures. Indians vented it directly upon the person of their victim, hacking and slashing at his body democratically with their own hands. Even old women would satisfy some horrid lust by thrusting firebrands at his genitals or chewing off the joints of his fingers. Their culture sanctioned what they did in the same way that local and regional cultures in nineteenth- and twentieth-century America sanctioned somewhat similar practices by white supremacists at lynching parties. In the more authoritarian seventeenth century the European populace in general was not allowed to participate except as spectators in the tortures prescribed for condemned per-

[49] Lescarbot, *History of New France*, trans. Grant, III, 13–15.

[50] *Ibid.*, III, 20–21.

[51] [Allen W.] Trelease, [*Indian Affairs in Colonial New York: The Seventeenth Century* (Ithaca, N.Y., 1960)], 41. But see a dissenting meaning for "Mohawk" given by Mohawk sachem Joseph Brant who held that it came from the Mahican word *munkwas*, meaning "fish dryed." Brant may have been a little sensitive on the subject. Boyce, ed., "Glimpse of Iroquois Culture History," Am. Phil. Soc., *Procs.*, CXVII (1973), 291.

[52] *Encyclopaedia Britannica*, 11th ed., s.v. "torture."

[53] Louis Hennepin, *A Description of Louisiana* (1683), trans. John Gilmary Shea, March of America Facsimile Series, No. 30 (Ann Arbor, Mich., 1966), 311–12.

sons. When we consider that crowds brought their lunch along to be enjoyed during such entertainments as disemboweling and slow immolation, we may wonder about the significance of the cultural difference. We have no way of knowing how many Europeans were prevented from soaking their own hands in blood only by the state's armed guards. Equally we have no way of knowing how many of the persons in an Indian village were active participants in the grim sport of torture, or how many just looked on. The diverse qualities of character that we recognize as distinguishing one European or Euramerican from another are ignored or denied among Indians. Savages are homogeneously cruel.

In America, Europeans sometimes turned captives over to allied Indians for torture in order to make hostility between two tribes irrevocable. Their own complicity was not felt keenly enough to shame the Europeans into silence; after having thus condemned a victim they would sometimes fastidiously deplore the sadistic appetites of the Indian torturers who were carrying out the Europeans' own desires.[54] One French officer, after "prudently" consigning an old Onondaga to the torture in 1696, considered that the *victim's* taunting defiance "will be found perhaps to flow rather from ferociousness, than true valour."[55]

One thing is not in doubt: as befitted its greater progress in technology, Europe had designed a variety of implements for the specific purpose of creating agony, not merely death, in human bodies. Their function was to make pain excruciating—a word that itself commemorates one of the pioneering inventions in that field and recalls its connection with European worship. Indians never achieved the advanced stage of civilization represented by the rack or the Iron Maiden. They simply adapted instruments of everyday utility to the purposes of pain. It may be worth a moment to reflect on the cultural traits imaged in the specialized torture technology of Europe. Something more than sudden emotional impulse will have to be taken into account.

I have an impression that about midway through the seventeenth century the outlook toward torture began to change in opposite directions among the two peoples. It seems to me from general reading that European attitudes toward mutilation of the human body began to turn negative. The old delight in hacking enemies' corpses in the public square and exposing their heads on palings went out of fashion—gradually and with conspicuous exceptions such as the displays made of sachem Philip and "squaw sachem" Weetamoo in "King Philip's War."[56] Slowly the

54 Heckewelder, *Account of the Indian Nations,* ed. Reichel, in Hist. Soc. Pa., *Memoirs,* XII, 343–44; [*Dictionary of Canadian Biography*], I (1966), s.v. "Buade de Frontenac et de Palluau, Louis de." Sir William Johnson followed the same practice but masked it under euphemisms. For example, he told Cadwallader Colden, Mar. 16, 1764, "I was obliged to *give* them People 5 Prisoners for their good behaviour." To General Gage, on the same day, Johnson wrote that the Indians had "kept" the five prisoners. *Sir William Johnson Papers,* IV, 365, 368–69 (emphasis added).

55 O'Callaghan, ed., *Doc. Hist. of N.-Y.*, I, 334.

56 [Samuel G.] Drake, *Biography and History of the Indians* [*of North America from its First Discovery* . . . , 11th ed. (Boston, 1856)], 189–90, 227.

use of torture for extracting information from political prisoners came under disapproval and ultimately under official ban. At the same time, torture was increasing among Indians as trade wars multiplied and European conflicts dragged Indian allies along. It is easy to understand why the Europeans, who were apparently trying to overcome their own worst traits, should have found relief and a sense of superior righteousness by rejecting torture and cruelty as things foreign to their own best impulses and therefore to civilization per se. No one dreamed at the time that the increase of torture by Indians could have come as the result of exposure to the uplifting influence of Europe, but the idea seems more credible nowadays after the revelations of German and Russian secret police practices, French policy in Algiers, Mississippi justice, and the ministrations of nice young American boys in Vietnam.

Every day brings revelations of secret tortures committed as deliberate instrumentation of governmental policy. Today's newspaper leads off an article with this paragraph: "Amnesty International, the organization dedicated to assisting political prisoners, has charged that torture as a systematic weapon of control is being used by almost half the world's governments and is spreading rapidly." The civilized world's response to this information is symbolized by the United Nations Educational, Scientific, and Cultural Organization. UNESCO withdrew from Amnesty International the offer of its facilities because the torture report implicated more than 60 of UNESCO's 125 member countries.[57] Clearly civilization is not a homogeneous whole, whatever it may otherwise be. Nor was it in the seventeenth century.

Apart from torture, some Europeans have domineered over Indians, when they could, with a reign of terror functioning through indiscriminate cruelty. In early Virginia the curtain was opened briefly on the reality behind self-serving and self-glorifying reports when Englishmen slew twelve Chickahominy Indians without cause and by treachery. Relatives of the victims retaliated against ten colonists and then fled into the woods. The rest of the villagers, abused by both sides, "much feared the English would be revenged on them"—a fear they had unquestionably been taught by the swaggering Virginians. Grand sachem Opechancanough "saved" the village from causeless slaughter, and incidentally revealed the motive behind the English menaces, by ceding the village to the colonists.[58] On a larger scale, after the much-provoked Virginia Indians rebelled in 1622, English writers fumed against the Indian massacre even as English soldiers multiplied their vengeance massacres beyond counting. Virginian Dr. John Pott became "the Poysner of the Savages thear" in some sort of episode so shocking that the earl of Warwick insisted it was "very unfitt" that Pott "should be imployed by the State in any business." But Pott became governor.[59]

[57] *New York Times,* Dec. 16, 1973: "64 Nations Charged in Report as Users of Torture."

[58] John Smith, *Generall Historie of Virginia,* in Arber and Bradley, eds., *Travels and Works of Smith,* II, 528, 538–39.

[59] See [Wesley Frank] Craven, "Indian Policy in Early Virginia," [*William and Mary*

Virginia was not exceptional. Puritan New England initiated its own reign of terror with the massacres of the Pequot conquest. David Pieterszoon de Vries has left us an unforgettable picture of how Dutch mercenaries acted, under orders of New Netherland's Governor Willem Kieft, to terrorize Indians into paying tribute.

> About midnight, I heard a great shrieking, and I ran to the ramparts of the fort, and looked over to Pavonia. Saw nothing but firing, and heard the shrieks of the Indians murdered in their sleep. . . . When it was day the soldiers returned to the fort, having massacred or murdered eighty Indians, and considering they had done a deed of Roman valour, in murdering so many in their sleep; where infants were torn from their mother's breasts, and hacked to pieces in the presence of the parents, and the pieces thrown into the fire and in the water, and other sucklings being bound to small boards, and then cut, stuck, and pierced, and miserably massacred in a manner to move a heart of stone. Some were thrown into the river, and when the fathers and mothers endeavoured to save them, the soldiers would not let them come on land, but made both parents and children drown–children from five to six years of age, and also some old and decrepit persons. Many fled from this scene, and concealed themselves in the neighbouring sedge, and when it was morning, came out to beg a piece of bread, and to be permitted to warm themselves; but they were murdered in cold blood and tossed into the water. Some came by our lands in the country with their hands, some with their legs cut off, and some holding their entrails in their arms, and others had such horrible cuts, and gashes, that worse than they were could never happen.

And the sequel: "As soon as the Indians understood that the Swannekens [Dutch] had so treated them, all the men whom they could surprise on the farm-lands, they killed; but we have never heard that they have ever permitted women or children to be killed."[60]

Indians have often been charged with senseless bloodlust in their fighting, even to the point of treacherously murdering people who had befriended them. The variety of friendship claimed for the victims of such murders should always be investigated in particular detail. The purported friend often turns out to be no more than someone who lived close to the Indians in order to exploit them more efficiently than he could from a distance–his "friendship" is proved by nothing more than his toleration of their persons–or one who warded off other exploiters in order to preserve his own monopoly. For reasons of space and proportion, the subject cannot be fully discussed here, but examples can be cited of real discrimination by Indians in favor of persons that they

Quarterly], 3d Ser., I (1944), 73; Warwick to Sec. Conway, Aug. 9, 1624, C.O. 1/3, 94; C.O. 1/5, Pt. 2, fol. 206, Public Record Office.

[60] De Vries, *Voyages,* in N.-Y. Hist. Soc., *Colls.,* 2d Ser., III, 115–16.

recognized as friends. David de Vries, himself one such person, was able, after Kieft's massacre, to walk alone, unmenaced and unscathed, in the midst of the very Indians whose kinsfolk had been treated so cruelly.[61] The most startling example is to be found in eighteenth-century Pennsylvania, where the entire Religious Society of Friends, whose members were settled the length and breadth of the colony, was excepted from the raids of the Seven Years' War. In 1758 the Yearly Meeting held at Burlington for New Jersey and Pennsylvania recorded its "Thankfulness for the peculiar favour extended and continued to our Friends and Brethren in profession, none of whom have as we have yet heard been Slain nor carried into Captivity." In consideration of Indian willingness to reciprocate benevolence, the Yearly Meeting displayed an unusual form of racist thinking: it urged all Friends to show their gratitude practically by freeing their slaves.[62]

Indian war, like European war, changed with time and circumstance. The guerrilla raids of small war parties became more common after the introduction of firearms made massed attack suicidal. Firearms also reduced the value of stockades around villages even as they had destroyed the invulnerability of walled castles in Europe. The most militaristic of Indians, the Iroquois, adapted to fighting with guns by casting aside their encumbering wooden and leather body armor to gain greater mobility. The naked warrior of the savage stereotype became real enough, but among the Iroquois, at least, he was the product of acculturation rather than an aboriginal prototype.[63]

The influence of European contact on Indian warfare is quite plain. In New England, for instance, until the Pequot conquest, the tribes marched to war en masse, but the Pequots recognized that such tactics would be futile against English firepower. They therefore approached the Narragansetts to propose joint harassment of the English rather than confrontation. They would kill livestock, waylay travelers, and ambush isolated farmers. The Narragansetts rejected this proposal in favor of an English alliance and later fought a battle against the Mohegans with the traditional tactics of a large army; but when they were finally forced into open violence against the English in "King Philip's War," they adopted the Pequots' proposed guerrilla tactics, to New England's great distress. Cultural change in response to the contact situation was not one-sided, however. While Pequots and Narragansetts changed traditional tactics to cope with English colonials, the Englishmen were also modifying ancient military wisdom to meet the needs created by Indian guerrilla war. In James Axtell's words, "From these opponents the English gradually learned to fight 'Indian-style,' an ability that once again spelled

[61] *Ibid.*, 116–20.

[62] Minutes, 1758, Minutes of the Yearly Meeting Held at Burlington for New Jersey and Pennsylvania, Manuscripts, Bk. A3, 121, Department of Records, Philadelphia Yearly Meeting, Society of Friends, 302 Arch St., Philadelphia.

[63] Keith F. Otterbein, "Why the Iroquois Won: An Analysis of Iroquois Military Tactics," *Ethnohistory*, XI (1964), 57–59; Snyderman, *Behind the Tree of Peace*, in *Pa. Archaeol.*, XVIII (1948), 75–77.

the difference between their destruction and survival in the New World."[64]

Customs and practices changed from decade to decade, even in regard to the trait of scalping, which, while apparently Indian in origin, did not exist among many Indian tribes in the early seventeenth century. It seems to have been adopted in New England, for example, as a convenient way to collect provincial bounties for heads without having to lug about the awkward impedimenta attached to the scalps.[65]

Both Indians and Englishmen took heads as trophies and put them on show, and the practice of paying bounties for heads was well established among Englishmen. It had been conspicuous in the wars in Ireland in the thirteenth and fourteenth centuries.[66] In the sixteenth century Sir Humphrey Gilbert had terrorized the Irish by ordering that "the heddes of all those (of what sort soever thei were) which were killed in the daie, should be cutte off from their bodies and brought to the place where he incamped at night, and should there bee laied on the ground by eche side of the waie ledyng into his owne tente so that none could come into his tente for any cause but commonly he muste passe through a lane of heddes which he used *ad terrorem*. . . . [It brought] greate terrour to the people when thei sawe the heddes of their dedde fathers, brothers, children, kinsfolke, and freinds. . . ."[67]

As Europeans taught Indians many of the traits of "savage" war, so also their intrusion into Indian society created new situations to which the Indians responded by cultural change on their own initiative. The attritional warfare of the macrocontact era did indeed justify A. L. Kroeber's indictment of having become so integrated in the culture that escape from it had become impossible, but it was not the aboriginal culture that took such a grim toll. It was instead a culture in which European motives and objectives of war multiplied war's occasions and casualties. Four different kinds of war took place in the macrocontact era: European versus European, Indian versus Indian, intermixed allies versus other allies, and, rarely, European versus Indian. In all of them the influence of European political or economic institutions is apparent. Many of the Indian versus Indian combats were really European wars in which the Indians unconsciously played the role of expendable surrogates. The curbs and restraints of aboriginal custom held no power over Europeans, and particular tribes were in various states of dependency or "ambipendency" with regard to particular colonies. Continual European initiatives and pressures for war created a *macrocontact* system in which tribal bellicosity was indeed self-preservatory for particular

64 [William] Bradford, *Of Plymouth Plantation*, [*1620–1647*, ed. Samuel Eliot Morison (New York, 1952)], 294–95, 330–31; James Axtell, "The Scholastic Philosophy of the Wilderness," *WMQ*, 3d Ser., XXIX (1972), 340.

65 Hodge, ed., *Handbook of N. Am. Indians*, s.v. "scalping."

66 Lydon, *Lordship of Ireland*, 195.

67 [Nicholas P.] Canny, ["The Ideology of English Colonization: From Ireland to America," *William and Mary Quarterly*, 3d Ser., XXX (1973)], 582.

groups in particular circumstances, even though it worked general calamity upon the whole of Indian society.

There were no innate differences between Indians and Europeans in their capacity for war or their mode of conducting it. Their differences were matters of technology and politics.[68] Only a few generations before the invasion of America, Europeans had conducted war according to feudal rules very different from those of the nation-state but startlingly similar in many respects to the practices of Indian war. Admittedly Indian society was not class-stratified like feudal society, and the Indian warrior differed from the feudal knight by being an all-purpose man who turned his hand to peasant occupations between battles. Clearly, also, Indians did not build or besiege castles, or fight with metal weapons and armor. But let not reality disappear behind the knight's armor plate; there was a naked warrior within. From childhood he had received special training in the use of arms, and he spent much time in strenuous sports that would strengthen and condition his body for war. So did the Indian. Both were hunters, and in the hunt both maintained their skill in the use of weapons. Like the Indian the medieval knight hunted for food as well as for sport and training; and, as with the Indian's hunting territories, unauthorized persons were forbidden to hunt in the knight's domain.[69]

A special purification ritual admitted the European esquire into the status of warrior; so also for the Indian, although in his case the ritual was also an ordeal. Knight and warrior mobilized for war in similar ways: the knight responded, if he felt like it, to the call of a lord to whom he had commended himself as vassal; the warrior responded, if he felt like it, to the invitation of an admired chief. No warrior was conscripted against his will. In neither case was there a bureaucracy to recruit and organize a fighting force; such loyalty as existed was that of man to man and family to family. Naturally enough, such soldiers knew nothing of Prussian discipline. Knights and warriors were free men fighting in wars and battles of their own choosing, unlike the hireling standing armies of the nation-state, who accepted orders with their wages.

[68] The only extended discussion seems to be one without visible virtues: Henry Holbert Turney-High, *Primitive War: Its Practice and Concepts* (Columbia, S.C., 1949). This is an unreliable, superficial, Colonel Blimp sort of repetitive dogma and slippery semantics. The author repeatedly expresses his contempt of the social sciences and declares that any noncommissioned officer knows more than all the social scientists. He hastens to add that he was himself a commissioned officer.

[69] A. F. C. Wallace has erroneously extrapolated the American custom of freedom to hunt on unposted lands back into European times, and the error is repeated by Vaughan; but hunting in Europe was stringently limited to the nobility and to "stinted" limits of rights in commons for the lower orders. Wallace, "Political Organization," *Southwest. Jour. of Anthro.*, XIII (1957), 312, n. 7; [Alden T.] Vaughan, *New England Frontier: [Puritans and Indians, 1620–1675* (Boston, 1965)], 108; E. C. K. Gonner, *Common Land and Inclosure* (London, 1912), 14–16.

One of the most striking parallels between the customs of feudal knights and those of Indian warriors was a code of behavior that in Europe is called chivalry. The sparing of women and children in Indian warfare fits snugly into the doctrines of chivalry avowed by feudal knights (and even practiced by them when the women and children were of their own religion). The practice was abandoned by the more rational or efficient killing machines organized by the nation-states; chivalry belonged to the knights, and the knights belonged to the Middle Ages. Chivalry, in short, was barbarous.

Perhaps an opportunity exists here to use the parallel between America and Europe to learn more about Europe. A customary explanation of chivalry's rise has been that the sweet moan of minnesingers and troubadours softened the hearts and manners of the great hulks on horseback. This lacks persuasion. Indians had a different sort of explanation for their own variety of chivalry: they needed to rebuild their declining populations. Feudal Europe was a time of population uncertainty, and the damsels spared by gallant knights were prime breeding stock—a fact sometimes put to test by the knights. In this respect the Indians seem to have been the more chivalrous, for they were observed everywhere to refrain from sexual molestation of female prisoners; they took the women and girls, untouched, back to the captors' villages for assignment to families as wives and daughters.[70] The knight, however, though he served the public interest by preserving his prisoners' lives, served himself also by demanding ransom.

Knight and warrior both gave first allegiance to their kin. This reservation of loyalty from the monopoly demanded by the nation-state was the unforgivable sin that has roused nationalists to denounce the special barbarity of feudal Europe and the special savagery of Indian America. That all war is cruel, horrible, and socially insane is easy to demonstrate, but the nationalist dwells upon destiny, glory, crusades, and other such claptrap to pretend that his own kind of war is different from and better than the horrors perpetrated by savages. This is plainly false. The qualities of ferocity and atrocity are massively visible in the practices of European and American powers all over the world, quite recently in the assaults of the most advanced civilized states upon one another.

[70] Hodge, ed., *Handbook of N. Am. Indians,* s.v., "captives"; Heckewelder, *Account of the Indian Nations,* ed. Reichel, in Hist. Soc. Pa., *Memoirs,* XII, 339–40.

"It Was a Negro Taught Them": A New Look at African Labor in Early South Carolina

PETER H. WOOD

By the end of the seventeenth century the English colonies in southern North America had turned to the African slave and his descendants to solve the problems arising from a chronic shortage of labor. The English adapted for their own use the Spanish system of African enslavement, which had begun early in the sixteenth century in the Caribbean. Indian slavery, too, had been widely practiced in Latin America, to the point of bringing the native Indian populations close to extinction. But in North American colonies, although Indian captives were frequently enslaved in the early years of colonization, it appears that Indian slavery was never economically profitable. As a result, the African became **the** slave in the English colonies.

Slavery, in the sense of lifetime bondage, is an institution as old as human history. Almost every past civilization has had some system of involuntary service that may with some accuracy be called slavery. Throughout history, military conquest has been the most common means of enslavement. What distinguished North American slavery, however, was its racial character. By the beginning of the eighteenth century, any African in the English colonies was assumed to be a slave unless he could prove otherwise. Except in exceptional circumstances, not only the original African but his descendants forever were confined to slave status.

From the earliest days of settlement in North America, the historical record clearly shows that some blacks were free. What it does not show is the process by which African slavery became the widespread institution that it was by 1700. In fact historians have argued as to whether slavery produced racial prejudice or racial prejudice produced slavery—a question that could have vital significance for easing racial tensions in America today. If, for instance, slavery, as an absolute form of economic inequality, led to racial prejudice, then the elimination of economic inequality in the United States might contribute immensely to the elimination of racial prejudice. If, on the other hand, prejudice preceded slavery, then equal economic opportunity might not be expected for blacks until the roots of racial prejudice might have been identified and removed.

Historians are only now beginning to explore the nature of slavery and slave life in the earliest days of English settlement in North America. One of the persistent myths of that period is that the Africans imported to the New World were empty vessels culturally and had to be taught by the English all of those things they would be required to do in their new life. Peter Wood, of Duke University, has brilliantly exploded that myth in his extensive study of slavery in early South Carolina. In the article reprinted below, he suggests that the Africans were much better prepared for the environment of colonial South Carolina than were their masters and, in fact, brought with them skills that contributed significantly to the success of the colonial venture. Not only were these skills put to use by the Africans in the service of their masters, but they were also used in constructing forms of resistance that provided the slaves with some measure of protection against the abuses of the slave system.

When Col. John Barnwell of South Carolina laid siege to the stronghold of the Tuscarora Indians in the spring of 1712, he noticed a special ingenuity in the fortification. "I immediately viewed the Fort with a prospective glass and found it strong," the commander wrote. Not only were there impressive trenches, bastions, and earthworks to ward off attack, but heavy tree limbs had been placed around the fort making any approach difficult and hiding innumerable "large reeds & canes to run into people's legs." What struck Barnwell particularly was the fact that, according to the fort's occupants, "it was a runaway negro taught them to fortify thus." At that early date blacks and whites had lived in the region for scarcely a generation, and it is not likely that this slave, identified only as "Harry," had been born in Carolina. Instead it seems probable that he had grown up in Africa and had lived in South Carolina before he was "sold into Virginia for roguery & . . . fled to the Tuscaruros" (*Virginia Magazine*, July 1898, 44–45). If Harry's African

"'It Was a Negro Taught Them,' a New Look at African Labor in Early South Carolina," by Peter H. Wood. From *Journal of Asian and African Studies,* IX (1974), 160–79. Reprinted by permission of the publisher, E. J. Brill, Leiden, The Netherlands. An earlier version of this paper was read to the Organization of American Historians in 1972. Material appearing here is presented in a fuller context in Peter H. Wood, *Black Majority: Negroes in Colonial South Carolina from 1670 through the Stono Rebellion.* (New York 1974).

know-how caught the South Carolina commander off guard, it may also startle modern historians, for this obscure incident exemplifies an intriguing aspect of Afro-American history which has not yet been adequately explored.

Colonial South Carolina is an excellent place to begin searching the cultural baggage of early black immigrants for what anthropologists have termed "carryovers." More slaves entered North America through Charleston (called Charlestown until 1783) than through any other single port, and no other mainland region had so high a ratio of Africans to Europeans throughout the eighteenth century as did South Carolina. Early migrants from Barbados and other places where black slavery was well-established brought Negro workers with them when they could afford it. In the initial years after 1670, however, most English settlers hoped to meet the colony's intensive labor needs in other ways. Attempts were made to procure a steady supply of European workers and to employ neighboring Indians on a regular basis, but neither of these sources could meet the demand. Within half a century Negroes constituted a majority of the settlement's population, and additional black slaves were being imported regularly from Africa.

That such a large percentage of early South Carolinians were Negroes has never been thoroughly explained, though basic contributing factors have long been recognized: European racism, colonial precedent, and the proximity of the African trading routes. No other workers were available for such extended terms, in such large numbers, at so low a rate. Indeed, that such slave labor was so has always seemed almost inevitable. And perhaps for this very reason, the question of whether Negroes brought with them any inherited knowledge and practical skills from the African continent has seemed irrelevant to white historians. Though the anthropologist Melville Herskovits challenged "The Myth of the Negro Past" more than thirty years ago, the American historian has tended to uphold the legend that blacks had no prior cultures of any consequence, or that if they did, little could have survived the traumatic Middle Passage (Herskovits 1941). (McPherson [1971: 32–39] indicates that a few historians have considered some carryovers, but little attention has been given to the importation of any practical kinds of cultural information.) Africans, according to this approach, were imported *in spite* of being thoroughly unskilled (or perhaps in part *because* of it). And it followed from this that the central chore which faced European masters was one of patient and one-sided education, so that "ignorant" slaves could be taught to manage simple tasks.

Yet in actuality something very different seems to have taken place. In the earliest years of colonization slaves who had passed through the Creole culture of the West Indies demonstrated unsuspected talents. Within several decades the necessity for labor of any sort led to an increase in the size and diversity of the Negro population, and a further variety of African skills emerged which were strikingly appropriate to the lowland frontier. Slaves, therefore, were far from being the passive objects of white instruction. A process of mutual education took place among the slaves themselves, despite initial language problems. And many of these workers, regardless of legal status, occasionally ended up teaching their masters. Africans, as will be made clear, sometimes proved knowledgeable and competent in areas where Europeans remained disdainful or ignorant. Hence the problem faced by white Carolinians during the first and second generations of settlement was less one of imparting knowledge to unskilled workers than of controlling for their own ends black expertise which could, as in Harry's case, be readily turned against them.

Though hitherto unacknowledged, the comparative advantages which Africans possessed over Europeans in this New World setting can be seen in a variety of different ways. South Carolina, first of all, was in a different geographic zone from England and from all the earlier English colonies in mainland North America. This fact was pleasing to white settlers on one level, but disconcerting on another, and they were slow to make the adjustments necessary for life in a somewhat alien semitropical region. John Lawson, an amateur naturalist who explored the Carolinas at the start of the eighteenth century, commented that if English colonists "would be so curious as to make nice Observations of the Soil, and other remarkable Accidents, they would soon be acquainted with the Nature of the Earth and Climate, and be better qualified to manage their Agriculture to more Certainty." But he went on to admit, as would Jefferson and others after him, that Europeans seemed to become less careful and observant rather than more so in the unfamiliar environment of the American South (Lawson 1967 [1709]: 80, 81).

West Africans, on the other hand, were not only more accustomed to the flora and fauna of a subtropical climate generally, but they possessed an orientation toward what Lévi-Strauss has called "extreme familiarity with their biological environment, . . . passionate attention . . . to it and . . . precise knowledge of it" (Lévi-Strauss 1966: 5). Even prior to the 1600s black slaves had established a reputation for being able to subsist off the land more readily than Europeans in the Southeast. A century before the founding of Carolina, when Negroes were sent to work on the fortifications at St. Augustine, a Spanish official had written approvingly, "With regard to their food, they will display diligence as they seek it in the country, without any cost to the royal treasure" (*Colonial Records of Spanish Florida*, 1930: 315). In Carolina their ability to cope with this particular natural world was demonstrated, and reinforced, by the reliance Europeans put upon them to fend for themselves and others. Instances of black self-sufficiency (like instances of Indian assistance) made a lasting impression upon less well acclimated whites, and as late as 1775 we find an influential English text repeating the doctrine that in Carolina, "The common idea . . . is, that one Indian, or dextrous negroe, will, with his gun and netts, get as much game and fish as five families can eat; and the slaves support themselves in provisions, besides raising . . . staples" (Land 1969: 67).

By far the largest number of people entering South Carolina during the colonial period came from West Africa, and, in the course of a century of immigration, items indigenous to parts of that vast region were transported with them. For example, though white colonists would debate at length which European should receive credit for introducing the first bag of rice seed,[1] it is possible that successful rice cultivation, to be discussed separately later, followed the arrival of seeds aboard a ship from Africa.[2] Often the botanical imprecision of contemporary Englishmen makes it hard to say exactly which plants were introduced and when. Semantic confusion about Guinea corn and Indian corn provides a case in point. Maurice Mathews reported during the initial summer of settlement that along with Indian corn, "Guiney Corne growes very well here, but this being ye first I euer planted ye perfection I will not Aver till ye Winter doth come in" (South Carolina Historical Society, *Collections*, V, 333). This grain or some subsequent variety clearly took hold, for in the next generation Lawson reported Guinea corn to be thriving; he noted it was used mostly for hogs and poultry, while adding that many black slaves ate "nothing but" Indian corn (with salt) (Lawson 1967 [1709]: 81). A definition offered by Mark Catesby in 1743 reveals that Indian and Guinea corn had become interchangeable in English texts, if not in actual fact:

> *Milium Indicum.* Bunched Guinea Corn. But little of this grain is propagated, and that chiefly by negroes, who make bread of it, and boil it in like manner of firmety. Its chief use is for feeding fowls. . . . It was at first introduced from Africa by the negroes (Catesby 1743, appendix, xviii).

Catesby also recorded "The Leg-worm, or Guinea-worm" among the "insects" he found in Carolina, and Lawson listed among varieties of muskmelon a "guinea melon" which may have come from Africa. Others mentioned the "guinea fowl" or "guinea hen," a domesticated West African bird which was introduced into North America during the eighteenth century. Henry Laurens of Charleston (like George Washington of Mount Vernon) acquired seed for "guinea grass," a tall African grass used for fodder (Lawson 1967 [1709]: 81–83; Mathews, II, 1193).

The West African and Carolinian climates were similar enough so that even where flora and fauna were not literally transplanted, a great deal of knowledge proved transferable. African cultures placed a high priority on their extensive pharmacopoeia, and details known through oral tradition were readily transported to the New World. For example, expertise included familiarity with a variety of herbal antidotes and

[1] Landgrave Thomas Smith, Dr. Henry Woodward, an anonymous sea captain, and a treasurer of the East Indian Company all took or received the credit at some point. A letter of Nov. 4, 1726 (overlooked by historians), from Jean Watt in Neufchatel makes the claim "that it was by a woman that Rice was transplanted into Carolina." Records of the British Public Record Office Relating to South Carolina (hereafter abbreviated as BPRO Trans.), xii, 156–57.

[2] At the end of the eighteenth century the Abbé Raynal wrote: "Opinions differ about the manner in which rice hath been naturalized in Carolina. But whether the province may have acquired it by a shipwreck, or whether it may have been carried there with slaves, or whether it be sent from England, it is certain that the soil is favourable for it" (Raynal, London, 1798, VI, 59).
The first edition of this work, in 1772, offered only the shipwreck theory. The

abortives (Vansina 1971: 443; Curtin 1968: 215). A South Carolina slave received his freedom and one hundred pounds per year for life from the Assembly for revealing his antidote to certain poisons; "Ceasar's Cure" was printed in the *South Carolina Gazette* and appeared occasionally in local almanacs for more than thirty years (*S. C. Gazette*, May 9, 1750; Webber 1914: 78; On Caesar, cf. Duncan 1972: 64–66).

Although certain medicinal knowledge was confined to specially experienced slaves (some of whom were known openly as "doctors"), almost all blacks showed a general familiarity with lowland plants. Negroes regularly gathered berries and wild herbs for their own use and for sale. John Brickell noted of slaves in Carolina, for example, that "on Sundays, they gather Snake-Root, otherwise it would be excessive dear if the Christians were to gather it" (Brickell 1911 [1737]: 275). The economic benefits to be derived from workers with such horticultural skills were not lost upon speculative Europeans. In 1726 Richard Ludlam urged the collection and cultivation of special plants upon which the cochineal beetle (an insect used to produce red dye) might feed and grow. According to Ludlam:

> Two or Three Slaves will gather as many Spontaneous Plants in one day, as will in another Day regularly Plant Ten Acres, by the Same hands and for the Quantity of Plants Growing here on the Banks of Rivers & in the multitudes of Islands on the Sea Coasts, I can Safely Assure you . . . Thousands of Acres might, at a Little Charge, be Stock with them.[3]

Bringing a greater awareness of the environment with them, foreign slaves were better able to profit from contact with native Indians than were their equally foreign masters. A variety of plants and processes were known to both West African and southeastern American cultures, and such knowledge must have been shared and reinforced upon contact. Gourds, for example, served as milk pails along the Gambia River in much the same way calabashes had long provided water buckets beside the Ashley[4] (Grant 1968: 24; Lawson 1967 [1709]: 149). The creation of elaborate baskets, boxes, and mats from various reeds and grasses was familiar to both black and red (Lawson 1967 [1709]: 195–96), and South Carolina's strong basket-weaving tradition, still plainly visible on the roadsides north of Charleston, undoubtedly represents an early fusion of Negro and Indian skills (Smith 1936: 71).

---

tradition of a Madagascar origin has been popularized in Heyward 1937. On slaves from that region, see Platt 1969: 548–77.

[3] A copy of this letter (Jan. 10, 1726) is in volume II (labelled volume III) of the typescript marked, "Charleston Museum, Miscellaneous Papers, 1726–1730," South Caroliniana Library, Columbia.

[4] It is impossible to say whether it was Africans or Indians who showed white planters, around 1700, how to put a gourd on a pole as a birdhouse for martins (that would in turn drive crows from the crops) or who fashioned the first drinking gourd which would become the standard dipper on plantations.

The palmetto, symbol of the novel landscape for arriving Europeans, was well known to Africans and Indians for its useful leaf. They made fans and brooms from these leaves and may well have entered into competition with Bermudians who were already exporting baskets and boxes made of woven palmetto (Lawson 1967 [1709]: 14; Corry 1968 [1807]: 66). An authority on Carolina furniture writes that "The very early inventories frequently mention Palmetto chairs or Palmetto-bottom chairs" (Burton 1955: 36–37). The skill and labor behind these traditional items may well have been primarily African, as suggested by one surviving mortgage. In 1729 Thomas Holton, a producer of chairs and couches, listed as collateral three of his Negro slaves: "by name Sesar, Will, and Jack by trade Chairmakers (Wills, Inventories, and Miscellaneous Records, 1729–1731: 27).

Through the first two generations of settlement Indians were common among the Negroes in lowland Carolina, both as fellow slaves and as free neighbors (Cf. Dundes 1965: 207–19; Hudson 1971). But the number of Indians steadily declined, and as their once-formidable knowhow dissipated it was the Negroes who assimilated the largest share of their lore and who increasingly took over their responsibilities as "pathfinders" in the Southern wilderness. Blacks became responsible for transporting goods to market by land and water and for ferrying passengers and livestock. From the first years of settlement the primary means of direct communication between masters was through letters carried by slaves. Charleston set up a local post office at the beginning of the eighteenth century, and by 1740 there was a weekly mail going south toward the new colony of Georgia and a monthly post overland to the north via Georgetown and Cape Fear, but with the exception of these minimal services the responsibility for delivering letters in the region fell entirely to Negro boatmen and runners throughout the colonial period (Cooper and McCord, II, 188–89; *S. C. Gazette*, September 17, 1737; May 3, 1739; November 20, 1740).

There is no better illustration of white reliance upon black knowledge of the environment than the fact that slaves became quite literally the guides of their masters. Contemporary records give adequate testimony. John Lawson, travelling from the Ashley to the Santee by canoe at the start of the eighteenth century, relates that at one point a local doctor "sent his Negro to guide us over the Head of the Swamp" (Lawson 1967 [1709]: 20–21). A public official such as the Provost Marshal would sometimes be loaned a slave boy "to Show him the way" between plantations (*Journal of the Commons House Of Assembly, 1726–1727*, 119). In October 1745 a white traveller coming from Philadelphia recorded in his Journal: "had a Negro to guide us the Road being Intricate" (Pemberton *Diary*, 1745), and in the same month a minister of the Society for the Propagation of the Gospel wrote that his parishioners had urged him to purchase a family of three Negroes.

> I consented [he wrote] not knowing full well the ways and management of country affair[s] . . . , and was obliged also by extream necessity to buy 3 horses with bridles and saddles, one for

me, another for my wife, and the other for a Boy servant, for it would be impossible for me to go through the Parish between the woods without a Guide (Boschi 1949 [1745]: 185).

In 1770 William De Brahm would observe that slaves, besides being stationed at their masters' gates to offer hospitality to white travellers, were often sent with departing guests "to cut down small trees in the way of carriages, to forward and guide through unfrequented forrests, . . . [and] to set them over streams, rivers and creeks" (Weston 1856: 179). It is not an unrelated fact that ever since colonial times Negroes have commonly served as guides to white sportsmen in the Sea Islands and throughout the coastal South (Cf. Crum, Chapter IV).

It is striking to find black familiarity with the land more than matched by familiarity with the coastal sea. Although Europeans were unrivaled as the builders and navigators of oceangoing ships, there was little in the background of most white immigrants to prepare them for negotiating the labyrinth of unchanneled swamps and tidal marshes which interlaced the lowland settlement. Afro-Americans drew on a different heritage. Some slaves had scarcely seen deep water before their forced passage to America, and none had sailed in ocean vessels; yet many had grown up along rivers or beside the ocean and were far more at home in this element than most Europeans, for whom a simple bath was still exceptional (Cf. Turberville 1929: 126, for history of English bathing). Lawson, describing the awesome shark, related how "some Negro's, and others, that can swim and dive well, go naked into the Water, with a Knife in their Hand, and fight the Shark, and very commonly kill him" (Lawson 1967 [1709]: 158). Similarly the alligator, a fresh-water reptile which horrified Europeans (since it was unfamiliar and could not be killed with a gun), was readily handled by Negroes used to protecting their stock from African crocodiles (Grant 1968: 13, 23; see also Schaw 1922: 149–51).

Most importantly, a large number of slaves were more at home than their masters in dugout canoes, and these slender boats were the central means of transportation in South Carolina for several generations while roads and bridges were still too poor and infrequent for easy land travel.[5] Small canoes were hollowed from single cypress logs by Negroes or Indians, or by whites whom they instructed in the craft.[6] To make the

[5] In 1682 Thomas Newe found that horses brought from New England were still scarce and expensive, "so there is but little use of them, all Plantations being seated on the Rivers, they can go to and fro by Canoo or Boat as well and as soon as they can ride." Newe added that "the horses here like the Indians and many of the English do travail without shoes" (Salley 1911: 184).

[6] The English experience in Carolina must have been comparable to that of the French among the Island Caribs of the Antilles at the same time. Breton (1665, reprinted 1892), 331 states:

The French learned from the Savages to hollow out trees to make canoes; but they did not learn from them to row them, steer them, or jump overboard to right them when they overturned: the Savages are not afraid of overturning,

larger canoe known as a pettiauger two or three trees were used, giving the boat additional beam for cargo without significantly increasing its draft; fifty to one hundred barrels of tar or rice could be ferried along shallow creeks and across tidal shoals in such vessels.

These boats were frequently equipped with one or even two portable masts for sailing and often ventured onto the open ocean (Lawson 1967 [1709]: 103, 104, 107; Clontes 1926: 16–35; Cf. McKusick 1960). Their design may have represented a syncretic blend between European, Caribbean, and Indian styles on the one hand, and on the other hand diverse coastal traditions from West Africa, where cypress wood was used to fashion both round and flat bottomed craft (Batutah 1929 [1325–1354]: 333; Hakluyt 1904: 18; see also Wax 1968: 474, 478). Negro crews, directed by a black "patroon," managed these boats, and many of their earliest rowing songs were apparently remnants recalled from Africa (McCrady 1899: 516; Fisher 1953: 8).

The fact that dexterity in handling cypress canoes was an art brought from Africa is underscored by an advertisement for a runaway in the Virgina colony. The notice concerned "a new Negro Fellow of small Stature" from Bonny on the coast of Nigeria; it stated that "he calls himself Bonna, and says he came from a Place of that name in the Ibo Country, in Africa, where he served in the Capacity of a Canoe Man" (*Virginia Gazette*, December 24, 1772). In South Carolina slave men were often advertised in terms of their abilities on the water: "a very good Sailor, and used for 5 years to row in Boats, . . . a Lad chiefly used to row in Boats," "a fine strong Negro Man, that has been used to the Sea, which he is very fit for, or to go in a Pettiaugua," "all fine Fellows in Boats or Pettiau's." So many Negroes brought these skills with them, or learned their seamanship in the colony from other slaves, that black familiarity with boating was accepted as axiomatic among whites. In 1741, when Henry Bedon advertised two Negro men "capable to go in a Pettiauger" who had been "going by the Water above 10 Years," he added that the pair "understands their Business as well as most of their Colour" (*S. C. Gazette*, April 6, 1734; April 11, 1739; January 31, 1743; February 18, 1741).

"Their business" often included fishing, and it is not surprising that in the West Indian and southern colonies Africans quickly proved able to supply both themselves and their European owners with fish (Wax 1968: 475–76). In Charleston, an entire class of "fishing Negroes" had emerged early in the eighteenth century, replacing local Indians as masters of the plentiful waters (*S. C. Gazette*, November 5, 1737). (For an excellent discussion of fishing slaves as a privileged subgroup, see Price 1968.) "There is . . . good fishing all along this Coast, especially from October till Christmas," wrote James Sutherland who commanded Johnson's Fort overlooking Charleston harbor during the 1730s, adding (perhaps with fisherman's license), "I've known two Negroes take be-

---

wetting their clothes, losing anything, or drowning, but most French fear all of these things . . . Every day one sees disastrous accidents.

tween 14 & 1500 Trouts above 3 feet long, wch make an excellent dry fish" (Coe Papers, undated). A French visitor whose ship anchored not far from Johnson's Fort early in the next century found himself "in the midst of twenty-five dugouts,"

> each containing four Negroes who were having excellent fishing, such as one might well desire on the eve of Good Friday. Ten minutes doesn't go by without there being hauled into the dugout fish weighing from twelve to fifteen pounds. After they are taken on the line, they are pulled up to the level of the sea where one of the black fishermen sticks them with a harpoon (Montlzun 1948: 136; see also Price 1968: 1372).

Skill with hooks and harpoons was complemented by other techniques more common in Africa and the Caribbean than in Europe. The poisoning of streams to catch fish was known in West Africa (Fyfe 1964: 96), and fish drugging was also practised in the West Indies, first by Island Caribs and later by Negro slaves. They dammed up a stream or inlet and added an intoxicating mixture of quicklime and plant juices to the water. They could then gather inebriated but edible fish from the pool almost at will (Price 1968: 1366, 1372; Quigley 1956: 508–25). Inhabitants of South Carolina in the early eighteenth century exploited a similar tactic, for in 1726 the Assembly charged that "many persons in this Province do often use the pernicious practice of poisoning the creeks in order to catch great quantity of fish," and a public whipping was imposed upon any slave convicted of the act (*Statutes*, III, 270; the misdemeanor seems to have continued; cf. *S. C. Gazette*, April 6, 1734).

West African Negroes may also have imported the art of net casting, which became an established tradition in the tidal shallows of Carolina. The doctor aboard an American slaving vessel off the Gold Coast in the mid-eighteenth century recorded in his journal: "It is impossible to imagine how very dextrous the negroes are in catching fish with a net, this morning I watch'd one man throw one of 3 yards deep, and hale it in himself with innumerable fish" (Wax 1968: 474; see also Whitten and Szwed, pictorials, 11th p.). Weighted drawstring nets, like the dugout canoes from which they were cast, may have represented the syncretic blend of several ancient Atlantic fishing traditions (Price 1968: 1374). The men who could handle nets could also mend them; in 1737 a runaway named Moses was reported to be "well known in Charlestown, having been a Fisherman there for some time, & hath been often employed in knitting of Nets" (*S. C. Gazette*, November 5, 1737). The prevalence of Negro commercial fishermen in the Southeast, as in the Caribbean, continued long after the end of slavery, and blacks who man shrimpboats in present-day Carolina earn their living at a calling familiar to many of their West African forebears.[7]

[7] Frederic G. Cassidy (1967) points out that the Doulla-Bakweri language of the Cameroon River area provided the Jamaican Creole word for the crayfish or

No single industry was more important to the early settlement in South Carolina than the raising of livestock. While the first generation of Englishmen experimented unsuccessfully with such strange crops as grapes, olives, cotton, rice, indigo, and ginger in the hopes of finding an appropriate staple, their livelihood depended in large measure upon the cattle and hogs that could be raised with a minimum of labor. Beef and pork were in great demand in the West Indies, and these at least were items which the English had long produced. But even here there was an unfamiliar element. According to traditional European patterns of animal husbandry, farmers confined their cows in pastures, milked them regularly, and slaughtered them annually. Since winter fodder was limited, Europeans maintained only enough stock through the cold months to replenish their herds in the following spring. This practice made little sense in a region where cattle could "feed themselves perfectly well at no cost whatever" (Thibou 1683) throughout the year. Stock grew lean, but rarely starved in South Carolina's mild winters. Colonists therefore might build up large herds with little effort, a fact which could benefit the settlement but which dismayed the Proprietors in London. It has been "our designe," they stated indignantly, "to have Planters there and not Graziers" (South Carolina Historical Society, *Collections*, V, 437–38).

Africans, however, had no such disdain for open grazing, and many of the slaves entering South Carolina after 1670 may have had experience in tending large herds. Melville Herskovits, along with others, has pointed out that although domesticated cattle were absent from the Congo region due to the presence of the tse-tse fly, such animals were common along much of the African coast to the north and west. Stock was even traded for export on occasion. In 1651, for example, the English Guinea Company, precursor of the Royal African Company, instructed a captain to barter liquor at the Gambia River for a "Cargo of negers or Cattel" to be carried to Barbados. People of the Gambia region, the area for which South Carolina slave dealers expressed a steady preference, were expert horsemen and herders. English visitors expressed high admiration for their standards of cleanliness with respect to dairy products, and contemporary descriptions of local animal husbandry bear a striking resemblance to what would later appear in Carolina. Herds grazed on the savannahs bordering the river and in the low-lying paddy fields when the rice crop was off; at night stock was tethered within a cattlefold and guarded by several armed men (Herskovits 1930: 67, 72, 73; Donnan 1930–1935, I, 129; Grant 1968: 24–25).

As early as the 1670s there is evidence of absentee investors relying upon Negro slaves to develop herds of cattle in Carolina.[8] Even when

river prawn. "This part of Africa, indeed, took its name from the plentiful shrimp or prawns in the river: *Cameroon* is from Portuguese *camarao* 'shrimp.'"

[8] In 1673, for example, Edmund Lister of Northumberland County, Virginia, bought one hundred acres of land along the Ashley River on Oyster Point from an illiterate laborer named John Gardner. Lister sent three men south ahead of him to prepare the land (not an unusual practice), but he died the following year

the white owner lived within the province, the care of his livestock often fell to a black. The slave would build a small "cowpen" in some remote region, attend the calves and guard the grazing stock at night. When Denys Omahone sold a fifty-acre tract to a new white arrival in the 1680s the property contained, besides the Indians who still inhabited it, four calves, three steers, five sows, one boar and a "Negro man by name Cato" (South Carolina Archives, Miscellaneous Records A, 1682–1690: 318–19).

This pattern continued. In 1690 Seth Sothell gave his father-in-law one of several large landholdings "And thirty head of Cattle belonging to ye Said Plantation and one Neg^{ro} Man" (South Carolina Archives, Archdale Papers, item 26, January 25, 1690; cf. Dunbar). Upon the death in 1692 of Bernard Schenckingh, a well-to-do Barbadian migrant with four estates, the appraisers of his James Island holdings reported that "In sight and by account apeareth 134 head of Cattle [and] one negro man" (South Carolina Archives, Records of the Secretary of the Province, 1692–1700: 38). Half a century later the estate of Robert Beath at Ponpon included, "a Stock of Cattle . . . said to be from Five Hundred to One Thousand Head . . . Also a Man used to a Cow Pen and of a good Character" (*S. C. Gazette*, March 19, 1741).

At first the Carolina settlement occupied a doubly colonial status, struggling to supply provisions to other English colonies.[9] The development of a trade in naval stores soon enabled the settlement to become a staple producer in its own right, but it was the cultivation of rice as an export commodity which came to dominate Carolina life in the course of the eighteenth century. Despite its eventual prominence, the mastery of this grain took more than a generation, for rice was a crop about which Englishmen, even those who had lived in the Caribbean, knew nothing at all. White immigrants from elsewhere in northern Europe were equally

---

before taking up residence. One of those he had sent ahead to South Carolina was an indentured servant named Patrick Steward with only several months left to serve, but the others were apparently black slaves experienced with livestock, for in 1676 Lister's widow stated in a bill of sale that her "Dec^{d} Housband, did formerly Transport Severall Negros, out of this Colony of Virginia, into Carolina and did there Settle them upon a Plantacon, together w^{td} Some Cattle." The holding may have been considerable, for the widow received 10,000 pounds of good tobacco for the land, Negroes, and stock from a Virginia gentleman who was himself an absentee owner of slaves in Carolina (South Carolina Archives, Records of the Secretary of the Province, 1675–1695: 39–41; Salley 1944 (1671–1675): 59, 66–69). It was long ago suggested that the particularly numerous slaves in the Narragansett country of Rhode Island played an important role on the renowned stock farms of that region (Channing 1886: 9–10).

[9] A letter from the Reverend John Urmstone in North Carolina, July 11, 1711 (quoted in Land, 22–23), typifies conditions which had prevailed in South Carolina slightly earlier. Urmstone stated, "the planter here is but a slave to raise a provision for other colonies," adding:

> Men are generally of all trades, and women the like within their spheres, except some who are the posterity of old planters, and have great number of slaves, who understand most handicraft. . . .

ignorant, and local Indians who gathered small quantities of wild rice had little to teach them.

Though England consumed comparatively little rice before the eighteenth century, the cheap white grain was a dietary staple in parts of southern Europe by 1670, and Carolina's Proprietors were anticipating a profit from this crop even before the settlement began (S. C. Historical Society, *Collections*, V, 15). When the colonists could show nothing for their efforts after their first seven years, the Londoners wrote impatiently, "wee are Layinge out in Severall places of y[e] world for plants & Seeds proper for yo[r] Country and for persons that are Skill'd in plantinge & producings . . . Rice oyles & Wines" (BPRO Trans., I: 59). But there is no direct evidence that the Proprietors followed through on this promise, or that they responded helpfully to later requests for guidance (*Journal of the Commons House of Assembly*, 1698: 36).

Nevertheless, during the 1680s, perhaps after the arrival of a better strain of rice seed from Madagascar, the colonists renewed their efforts to grow rice, but with only marginal success through the 1690s (Salley 1919; Gray, I: 277 ff.; Clowse 1971: 123–32. See also *South Carolina Historical and Geneological Magazine*, January and April, 1931). An eighteenth-century Englishman recalled:

> the people being unacquainted with the manner of cultivating rice, many difficulties attended the first planting and preparing it, as a vendable commodity, so that little progress was made for the first nine or ten years, when the quantity produced was not sufficient for home consumption (*Gentleman's Magazine*, June, 1776, 278–79).

Similarly, Governor Glen would later claim that even after experimenters had begun to achieve plausible yields from their renewed efforts around 1690, they still remained "ignorant for some Years how to clean it" (Glen 1951 [1761]: 94).[10]

In contrast to Europeans, Negroes from the West Coast of Africa were widely familiar with rice planting. Ancient speakers of a Proto-Bantu language in the sub-Sahara region are known to have cultivated the crop (McCall 1964: 69). An indigenous variety (*Oryza glaberrima*)

[10] Glen added at this later date (p. 95): "The only Commodity of Consequence produced in South Carolina is Rice, and they reckon it as much their staple Commodity, as Sugar is to Barbadoes and Jamaica, or Tobacco to Virginia and Maryland."

In 1691 a Frenchman named Peter Jacob Guerard received a two-year patent on "a Pendulum Engine, which doth much better, and in lesse time and labour, huske rice; than any other [that] heretofore hath been used within this Province," but there is no indication that the device itself succeeded, or that it helped to spur further invention as hoped (*Statutes*, II, 63). Guerard came to South Carolina in April 1680 aboard the *Richmond* with a group of French Huguenots. He was a goldsmith by trade and served as collector of the port in 1696 (*South Carolina Historical and Genealogical Magazine*, XLIII (Jan., 1942), 9–11). His pendulum device may have been nothing more than a pestle attached to the limb of a tree so that it would swing back up after each stroke into the mortar below.

was a staple in the western rain-forest regions long before Portuguese and French navigators introduced Asian and American varieties of *O. sativa* in the 1500s. By the seventeenth and eighteenth centuries, West Africans were selling rice to slave traders to provision their ships. The northernmost English factory on the coast, James Fort in the Gambia River, was in a region where rice was grown in paddies along the riverbanks (Herskovits 1930; Donnan 1930–1935: I; Grant 1968: 24–25). In the Congo-Angola region, which was the southernmost area of call for English slavers, a white explorer once noted rice to be so plentiful there as to bring almost no price (Grant 1968: 24–25; Parrish 1942: 227n.).

The most significant rice region, however, was the "Windward Coast," the area upwind or westward from the major Gold Coast trading station of Elmina. An Englishman who spent time in Sierra Leone on the Windward Coast at the end of the eighteenth century claimed that rice "forms the chief part of the African's sustenance." He went on to observe, "The rice-fields or *lugars* are prepared during the dry season, and the seed sown in the tornado season, requiring about four or five months growth to bring it to perfection" (Corry 1968 [1807]: 37; cf. Fyfe 1964: 20, 29, 77). Throughout the era of slave importation into South Carolina references can be found concerning African familiarity with rice. Ads in the local papers occasionally made note of slaves from rice-growing areas (Donnan, I: 375, 377–80, 413, 428, 438, 442. See also Mannix and Cowley 1962, opp. 146), and a notice from the *Evening Gazette*, July 11, 1785, announced the arrival aboard a Danish ship of "a choice cargo of windward and gold coast negroes, who have been accustomed to the planting of rice."[11]

[11] The most dramatic evidence of experience with rice among enslaved Africans comes from the famous rebels aboard the *Amistad* in the nineteenth century. Thirty-six slaves from the Sierra Leone region were shipped illegally from Lomboko to Cuba, and in the wake of their successful shipboard uprising they eventually found themselves imprisoned in New Haven. There they were interrogated separately, and excerpts from the interviews drive home this familiarity with rice in personal terms:

> He was a blacksmith in his native village, and made hoes, axes and knives; he also planted rice.
>
> There are high mountains in his country, rice is cultivated, people have guns; has seen elephants.
>
> He was caught in the bush by four men as he was going to plant rice; his left hand was tied to his neck; was ten days going to Lomboko.
>
> He was seized by four men when in a rice field, and was two weeks in traveling to Lomboko.
>
> He is a planter of rice.
>
> His parents are dead, and he lived with his brother, a planter of rice.
>
> He was seized by two men as he was going to plant rice.
>
> 5 ft. 1 in. high, body tattoed, teeth filed, was born at Fe-baw, in Sando, between Mendi and Konno. His mother's brother sold him for a coat. He was taken in the night, and sold to Garlobá, who had four wives. He staid with this man two years, and was employed in cultivating rice. His master's wives and children were employed in the same manner, and no distinction made in regard to labor (Barber 1969 [1840]: 9–15).

Those Africans who were accustomed to growing rice on one side of the Atlantic, and who found themselves raising the same crop on the other side, did not markedly alter their annual routine. When New World slaves planted rice in the spring by pressing a hole with the heel and covering the seeds with the foot, the motion used was demonstrably similar to that employed in West Africa (Herskovits 1937: opp. 100; Bascom 1941: 49). In summer, when Carolina blacks moved through the rice fields in a row, hoeing in unison to work songs, the pattern of cultivation was not one imposed by European owners but rather one retained from West African forebears (Bascom 1941: 45; Glassie 1968: 117). And in October, when the threshed grain was "fanned" in the wind, the wide flat winnowing baskets were made by black hands after an African design (Huggins, Kilson, Fox 1971: opp. 128; Herskovits 1958: 147).

Those familiar with growing and harvesting rice must also have known how to process it, so it is interesting to speculate about the origins of the mortar and pestle technique which became the accepted method for removing rice grains from their husks. Efforts by Europeans to develop alternative "engines" proved of no avail, and this process remained the most efficient way to "clean" the rice crop throughout the colonial period. Since some form of the mortar and pestle is familiar to agricultural peoples throughout the world, a variety of possible (and impossible) sources have been suggested for this device (Glassie 1968: 116–17). But the most logical origin for this technique is the coast of Africa, for there was a strikingly close resemblance between the traditional West African means of pounding rice and the process used by slaves in South Carolina. Several Negroes, usually women, cleaned the grain a small amount at a time by putting it in a wooden mortar which was hollowed from the upright trunk of a pine or cypress. It was beaten with long wooden pestles which had a sharp edge at one end for removing the husks and a flat tip at the other for whitening the grains. Even the songs sung by the slaves who threshed and pounded the rice may have retained African elements (Herskovits 1958: 147; Parrish 1942: 13, 225–33, plates 7 and 8).

In the establishment of rice cultivation, as in numerous other areas, historians have ignored the possibility that Afro-Americans could have contributed anything more than menial labor to South Carolina's early development. Yet Negro slaves, faced with limited food supplies before 1700 and encouraged to raise their own subsistence, could readily have succeeded in nurturing rice where their masters had failed. It would not have taken many such incidents to demonstrate to the anxious English that rice was a potential staple and that Africans were its most logical cultivators and processors. Some such chain of events may even have provided the background for Edward Randolph's report to the Lords of Trade in 1700 that Englishmen in Carolina had "now found out the true way of raising and husking Rice" (BPRO Trans., IV, 189–90). Needless to say, by no means every slave entering South Carolina had been drawn from an African rice field, and many, perhaps even a great majority, had never seen a rice plant. But it is important to consider the fact that literally hundreds of black immigrants were more familiar with the planting, hoeing, processing, and cooking of rice than were the European settlers who purchased them.

Despite the usefulness of all such African skills to the colony's development, there existed a reverse side to the coin. While it is clear that Negro South Carolinians made early contributions to the regional culture, it is also clear that they received little recompense for their participation and that they were bound to respond to this fact. Slaves quickly proved that the same abilities which benefitted Europeans, such as gathering herbs and guiding canoes, could also be used to oppose and threaten them. The connection between black expertise and black resistance, suggested by the story of Harry's skill in protecting a fort against white soldiers, can be illustrated in a number of areas.

The raising of livestock provides a case in point. As cattle and hog production grew, it provided numerous whites with the substance for increasing their holdings in Negroes (Salley 1911: 172), and European observers marvelled at this growth (Nairne 1710: 13). Slaves, on the other hand, benefitted little from this enterprise in which they were involved. Consequently they began to utilize their skills to the disadvantage of the white society. Negroes often helped themselves to the livestock which they tended, and the regulations for branding stock which were introduced by the government before 1700 did little to deter this practice. Slaves altered brands with such dexterity that in the Negro Act of 1722 their owners denied them the right to keep and breed any horses, cows, or hogs whatsoever (*Statutes* II, 106; VII, 382). Nevertheless, livestock rustling by Negroes continued, and in 1743 the Assembly was obliged to draft "An Act to prevent Stealing of Horses and Neat Cattle," which went so far as to declare, "it shall not be lawfull hereafter for any Slave whatsoever to brand or mark any horses or neat Cattle but in the Presence of some white Person under the penalty of being severely whip[p]ed" (*Statutes* III, 604; cf. IV, 285 (1768)).

A law passed the following year required that Negro ferrymen, suspected of transporting fellow slaves, were to be accompanied by a freeman at all times (*Statutes* III, 626; ix, 72 (1731)). By then it had been apparent for decades that the skills of black boatmen could be a liability as well as a source of profit to white colonists. As early as 1696 an act had been passed, patterned on laws already in force in the West Indies, which threatened any slave who "shall take away or let loose any boat or canoe" with thirty-nine lashes for the first offense and loss of an ear for repetition (*Statutes* II, 105. See Higham for a similar law on Antigua). Related acts in the eighteenth century prohibited unfree Negroes from owning or using any boat or canoe without authorization (*Statutes* VII, 368 (1714), 382 (1722), 409–10 (1740)). Such repeated legislation underscores the fact that slaves who were involved in building and manning these boats inevitably found occasions to use them for travel or escape.

Among the Negroes whose seamanship was most valuable and also most problematical for whites were those who served aboard Charleston pilot boats or were otherwise knowledgeable in local navigation. The possibility that slaves would make such strategic skills available to an international rival was always a source of concern for English settlers. There was alarm, for example, during hostilities with Spain in 1741 when the Negroes from Thomas Poole's pilot boat were carried to St. Augustine by a Spanish privateer (*Journal of the Commons House of Assembly, 1741–1742*, 272). At that time colonists were well aware that for several decades Bermuda had suffered serious depradations from Spanish vessels piloted by Bermuda Negroes who had defected (Wilkinson 1950: 112; cf. Wood: 350). Four years later a slave named Arrah was seized from Hugh Cartwright's schooner and "great encouragement was offered to be given him by the enemy if he would join with them against the English, and assist them as a pilot for . . . Carolina." When he stoutly refused and succeeded in making his way back to Charleston after several years, the grateful Assembly granted him his freedom by a special act (*Statutes* VII, 419–20).

Black knowledge of herbs and poisons was the most vivid reminder that Negro expertise could be a two-edged sword. In West Africa, the obeah-men and others with the herbal know-how to combat poisoning could inflict it as well, and this gave slaves a weapon against their new white masters. In Jamaica, poisoning was a commonplace means of black resistance in the eighteenth century, and incidents were also familiar in the mainland colonies (Patterson 1967: 265–66; Mullin 1972). In South Carolina the administering of poison by a slave was made a felony in the stiff Negro Act of 1740 which followed in the wake of the Stono Rebellion (*Statutes* VII, 402). Eleven years later an additional law was written, stating that "the detestable crime of poisoning hath of late been frequently committed by many slaves in this Province, and notwithstanding the execution of several criminals for that offence, yet it has not been sufficient to deter others from being guilty of the same" (*Statutes* VII, 422–23).

The statute of 1751 suggests the seriousness with which white legislators viewed the poisoning threat, for they attempted belatedly to root out longstanding Negro knowledge and administration of medicinal drugs. It was enacted, "That in case any slave shall teach or instruct another slave in the knowledge of any poisonous root, plant, herb, or other poison whatever, he or she, so offending, shall, upon conviction thereof, suffer death as a felon; and the slave or slaves so taught or instructed" were to receive a lesser punishment. "And to prevent, as much as may be, all slaves from attaining the knowledge of any mineral or vegetable poison," the act went on, "it shall not be lawful for any physician, apothecary or druggist, at any time hereafter, to employ any slave or slaves in the shops or places where they keep their medicines or drugs." Finally, the act provided that "no negroes or other slaves (commonly called doctors,) shall hereafter be suffered or permitted to administer any medicine, or pretended medicine, to any other slave; but at the instance or by the direction of some white person." Any Negro disobeying this law was subject to the most severe whipping which the colony's Assembly ever prescribed. Yet even this strict legislation was apparently not enough to suppress such resistance, for in 1761 the

Gazette reported that "The negroes have again begun the hellish practice of poisoning" (*S. C. Gazette*, January 17, 1761; Aptheker 1969: 143–44; Marburg and Crawford 1802: 430).

The matter of poisoning was discussed at length in a letter which Alexander Garden (the Charleston physician after whom Linnaeus named the gardenia) sent to Charles Alston, his former teacher in Edinburgh, in 1756 (Waring 1964: 225–26). Garden stated his candid belief that while some masters had been "actually poisoned by their slaves," numerous other deaths were listed as poisonings by local doctors as a device to "screen their own ignorance." Nevertheless, actual instances of poisoning intrigued him, and he put forward a scheme "To examine the nature of vegetable poisons in general." Garden took most seriously the implications that black proficiency derived from Africa. He requested from Alston, "assistance in giving me what information you could about the African Poisons, as I greatly and do still suspect that the Negroes bring their knowledge of the poisonous plants, which they use here, with them from their own country." He even went so far as to state explicitly that it was part of his plan, "To investigate the nature of particular poisons (chiefly those indigenous in this province and Africa)." But his scheme was of little avail at a time when European knowledge of African flora was still so limited.

Europeans entering South Carolina did not anticipate black skills or the uses to which they might be put. Indeed, most were ignorant of the environment they entered and of the labor they purchased. But white settlers soon realized that African workers possessed expertise which could be exploited and knowledge which was to be feared. Within several generations, the Europeans had imparted aspects of their culture to the slaves and had themselves acquired practical knowledge in matters such as ricegrowing (Corry 1968 [1807], 65–66). Consequently, Negro skills rapidly lost distinctiveness during the middle decades of the eighteenth century. By that time, however, black South Carolinians had already contributed significantly to the colony's initial growth, and ironically these early contributions, although threatening at times, served to strengthen rather than to weaken the European rationale for perpetuating an African labor force. A full generation before the American Revolution, race slavery had become a firmly established institution in the region, and white patterns of exploitation and fear were destined to run their lengthy course.

REFERENCES

1775 *American Husbandry*. London. (Reprinted in Aubrey C. Land.)

Aptheker, Herbert
1969 *American Negro Slave Revolts*. 2nd ed. New York.

Baker, H. G.
1962 "Comments on the thesis that there was a major centre of plant domestication near the headwaters of the River Niger." *Journal of African History* 3: 229–34.

Barber, John Warner
1840 *A History of the Amistad Captives*. New Haven. (Reprinted, New York, 1969.)

Barnwell, J.
1898 *Virginia Magazine of History and Biography*, VI (July): 44–45.

Bascom, William R.
1941 "Acculturation among the Gullah Negroes." *American Anthropologist* XLIII: 43–50.

Batutah, Ibn (Muhammed ibn abd Allah)
1929 *Travels in Asia and Africa, 1325–1354*. Translated and selected by H. A. R. Gibb. London.

Boschi, Charles
1949 To S. P. G. Secretary, Oct. 20, 1745. *South Carolina Historical and Genealogical Magazine* L (October): 185.

Brenton, R. P. Raymond
1892 *Dictionnaire Caraibe-Francais, 1665*. (Reprinted, Leipzig, 1892.)

Brickell, John
1737 *The Natural History of North-Carolina*. London. (Reprinted, Raleigh, 1911.)

Burton, E. Milby
1955 *Charleston Furniture, 1700–1825*. Charleston.

Cassidy, Frederic G.
1967 "Some New Light on Old Jamaicanisms." *American Speech* XLII: 191–92.

Catesby, Mark
1743 *The Natural History of Carolina, Florida and the Bahama Islands*. London.

Channing, Edward
1886 "The Narragansett Planters." Johns Hopkins University Studies in Historical and Political Science, Series 4, No. 3. Baltimore.

Clark, J. D.
1962 "The spread of food production in Sub-Saharan Africa." *Journal of African History* 3: 211–28.

Clontes, F. W.
1926 "Travel and Transportation in Colonial North Carolina." *North Carolina Historical Review* III (January): 16–35.

Clowse, Converse D.
1971 *Economic Beginnings in Colonial South Carolina, 1670–1730*. Columbia.

Conner, Jeanette Thurber, trans. and ed.
1930 *Colonial Records of Spanish Florida* III (June 4, 1580). Deland, Florida.

Cooper, Thomas and David J. McCord, eds.
1836–1841 *The Statutes at Large of South Carolina*. 10 vols. Columbia.

Corry, Joseph
1807 *Observations upon the Windward Coast of Africa.* London. (Reprinted, London, 1968.)

Crum, Mason
1940 *Gullah: Negro Life in the Carolina Sea Islands.* Durham, North Carolina.

Curtin, Philip D.
1968 "Epidemiology and the slave trade." *Political Science Quarterly* LXXXIII (June): 119–216.

Donnan, Elizabeth, ed.
1930–1935 *Documents Illustrative of the Slave Trade to America.* Washington.

Dunbar, Gary S.
1961 "Colonial Carolina Cowpens." *Agricultural History* XXXV: 125–30.

Duncan, John D.
1972 "Slave emancipation in colonial South Carolina." *American Chronical, A Magazine of History* I (January): 64–66.

Dundes, Alan
1965 "African Tales among the North American Indians." *Southern Folklore Quarterly* 29 (September): 207–19.

Fisher, Miles Mark
1953 *Negro slave songs in the United States.* New York.

Fyfe, Christopher
1964 *Sierra Leone inheritance.* London.

Glassie, Henry
1968 "Patterns in the Material Folk Culture of the Eastern United States." University of Pennsylvania Monographs in Folklore and Folklife, No. 1. Philadelphia.

Glen, James
1761 *A Description of South Carolina.* London. (Reprinted in Chapman J. Milling, ed., *Colonial South Carolina: Two Contemporary Descriptions.* Columbia, 1951.)

Grant, Douglas
1968 *The Fortunate Slave, An Illustration of African Slavery in the Early Eighteenth Century.* London.

Gray, Lewis Cecil
1933 *History of Agriculture in the Southern United States to 1860.* Washington.

Hakluyt, Richard
1904 *The Principal Navigations, Voyages, Traffiques & Discoveries of the English Nation,* X. Glasgow.

Herskovits, Melville J.
1930 "The culture areas of Africa." *Africa* III: 67–73.
1937 *Life in a Haitian Valley.* New York.
1941 *The Myth of the Negro Past.* Boston.

Heyward, Duncan Clinch
1937 *Seed from Madagascar.* Chapel Hill.

Higham, C. S. S.
1921 *The Development of the Leeward Islands, 1660–1688.* Cambridge, England.
Hudson, Charles M., ed.
1971 "Red, White, and Black, Symposium on Indians in the Old South." Southern Anthropological Society, *Proceedings,* No. 5. Athens, Georgia.
Huggins, Nathan I., Martin Kilson, Daniel M. Fox, eds.
1971 *Key Issues in the Afro-American Experience.* New York.
Journal of the Commons House of Assembly, 1726–1727.
Land, Aubrey C.
1969 *Bases of the Plantation Society.* Columbia.
Lawson, John
1709 *A New Voyage to Carolina.* London. (Republished with introduction and notes by Hugh Talmage Lefler, Chapel Hill, 1967.)
Lévi-Strauss, Claude
1966 *The Savage Mind.* London.
McCall, Daniel F.
1964 *Africa in Time-Perspective.* Boston.
McCrady, Edward
1899 *The History of South Carolina Under the Royal Government, 1719–1776.* New York.
McKusick, Marshall B.
1960 "Aboriginal canoes in the West Indies," in Sidney W. Mintz (comp.), *Papers in Caribbean Anthropology.* Yale University Publications in Anthropology, No. 57. New Haven.
McPherson, et al., eds.
1971 "African cultural survivals among Black Americans," in *Blacks in America: Bibliographical Essays.* Garden City.
Mannix, Daniel P. and Malcolm Cowley
1962 *Black Cargoes: A History of the Atlantic Slave Trade, 1518–1865.* New York.
Marburg, H. and W. H. Crawford
1802 *Digest of the Laws of Georgia.* Savannah.
Mathews, Mitford
1938–1944 *A Dictionary of American English.* Chicago.
Montlzun, Baron de
1948 "A Frenchman Visits Charleston, 1817." *South Carolina Historical and Genealogical Magazine* XLIX (July): 136.
Morgan, W. B.
1962 "The forest and agriculture in West Africa." *Journal of African History* 3: 235–40.
Mullin, Gerald W.
1972 *Flight and Rebellion: Slave Resistance in Eighteenth-Century Virginia.* New York.
Nairne, Thomas
1710 A Letter from South Carolina. London.

Parrish, Lydia
1942 *Slave Songs of the Georgia Sea Islands.* New York.

Patterson, Orlando
1967 *The Sociology of Slavery, An Analysis of the Origins, Development and Structure of Negro Society in Jamaica.* London.

Pemberton, James, *Diary of a trip to South Carolina, 1745*, entry for October 17, original in Library of Congress, mfm. in South Caroliniana Library, Columbia.

Platt, Virginia Bever
1969 "The East India Company and the Madagascar slave trade." *William and Mary Quarterly*, 3rd ser., XXVI (October): 548–77.

Price, Richard
1968 "Caribbean fishing and fishermen: a historical sketch." *American Anthropologist* LXVIII: 1363–83.

Quigley, Carroll
1956 "Aboriginal fish poisons and the diffusion problem." *American Anthropologist* LVIII: 508–25.

Raynal, Abbé
1798 *Philosophical and Political History of the Possessions and Trade of Europeans in the Two Indies.* 2nd ed. London.

Records of the British Public Record Office Relating to South Carolina, 36 vols. (1663–1782). (In the South Carolina Department of Archives and History.)

Salley, Alexander S., ed.
1911 *Narratives of Early Carolina, 1650–1708.* New York.
1919 "The Introduction of Rice Culture into South Carolina" (Bulletins of the Historical Commission of South Carolina, No. 6). Columbia.
1944 *Records* of the Secretary of the Province and the Register of the Province of South Carolina, 1671–1675. Columbia.

Schaw, Janet
1922 *Journal of a Lady of Quality*, edited by Evangeline W. Andrews and Charles M. Andrews. New Haven.

Smith, Alice R. Huger
1936 *A Carolina Rice Plantation of the Fifties.* New York.

South Carolina Historical Society, *Collections*, in the South Carolina Department of Archives and History.

Sutherland, James
Undated letter in the Coe Papers (Documents of the Lords Commissioners, 1719–1742.) South Carolina Historical Society.

Thibou, Louis
Letter in French dated September 20, 1683 and typescript translation in the South Caroliniana Library, Columbia.

Turberville, A. S.
1929 *English Men and Manners in the Eighteenth Century.* 2nd ed. London.

Vansina, Jan
1971 "Once upon a time: oral traditions as history in Africa." *Daedalus* C (Spring): 442–68.

Waring, Joseph I.
1964 *A History of Medicine in South Carolina, 1670–1825*. Charleston.

Wax, Darold D.
1968 "A Philadelphia surgeon on a slaving voyage to Africa, 1749–1751." *Pennsylvania Magazine of History and Biography* XCII (October): 474–78.

Webber, Mabel L., comp.
1914 "South Carolina Almanacs, to 1800." *South Carolina Historical and Genealogical Magazine* XV (April): 78.

Weston, P. C. J., ed.
1856 Documents Connected with the History of South Carolina. London.

Whitten, Norman E., Jr., and John F. Szwed
1970 *Afro-American Anthropology: Contemporary Perspectives*. New York.

Wilkinson, Henry C.
1950 *Bermuda in the Old Empire*. London.

Wills, Inventories and Miscellaneous Records, in the South Carolina Department of Archives and History.

Wood, Peter H.
1972 "Black majority: Negroes in colonial South Carolina from 1670 through the Stono Rebellion." Ph. D. dissertation, Harvard University.

White Servitude

RICHARD HOFSTADTER

Though African slavery was to become the most important form of unfree labor in North America in the eighteenth and nineteenth centuries, during the first hundred years of English colonization the labor force was primarily made up of indentured servants from England—men, women, and children who sold themselves into temporary bondage in return for passage to the New World. It is estimated that from one-half to three-fourths of the immigrants to the English colonies in the seventeenth century fit into this category.

In view of the many hazards faced by New World settlers, the reluctance of prosperous tradesmen or skilled craftsmen to journey from Europe to North America is understandable. The three thousand miles that separated it from England, the strangeness of the land, and the danger of conflict with the Indians made the attraction of the New World slight for those with any degree of comfort in the old. Apart from a few daring speculators, most of the prosperous immigrants were men seeking religious freedom. Most of these immigrants settled in New England and Pennsylvania.

There was, however, a great demand for new population in America. Laborers were needed to grow food for the colonists and to develop commerce. Moreover, additional manpower was needed to defend the settlements against increasingly hostile Indians as well as against the French and the Spanish.

Fortunately for the development of the colonies, several conditions made labor available. First, there was a growing surplus of population in England. Farmland, which had hitherto been divided into individually owned strips and farmed communally, was increasingly consolidated into large tracts of land, thereby forcing the English peasants either to become tenant farmers or to look for new means of livelihood. Industrialization, which might have absorbed these landless peasants, was more than a century away, and city life held little promise for them. Many turned to indentured servitude in the colonies as a solution to their problems, to the relief of both England and

America. Other servants came to the colonies as a result of the civil wars in the British Isles during the seventeenth century. James I, Oliver Cromwell, and the later Stuart kings sent Scottish and Irish prisoners to the colonies—chiefly to the West Indies but also to the North American mainland.

In the following selection, the late Richard Hofstadter describes still other sources of the dependent labor class that grew up in the New World. He also demolishes the myth that these servants, when freed, moved for the most part into the yeoman farmer class.

Except during brief periods of recession, the shortage of labor in the colonies and then in the United States continued until the enormous mid-nineteenth-century influx of poor Irish and German immigrants. Skilled labor was always scarcer, and craftsmen were among the most favored of immigrants.

1

The transportation to the English colonies of human labor, a very profitable but also a very perishable form of merchandise, was one of the big businesses of the eighteenth century. Most of this labor was unfree. There was, of course, a sizable corps of free hired laborers in the colonies, often enjoying wages two or three times those prevalent in the mother country. But never at any time in the colonial period was there a sufficient supply of voluntary labor, paying its own transportation and arriving masterless and free of debt, to meet the insatiable demands of the colonial economy. The solution, found long before the massive influx of black slaves, was a combined force of merchants, ship captains, immigrant brokers, and a variety of hard-boiled recruiting agents who joined in bringing substantial cargoes of whites who voluntarily or involuntarily paid for their passage by undergoing a terminable period of bondage. This quest for labor, touched off early in the seventeenth century by the circulars of the London Company of Virginia, continued by William Penn in the 1680's and after, and climaxed by the blandishments of various English and continental recruiting agents of the eighteenth century, marked one of the first concerted and sustained advertising campaigns in the history of the modern world.

If we leave out of account the substantial Puritan migration of 1630–40, not less than half, and perhaps considerably more, of all the white immigrants to the colonies were indentured servants, redemptioners, or convicts. Certainly a good many more than half of all persons who went to the colonies south of New England were servants in bondage to planters, farmers, speculators, and proprietors.[1] The tobacco economy of Virginia and Maryland was founded upon the labor of gangs of indentured servants, who were substantially replaced by slaves only during the course of the eighteenth century. "The planters' fortunes here," wrote the governor of Maryland in 1755, "consist in the number of their servants (who are purchased at high rates) much as the estates of an English farmer do in the multitude of cattle." Everywhere indentured servants were used, and almost everywhere outside New England they were vital to the economy. The labor of the colonies, said Benjamin Franklin in 1759, "is performed chiefly by indentured servants brought from Great Britain, Ireland, and Germany, because the high price it bears cannot be performed in any other way."[2]

Indentured servitude had its roots in the widespread poverty and human dislocation of seventeenth-century England. Still a largely backward economy with a great part of its population permanently unemployed, England was moving toward more modern methods in industry and agriculture; yet in the short run some of the improvements greatly added to the unemployed. Drifting men and women gathered in the cities, notably London, where they constituted a large mass of casual workers, lumpenproletarians, and criminals. The mass of the poverty-stricken was so large that Gregory King, the pioneer statistician, estimated in 1696 that more than half the population—cottagers and paupers, laborers and outservants—were earning less than they spent. They diminished the wealth of the realm, he argued, since their annual expenses exceeded income and had to be made up by the poor rates, which ate up one-half of the revenue of the Crown.[3] In the early seventeenth century, this situation made people believe the country was overpopulated and emigration to the colonies was welcomed; but in the latter part of the century, and in the next, the overpopulation theory gave way to the desire to hoard a satisfactory labor surplus. Yet the strong outflow of population did not by any means cease. From the large body of poor drifters, many of them diseased, feckless, or given to crime, came a great part of the labor supply of the rich sugar islands and the American mainland. From the London of Pepys and then of Hogarth, as well as from many lesser ports and inland towns, the English poor, lured, seduced, or forced into the emigrant stream, kept coming to America for the better part of two centuries. It is safe to guess that few of them, and indeed few persons from the other sources of emigration, knew very much about what they were doing when they committed themselves to life in America.

Yet the poor were well aware that they lived in a heartless world. One of the horrendous figures in the folklore of lower-class London in

[1] Abbott E. Smith, *Colonists in Bondage* (1947), 3–4; Richard B. Morris, *Government and Labor in Colonial America* (1946), 315–16.

[2] Smith, 27; M. W. Jernegan, *Laboring and Dependent Classes in Colonial America* (1931), 55; see also K. F. Geiser, *Redemptioners and Indentured Servants in . . . Pennsylvania* (1901), 24–5.

[3] Christopher Hill, *The Century of Revolution* (1961), 206.

the seventeenth and eighteenth centuries was the "spirit"–the recruiting agent who waylaid, kidnapped, or induced adults to get aboard ship for America. The spirits, who worked for respectable merchants, were known to lure children with sweets, to seize upon the weak or the gin-sodden and take them aboard ship, and to bedazzle the credulous or weak-minded by fabulous promises of an easy life in the New World. Often their victims were taken roughly in hand and, pending departure, held in imprisonment either on shipboard or in low-grade hostels or brothels. To escaped criminals and other fugitives who wanted help in getting out of the country, the spirits could appear as ministering angels. Although efforts were made to regulate or check their activities, and they diminished in importance in the eighteenth century, it remains true that a certain small part of the white colonial population of America was brought by force, and a much larger portion came in response to deceit and misrepresentation on the part of the spirits.

With the beginnings of substantial emigration from the Continent in the eighteenth century the same sort of concerted business of recruitment arose in Holland, the Rhenish provinces of Germany, and Switzerland. In Rotterdam and Amsterdam the lucrative business of gathering and transshipping emigrants was soon concentrated in the hands of a dozen prominent English and Dutch firms. As competition mounted, the shippers began to employ agents to greet the prospective emigrants at the harbor and vie in talking up the comforts of their ships. Hence the recruiting agents known as *Neülander*–newlanders–emerged. These newlanders, who were paid by the head for the passengers they recruited, soon branched out of the Dutch ports and the surrounding countryside and moved up the Rhine and the Neckar, traveling from one province to another, from town to town and tavern to tavern, all the way to the Swiss cantons, often passing themselves off as rich men returned from the easy and prosperous life of America in order to persuade others to try to repeat their good fortune. These confidence men–"soul sellers" as they were sometimes called–became the continental counterparts of the English spirits, profiteers in the fate of the peasantry and townspeople of the Rhineland. Many of the potential emigrants stirred up by the promises of the newlanders were people of small property who expected, by selling some part of their land or stock or furnishings, to be able to pay in full for their passage to America and to arrive as freemen. What the passage would take out of them in blood and tears, not to speak of cash, was carefully hidden from them. They gathered in patient numbers at Amsterdam and Rotterdam often quite innocent of the reality of what had already become for thousands of Englishmen one of the terrors of the age –the Atlantic crossing.

2

In 1750 Gottlieb Mittelberger, a simple organist and music master in the Duchy of Württemberg, was commissioned to bring an organ to a German congregation in New Providence, Pennsylvania, and his journey inspired him to write a memorable account of an Atlantic crossing. From Heilbronn, where he picked up his organ, Mittelberger went the well-traveled route along the Neckar and the Rhine to Rotterdam, whence he sailed to a stopover at Cowes in England, and then to Philadelphia. About four hundred passengers were crowded onto the ship, mainly German and Swiss redemptioners, men pledged to work off their passage charges. The trip from his home district to Rotterdam took seven weeks, the voyage from Rotterdam to Philadelphia fifteen weeks, the entire journey from May to October.

What moved Mittelberger, no literary man, to write of his experiences was first his indignation against the lies and misrepresentations used by the newlanders to lure his fellow Germans to America, and then the hideous shock of the crossing. The voyage proved excruciating and there is no reason to think it particularly unusual. The long trip down the Rhine, with constant stops at the three dozen customs houses between Heilbronn and Holland, began to consume the limited funds of the travelers, and it was followed by an expensive stop of several weeks in Holland. Then there was the voyage at sea, with the passengers packed like herring and cramped in the standard bedsteads measuring two feet by six. "During the journey," wrote Mittelberger, "the ship is full of pitiful signs of distress–smells, fumes, horrors, vomiting, various kinds of sea sickness, fever, dysentery, headaches, heat, constipation, boils, scurvy, cancer, mouth-rot, and similar afflictions, all of them caused by the age and the highly salted state of the food, especially of the meat, as well as by the very bad and filthy water, which brings about the miserable destruction and death of many. Add to all that shortage of food, hunger, thirst, frost, heat, dampness, fear, misery, vexation, and lamentation as well as other troubles. Thus, for example, there are so many lice, especially on the sick people, that they have to be scraped off the bodies. All this misery reached its climax when in addition to everything else one must suffer through two or three days and nights of storm, with everyone convinced that the ship with all aboard is bound to sink. In such misery all the people on board pray and cry pitifully together."[4]

Even those who endured the voyage in good health, Mittelberger reported, fell out of temper and turned on each other with reproaches. They cheated and stole. "But most of all they cry out against the thieves of human beings! Many groan and exclaim: 'Oh! If only I were back at home, even lying in my pig-sty!' Or they call out: 'Ah, dear God, if I only once again had a piece of good bread or a good fresh drop of water.'" It went hardest with women in childbirth and their offspring: "Very few escape with their lives; and mother and child, as soon as they have died, are thrown into the water. On board our ship, on a day on which we had a great storm, a woman about to give birth and unable to deliver under the circumstances, was pushed through one of the portholes into the sea because her corpse was far back in the stern and could not be brought forward to the deck." Children under seven, he thought

[4] For the voyage, Mittelberger, *Journey to Pennsylvania* (edn. 1960), ed. and trans. by Oscar Handlin and John Clive, 10–7.

(though the port records show him wrong here), seldom survived, especially those who had not already had measles and smallpox, and their parents were condemned to watch them die and be tossed overboard. The sick members of families infected the healthy, and in the end all might be lying moribund. He believed disease was so prevalent because warm food was served only three times a week, and of that very little, very bad, very dirty, and supplemented by water that was often "very black, thick with dirt, and full of worms . . . towards the end of the voyage we had to eat the ship's biscuit, which had already been spoiled for a long time, even though no single piece was there more than the size of a thaler that was not full of red worms and spiders' nests."

The first sight of land gave heart to the passengers, who came crawling out of the hatches to get a glimpse of it. But then for many a final disappointment lay in wait: only those who could complete the payment of their fare could disembark. The others were kept on board until they were bought, some of them sickening within sight of land and, as they sickened, losing the chance of being bought on good terms. On landing some families were broken, when despairing parents indentured their children to masters other than their own.

Not even passengers of means who paid their way, moved more or less freely about ship, occupied cabins or small dormitories, and had superior rations could take an Atlantic crossing lightly. In addition to the hazards of winds too feeble or too violent, of pirates, shipwrecks, or hostile navies, there were under the best of circumstances the dangers of sickness. Travelers in either direction frequently died of smallpox or other diseases on board or soon after arrival. Anglican colonials often complained of the high mortality rate among their young would-be clergymen crossing to England to be ordained. The Dutch Reformed preacher Theodorus Frelinghuysen lost three of his five sons on their way to be ordained in Amsterdam. The evangelist George Whitefield on his first crossing to the colonies in 1738 saw a majority of the soldiers on board afflicted with fever and spent much of his time "for many days and nights, visiting between twenty and thirty sick persons, crawling between decks upon his knees, administering medicines and cordials" and giving comfort. On this voyage the captain's Negro servant died, was wrapped in a hammock and tossed into the sea. In the end all but a handful of the passengers took the fever, including Whitefield, who survived treatment by bleeding and emetics. The ship on which he returned a few months later was afflicted by a "contrary wind," drifted for over a week to the point at which crew and passengers were uncertain where they were, and took so long to arrive at Ireland that water rations, which had been cut to a pint a day, were just about to run out.[5]

When paying passengers were exposed to such afflictions, how much worse must have been the sufferings of the servants and redemptioners packed into the holds, frequently at a density that violated the laws, and without adequate ventilation. Food provisions were calculated to last

[5] Quoted in Luke Tyerman, *The Life of the Rev. George Whitefield* (1876), I, 124–5, 144–5.

fourteen weeks, which was normally sufficient, but the rations deteriorated rapidly, especially in summer. Water turned stale, butter turned rancid, and beef rotted. If Mittelberger's voyage ranked among the worst, Atlantic crossings were frequently at or near the worst, and many more disastrous ventures were recorded.[6] With bad luck, provisions could give out. The *Love and Unity* left Rotterdam for Philadelphia in May 1731 with more than 150 Palatines and a year later landed with 34, after having put in toward the end at Martha's Vineyard for water and food. On the way rations became so low that water, rats, and mice were being *sold*, and the storage chests of the dead and dying were broken open and plundered by the captain and crew. A ship called the *Good Intent*—the names of eighteenth century vessels often reek with irony—arrived off the American coast in the winter of 1751 but found herself unable to make port because of the weather; she was able to put in to harbor in the West Indies only after twenty-four weeks at sea. Nearly all of the passengers had died long before. The *Sea Flower*, which left Belfast with 106 passengers in 1741, was at sea sixteen weeks, and lost 46 passengers from starvation. When help arrived, six of the corpses had been cannibalized.

It is true that given adequate ventilation, a stock of lemon juice and vegetables, and good luck with the winds, decent sanitary arrangements were possible. The philanthropic Georgia Trustees, who were concerned about the health of their colonists, "put on board turnips, carrots, potatoes, and onions, which were given out with the salt meat, and contributed greatly to prevent the scurvy." Out of some fifteen hundred people who had gone to Georgia at the public expense, it was claimed in 1741, not more than six had died in transit. A traveler to Jamaica in 1739 reported that the servants on his ship "had lived so easily and well during the voyage, that they looked healthful, clean and fresh, and for this reason were soon sold," yet he saw another vessel arrive not long afterward with "a multitude of poor starved creatures, that seemed so many skeletons: misery appeared in their looks, and one might read the effects of sea-tyranny by their wild and dejected countenances."[7]

3

The situation in which the indentured servant or the redemptioner found himself upon his arrival depended in large measure upon his physical condition. There would be a last-minute effort to clean up and appear presentable, and in some ports the healthy were separated from the sick, once colonial officials adopted quarantine measures. Boston, the most vigilant of the ports, had long kept a pesthouse on an island in the harbor and fined captains who disregarded the regulations. "As Christians and men," the governor of Pennsylvania urged in 1738, "we are obliged to make a charitable provision for the sick stranger, and not by confining

[6] See Geiser, chapter v; F. R. Diffenderfer, *German Immigration into Pennsylvania* . . . (1900), chapter v, esp. 63–7.

[7] Smith, 217–8.

him to a ship, inhumanly expose him to fresh miseries when he hopes that his sufferings are soon to be mitigated."[8] Pennsylvania then designated Province Island for quarantine and built a pesthouse to harbor sick immigrants. In 1750 and again in 1765 it passed laws to bar overcrowding on ships. Laws passed by Virginia and Maryland in the 1760's providing for the quarantine of convict ships were frowned upon in London, and Virginia's law was disallowed.

Buyers came on shipboard to take their pick of the salably healthy immigrants, beginning a long process of examination and inspection with the muscles and the teeth, and ending with a conversational search for the required qualities of intelligence, civility, and docility. At Philadelphia buyers might be trying to find Germans and eschew the Scotch-Irish, who were reputed to be contumacious and work resistant and disposed to run away. Some buyers were "soul drivers" who bought packs of immigrants and brutally herded them on foot into the interior where they were offered along the way to ready purchasers. On the ships and at the docks there were final scenes of despair and frenzy as servants searched for lost articles of indenture, or lamented the disappearance of baggage, unexpected overcharges, the necessity of accepting indentures longer than their debts fairly required, the separation of families.

The final crisis of arrival was the process we would call acclimatization, in the eighteenth century known as "seasoning." Particularly difficult in the tropical islands, seasoning also took a heavy toll in the Southern colonies of the mainland. People from cities and from the mild English climate found the summer hard going in any colony from Maryland southward, especially on plantations where indentured servants were put to arduous field labor by owners whose goal it was to get a maximum yield of labor in the four or five years contracted for. Fevers, malaria, and dysentery carried many off, especially in their first years of service. Seasoning was thought to be more or less at an end after one year in the new climate, and servants who had been wholly or partly seasoned were at a premium.

During the voyage, thoughtful servants might have recalled, quite a number of persons had battened on their needs—the spirit or the newlander, the toll collectors and the parasites of the seaports, the ship captain or merchant; now there was the master. Any traffic that gave sustenance to so many profiteers might well rest on a rather intense system of exploitation. A merchant who would spend from six to ten pounds to transport and provision an indentured servant might sell him on arrival—the price varied with age, skill, and physical condition—for fifteen to twenty pounds, although the profits also had to cover losses from sickness and death en route. The typical servant had, in effect, sold his total working powers for four or five years or more in return for his passage plus a promise of minimal maintenance. After the initially small capital outlay, the master simply had to support him from day to day as his services were rendered, support which was reckoned to cost about thirteen or fourteen pounds a year. In Maryland, where exploitation was as intense as any-

[8] Diffenderfer, 82.

where, the annual net yield, even from unskilled labor, was reckoned at around fifty pounds sterling.[9] The chief temptation to the master was to drive the servant beyond his powers in the effort to get as much as possible out of him during limited years of service. The chief risk was that the servant might die early in service before his purchase price had been redeemed by his work. That he might run away was a secondary risk, though one against which the master had considerable protection. Still, hard as white servitude bore on servants, it was nevertheless not always a happy arrangement for owners, especially for those with little capital and little margin for error: shiftless and disagreeable servants, as well as successful runaways, were common enough to introduce a significant element of risk into this form of labor.

Indentured servants lived under a wide variety of conditions, which appear to have softened somewhat during the eighteenth century. Good or bad luck, the disposition of the master, the length of the term of work, the size of the plantation or farm, the robustness or frailty of the worker—all these had a part in determining the fate of each individual. Servants in households or on small farms might be in the not uncomfortable situation of familiar domestic laborers. Tradesmen who were trying to teach special skills to their workers, or householders who wanted satisfactory domestic service, might be tolerable masters. The most unenviable situation was that of servants on Southern plantations, living alongside—but never with—Negro slaves, both groups doing much the same work, often under the supervision of a relentless overseer. One has to imagine the situation of a member of the English urban pauper class, unaccustomed to rural or to any sustained labor, thrust into a hot climate in which heavy field labor—including, worst of all, the backbreaking task of clearing new land of rocks, trees, and shrubs—was his daily lot. Even as late as 1770 William Eddis, the English surveyor of customs at Annapolis, thought that the Maryland Negroes were better off than "the Europeans, over whom the rigid planter exercises an inflexible severity." The Negroes, Eddis thought, were a lifelong property, so were treated with a certain care, but the whites were "strained to the utmost to perform their allotted labour; and, from a prepossession in many cases too justly founded, they were supposed to be receiving only the just reward which is due to repeated offenses. There are doubtless many exceptions to this observation, yet, generally speaking, they groan beneath a worse than Egyptian bondage." Yet in Virginia, as the blacks arrived in greater numbers, white laborers seemed to have become a privileged stratum, assigned to lighter work and more skilled tasks.[10]

The status and reputation of Southern indentured laborers were no doubt kept lower than elsewhere because there were a considerable number of transported convicts among them. Colonies to the north were not completely free of convict transportees, but the plantation system regu-

[9] Raphael Semmes, *Crime and Punishment in Early Maryland* (1938), 80, 278; *cf.* Samuel McKee, Jr., *Labor in Colonial New York* (1935), 111.

[10] William Eddis, *Letters from America* (1777), 69–70; J. C. Ballagh, *White Servitude in the Colony of Virginia* (1895), 89–92.

larly put honest unfortunates alongside hardened criminals and lumped them all together as rogues who deserved no better than what was meted out to them. Among the by-products of English social change of the seventeenth and eighteenth centuries was a very substantial pool of criminal talents. The laws devised to suppress the criminal population were so harsh—scores of crimes were defined as felonies and hanging was a standard punishment for many trivial offenses—that England would have been launched upon mass hangings far beyond the point of acceptability had it not been for two devices that let many accused off the penalties prescribed for felons. One was the benefit of clergy—a practice inherited from the Middle Ages and continued until the early nineteenth century—which permitted a convicted felon to "call for the book" and prove his literacy. On the ancient assumption that those who could read were clerics and thus exempt from severe punishments by the secular state, the relatively privileged class of literate felons could be permitted to escape with the conventional branding on the thumb.

A second practice, the predecessor of convict transportation, was to secure royal pardons for ordinary offenders deemed by the judges to be worthy of some indulgence. Until the end of the French wars in 1713 it was customary to send them into the army, but in peacetime England did not know what to do with felons and drifters. In 1717 Parliament passed an act which in effect made royal clemency contingent upon transportation to the colonies for a term of labor; in consequence the large-scale shipping of convicts began which continued to the time of the American Revolution. To America at large, including the island colonies, around thirty thousand felons were transported in the eighteenth century, of whom probably more than two-thirds reached Virginia and Maryland, where they were readily snapped up by the poorer planters.[11]

The whole procedure, though clearly intended to be a humane and useful alternative to wholesale hangings, was dreadfully feared by convicts, who may have guessed, quite rightly, that whoever bought their services would try to get the most out of them during their seven-year terms (fourteen years in the case of transmuted death penalties) of hard labor. In transit felons probably were fed somewhat better than they were used to, but usually they were kept below deck and in chains during the entire voyage, and on the average perhaps one in six or seven would die on the way. "All the states of horror I ever had an idea of," wrote a visitor to a convict ship, "are much short of what I saw this poor man in; chained to a board in a hole not above sixteen feet long, more than fifty with him; a collar and padlock about his neck, and chained to five of the most dreadful creatures I ever looked on."[12] Mortality could run very high: on one ship, the *Honour*, which arrived in Annapolis in 1720, twenty of the sixty-one convicts had died. Merchants transporting felons on government contracts pleaded for subsidies to cover losses that hit them so hard.

[11] See Smith, 116–9; *cf.* Lawrence H. Gipson, *The British Empire before the American Revolution,* II (1936), 69, 79.

[12] Smith, 125.

While some planters rushed to the seaports to find convicts for their field labor supply, others were disturbed by the effect they expected criminals would have on the character of the population. These hazardous importations caused most anxiety in the colonies that received masses of transported felons. Pennsylvania subjected the importation of convicts to constant statutory harassment after 1722. Virginia at mid-century seems to have thought herself in the midst of a crime wave. The Virginia *Gazette* complained in 1751: "When we see our papers fill'd continually with accounts of the most audacious robberies, the most cruel murders, and infinite other villainies perpetrated by convicts transported from Europe, what melancholy, what terrible reflections it must occasion! What will become of our posterity? These are some of thy favours Britain. Thou art called our Mother Country; but what good mother ever sent thieves and villains to accompany her children; to corrupt some with their infectious vices and murder the rest? What father ever endeavour'd to spread a plague in his family? . . . In what can Britain show a more sovereign contempt for us than by emptying their jails into our settlements; unless they would likewise empty their jakes [privies] on our tables!"[13] The concluding metaphor seems to have come quite naturally to the colonials: Franklin also used it, although he is better remembered for his suggestion that the Americans trade their rattlesnakes for the convicts.[14] But all laws rejecting transported convicts were disallowed in England by the Board of Trade and the Privy Council, while subterfuge measures designed to impede or harass the trade were looked at with suspicion.

4

The system of indenture was an adaptation, with some distinctively harsh features, of the old institution of apprenticeship. In fact, a few native-born colonials, usually to discharge a debt or answer for a crime but sometimes to learn a trade, entered into indentures not altogether unlike those undertaken by immigrants. In law an indenture was a contract in which the servant promised faithful service for a specified period of time in return for his housing and keep and, at the end of his term of work, that small sum of things, known as "freedom dues," which his master promised him upon their parting. The typical term was four or five years, although it might run anywhere from one or two years to seven. Longer terms were commonly specified for children, and were calculated to bring them to freedom at or just past the time they reached majority. Most indentures followed a standard pattern: as early as 1636 printed forms were available, needing only a few details to be filled out by the contracting parties. Often an emigrant's original indenture was made out to a merchant or a ship's captain and was sold with its holder to an employer on arrival. Indentures became negotiable instruments in the colo-

[13] Ibid., 130.

[14] Cheesman A. Herrick, *White Servitude in Pennsylvania* (1926), 131–2.

nies, servants bound under their terms being used to settle debts, even gambling debts. In theory the contract protected the servant from indefinite exploitation, but in practice it had quite limited powers. It was a document vulnerable to loss, theft, or destruction, and when one considers both the fecklessness and inexperience of most indentured servants and the lack of privacy under which they lived, it is little wonder that their contracts often disappeared.

During the eighteenth century, however, circumstances began to alter the prevailing system of indentures and to lessen its severities, particularly when a special class of bonded servants, the redemptioners, became numerous. The redemptioner appeared at the beginning of the century, coming largely from the Continent, often emigrating with a family and with a supply of tools and furnishings. The passengers who traveled with Mittelberger were mostly redemptioners. Indentured servants were simply a part of a ship's cargo, but redemptioners were low-grade, partially paid-up passengers. The redemptioner embarked without an indenture, sometimes having paid part of the money for his own and his family's passage, and arranged with the shipping merchant to complete payment within a short time after landing. Once here, he might try to find relatives or friends to make up his deficit; failure to pay in full meant that he would be sold to the highest bidder to redeem whatever part of his fare was unpaid. The length of his servitude would depend upon the amount to be redeemed. It could be as short as one or two years, although four years seems to have been much more common. Redemptioners would try to go into service as a whole family group. Although redemptioners were often swindled because of their lack of English and were overcharged for interest, insurance, and the transportation of their baggage, it was less profitable to carry them than indentured servants. Still, merchants were eager to fill their ships as full as possible with a ballast of redemptioners.[15]

All bonded servants, indentured and redemptionist, were chattels of their masters, but the terminability of their contracts and the presence of certain legal rights stood between them and slavery. A servant could be freely bought and sold, except in Pennsylvania and New York where laws required the consent of a court before assigning a servant for a year or more. His labor could be rented out; he could be inherited on the terms laid down in his master's will. Yet he could own property, although he was forbidden to engage in trade. He could also sue and be sued, but he could not vote. It was expected that he would be subject to corporal punishment by his master for various offenses, and whipping was common; but a master risked losing his servant on the order of a court for a merciless or disfiguring beating. The right of a servant to petition the courts against abuse was more than a negligible protection. Penniless servants were, of course, at a disadvantage in courts manned by representatives of the master class: in effect they were appealing to the community pride, compassion, or decency of the magistrates, and the sense that there were certain things that ought not be done to a white Christian. Yet the

[15] Smith, 41.

frequency of complaints by servants makes it clear that the prerogative of appeal was widely used, and the frequency of judgments rendered for servants shows that it was not used in vain. No colony recognized the validity of agreements between master and servant made *during* servitude unless both parties appeared before a magistrate and registered their consent. Statutes regulated the terms of servitude in cases in which no papers of indenture existed.

For many thousands of servants their term of indentured servitude was a period of enforced celibacy. Marriage without the consent of the master was illegal, and the crimes of fornication and bastardy figure importantly in the records of bound servitude—not surprisingly, when we realize how many of the servant population were between the ages of eighteen and thirty. The sexuality of redemptioners, since they commonly came in families, was a much less serious problem for them and their masters. Among indentured servants as a whole, however, there were many more men than women. The situation of maidservants was full of both opportunities and hazards. Their services were considerably prized, and a clever or comely woman, as mistress or wife, might escape from the dreariest exactions of servitude. Still, women were also vulnerable to sexual abuse, and the penalties for simply following their own inclinations were high. Masters were unwilling to undergo the loss of time, the expense of rearing a child, or the impairment of health or risk of death in childbirth, and thus were unlikely to give consent to marriage. But the laws contrived to give masters the chance to turn such events to their own account. For fornication and bastardy there were ceremonial whippings, usually of twenty-one lashes; more to the point, sentences of from one to two or three years of extra service were exacted, an overgenerous compensation for the loss of perhaps no more than a few weeks of work. From Pennsylvania southward, Richard B. Morris has concluded, the master was often enriched far beyond his actual losses. Where a manservant fathered a child, he could be required to do whatever extra service was necessary to provide for its maintenance. Merely for contracting unsanctioned marriages, servants could be put to a year's extra service. If a maidservant identified her master as the father of her child, he could be punished for adultery, and she removed from him and resold. A keen disrelish for miscegenation provided an additional term of punishment: for bearing a mulatto bastard a woman might get heavy whipping and seven years of extra service. Despite such restraints, there were a substantial number of illegitimate births, mulatto and otherwise.

However, the commonest crime committed by servants, not surprisingly, was running away—not an easy thing to get away with, since in the colonies everyone had to carry a pass, in effect an identity card, and stiff penalties ranging from fines and personal damages to corporal punishment were imposed upon persons harboring fugitives. Runaways were regularly advertised in the newspapers, rewards were offered, and both sheriffs and the general public were enlisted to secure their return. Returned they often were, and subjected to what were regarded as suitable penalties; captured servants who were unclaimed were resold at public auction. On the whole, and especially in Pennsylvania and colonies to the south, the laws turned the punishment of the recovered runaway into an advantage for the master. The standard penalty in the North, not always rigorously enforced, was extra service of twice the time the master had lost, though whipping was also common. In Pennsylvania, a five-to-one penalty was fixed and commonly enforced, while in Maryland, the harshest of all the colonies, a ten-to-one penalty was authorized by a law of 1661 and very often enforced to the letter. A habitual runaway, or one who succeeded in getting away for weeks, could win himself a dreary extension of servitude. There was one horrendous case of a maidservant in Anne Arundel County, Maryland, who ran off habitually for short terms, and whose master quietly kept a record, true or false, of her absences. Finally taking her to court, the master rendered an account of 133 accumulated days of absence. Since it was impossible for her to deny her frequent absences, she had no shadow of an answer, and was booked for 1,330 days of extra service.[16] Hers was an unusual but not a singular case: there are recorded penalties of 1,530 days, 2,000 days, and even one of 12,130 days, which the master handsomely commuted to an even five years.[17] Virginia assessed double time, or more if "proportionable to the damages" which could be high in tobacco-harvesting time, plus an additional punishment, more commonly inflicted in the seventeenth than the eighteenth century, of corporal punishment. On the eve of the Revolution, Negro slavery had largely replaced indentures in the tidewater plantations but indentures were still important on the accessible and inviting edges of settlement, and there runaways became a critical problem. In South Carolina, where fear of insurrection had been a dominant motive, a law of 1691 had authorized a week's extra service for a day of absence, and for absences that ran as long as a week, a year for a week—a fifty-two-to-one ratio that made Maryland seem relaxed. In 1744 the week-for-a-day ratio was still kept, but the maximum penalty was set at a year's service. Whipping was also routine.

The problem of preventing and punishing runaways was complicated by what was held to be the "pirating" of labor by competing employers —and it became necessary to establish a whole series of penalties for enticing or distracting indentured labor. Plainly, if neighbors could entice bound laborers from their owners for occasional or even permanent service by offering money or promising better treatment, a rudimentary subterranean labor market would begin to replace servitude, and property in servants would become increasingly hazardous. Pirating was not taken lightly in the law, and enticers of labor were subject to personal damage suits as well as to criminal prosecution, with sentences ranging from whipping or sitting in the stocks to fines. The penalties were so heavy in the tobacco colonies that law-abiding planters might even hesitate to feed or shelter a servant who had apparently been deserted by his master. Indeed, innkeepers in these colonies were often fined simply for entertaining or selling liquor to servants. Suits for damages for brief enticements were hardly worth the trouble in the case of servants whose work was valued at a few pence a day. But in New York a skilled cabinetmaker

[16] Ibid., 268–9.
[17] Morris, 452.

and chair carver indentured in 1761 was lured away by a competitor at frequent intervals, and a few years later his master won a smashing judgment of £128.[18]

Plots hatched by several servants to run away together occurred mostly in the plantation colonies, and the few recorded servant uprisings were entirely limited to those colonies. Virginia had been forced from its very earliest years to take stringent steps against mutinous plots, and severe punishments for such behavior were recorded. Most servant plots occurred in the seventeenth century: a contemplated uprising was nipped in the bud in York County in 1661; apparently led by some left-wing offshoots of the Great Rebellion, servants plotted an insurrection in Gloucester County in 1663, and four leaders were condemned and executed; some discontented servants apparently joined Bacon's Rebellion in the 1670s. In the 1680s the planters became newly apprehensive of discontent among the servants "owing to their great necessities and want of clothes," and it was feared they would rise up and plunder the storehouses and ships; in 1682 there were plant-cutting riots in which servants and laborers, as well as some planters, took part.

By the eighteenth century, either because of the relaxed security of the indenture system or the increasing effectiveness of the authorities, disturbances were infrequent, although in 1707 a gang of runaways planned to seize military stores, burn Annapolis, steal a ship, and set up as pirates, but were stopped. Again in 1721 a band of convict servants conspired unsuccessfully to seize military stores at Annapolis. An insurrection of some consequence did actually break out among white servants under the British regime in East Florida during the summer of 1768, when three hundred Italians and Greeks in that very heterogeneous colony revolted against hard work and stern treatment, seized the arms and ammunition in the storehouse, and prepared to set sail from a ship at anchor in the river at New Smyrna. They were intercepted by a government vessel and promptly surrendered. Three leaders were convicted of piracy, one of whom was pardoned on condition that he execute his two comrades. Discontent and dissension, reaching into the local elite, were still rife in Florida at the time of the Revolution.[19]

A serious threat to the interests of masters, one which gives testimony to the onerousness of servitude, was the possibility of military enlistment. In New England, where there were not many servants, military service was obligatory and seems to have posed no major temptation to escape servitude, but in Pennsylvania and the tobacco colonies, where servants were numerous and essential, the competing demand by the army for manpower in the intercolonial war of the 1740s, and, even more, in the French and Indian War of the 1750s, aroused great anxiety among the masters. In the 1740s, more than a third of the Pennsylvania enlistments were from men in the servant class whose masters were compensated at the colony's expense; in Maryland, during the French and Indian War, Governor Horatio Sharpe reported not only that "servants immediately flocked in to enlist, convicts not excepted," but also that recruits among

[18] Ibid., 416–29, esp. 421–3.

[19] On insurrections, see ibid., 169–81.

freemen were extremely scarce, and in Virginia George Washington urged that servants be allowed to enlist in the Virginia volunteers lest they seize the alternative and join the regular army.[20] The resistance of the Pennsylvania Assembly to enlistments during the 1750s became provocatively stubborn and in Maryland there was armed resistance and rioting against recruitment. Parliament, whose interest it was to increase the army, passed a measure in 1756 authorizing officers to enlist indentured servants regardless of restraining colonial laws or practices. The best that masters could hope for was compensation from their colony's legislature, a practice that was repeated in Pennsylvania in 1763, or suing the recruiting officer for civil damages. During the Revolution, the Continental Congress and some of the states encouraged the enlistment of servants, but Pennsylvania and Maryland exempted them from military service. When despite this recruiting officers in Pennsylvania continued to enlist servants, a group of Cumberland County masters complained with magnificent gall that apprentices and servants "are the property of their masters and mistresses, and every mode of depriving such masters and mistresses of their property is a violation of the rights of mankind. . . ."[21] A good number of servants ran off to the British forces, especially in Virginia, but neither the wars nor the Revolution ended the practice of servitude, which declined but did not die until the nineteenth century.

5

Numerous as are the court records of penalties which lengthened service, most servants did not run afoul of the law; their periods of servitude did at last come to an end, entitling them to collect "freedom dues" if they could, and to start in life for themselves. Freedom dues were usually specified by law, but little seems to be known about their payment. Virginia and North Carolina laws of the 1740s required £3 in money, and North Carolina added an adequate suit of clothes. The Crown provided 50 acres of land, free of quitrent for ten years, in South Carolina. A Pennsylvania law of 1700 specified two complete suits of clothes, one of which was to be new, one new ax, one grubbing hoe, and one weeding hoe. Massachusetts long before in the seventeenth century had provided in biblical fashion that servants after seven years' labor should "not be sent away empty," but what this maxim was actually worth to servants is difficult to say. Like the dues of ordinary apprentices, freedom dues may have functioned most importantly as a kind of inducement to servants to carry out in good faith the concluding months and weeks of servitude. Where the labor of a servant was particularly valuable, his master might strengthen that inducement by a cash payment considerably beyond what had been promised.[22]

[20] Ibid., 284n, 286; E. I. McCormac, *White Servitude in Maryland* (1904), 90.

[21] Morris, 292; on the enlistment problem generally, see ibid., 278–94; Geiser, 94–101; Smith, 278–84; McCormac, 82–91.

[22] McKee, 95–6.

What was the economic situation of the servant after completing his servitude? It varied, no doubt, from colony to colony, and with the availability of lands. In the mainland colonies, it appears to have been assumed that an ex-servant was to be equipped for work as a free hired man with enough clothes and tools or money to give him a small start. It was assumed that wages for a freeman were high enough to enable him to earn an adequate competence or to provide himself with a plot of land within a fairly short time. Some ex-servants no doubt went westward and took up new lands. "The inhabitants of our frontiers," wrote Governor Alexander Spotswood of Virginia in 1717, "are composed generally of such as have been transported hither as servants, and being out of their time, settle themselves where land is to be taken up that will produce the necessaries of life with little labour."[23] But it is quite likely that Spotswood erred considerably on the side of optimism. For example, in Maryland, where a freed servant in the seventeenth century was entitled to 50 acres of land upon showing his certificate of freedom at the office of the land office secretary, the records show that relatively few became farmers, though many assumed their land rights and sold them for cash. Abbott E. Smith, in one of the most authoritative studies of colonial servitude, estimates that only one out of ten indentured servants (not including redemptioners) became a substantial farmer and another became an artisan or an overseer in reasonably comfortable circumstances. The other eight, he suggests, either died during servitude, returned to England when it was over, or drifted off to become the "poor whites" of the villages and rural areas. There is reason to think that in most places servants who had completed a term of bondage and had a history of local residence met the prevailing parochial, almost tribal qualifications for poor relief, and were accepted as public charges.[24] Redemptioners, Smith remarks, did a good deal better, but the scrappy evidence that has thus far been found does not yet allow much precision. Sir Henry Moore, governor of New York, thought them so anxious to own land that they made great sacrifices to do so: "As soon as the time stipulated in their indentures is expired, they immediately quit their masters, and get a small tract of land, in settling which for the first three or four years they lead miserable lives, and in the most abject poverty; but all this is patiently borne and submitted to with the greatest cheerfulness, the satisfaction of being land holders smooths every difficulty, and makes them prefer this manner of living to that comfortable subsistence which they could procure for themselves and their families by working at the trades in which they were brought up."[25] An Englishman who traveled in America in the opening years of the nineteenth century noticed "many families, particularly in Pennsylvania, of great respectability both in our society and amongst others, who had themselves come over to this country as redemptioners; or were children of such."[26]

As for the indentured servants, the dismal estimate that only two out of ten may have reached positions of moderate comfort is an attempt to

[23] Smith, 297.
[24] See ibid., 251–2.
[25] McKee, 112–3.
[26] Geiser, 108–9.

generalize the whole two centuries of the experience of English servitude, taking the seventeenth century when the system was brutal and opportunities were few with the eighteenth, when it became less severe.[27] In the early years more servants returned to England, and mortality was also higher. But it will not do simply to assume that freed servants, especially those from the tobacco fields, were in any mental or physical condition to start vigorous new lives, or that long and ripe years of productivity lay ahead for them. If we consider the whole span of time over which English indentured servitude prevailed, its heavy toll in work and death is the reality that stands out.

The Horatio Alger mythology has long since been torn to bits by students of American social mobility, and it will surprise no one to learn that the chance of emergence from indentured servitude to a position of wealth or renown was statistically negligible. A few cases to the contrary are treasured by historians, handed down from one to another like heirlooms—but most of them deal with Northern servants who came with education or skills. The two most illustrious colonial names with servitude in their family histories are Benjamin Franklin and the eminent Maryland lawyer Daniel Dulany. Franklin's maternal grandfather, Peter Folger of Nantucket, a man of many trades from teacher and surveyor to town and court clerk and interpreter between whites and Indians, had bought a maidservant for £20 and later married her. Dulany, who came from a substantial Irish family, arrived in 1703 with two older brothers; the brothers melted into the anonymity that usually awaited indentured arrivals, but Daniel was picked up by a lawyer who was pleased to buy a literate servant with some university training to act as his clerk and help with his plantation accounts. The closest thing to a modest, American-scale family dynasty to come out of servitude was that of the New England Sullivans. John Sullivan and Margery Browne both came to Maine as indentured servants in the 1720's. After Sullivan earned his freedom he became a teacher, bought Margery out of servitude, and married her. Their son John became a lawyer, a Revolutionary patriot, one of Washington's leading generals, and governor of New Hampshire. His younger brother, James, also a lawyer, became a congressman from Massachusetts and in time governor of the state. In the third generation, John's son, George, became a Federalist congressman and the attorney general of New Hampshire; James's son, William, pursued a successful legal career in Boston, played a prominent role in state politics, and was chosen to be one of the three delegates to take the manifesto of the Hartford Convention to Washington. John Lamb, a leader of the Sons of Liberty and later an officer in the Revolution, was the son of Anthony Lamb who had followed an improbable career: an apprentice instrument maker in London, Anthony became involved with a notorious burglar who ended on the gallows at Tyburn; as a first offender, Lamb was sentenced to be transported, served out an indenture in Virginia, moved to New York, and became a reputable instrument maker and a teacher of mathematics, surveying, and navigation. Charles Thomson, one of six children orphaned

[27] See Smith, 288–9, on later conditions.

by the death of their father on shipboard in 1739, began his American life as an indentured servant and became a teacher in Philadelphia, a merchant, a Revolutionary patriot, and Secretary of the Continental Congress. Matthew Thornton, whose parents came to Maine in the Scotch-Irish emigration of 1718, began life under indenture, became a physician, a patriot leader in New Hampshire, and a signer of the Declaration of Independence. Matthew Lyon, who won notoriety as a peppery Republican congressman from Vermont and as a victim of the Sedition Act, emigrated from Ireland in 1765 and paid off his passage by three years of indentured service on farms in Connecticut before he bought his own farm in Vermont. And there were others, brands snatched from the burning, triumphs of good fortune or strong character over the probabilities.

6

Thoreau, brooding over the human condition in the relatively idyllic precincts of Concord and Walden Pond, was convinced that the mass of men lead lives of quiet desperation. His conviction quickens to life again when we contemplate the human costs of what historians sometimes lightly refer to as the American experiment. It is true that thousands came to the colonies in search of freedom or plenty and with a reasonably good chance of finding them, and that the colonies harbored a force of free white workers whose wages and conditions might well have been the envy of their European counterparts. Yet these fortunate men were considerably outnumbered by persons, white or black, who came to America in one kind of servitude or another. It is also true that for some servants, especially for those who already had a skill, a little cash, or some intelligence or education or gentility, servitude in America might prove not a great deal worse than an ordinary apprenticeship, despite the special tribulations and hazards it inflicted. But when one thinks of the great majority of those who came during the long span of time between the first settlements and the disappearance of white servitude in the early nineteenth century—bearing in mind the poverty and the ravaged lives which they left in Europe, the cruel filter of the Atlantic crossing, the high mortality of the crossing and the seasoning, and the many years of arduous toil that lay between the beginning of servitude and the final realization of tolerable comfort—one is deeply impressed by the measure to which the sadness that is natural to life was overwhelmed in the condition of servitude by the stark miseries that seem all too natural to the history of the poor. For a great many the journey across the Atlantic proved in the end to have been only an epitome of their journey through life. And yet there must have seemed to be little at risk because there was so little at stake. They had so often left a scene of turbulance, crime, exploitation, and misery that there could not have been much hope in most of them; and as they lay in their narrow bedsteads listening to the wash of the rank bilge water below them, sometimes racked with fever or lying in their own vomit, few could have expected very much from American life, and those who did were too often disappointed. But with white servants we have only begun to taste the anguish of the early American experience.

Women in Colonial America

CAROL RUTH BERKIN

When the British began settling their American colonies, they brought with them few women. The early settlements in Virginia were speculative ventures in which gentlemen intended to turn a quick profit and return home. Colonists farther to the north, and later settlers in this region, did intend to stay. Nevertheless, women remained in short supply. The rigors of frontier life and the dangers of continuous childbirth without proper hygienic or medical care made the female mortality rate extremely high. Indeed, it was not unusual for a hardy male settler to outlive three or four wives.

This scarcity of women accounts in great part for the relative independence granted them in both law and custom in the early period. Women could insist on certain rights and privileges as conditions of marriage. Although under British common law a woman lost her legal rights as an individual when she married, the colonies allowed some wives to sign contracts, to own property, and to operate businesses in certain cases.

This breach of the common law was made not only to secure women in the home, but also because the nascent society was reluctant to follow a course that might reduce some individuals to poverty and thus make them dependent on the community for subsistence. By granting women certain legal rights, usually exercised by them as widows, the society protected itself from what might have become an economic burden.

In the following selection, Carol Ruth Berkin, of Baruch College of the City University of New York, provides a description of the conditions in which women found themselves in the colonies. In viewing this material from a feminist perspective, Berkin provides an analysis of the ideology of oppression that has been at work in society since the beginning of recorded history. At the same time she points out how extraordinary women struggled within the confines of that oppression to assert their individuality and realize fully their talents.

The patriarchal ideology continues to impress itself upon American society today in much the same form as it was found during the Colonial period. But perhaps more than in the past, the tradition is being challenged head-on by increasing numbers of women and men. It remains to be seen whether this most long-lived of discriminatory patterns can be overturned and all mature human beings, regardless of sex, allowed, even encouraged, to develop themselves in whichever directions and to whatever extent they choose.

INTRODUCTION

As women become more conscious of themselves as individuals and as a distinct group within society, they also become more curious about their collective past. But the written history they encounter tells them all too little. It presents, if not a conspiracy of silence about women, at least a persistent sin of omission. Where women do appear in traditional accounts of the past, they emerge as adjuncts of the masculine world being recorded, as supporting players, seen only in their male-related roles as wife, mother, daughter, or mistress. History thus related occurs around them rather than with them.

Of necessity, then, women have turned to the writing of their past. Their primary goal is self-knowledge rather than self-glorification. No honest search for a history of women, or a reconstruction of the past as it developed with women, will be an attempt to find matriarchy in a patriarchal world. Little major social policy was shaped by women, and no new search, for example, into our own American past, will stand the pyramids of power and leadership on their heads, revealing women as the dominant force in political, economic, or social decision-making.

But self-knowledge is more readily accepted today as a legitimate pursuit of the subordinate as well as the dominant groups in society. There is therefore a history to be written of how and why women came to play a subordinate role in society; of what that role was, its inner dynamics as well as its contribution to the male society; how the role was justified and maintained; and what challenges were made to it.

THE IDEOLOGY OF SUBORDINATION

The history of the American colonial woman is not a chronicle of transcendence above circumstance. Her story, though distinguished by

Berkin, Carol Ruth, *Within the Conjurer's Circle: Women in Colonial America* (General Learning Press, Morristown, N.J.), pp. 1–15

its many variations on the theme, conforms to that of most women in the patriarchal societies of Europe. This American woman, no less than her English sisters, was part of a social structure that locked her into a subordinate position within her society. Its basic social and economic unit was the family, headed by father and husband. The larger units of community and colony were correspondingly masculine domains.

Such a patriarchal system was centuries old when American colonial history began, and in justification or explanation of this patriarchy the colonists and their English brothers had at readiness hallowed assumptions about the "right ordering of things." These assumptions, woven together into a whole, constituted the ideology of women's subordination, which prevailed in Mother Country and New World throughout the seventeenth and eighteenth centuries. This ideology eliminated the possibility of debate on the "woman question" by pronouncing woman's destiny, her nature, and her proper place in society as matters of fact, not debate. Perhaps, then, the story of women in colonial America should begin with an examination of this ideology.

The surety that characterized pronouncements upon women rested above all upon divine revelation. And, God's most explicit statement was to be found in the Biblical account of creation. Traditional interpretation located in the Genesis story an explanation for generic man's superiority over all other animals, and an explanation for Adam's superiority to Eve. It was the gift of a soul, through which man enjoyed a direct and conscious relationship with his creator, which set him apart from his fellow creatures in Eden. In this gift of superiority woman also shared. Yet, unlike his creation, hers had not flowed from the direct Will of God. It was for Adam's sake, and out of his very body, that God made Eve. Woman therefore owed her existence to man and to his need for companionship. Appropriately, her soul's relationship to God was less direct than man's: woman celebrated her Creator by fulfilling her purpose as companion or "helpmeet" to man. Many centuries after creation, the English poet Milton expressed this most basic difference in human destinies by declaring, "He for God only, She for God in him." [Milton 1669, Book iv, Line 294] Certainty of woman's subordination to man also rested upon her role in the exile from Paradise. The divine injunction to obedience to her husband was "the mulct that was laid upon the first Woman's disobedience to God. . . ." [*The Ladies Calling* 1673, p. 191]

If the Bible revealed human destinies, nature also offered its own discernible laws on the proper relationship between men and women. Anatomy was viewed as the natural determinant of destiny, and man's superior strength and woman's physical weakness were natural echoes of the supernatural design. Such obvious physical differences were not, however, nature's only statements on the subject. For the seventeenth century European man, nature encompassed psychology as well as physiology. Personality traits were looked upon as phenomena of nature, and like physical characteristics, they were believed to be inherent in the individual rather than shaped by society. In their efforts to understand "human nature" seventeenth century men applied theological patterns of thought. English Puritanism, for example (and its American offspring in particular), perceived symmetry to be the organizing principle of the world: endless dichotomies, exact opposites which attracted each other, came together to form the whole. [Morgan 1966] Accordingly all personality characteristics were dichotomized, producing complementary pairings such as strong–weak, rational–emotional, bold–meek. These inherent and dichotomous characteristics were not, however, found to be distributed to men and women at random. Instead they followed a sex-based pattern, a pattern which conformed to the Biblical and physiological divisions already distinguished. Women proved to be endowed—naturally and permanently—with the passive or weaker characteristic of each pairing.

In sum, God had decreed separate destinies and Nature provided appropriately separate endowments for the sexes. It was from these separate fates that a division of activity in society into two mutually exclusive, but complementary spheres was said to arise: for women, the circle of domesticity; for men, the larger sphere of the organization and management of society. These spheres were complementary, not comparable; unbreachable, but mutually beneficial in their exclusivity.

Over time, it was expected that a society's laws and customs might define or clarify the particulars of the two spheres. This process, however, was not held responsible for woman's subordination nor for the differences in ability or interests evident in the two sexes. Such human laws merely conformed to divine and natural imperatives. Thus the seventeenth century Englishman would explain women's exclusion from political and legal rights in these terms: "the reason why women have no control in Parliament, why they make no laws, consent to none, abrogate none, is their original sin. . . ." [Calhoun 1945, p. 42]

The American colonial patriarchy took both the reality and the ideology of its social organization from the Mother Country. Thus, the basic organizing unit of the new society, like the old, was the family. And within the family—in the roles of wife, mother, and daughter—a woman fulfilled her obligations to domesticity. Yet, American circumstances revised, reshaped, and often added to the traditional "particulars" of the woman's sphere. Although her subordination remained constant, the actual range of acceptable and even required female activities broadened, and sometimes breached, the boundaries of domestic life. The frontier conditions of seventeenth century America, the scarcity in colonial society of trained and even unskilled labor, and the scarcity of women themselves recast the nature of the "helpmeet's" role. The history of the colonial woman is the history of the shifting and changing particulars of the woman's role, her range of activities expanding and contracting as the men who directed her world built theirs.

THE VALUE OF WOMEN: MOTHER AND HOMEMAKER

The English colonial world was, by virtue of numbers alone, a man's world. There were no women in the original Jamestown settlement parties, and, although no other colony followed this Virginia example of exclusivity, the ratio of women to men remained unbalanced for over a century and a half. In 1708 South Carolina's population showed 148 men for every 100 women; in Maryland, men still outnumbered women by 13 per hundred on the eve of the American Revolution. [Degler 1959] Observers of the colonial scene wrote of this scarcity of women as a boon to the female sex. One Maryland gentleman went so far as to declare America a "paradise for women." [Degler 1959, p. 58] The Marylander's judgment bears some scrutiny. America was perhaps a paradise for women seeking matrimony. There was however far less enthusiasm for women as independent settlers. Even in colonies like Massachusetts, where "maiden lots" were granted to single women immigrants, leaders discouraged rather than encouraged this means of independent support for adventurous women. [Earle 1962] What American male settlers wanted, and actively sought, were wives.

The men of Jamestown reflect the American eagerness for matrimony. These bachelors actually imported their brides, sight unseen, by the boatload. In that struggling colony, the only true profits made in the year 1619 went to the sea-going entrepreneurs who shipped eligible young girls to Virginia and sold them in marriage at 80 pounds of tobacco a head. [Earle 1962] In other colonies, single men eagerly wooed eligible neighbors. Neither homeliness nor slowness of wit—not even poverty—seemed to decrease a girl's stock in the marriage market. Her very presence in the new world guaranteed her a proposal. [Smith 1970]

The settlers' desire for wives reflected more than the human need for companionship. Most of the expectant bridegrooms were farmers, and to manage a self-sustaining farm unit, a man needed the traditional housewifely skills which could be expected from a woman. To his wife the farmer could allocate the responsibilities of processing what his labor in field and forest produced. Thus, in Virginia, and in all other agricultural communities of early America, women as wives were necessary to transform the farmers' homes into full-time domestic factories, where raw materials were changed into goods essential for survival.

If, then, America was a "paradise" for the eligible and willing bride, it was also a land of constant and grueling domestic duties for the wife. Her activities required more than time; strength, skill, and an ability for improvisation were needed for her tasks. Cooking utensils were heavy and crude [Demos 1971]; household work-space was cramped; and all necessities in a cooking or cleaning process must be produced by the housewife before she could complete the task or assemble the meal. In the course of her day she cooked, pickled, and preserved the food that entered her home. She combed wool, spun it into thread, wove this thread into cloth, and mended the clothing she had earlier made. She made soap, dipped candles, and did the routine housework necessary to keep her home-factory in working order. At the same time, the colonial wife saw to the daily needs of her husband and family.

"Woman's work" in this colonial setting was physical and difficult. But no social judgment labeled physical activity unfeminine. In the farmhouse, femininity emanated from a cheerful acceptance of the helpmeet role and the fulfillment of its many domestic duties, not from a style of behavior within that domestic role. The helpless or idle female was of no more value to the seventeenth century settler than his continued bachelorhood would be; nor would she be valued by the urban poor or the frontiersman of the next century.

As a wife, the woman of colonial America served a second, and even more basic, function. As one historian of the period has put it, the colonial woman's chief obligation seems to have been to populate the country. [Douglas 1966] In more personal terms, she was expected to give the farmer a family. And, because children were valued assistance in the success of the farming venture, large families were desired.

High infant and child mortality made the colonial wife's obligation more difficult to fulfill. Repeated pregnancy was her only antidote to the inadequate medical care which filled colonial cemeteries with small graves. Thus, pregnancy and childbirth were a cycle in which some women spent the major portion of their married life.[1] Their very speech was rich with the vocabulary of birth, and "laying in" was a process regular and repetitious enough for many households to acknowledge its permanence with separate pillows, bed linen, and accessories accumulated for the delivery tasks. [Spruill 1938]

Colonial mothers as well as their children frequently died in childbirth, victims of the perils of home-delivery and of the physical toll of many pregnancies. Surviving children lived in the shadow of sibling death. Mothers, as historian Julia Spruill points out, often lacked both the physical and emotional energy they might wish to bring to the care of these survivors. [1938] Colonial women seemed, however, to accept their circumstances with resignation. Motherhood was believed to be woman's ultimate purpose, and death in childbirth to be the "will of Providence."

WOMEN'S EDUCATION: TRAINING TO BE AN "ORNAMENT OF ZION"

The importance to the settlers of the woman's role—both as wife and as mother—accounts in large part for the pressures, both formal and informal, upon women to marry. Wife-and-mother were lauded as the most desirable identities for women by community leaders, especially by the religious hierarchy. Leading ministers like Massachusetts clergyman Cotton Mather consistently declared the married mother to be the most prized of God's "ornaments of Zion." [Mather 1692] And, single women were urged by their religious leaders to display their virtue by devoting the maiden years to preparation for marriage and motherhood. Thus the learning of housewifely skills was elevated from a necessity to a virtue,

[1] There is a debate among modern demographers as to the number of children born to the average woman, and the mortality rate for both mothers and children. While earlier historians of this century have estimated the typical surviving family group to include 10 or 12 children [Spruill 1938], John Demos has recently judged this figure inaccurate for areas of New England. His findings for Plymouth colony [Demos 1965] show the average surviving family to be considerably smaller.

and the unmarried years were defined as without meaning except as a training period for matrimony and maternity.

If positive social status was acquired by a woman through marriage and motherhood, strongly negative status was conferred upon women who refused or failed to marry. Social disapproval increased in intensity over time: single women over the age of twenty might be viewed with a sympathetic admixture of alarm and pity, but this sympathy turned to ridicule with the passing of additional maiden years. New England spinsters of thirty, for example, were openly labeled "thornbacks," a crudely put judgment on their desirability. [Calhoun 1945]

Perhaps what gave the social pressures upon women their true persuasiveness was the legal and economic reality which they reflected. The average colonial woman had limited options. Few, if any, viable alternatives were available to her save marriage. Both legal and customary prohibitions against self-support made spinsterhood an undesirable state, and it was perhaps the contempt for the "thornback's" future which made her critics bold. Most unmarried women could expect to live as permanent dependents in the homes of brothers or sisters. And in these homes they were expected to perform most of the same domestic chores that they would otherwise have performed as mistresses of their own house. If there was no independence from the domestic duties, marriage at least gave a woman a domain over which she could preside.[2]

Whether she ultimately chose marriage or spinsterhood, the colonial woman's childhood was devoted to preparation for marriage. Within her mother's home she learned the womanly skills of cooking, sewing, and cleaning. But her education also focused upon behavior and attitude. She was taught, in short, "womanly virtues" as well as womanly skills. Cotton Mather had catalogued the appropriate virtues for the New England woman: modesty, silence, industriousness, humility, thrift, discretion, and obedience. [1692] But girls in New York and Virginia, not subject to Mather's Puritan influence, had the same virtues held up to them.

Little importance was placed upon academic or formal education for the colonial girl. Few women of early seventeenth century Virginia were even literate. [Spruill 1938] In New England, where a public school system was traditional, women fared better than their southern counterparts, and many were probably taught to read, to write, and to do sums. Ultimately, the family's economic and social status had much to do with a daughter's chance to acquire academic skills. In prosperous families, daughters sometimes received elementary lessons in geography, arithmetic, and even Latin from their brothers' tutors. The rule of formal ignorance had its exceptions, of course, and women like Anne Bradstreet and Anne Hutchinson, both of Massachusetts, were as well educated as their male contemporaries. However, their educations were the gifts of learned

[2] The privilege of *femme sole,* discussed later, did ease this dependence for some spinsters. After about 1670 New England spinsters could keep school rather than depend entirely upon the charity of relatives. It is doubtful, however, that many could afford to live alone in independent households. Boarding with relatives continued to lay the burden of household chores upon the schoolteacher. [Dexter 1924]

fathers; their academic accomplishments were tributes to special familial relationships, not to colonial educational priorities.

The denial of formal education to girls did not rest solely upon its apparent inapplicability to their future life. The truth was that colonial society held women to be naturally unsuited for intellectual training. While many women were allowed and even encouraged in adulthood to master the practical mathematical skills of budget-balancing and bookkeeping for their husbands [Morgan 1966], the feminine brain was said to be too weak to bear the strains of logic or abstract thought. [Calhoun 1945] Nor, it was argued, could women endure *sustained* thinking. These assumptions of constitutional weakness were borne out to community leaders' satisfaction in case after case. In Massachusetts, for example, Governor John Winthrop attributed an instance of mental derangement to the woman's excessive reading of books. On the woman's condition Winthrop offered this post mortem:

> If she had attended to her household affairs and such things as belong to women, and not gone out of her way and calling to meddle in such things as are proper for men, she had kept her wits, and might have improved them usefully and honorably in the place that God had set her. [Winthrop 1908, II, 225]

The intellectually presumptuous woman was believed to be a woman who had overstepped natural boundaries, and such women were almost predictably disruptive to society. When, for example, a Puritan woman produced a book on theology, she was immediately discovered to have fallen into heresy. Her own brother publicly rebuked her, declaring "Your printing of a Book, beyond the custom of your sex, doth rankly smell." [Morgan 1966, p. 44]

Perhaps the most striking example of such a presumptuous woman was Anne Hutchinson, who came to the Massachusetts Bay Colony in 1636. Anne Hutchinson was in her forties, married, and the mother of fourteen children. But in her own girlhood she had been educated in more than cooking and sewing. Her father gave her the training of a son, and like any educated Puritan, she was keen in the discussion of Calvinist theology. She exhibited in theological debate all that the Puritan community admired: intelligence, quickness of mind, a provocative style, and above all, a relentless logic. Had Anne Hutchinson been a man, she might well have found her way into the ministry. But church leadership was closed to her sex. In fact, a "rule of silence" lay upon women while in the church sanctuary. But Mrs. Hutchinson *was* a theologian, and to her delight she found in Massachusetts that her interest in theology, if not her interpretive skill, was matched by her Boston neighbors. These Puritans soon flocked to the Hutchinson home to enjoy Anne's "nimble wit & spirit." Her parlor became, as historian Kai Erikson put it, "a kind of theological salon," where the minister's sermon was laid open to discussion–and, increasingly, to criticism. [Erikson 1966, p. 77]

The thrust of Mrs. Hutchinson's criticisms went directly to the heart of ministerial authority. In a society which believed that good works, or moral behavior, was not a guarantee of salvation, Anne Hutchinson challenged the holiness of the local clergy themselves. Although these might indeed be moral men, she conceded, they had not persuaded her that they were among the saved. If they could not, as she feared, definitely be counted among God's "elect," what legitimate authority over the religious life of the community did they enjoy?

Even were the ministers' religious credentials in order, Mrs. Hutchinson was not certain that the true, elected saints of Massachusetts (of which she was certain she was one) needed any earthly church or church authorities at all. What purpose, she asked in her Sunday afternoon discussions, did the earthly church serve for souls in direct communion with God?

The questions Anne Hutchinson raised were basic, but they were not new; Puritan ministers before her had raised them, and, as supporters of the church as an institution, had laid them to an uneasy rest. Nor were they purely theological questions in the Massachusetts of 1636, for here all political policy was legitimated by religious authorities. Thus Mrs. Hutchinson's revival of the debate was embarrassing and dangerous to the colonial government as well. In fact, when the leaders of the colony moved to silence Anne Hutchinson, they charged her not with heresy, but with sedition. Within a year after she had raised her challenge, she had been tried, found "unfit for our society," and exiled from the colony. [Erikson 1966]

The boldness of an Anne Hutchinson was not common. More typically the women who displayed uncommon talents, intelligence, or commitment to religious or secular causes adopted a defensive posture. When the poetess Anne Bradstreet published her work, she asked for toleration of her foray into masculine endeavors. In "The Prologue" to her first volume of poetry she carefully paid homage to masculine superiority:

> . . . I am obnoxious to each carping tongue,
> Who sayes, my hand a needle better fits,
> A Poets Pen, all scorne, I should thus wrong;
> For such despight they cast on female wits:
> If what I doe prove well, it wo'nt advance,
> They'l say its stolne, or else, it was by chance.
> But sure the antick Greeks were far more milde,
> Else of our Sex, why feigned they those nine,
> And poesy made, Calliope's owne childe,
> So 'mongst the rest, they plac'd the Arts divine:
> But this weake knot they will full soone untye,
> The Greeks did nought, but play the foole and lye.
> Let Greeks be Greeks, and Women what they are,
> Men have precedency, and still excell,

> It is but vaine, unjustly to wage war,
> Men can doe best, and Women know it well:
> Preheminence in each, and all is yours,
> Yet grant some small acknowledgement of ours . . .
> [Bradstreet 1650, p. 4]

Although one of Anne Bradstreet's poems chided Englishmen to remember that a woman named Elizabeth had once ruled them, most of her work was gently lyrical, romantic, and orthodox in point of view.

Little effort was made to reconcile the reality of an Anne Bradstreet or an Anne Hutchinson with the assumptions of female intellectual inadequacies. The educated and intellectually powerful woman remained an anomaly within her culture, and was not exempt from the domestic duties of her sex.

THE CHOICE OF A HUSBAND: THE RULES AND THEIR EXCEPTIONS

Trained as a daughter in the womanly skills, taught the passive womanly virtues, discouraged from intellectual activity, and encouraged to expect her ultimate fulfillment in marriage and motherhood, the average colonial woman led a life of narrow focus. And, although her husband was to be the central figure of her life, she had little formal say in his selection. The adventurous women imported to Jamestown may have enjoyed a free choice amongst eager suitors, but colonial girls from prosperous and proper families often entered marriages made for them rather than by them.

This exclusion of a woman from the choice of her husband was a logical consequence of seventeenth and eighteenth century views of marriage. Marriage not only provided a man his domestic assistant and his emotional companion; as a legal institution, it operated as a vehicle for the redistributing and securing of wealth between two families. Thus it was, among the prosperous and among those on their way to prosperity, a matter of economics.

No attempt was made to hide this bookkeeping quality of marriage among the monied. Wealth was acknowledged to count for more than beauty in a wife, and men were in no way embarrassed to discuss matrimony as a means of shoring-up their fortunes or of making them. The diaries of a man as distinguished as Judge Samuel Sewall of Massachusetts give frank evidence of the colonial gentleman's shrewdness in marital negotiations. [Sewall 1927]

Premarriage negotiations in such circumstance were largely concerned with the transfer and pledge of wealth, and such negotiations required consent between legal adults; father and prospective son-in-law. Seen in its coldest light, such a marriage was a sophisticated means of barter in which the bride was not so much the currency but its conveyance.

How neatly reality conformed to this model is difficult to measure. Informally, favorite or loved daughters may well have chosen the man with whom their father negotiated. "Understandings" between lovers may have preceded and prompted those exclusively masculine contract discussions. However, formal power was never relinquished by the men, and even among the liberal Puritan societies of New England no proper marriages took place without the father's consent.[3]

The retention of formal power may have reflected parental desire to check unions undesirable for reasons of class rather than personal character. Even within the Puritan culture, which held love between husband and wife an obligation to God, economic and social compatibility was stressed as a major consideration for a successful marriage. Puritan ministers were careful to preach that an equality of social rank was the most important factor in choosing a mate. In the 1670s, for instance, a Boston minister reminded those attending a wedding that "the happiness of marriage (sic) life consists much in that Persons being equally yoaked draw together in a holy yoak . . . there must be sutable fittness (sic) for this Condition equality in birth, education, and religion." [Morgan 1966, p. 55]

Perhaps then the greatest freedom of choice for women existed among the poor, for in their marriages little of material value was to be transferred or absorbed, and no class barriers were to be overcome.

LEGAL ABSORPTION IN MARRIAGE: THE FEMME COVERT

Whatever the process of acquiring their husbands had been, whatever the bases of marriage, women once married were expected to show complete devotion to their husbands. Held up to them as models were the ideal wives of men's fact and fantasy, women invariably meek and humble, who, like Mrs. R--, was praised because "the hyacinth follows not the sun more willingly than she her husbands's pleasure." [Calhoun 1945, p. 86] Of the truly perfect wife it would not be too much to say, as William Habington did, that she looked upon her husband "as Conjurers upon the Circle, beyond which there is nothing but Death and Hell; and in him shee beleeves Paradice circumscrib'd." [Spruill 1938, p. 164]

This domestic "conjurer's circle" was drawn by law as much as by precept. Husbands escaped such limitations of identity, for the legal and political rights conferred upon them in adulthood provided them identities independent of husband and father. Traditionally these rights were

[3] Puritan parents permitted their children considerable freedom of choice in courtship, and the pattern of courtship itself was quite liberal. Customs peculiar to New England, such as "bundling," aided a young woman in making her choice: lying together in a coal-heated bed, the bundling couple indulged in a courtship more intimate than most. Puritan girls undoubtedly knew their new husbands better than other colonial brides, especially since it was customary in New England to permit premarital sex between formally pledged couples. [Smith 1970]

denied a woman, and marriage itself sealed her exclusion from most of them. No rite of passage from child to adult member of the society actually existed for women, although the less sophisticated and more pragmatic legal and political structure of early America did make the colonial wife less the permanent child her English sister was.

In England legal absorption of the woman in marriage was strikingly complete. In 1632, an English legal scholar compared marriage to the merging of a small brook and a major river: "the poor rivulet looseth her name; it is carried and recarried with the new associate; it beareth no sway; it possesseth nothing. . . ." [Spruill 1938, p. 340]

So too a woman was absorbed. Her inheritance, her possessions, even her personal items became his by law. After marriage, she owned no property, nor could she acquire any by purchase. The profits from her labor belonged to her husband.

As with all rules, there were exceptions to this one. In the sixteenth and seventeenth centuries prosperous men grew anxious to insure that their wealth passed to their blood heirs. These men arranged prenuptial contracts with each daughter's suitor, contracts that set outside the husband's reach a portion of the wealth the daughter brought to the marriage. This land or money was held in trust for her and her children. But this prenuptial contract was a device of the wealthy; ordinary women were left in total dependence upon their husbands. [Morris 1930; Goodsell 1934]

Rich or poor, all women shared in the exclusion from political and general legal rights which indeed circumscribed their life in marriage. A married woman could not sue or be sued. She could not make contracts or sign deeds. If she broke the law, her husband was legally responsible. Even the debts she incurred were his, not hers. [Spruill 1938] His responsibility for her entitled him to discipline powers over her, and husbands were within their legal rights when meting out physical punishments to their wives. Many relationships were tempered by respect and affection, but the power of the husband made this warmth his initiative alone.

Colonial wives fared better than their English sisters. For in the colonies a general policy on marriage evolved over time which was based, as Professor Richard B. Morris has noted, on the recognized social value of increased population. [1930] This policy gave women some improvement in, and power over, the conditions within their marriages. The treatment of the wife became, increasingly, a public rather than a private matter. The scarcity of women, and their value to the new settlements, won them legal guarantees of some physical protection within marriage. Massachusetts' earliest codification of laws, the 1641 Body of Liberties, insured that "everie marryed woeman shall be free from bodily correction or stripes by her husband, unless it be in his own defence upon her assault. . . ." [Calhoun 1945, p. 93] Southern authorities, too, were careful to limit a man's absolute power over his wife. Although punishment was allowed, no wife could be beaten to the point of permanent injury or death. [Spruill 1938]

Colonial authorities expanded their jurisdiction over other marital abuses as well. Courts ordered cohabitation in marriage, although traditionally desertion had not been subject to judicial ruling. [Morris 1930]

The colonial policy favoring fruitful marriage produced, interestingly, striking changes in divorce law. New England, for example, granted to women as well as to men the right to sue for divorce. The major grounds were incest, bigamy, malicious desertion, "criminal uncleanliness" (sodomy), and male sterility. [Morgan 1966] All these legal "sins" undermined the stability of the family unit within the society, and it is this fact which explains the innovation in divorce law. Civil and religious authorities desired stable family situations, and the liberalization of the divorce law did not, as it might first appear, contradict this goal. It was to facilitate dissolution of unsuccessful marriages so that successful remarriage might occur, that New England legislators gave women the power to initiate divorce proceedings. [Morris 1930]

Some measure of economic security was assured the colonial wife through the adoption and expansion of the English upper class device of contracting. Not only premarriage agreements but postnuptial contracts as well were drawn up in marriages among the colonial wealthy and the middle classes. The novel postnuptial contracts were usually a form of separation agreement which assured the estranged wife some financial support. [Morris 1930]

If colonial law made a woman less powerless within her marriage, there were also some indications that limited legal powers within the larger society were to be conferred upon her. Most of these powers centered, however, upon the transfer of property brought by her to the marriage. In efforts to expedite sale and purchase of land, several colonies bypassed the complicated legal maneuvers necessary in English law for the release of trust property and simply allowed the wife to sign the deed with her husband. [Morris 1930] Some colonies went so far as to grant a wife the *femme sole* status (discussed later) so that, in her husband's absence, she could execute the deed herself. [Morris 1930] Such legal innovations, however, seemed to have been designed to aid husbands in their business transactions rather than to expand women's rights. And, many promising innovations proved to be temporary in nature. In the earliest days of colonial settlement, for example, a wife was allowed to represent an absent husband's interests in court. It was a practical concession in an era without professional lawyers to substitute for a man in time-consuming legal proceedings. But this "right" did not outlive its practicality; it was revoked as easily as it was instituted. [Morris 1930]

THE COLONIAL WIDOW AND SPINSTER: THE RIGHTS OF FEMME SOLE

Although conditions within marriage improved, and some limited and specific legal identity was allowed, law no less than ideology bound a wife within the "conjurer's circle." It was only the total absence of a husband which released the colonial woman from circumscription.

The existence of widows and spinsters compelled special legal provisions to be devised in order to accommodate their circumstances. These were women not under the protection and care of a man; their condition was recognized in law as that of "woman alone" (*femme sole*) rather than "woman covered" (*femme covert*). Necessity was therefore accommodated by law, and the widow and spinster were allowed to operate as legal individuals in the competitive world outside the home. In short, the femme sole status conferred upon a woman those legal rights denied her as unnecessary in marriage. She could buy and sell property, make binding contracts, sue and be sued.

The device of femme sole served the community at large as well as the individual woman granted this privileged status. First, femme sole removed the burden of a nonproductive, dependent group from the shoulders of the public. It also released and channeled into the society skills and talents needed in the colonial economy: through femme sole woman-power provided goods and services when man-power was lacking.[4] Finally, in instances where the widow or spinster was not destitute, but held an inheritance from husband or father, the femme sole device had yet another practical social value. The colonial economy was a developing economy, dependent upon the flow of capital. Such a society could not afford to see private inheritance frozen outside the marketplace. A single or widowed woman must be given the legal powers necessary to employ her husband's or father's fortune, not only for her sake and for the sake of her husband's heirs, but for the economic well-being of her community. [Morris 1930] The money held by women was thus infused into the economy. Colonial widows invested in land, in business enterprises, and in commercial ventures such as shipping. [Earle 1962] Ordinarily women did not direct these enterprises but simply helped finance them. There were however women who managed their own speculative interests, their own businesses, or their own professional enterprises. [Dexter 1924; Earle 1962]

Most women who made their own business fortunes began with a generous and prosperous husband or father. When for instance, New Yorker Peter de Vries died, he left his wife Margaret Hardenbroeck de

[4] This substitution quality can be seen more clearly if we trace developments as sectors of the economy mature. For, as the economy matures, *femme sole* activities contract. For example, a slow process of professionalization in many service fields previously open to women worked toward their exclusion. As long as these careers had been of low status, and required no formal education or technical skills, women had dotted their ranks. But the upgrading of vocations like the law, and the accompanying influx of men to the field, made it impossible for women to compete, even if public legislation did not bar them. It was not necessary, in many cases, to declare exclusion based on sex; it was sufficient to set training standards which other sex-based discriminations would make impossible for women to meet. Thus, the Massachusetts Bar Association required a college degree or, in special instances, an extended clerkship with one of its members. Women, barred from the former by law and the latter by custom, were thus eliminated from the profession. [Wroth and Zobel 1965]

Vries considerable property. Margaret, employing her powers granted her as *femme sole,* sold this property and invested her money in shipping. The widow de Vries proved herself more than a judicious investor; she was an innovative businesswoman as well. Recognizing the importance of New York City as an entrepôt, she established the first packet line between Europe and America. To supervise her business, Margaret Hardenbroeck de Vries often made the transatlantic voyage herself, serving as the packet's supercargo.

With her packet line thriving, Margaret de Vries remarried. But in remarriage she was not required to sign away the de Vries-based fortune she had built. A widow could require a prenuptial contract with her new husband which guaranteed her possession of her own wealth. Nor did her new husband, Frederick Philipse, make any effort to put an end to Margaret's business activities. As Margaret Hardenbroeck de Vries Philipse, she continued her operations under a special femme sole status and even assisted her husband in the investment of his own fortune. [Dexter 1924]

The majority of the colonial businesswomen were not so independent as Margaret Philipse. These women entered the business world in search of a livelihood. Most turned to occupations which drew upon their domestic training, turning the chores of marriage into marketable skills. Typical of this sort of enterprise was the transformation of housekeeping into tavern-keeping. A widow with a roomy house began her career as tavernkeeper simply by opening her home to travellers. In her "Plume of Feathers" or her "Blue Anchor" she performed the familiar domestic routine of bed-making, sweeping, and cooking for paying guests, while employing a man to supervise the tavern taproom. [Dexter 1924]

In the eighteenth century widows branched out into coffee houses as well as taverns and inns. Modelled on the English coffeehouses, these were establishments "For the Entertainment of Gentlemen, Benefit of Commerce, and Dispatch of Business"; in short, meeting places and unofficial offices for the merchants, lawyers, and shipping magnates of Boston, New York, Philadelphia, or Charlestown. [Dexter 1924]

Many women simply marketed a particular domestic skill. Colonial newspapers carried advertisements for dressmakers, seamstresses, silkdyers, starchmakers, and laundresses. In the South, wet nurses were for hire. There were amongst these enterprising women specialists like "Mary Morcomb, Mantua Maker from London." [Dexter 1924, p. 42] Some, like Jane Moreland, catered to refined tastes, offering Philadelphia women gourmet treats like "sausages, Black and White Pudding, Tripes, & Cow Heels, likewise pickled Sheeps Tongues. . . ." [Dexter 1924, pp. 46–47] Some, like Mary Bannister, catered instead to human gullibility. Mary made her fortune from quack medicines, offering "Drops of Venice Treacle" as cure for 101 ills. And yet others catered to human vanity. Among them, a Mrs. Edwards, who offered for sale

> an admirable Beautifying Wash, for Hands, Face, and Neck, it makes the Skin soft, smooth and plump, it likewise takes away

> Redness, Freckles, Sun-burnings, or Pimples, and cures Postules, Itchings, Ring-Worms, Tetters, Scurf, Morphew, and other like Deformities of the Face and Skin, (Intirely free from any Corroding Qualities) and brings to an exquisite Beauty, with Lip Salve, and Tooth Powder, all sold very Cheap. [Dexter 1924, p. 71]

Many of these colonial businesswomen were in fact new arrivals to the colonies from England, and may well have been spinsters rather than widows. Native spinsters favored school-keeping as a livelihood, although only the common schools, where rudimentary skills were taught, were open to them. New England's famous Latin schools and college preparatory academies remained outside a woman teacher's reach. By the late seventeenth century, boarding schools for girls were the woman teacher's best opportunity. Like tavern-keeping, managing a boarding school enabled a woman to transform familiar domestic duties into profit-making ones. These schools were much publicized. A typical advertisement, appearing in the *Boston Gazette* on May 24, 1736, announced that "Mrs Sarah Todd has now opened a school to teach young Women Writing, and Cyphering . . . at the same house young Gentlewomen are boarded and all sorts of Needle Work is taught." [Dexter 1924, p. 90]

But not all women were bound by their domestic experiences. Colonial widows tried their hand in the mercantile world as grocers, tobacconists, wine merchants, booksellers, and owners of hardware and dry goods shops. Perhaps more surprising were the occasional women blacksmiths, tinworkers, shoemakers, shipwrights, tanners, butchers, and even gunsmiths. These women rarely started businesses of their own; instead most stepped into their husband's place at his death. They had inherited their unusual profession rather than chosen it.

Despite the wide economic freedoms it granted, femme sole remained a carefully circumscribed status. The femme sole's "stake in society" was not allowed political expression: no political rights flowed, as they did for men, from a woman's ownership of property or accumulation of wealth. She, like her married sisters, lived in a society shaped by the decisions of men.

Most married women had no meaningful frame of reference in which to perceive political discrimination; it was simply one in a host of factors which created and insured her dependency. But the woman dealing in the marketplace was in a position to perceive the relationship between political and economic power. She felt immediately and directly the effects of legislative decision-making upon her enterprises, whether it was a matter of tax rates, land policy, or the location of a new road or wharf. It was only from her that any opposition to the political rules could reasonably be expected to originate. But those few women who did challenge their political exclusion did not do so in the name of their entire sex. They acted as individuals, or as the special economic interest groups they were. Yet the response to their demands *were* sex-based. If they did not ask for political rights as women, they were nevertheless denied them by a reference to their sex.

One of the women to make such a demand for political rights was Margaret Brent, who settled in Maryland with her sisters and brothers in 1638. Margaret, and her sister Mary Brent, both unmarried, purchased Maryland land, sponsored other settlers, and built homes for them. Margaret Brent soon established herself as a leading land speculator, shrewd businesswoman, and competent lawyer, serving as her brother's attorney before the courts. Her success was not, of course, a rags-to-riches story. She had arrived in the colony with considerable wealth and had enviable connections as a friend (and probably a relative) of the colony's founder, Lord Baltimore. Her accomplishments were, nevertheless, outstanding, and won for her the respect of leading Marylanders like Governor Leonard Calvert. Calvert, in fact, appointed Margaret Brent sole executrix of his vast estate after his death.

Margaret Brent could not have doubted her abilities to handle such a responsibility, but in her efforts to manage Calvert's interests she found herself handicapped. Legislative land policy affected the Calvert holdings; but Margaret Brent could not participate in decisions crucial to the Calvert interests. To rectify this situation she went before the colonial assembly on January 21, 1647–48:

> Came Mrs Margaret Brent and requested to have a vote in the House for herself & voyce allsoe, for that on the last Court 3d January it was ordered that the said Mrs Brent was to be looked upon & received as his Ldp's attorney. The Governor deny'd that the s'd Mrs Brent should have any vote in the house. And the s'd Mrs Brent protested against all proceedings in this present Assembly unlesse she may be present and have vote as afores'd. [Earle 1962, pp. 45–46]

Her protests were in vain. And, only a decade after Margaret Brent's unsuccessful challenge a Maryland proclamation ended the right of women to represent a client in a court of law. [Morris 1930]

Women based their demands for political rights upon satisfactory compliance with the traditional qualifications of property or wealth, not upon any appeal to radical notions of universal suffrage. When, for example, the women merchants of New York begged for a redress of grievances in 1733, they phrased their appeal to read:

> We, widows of this city, have had a meeting as our case is something deplorable, we beg you will give it place in your Weekly Journal, that we may be relieved, it is as follows. We are house keepers, pay our taxes, carry on trade and most of us are she merchants, and as we in some measure contribute to the support of the government, we ought to be entitled to some of the sweets of it [Morris 1930, pp. 133–34; Smith 1970, p. 54]

No concessions were made to these women merchants and taxpayers. The principle of political exclusion based on sex outlasted all others, including property and race.

NON-FREE WOMEN IN THE COLONIAL WORLD: INDENTURED SERVANTS AND SLAVES

There were many women under constraints different from those of the colonial housewife or businesswoman. For the white indentured servant, these were the result of a temporary arrangement in law; for the black slave woman, they were permanent realities.

Indentured servants, historian Richard Hofstadter estimates, made up at least half of the white immigration to colonial America. [Hofstadter 1973] These colonists, unable to pay the expense of the transatlantic voyage or the costs of self-support in the new world, sold their only asset–their labor–for four to seven years in return for travel costs or maintenance. There were many more men who bound themselves out than there were women, but houses and farms throughout the colonies enjoyed the domestic toil of female servants.

Perhaps the most striking characteristic of indenture for the woman was the reversal in expectations it laid upon her. In a milieu of marriage and fecundity, she was enjoined to celibacy. Her value to her master or mistress lay in her capacity for work, and the disability of pregnancy was interpreted as a breach of her contract. An indentured woman could find her term of servitude legally extended if childbearing interfered with fulfillment of her duties.

For the woman servant whose master had fathered her child, the colonial bastardy laws were a unique form of double jeopardy. The threat of physical punishment by her master hung over her head if she revealed his paternity; yet at the same time, the courts awarded the master added years of her service if she did not speak up. When, in 1692, legislators of colonial Virginia conceded the injustice of the servant woman's situation, she gained little by the reform of the law. The penalty of extended service remained, although her additional two years' work was sold for the benefit of the parish church rather than granted to her guilty master. [Spruill 1938]

Once free of her indentured condition, the white servant woman was subject to the laws and the ideology of the society she had entered.

The unfree black woman, like her male counterpart, was above all else, property. If the laws of marriage or indenture restricted women's legal or political identity, the institution of chattel slavery removed much of the human identity of its victims as well. Many of the social and moral divisions drawn between the behavior and the treatment of the sexes in white society vanished in a system which made of both male and female possessions rather than persons. The slave woman of the South thus enjoyed an ironic emancipation from the ideology of separate spheres: she could be sent to labor in the fields, for example, although the laws governing white servants followed social custom and prohibited the use of women in nondomestic or "masculine" chores. [Jordan 1969]

In the fields, the slave's femininity commanded no special legal or practical distinction in treatment. Her workday, like the male's, was sunup to sundown. Only pregnancy altered the sex-blind requirements upon slave labor. [Lerner 1972]

The realities of sex differences did, however, enter into the bookkeeping of slavery. Women field workers were worth less in the marketplace than men, because their productivity was lower. A woman's value–or price–increased, however, if she was able to perform in the more specialized area of childbearing. Advertisements like the following–"Pat, 'with child'–lame on one side, and a 'fine breeding woman' "–were common in colonial newspapers. [Mullin 1972, pp. 8–9]

Within the slave subculture itself, the traditional roles of male and female, emanating from the family unit organization, could not be fully sustained. Slave women did perform the domestic chores–sewing, mending, preparation of meals, child rearing–but the basic exchange of male support and protection for female obedience and assistance was not possible within slavery. [Lerner 1972] The complete dependence of all slaves upon the plantation master vitiated the social function of marriage and the family unit.

The family, as a social and legal institution, was itself incompatible with the requirements of slavery. For example, the rule of monogamy, central to white marriage, could run counter to the profitability of slave breeding. The sense of obligation of parent to child, also stressed in the free white society, could act as a hindrance in a system in which profitable allocation of resources often led to the sale of either parent or of child.

The nature of the male-female relationship was ultimately determined by the master. Frequently the resulting arrangements reflected the master's arbitrary selection of certain conventions of white society. In many instances, slave "marriages" were sanctioned and encouraged, and masters often acted as guardians of morality, interfering in the slaves' domestic life with punishments for quarreling, infidelity, or for physical abuse of one another. [Mullin 1972] These slave marriages thus incorporated the *moral* aspects of the white institution, but they lacked its legal and social function.[5]

As slaves were dependent upon masters for the shaping of their own sexual relationships, so too were they dependent in the shaping of sexual relationships with white society. Although intermarriage between the

[5] In the northern colonies, the slave subculture conformed more closely to the white society in which it was more diffusely integrated. Laws and customs regarding marriage were in force for blacks as well as whites and New England slaves were compelled to marry according to the rules of the predominant culture. Wedding bans were publicly read or published, marital fidelity expected, and the marriage recorded in civil records. [Greene 1966]

races was forbidden by the year 1700 in most southern colonies [Jordan 1969], sexual intercourse was not. Masters who chastised their slaves for marital infidelity apparently saw no moral contradiction in demanding submission from black slave women. Widespread, almost institutionalized, miscegenation in the South was noted by colonial figures themselves. "The enjoyment of a negro or mulatto woman is spoken of as quite a common thing," observed Bostonian Josiah Quincy, on a visit to Charlestown, South Carolina. "No reluctance, delicacy, or shame is made about the matter." [Jordan 1969, p. 145] Historian Gerald Mullin points out that slave masters certainly knew their slave women better than they knew their men. Descriptions of female fugitive slaves often revealed intimate anatomical knowledge, citing a large scar "as long as one's Finger above her Breast," or "Milly with Grey eyes and very large Breasts." [Mullin 1972, p. 104]

Often sexuality was the slave woman's only effective weapon in resistance to her enslavement. Fugitive black women, unable to survive alone in the outside world, exchanged sexual freedoms for freedom from slavery. They ran off with white men, or, in the revolutionary era, they fled the plantation to the "shelter" of troop barracks. [Mullin 1972] Even for the freed black woman the dependent sexual relationship with a white man was often her best of limited options in southern society. For her, economic independence was possible only through employment as a seamstress or as a wet nurse. [Lerner 1972]

The few instances on record in which individual achievement and personal growth were encouraged in slave women occur within the domestic slavery of New England. There the thin ranks of black poetesses and authors were filled, and women like Lucy Terry of Deerfield, Massachusetts or Phyllis Wheatley of Boston were given the opportunity to express themselves. Few female slaves received the special attention accorded a Phyllis Wheatley, however; few had a mistress like Mrs. Wheatley who taught a seven-year-old African girl to read and write English and Latin, encouraged her creativity, and treated this slave as a daughter rather than a servant. [Dannett 1964] Thus, few records remain of the individual lives of the colonial black women.

ANGLICIZING AMERICA: NEW IDEAS OF FEMININITY AND A CALL FOR WOMEN'S EDUCATION

As the American colonies matured, a process that historian John Murrin has called "anglicization" took place. This was a movement, sometimes conscious, sometimes not, toward uniformity of law and custom with the Mother Country. The process has been most clearly traced in the colonial legal systems, which had been flexible and adaptable to local circumstances, but grew more rigid and less individualistic as they were brought into conformity with English law. [Murrin 1966; Morris 1931] But anglicization was also reflected in the urge among the more comfortable classes to imitate their English social superiors. [Smith

1970] New social attitudes and styles from the Mother Country began to shape American upper and middle class life. Often, however, the gap between English realities and American realities made the colonial imitation imperfect.

In seventeenth century England, mores and morals had undergone a revolution and restoration no less drastic than their political counterparts. If the mid-century social style was set by the sombre Puritan regime, the return of royal rule in 1660 heralded an era in which frivolity was raised to an art form. Morality, as conventionally defined, was sacrificed to pleasure, and a cheerful decadence settled upon the English upper classes.

A key element of this new lifestyle was the emphasis upon leisure and nonproductive activities among women. Wealthy Englishwomen foreswore any useful activities, thus ending that participation in the management of their fortunes which had been the model for colonial businesswomen like Margaret Philipse and Margaret Brent. Unlike Reverend Cotton Mather's "ornaments"–women who practiced the commendable virtues of thrift and industry–these women became decorative "ornaments," good only for show and pleasures. Their outer appearance reflected the new values, for the exaggerated hairdos, wide hoopskirts, and tightly laced waists all restricted movement for the sake of presenting beauty.

Within a decade a modest campaign to curb these Restoration extravagances had been mounted. Several books, written before the turn of the century, were addressed to this crisis in morality. Their authors begged Englishwomen to return, not to productive activity, but to a role as moral leaders in their society. This appeal was based on the revival of a corollary to the traditional ideology of woman's subordination to man. It was now argued, as it had been earlier by religious leaders as prestigious as Cotton Mather, that one privileged result of women's passivity, submissiveness, and necessary habit of obedience was their sex's greater receptivity to piety and to the morality which flowed from sincere commitment to one's faith. Women who embraced the submissive role were thus raised to the exalted position of moral leaders of society.

Because no effort was made to distinguish social conditioning from innate capacity, all women were assumed to share the basic affinity for virtue or morality. Yet if the capacity were innate, the actual realization of its potential appeared to require training. A woman, it seemed, must prepare herself to receive this special grace. Virtuous *behavior* was prescribed as the best preparation for the growth within the woman of true virtue. Thus, the morality tracts of the late seventeenth century were, in large part, "how-to" books, instructing a woman in how to develop and employ her gifts of submission, passivity, obedience, and compassion through the perfection of a certain feminine pattern of thought and feminine style of behavior. The display of virtue was assumed to prompt real virtue to flourish within her, and her virtue, in turn, would encourage imitation by the men around her.

These morality tracts were widely read in the colonies, although they spoke to a social problem not really crucial in American culture. American society lagged far behind in the race to decadence, for the colonial rich could not equal the English extravagances. Nevertheless, these books had great impact in America, and their reception was not merely a case of a cure being embraced before the contagion set in.

These books spoke to the colonial audience because their theme was filtered through the American experience. English authors urged a return to virtue as an antidote to decadence. But the colonists found it possible to read into the authors' emphasis on passivity and meekness a call from colonial rough-and-ready female behavior to a more refined, "lady-like" or feminine behavior suitable to a prosperous class. Thus, the colonists approached the books from exactly the opposite direction their authors intended. Not yet decadent, the prosperous Americans heeded a call to gentility. They took for granted many of the virtues the authors espoused and focused their attention upon the style of behavior called for rather than its moral purpose. It was not to the philosophical arguments but to the etiquette of books like *The Ladies Calling* [1720] that colonists turned their attention; it was not the author's praise of modesty as a supreme virtue which educated American readers, but his explanation of how a quiet voice—"like the imaginery Musick of the Spheres, sweet and Charming; but not to be heard at a distance"—would proclaim that virtue. [*The Ladies Calling* 1720, pp. 6–7] Passivity, sensitivity, and especially delicacy were components of a style now possible among the colonial well-to-do, a style which would help set them apart from their poorer neighbors. The idle but gracious wife it produced would serve to highlight a colonial husband's own success.

If then the morality tracts served primarily as etiquette books for the new colonial woman, they pointed the way to some radical developments in English thought. The central notion of books like *The Ladies Calling* was, after all, that women's behavior was a matter of training rather than natural impulse. The elaborate etiquette and moral discipline prescribed for women in these books made no sense unless the authors of such tracts conceded this point. While they were careful to stress that the training was devised only to bring to fruition certain "natural" tendencies in the female sex, nevertheless their operating assumption was that nurture, not nature determined sex-exclusive behavior.

The implications of this assumption were perhaps only vaguely understood by those who brought it forth. If a good program of training was guaranteed to produce the moral leaders society needed, then the absence of such a program, or a negative program, must account for much of the frivolity and immorality exhibited by this post-Restoration generation of women. Likewise men's productive activities, their superior talents and abilities—these must be explained in some measure by their training or education. In the end, the author of *The Ladies Calling* thoughtfully concluded: "Men have their parts cultivated and improv'd by Education . . . And truly had Women the same advantage, I dare not say but they would make as good returns of it. . . ." [preface]

If in fact education or training shaped human behavior, and if a woman had been deprived of positive training, what then was her potential if, for example, she were to receive the education reserved for a man? Was the inequality of talent also a result of the inequality of training? If the author of *The Ladies Calling* had lifted this lid to the Pandora's box of the relationship of the sexes, he quickly slammed it tight again. Only occasionally did someone follow to its logical conclusions the notion that nurture not nature determined the human product. The eighteenth century educator Mary Astell, for example, argued that the sexes were equal in abilities, and only deprivation and repression held women in their subordinate condition. Yet even Astell refused to let this discovery of equality in human potential interfere with the appropriate destinies of the respective sexes. Woman's ultimate fulfillment remained, biologically as mother, socially as wife. [Benson 1935]

Neither English nor American society was willing to grapple with these questions of first cause in the relationship of the sexes. The notion of inequality as a result of education was lost, overshadowed by the enthusiastic movement to apply its one acceptable implication: women could be, and ought to be, better educated in order that they might be better helpmeets in marriage. Formal education was espoused for women, with reading, writing, arithmetic, and theology given in doses not powerful enough to disturb the inequality between the sexes, but sufficient to help women perform their various duties as wife and mother more satisfactorily. Education was advocated for a woman not in the name of her own individual growth but as a means to make her a more agreeable companion to her husband and a better mother to her children.

In the years that followed, education was espoused as a corrective to all feminine vices. Studying was deemed an excellent preventive of mischief. If the idle hands of the rich could no longer be fitly employed in common housework, then idle minds would be employed in learning. In short, as physical work within the domestic sphere diminished, as women withdrew from helpmeet activities outside the home, emphasis upon a feminine style and attitude—both to be learned from books—increased.

The champions of women's education were readily received by the eighteenth century colonists. Among the most popular of the enlightened English reformers was Mrs. Eliza Haywood, whose novels and magazine, the *Female Spectator*, popularized the ideas of the drier treatises on education. Indeed, the most effective teaching device proved to be the novel. American women, like their English sisters, found models of femininity for themselves in the pages of books by Richardson and Mrs. Haywood. Such novelists showed a sensitivity to the potential incompatibility of education and submissive behavior; as if to offset any boldness which education might unleash, they made their heroines submissive creatures, who bent to circumstances as well as to men with womanly resignation. In the end, the heroine's beauty (style) and goodness (attitude), not her skill or intelligence saved her. And, as just reward, she inevitably lived happily ever after. [Benson 1935]

The emphasis in the early eighteenth century was thus on education as a tool for insuring feminine women, women whose attitudes and personal style, rather than any actual usefulness, made them good wives and mothers. Such a context for education threatened no radical alteration in the male–female relationship. Yet there were those who continued to fear that education was a threat to this relationship. It was these conservative thinkers of the second quarter of the eighteenth century who reraised, in order that they might put to rest, the questions of nature and nurture.

The two leading spokesmen of the conservative counterattack were Reverend James Fordyce and Dr. John Gregory. Through their writings both men hoped to firmly reestablish the primacy of physical rather than intellectual endowments in the ordering of the sexual relationship. The crux of their argument was that women were inferior to men, and dependent upon them, because of their physical weakness. This physical inferiority was the determining factor for woman's behavior; as a weak being, her survival in the world depended upon her ability to acquire male protection. A woman must, therefore, of the most basic necessity cultivate behavior which activates the protective impulse in men. Timidity, delicacy, piety, a sweetness of manner and voice–a display of these qualities, rather than a quick wit or a well-trained mind, awakened that impulse. A woman could, it was true, become a man's intellectual equal (although Fordyce retains doubts on this score), but in doing so she endangers her existence. "You yourselves," Fordyce coaxed the ladies, "will allow that war, commerce, politics, exercises of strength and dexterity, abstract philosophy, and all the abstruser sciences, are most properly the province of men. . . ." But in case the ladies would not allow this, he added as a warning: "those masculine women that would plead for your sharing any part of this province equally with us do not understand your true interests." [Spruill 1938, p. 221] The educated "masculine woman"–she was, if not unnatural, highly dangerous to the survival of her sex.

What Fordyce and Gregory had developed was a teleological explanation for the traditional sexual relationship. Their opposition to the education of women in other than the feminine arts of pleasing men rested on a conviction that the resulting independent behavior in the educated female would cause the vital male protective instinct to atrophy.

Both authors found a receptive audience among the American well-to-do. But it is not likely that the American interest centered on the Englishmen's shared nightmare vision of a breakdown in the established sexual relationship. American society had survived intact the independent behavior of femme sole businesswomen and pioneer wives. Fordyce and Gregory wrote books that were valued, as *The Ladies Calling* had been, for their full descriptions of behavior producing "exquisite sensibility and delicacy." It was these descriptions which, if imitated in daily life, would aid in the refining of the colonial lady.

THE AMERICAN REVOLUTION: A SUSPENSION OF "EXQUISITE DELICACY"

Ironically, it was the thrust for national independence which jolted this new pattern of gentility, with its complete withdrawal of women from public life or serious concerns. The participation of women in political protest, a participation which once again expanded the boundaries of the domestic circle, was valuable to radical organizers of the American protest. Not retiring modesty but active zeal became the greatest virtue of the helpmeet in prerevolutionary America.

The exigency of political struggle seemed to suspend the carefully established rules of behavior. Women were called upon to look outside their immediate family circle, to take a stand on public issues, and even to organize appropriate protests themselves. When, in the early 1770s, Philadelphia women and Boston women announced their organization of associations to ban tea, sympathetic colonial newspaper editors praised the women for initiative and courage. No mention of unseemly behavior was made. Yet, conservative Englishmen, finding traditional attitudes in accord with their political positions, ridiculed the women's organizations on exactly those grounds of unnatural, unfeminine behavior. [Benson 1935]

During the war itself, most patriotic women made their sacrifices to national interest along traditional lines. They remained in their homes, knitting socks for the soldiers, weaving linsey-woolsey, rolling bandages. Yet there were women who organized fund drives, and made door-to-door canvassings through the streets of Philadelphia or New York. Clearly these activities outside the home defied the century's conventions of exquisite delicacy and retiring modesty. [Douglas 1966]

For other women the strict division of roles seemed to break down completely, and they took up arms in battle. Some did so as individuals: women like Deborah Samson, who, disguised as a man, enlisted in Washington's army and took her place on the front lines. [Douglas 1966] But most of these women who fought had not come to the war as individuals. They came as faithful wives. They had joined the army's entourage as cooks and nurses, performing their domestic chores in a military setting. When these "Molly Pitchers" took up arms it was to replace a soldier-husband who had been killed or wounded in his wife's presence. This military participation by "Molly Pitchers" was no myth born of postwar reminiscences; the records of the Continental Congress attest to the reality of fighting women. The government granted pensions to women soldiers like Margaret Corbin, "wounded and disabled at the attack on Fort Washington, while she heroically filled the post of her husband." [Ellet 1969, pp. 123–24]

With the war's end, political and military activities by women ceased and women soldiers and community organizers returned to the narrowly defined feminine, or domestic, concerns. It did not appear that the revolutionary credo of individual liberty would alter the status of women in the new nation.

BIBLIOGRAPHY

Mary Summer Benson, *Women in Eighteenth Century America: A Study of Opinion and Social Usage*. Columbia University Press, 1935.

Anne Bradstreet, "The Prologue," *The Tenth Muse Lately Sprung Up in America.* Printed for Stephen Bowtell, London, 1650.

Arthur W. Calhoun, *A Social History of the American Family from Colonial Times to the Present, Volume I.* Barnes and Noble, 1945.

Sylvia Dannett, *Profiles of Negro Womanhood, Volume I, 1619–1900.* Educational Heritage Inc., Negro Heritage Library, 1964.

Carl Degler, *Out of Our Past: The Forces That Shaped Modern America.* Harper-Colophon, 1959.

John Demos, "Notes on Plymouth Colony." *William and Mary Quarterly*, 3rd Series, 1965, 264–286.

John Demos, *A Little Commonwealth: Family Life in Plymouth Colony.* Oxford University Press, 1971.

Elizabeth Dexter, *Colonial Women of Affairs; A Study of Women in Business and the Professions in America Before 1776.* Houghton Mifflin, 1924.

Emily Douglas, *Remember the Ladies: The Story of Great Women Who Helped Shape America.* Putnam's, 1966.

Alice Morse Earle, *Colonial Dames and Good Wives.* Frederick Ungar, 1962.

Elizabeth F. Ellet, *The Women of the American Revolution, Volume I.* Haskell House, 1969.

Kai T. Erikson, *Wayward Puritans: A Study in the Sociology of Deviance.* John Wiley & Sons, 1966.

Willystine Goodsell, *A History of Marriage and the Family.* Macmillan, 1934.

Lorenzo J. Greene, *The Negro in Colonial New England, 1620–1776.* Kennikat, 1966.

Richard Hofstadter, *America at 1750: A Social Portrait.* Vintage, 1973.

James K. Hosmer, ed., *John Winthrop, Winthrop's Journal, "History of New England, 1630–1649," Volume II.* Scribner's Sons, 1908.

Winthrop Jordan, *White Over Black.* Pelican, 1969.

Gerda, Lerner, *The Woman in American History.* Addison-Wesley, 1972.

Cotton Mather, *Ornaments for the Daughters of Zion.* Samuel Phillips, 1692.

John Milton, *Paradise Lost.* S. Simmons, London, 1669.

Edmund S. Morgan, *The Puritan Family, Religion and Domestic Relations in Seventeenth Century New England.* Harper & Row, 1966.

Richard B. Morris, *Studies in the History of American Law.* Columbia University Press, 1930.

Richard B. Morris, "Legalism versus Revolutionary Doctrine in New England." *New England Quarterly*, 1931, 4: 195–205.

Gerald W. Mullin, *Flight and Rebellion, Slave Resistance in Eighteenth Century Virginia.* Oxford University Press, 1972.

John Murrin, "Anglicizing an American Colony: The Transformation of Provincial Massachusetts." Unpublished doctoral dissertation. Yale University, 1966.

Page Smith, *Daughters of the Promised Land.* Little, Brown, 1970.

Julia Cherry Spruill, *Women's Life and Work in the Southern Colonies.* University of North Carolina Press, 1938.

The Ladies Calling, in Two Parts. Printed at the Theater, Oxford, England, 1720.

Mark Van Doren, ed., *Samuel Sewall's Diary.* Macy-Marius, 1927.

L. Kinvin Wroth, Hiller B. Zobel, eds., *Legal Papers of John Adams, Volume I.* Harvard University Press, 1965.

1

Suggestions for Further Reading

Gary Nash provides an excellent introduction to the various cultures in the colonies in *Red, White and Black: The Peoples of Early America** (Prentice-Hall, 1974). For Virginia, see Wesley Frank Craven, *White, Red, and Black: The Seventeenth Century Virginian* (University Press of Virginia, 1971).

Good introductions to American Indian life are Alvin M. Josephy, Jr., *The Indian Heritage of America** (Knopf, 1968); Peter Farb, *Man's Rise to Civilization as Shown by the Indians of North America from Primeval Times to the Coming of the Industrial State** (Dutton, 1968); Angie Debo, *A History of the Indians in The United States* (University of Oklahoma Press, 1970); and Wilcomb E. Washburn, *The Indian in America** (Harper and Row, 1975). Relations between Indians and whites throughout American history are treated in Francis Paul Prucha, *A Bibliographical Guide to the History of Indian-White Relations in the United States** (University of Chicago Press, 1977); William T. Hagan, *American Indians** (University of Chicago Press, 1961); Roy Harvey Pearce, *The Savages of America: A Study of the Indian and the Idea of Civilization** (Johns Hopkins Press, 1953); and two works by Wilcomb E. Washburn, *Red Man's Land/White Man's Law: A Study of the Past and Present Status of the American Indian* (Scribner, 1971) and *The Indian and the White Man** (Doubleday, 1964), a collection of documents. Special problems are confronted in Alfred W. Crosby, Jr., *The Columbian Exchange: Biological and Cultural Consequences of 1492** (Greenwood Press, 1972); William M. Denevan, *The Native Population of the Americas in 1492* (University of Wisconsin Press, 1976); and Wilbur R. Jacobs, *Dispossessing the American Indian: Indians and Whites on the Colonial Frontier** (Scribner, 1972).

American slavery is placed in the context of world history in David B. Davis' works, *The Problem of Slavery in Western Culture** (Cornell University Press, 1966) and *The Problem of Slavery in the Age of Revolution, 1770–1823** (Cornell University Press, 1975). On the origin of slavery in the United States, see Winthrop D. Jordan, *White Over Black: American Attitudes Toward the Negro, 1550–1812** (University of North Carolina Press, 1968) and Edmund S. Morgan, *American Slavery, American Freedom: The Ordeal of Colonial Virginia** (Norton, 1975). The basic primary source on the slave trade is Elizabeth Donnan, ed., *Documents Illustrative of the Slave Trade to America*, 4 vols. (Carnegie Institution, 1930–1935). Philip D. Curtin's book *The Atlantic Slave Trade: A Census** (University of Wisconsin Press, 1969) is a provocative study of the numbers of slaves imported to the various

* Available in paperback edition.

parts of the New World. A good secondary treatment of the trade is Daniel P. Mannix and Malcolm Cowley, *Black Cargoes: A History of the Atlantic Slave Trade, 1518–1865** (Viking, 1962). On slavery in the individual colonies see Lorenzo Greene, *The Negro in Colonial New England** (Columbia University Press, 1942); Thaddeus Tate, Jr., *The Negro in Eighteenth-Century Williamsburg** (University of Virginia Press, 1965); Gerald W. Mullin, *Flight and Rebellion: Slave Resistance in Eighteenth Century Virginia** (Oxford University Press, 1972), and Peter H. Wood, *Black Majority: Negroes in Colonial South Carolina from 1670 through the Stono Rebellion** (Knopf, 1974).

The standard works on white servants and laborers in the colonies are Abbot E. Smith, *Colonists in Bondage: White Servitude and Convict Labor in America, 1607–1776** (University of North Carolina Press, 1947), and Richard B. Morris, *Government and Labor in Early America** (Columbia University Press, 1946). Warren B. Smith examines the situation in a single state with *White Servitude in Colonial South Carolina** (University of South Carolina Press, 1961). John Barth's novel *The Sot-Weed Factor** (Doubleday, 1960) gives a hilarious, bawdy, and generally correct picture of life in colonial Maryland, in the process conveying a good deal of information about white servitude.

Works which provide an overview of the history of women in America are Mary Ryan, *Womanhood in America: From Colonial Times to the Present* (New Viewpoints, 1975); Jean E. Friedman and William G. Shade, eds., *Our Sisters: Women in American Life and Thought** (Allyn and Bacon, 1973); and Carol Ruth Berkin and Mary Beth Norton, eds., *The Women of America: Original Essays and Documents** (Houghton-Mifflin, 1978). For an older but still valuable study of Southern women see Julia Cherry Spruill, *Women's Life and Work in the Southern Colonies** (University of North Carolina Press, 1938). Most studies of family life in the colonies provide insight into the role of women. See, for example, Edmund S. Morgan, *The Puritan Family** (Harper and Row, 1966); John Demos, *A Little Commonwealth: Family Life in Plymouth Colony** (Oxford University Press, 1970); and Philip J. Greven, Jr., *Four Generations: Population, Land, and Family in Colonial Andover, Massachusetts** (Cornell University Press, 1970).

2 The New Nation

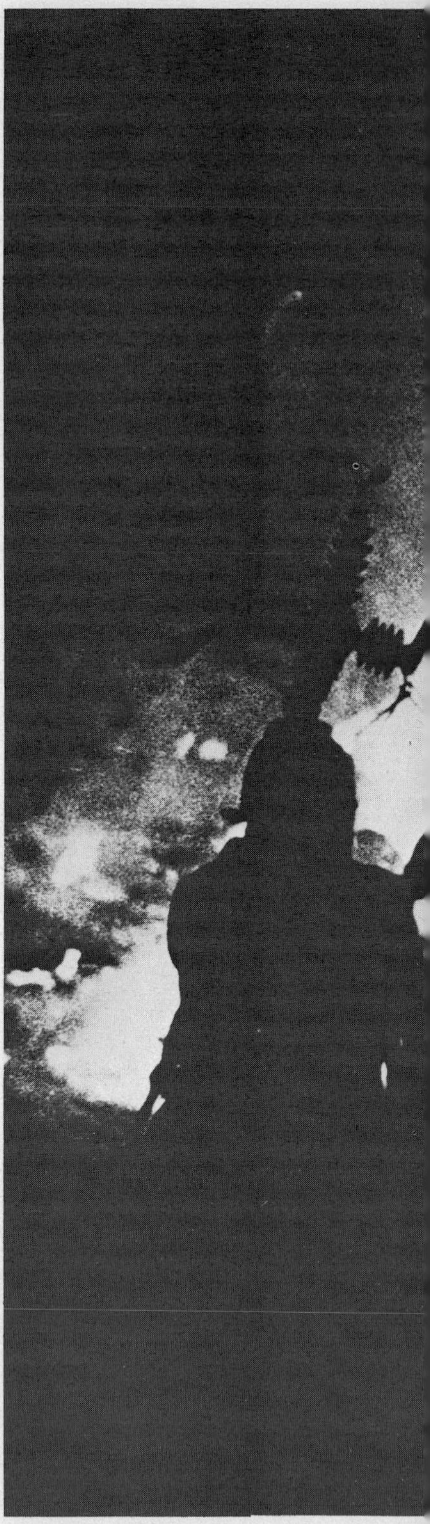

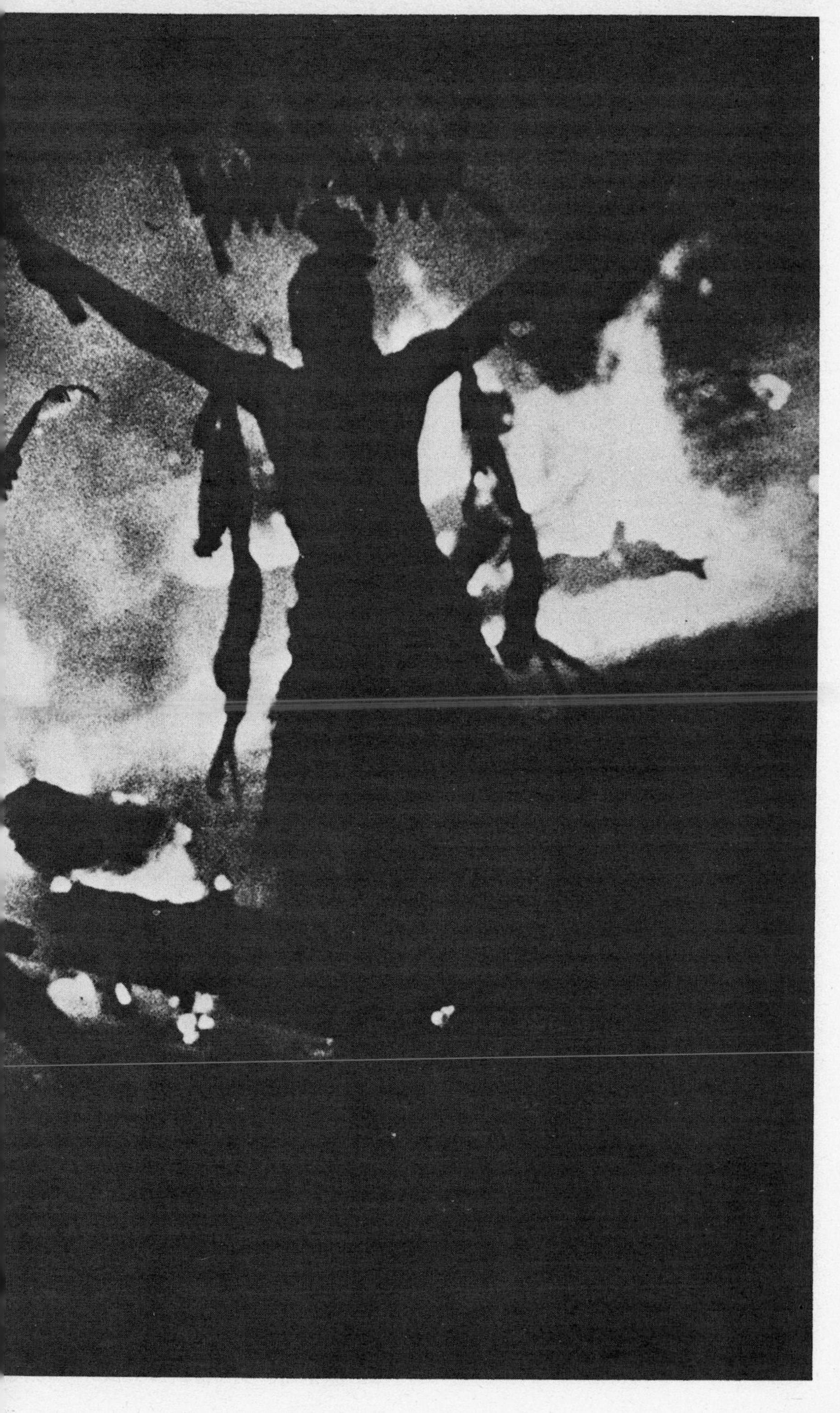

The Rebirth of the Seneca

ANTHONY F. C. WALLACE

The Indians met the advance of white settlers in various ways. During the colonial period and in the early years of the American nation, some Indians must have have hoped to halt the white man through military action. However, the peace treaties that followed military skirmishes were regularly ignored by whites, and endless armed conflict was obviously out of the question. Some Indians must have considered the possibility of seeking admission to the Union as separate Indian states. Although in retrospect this may seem a vain hope, it did not appear to be so at the time. Article VI of the Delaware Treaty of September 17, 1778, for example, contained the following statement:

> The United States do engage to guarantee to the aforesaid nation of Delawares, and their heirs, all their territorial rights in the fullest and most ample manner as it hath been bound by former treaties, as long as they the said Delaware nation shall abide by and hold fast the chain of friendship now entered into. And it is further agreed on between the contracting parties should it for the future be found conducive for the mutual interest of both parties to invite any other tribes who have been friends to the interest of the United States, to join the present confederation, and to form a state whereof the Delaware nation shall be the head, and have a representation in Congress: Provided, nothing contained in this article to be considered as conclusive until it meets with the approbation of Congress.

Indian unity also seemed to some to hold out genuine possibilities. On the other hand, the history of the Indian nations in America is anything but the story of increasing cooperation. Although there were some confederations among Indian groups, such as those of the Creek and the Iroquois, not even the presence of a common enemy led to the formation of permanent alliances. Pan-Indianism met the fate of similar movements the world over—Pan-Slavism, Pan-Arabism, Pan-Africanism, all have demonstrated a low degree of cohesiveness and effectiveness.

The Six Nations of the Iroquois, the most powerful Indian organization in the Northeastern United States, suffered disastrously after the War for American Independence. They had fought, for the most part, on the side of the English but had been left out of the peace proceedings. The United States was determined to have much of the land that the Iroquois controlled and by the turn of the century had succeeded in restricting the nations of the once proud confederacy to a few reservation areas.

As the Iroquois confederacy disintegrated, one small group of Seneca Indians, under the leadership of their chief, Cornplanter, settled in the Allegheny Mountains of New York State. They found themselves in a profound malaise, their confidence destroyed as a result of their multiple defeats at the hands of a clearly more highly developed civilization. The major question they confronted was the direction in which the tribal group should move in the face of this challenge. Should they retreat as far as possible from contact with the white man's culture and seek to preserve what little they had left until they and the traditions died, or should they seek to make an adjustment to the dominant culture, changing certain of their practices in an attempt to rebuild their tribal life in a way that would enable them to live in the midst of the white men without losing their distinctiveness? It was at this point, in 1799, that Handsome Lake, the brother of Cornplanter, began to have the series of visions that would provide for the revitalization of the Seneca culture and the establishment of a new religion which is still practiced among many of the Iroquois.

Anthony F. C. Wallace, an anthropologist at the University of Pennsylvania, has described this process of disintegration and revitalization in his brilliant book on the history of the Seneca. The selection from that work reprinted below describes the major themes in Handsome Lake's preaching that contributed to the rebirth of the Seneca culture. In this example of acculturation can be clearly seen the possibility of a blending of cultural practices that stops well short of assimilation, and allows for the continuance of many valuable traditional practices in the midst of modernization.

Handsome Lake's preaching was remarkably effective. Inspired by their prophet and taking advantage of the educational and technological aid offered by religious and government organizations, the Iroquois quickly began to implement the recommendations of the social gospel. A true renaissance occurred on many of the reservations in the years between 1799 and 1815. This renaissance affected the lives of the Iroquois most conspicuously in matters of temperance, technology, and religious observance.

Thus, long before his death in 1815, Handsome Lake was able to see both a spiritual and a profane reformation among his people. But the political strife that had plagued his own career continued and intensified after his death. It was not until after a generation of political disorder that his old disciples, sickened by the endless contention and threatened by the aggressive proselytizing of the Christian missions, collated and revived his words and made them into the code of a new religion, a religion that survives today as *Gaiwiio*—The Old Way of Handsome Lake.

TEMPERANCE

The implementation of the prophet's demand for temperance was not left to individual conscience. The political structure of the several communities and of the Great League itself was mobilized to exact conformity to the discipline of sobriety. As we have seen, village, tribal, and League councils early met to discuss the prophet's Code and uniformly supported the condemnation of alcohol. At Allegany it was said that "they . . . seldom held a council without some animadversions of their baneful effects" (i.e., of spiritous liquors).[1] At many of these councils Handsome Lake appeared to exhort the people to follow the Code, but his presence was not necessary for his views were widely known and his revelations constantly cited. The Quaker journals and letters and the minutes of their meetings with the Indians were filled with formal declaration of the intention of the chiefs and principal men and women of individual communities to oppose the drinking of liquor. These council resolutions did not, to be sure, have the force of law in the European sense, for there were no police or courts to enforce the resolution; but the council members made it their business to harass nonconformists into sobriety. If the chiefs found out that someone had gotten drunk "when

[1] [Halliday] Jackson, [*Civilization of the Indian Natives*, Philadelphia, Gould,] 1830, p. 51.

they were out in the white settlements, they were sharply reproved by the chiefs on their return, which had nearly the same effect among Indians, as committing a man to the workhouse among white people."[2]

The temperance program moved ahead most rapidly, of course, in the Seneca towns along the Allegheny River, where drunkards were continually under the watchful and reproving eye of Handsome Lake himself. The Quaker reports provide a year-by-year monitoring of the situation there. In May 1799, even before Handsome Lake's first vision, a council in Cornplanter's settlement had resolved not to permit any more whiskey to be imported into the town, and two young men had been appointed "petty chiefs" to enforce the resolution. By the month of September, after the vision, Cornplanter was able to report that the Allegany Seneca "now drank much less than formerly." By 1801 it was reported that "the Indians," including Handsome Lake himself, "now became very sober, generally refraining from the use of strong liquor, both at home and when abroad among the white people. One of them observed to Friends, 'no more get drunk here, now this two year.' "[3] By 1802 under the pressure of the charge that "the Whiskey is the great Engine which the bad Spirit uses to introduce Witchcraft and many other evils amongst Indians," sobriety was "in some degree spreading to other settlements of the Seneca Nation."[4] In 1803 Handsome Lake was praised as being principally responsible for curing the Seneca of "the misuse of that dreadful manbane, distilled spirits."[5] When the Quakers visited the Allegany in 1806, they learned that the surrounding white settlers were amazed by the fact that the Seneca would "entirely refuse liquor when offered to them. The Indians said, that when white people urged them to drink whiskey, they would ask for bread or provisions in its stead."[6] Blacksnake informed the Quakers that the Indians still refused to drink whiskey and were "determined never to let the Whisky rise again."[7] Next year the Allegany chiefs, including Handsome Lake, reported again that their young men had generally given up the drinking of whiskey.[8]

The profit motive, however, which the Quakers were endeavoring to encourage, had mixed effects in regard to the general question of drinking. Two young chiefs in 1807 bought some whiskey and hid it, not for their own use, but for the purpose of selling it to the white people. But this conduct was "much disapproved by the Indians generally."[9] In

[2] Jackson, 1830, pp. 45–46.

[3] [Swarthmore College, Friends' Historical Library, Henry] Simmons Journal, entries under "5th Month" and "9 Mo. 11th," 1799; Jackson, 1830, pp. 35–44.

[4] [Historical Society of Pennsylvania], Logan Papers, Vol. XI, p. 70 (unsigned letter from a Friend at Genesinguhta, January 18, 1802).

[5] [Library of Congress], British Archives, Gilbert's Journal.

[6] Jackson, 1830, p. 51.

[7] [Chester County Historical Society, Halliday] Jackson Journal, 1806; SC, Jackson Journal (published in Snyderman, 1957), September 16, 1806.

[8] [Philadelphia Yearly Meeting, Archives], Indian Committee, Box 2, Speech to Indian Committee by Conudiu *et al.*, November 6, 1807.

[9] [Clements Library, University of Michigan], Isaac Bonsall Journal, 1806–07, entry of September 18, 1807.

1809 it was reported by Allinson that an enterprising white trader, who succeeded in making a number of Seneca drunk on cider royal, was driven away from the Indian settlements: "A White Trader about 5 Months back had bought a Load of Goods up the River and among the rest some Cyder and Cyder Royal–stopping at Cold Spring he offered them for sale and the Indians not aware of the effects of Cyder Royal many of them purchased & Drank particularly a few of their chiefs who collecting in their council Houses alarmed many of the Sober Indians–who threatened to Stave his Casks & let out the Liquor if he did not go away–they however thought it best first to come & advise with Friends & with this View several of their Warriors Came down to Tunassasa–on their Representation Joel Swain & Jacob Taylor went with them to their Town but the Trader probably alarmed with the threats of the Indians and removed his Canoe Further up the River where it is expected he disposed of his Liquors among the White People." Allinson included his observations on Allegany Seneca drinking in 1809 on a positive note: "The Indians of this Settlement generally abstain from the use of Spiritous Liquors so that it has become very rare to see one of them Intoxicated–since which they seldom quarrel or fight among themselves but live in Harmony together–this disposition they endeavour to Cultivate among the Children & hence they rarely differ as is very common with Boys. . . . They are naturally avaricious and saving & not being so liable to Imposition as when they drank Spirits, some of them are growing rich."[10]

Indian storekeepers continued to contribute to backsliding from temperance for many years, and Handsome Lake was unable completely to suppress the traffic in liquor. His prophecies of doom and damnation were used to good effect in reducing it to minor proportions, however. In the fall of 1811 the prophet had been issuing grave warnings of divine retribution "if they fell into their former bad practices." During the winter several earthquake shocks were felt along the borders of Lake Erie and the Niagara frontier "which gave the Indians such alarm that they believ'd the predictions of their prophet was going to be fulfil'd upon them. . . . They believ'd it to be the voice of the great Spirit, that he had now spoken so loud as to be heard and that some great event would follow." Resolutions against whiskey-selling were immediately reasserted. And in 1814 one of the principal Indian whiskey-sellers died of a lingering illness. He had kept a "kind of store" where "from the love of gain" he kept liquor to sell. "In a time of great affliction of body, and distress of mind, he acknowledged that Selling whisky and other bad practices had brought him to that situation–this with the more thoughtful part of the Indians had a serious effect, and in consequence thereof many of their leading characters became again animated to discourage the use of strong drink among them."[11]

On other Seneca reservations, particularly at Cattaraugus and Tonawanda, the temperance movement was also notably successful. In 1801 Red Jacket, as "Chief Speaker of the Seneker Nations," declared that

[10] [Haverford College], William Allinson Journal, Vol. I, p. 26, 38–39, September 17, 1809.

[11] CCHS, Jackson Journal 1810–18, pp. 14–15, 41.

"we have all agreed to quit the use of liquor which you must be in some measure convinced of from what you see at the present meeting" (which was for the purpose of receiving the annuities, and was held at the Genesee River).[12] At Cattaraugus the Quakers were told in 1806 that the chiefs' council "had taken up strong resolutions against the use of Whisky and Strong drink & that all that was then present were Chiefs & each of them kept a daily watch over the rest of the Indians to caution them against drinking Whisky playing ball or other Bad practices which they believ'd was not pleasing to the Great Spirit—but were of the mind that the Great Spirit was better pleas'd when they took hold of the ax or the hoe and set to work—that since they had got their eyes open to see they were sensible that strong drink had done them a great deal of mischief and kept them poor but now they had got hold of it and was determined never to let it rise again & that they were in hopes that the Indians of the Six Nations would in time become master of it."[13] Even more direct was the information given the Quakers at the same settlement in 1809: the Cattaraugus Seneca "had done with the use of spiritous liquors every man, but there were yet three women who would sometimes become intoxicated, yet they did not intend to cease labouring with them till they became reformed."[14] At a council of Seneca from various reservations held at Jenuchshadago in January 1803, it was announced by a chief from Tonawanda that his people too had renounced the use of strong drink.[15]

The other tribes also joined in temperance, inspired by Handsome Lake. In 1803 a missionary reported of the Onondaga that they had "for two years greatly reformed in their intemperate drinking. . . . The Impression he made was so powerful, that different tribes held several councils on the subject, and finally agreed to leave off the intemperate use of strong liquors."[16] The effect of the prophet's preaching on the Onondaga is vividly described in the recollections of a trader and whiskey-seller named Webster. One day eighteen of the principal chiefs and warriors of the Onondaga nation called at the trading post saying that they were just setting out to attend "a great council of the six nations, to be held at Buffalo." Mr. Webster treated them to a drink all round, and they left in high spirits. In due time the delegates returned and again stopped off at Webster's trading post. The trader put a bottle of liquor before them, but to his "utter astonishment . . . every man of them refused to touch it." At first he thought that this was a sign of hostility and feared for his life, "for he could imagine that nothing short of the most deadly resentment (or a miracle), could produce so great a change." But he was quickly reassured. "The chiefs explained, that they had met at

12 [New-York Historical Society, O'Reilly Collection], Vol. XIV, p. 12 (Council at Genesee River, November 12, 1801).

13 CCHS, Jackson Journal, 1806; SC, Jackson Journal (published in Synderman, 1957), pp. 60–66.

14 HAVC, William Allinson Journal, Book 3, p. 7, September 29, 1809.

15 PYM, [John] Pierce Journal, 1801, entry of October 16, p. 42; and Indian Committee, Box 2, 1803–15, Letters of August 30, 1803, and June 4, 1811.

16 *Massachusetts Missionary Magazine*, 1804, Vol. I, pp. 68–69.

Buffalo, a Prophet of the Seneca nation, who had assured them, and in this assurance they had the most implicit confidence, that without a total abstinence, from the use of ardent spirits, they and their race would shortly become extinct; that they had entered upon a resolution, never again to taste the baneful article, and that they hoped to be able to prevail on their nation to adopt the same salutary resolution. Many at this early day adopted the temperance principles, it is said at least three fourths of all the nation; and of all those who pledged themselves to the cause, not an instance was known of alienation or neglect; but to a man, they religiously adhered to their solemn pledge. The consequence was, that from a drunken, filthy, lazy, worthless set of beings, they became a cleanly, industrious, sober, happy, and more prosperous people. At this period, it was considered one of the most temperate communities in the land; only a very few of the nation indulging in the intoxicating cup, and these were treated with contempt by their more sober companions."[17] On another occasion an Onondaga, on being asked why they had not abandoned their drunken habits before (as they had often been urged to do by white missionaries and others, and which they knew to have ruinous consequences), explained that earlier "they had no power but when the Great Spirit forbid such conduct by their prophet, he gave them power to comply with his request."[18] In 1809, Quakers reported, the Onondaga "had totally refrained from the use of ardent spirits for about 9 years, and . . . none of the natives will touch it."[19]

The effect on the Oneida was equally striking. The Oneida had for many years been served by a harried schoolmaster, by Quaker missionaries, and by Samuel Kirkland, who had formed a congregation of more or less loyal Christians. In 1799, as we remarked earlier, the Oneida had been swept by a revival of the pagan religion recommended by a Mohawk prophet from the Grand River. But by August 1806, the full import of Handsome Lake's revelation had been communicated to them, even to the Christians, by a member of the Christian congregation, the Reverend Mr. Kirkland's Oneida helper, Doctor Peter. After Kirkland's sermon Doctor Peter stood up and spoke about "the late revelations from the Seneka prophet, or man of God, as they stile him." Doctor Peter spoke "with great zeal and eloquence."

> He said the prophet enjoined the strictest temperance and sobriety upon all Indians, and commanded them to abstain from the use of ardent spirits, which was never made for Indians; and for any Indian to drink a single glass or one swallow would be a deadly sin if not repented of. (Here in his great zeal he overstepped the mark, and this bold assertion was apparently displeasing to many.) He then exhorted them to live in peace and love one another and

[17] [Joshua V. H.] Clark, [*Onondaga; or Reminiscences of Earlier and Later Times*, Syracuse, Stoddard and Babcock], 1849, Vol. I, pp. 103–09.

[18] [*General Assembly's Missionary Magazine* or] *Evangelical Intelligencer*, 1807, Vol. I, pp. 92–93.

[19] *The Friend*, 1844, p. 163.

> all mankind, white people as well as Indians. He then spoke upon the duties of husbands and wives, and the great sin of divorce.

The pagans, according to Kirkland, although they became converts to Handsome Lake's Code, were not overly successful in their adherence to the rule of temperance; but Kirkland's flock of Christians were not always sober either. In any case, the Seneca prophet was quoted in December 1806, as insisting that total temperance was necessary to salvation. "He forbids their feeling envious or resentful towards the white people because they so generally and freely use it, forbids them to reproach the white people with being the inventors of rum. This would be very offensive to the Great Spirit, for it was God who made rum, and made it for the white people to be used as a medicine to strengthen them after labor!" But he reported that fewer among the pagan Oneida were temperate than among the Onondaga. Despite the uncertainty of their sobriety, however, even Kirkland certified that the pagan party "absolutely forbid the use of rum, and assert that no Indian can be a good man who takes even a spoonful."[20]

The temperance movement was least effective at Buffalo Creek, at Tuscarora, and on the Genesee, where Iroquois settlements were closest to major white population centers. Buffalo Creek, furthermore, was the headquarters of Red Jacket, who although a defender of the old pagan religion of the Iroquois and an opponent of demon rum, was not favorably disposed toward the pretensions to power of Handsome Lake. Red Jacket himself drank, and so did Young King, another Buffalo Creek resident, one of the most influential of the Seneca chiefs, before his conversion to Christianity in the 1820s. In 1807 Handsome Lake and other Allegany Seneca leaders declared, "We are almost discouraged about our Brothers at Buffalo and Genesee River," on account of their persistence in intemperate habits.[21] And in 1809 Allinson on his visit to Buffalo said: "There are several Indian Towns within a few miles & the Indians are too often here to give hope, on National Ground, of their general reformation from the use of Spiritous Liquors, & yet we were told that many of them have abandened this Destroyer & stand firm against Temptation." At Tuscarora nearby, where by 1809 the chiefs had committed the nation to Christianity, the council declared "we mean to keep sabath, and hear Gospel, and try to persuade all our Nation not Drunk Whiskey —we shamed any of our People get Drunk."[22]

The overall impression provided by many observers between 1800 and 1810 is that the Iroquois in New York had substantially reduced their consumption of alcohol. In 1806 Halliday Jackson was able to sum up his impressions to this effect: "I . . . have noted with satisfaction that in the course of our travels among all the Indians on the Allegheny River, or either of the Villages at Cataraugus we have not seen a Single individual

[20] [Hamilton College, Samuel] Kirkland Papers, Journal for August 3 and December 27, 1806.

[21] PYM, Indian Committee, Box 2, Speech to Indian Committee by Conudiu *et al.*, November 6, 1807.

[22] HAVC, William Allinson Journal, 1809, Book 2, pp. 34–35, and Book 3, p. 20.

the least intoxicated with Liquor—which perhaps would be a Singular Circumstance to Observe in traveling among the same number of white Inhabitants."[23] And Jacob Taylor in 1809, when he was at Buffalo Creek to attend a meeting of the Council of the Six Nations, remarked, "I think I never saw so many Indians together before that conducted with so much propriety—the number could not be well ascertained, but it was thought there were about One Thousand, and I dont remember to see one Drunken Indian amongst them."[24]

TECHNOLOGY

By 1799 the Iroquois had for a generation been living in a state of economic limbo, unable any longer to hunt extensively or even very effectively to continue the traditional agriculture. During the war years, they had been largely dependent upon military stores for rations, clothing, and equipment; after the war, they had relied heavily on handouts from Indian agents and missionaries and on the annuities paid to the tribes and to individual chiefs. Now, and suddenly, they embraced the rural technology of the white man and became a nation of farmers. The effective causes for this cultural transition were, as in the case of the relinquishment of alcohol, certainly multiple. Advice and general example had been provided for many years, but agriculture by men had been resisted as an effeminate occupation with the women themselves taking the lead in ridiculing male farmers as transvestites. "If a Man took hold of a Hoe to use it the Women would get down his gun by way of derision & would laugh & say such a Warrior is a timid woman."[25] The final realization of the irrevocability of reservation life, occurring simultaneously with Handsome Lake's explicit sanctioning of the farmer's role for men and the provision of tools and instruction in their use by Quakers and other whites, made the change possible.

The Quaker observers provide anecdotal, and sometimes even statistical, measures of the pace of agricultural reform among the Iroquois. The initial approach of the Allegany Seneca to the proposed new methods was cautious and sometimes even rigorously scientific. "It was in the spring of 1801, that the Indians first began to use the plough for themselves. They took a very cautious method of determining whether it was likely to be an advantageous change for them or not. Several parts of a large field were ploughed, and the intermediate spaces prepared by their women with the hoe, according to former custom. It was all planted with corn; and the parts ploughed (besides the great saving of labour), produced much the heaviest crop; the stalks being more than a foot higher, and proportionably stouter than those in the hoed ground."[26] The support that the chief women at this time gave to Handsome Lake and

[23] CCHS, Jackson Journal, 1806; SC, Jackson Journal (published in Snyderman, 1957), p. 72, September, 1806.

[24] HAVC, William Allinson Journal, Book 2, p. 32, letter of September 19, 1809.

[25] HAVC, William Allinson Journal, 1809, Book 1, p. 42.

[26] Jackson, 1830, pp. 43–44.

to the Quakers was indispensable, for it released the men from the embarrassment of being called effeminate when they worked in the fields. By the end of the year 1801 the agricultural revolution along the Allegheny was well underway. Individual fields were being fenced (about 18,000 fence rails were sawed and split in that year alone). Instead of clusters of cabins near the river, now there were well-made log houses with shingled roofs scattered among the fields and meadows. The trail along the river was widened, and soon some twenty miles of roads, usable by wagons, connected all settled parts of the reservation. The tinkling of cowbells could be heard in all directions, and corn fodder and mown hay were stored to feed the cattle through the winter. In 1801 thirteen or fourteen new farming lots were laid out, and in 1803 some seventeen new houses were constructed. By 1806, when a Quaker inspection team arrived to survey the work of the preceding eight years, they found that both the settlement pattern and house type had dramatically changed. Now the Allegany Seneca lived in a hundred or so log cabins, of which about thirty were concentrated at Cold Spring village and the rest distributed among approximately one hundred individually fenced farms. Many of the houses were roofed with shingles and had panel doors and glass windows. A number of these farms had barns and were equipped with carts and wagons. The fencing was a good eight to ten rails high. The carpentry work had been mostly done by Indians, including the corner-notching of the logs; "scarcely a vestige remained of the cabins they occupied when Friends first settled among them [in 1798]."[27] Standards of cleanliness had improved, and there was some modern furniture. The Quaker inspection team was entertained in the house of Cornplanter's son Henry. It was the local showpiece: "It was a good house and well finished with a Piazza in front pallisaided round, and altho' its internal furniture still bore some marks of Indian hous-Wifery, they were furnished with a good feather bed enclosed with Callico Curtains."[28] The Minister's house, up the river from Cold Spring, was painted red and white and surrounded by a red paling fence "& at a Distance looks very smart."[29] Many of the chiefs at both Allegany and Cattaraugus built two-story houses. The council-house, at the center of Cold Spring village only a few yards from Handsome Lake's house, was forty feet long by twenty wide and the largest structure in the town. It was built of boards. All dwelling houses, however, still had earthen floors and were infested with fleas, bedbugs, and other insects, and dogs and pigs wandered through the open doors.

In 1826 the total Seneca population of 469 persons in the Allegany band was assigned by the Quakers to one or another of 80 "families" (presumably meaning nuclear households); thus the average family size was approximately six persons.[30] This suggests that the combined effect of the new settlement pattern dictated by the needs of rural technology

[27] Jackson, 1830, p. 52.

[28] CCHS, Jackson Journal, 1810–18, p. 54.

[29] HAVC, William Allinson Journal, 1809, Book 1, p. 35.

[30] Jackson, 1830, p. 89.

and of the social gospel preached by Handsome Lake, emphasizing the focal moral importance of the nuclear household, had within a generation been able to complete the transition from the ancient matrilineal household to the nuclear family. Eventually, also, these families became patrilineal with respect to name and inheritance, the Indian men taking on an English name, or an English translation of an Indian name, as a surname, and transmitting this name, along with inheritance rights to real estate, in the white style.

The new agriculture was productive and diversified. By 1801 the yield of corn had been increased tenfold. Spring wheat was planted between 1801 and 1806, and by 1806 the Indian farmers were adding to the traditional staples (corn, squash, beans, and tobacco) such other new crops as oats, buckwheat, potatoes, turnips, and flax. Grain was ground at the Quaker mill; the old wooden mortars fell into disuse. The production of flax was tied to the arts of spinning and weaving, which took hold firmly about 1807; by 1813 many of the Indian women were operating their own spinning wheels and producing over the winter sufficient thread to keep two Indian weavers busy making some two hundred yards of cloth, including both linen and wool, from which they made blankets and other useful cloth; some surplus was even sold to whites off the reservation. So profitable were the farms that some Seneca were able to invest in livestock. By 1803 there were well over a hundred head of cattle and by 1806 over a hundred horses; by 1810 there were at least five yoke of oxen available for heavy farm labor, such as hauling firewood and clearing fields of stones and stumps; by 1814 there was a considerable stock of swine being kept. By 1816 all but four families had "horned cattle," and the number of such cattle in the community reached four hundred. The Indians were learning to tan hides and salt the beef. Sheep still could not be managed because of the incursions of wolves.

Inevitably, various cultural consequences flowed from the fundamental new economic transformation. Progress in public health measures was an early effect. By 1805 the Indian women were learning to make soap, and standards of personal and household cleanliness were rising. During the War of 1812 the Quakers were able to avert a threatened epidemic of smallpox by vaccinating over a thousand Seneca at Allegany and Cattaraugus.[31] The Quakers emphasized the virtue of cleanliness so strongly that some of the Indian women, when white visitors approached "would immediately begin to sweep their houses, and appear somewhat disconcerted if friends entered their doors before they got their apartments in order." But the absence of surgeons to mend broken bones and stitch cuts and the general inability of both Indian and white medicine of the day to cope effectively with infectious and degenerative diseases meant that there were relatively large numbers of older people whose bodies bore the scars and deformities of a lifetime without effective medical care. Battered, aging hulks, half blind, or lame, or crippled in

[31] [Arthur C.] Parker, ["The Life of General Ely S. Parker: Last Grand Sachem of the Iroquois and General Grant's Military Secretary," *Publications of the Buffalo Historical Society*, XXIII], 1919, p. 297.

hand or foot or disfigured from the lack of minor surgery, they nonetheless worked as their infirmities allowed.

A specialization of labor among Indian artisans developed, with individual Indian men setting up shop as weavers, blacksmiths, shoemakers, and carpenters. Some Indian farmers were said to be getting rich, and others, who for a time had clung to hunting as their means of support, had with the decline of the small remaining local fur trade about 1810 been forced to hire themselves out as farm laborers to the well-to-do. A few of the men were adding to their income by renting out their land and by working part time as smiths, carpenters, and shoemakers, and everyone, of course, had access to timber and grazing meadows on the "national land," which was held in common by the tribe and could be used by anyone so long as he did not interfere with anyone else's use. Some of the Indians even complained of the pace of work and resented the comparative leisure of their domestic animals. "An Industrious Indian" at Cattaraugus testified that "he had become very uneasy on thinking he had so much to do to provide for his horses and that they had done nothing to assist him that he had lost considerable of Sleep on the occasion and was determined in future to make them assist him work."[32] The Quakers were well pleased with the progress made at Allegany, and in 1814 observed that "their improvements rather exceeded, in divers respects, those made in some new settlements of white people on the frontiers, in the same length of time."

The economic structure of the Indian farm household was described in detail in 1820 by the Quaker historian of the Tunessassa mission. He compiled individual data on a sample of thirty-five families (nearly half of the community). His figures showed that the average Indian family had cleared and fenced ten acres of ground, putting four in corn, two in oats, one in potatoes, and using the rest for meadow, orchard, or vegetable garden; owned a plow and either a pair of horses or a yoke of oxen; and kept five cows and eleven pigs. Only four households had less than five acres of cleared ground and only three more than fifteen. By 1826 the eighty families at Allegany were working 699 acres of improved land, raising thereon corn (239 acres), oats (116), hay (70), potatoes (42), wheat (38), besides a quantity of buckwheat and various vegetables. These families possessed 479 head of cattle, 58 horses, and 350 hogs. The agricultural revolution had become the way of life for the next generation.[33]

Although the Quaker vocational school, conducted in the Seneca language, thus was remarkably effective in transforming the economic basis of Seneca society, comparable progress was not made in academic instruction. The Friends had in the winter of 1798–99 opened their school to instruct Indian children—in English—in reading, writing, and arithmetic, and although about twenty pupils had attended on and off, they

[32] CCHS, Jackson Journal, 1810–18, pp. 37–38.

[33] The statistical information about Seneca agricultural technology and other aspects of their economic transformation is given in systematic and detailed form in Jackson, 1830, pp. 85–89 *et passim*.

proved irregular scholars. The project of academic, as opposed to vocational, education, was abandoned for ten years, and instead a few—perhaps half a dozen—Indian youths were sent from time to time to live with Friends in Philadelphia for several years, there to absorb English letters, Quaker values, and the manual arts. In 1810 a census of the households revealed that most of the parents wanted their children to attend a summer school. But still very few of the Allegany Seneca spoke English, and instruction in reading, writing, and arithmetic could be conducted only with great difficulty. A Quaker school at Tunessassa was not firmly established until 1822. Throughout the period from 1799 to about 1825, despite the occasional presence of a schoolmaster, not more than twenty children were regular pupils at any one time, and it may be doubted whether the schools accomplished much more than rudimentary instruction in English speech. As the Quakers observed about 1811, "very few of them had yet acquired the English language so as to be able to understand what they did learn."[34]

Technological progress was faster at Allegany, which received the concentrated attention of both Handsome Lake and the Quakers, than it was on the other reservations. But all were moving in the same direction. The Quakers frequently visited Cattaraugus and donated mill irons and plows; the Cattaraugus Seneca soon were building two-story board houses, fencing their farms, and keeping livestock. The Quakers also gave sawmill irons to Red Jacket for building a mill at Buffalo Creek, and they and Kirkland's mission had earlier helped the Oneida. And Handsome Lake was urging economic acculturation everywhere. Allegany was merely the spearhead of the movement to abandon the traditional technological and economic structure and to adopt the white man's customs.

RELIGIOUS OBSERVANCE

Handsome Lake did not consider that his revelations and the gospels that issued from them constituted a new religion. He believed rather that he was commissioned to revive in a pure, full, and correct form the traditional religious observances of the Iroquois and thereby to guide his people toward a better life in this world and salvation in the next. Although later his disciples, in codifying the prophet's teachings, did in effect create a new religious institution, during his lifetime such innovations as he proposed were added to the body of Iroquois belief in the spirit of free incorporation of dream-inspired religious observance that was characteristic of Iroquois culture. At no time, despite his difficulties in political affairs, did he have to confront a conservative *religious* opposition except in the matter of the medicine-societies.

The religious renaissance among the Iroquois thus was essentially a renewal of popular observance of the traditional communal religious rituals. The major innovations in belief—the idea of divine judgment and an afterlife in heaven or hell—was readily palatable and quickly and

[34] CCHS, Jackson Journal, 1810–18, pp. 11–13.

widely accepted because it was similar in form to the old belief in the cosmic bargain between the Good Twin and the Evil Twin. There were few important innovations in ritual adopted as a result of the prophet's teaching. The old annual calendar—including the white dog ceremony—was celebrated without any modification except, at Allegany, the abandonment of the statue of Tarachiawagon.[35] The old medicine-societies—including the False Faces—continued their rituals despite the prophet's qualms about them.[36] His emphasis upon the four sacred ceremonies—Thanksgiving Dance, Great Feather Dance, Personal Chants, and Bowl Game—did not imply that all other observances should be abandoned; it was merely an endorsement of the central themes in existing ritual. The pantheon remained unchanged except for the addition of a new scene of action for the struggle between the creative and destructive principles, represented traditionally by the Good Twin and the Evil Twin, Tarachiawagon and the Great World Rim Dweller, in the domain of heaven and hell, where the same protagonists bore different names (Haweniyu or the Great Spirit, and Ganosge' or the Tormentor). The ritual of confession, which later became a central feature of the religion of Handsome Lake, was in his own time simply an application of the traditional practice of requiring confession of a suspected witch, and Handsome Lake's central role as accuser and confessor was an amplification of the old responsibility of the shaman. The prophet directly supported the Minister at Cold Spring who for years had been calling the people together for the ceremonies, and he indirectly supported any other traditional religious leader whom he could find. Even his own temporary position as great leader was an extension of custom, for in times of crises the Iroquois were used to the nomination of powerful war-captains or political leaders (like Brant among the Mohawk and Cornplanter among the Seneca) who were made responsible for mobilizing the village, tribe, or League to action.

Thus, in the first decades of the nineteenth century, when the Quaker missionaries and Mary Jemison, the white captive, described the religious rituals among the Seneca and Kirkland wrote his accounts of the pagan ceremonies of the Oneida, they delineated a ceremonial and belief system already hundreds of years old with minor modifications of content, emphasis, and terminology recently suggested by Handsome Lake. Furthermore, each Iroquois tribe, and even each band or reservation community, maintained its own more or less variant form of this general system. Handsome Lake, under the circumstances, simply could not in-

[35] Although the white dog is not burned today by Handsome Lake followers, and some of them say that he disapproved of it, the sacrifice was still being carried out under his direct sponsorship at Allegany in 1809 (HAVC, William Allinson Journal) and was continued in the "pagan" communities in New York and Canada until it died out under the pressure of white disapproval late in the nineteenth and early in the twentieth centuries.

[36] Again, although the prophet criticized the conduct of the societies and purged them of their ritual use of alcohol, their ceremonies were publicly practiced under his eyes at Allegany in 1809 (HAVC, William Allinson Journal) and have been continued by his followers ever since.

troduce a new religious system standardized for all the reservations. As we shall see, it was not the prophet but the prophet's disciples who created the new, relatively uniform institution known as the Longhouse Religion or the New Religion of Handsome Lake, with its own unique beliefs, rituals, organization, and ceremonial paraphernalia, and who determined the relation this new institution should have to the old religion that Handsome Lake himself had practiced.

There was, for a time, some religious doubt expressed by various critics of the prophet who, as he put it, would say, "We lack an understanding of this religion." Most of this doubt did, as one might expect, focus on the introduction of the concept of divine judgment and an afterlife in heaven or hell. Handsome Lake answered the critics who asked why no one had known these things before by suggesting that not everything was known even to the angels, who told him "even we, the servants of the Creator, do not understand all things." When asked where the ancestors had gone, he replied,

> Now it is said that your fathers of old never reached the true lands of our Creator nor did they ever enter the house of the tormentor, Ganosge'. It is said that in some matters they did the will of the Creator and that in others they did not. They did both good and bad and none was either good or bad. They are therefore in a place separate and unknown to us, we think, enjoying themselves.[37]

But rather than propose new ritual, Handsome Lake applied these new principles of belief as sanctions for the observance of old custom. It was, he said, man's duty to follow the traditional ceremonies; it was the Evil Spirit who kept him away from performing the ancient religious observances of the Iroquois.

Thus the religious innovations of Handsome Lake were modifications of belief whose function was to ensure the dedication of the people to conservative ritual. He was in his own eyes as the messenger of God, necessarily the defender of the faith. And at his behest hundreds of lukewarm pagans and half-converted Christians returned to the council-house to hear once again the prayers of thanksgiving, to burn the white dog, to tell their dreams, and play the Sacred Bowl Game—the cosmic game of chance forever being renewed in the endless and balanced struggle between the Spirit of Good and the Spirit of Evil.

[37] Parker, 1913, p. 56.

The Treatment of Delinquent Children

JOSEPH M. HAWES

A continuous problem of human society is the conflict between the adult and the young. Going back to the beginnings of human history we find references in literature to the disrespect that children and young people showed toward their elders. While this conflict is pervasive on all socioeconomic levels, societies have always been particularly disturbed by the recalcitrance of the youthful poor, and it is out of that segment of society that the "juvenile delinquent" first emerged.

In early American history the government assumed that the middle-class family would take the responsibility for the antisocial behavior of its children. When the family could not control its children, the government might take those children from their homes and place them in another, which was supposed to have greater control. Often recalcitrant children were placed in apprenticeships with notably tough masters who had developed reputations for breaking even the most willful youths.

Colonial Virginia, in an attempt to increase its population, requested that the authorities in London send several hundred young vagrants to the colony. London obliged readily, eager to rid her streets of young troublemakers. These young people were then indentured and put to work on the plantations of the New World, where it was assumed their undesirable habits would be curbed. They were not, so London's problem became Virginia's.

Massachusetts Bay, always the extremist on moral matters, passed a law stating: "If any child, or children, above sixteen years old, and of sufficient understanding, shall CURSE or SMITE their natural FATHER, or MOTHER, he or they shall be putt to death" unless that behavior had been deliberately provoked. While this law was never applied, it indicates the seriousness with which the authorities viewed the problem of youthful disrespect.

When a foster home or apprenticeship seemed inadequate for rehabilitating a young person, he might be placed in the common jails where all classes and categories of "criminals" were herded together in large rooms that became the breeding grounds for more overtly criminal behavior.

When the prison reform movement of the late eighteenth century began to change the conditions of prison life, it was not unexpected that a movement began to try to deal with youthful offenders in an altogether different way. The selection reprinted below, by Joseph M. Hawes, of Kansas State University, describes one of the first of such attempts. These reformers dealt with the urban poor youth, not so much hardened criminals as footloose and undisciplined pauperized children. The juvenile delinquency problem of our own time is concerned with these same poor children and the attempts to deal with it today are no more successful and only a little less inhumane than those made one hundred and fifty years ago.

In the fall of 1822 two men met in one of New York City's parks. They were James W. Gerard, a young lawyer, and Isaac Collins, a Quaker, and both were members of the Society for the Prevention of Pauperism. Every year this Society presented a public report to suggest ways of carrying out its purposes. Usually, one man, with the assistance of two others "for form's sake," wrote this report. Gerard was talking to Collins about the street children of New York because he was going to write the report for 1822 on "the reformation of juvenile delinquents." Collins, whose father was a Philadelphia printer, became interested in the treatment of juvenile delinquents after reading the annual report of an English institution for young offenders. Gerard had become interested in juvenile crime as a result of the very first case he tried, that of a fourteen-year-old boy accused of stealing a bird. The young lawyer won acquittal for his client by arguing that prison would corrupt the boy. The case so interested Gerard that he began to investigate the facilities for detaining prisoners in New York. He also decided to join the Society for the Prevention of Pauperism.

Gerard presented his report at a public meeting held in the ballroom of the City Hotel in February, 1823. "Those who are in the habit of attending our criminal courts, as jurors or otherwise," Gerard said,

> must be convinced of the very great increase of juvenile delinquency within these few years past, and of the necessity of im-

> mediate measures to arrest so great an evil. . . . Those whose walks are limited to the fairer parts of our city know nothing of the habits, the propensities and criminal courses, of a large population in its remote and obscure parts. . . . it is with pain we state that, in five or six years past, and until the last few months, the number of youth under fourteen years of age, charged with offenses against the law, has doubled; and that the same boys are again and again brought up for examination, some of whom are committed, and some tried; and that imprisonment by its frequency renders them hardened and fearless.

This was hardly surprising, Gerard said, if one knew the conditions of the prisons and the Bridewell. (A Bridewell then had about the same functions as a county jail in twentieth-century America.) At the Bridewell persons awaiting trial because they could not afford to pay bail were all packed into one large room, "the young and the old . . . promiscuously crowded together. . . . Boys who have been charged with picking pockets, stealing watches, and the like crimes," Gerard continued, "have declared before the police when [asked] how they came to such things, that they learned the art from the experienced offenders they met in [the] Bridewell. . . ."

Every year one to two hundred children between the ages of seven and fourteen appeared in the criminal courts of New York City. Some were homeless and most of them were "the children of poor and abandoned parents" whose "debased character and vicious habits" caused them to be "brought up in perfect ignorance and idleness, and what is worse in street begging and pilfering." Gerard concluded with a recommendation that a "house of refuge" for young convicts be established where juvenile delinquents might be reformed. "Unless the heart is corrupt indeed, and sunk deep in guilt," Gerard said, "the youth would undergo a change of feeling and character, and he would look on crime with greater abhorrence, because he himself had been a criminal."[1] Gerard's report led to the creation of the first separate institution for juvenile delinquents in the United States, the New York House of Refuge.

II

Even before the end of the second decade of the nineteenth century, the City of New York was well on its way to becoming the largest and

[1] Isaac Collins to James W. Gerard, March 4, 1850, in New York House of Refuge, *Thirtieth Annual Report* (1855), p. 73; Gerard to Collins, March 6, 1850, *ibid.*, p. 75; "Reminiscences of James W. Gerard, Esq.," in *Proceedings of the First Convention of Managers and Superintendents of Houses of Refuge and Schools of Reform in the United States of America, Held in the City of New York, on the Twelfth, Thirteenth and Fourteenth Days of May, 1857* (New York: Wynkoop, Hallenbeck & Thomas, 1857), pp. 75–78; "Extracts from the Annual Report of the Society for the Prevention of Pauperism in the City of New York for the Year, 1822," *ibid.*, pp. 79–82.

most prosperous city in the United States. But as the city increased in wealth and size, some of its most prominent citizens worried about the depressing conditions of the city's poor.[2] The nationally known chemistry teacher, John Griscom, his neighbor, Thomas Eddy, and a set of like-minded friends began meeting to discuss what they called "the perishing and dangerous classes," the impoverished and criminal elements among the city's population. Somehow, it did not seem right that an American city should have the same kind of discouraging problems which beset the cities of the Old World. The informal gatherings at Griscom's house set the stage for the creation of a formal organization to do something about the problems of the lowest classes of society.

On December 16, 1817, Griscom's friends and other philanthropic citizens formed the Society for the Prevention of Pauperism in the City of New York. They elected a veteran of the Revolutionary War, General Matthew Clarkson, as chairman and appointed a committee to draw up a constitution, to study the "causes" of pauperism and continual and hereditary poverty, and to suggest remedies. The Society met again in February of the following year to hear the committee report on the causes of pauperism. The committee listed "juvenile delinquency" as one of the major causes of pauperism. To alleviate the threat of youthful crime the committee suggested that child convicts be confined in a building separate from the regular prison for adult criminals. For the next three years the Society for the Prevention of Pauperism continued to recommend the complete separation of youthful offenders from older convicts in prisons and jails.[3]

In the meantime John Griscom had gone to Europe to visit the Continent's charitable institutions, particularly those devoted to children. One of the most important of the institutions Griscom saw was that maintained by the Philanthropic Society at Hoxton, England. The Society had been organized in London in 1788 as a means of preventing the children of convicts from growing up in idleness and crime. In 1804 the directors moved their Society's operation to Hoxton and began accepting other children, especially juvenile offenders, who seemed likely to grow up into a criminal life. Griscom noted that "it is the peculiar distinction of this society, to seek for children in the nurseries of vice and iniquity, in order to draw them away from further contamination, and to bring them up to the useful purposes of life." The Society received both boys and girls, although it kept them separated "by a high wall which prevents all intercourse." The chemistry teacher from New York thought that the boys received "a sufficient share of school learning," and described the various trades which master workmen taught the boys: printing, bookbinding,

[2] Constance McLaughlin Green, *American Cities in the Growth of the Nation* (London: Univ. of London, Athlone Pr., 1957), p. 9.

[3] Bradford Kenny Pierce, *A Half-Century with Juvenile Delinquents, or The House of Refuge and its Times* (New York: D. Appleton and Co., 1869), pp. 32–42; Grace Abbott, *The Child and the State*, 2 vols. (Chicago: Univ. of Chicago Pr., 1938), II, 345–46; Samuel L. Knapp, *The Life of Thomas Eddy; Comprising an Extensive Correspondence with many of the most Distinguished Philanthropists and Philosophers of this and other Countries* (New York: Connel and Cooke, 1834), p. 23.

shoemaking, tailoring, rope-making, and twine spinning. The girls learned domestic skills, "so as to qualify . . . for useful and respectable service." In passing through the workshops of this beneficent institution, "where industry and skill were apparent," Griscom concluded, "it was cheering to find that so many wretched children were 'snatched as fire brands' from criminality and ruin, and restored to the prospects of respectable and honourable life."[4]

On the Continent Griscom was especially impressed by "Hofwyl," an institution in Switzerland devoted to "problem" children. M. Philip Emanuel Fellenberg had founded this complex of schools only a few years earlier. Fellenberg and Heinrich Pestalozzi, one of the seminal minds in the history of education, had worked together in an effort to teach the orphans, the homeless, and the delinquent children of Switzerland how to make a living for themselves. In 1774, Pestalozzi, who had been brooding about the failures of the institutions society had developed to aid the poor—orphan asylums, poor-houses, prisons, and the like—brought a group of vagrant children to his farm at Neuhof. He treated the children as if they were members of his own family, worked with them in the fields, and tried to give them the rudiments of an education. But Pestalozzi was a poor manager and, despite a number of appeals to the public for funds, was forced to abandon the project in 1780. In one of his appeals he had written: "I have for a long time thought it probable that, under favorable circumstances, young children might be able to earn their own living without undue labor, provided that enough capital were advanced to organize an establishment, in which they would not only live, but at the same time receive a certain elementary education." Pestalozzi tried in vain to attract the necessary finances to promote his ideas until Fellenberg invited him early in the nineteenth century to help at the experimental establishment at Hofwyl, Fellenberg's estate. In 1807 Fellenberg had founded the "Literary Institution" for the sons of the nobility and upper classes. The next year he founded the "Agricultural Institution," or "Poor School" for the children of the common people. Pestalozzi's gentle and abstract ways led to conflict with the stricter and more businesslike Fellenberg and they soon parted, but the teacher of the poor school, Joseph Vehrly, conducted his school on Pestalozzi's principles.[5]

Soon after he arrived at Hofwyl, Griscom had a brief interview with Fellenberg, who discussed the principles of his institution and his own particular philosophy of education. Briefly he explained that Hofwyl's

[4] Edouard Ducpetiaux, *Des Progrès et de l'état actuel de la réform pénitentiaire et des institutions préventives, aux Etats-Unis, en France, en Suisse, en Angleterre et en Belgique* (Bruxelles: Hauman, Cattari and Co., 1838), p. 323; Henry Barnard, *Reformatory Education; Papers on Preventative, Correctional, and Reformatory Institutions in Different Countries . . .*, 3 vols. (Hartford, Conn.: F. C. Brownell, 1857), III, 295; John Griscom, *A Year in Europe: Comprising a Journal of Observations in England, France, Switzerland, the North of Italy and Holland, In 1818 and 1819*, 2 vols. (New York: Collins and Co., 1823), I, 121–23.

[5] Charles A. Bennett, *A History of Manual and Industrial Education up to 1870* (Peoria, Ill.: Manual Arts Press, 1926), pp. 111, 112, 131–35; Barnard, *Reformatory Education*, pp. 34–35, 55.

two schools were designed to give the two extreme classes of society a better understanding of each other. The rich, observing the poor, would learn to respect their industry and skill; the poor would regard the rich as benefactors by experiencing their kindly influence. All of this would be accomplished without any mingling of the classes, since the two schools—though conducted in close proximity—were separate.

The school for the poor boys particularly impressed Griscom. "Their teacher [Vehrly]," he wrote, "is a young man of very extraordinary qualifications. . . . He lives with them, eats, sleeps, and works with them, dresses as they do, and makes himself their friend and companion, as well as their instructor." Vehrly had clearly borrowed his principles from Pestalozzi: "Much pains are taken to impress on the minds of the pupils, a deep sense of the importance of time, and of habits of industry," Griscom recalled, "and from the reports that have been published by commissioners appointed to examine the establishments, it is evident that the most favourable results had attended these endeavors." Vehrly taught his young charges traditional and vocational matter. He concentrated on agriculture, and each boy had his own plot to cultivate. Those who wished could also learn a trade in one of the several workshops on the grounds. Both Vehrly and Fellenberg were "strongly imbued with a sense of religious obligation, and unremittingly attentive to awaken those sentiments in the minds of the pupils." The New York philanthropist was so impressed with what he had seen at Hofwyl that he recommended that the United States adopt a similar approach: "The greatest recommendation of the Pestalozzian and Fellenberg plan of education is the moral charm which is diffused throughout all its operations." Griscom knew that many of Fellenberg's notions—especially those of his upper-class school—were alien to American traditions, but he argued that poor schools like the one Vehrly taught "would soon impart to a large and populous district . . . a moral tone of incalculable importance to its highest interests and welfare." If white children could not be induced to attend such a school, he suggested that the school accept Negro children. "Such an experiment, with persons of this description, would be highly interesting," he added, for "it would put to flight the ridiculous theory of those who contend for an organic inferiority on the part of the blacks." Finally, he noted that to succeed such an institution needed a man of unusual talents to run it—a man like Vehrly.[6]

When Griscom returned to New York, he found that the Society for the Prevention of Pauperism was still discussing the causes of pauperism, although the members of the Society found their attention turning increasingly to the question of juvenile delinquency. To them a juvenile delinquent was a young person (under twenty-one) who had broken the the law, or who wandered about the streets, neither in school nor at work and who obviously lacked a "good" home and family. Such a criminal or vagrant youth would probably lack the skills of a trade and would be illiterate as well. Most such children would certainly grow up to be paupers or criminals, persons which the community would have to

[6] Griscom, *A Year in Europe,* pp. 384–400.

maintain with charity or tax money. By the second decade of the nineteenth century this dependent class had grown large enough to disturb the prosperous middle-class members of the Society for the Prevention of Pauperism. The members reasoned that adult paupers and criminals had been delinquents in their youth and that the best way to eliminate pauperism was to reform juvenile delinquents. The Society's *Annual Report* for 1819 discussed conditions in the New York penitentiary—particularly the fact that there were many children confined there—and asked: "Shall we send convicts in the morning of life, while the youthful mind is ardent and open to vivid and durable impressions, to this unhallowed abode, to be taught in all the requisites that will enable them to come forth when their terms of imprisonment expire, more prepared to invade the peace of cities and communities?" No, the report concluded, "to say that this is not a great source of pauperism and nursery of crime and outrage, is denying the fairest deductions of reason."[7]

Meanwhile, the problem of wayward and criminal children had been taken up by other groups and individuals in New York. In 1803 Edward Livingston, the Mayor of the city who later became one of the country's leading penal reformers, attempted to form a society to help young ex-convicts, but he was unable to find enough people interested to initiate his project. On August 14, 1809, the Common Council of New York City designated the Almshouse as "an asylum for lost children." But the Almshouse and the penitentiary seemed inappropriate places for children, and in March, 1812, the Council reported that it had received "a communication of John Stanton on the subject of erecting an asylum for the protection of profligate orphans of the city." "Stanton" in this case was undoubtedly the Reverend John Standford, chaplain of the Almshouse, who asked the Council to "make an attempt to rescue from indolence, vice, and danger, the hundreds of vagrant children and youth, who day and night infest our streets." He recommended the creation of "an asylum for vagrant youth," but beyond noting the receipt of his letter, the Council took no action on his request.[8]

Seven years later, in June, 1819, Mayor Cadwallader Colden, Jr., who was also a member of the Society for the Prevention of Pauperism, and the Recorder, Peter Augustus Jay, went on an inspection tour of the city's charitable institutions and reported their findings to the board in charge of the prison and the Bridewell. They complained about the mixing of young and old convicts in the penal institutions and noted that young criminals posed a difficult problem. "The members of the board, who are judges of the Criminal Court," the Mayor and the Recorder said, "must often have felt how difficult it is, satisfactorily to dispose of these

[7] Quoted in Abbott, *Child and State*, II, 346.

[8] Peirce, *Half-Century*, pp. 32–42; Abbott, *Child and State*, II, 345–46. The actions of the New York City Common Council relevant to the creation of the New York House of Refuge may be found in New York, Common Council of the City of New York, *Minutes of the Common Council of New York* (New York: Published by the City of New York, 1917), V, 641; VII, 65; X, 467–68, 556, 747; XI, 722. See also *New York Spectator*, Jan. 23, 1824; and Charles G. Sommers, *Memoir of the Rev. John Stanford, D.D.* (New York: Swards, Stanford and Co., 1835), pp. 272–77.

young culprits." If the judge turned them loose, they would soon be back on another charge, but if the judge sentenced them to prison, they would mingle with older convicts and be encouraged in a life of crime. "The jury, as well as the Court," the report continued, "feel a reluctance to convict and condemn them when it is believed that the infliction of punishment, by confinement in the Penitentiary, will tend to harden them in vice." In their conclusion Colden and Jay argued that if the boys could be effectively isolated from the other convicts and then taught a trade, "imprisonment would sometimes produce reformation."

In September of the same year, two more members of the Common Council, the Alderman for the Second Ward and his assistant, visited the Almshouse, the Bridewell, and the penitentiary, and found that conditions had slightly improved. The children were now kept separate from the older convicts, and "considerable attention" was devoted to teaching them "the common branches of education." But the Council members complained that the children were not learning a trade.

In February, 1820, the Grand Jury included among the presentments which it forwarded to the Common Council the recommendation that "all persons under 15 years of age who may be committed to Bridewell be confined in a separate apartment to preclude intercourse with persons of mature age." The following year, in June, the Reverend John Standford sent the Council another letter, again suggesting that it establish "an asylum for vagrant youth." The Council referred the letter to the Mayor and the Commissioners of the Almshouse, who endorsed the chaplain's recommendation and indicated that they had already ordered the boys in the penitentiary charged with vagrancy transferred to the Almshouse. Shortly after this step, the Commissioners of the Almshouse decided to take the remainder of the boys in the penitentiary into the Almshouse, even though more than half of the boys moved there originally had escaped. The boys could stay only for the summer, however, since the building usually filled up with adults during the winter months.

By the spring of 1823 several different efforts to create a separate institution for wayward and criminal children in New York had coalesced into a movement. The Mayor and Almshouse Commissioners had endorsed the Reverend John Standford's suggestion to establish an asylum for vagrant youth, and in June the members of the Society for the Prevention of Pauperism, probably in response to the paper James Gerard had given in February, established a committee "to prepare a report on the subject of establishing a House of Refuge, or prison for the reformation of juvenile delinquents." Among the committee members were John Griscom, Isaac Collins, and Gerard. As the committee prepared its report, Griscom's account of his travels in Europe appeared and probably helped to publicize the movement on behalf of an institution for juvenile delinquents.[9]

The Society called a public meeting in the ballroom of the City

[9] Society for the Prevention of Pauperism in the City of New York, *Report on the Expediency of Erecting an Institution for the Reformation of Juvenile Delinquents* (New York: Mahlon Day, 1823), title page; Peirce, *Half-Century*, pp. 45–48.

Hotel in December, 1823, and John Griscom read the committee's report. "It will be admitted by every person conversant with human nature, and with the great objects of political association," Griscom said, "that there are few judicial considerations of greater importance than the wise adaptation of punishment to crime." Then Griscom stressed the idea that punishment deters criminals and thereby protects property. One of the purposes of this public meeting, then, was to find new, better, and possibly cheaper ways of defending society against the threat of crime–including juvenile crime.[10]

Griscom went on to charge that most penitentiaries had not lived up to their original promise, because their officers now lacked "the same intelligent and disinterested zeal" which their founders had possessed. The greatest deficiency in the penitentiaries was inadequate classification, the separation of prisoners by offenses and ages. Consequently, convicts "of all ages and degrees of guilt" found themselves thrown together and the penitentiaries were fast becoming "schools and colleges of crime." Perhaps, Griscom continued, the old system of "whipping posts, pillories, and croppings" would be better. In some states, however, there were penal institutions, "where classification is an object of careful attention." These were penitentiaries "directed with a constant reference to the moral faculties" and "clothed in the spirit which seeks to restore, in order that it may safely forgive." Thus, Griscom argued, governments should recognize that "those who are guilty of crime should receive the chastisement due to their offenses," and that "no pains should be spared to remove the causes of offense, and to diminish, as far as possible, the sources of temptation and corruption." Such an approach was particularly appropriate for juvenile delinquents–"a class whose increasing numbers, and deplorable situation in this city, loudly call for the more effective interposition of its police, and the benevolent interference of our citizens in general."

Following Gerard's earlier report, Griscom turned to a discussion of the byways of the city where one could see "the ragged and uncleanly appearance, the vile language, and the idle and miserable habits of great numbers of children, most of whom were of school age or capable of some useful employment." Many of these children had no parents, and many had parents who were "too poor or too degenerate" to provide their children with the clothing necessary to go to school or to work. It was no surprise that many of these children turned to vagrancy and crime:

> Accustomed, in many instances, to witness at home, nothing in the way of an example, but what is degrading; early taught to observe intemperance, and to hear obscene and profane language without disgust; obliged to beg, and even encouraged to acts of dishonesty, to satisfy the wants induced by the indolence of their parents—what can be expected, but that such children will, in due time, become responsible to the laws for crimes, which have thus, in a man-

[10] Society for the Prevention of Pauperism, *Report on Expediency*, pp. 3–36; *New York Spectator*, Dec. 25, 1823, Jan. 23, 1824.

> ner, been forced upon them? Can it be consistent with real justice, that delinquents of this character, should be consigned to the infamy and severity of punishments, which must inevitably tend to perfect the work of degradation, to sink them still deeper in corruption, to deprive them of their remaining sensibility to the shame of exposure, and establish them in all the hardihood of daring and desperate villainy?

To gain further evidence, the members of the committee had asked both the District Attorney and the keeper of the Bridewell about the treatment of juvenile offenders. The District Attorney gave them a list of "more than 450 persons" under twenty-five who had been sentenced either to the Bridewell or the penitentiary. "A very considerable number" of them were between nine and sixteen years old. These were vagrants; none of them had been charged with a specific offense. The list included "children who profess to have no home, or whose parents have turned them out of doors and take no care of them." The committee believed that children in such circumstances would "eventually have recourse to petty thefts." If they were girls, they would "descend to practices of infamy, in order to save themselves from the pinching assaults of cold and hunger." The members of the committee decided to visit the Bridewell themselves. There the keeper told them that the old and young spent a part of every day together, "because the prison is so constructed that it will not admit of keeping them otherwise." Two-thirds of the young people in the Bridewell had been there before. "It may well be submitted to the judgment of a discerning public," they wrote, "whether an exposure of a few days to such company and fare as here represented, is not sufficient to suppress, in youthful minds, all virtuous emotions." Having noted these facts, they concluded that it was "highly expedient" that a "house of refuge" for juvenile delinquents be established near the City of New York "as soon as practicable."

According to the committee, a house of refuge would be "an asylum in which boys under a certain age, who become subject to the notice of the Police, either as vagrants, or homeless, or charged with petty crimes, may be received, [and where they may be] judiciously classed according to their degrees of depravity or innocence, [and then] put to work at such employments as will tend to encourage industry and ingenuity." The committee also proposed to teach the boys "reading, writing, and arithmetic, and . . . the nature of their moral and religious obligations." The primary purpose of the treatment of the boys was "to afford a prompt and energetic corrective of their vicious propensities and hold out every possible inducement to reformation and good conduct."

The proposed house of refuge would also have a department for girls "either too young to have acquired habits of fixed depravity, or those whose lives have in general been virtuous, but who, having yielded to the seductive influence of corrupt associates, have suddenly to endure the bitterness of lost reputation, and are cast forlorn and destitute upon a cold and unfeeling public." The committee realized that this was a controversial proposal, but indicated that they thought a girls' department would be an "advantage to the institution." They also pointed out that "similar institutions in Europe" included departments for girls. The committee thought that the institution maintained by the Philanthropic Society near London appeared "to come nearest in its general system to that which we would recommend."

Griscom finished the report and turned the platform over to Mayor Colden. The assembly, probably at the committee's suggestion, then passed a series of resolutions. The first endorsed the creation of a house of refuge, and the second urged "that a society be now formed under the appelation of the 'Society for the Reformation of Juvenile Delinquents.' " Successive resolutions named the board of managers and the treasurer of the new society and outlined rules for membership. Once these resolutions passed, Peter Augustus Jay, the City Recorder, James W. Gerard, and others gave brief speeches in support of the proposed house of refuge. They touched themes which were now familiar: that prison corrupted young people who were sent there, that there were as many as four hundred boys under sixteen arrested annually, and that such an arrest almost always meant the beginning of another criminal career. The speakers also said that society now made it practically impossible for a criminal to reform, and claimed that the house of refuge might save as many as two hundred children a year from crime and infamy. At the conclusion of the meeting the officers of the new Society collected over $800 and announced that they would canvass the entire city for funds.

Shortly after this meeting the Reverend Mr. Standford wrote to the Common Council for the third time about the city's vagrant youth. He reminded the Council of his interest in an asylum for them and concluded: "If I may be permitted to name a permanent spot for such an establishment, it is the premises now occupied as the U.S. Arsenal, at the fork of the Bloomingdale Road. . . . In my estimation, it could not be appropriated to a more useful purpose, or prove more honourable to the city."

In February the newly formed Society for the Reformation of Juvenile Delinquents sent a memorial to the Common Council stating that they were "desirous of establishing an institution which shall serve at once as a refuge for neglected or depraved children . . . and praying the aid of the corporation in donations of lands or otherwise." The Council referred the request to a special committee, which wholeheartedly endorsed the proposal: "The committee believes that such an institution, properly regulated and conducted, would not only tend to improve the condition of society by lessening the commission of crime, and the number of convicts sent to our prisons, but would have a tendency to diminish the expences [*sic*] of the city incurred on that account." The Common Council arranged to have the land on which the Arsenal was located returned to the city's jurisdiction. The city then gave the land to the Society, and the Society paid the federal government $2000 for the buildings and the wall.[11]

[11] *Minutes of Common Council*, XIII, 538, 578–81; "Daybook No. 1," New York House of Refuge Records, Manuscript Collections, Carnegie Library, Syracuse University. Hereafter, these records will be cited as NYHR.

The Society now sought state financial aid and sent a memorial to the New York legislature in Albany. John Griscom's report, read at the City Hotel in December, formed the main part of the memorial. The managers of the Society explained that they had obtained land and buildings for the proposed house of refuge, but they did not have enough money to keep the project going. While the members of the new Society waited to learn if the legislature would appropriate money for their institution, the Secretary of State for New York, J. V. N. Yates, in a report on pauperism in the state, noted that a great many paupers were children under fourteen, who might "at no distant day form a fruitful nursery for crime unless prevented by the watchful superintendence of the legislature."[12]

Meanwhile, a select committee of the legislature met to draft a bill to charter the New York House of Refuge and place it under state supervision. The bill passed without a negative vote on March 29, 1824. The question of state financial aid remained unsettled, however, and the Society for the Reformation of Juvenile Delinquents asked the Common Council of New York to endorse a request for the proceeds of a tax on public amusements in the City of New York. The Common Council agreed and sent a memorial of their own to Albany along with the request from the Society. But the state granted no money to the House of Refuge in 1824, and it was not until 1829 that the Society received a substantial and steady income from public funds.[13]

III

The act incorporating the Society for the Reformation of Juvenile Delinquents in the City of New York outlined the procedures for membership in the Society and made the Board of Managers responsible for the operation of the House of Refuge. Thus, America's first institution for juvenile delinquents was a "mixed" institution. That is, a private philanthropic group established and operated it, but the state had chartered it and provided for the conditions of its operation. The act of incorporation also contained the first statutory definition of juvenile delinquency in the United States. It authorized the Managers "to receive and take into the house of refuge to be established by them, all such children who shall be taken up or committed as vagrants, or convicted of criminal offenses" if a judge thought they were "proper objects." The Managers could also "place the said children committed to their care, during the minority of such children at such employments, and cause them to be instructed in such branches of useful knowledge, as shall be suitable to their years and capacities." The Managers had the power to bind out children (with their consent) as apprentices until they reached legal maturity. The children remained under the control of the Managers

[12] *New York Spectator*, Feb. 3, March 30, 1824; New York Legislature, Senate, *Journal* (1824) App. A., p. 96.

[13] *New York Spectator*, March 30, 1824; *Minutes of Common Council,* XIII, 648; Abbott, *Child and State*, II, 351.

until the boys were twenty-one and the girls were eighteen, or until the officials at the House of Refuge decided that they were "reformed" and agreed to their discharge. Thus, the New York House of Refuge began the use of the indeterminate sentence long before penal reformers advocated it in the late nineteenth century as a necessary innovation in American penology.[14]

The House of Refuge began its operations in the old arsenal building on January 1, 1825, with six boys and three girls. By the end of the first year, a total of seventy-three children had come to the Refuge, fifty-four boys and nineteen girls, and fifty-six remained in the institution. Of the seventeen children who left during the first year, nine had been indentured as apprentices or servants, four had been discharged, and four boys had "absconded."[15]

Most of the children who came to the House of Refuge that first year and most of the ones who came later were "very ignorant." Even those few who had learned to read "had acquired no relish for intellectual improvement. Their habits, as it [*sic*] respects skill and useful industry, were still more deplorable." Particularly surprising was the fact that the girls could not perform any of the standard feminine tasks; they could not cook, sew, or iron. For the first year the boys spent most of their time cleaning up the grounds and helping to erect a new building and make the wall higher. When they were not busy with their newly learned domestic tasks, the girls planted grass. Once the maintenance tasks were finished, the boys began to learn shoemaking and tailoring, and the girls found themselves doing all of the mending and laundry for the institution.

The schedule, which the superintendent had worked out, allowed two hours a day, one in the morning and one in the evening, for formal instruction. The curriculum included spelling, reading, writing, and cyphering (arithmetic). To some extent the inmates taught themselves, since the Lancastrian or monitorial system was used. Apparently, the combination of labor and instruction and the system of discipline at the House of Refuge were effective. The *Annual Report* for the first year noted that "of the whole number in the house, the superintendent reports that [only] eleven are still restless and refractory." Four of the boys had run away, but the Managers and the superintendent were apparently satisfied with the other children, who had been in the House of Refuge at one time or another in 1825.[16]

Methods of discipline varied; the superintendent sometimes put the "subjects" on a ball and chain. He also used handcuffs, leg irons, and the "barrel." On January 28, 1825, Superintendent Curtis noted in his daily journal that six subjects, two of whom were girls, had been talking during a meal. He "took each of them to the barrel which supports them while

[14] New York, *Laws of 1824*, c 126.

[15] "Case Histories No. 1," NYHR.

[16] Society for the Reformation of Juvenile Delinquents in the City of New York, First Annual Report (1825) in New York, Legislature, House, *Documents Relative to a House of Refuge* (New York: Mahlon Day, 1832), pp. 38, 42–49; hereafter the Society is cited as SRJD.

the feet are tied on one side and the hands on the other. . . . With the pantaloons down [this device] gives a convenient surface for the operation of the 6 line cat." On that same day a boy wearing handcuffs made himself a key. The superintendent "put him in prison," locked his leg iron to the wall, and instructed the staff to feed him on bread and water. In spite of these restraints, however, the boy broke out of "prison," but the police soon recaptured him. Curtis refused to have this boy back at the House of Refuge, and so he went to the penitentiary. Corporal punishment was not confined to boys. On March 13, 1825, the superintendent put leg irons on a girl who "does not obey the orders of coming when called, and neglects her work for playing in the yard." Curtis also gave one "sullen, ill-natured and disobedient" girl "a dose of salts"—apparently aloes, a purgative. She came to the House of Refuge in March, 1825, and was "very trying." She did not "transgress in things of importance" but she was "artful and sly" and told "many equivocating stories." Her conduct exasperated Superintendent Curtis and he "gave her a ball and chain and confined her to the house." She escaped twice; once the police recaptured her, and once she returned on her own. She went out as a servant, but voluntarily returned to the House of Refuge. Another indenture took the girl to her majority, but on December 26, 1829, the superintendent wrote that "she is said to be on the town."[17]

The situation at the Refuge made some of these punishments necessary. The walls presented no real barrier, and the superintendent had to appoint some of the boys as guards. There were, consequently, a number of escapes. On October 4, 1825, Superintendent Curtis noted in the daily journal that "this evening has been spent in making confessions on the repeated attempts of escaping." As a result,

> great freedom of speach [*sic*] and frankness appeared to our entire satisfaction, all the movements and plans as well as the persons who have manifested a desire to go has [*sic*] been fully exposed. . . . It tells us that the insecurity which we have daily felt on this subject has been well grounded; and that there is no security with our present encumbrances.

The fact that the magazine of the old arsenal still contained powder also added to the superintendent's worries. In addition many of the inmates in the House of Refuge were boys over sixteen, for legally any boy under twenty-one could be sent there. In September, 1826, the superintendent complained about the "large notorious & hardened villains" who came to the Refuge. "I fear," he said, "that our extended wish to do good will in consequence of introducing these ill bred hardened boys among the first and young offenders, will prove a curse rather than a blessing." Since the old arsenal building was clearly inadequate, the Acting Committee (which functioned as a board of trustees for the House of Refuge) decided to erect a new building which would provide "greater security."

[17] "Daily Journal, No. 1," NYHR, Jan. 28, March 13, 1825; "Case Histories No. 1," NYHR.

In April, 1825, the Committee resolved to add workshops and small utility buildings to their construction plans and decided that the new main building should contain "cells and accommodations for a number of delinq'nts not exceeding one hundred." In that same month the United States Army sent a man to remove the powder from the magazine, which somewhat reduced the "insecurity."[18]

To pay for the new building the managers of the Society appealed to the public for more money. In May, 1825, they issued an *Address to Annual Subscribers* in which they claimed that "already the number of vagrant children who beg and steal in our streets is perceptibly diminished." There were thirty-five boys and eleven girls in the House of Refuge at that time "in a situation where there is no temptation to vice . . . and, where, instead of being left to prey on the public, they will be fitted to become valuable members of society." To continue this important work the managers felt compelled "to erect . . . an additional stone building with separate dormitories for each child, on a plan somewhat resembling the State Prison at Auburn. . . ." To be sure that their contributions were worthwhile "subscribers and the public" were invited "to call at the House of Refuge, and see that idleness has become changed to industry, filth and rags to cleanliness and comfortable appearance, [and] boisterous impudence to quiet submission. . . ."

The Acting Committee directed the superintendent to employ a foreman and four to six masons to erect the building with the assistance of the boys. The masons and the boys finished the new cell-house in April, 1826. It was a two-story stone building with barred windows and heavy doors. Inside were small "dormitories"–three feet, three inches wide–for each boy. The new building did make it more difficult to escape and brought about the complete separation of the male and female departments. "We find ourselves in possession and enjoyment of all the long wished advantages of the new building," Superintendent Curtis wrote, "and we also find (as we may allways [*sic*] expect) that our anticipations are not realised." The boys now had to do their own cooking, and for a time they proved less adept than the girls.[19]

From the first the House of Refuge attracted a stream of visitors, distinguished and otherwise. Soon after the Refuge opened, a father appeared and demanded the return of his son. Only after he had secured a writ of habeas corpus did the superintendent permit the man to take his boy. In May, 1826, Governor De Witt Clinton of New York, the Governor of Ohio, the Mayor of New York, "and various other dignitaries and their wives" came to the House of Refuge and left apparently "well-pleased." In July three men from Pennsylvania came to study the House of Refuge because they were planning to establish a similar institution in Philadelphia. "They left us highly gratified," the superintendent noted in

[18] "Minutes of the Acting Committee, No. 1," NYHR, April 30, 1825; "Daily Journal, No. 1," NYHR, Oct. 4, 1825, Sept. 22, 1826.

[19] "Minutes of the Acting Committee, No. 1," NYHR, May 10, May 21, 1825; "Daily Journal No. 1," NYHR, April 14, 1825, [March ?] 1826; For a sketch of the new building see SRJD, *Fifth Annual Report* (1830), frontispiece.

the daily journal, "with a determined resolution to advance the same good cause they had witnessed. . . ." A week later, the sister of a former inmate came by to see some of her old friends. She was wanted by the police, however, and the superintendent arranged to have her detained. Such guests must have appeared frequently for on July 26, 1826, Superintendent N. C. Hart (Joseph Curtis had resigned on July 11, 1826) noted in the daily journal that "it is found that now and then improper persons get into our yard on visiting days. I have given direction to the gatekeeper not to permit any to enter (even on visiting days) Unless they are very respectable looking persons. . . ."[20]

On Sundays many of the Managers drove out to the House of Refuge to attend the worship services. Two of the most regular visitors were John Griscom and Isaac Collins, both of whom figured prominently in the founding of the refuge. Griscom sometimes talked to the boys about science. On August 13, 1826, for example, he spoke on "the creation of man and matter," and on New Year's Day, 1827, he illustrated his talk with a magic lantern. Collins gave some books for the library. Among the titles were *Essays on Virtue*, the *Life of Captain Cook*, a *Report* of the British and Foreign School Society, *Robinson Crusoe*, and *Wonderful Escapes*.[21]

At the end of the second year, in the *Annual Report* the Managers explained the theories which guided the efforts to reform juvenile delinquents at the House of Refuge. "The young offender," they said, "should, if possible, be subdued by kindness. His heart should first be addressed, and the language of confidence, though undeserved, be used towards him." They added that the young inmate should be taught that "his keepers were his best friends and that the object of his confinement was his reform and ultimate good. If he is made to believe that he is still of some use and value, he will soon endeavor to act up to the character which is set upon him." This kind of discipline, the managers argued, "will be willing, cheerful and lasting." The remarkably gentle–and from the lights of modern psychology, appropriate–methods espoused by the Managers of the New York House of Refuge came from a nineteenth-century theory about children and the development of their personalities. As the Managers explained, men of the early nineteenth century believed that "the minds of children, naturally pliant, can, by early instruction, be formed and moulded to our wishes. An inclination can there be given to them, as readily to virtuous as to vicious pursuits." Not only can the plastic minds of children be turned to vice or virtue, but earlier inclinations can be altered if the child is not too old: "The seeds of vice, which bad advisers may have planted, if skill is exercised, can yet be extracted . . . and on the mind which appeared barren and unfruitful may yet be engrafted those principles of virtue which shall do much to retrieve the errors of the past, and afford a promise of goodness and usefulness for the future."

[20] "Daily Journal, No. 1," NYHR, April 25, 1825, May 26, July 11, July 12, July 19, July 28, 1826.

[21] *Ibid.*, Aug. 8, 1825, Aug. 13, 1826, Jan. 1, 1827.

The Managers also reminded their readers that "these little vagrants, whose depredations provoke and call down upon them our indignation are yet but children, who have gone astray for want of that very care and vigilance we exercise towards our own." They were nonetheless, misbehaving children, whose actions had to be condemned. Furthermore, "a regard for our property and the good of society, requires that they should be stopped, reproved and punished. . . . But," the Managers continued, "they are not to be destroyed. The public must in some measure take the place of those who ought to have been their natural guardians and protectors." Here the Managers of the New York House of Refuge anticipated one of the key concepts of the Illinois Juvenile Court Act of 1899—the idea that the public (in the Illinois law it was the state) has a collective responsibility to and for society's misbehaving children. Ironically, this provision of the Illinois law was hailed as a great innovation in the legal treatment of delinquent children.[22]

In order to carry out their theories, the officials at the New York House of Refuge adopted rules which prescribed continuous activity for the inmates during their waking hours. They were to be employed "every day in the year, except Sundays, at such labor, business, or employment as from time to time [would] be designated by the Acting Committee." Other rules indicated that all the children wore "coarse but comfortable apparel of the cheapest and most durable kind," which was made on the premises. Inmates who refused to work or who used profane or indecent language, or who fought with their fellow delinquents, would be punished. Punishments included deprivation of play periods, being sent to bed without supper, and bread and water. In more serious cases, the officials might force the recalcitrant boy or girl to drink a bitter herb tea which caused them to sweat profusely, or they might put the offender in solitary confinement. In extreme cases, corporal punishment or iron fetters might be used. The rules provided that corporal punishment could only be inflicted in the presence of the superintendent (or the matron in the case of misbehaving girls). The rules also indicated that "the females shall eat their meals and lodge in a separate building from the males, with whom they shall have no intercourse or communication, except at family or public worship."[23]

Scarcely a week passed without some sort of incident. On September 5, 1826, one of the worst troublemakers in the girls' department returned of her own accord after having escaped. She and the school teacher got into an argument, and he began whipping her. According to Superintendent Hart,

> She commenced swearing most bitterly, tore his shirt considerable & made battle with her fists—having a pen knife secreted about her, she succeeded in opening it with her mouth, & made several attempts to stab him in his breast—to no purpose, but finally got it in

[22] SRJD, *Second Annual Report* (1826), in *Documents Relative to a House of Refuge*, p. 80.

[23] *Documents Relative to a House of Refuge*, pp. 106–8.

> the flesh of his arm and ripped a gash at least 1½ inches long and very deep.

The superintendent put the girl in irons. In December, 1826, two boys escaped through the attic of the male cell house, and an officer went to town to look for them. He found one of the boys "in a small rum hole in Anthony St. with girls and other company of ill fame." The boy drew out a knife, while one of the patrons of the establishment shouted "Stick him [!] Stick him [!]." The boy cut the officer severely on the arm and on the neck "near the jugular vein." When the police had returned this boy to the House of Refuge, the superintendent punished him "with a cowskin up on his bare back" and then put him in solitary confinement "without a book to divert his mind" on a bread and water diet. The boy remained in solitary for three days, after which the superintendent put him in a cell in the upper tier. The boy then attempted another escape:

> [He] tied three sheets & a cord together—broke through the plastered wall into the garret—again fastened the cord to the same place where he had been successful in making his escape but a few evenings since—but alas! no sooner than he had . . . [placed] his weight upon the cord thus fastened, it broke & he fell about 30 feet upon frozen ground & stones—broke his foot badly—pitched upon his face cut a hole over his eye to the skull bone & fractured it, broke his nose & drove the bones so deep as to endanger his life—cut his lip through nearly up to his nose. Thus he rolls in agony.

To prevent similar escape attempts the officers moved the older boys to the first tier and put the younger boys in their place.[24]

The House of Refuge, following the penal theories of men like Thomas Eddy, also instituted a rudimentary classification system. When they entered, the officials placed the inmates in one of four grades, ranging from "those who are vicious, bad and wicked" in class four to "the best behaved and most orderly boys and girls; those that do not swear, lie, or use profane, obscene or indecent language or conversation," in class one. Every Sunday, the superintendent, his assistant, and the teacher reclassified the children according to their behavior. The upper classes enjoyed extra recreation, and the lower classes found themselves on a reduced diet and suffered from the loss of other privileges. The system of treatment at the New York House of Refuge, rudimentary as it was, is another example of an improvement in penal practice made in a juvenile institution which would later be hailed as an "innovation" in adult reformatories.

A typical day in the Refuge illustrates this system. A bell would ring at sunrise to arouse the sleeping children. They had fifteen minutes to dress, make their beds, and straighten up their cells; then they assembled in the corridors and marched off to the washrooms. After washing, the inmates lined up for a personal inspection. They were at best a motley

[24] "Daily Journal, No. 1," NYHR, Sept. 5, Dec. 18, Dec. 21, Dec. 24, 1826.

group. Their clothing had been cut from "a coarse, cheap material" to six standard sizes. In 1848 Elijah Devoe, formerly an assistant superintendent, recalled that they had "collectively a slovenly and untidy appearance." From inspection the children went to morning prayers, after which they went to school for an hour and a half. Then they sat down to a breakfast which usually consisted of bread, molasses, and rye coffee. After breakfast, the inmates trooped off to their various workshops, where they worked until noon. Washing up again and the noon meal occupied the next hour, after which the children returned to work. During this afternoon work period the children could gain extra recreation time if they finished their assigned tasks early. The work period ended at five o'clock; then there was a half-hour for supper and another hour and a half of school. Following the evening school session, there were evening prayers; the inmates then marched back to their cells, turned in, and followed a rule of silence for the night.[25]

The labor of the children in the House of Refuge was let out to contractors, who then paid the institution for the value of the work done by the children. While the contractors taught the children the skills necessary to perform their tasks, the officials of the House of Refuge maintained discipline. The girls worked mostly at sewing; and the boys made cane bottoms for chairs, various kinds of brushes, shoes, and boxes for soap and candles. The contractors represented an outside presence in the House of Refuge and an unending source of difficulty. On July 22, 1826, for example, two girls claimed that the shoemaker took them "into his dwelling & there perpetrated that heinous crime of seduction." An investigation quickly followed and on August 6, Superintendent Hart wrote that the shoemaker had "closed his business with us." On October 16, 1827, Hart noted in the daily journal that the parents of some of the boys in the House of Refuge had complained that their sons were not learning a trade since the shoemaker had set up an assembly line, assigning a separate task to each boy. "The remarks are in considerable degree true," Hart wrote, "& how the difficulty is to be obviated I cannot tell." It would take nearly half a century to eliminate the contract system.[26]

When the officials at the New York House of Refuge concluded that a boy or girl had sufficiently reformed to be trusted outside the institution itself, they often bound them out as apprentices. Some of the boys signed on as sailors in whaling ships, a practice which the managers endorsed heartily in the *Fifth Annual Report* because such a boy would find himself under "wholesome restraint and discipline" and would have the examples of "moral, industrious, and religious companions." Most of the boys, however, were apprenticed to farmers, including some in the West—a practice which anticipated the placing out system of Charles

[25] SRJD, *Sixth Annual Report* (1831), in *Documents Relative to a House of Refuge*, pp. 219–52; Elijah Devoe, *The Refuge System, or, Prison Discipline Applied to Juvenile Delinquents* (New York: J. R. M'Gown, 1848), pp. 36, 46, 56; SRJD, *Seventh Annual Report* (1832), in *Documents Relative to a House of Refuge*, pp. 253–302.

[26] "Daily Journal, No. 1," NYHR, July 22, Aug. 6, 1826, Oct. 16, 1827.

Loring Brace and the Children's Aid Society. Generally, the girls became servants in families not too distant from the House of Refuge. Boys were indentured until they were twenty-one, girls until they reached eighteen. To explain the purposes and methods of the New York House of Refuge, the superintendent sent a form letter to the masters of the apprentices, which warned against the overuse of corporal punishment and reminded the masters that "it has not been concealed from you, that this child has been a delinquent." The superintendent also addressed a form letter to the apprentice. "We should not have consented to part with you at this time," it began, "had not your conduct given us reason to hope, that the religious and moral instruction you have received since you have been under our care, have disposed you to lead an honest, industrious, and sober life." The letter to the apprentice also cautioned him against bad company, especially his former associates.[27]

IV

In 1820 a committee of the Massachusetts legislature began investigating the causes of poverty. In 1821 the committee recommended that the system of alms-giving then practiced throughout Massachusetts be abandoned and that cities and towns build work houses or houses of industry. As a result of this report, the town fathers of Boston launched an investigation of poverty in their city. They found the Boston Almshouse to be in deplorable condition. Crowded together were the poor who could not work, the able-bodied who were given make-work such as picking oakum, and those convicted of minor offenses such as drunkenness. The Boston investigators recommended the erection of a work house or industry for the able-bodied poor and a house of correction for minor offenders. By the summer of 1823 these new institutions were in use, but the south wing of the House of Correction remained empty. As in New York, hundreds of undisciplined and apparently homeless children roamed the streets of Boston. Their disturbing presence—the prosperous people of Boston also saw these waifs as a threat to society—and the creation of the New York House of Refuge stimulated the town fathers of Boston to do something about juvenile delinquency. Early in 1826 a committee of the City Council recommended that the unused wing of the House of Correction be converted to "a house of reformation for juvenile offenders."[28]

In March of 1826 the legislature passed an act authorizing the Boston City Council to use the House of Correction or any other building as an institution for juvenile offenders. This statute also gave the Commonwealth of Massachusetts a definition of juvenile delinquency. Like the

[27] SRJD, *Fourth Annual Report* (1829), in *Documents Relative to a House of Refuge*, pp. 179–80; SRJD, *Fifth Annual Report* (1830); Homer Folks, *Care of Destitute, Neglected, and Delinquent Children* (New York: Macmillan, 1902), p. 203.

[28] Josiah Quincy, *A Municipal History of the Town and City of Boston, during Two Centuries* (1630–1830) (Boston: Little and Brown, 1852), pp. 35–106.

act passed two years before in New York, the Massachusetts law defined juvenile delinquents as "all such children who shall be convicted of criminal offenses, or taken up and committed under and by virtue of an act of this Commonwealth, 'for suppressing and punishing of rogues, vagabonds, common beggars, and other idle, disorderly and lewd persons.'" In addition, the Massachusetts General Court also provided that the house of reformation could receive "all children who live an idle or dissolute life, whose parents are dead, or if living, from drunkenness, or other vices, neglect to provide any suitable employment, or exercise any salutary control over said children." The Massachusetts law was the first legislative recognition of the idea of preventing juvenile delinquency.[29]

The early years of the Boston House of Reformation were difficult. Ordinary citizens and members of the Boston City Council disagreed about its design, and, as Mayor Josiah Quincy indicated in his *Municipal History of Boston*, "the expenditures were immediate and considerable; the advantages distant and problematical." Many Bostonians felt that the institution should have been supported by the state instead of the city. Mayor Quincy also complained about parents who tried to have their sons removed from the institution and about "tender-hearted philanthropists, who regarded the length and nature of the restraint as severe, notwithstanding [the fact that] the boys were committed by a court of justice for serious offenses." The new institution was very fortunate, however, in the selection of its second superintendent, the Reverend E. M. P. Wells. According to Mayor Quincy, "Strictness without severity, love without indulgence, were the elements of his system of management." Quincy was not alone in his praise of Wells. In 1832 two French noblemen, Alexis de Tocqueville and Gustave Beaumont, came to the United States on an official mission for the French government to study American prison systems. They inspected several American prisons and the houses of refuge at New York and Philadelphia, and naturally they came to Boston and visited the House of Reformation. They were particularly impressed by Superintendent Wells and his administration of the Boston institution. "It is possible to find superintendents who are fit for the Philadelphia system," they wrote, "but we cannot hope to meet often with such men as Mr. Wells."[30]

What distinguished the House of Reformation in Boston from the New York House of Refuge and the House of Refuge established in Philadelphia in 1828 was its system of discipline. As Tocqueville and Beaumont noted, "the Boston discipline belongs to a species of ideas much more elevated than that established in New York and Philadelphia"; but it was difficult to practice because it was "entirely of a moral character." The Boston House of Reformation used a classification system based on the conduct of the inmates, but unlike the New York House of Refuge

[29] Massachusetts, "Laws of 1826," in *Private and Special Statutes of the Commonwealth of Massachusetts from May, 1822 to March, 1830* (Boston: Dutton and Wentworth, State Printers, 1837), c 182.

[30] Quincy, *Municipal History*, pp. 106–7; Alexis de Tocqueville and Gustave Beaumont, *On the Penitentiary System in the United States*, ed. by Thorstein Sellin (Carbondale, Ill.: Southern Illinois Univ. Pr., 1964), p. 121.

it required each child to evaluate his own conduct, and a jury composed of children in the institution tried cases of serious misconduct. In the House of Reformation there were six grades of conduct—three good ones and three bad ones. Each of the good grades carried with it certain privileges; boys in the highest grade could go outside the bounds of the House of Reformation by themselves. Conversely, each of the bad grades carried a degree of privation; boys in the two lowest grades were not allowed to speak unless it was absolutely necessary. Before the boys could participate in this system of discipline, they went through a period of probation. A new arrival met with the superintendent who interviewed him to determine his moral condition. Then, if the new inmate had been found guilty of a serious offense, he was placed in solitary confinement for two weeks so that he could reflect on his vices. Superintendent Wells then told him why he was in the Boston House of Reformation and explained the system of discipline. If the boy rebelled against the officials during his probationary period, they whipped him. Only at this first stage did the superintendent permit corporal punishment. At the end of the probationary period, the superintendent assigned the child one of the bad grades and encouraged him to move up.[31]

While the Society for the Prevention of Pauperism in the City of New York began concentrating on the problem of youthful offenders in its city, the Society for Alleviating the Miseries of Public Prisons met in Philadelphia and appointed a committee to investigate the conditions of vagrant children in the prisons of the city. At that time, juvenile vagrants and young offenders in Philadelphia were placed in the Walnut Street jail along with adult criminals. In May, 1824, the committee recommended that the Guardians of the Poor provide a suitable place for the reception of juvenile vagrants. In the meantime the Society had appointed another committee to consider what should be done about juvenile offenders. This committee recommended the creation of a House of Refuge for discharged prisoners, but soon after they filed their report "an association of females" petitioned the Society to create a House of Refuge for Juvenile Offenders. So the committee investigated again and decided that such an institution was desirable but beyond the means of the Society for Alleviating the Miseries of Public Prisons. The Society then called a public meeting in February, 1826, to find additional support for the proposed House of Refuge. The assembly adopted a resolution calling for the creation of such an institution for juvenile offenders and appointed a committee to draw up "articles of association" for that purpose and to ask the legislature for "such powers in law, as may be necessary to carry the designs of the association into full effect when it may be organized." The legislature readily acceded to the request and passed an act of incorporation for the Philadelphia House of Refuge in March, 1826. This act, like those statutes creating the New York House of Refuge and the Boston House of Reformation, provided that the Managers of the Philadelphia House of Refuge could receive "such children who shall be taken up as vagrants, or

[31] Tocqueville and Beaumont, *On the Penitentiary System*, pp. 119–21; "The House of Reformation," *New England Magazine*, III (Nov. 1832), 386–87.

duly convicted of criminal offenses," but it also gave the managers the authority to receive children "who shall be taken up . . . upon any criminal charge." Thus, by law, children suspected of crime could be placed in the Philadelphia institution.[32]

To accomplish their goals the Managers of the Philadelphia House of Refuge expected to rely on a combination of strict discipline, a classification similar to that used at the House of Reformation in Boston, work at a useful occupation, education, and moral instruction. The first step in such a program was "to raise the delinquent in his own estimation . . . to change his whole course of thought: to awake his latent pride and sensibility: to direct his ambition to useful and honorable pursuits: and thus to conduct him unconsciously as it were to the practical charms and advantages of a virtuous life." The managers expected to retain control over delinquents who entered the House of Refuge until they reached a majority, but the managers hoped to place the children out as apprentices well before they reached the upper age limit.[33]

V

The public image of an institution, derived in part from the reports of well-publicized visitors and investigations and also from the institution's own annual reports, is rarely a complete picture of its daily life. In a book that amounted to a polemic against the New York House of Refuge, Elijah Devoe, a discharged assistant superintendent, contended that the New York institution had deliberately falsified its public face. He charged that officials had altered the records to give a higher rate of reformation and that the day-by-day practices in the institution were far more cruel than any outsider realized. The routine was "a stern, brutal, coercive government and discipline, entirely the opposite of that paternal establishment so amiable and ingeniously pictured in the 'annual reports.' " Devoe also indicated that the rule prohibiting corporal punishment unless in the presence of the superintendent was a dead letter: "Corporal punishments are usually inflicted with the cat or a ratan. The latter instrument is applied in a great variety of places, such as the palm and back of the hands, top and bottom of the feet, and lastly, but not rarely or sparingly, to the posteriors over the clothes, and also on the naked skin." Ratans were readily available and "liable to be used everywhere and at all times of the day." In addition, Devoe deplored the mixing of "hardened culprits over fifteen years" of age with "small, younger, and less corrupt children." The older boys were just as likely to corrupt the younger ones as hardened adult criminals were to corrupt juveniles in prison; it was therefore an injustice that "boys under a certain age, who become subject to the notice of our police, either as vagrants or houseless, should be thrust into

[32] Negley K. Teeters, *They Were in Prison; A History of the Pennsylvania Prison Society, 1787–1937* (Philadelphia: John C. Winston Co., 1937), pp. 161–68; Pennsylvania, *Laws of 1826–27*, c XLVII.

[33] Philadelphia House of Refuge, *An Address from the Managers of the House of Refuge to their fellow Citizens* (Philadelphia: D. & S. Neall, 1826), pp. 9–12.

the society of confirmed thieves, burglars, and robbers, and subjected to the same discipline and punishments."[34]

Devoe's account, which was the work of an unhappy former employee, nonetheless provides an "inside view" of an early nineteenth-century juvenile institution. It seems probable that the annual reports of these institutions, which were made in response to state law and which represented to some extent arguments for state appropriations, presented only the most favorable aspects of houses of refuge and ignored the day-to-day activities which deviated from the high ideals set by the managers. In some respects, however, the view of juvenile institutions presented in their annual reports is more valuable than the "inside story," because the annual reports gave the public its only look at juvenile institutions. Thus, they are a rudimentary index to what nineteenth-century Americans knew about institutions for juvenile delinquents.

The creation of special institutions for juvenile offenders in the second decade of the nineteenth century indicated a growing awareness on the part of American city-dwellers of the problem of juvenile delinquency, and the new institutions also represented a modification in the application of criminal laws to young people. Under the common law as Blackstone explained it, children under seven were presumed to be unable to distinguish between right and wrong. Between the ages of seven and fourteen, "though an infant shall be *prima facie* adjudged to be *doli incapax* [not mentally competent]; yet if it appear to the court and jury that he was *doli capax*, and could discern between good and evil, he may be convicted and suffer death." That this understanding of the common law was generally adopted in the United States may be illustrated by a case involving a twelve-year-old Negro boy in New Jersey in 1828. The boy had been found guilty of the murder of a sixty-year-old woman by a lower court, and the case had been appealed to the New Jersey Supreme Court on the grounds that the boy was too young to be found guilty of such an offense. The Supreme Court upheld the verdict of the lower court, finding that the judge had correctly charged the jury with the relevant points of law in the case. The lower court judge had told the jury that "with respect to the ability of persons of his age, to commit crimes of this nature, the law is, that under the age of seven, they are deemed incapable of it. Between seven and fourteen, if there be no proof of capacity, arising out of this case, or by testimony of witnesses, the presumption is in their favor; a presumption however, growing weaker and more easily overcome, the nearer they approach to fourteen." The judge went on to explain that a twelve-year-old boy in New Jersey at that time probably possessed "sufficient capacity" to commit murder. Finally he told the jury: "you call to mind the evidence on this subject; and if you are satisfied that he was able, in a good degree, to distinguish between right and wrong; to know the nature of the crime with which he is charged; and that it was *deserving* of *severe* punishment, his infancy will furnish no obstacle, on the score of incapacity, to his conviction."[35]

[34] Devoe, *Refuge System,* pp. 11, 28–29, 50–51.

[35] Sir William Blackstone, *Commentaries on the Laws of England,* 4 vols. (Dublin: John Exshaw *et al.,* 1773), IV 23; *State* v *Guild,* 5 Halstead 163 (New Jersey

None of the statutes which established the houses of refuge in New York, Boston, and Philadelphia changed the basic premises of the common law, but in effect they raised the age below which a child could expect to receive some kind of preferential treatment from the law. The sentiment behind the creation of the new institutions for juvenile delinquents recognized that children—even children over fourteen—required different treatment from adults. The new laws, although they did not mention any ages except those for the end of minority, created institutions which would provide that treatment. The laws also provided a legal definition of juvenile delinquency. A juvenile delinquent was a child who broke the law, or who was in danger of breaking the law, and the community hoped to keep him from becoming an adult criminal by providing reformatory treatment in a house of refuge.

The creation of the House of Refuge, a unique institution in the United States, posed some new legal problems, which soon led to court action. In the case of *Commonwealth* v *M'Keagy*, heard before the Court of Common Pleas in Philadelphia in 1831, the issue was a plea for a writ of habeas corpus on behalf of one Lewis L. Joseph, who had been convicted on evidence supplied by his father of being "an idle and disorderly person" and sent to the Philadelphia House of Refuge. After reciting the relevant sections of the statute establishing the Philadelphia House of Refuge, the court noted that "great power is given to the managers of this institution, a power which could only be justified under the most pressing public exigencies, and whose continuance should depend only on the most prudent and guarded exercise of it." Particularly unusual, according to the court, was the power given to any magistrate or justice of the peace, "on a charge of vagrancy or crime . . . to take a child from its parent and consign it to the control of any human being, no matter how elevated or pure." The overseers of the poor generally had the power to provide for orphans and dependent children and even to bind them out as apprentices until they reached their majority. "Why is it that in some shape, and if necessary, in a more decided shape," the court asked, "the public cannot assume similar guardianship of children whose poverty had degenerated into vagrancy?" The court agreed that the House of Refuge indeed did have the power to receive and control children whose vagrancy fell within the categories the court had outlined. However, the court continued, "it is when the law is attempted to be applied to subjects who are not vagrants in the just and legal acceptation of the term"; when "preservation becomes mixed with a punitory character, that doubts are started and difficulties arise, which often and necessarily involve the most solemn questions of individual and constitutional rights."

Having thus stated its position, the court proceeded to find that Lewis Joseph was not a vagrant. His father, who had committed him, was not a pauper, and the boy, while he had misbehaved, was not a fit subject for the House of Refuge. The Superintendent of the House of Refuge had

State Law Reporter). Although the fact that the defendant was black may have affected the original decision, the appeal did establish a precedent for the application of the English Common Law to infants in American courts.

told the judge that the boy had been very well behaved there and had been very receptive to discipline. As the court said, "it is manifest, that gentle but firm discipline was all that was necessary to root out from his mind the luxuriant weeds produced by weak indulgence, bestowed by an erring parent of a sportive and volatile disposition." In opposing the petition for a writ of habeas corpus the lawyer for the House of Refuge had argued that the boy's father had transferred his parental authority to the managers of that institution, which now acted *in loco parentis*. But the court rejected this view, saying that the House of Refuge could only receive vagrant and criminal children; it was not "a place to correct refractory children." Accordingly, the court ordered Lewis L. Joseph released from the Philadelphia House of Refuge.[36]

In a later case, *Ex parte Crouse*, which the Pennsylvania Supreme Court heard in 1839, a similar petition for a writ of habeas corpus challenged the constitutionality of the statute which created the Philadelphia House of Refuge. The petition had been filed on behalf of Mary Ann Crouse by her father. "The House of Refuge is not a prison, but a school," the court said in opening its argument. The use of the House of Refuge "as a prison for juvenile convicts who would also be committed to a common gaol" is clearly constitutional, but in the case of juveniles admitted as vagrants or potential criminals, the constitutionality was open to some question. The main purpose of the House of Refuge was clearly reformation and not punishment; education was one of its principal activities. If a child's parents did not, for one reason or another, provide it with adequate education, the state by virtue of its power of *parens patriae* could provide the child with the necessary education. Such was Mary Ann Crouse's case: "The infant has been snatched from a course which must have ended in confirmed depravity; and not only is the restraint of her person lawful, but it would be an act of extreme cruelty to release her from it."[37]

These two cases illustrate that the House of Refuge was a legal institution with certain well-defined powers. Primarily, it was an institution designed to reform youthful criminals, but it also functioned to prevent crime by accepting young vagrants who were potential juvenile criminals. Once a house of refuge received a child, the managers had a wide latitude of authority over him. In effect, they had the same powers over their charges that a natural parent had over his own children. Thus the state, by chartering a private or municipal association to take the place of inadequate or missing parents, had taken a bold step in the direction of providing for the welfare of its children. In addition, such a step appeared almost too attractive to resist. When houses of refuge first appeared, they seemed to have a good chance of preventing or drastically reducing the rate of adult crime. They not only gave the community something to do with juvenile offenders and vagrant children, they promised to cut future welfare and prison costs. When they insisted that the inmates of houses of

[36] *Commonwealth* v *M'Keagy*, 1 Ashmead (1831), 248 (Pennsylvania State Law Reporter).

[37] *Ex parte Crouse* 4 Wharton (1839), 9 (Pennsylvania State Law Reporter).

refuge be taught a useful trade, the managers shrewdly responded to a community prejudice which not only condemned idleness as a sin but also linked it with serious crime. By teaching juvenile offenders how to work then, houses of refuge were exorcising sin and providing for the future security of life and property. The creation of the New York House of Refuge and similar institutions in Boston and Philadelphia marked the beginning of nineteenth-century America's concern for wayward children. It also marked the beginning of the process of separating juvenile delinquents from adult criminals—a process that would not be complete until the creation of the juvenile court in 1899. But the house of refuge had one essential weakness as an institution—it was a charity, which, although chartered by the state, private citizens operated. The involvement of private citizens had been necessary to launch the first institutions for juvenile delinquents, but once their worth had been proved, many philanthropists felt that the reformation of juvenile offenders was a duty for which the state should take full responsibility.

Rioting in Its Jacksonian Setting

DAVID GRIMSTED

From the Stamp Act revolts of 1765 to the ghetto uprisings of the 1960s, mob violence has been a powerful influence in American history. Although the specific intent of the mobs has varied, the process by which they formed has tended to be much the same, and the uprisings have generally had certain characteristics in common.

First, mobs rarely see the purpose of their action as illegal, although on occasion they see it as supralegal—that is, as carrying the enforcement of the law beyond its stated limits. A lynch mob, for example, may be unwilling to wait for or to trust the court system to reach what they consider a just verdict; thus the mob may see itself as the executor of proper justice. Similarly, the vigilante groups that administered dubious justice in the old West joined together in posses allegedly to enforce the law.

Generally, mobs tend to rally around some real or imagined grievance that they have reason to believe the recognized authorities will not deal with properly. This is especially apt to be the situation when the ultimate authorities are far away or unsympathetic to local conditions, as in Colonial America, the old West, or the pre–Civil War South; when authorities are nearby and repressive, as in urban ghettoes; or when local authorities side with citizen groups in opposition to higher authorities, as in Colonial America or the South during the school desegregation crisis of the late 1950s and early 1960s.

Mob action is rarely directed against the **idea** of authority or order, but rather against some particular condition that the authority has either caused or allowed to exist. Studies of mob action in Europe in the eighteenth and nineteenth centuries as well as studies of more recent riots in the United States have shown that the targets of mob violence are limited and selective. This has been the case in the twentieth-century ghetto revolts in Northern cities, for instance, in which attacks have been primarily on property and few deaths have occurred at the hands of the rioters.

In the article that follows, David Grimsted, of the University of Maryland, discusses rioting during the Jacksonian era, when democratic ideas were in ferment and the nation was struggling to find the proper balance between individual freedom and the requirements of social order. The riots studied here do not fit neatly into the paradigm mentioned above because the government on all levels was testing the nature and limits of its authority and was reluctant to use excessive force against the citizens who were expressing their grievances, particularly when the victims of mobs were weak or unpopular.

"Americans have always been a beneviolent people." As the Romantics argued the kinship of madness and genius, so it is difficult clearly to segregate student inspiration from imbecility. And if not the student who wrote the comment in that eternal source of peculiar wisdom, last year's exam books, perhaps Providence acting through the student spoke suggestively, especially considering the root of the word: if *bene-volo* means to will good, "beneviolent" would suggest the willing of good in notably vigorous form. And here perhaps lies a clue to some of the paradoxes of both the origin and significance of social violence in its American contexts.[1]

Social violence has obvious roots in both the psychology of its participants and their socioeconomic situation, and analysts of crowd behavior understandably have concentrated their examinations around such causes. Yet the extent, nature, and direction of mob violence depend equally on shared cultural assumptions about the nature of power and law,

[1] As recent popular books have stressed the peculiar violence of American society, more scholarly ones have suggested the limits as well as the extent of disruptiveness in the United States. Irving J. Sloan, *Our Violent Past* (New York, 1970); David Abrahamsen, *Our Violent Society* (New York, 1970); Ovid Demaris, *America the Violent* (New York, 1970); Hugh Davis Graham and Ted Robert Gurr, eds., *The History of Violence in America* (New York, 1969); Richard Hofstadter, introd. to Hofstadter and Michael Wallace, eds., *Violence in America: A Documentary History* (New York, 1970).

"Rioting in Its Jacksonian Setting," by David Grimsted. From *American Historical Review,* LXXVII (April, 1972), 361–97. Reprinted by permission of the author.
An earlier version of this paper was read at the joint session of the American Studies Association and the Southern Historical Association at the annual meeting of the Southern Historical Association, November 13, 1970, in Louisville. This study has been supported in part by fellowships from the National Endowment for the Humanities and the Charles Warren Center for Studies in American History and summer grants from the Social Science Research Council, the American Council of Learned Societies, and the University of Maryland.

and the relation of the individual and the group to them.[2] For the Jacksonian period, the diversity of type and circumstance of riot offers presumptive evidence that social violence owed less to local and particular grievances than to widely held assumptions and attitudes about the relation of the individual to social control. Only a cause that was "general in its operation," wrote a Baltimore newspaper, could explain the variously directed outbursts of social violence in the mid-1830s.[3]

Historians of eighteenth-century America have shown that mobs in that period functioned more as an accepted part of the political structure than an attack on it, largely because authorities unofficially recognized their legitimacy so long as they acted within certain bounds.[4] This reflected in part English preference for granting the lower classes occasional informal sway to giving them any established influence on government and in part colonial willingness to use the mob to make imperial authorities heed local interests. With the achievement of independence both of these justifications of the mob were undercut. Power was no longer imperially centered, nor were there large groups of white males denied a measure of political influence through established channels. Royall Tyler's play, *The Contrast*, written partly as a Federalist political document in 1787, marked the change clearly. Tyler, who had been active in putting down Shays's Rebellion, has his likably naive American democrat, Jonathan, admit that he was talked out of siding with Shays only by the natural aristocrat, Colonel Manly, who explained to him, "It was a burning shame for the true blue Bunker Hill sons of liberty, who had fought Governor Hutchinson, Lord North, and the Devil to have any hand in kicking up a cursed dust against the government which we had, every mother's son of us, a hand in making."[5] The strong though unvindictive action of the authorities toward Shays's and Fries's and the Whisky rebellions—even the fact that these incidents were labeled "rebellions"—made clear that the eighteenth-century role of the riotous crowd had ended.

[2] Ted Robert Gurr, who has constructed the most complex and satisfactory sociological model for violence, argues that ideological sanctions for violence are important, but in "a secondary, rationalizing" way. Because "relative deprivation" is his key concept, Gurr claims that social tensions develop first, and from these grow intellectual sanctions for violence. One could argue equally well that deprivation relative to something or other is always with us, and violence depends more on ideological or cultural channeling. *Why Men Rebel* (Princeton, 1970), 13–15, 155–231.

[3] Baltimore *Republican*, Aug. 20, 1835.

[4] Pauline Maier, "Popular Uprisings and Civil Authority in Eighteenth-Century America," *William and Mary Quarterly*, ser. 3, vol. 27 (1970): 3–35; Maier, "The Charleston Mob and the Evolution of Popular Politics in Revolutionary South Carolina, 1765–1784," *Perspectives in American History*, 4 (1970): 173–96; Gordon Wood, "A Note on Mobs in the American Revolution," *William and Mary Quarterly*, ser. 3, vol. 23 (1966): 635–42; William Ander Smith, "Anglo-American Society and the Mob, 1740–1775" (Ph.D. dissertation, Claremont Graduate School, 1965).

[5] Royall Tyler, *The Contrast* (Boston, 1920), 55–56.

The United States in the first quarter of the nineteenth century was relatively free of internal group violence, but in the 1830s riot once again became frequent. Between 1828 and 1833 there were some twenty incidents of riot, in 1834 at least sixteen riots took place, and in 1835 the number increased to thirty-seven, most of them concentrated in the summer and fall of that year.[6] The Philadelphia *National Gazette* echoed the sentiments of many when it wrote in August 1835, "The horrible fact is staring us in the face, that, whenever the fury or the cupidity of the mob is excited, they can gratify their lawless appetites almost with impunity; and it is wonderful with all the evidence of the facts that have been furnished in such abundance, to behold the degree of supineness that exists."[7] Never again in the antebellum period was rioting this concentrated, but it remained a regular social phenomenon to be accepted with a degree of "supineness." Some of these incidents were in result minor—for example, the anti-Garrison mob, which resulted in one torn coat and one broken sign—but property damage was often extensive, and numerous lives were lost. By 1835 at least 61 people had been killed in riot; by 1840 that figure goes above 125, and the worst destructiveness was yet to come. Certainly over one thousand people were killed in antebellum riots, and the draft riots of 1863 added probably another thousand to that roll.[8] Even when the riots were comparatively undestructive, they revealed major tensions in the society: ethnic hatreds; religious animosities; class tensions; racial prejudice; economic grievances; moral fears over drinking, gaming, and prostitution; political struggles; the albatross of slavery.

That these incidents had been largely forgotten until the last few years tells us something, as current violence experts have said, about the way Americans have accentuated the positive in their past. More important, it reflects the way in which American democracy has been able to absorb quantities of violence in its structure without fundamentally shaking it.[9] Historians have neglected the topic in large part because people so quickly forgot about the incidents. At times between 1834 and 1837 there was in some men's minds a sense of real possibility of social disintegration, but even during these years there was always a quick return to placidity after the outbreaks. And as resort to violence proved not a steadily spreading disease but a kind of periodic social virus, unpleasant perhaps but also unthreatening to the social organism, fearful responses became shorter and more ritualistic. For a day or two after a riot some papers explored the specific situation and the general problem; a week later, unless a trial or coroner's inquest reawoke interest, it would be pub-

[6] Incidents of riot were compiled from secondary sources, particularly local histories, from a complete reading of *Niles' Register* and the *National Intelligencer*, and from scattered reading in other newspapers, journals, and manuscripts.

[7] Philadelphia *National Gazette*, Aug. 11, 1835.

[8] Accounts about the number of deaths in particular incidents are frequently vague, unconvincing, or contradictory, but these figures are minimal, except possibly for the New York Draft Riot.

[9] Richard E. Rubenstein, *Rebels in Eden* (Boston, 1970); Hugh Davis Graham, "The Paradox of American Violence: A Historical Approach," *Annals of the American Academy of Political and Social Science*, 391 (1970): 75–82.

licly forgotten. Riot had regained its eighteenth-century status as a frequent and tacitly accepted if not approved mode of behavior.

Acquiescence in riot owed much to the fact that rioting was not basically an attack on the social system itself. Francis Grund, the Jacksonian publicist, wrote that lynch law, a term often used interchangeably with riot in these years, "is not properly speaking an opposition to the established laws of the country . . . , but rather . . . a supplement to them—as a species of *common law*."[10] A working definition of riot would be those incidents where a number of people group together to enforce their will immediately, by threatening or perpetrating injury to people or property outside of legal procedures but without intending to challenge the general structure of society. Such a definition, in its psychological and social basis, distinguishes riot in a rough way from revolutionary violence, which aims at the destruction of the existing political structure; or insurrection, the uprising of people essentially excluded from political participation; or group criminality, where people act in defiance rather than alleged support of accepted communal standards; or acts of civil disobedience, which involve lawbreaking to dramatize a cause but without threatening injury or destruction; or acts of disruption or symbolic violence such as burning in effigy where no real threat is involved. Such a definition of riot would include some types of social violence—like lynchings or vigilance committees in areas where there were existing legal structures—often given other labels. Here, aside from some very quasi-judicial procedure, the main difference from riot was the unusual inactivity of the constituted power.[11]

Defenders of specific riots in the period talked of the action not as revolution or even illegality but as an enforcement of justice within the bonds of society—an immediate redressing of moral wrongs or a removal of social dangers that for various reasons could not be handled by ordinary legal process. Justifications of riots and vigilance committees often invoked the precedents of 1776 in their defense, but such invocations invariably implied no intention to destroy society, suggesting instead that existing society entailed the right of popular correction of social abuses in instances when the legal system was unable or unwilling to act. In the United States the "right of revolution" justified not overthrowing the government but considerable group violence within its structure.[12]

[10] Francis Grund, *The Americans in Their Moral, Social and Political Relations* (Boston, 1837), 180.

[11] Some other things have been suggested to distinguish riotous violence from vigilance committees: that they were composed of respectable citizens, that they were extralegal rather than antilegal organizations, and that they did not act "spontaneously" as rioters did. In truth the composition of some riotous mobs—especially those against abolitionists or Mormons—rivaled in respectability that of vigilance organizations. Both groups saw their actions as extralegal, and both acted usually with some preparation but with much responsiveness to chance developments and moods.

[12] Eugene Dumez, introd. to Alexandre Barde, *Histoire des Comités de Vigilance aux Attakapas* (Saint-Jean-Baptiste, La., 1861), iii, 36–37; Leonard L. Richards, *Gentlemen of Property and Standing: Anti-Abolition Mobs in Jacksonian America* (New

Observers realized that the traditional justifications of riot in colonial America or in Europe were absent, and they puzzled over explanations of why rioting re-established itself in the United States. In pondering the "disorganizing, anarchical spirit" of 1835, the editor of the Boston *Evening Journal* claimed, "There are strong reasons why the laws should be implicitly obeyed in this country for they are but the echo of public opinion. . . . Our laws are not made as in many countries abroad, by the few for the suppression of the many, but by the many for the advantage of the whole." Governor James F. Thomas of Maryland put the case most succinctly:

> In governments not formed in the principles of republicanism . . . these popular commotions may sometimes be palliated or excused. . . . But in a country like ours where the people are acknowledged to be supreme, and are in fact in the constant practical exercise of absolute sovereignty there can be no apology, there is no extenuation or excuse for such commotions, and their occurrence stains the character of the government and wounds deeply the cause of equal government.[13]

The irony in these observations was that the reason for denying the old justification of riot—the institutionally clear power of the individual to influence the state—had become central to the new. The ideological tenets and political emotions of the age of Jackson, focusing on the centrality and sovereignty of the individual, both encouraged riotous response to certain situations and made it difficult to put riot down when it broke out. Jacksonian political notions were in no sense new, but the intensity, the immediacy, indeed the simplicity with which they were held gave them a fresh cast and social significance.

American political theory had long stressed the centrality in the social structure of the individual rather than the state: here the state was to have little power, no more than was needed to safeguard, or if broadly construed, to promote the individual's pursuit of happiness and search for fulfillment. Authority was subdivided among federal, state, and local groups; it was checked and balanced on each level and bound by constitutional, natural, and democratic controls to prevent tyranny over the individual. "In contrast to Europe, where society is everything and the individual nothing, and where society crushes without pity all who stand in its way," wrote one of the ablest defenders of early vigilante groups, "in America the individual is all and society nothing. There an admirable system of laws protects the feeble, the poor, the accused; there especially is the jury favorable to the defense; and finally, there all aspects of the

---

York, 1970), 69, 97–98; Richard Maxwell Brown, "The American Vigilante Tradition," in Graham and Gurr, *History of Violence*, 181.

[13] Boston *Evening Journal*, Aug. 7, 1835; Governor Thomas's message, Dec. 30, 1835, quoted in the Baltimore *Republican*, Jan. 4, 1836; see also the Baltimore *Republican*, Aug. 10, 1835; and Francis Wyse, *America, Its Realities and Resources* (London, 1846), 1: 199–200.

law are subordinated to individual right, which is the basis and essence of the republic."[14] Democratic government was not only to reflect the will of the people but also was not to interfere with the proper private will of the individual.

Historians have generally seen the Jacksonian period as marking the fruition of the nation's democracy—a notion upheld even as the evidence mounts that most of the legal changes toward democracy occurred earlier and that the major techniques of the second party system had been prefigured in the first.[15] The answer may lie in seeing democracy less as a legal and technical system than as a psychological construct: Everyman's sense of his equality of right to participate and of his ability to decide. Democracy in this psychological sense reaffirms the importance of Jackson on the political scene: his lack of formal education, his intuitive strength, his belief that anyone had the ability to handle government jobs, his transformation of the presidency from that of guide for the people to a personalized representative of the Democracy, all helped create a sense of power justly residing in the hands of each man rather than in the state and a sense of the need for democratic citizens to pursue the right comparatively free from mere procedural trammels and from deference to their social and intellectual betters.

Andrew Jackson himself deplored the rioting that accelerated during his second administration. In at least three instances he sent federal troops to quell riots, and at the height of rioting in 1835 he wrote Amos Kendall, "This spirit of mob-law is becoming too common and must be checked or, ere long, it will become as great an evil as servile war, and the innocent will be much exposed." Yet in this same letter he showed his willingness to circumvent laws that he thought were protecting the guilty. He approved of Kendall's decision to let postmasters withhold abolitionist literature from the mail if they chose on the grounds that, in Kendall's words, citizens owed "an obligation to the laws but a higher one to the communities in which we live." Jackson thought Kendall had perhaps not gone far enough and suggested that postmasters be ordered to deliver abolitionist mail only at the receiver's request and that the names of all those accepting the material be published to "put them in coventry."[16]

[14] Dumez, introd., iv. Dumez concluded that the great advantages of the American system had their reverse in the difficulties of punishing wrong doers, especially among "un peuple né d'hier."

[15] Richard P. McCormick, "New Perspectives on Jacksonian Politics," *AHR*, 65 (1959–60): 288–301; McCormick, *The Second American Party System: Party Formation in the Jacksonian Era* (Chapel Hill, 1966), 19–31; William Nisbet Chambers and Walter Dean Burnham, eds., *The American Party Systems: Stages of Political Development* (New York, 1967).

[16] Andrew Jackson to Amos Kendall, Aug. 9, 1835, Andrew Jackson Papers, Library of Congress; Amos Kendall to Alfred Huger, Charleston postmaster, Aug. 4, 1835, printed in the Washington *Globe*, Aug. 12, 1835. Richard Maxwell Brown suggests Jackson once advised settlers to punish a man by lynch law; actually Jackson said only that he had no right to pardon a man convicted by an informal jury in Iowa territory prior to the extension of United States law to the area and urged that pardon be sought from the informal authority. "Legal and Be-

Jackson's personality and actions rather than his ideas made him seem, more than any other American political figure, the anarchic hero, a man who when he decided something went ahead untouched by popular clamor in favor of the national bank, or judicial decisions supporting the Cherokees, or mere legal technicalities regarding bank deposits. The Whigs felt real fear at the implications of King Andrew's highhandedness, but their attempts to make political capital out of it foundered on popular acceptance of Jackson's own sense of his role: that he was the disinterested spokesman of the people and the Democracy and as such his actions could not abridge but only perfect democratic procedure.

Jackson fitted perfectly the popular American image of the man who need not follow accepted procedures because of the rectitude of his own character, which insured proper action in a world neatly segregated between the innocent and the guilty, the righteous and the monstrous. Jackson's popularity was rooted in his embodiment of the deepest American political myth: that man standing above the law was to be not a threat to society but its fulfillment. "Trust thyself. Every heart vibrates to that iron string," wrote Emerson in his exhortation to his countrymen to be truly self-reliant and hence to become truly representative men. And James Fenimore Cooper, intending to write a story glorifying the ways of his patrician father, created a subsidiary character who stole the novel and the affections of American and world readers. Natty Bumppo came into being as the representative of natural justice in contrast to the legal justice of the good Judge Temple, and Cooper intended to preach of the sad need for the latter to prevail. But the author himself, much less his democratic audience, had small enthusiasm for the formal dogma that Natty ought to be punished for illegally shooting a deer in a community where the respectable citizens killed maple trees for sugar and slaughtered passenger pigeons and fish for fun—legally, of course. And after Natty comes Henry David Thoreau and Huck Finn and William S. Hart and Gary Cooper and Humphrey Bogart and John Wayne and the Hemingway heroes—all men whose stature comes from their standing outside of society and the law in order to live by an individual code, which peculiarly does not threaten the social good but offers its best protection. "Self-interest rightly understood" was the term Americans used to suggest that there was no disjunction between individualism and social responsibility but rather perfect union, Alexis de Tocqueville reported—with great skepticism about how well this worked in fact.[17]

The anarchistic implications of these tenets of Jacksonian democracy influenced but never seriously undermined that social force which most

---

havioral Perspectives on American Vigilantism," *Perspectives in American History*, 5 (1971): 121–25.

[17] Ralph Waldo Emerson, "Self-Reliance," in *Complete Works* (London, 1873), 1: 19; James Fenimore Cooper, *The Pioneers* (New York, 1823), chs. 20–36; Alexis de Tocqueville, *Democracy in America*, ed. Phillips Bradley (New York, 1957), 2: 129–35.

affected the lives of citizens, the legal system. Foreign observers agreed that the United States in the 1830s and 1840s was characterized less by anarchy than by a strong conformity to accepted standards and a general adherence to laws with little external pressure.[18] Yet there were paradoxes here too: in the willingness of Americans to disregard law on particular occasions with no sense of striking at society itself, their frequent scorn of the legal process to which they had such frequent recourse, and their vehement dislike for lawyers, the "necessary evil" to which the populace nevertheless consistently gave political power.[19]

Richard Rush wrote in 1815 that "here law is everything," and he explained that this was so because of "an alliance between an active and restless spirit of freedom and the comfortable conditions of all classes." This contentious sense of liberty and the widespread ownership and transfer of property described by Rush have generally been seen as the main impetus to law in American society. But these essentially stand as symbols for a larger truth: that as people move from a traditional society their relations must be controlled less by inherited patterns and more by formalized law. Roscoe Pound's seeing the origin of law in "codified tradition" is clearly correct, but equally important is the fact that it need be codified only when or in those areas where tradition itself is no longer strong enough to hold sway in disputes.[20] In the United States both abundant resources and democratic traditions allowed the benefits of the new bourgeois order to be widely shared, and it also served, as did the nation's conglomerate population, to disintegrate traditional mores quickly. Tocqueville's study of the United States revealed to him essentially how democracy tended to destroy the traditional trammels, or human bonds, of aristocracy–the historical family, the permanent community, the established church, the inherited profession and social class–both to free man and to isolate him. Man in America, except for the network of voluntary associations with which he protected himself and the mass in general with which he identi-

[18] Michael Chevalier, *Society, Manners and Politics in the United States: Letters on North America* (New York, 1961), 321–29; Harriet Martineau, *Society in America* (Paris, 1837), 1: 83–93; 2: 103–16; Tocqueville, *Democracy in America*, 1: 269–78; Grund, *Americans*, 155–80.

[19] Thomas Low Nichols, *Forty Years of American Life, 1821–1861* (New York, 1937), 223–24; James Willard Hurst, *The Growth of American Law* (Boston, 1950), 3–15, 249–55, 276–85; Perry Miller, *The Life of the Mind in America from the Revolution to the Civil War* (New York, 1965), 99–116. Richard E. Ellis explores the political ramifications of antilegalism in an earlier period in *The Jeffersonian Crisis: Courts and Politics in the Young Republic* (New York, 1971). Americans' mixed feelings toward the law, although felt with a certain democratic acuteness, were of course part of man's larger ambiguous hostility to authority. The connections between this hostility and social violence are intriguingly explored in Jacob Bronowski, *The Face of Violence* (New York, 1955), and Elias Canetti, *Crowds and Power* (New York, 1963).

[20] Richard Rush, *American Jurisprudence* (Washington, 1815), 7–10; Roscoe Pound, *Introduction to the Philosophy of Law* (New York, 1945), 4–7. The relationship between "made" and "implicit" law is ably explored in Lon L. Fuller, *Anatomy of the Law* (New York, 1968), 43–119.

fied, was man alone. Because of the identification with the mass, public opinion was an effective police force ensuring general compliance with accepted standards. But in subtler and especially commercial areas of human dealing, there were neither accepted familial, communal, religious, nor traditional authorities to settle disputes. A bourgeois society, as America fairly was by 1830, must elevate law both because of what it is creating and what it has to destroy.

Americans knew they needed law and even in frontier areas tended quickly to set up legal systems and generally to respect them. The *Spirit of the Times* reported, "One of the first wants of our new settlements is a regular administration of justice, for the privilege of litigation, so far as being considered, as a witty writer has termed it, an expensive luxury, is by our free and enlightened citizens regarded as one of the prime necessaries of life."[21] Chaotic or ridiculous instances occurred in frontier law, but these were the exceptions rather than the rule and were cherished in American folklore and memory because they corroborated the illusion of freedom from oppressive technicalities.[22] The heavy dependence of Americans on law stimulated a need to remember circumventions of it because the very use of the system denied the personal independence that was the American ideal.

Covert public dislike for the legal system commonly took the form of scorn of lawyers, the intellectual elite upon whom litigious Americans depended most directly.[23] Timothy Walker's defense of the profession in his *Introduction to American Law*, long a textbook in American law schools, canvassed the common charges against lawyers. People complained of the undue complexity of the law, but Walker professionally exulted in it. "Whatever . . . may be my feelings as a man and as a citizen, as a lawyer, I am bound to rejoice in those difficulties which render our profession

[21] *Spirit of the Times*, 10 (Jan. 9, 1841): 543; James Willard Hurst, *The Law and Conditions of Freedom in the Nineteenth Century United States* (Madison, 1856), 3–32; Robert R. Dykstra, *The Cattle Towns* (New York, 1968), 112–48; Elizabeth Gaspar Brown, "The Bar on the Frontier: Wayne County, 1796–1836," *American Journal of Legal History*, 14 (1970): 136–56. Daniel Boorstin has argued that settlement in the United States featured community preceding legal system, but his evidence points to a different conclusion: Americans manufactured temporary legal structures whenever they ventured beyond the pale of the established system because they were not communities but simply groups of individuals held together by temporarily common objectives. *The Americans: The National Experience* (New York, 1965), 65–87.

[22] Anton-Hermann Chroust, *The Rise of the Legal Profession in America* (Norman, 1965), 2: 92–128. Joseph G. Baldwin, himself a Southwest lawyer between 1836 and 1854, chronicled during these years both the amusing exceptions and the stability of general rules of frontier legal development in *The Flush Times of Alabama and Mississippi*, ed. William A. Owens (New York, 1957), 34–51, 163–82.

[23] For various kinds of popular objections to lawyers, see the *Working Man's Advocate*, Dec. 19, 1829; *Niles' Register*, 37 (Nov. 7, 1829): 169; Cincinnati *Chronicle*, Aug. 5, 1837; *North American Review*, 51 (July 1840): 234; Harriet Beecher Stowe, *Dred, A Tale of the Great Dismal Swamp* (Boston, 1856), 1: 20–21; 2: 99–110; Gerard W. Gawalt, "Sources of Anti-Lawyer Sentiment in Massachusetts, 1740–1840," *American Journal of Legal History*, 14 (1970): 283–307.

so arduous, so exclusive, so indispensable." Walker added "respectable" to his list of traits resulting from legal technicality, but he might better have included "profitable." The lawyer's function, Walker continued, was "to vindicate rights and redress wrongs," but in the next sentence he added, "The guilty and the innocent, the upright and the dishonest, the wronging and the wronged, the knave and the dupe, alike consult him, and with the same unreserved confidence." That guilty, dishonest, wronging knaves could place "unreserved confidence" in lawyers might for some confirm the idea that the profession delighted in chicanery and hired "out their conscience as well as their skill, to any client who will pay the fee." Of those charges, Walker told young law students, "I, for one, am willing to admit their truth to some extent. . . . We also take refuge behind the principle that supply corresponds to demand. If there were no dishonest or knavish clients there would be no dishonest or knavish lawyers. Our profession, therefore, does but adapt itself to the community." This adaptability, the moral ambiguity and sophistry, the seemingly purposeless complexity, the expensiveness charged to lawyers were all in truth a part of the legal system they represented. The attempts of legislators to make every man his own lawyer were as telling of social desires as they were futile.[24]

Vice Unmasked, a book written in 1830 by P. W. Grayson, presents most coherently the intellectual structure of uneasiness with the law that ran through Jacksonian life. Little is known about Grayson except what he himself reveals in the book: that his criticism of lawyers is knowledgeable, he himself having been one before he repented. When the book was published, Grayson apparently had connections with the New York Workingmen's party; George Henry Evans published his book, and the *Working Man's Advocate* advertised it and reprinted a review of it from the *Daily Sentinel*, which judged *Vice Unmasked* an important study if "a little enthusiastic perhaps."[25]

Grayson was unenthusiastic about law because he considered it the greatest obstacle to the realization of the promise of American life. That promise for Grayson, as for many Americans, had been to free man's potential by lifting from him the weight of the superstitions and repressive institutions of the past. The American government was the beginning of improvement, but progress was still slight, as the injustices and inequalities and unhappiness of America amply showed. What had gone wrong? Grayson's answer was simple: the United States had ended repressive government but had left untouched a legal system that impeded man's freedom and hence tarnished his natural integrity. Grayson fervently summarized the complaints against lawyers: they were a class of men who had a vested interest in fomenting and prolonging disputes; who were es-

[24] Timothy Walker, *An Introduction to American Law, Designed as a First Book for Students* (2d ed.; Boston, 1844), 15–19.

[25] P. W. Grayson, *Vice Unmasked, An Essay: Being a Consideration of the Influence of Law on the Moral Essence of Man* (New York, 1830); *Working Man's Advocate*, Mar. 6, 1830. The paper reported that Grayson had at one time been a member of the Kentucky state legislature from Louisville.

sentially social prostitutes willing to take any position that the highest bidder for their talents desired; who eschewed any concern for pursuing truth in order to pursue their client's interest; and who exulted in the complexities of their profession because these prevented honest men from acting in their own interests. Yet Grayson's prime target was not lawyers but the system that encouraged their moral degradation. The law itself was a jumble of old formulas inherited from feudal times, rarely suited to modern instances, and always more helpful in telling the cunning man how much he could get away with than in setting positive standards of human conduct. And whatever was done to improve it only changed its façade; one passed bankruptcy laws to protect the poor debtor, but the speculative stockjobber made use of them to defraud his honest creditors. Weaving together Thomas Paine's and a transcendental vision of man's potential, Grayson centered his indictment on the effects of law on the "moral essence of man," the way it debased man's sense of self and social responsibility by turning him from his high moral potential to a tricksy tailoring of conduct to avoid legal prosecution. In short, law was generally a tool of the cleverly vicious, a snare for the simply virtuous, and a burden on everyone, crippling human decency and progress.

Practically, Americans were not about to accept Grayson's program that law should deal only with instances of gross physical attack and in all other areas let man "seek, by the light of his own conscience, in the joyous genial climate of his own free spirit, for all the rules of his conduct." But Grayson's thinking paralleled that of many other Jacksonians.[26] Indeed his major premise was perfectly correct: from a tough-minded point of view, law, as Oliver Wendell Holmes, Jr. argued later on, has much less to do with man's highest responsibilities than it does with telling bad men just how much they can get away with; in any legal system decisions must be based as much on technical requirements as on the unfettered pursuit of justice. "Law and right," wrote John Quincy Adams, "we know but too well by the experience of mankind, in all ages, including our own, are not convertible terms."[27] Such was the paradox of legal development: the desire to be free from individual power and whim impelled rational man to set up a judicial structure that inevitably impeded almost as much as it promoted perfect justice. And so mankind's favorite myths of justice once again enthroned personal wisdom: the judgment of Solomon, Louis IX under the oaks, Cervantes' Sancho Panza, and any number of wise men ensuring the triumph of right in fairy tales or melodramas.[28]

[26] Grayson, *Vice Unmasked,* 168. For other pleas for near-legal anarchism see the speech of 1837 by John M. Hunt quoted in Fitzwilliam Byrdsall, *The History of the Loco Foco or Equal Rights Party* (New York, 1842), 149–50; and the *Democratic Review,* 6 (Dec. 1839): 466–72 and 18 (Jan. 1846): 26–30.

[27] Oliver Wendell Holmes, Jr., *Collected Legal Papers* (New York, 1952), 169–74; John Quincy Adams, "On the Opium War" (1841), *Massachusetts Historical Society Proceedings,* 43 (1910): 304. Roscoe Pound describes the inevitable judicial tension between doing justice in the immediate case and establishing desirable precedents for future ones. *The Formative Era of American Law* (New York, 1938), 119–24.

[28] The plays of the early nineteenth century, fairly accurate reflectors of popular

Both popular animus to the law and its importance in the lives of citizens helped to make the Jacksonian period, in Pound's phrase, "the formative era" of American law. The militant majoritarianism of Jacksonian rhetoric also spurred the efforts of conservatives to strengthen what seemed to be the only brake on untrammeled popular will. Francis Bowen wrote, "Here, nothing stands between the individual citizen and *his* sovereign—the majority of the people—but the majesty of the law and the independence of the courts." Conservatives like Joseph Story, Lemuel Shaw, Timothy Walker, and a host of lesser figures were so successful in increasing legal learning, dignity, and responsiveness to social needs that legal antipathy was never able to become programmatic. Even the codification issue, which drew on many of Grayson's ideas in "practical" form, was neutralized by conservative judicial skill and flexibility.[29] Such efforts ensured that Jacksonian America became increasingly a government of laws not men, but democratic man was not entirely happy about it.

Within the legal structure, popular wariness about law appeared in the leniency with which juries tended to view offenders for whose crimes there were extenuating circumstances.[30] Such legal actions, if technically irregular, often provided a kind of rough equity that the law could not formally incorporate. For instance, a St. Louis jury acquitted an actress who had stabbed her faithless lover to death in the theater one night. The argument that the man had a bad heart that might have given way before the knife got there was something of a blow to technical justice, but who knows if eternal justice would have been better served by a conviction? And one sympathizes with the California judge who concluded his charge to a jury: "Well, gentlemen, that's the law, but I don't really think it's God Almighty's justice, and I guess you may just as well find for the defendant."[31] Democratic man admitted that a legal system was needed,

---

ideals, often used the motif of justice ensured by personal wisdom. The first popular melodrama in the United States, William Dunlap's translation of Louis Charles Caigniez's *The Voice of Nature* in 1803, was an updating of the Solomon and true motherhood story; and Royall Tyler, at one time chief justice of the Vermont Supreme Court, wrote plays glorifying the judicial wisdom of both Solomon and Sancho Panza. *Four Plays*, ed. Arthur W. Peach and George F. Newbrough (Princeton, 1941). The most successful American comedy of the 1840s showed a simple farmer distributing justice in the end to avoid mere legal solution for criminal acts. Anna Cora Mowatt, *Fashion; or Life in New York* (London, 1850), act 5.

[29] Francis Bowen, "The Independence of the Judiciary," *North American Review*, 57 (Oct. 1843): 420; William W. Story, *Life and Letters of Joseph Story* (Boston, 1851), 1: 448; 2: 241–51, 570–600; Leonard W. Levy, *The Law of the Commonwealth and Chief Justice Shaw: The Evolution of American Law* (New York, 1967), 303–36.

[30] Dumez, introd., iii–vi. Francis Bowen chided James Fenimore Cooper for his novelistic attack on the jury system, *The Ways of the Hour*, on the grounds that the central argument of the book was mistaken: American juries did not tend to convict unfairly but were notorious for their leniency even when evidence of guilt was substantial. "Cooper's *Ways of the Hour: The Trial by Jury*," *North American Review*, 71 (July 1850): 121–35.

[31] Noah M. Ludlow, *Dramatic Life as I Found It* (St. Louis, 1880), 550; Sol Smith, *Theatrical Management in the South and West for Thirty Years* (New York,

but he had an active responsibility to see that it did not contradict the will of God Almighty, as interpreted by himself, of course.

This refusal to accept the sanctity of the law had its most disruptive manifestations in the long series of riots in the Jacksonian period. These were very diverse in origin and goal, but patterns do emerge about the structure of rioting, its social and psychological results, the type of person who rioted, and the problems of riot control in the period. A consideration of two incidents and of an ethnic category of riot suggests something of the nature of social violence in Jacksonian America and its implications for riot theory in general. The Bank Riot in Baltimore and the Snow Riot in Washington, D.C., took place within a week of each other in early August 1835. The Baltimore riot was highly unusual in that the mob attacked their social and economic superiors; partly for this reason information on it is unusually abundant. The Washington riot is more typical both in its direction and in the sketchiness of the material available on it. Together the two constitute an introduction to Jacksonian social violence.

Both riots took place in a climate of national near-hysteria. Instances of riot and lynching around the country filled the Baltimore and Washington newspapers throughout July and August. The same day that major rioting broke out in Baltimore, its leading periodical, *Niles' Register,* began with "a great mass of curious and important matter" showing that "the state of society is awful. Brute force has superseded the law, at many places, and violence become the 'order of the day.' The time predicted seems rapidly approaching when the mob shall rule." Niles blamed both lawless mobs and "fanatics who . . . have set their presses at work to spread desolation and death through the whole south" for the trouble.[32] The most obvious precipitant of these "various excitements" was the growing effectiveness of abolition organization in the North and the sending of abolitionist literature southward. The South responded with fear and fury, claiming that these movements would create slave insurrection. The South threatened economic boycott against the North, and Northern commercial centers responded with huge public meetings condemning abolitionism and declaring that the North had no proper business even discussing slavery. Such declarations of sentiment failed to satisfy the South, which demanded "works" not "words"—specifically laws prohibiting the discussion of slavery and legal or illegal action to silence those promoting abolition. Laws curtailing freedom of speech or mobs seemed the only possible response to appease extreme Southern feeling.[33]

1868), 165, 192; George Templeton Strong, *Diary*, ed. Allan Nevins and Milton Halsey Thomas (New York, 1952), 2: 81.

[32] *Niles' Register*, 48 (Aug. 8, 1835): 397. A survey of shocked reaction to mobs from newspapers around the country appears in the *National Intelligencer,* Aug. 14, 1835.

[33] *Niles' Register* between July and November gives a vivid picture of this controversy, complete with the proceedings of the various meetings and a rich selection of editorial comment from all sections and parties. Until mid-September sentiment was almost wholly antiabolitionist, but this changed as the implications of Southern

The political situation of the nation further heated these passions. Martin Van Buren, running for the presidency as Jackson's chosen successor, was politically vulnerable in the South, while the leading opposition candidate, Jacksonian renegade Hugh Lawson White of Tennessee, had great strength there among both Jacksonians and Whigs. Since the South promised to be the central battleground for supremacy, the Whig and Democrat partisan press competed in rabid attacks upon the abolitionists. In many instances the press and leading politicians promoted proslavery mob action;[34] more commonly they condoned them with open expressions of approval or quiet toleration. No Baltimore or Washington newspaper directly encouraged these particular riots, but even nonpartisan papers edited by men deeply disturbed by riot tended to print without comment incidents of proslavery violence or to deplore them while laying major blame on "those unprincipled incendiaries," the abolitionists who were their victims.[35] Well over half of the riots in July and August of 1835 had no immediate connection with abolition, but they all sprang from a social climate with an extraordinary tolerance for riot. Circumstances allowed only a very few newspapers or public figures to take a strong stand against the best known of popular outbursts.

The Baltimore riot was an attack on those connected with the failure to settle the affairs of the Bank of Maryland, which had ceased operation

---

demands became clear and the Northern nonparty press became truculent against Southern extremism. Niles himself marks the shift. On September 19 he wrote that Southern willingness "to have *mob-law*—or accept of *regulations* that monarchs would 'turn pale' to think of" was a remedy considerably "worse than the disease" of abolitionism. 49 (Sept. 19, 1835): 33.

34 The clearest case of politically instigated riot was the antiabolitionist mob in Utica in late October 1835. Van Buren, embarrassed by the comparatively mild New York City resolutions damning abolitionists, had his friends organize an Albany meeting, which passed stronger pro-Southern resolutions than those of any other city. The administration Richmond *Enquirer* praised them as "free from all qualification and equivocation—no idle denunciations of the *evils of slavery*—no pompous assertions of the *right of discussion*," but the Richmond *Whig* pointed out that they wanted only "the recognition of the power of the legislature to suppress the fanatics, and the recommendation to do so," and without this they were meaningless. Niles reported much Southern pressure on Van Buren to add legislative proposals to the resolves, and omission of these proposals was, for Niles, conclusive proof that nothing legally would be done. *Niles' Register*, 49 (Oct. 3, 1835): 75. About three weeks later, Samuel Beardsley, a Jacksonian congressman, led a mob that drove the New York Anti-Slavery Society out of Utica and sacked a press that embarrassed the Democratic party by being both antislavery and pro–Van Buren. Administration papers immediately touted this as proof of the purity of Van Buren's Southern feelings, and hinted that Beardsley would be appointed governor of New York if Van Buren were elected and could find a place in Washington for Governer William Marcy. Marcy stayed in New York after Van Buren's victory, but quickly appointed Beardsley the state's attorney-general. Another Democratic governer appointed him to the New York Supreme Court, and he became chief justice briefly in 1845.

35 Georgetown *Metropolitan*, Aug. 12, 1835; Washington *Mirror*, Aug. 1, 1835; Baltimore *Gazette*, Aug. 3, 1835; *Niles' Register*, 49 (Oct. 31, 1835): 149.

almost a year and a half earlier. "Considerable numbers of people, 'good, bad, and indifferent' " congregated in Monument Square during the clear and pleasantly cool evenings between August 5 and 7.[36] The general topic of conversation was the action of the trustees and the "secret partners" of the bank, and the mood was one of frustration and anger at the prolonged legal obstacles to settlement. On Friday afternoon Mayor Jesse Hunt called a public meeting, which pledged itself to keep the peace and try to discover the source of the inflammatory handbills posted on walls, but which also requested that the bank's books be immediately opened for public investigation. A crowd of ten thousand gathered on Friday night, but, aside from minor rock throwing, the peace was kept. On Saturday the trustees announced that the bank's books were impounded by the Harford County Court, and the mayor organized a citizens' guard armed with two-foot long poplar sticks. That evening the guard managed to keep the mob from their main objective, the home of the leading "partner," Reverdy Johnson, but were unable to prevent the sacking of the house of another "partner." When the crowd bombarded the guard with stones and brickbats and wounded several guards seriously, some of the guard's leaders demanded the right to use guns, and the mayor reluctantly consented. At least five people were killed, and some ten or twenty were wounded by shooting. Sunday morning the mayor announced that the firing had been done "against my will and advice," and the leaders of the citizens' guard decided that prudence dictated leaving town. The mob was left unopposed. That evening and night hundreds systematically sacked and damaged the homes of the mayor and of four men connected with the bank and did minor damage to property of certain leaders of the citizens' guard, while thousands watched.[37] At about noon Monday, eighty-three-year-old Samuel Smith drove through the streets in a carriage flying an American flag to a large meeting where he effectively organized the citizens into an armed force to handle any further troubles. The destruction, which was still going on, immediately ceased, and the citizen patrols that guarded the city for well over a week met no opposition.[38]

Federal troops were dispatched to Fort McHenry near Baltimore shortly after Smith and his fellow citizens had the situation under control, but most troops were quickly withdrawn to Washington, D.C., to overawe a riot that flourished between August 12 and 14 and sputtered on for several days thereafter. This riot resulted primarily in an attack on the property of free blacks. The mob congregated on Tuesday when it be-

[36] William Bartlett to Edward Stabler, Aug. 12, 1835, printed in *Maryland Historical Magazine*, 9 (1914): 157. The weather reports are in Henry Thompson's diary, in the Maryland Historical Society, Baltimore.

[37] This account is constructed from newspaper descriptions in the Baltimore *American*, *Republican*, and *Gazette*, from accounts in other papers reprinted from the Baltimore *Chronicle* and *Patriot*, and the testimony taken by the Maryland General Assembly on the riots, published in 1836. There are no major discrepancies about the facts of the incident and no probing considerations of its structure.

[38] When James Gordon returned to Baltimore a week after the riot, he reported the "military arrangement of cannon and soldiers" looked "more warlike" than anything he had ever seen. Diary, Aug. 17, 1835. Maryland Historical Society.

came known that abolitionist literature had been found in a trunk owned by Reuben Crandall, who was staying in Georgetown and was the brother of Prudence Crandall, already well known as a victim of riot when she had attempted to teach black girls in her school in Canterbury, Connecticut.[39] Crandall was quickly arrested and arraigned in jail to prevent his falling into the hands of the mob, who then turned their attention to a restaurant, the Epicurean House, which was run by a mulatto, Beverly Snow. Before the mob arrived, Snow had wisely disappeared; after a fruitless search for antislavery writings, and some more successful drinking, the mob left. The next day they returned to "get Snow," but again he escaped. A search of the homes of other free Negroes resulted in finding some abolition newspapers in the house of James Hutton, who was hustled to jail to protect him from the mob. The crowd, after staging a public meeting the proceedings of which no newspaper reported, returned to Snow's to destroy his property, "not forgetting to crack a bottle of hock, 'now and then.' " That night, and intermittently during the next week, the crowd burned or stoned several black-owned buildings.[40]

Such is the skeletal history of the two events. A closer examination of these two riots shows much not only about their own structure but about the nature of rioting in the Jacksonian period. The central question, of course, concerns what motivates riot. Seventy-five years ago Gustave Le Bon began the sociological study of crowd behavior with a discussion that can hardly be taken seriously today but that still informs much thinking about the problem. Man acting singly, Le Bon argued, acts rationally, but acting in groups—he lumps together such things as parliamentary bodies and riotous mobs—they revert to instinctual behavior; "bestial," "primitive," "childlike," "feminine" were Le Bon's favorite adjectives for it. Le Bon's explanatory devices are largely funny; the most irrational of crowds, Latin ones, he tells us, are so because they are "the most feminine of all." Yet his ideas have remained provocative because behavior within mobs suggests disruption more than continuity in the character of the participants, and aspects of his description are still convincing, particularly his emphasis on the emotive volatility, psychological release and anonymity, and the sense of total and totally justified power that comes from being part of a riotous crowd.[41]

39 *The Trial of Reuben Crandall Charged with Publishing and Circulating Seditious and Incendiary Papers* (Washington, 1836).

40 The Washington papers all reported the riot, but were very reticent about the destruction, particularly in the month following its supposed settlement. They agreed in what they reported. Duff Green's *U.S. Telegraph*, August 13, and Francis Blair's *Globe*, August 19, expressed some regret that Crandall was not hung, but the other papers—the *National Intelligencer*, Washington *Sun*, *Mirror*, Georgetown *Metropolitan* and Alexandria *Gazette*—regretted the rioting without condemning the rioters.

41 Gustave Le Bon, *The Crowd: A Study of the Popular Mind*, ed. Robert K. Merton (New York, 1960), 35–59. A pervasive problem in the book is that Le Bon treats three groups as identical—mobs, for which his description is most valuable;

Sociologists have long raised questions about Le Bon's arguments, especially his emphasis on the irrationality of crowd behavior.[42] Historians, particularly Eric Hobsbawm and George Rudé, first directly attacked the irrationality hypothesis in regard to riotous violence and suggested that rioters tend to act not irrationally but in ways made understandable by their social situation and related integrally to their social needs and desires.[43] Certainly Rudé and Hobsbawm win the argument if rationality means simply an understandable response to a social situation that made people discontented. Such a criterion, however, excludes irrationality by definition, for no action can be wholly unrelated to man's unhappiness stemming from objective social experience; the lunatic who thinks he is Napoleon obviously does so because this illusion fulfills certain needs caused by real deprivations and traumas in his social history.[44]

Jacksonian riots do not readily fall into categories of either "irrational" or "socially purposive" behavior. The mobs in Baltimore and Washington were not particularly wanton or vicious. In both cases the action taken was sensibly directed toward the social source of riotous anger—the financial manipulations of some rich men in one case and the pretensions to social dignity of blacks in the other. The Baltimore mob was particularly fastidious. They refused to sack houses of intended victims when they were informed that they were still officially owned by the contractor or were the property of the would-be victim's mother; they put out fires in houses that they were busy demolishing so adjoining property would not be endangered; they reprimanded some people for

---

a mass society, about which his comments are inferior to Tocqueville's in complexity and suggestiveness; and decision-making bodies such as juries and parliaments, for which his analysis is at best quaint.

[42] A good survey of the sociological theories of crowd behavior is Stanley Milgram and Hans Toch, "Collective Behavior: Crowds and Social Movements," in Gardner Lindzey and Elliot Aronson, eds., *Handbook of Social Psychology* (2d ed.; New York, 1968), 4: 542–84.

[43] Eric J. Hobsbawm, "The Machine Breakers," *Past and Present*, no. 1 (1952): 57–70; Hobsbawm, *Primitive Rebels: Studies in Archaic Forms of Social Movements in the Nineteenth and Twentieth Centuries* (Manchester, 1959); George Rudé, *The Crowd in the French Revolution* (Oxford, 1959); Rudé, *The Crowd in History: A Study of Popular Disturbances in France and England, 1730–1848* (New York, 1964); Hobsbawm and Rudé, *Captain Swing* (New York, 1968). Rudé in his two books both defends his crowds' general social purposiveness and also argues that the crowds that followed—those after the French Revolution in the first book (pp. 209, 238–39) and in the "industrial" age that had fully arrived by 1848 in the second (pp. 218–34, 266–68)—were purged of certain backward qualities through the development of "a stable social-ideological content" (p. 234). The opposite may be the case: as popular movements developed ideological content and as Western governments opened channels of influence to a broader segment of their population, significant social protest took less violent and destructive forms, and riotous mobs became commonly more backward looking or self-indulgent.

[44] R. D. Laing, in his *Politics of Experience* (New York, 1967), suggests that insanity is often reasonable response to social inconsistencies in an existential reworking of the Romantic preference for madness to bourgeois normality.

stealing rather than destroying property; and they voted by a slim majority not to burn a lumber yard because it threatened an adjacent one. (The minority had argued that it could be safely burned if the fire trucks were called out to keep the flames in bounds.) Their chief victims were rationally chosen: four men—Reverdy Johnson, John Glenn, Evan T. Ellicott, and Hugh McElderry—who had been "secret partners" in the Bank of Maryland and who had avoided settlement of the bank's affairs through legal prosecution of its former president and his relatives; John B. Morris, one of the trustees of the bank since its failure, who had steadily supported the nonsettlement policy; and Mayor Hunt, who was blamed for the firing into the crowd on Saturday. None was guilty of indictable offenses, and Hunt and Morris had not obviously profited from the situation, although the latter had lent himself to the delay and to the publication of a very inaccurate report of the bank's situation under the influence of his legal counsel, Reverdy Johnson. This unconscionable postponement worked a great hardship on the unusual number of people of modest means—"widows and orphans, small dealers and thrifty persons, mechanics and others"—who were the bank's creditors, while its debtors, including the partners, profiteered shamelessly.[45] Given the complexity of the affairs of the Bank of Maryland, and judging by the mob's choice of victims, the Baltimore mob was not only rational but financially astute.[46] Less is known about the specific mob actions in Washington, but there is evidence of similar restraint and selectivity. When told that the building and many of the furnishings of Snow's restaurant were actually owned by others, the mob confined itself to destroying the sign and a few things of minor value. And the property they attacked—black businesses, schools, churches, and homes—were those things most contributive to the free Negroes' sense of status and dignity, however tenuous, in the community.[47]

Yet are selectivity and aspects of moderation incompatible with the

[45] *Niles' Register*, 46 (Mar. 29, 1834): 65. The bank had attracted small investors by offering interest on short term deposits. A letter of a retired sea captain, Thomas Williams, gives a vivid sense of the suffering the bank's prolonged trusteeship caused its unfortunate creditors. Baltimore *Republican*, Mar. 19, 1836.

[46] The conflicting accounts of the affairs of the Bank of Maryland were presented in two pamphlets by its former president, Evan Poultney, and in two replies by Reverdy Johnson and John Glenn, the second reply appearing a few days prior to the riot. Poultney argued that he and five other men had secretly controlled the bank, that there were sufficient funds to meet, or almost meet, all debts, and that the legal cases against him and his brothers were all ruses. Poultney's story was borne out by the bank's books, the results of the criminal cases, and the final settlement of the trust over four years after the bank's failure, when the full amount of debts was paid plus a ten cent dividend per dollar. This almost all went to speculators who had bought the credits at about a quarter of their value. The best accounts of these financial manipulations are a long letter from George Gibbs to the Union Bank of Tennessee, July 1834, in the Jonathan Meredith Papers, Library of Congress, and Thomas Ellicott's self-serving but generally accurate, *The Bank of Maryland Conspiracy* (Philadelphia, 1839).

[47] The Washington papers talked most of the burning of a house of prostitution to suggest the riot had a moral tone; presumably it was owned or run by blacks.

idea that a riotous crowd unleashes elements of emotion that in important ways distort reality and allow individuals to act in a manner at variance with their usual behavior? The ablest defender of the Baltimore mob stressed its restraint and the justice of its social position: "fraud produced violence," and the people "operated upon the republican maxim 'resistance to tyrants is obedience to God.' " But he also stressed the emotive quality of the crowd situation. When the mob in Monument Square became active "every countenance was flushed with the spirit of destruction —reason had thrown down the reins and ungovernable fury had taken them up," and the retreat of the city guard led to Sunday's "anarchical desolation and mournful paralysis of reason."[48] The handbills, which were sent through the mails and posted on the walls of Baltimore during the week preceding the riot, reveal this tying of highly irrational emotionalism to very real grievances:

> Arm! Arm! . . .—my Countrymen—Citizens of this Republic, and of this City, will you suffer your firesides to be molested—will you suffer your beds to be poluted—will you suffer your pockets to be riffled and your wives and children beggared. . . . Then arouse, and rally around the free and unbiass'd judge Lynch who will be placed upon the seat of justice and the people enmasse will be the members of the Bar, and these lions of the law shall be made to know that the people will rise in their majesty and redress their own grievances. . . . Have not the whole Bar and the judges linked in a combination together, and brow-beaten these very people out of their just rights, with a full determination to swindle and rob the industrious and poor part of the community out of their hard earnings. . . . Designing lawyers and lazy greedy peculators . . . , these smiling villains nearly all of them are building palaces and riding in their carriages with the very money taken from the poor laborer, orphans and honest hard working mechanics. . . . Want staring your poor heart broken wives in the face—your little children clinging around their mother, crying mother, mother a piece of bread—I say mother bread—O! mother give me some bread,—while these protected villains are roling in luxury and ease, laughing to scorn the people they have just robbed. These very villains stroll the streets with a bold and impudent assurance and pass for honest men—not satisfied with robbing you of your money, but treat you as Vassals to their noble lordships—to gratify their Venery desires hire pimps and procuresses to go polute your wives and prostitute your daughters—Gracious God! —is this our fair famed Baltimore—is our moral city come to this. . . . We have a remedy, my fellow citizens—Judge Lynch will be notified that he is at our head, and will take his place upon the bench—his maxims are Virtue, honesty, and good decent behavior —his remedies are simple, Tar and Feathers, effigys, gallowses and extermination from our much injured city—the victims that fall

[48] "Junius" to the Baltimore *Republican* Jan. 4, Feb. 26, Mar. 5, 31, 1836.

> under this new law, I hope will be Johnson, Morris, Glenn, McElderry, Freeman and that dirty fellow Bossier etc., etc., etc.—
>
> Let the warhoop be given . . . Liberty, Equality, Justice or Death!!![49]

Here a generalized social fury melted justified anger and real economic hardship into an amalgam of major democratic grievances and fears: resentment at the deviousness and elitism of the law; a hatred of the powerful, the pretentious, the learned, the rich; uncertainties about economic status and the moral stability of the family. All these fears could be welded together and expressed because they resulted not from any intrinsic flaws in society but from the machinations of specific villains–in this case five men and three etceteras. When Judge Lynch had those people "exterminated from the city," supposedly Baltimore and the United States could return to their "fair fame" and purity.

The talk in the circular of "Venery desires" shows how the anger of the mob also united wholly separate incidents. The inclusion of "Bossier" in the list of intended victims makes clear that the author joined a recent Baltimore scandal with the long-brewing Bank of Maryland controversy. Over a week before the riot, Joseph Bossière was assaulted by an irate guardian who found his ward in Bossière's house. Rumor had it that Bossière had seduced her and that the directress of the exclusive school where the girl boarded had acted as procuress. The moralistic anger over this incident, totally unconnected with the bank controversy, nonetheless merged with it in the minds of the rioters. The mob attacked the house where Bossière was staying, and to save it he gave himself up to the crowd; what was done to him was not reported.[50]

In the Washington riot a similar event that had occurred about a week prior to the disturbance influenced the emotion of the mob. The slave of a prominent Washington widow entered her bedroom at night with an ax and drunkenly threatened to kill her. Newspapers soon had him spouting "abolitionist jargon" as he made the attack, and the conservative *National Intelligencer* labeled the story "The First Fruits."

[49] Handbill, in vertical file, Maryland Historical Society. Other handbills are in the David M. Perine Papers, Maryland Historical Society, and one is copied in William Bartlett's letter in the *Maryland Historical Magazine*, 9 (1914): 161–62. The "Freeman" mentioned in the circular was W. H. Freeman, another Baltimore banker, to whom the Union Bank of Tennessee sold its credits of some $275,000 on the Bank of Maryland for $60,000. Freeman owed the bank $50,000, so for an additional $10,000 he bought over $200,000 worth of credits. The mob leaders must have learned of the transaction even before the Baltimore *Gazette* announced on August 8 that the claims of the Union Bank of Tennessee had been "satisfactorily adjusted." John Bass to Jonathan Meredith, July 30, 1835; A. Van Wyck to Jonathan Meredith, Nov. 6, 1835, Meredith Papers; "One of the Mob" to Brantz Mayer, Aug. 12, 1835, Brantz Mayer Papers, Maryland Historical Society.

[50] Bossière's statement about his treatment during the riot appeared in the Baltimore *Gazette*, Aug. 21, 1835, and in the Baltimore *American*, Sept. 16, 1835. Reports of extreme excitement over the alleged seduction appeared in the Baltimore *Republican*, July 24, 1835, and in the Georgetown *Metropolitan*, Aug. 1, 1835.

While the widow, convinced that the slave had simply been drunk, hid him in her home and tried to sell him to safety, the press flaunted the incident as proof of coming terrors if abolitionists were not muzzled.[51] Hence Crandall's supposed activities could be seen as part of a plot threatening widows with violent death, and the attack on Negroes could then go forth in the guise of saving society from servile war. The purity of the family motif was also strangely tied to the attack on Snow. When no abolitionist literature was found in his restaurant, the official charge against him became that he had insulted the honor of mechanics' wives and daughters.[52]

In addition to a triggering generalized moral fury, another emotional set characterized Jacksonian riots. Once action began, anger was replaced by joy and release if the mob was not seriously opposed. The few reports of the Washington mob suggest great good humor, almost Bacchanalia, as the crowd destroyed, partly by drinking, the contents of Snow's Epicurean House. The reports of the Baltimore riot trials give a vivid sense of their saturnalian quality. Several rioters were convicted largely because they had lustily bragged about their riot exploits. James Spencer, furious against Mayor Hunt because Spencer had had his "knuckles shot off" on Saturday, amused the crowd as he broke Hunt's dinnerware on the street: "Gentlemen, who wants to go to a tea party, but stop I'll go and get the plates." Particular care and delight was taken in burning Reverdy Johnson's law library. The mob emptied Johnson's and Glenn's wine cellars and referred to the wine they abundantly drank as "American blood," perhaps suggesting that it was squeezed from their townsmen's labors as well as evoking old rituals of saturnalia, in which the continuance of patterns of authority was made acceptable by their brief ritual cessation. One rioter on Monday, before order was restored, went around saying "damned if he wasn't Mayor of the city" and appointing various friends to official positions. Such precise parallels to saturnalia's mock king were doubtless rare, but the mood often suggested the joy that comes from the destruction of official authority and its brief bestowal on self. Fifes and drums played and crowds of thousands watched the destruction, laughing and cheering on the rioters.[53] The moral or social issues that gave mobs life always circumscribed their action, but such restraints coexisted with a high degree of emotive fury and joy in power

[51] Mrs. William Thornton, diary, Aug. 5–8, 1835, Library of Congress; *National Intelligencer*, Aug. 8, 1835. The slave was sentenced to death, but Mrs. Thornton's ceaseless lobbying for him among her influential friends gained him a pardon from Jackson. See her diary, July 6–7, 1836.

[52] Snow begged for a hearing from a jail in Fredericksburg where he had gone for protective custody; the *National Intelligencer* published it, but apologized abjectly when a "respectable citizen" wrote a diatribe against the paper's so honoring one of Snow's "insolent class." "Let all blacks become subordinates and laborers," concluded the citizen, or leave Washington. Aug. 27, 28, 1835.

[53] Hester Wilkins to her sister Mrs. John Glenn, Aug. 11, 1835, John Glenn Papers, Maryland Historical Society. The quotations are all taken from the riot trials in the Baltimore City Court, published in the Baltimore *Gazette* between late November 1835 and the end of January 1836.

that transfigured social reality. Total self-righteousness, well or ill founded, joined with the unity and anonymity of the crowd to allow a saturnalia where social man's usual restraints could be shucked.

A bank clerk, witnessing a riot in 1843, was surprised that so little was done to protect the black victims:

> But the mob of Cincinnati must have their annual festival—their Carnival, just as at stated periods, the ancient Romans enjoyed the Saturnalia, and our city dignitaries must run no risk of forfeiting their "sweet voices" at the next charter election by any unceremonious interference with their "gentle violence"—their practical demonstrations of sovereignty.[54]

The cross-examination of a Baltimore defense witness is telling. Asked if he had been in Morris's house, the reporter recorded the witness as saying, "Not sure–thinks he went in–don't know if he went upstairs, if he did he might have been insane–drank two or three glasses from a decanter –was 'pretty warm.'" Had he been at Hunt's? "Might have been in the house, didn't know–thinks he was sober–was a 'little warm,' might have been insane–a great many passions make a man insane beside liquor–excited to see so much property destroyed."[55]

Most Jacksonian rioters were neither the "dregs of society," as Reverdy Johnson called the Baltimore mob, nor so much of a social elite as Richard M. Brown and Leonard Richards have found composing vigilante or antiabolition mobs.[56] Of the twelve people convicted of riot in

[54] James W. Taylor, *"A Choice Nook of Memory": The Diary of a Cincinnati Law Clerk, 1840–42*, ed. James Taylor Dunn (Columbus, 1950), 40. Ralph W. Conant suggests the idea of riot as saturnalia, but treats it as a largely benign phenomenon. "Rioting, Insurrection and Civil Disobedience," *American Scholar*, 37 (1968): 425–26. Jacob Bronowski's stress on the vicious possibilities of saturnalia makes the comparison truer. *Face of Violence*, 18–19.

[55] Testimony of Mr. Blakely, a carpenter, in the third mob case, Baltimore *Gazette*, Dec. 12, 1835.

[56] Reverdy Johnson, *Memorial to the Legislature of Maryland* (Annapolis, 1836), 8; Brown, "American Vigilante Tradition," 167–71; Richards, *Gentlemen of Property and Standing*, 131–55. The mobs Brown and Richards ably discuss were more "respectable" than most, but perhaps not generally so "upper class" as they suggest. Richards, for example, bases his key samples on the names of people who attended meetings that resolved basically that violence would occur if abolitionist editor James Birney stayed in Cincinnati or if the New York Slavery Society tried to meet in Utica. Such resolutions could be supported by a wide spectrum of citizens, from those who favored a mob to those who wished to avoid trouble, to those genuinely concerned for the safety of those threatened. That their action as it turned out supported the mob is clear, but that they intended it to do so is dubious. Participants in such meetings did not necessarily countenance riot, much less participate in it. In Cincinnati many citizens must have had in mind Birney's experience in Danville, Kentucky, where a similar public meeting had caused him to leave peaceably.

Baltimore, eight can be identified as to profession: three carpenters, two pavers, one blacksmith, one hatter, and one laborer. Of the ten people acquitted, four clearly did some rioting; two of these were carpenters, one a merchant, and one probably a farmer. Testimony revealed the names of nine other rioters, only two of whom were professionally identified, both as carpenters. Thus half of the fourteen rioters identified by job were carpenters and eleven (or 78.6 per cent) were "mechanics," that is workingmen with a particular skill.[57] No ages were given, but in about one-third of the cases the rioter's youth was mentioned. The evidence is sketchy but corresponds with the usually even less certain data on other riots. Rioters were predominantly lower-middle-class people with a skill or some property and some position in the community; the majority also tended to be young, in their late teens or twenties, and to have ties with the Jacksonian equivalent of the modern urban gang, the fire companies.

In Washington twenty-some persons were arrested, but the press mentioned only two names: John Laub, a ship carpenter from the Navy Yard, and a "Mr. Sweeting, of Philadelphia," possibly of the same vocation. The diary of Andrew Shiner, a black worker at the Navy Yard, offers the most helpful clues about who participated. A large group of out-of-town workers had been hired to refurbish the frigate *Columbia.* Late in July one mechanic was caught stealing copper, and the commander of the Navy Yard, Commodore Isaac Hull, ordered that workers be barred from eating in the storeroom. Considering this order an assault on their honor, the workers went on strike and ten days later eased their offended dignity and relieved their enforced leisure by terrorizing blacks. At some points the mechanics considered attacking the Navy Yard, but prudence and the fortifications kept the riot racial.[58] The strike explains how mechanics could spend Tuesday afternoon and all day Wednesday working at riot. The clearest evidence that the rioters were of this class grew from a meeting of "very respectable" mechanics called specifically to disavow such ties. The formal resolutions expressed resentment that mechanics should be thought involved with the riot and asked for the removal of federal troops from the streets, but several volunteer amendments, all adopted, revealed more than the meeting's sponsors wished. "Riotous" was changed to "excited," a resolution calling the presence of troops "an insult to freemen" was added, and finally the commander of the troops was damned "for stigmatizing those citizens of Washington who assembled . . . to inflict summary punishment on B. Snow as 'a set of ragamuffins.' " Little wonder that the Jacksonian journal, the *Globe,*

[57] Job identifications were made from the trial records and *Matchett's Baltimore Directory* (Baltimore, 1835–36). The possibilities of mistake are, of course, rife; the only Peter Harman listed for Baltimore in 1835 was a Lutheran or German Reformed minister, while the riotous Peter Harman was best known as a fireboy among whose favorite phrases were "damned" and "son of a bitch." The evidence against the only convicted laborer was very dubious as to his rioting, although he certainly took home a part of one of John Glenn's carpets.

[58] Andrew Shiner, diary, 1813–65, ff. 58–61, Library of Congress; Isaac Hull, *Papers of Isaac Hull, Commodore United States Navy,* ed. Gardner Weld Allen (Boston, 1929), 68–77.

an active sponsor of the meeting, had reservations about "the mode adopted to repel" those "unfounded" charges that mechanics had countenanced the riot.[59]

The question of leadership of Jacksonian riots is even harder to answer. In the Snow Riot no evidence remains of leadership, although John Laub was labeled a "ring leader." Those arrested in Baltimore were also called ringleaders, but their trials made clear that only two of them might have been influential even in a secondary way. Yet certainly someone wrote the hundreds of handbills inciting to riot, and witnesses testified that the mob had clear leadership from time to time. The identity of "Red Jacket," "Black Hawk," and "the Man in the Speckled Hat"—names given to alleged leaders—is unknown; perhaps people thought they were leaders only because of their notable costumes.[60] The riot testimony suggests that Leon Dyer was active in the crowd; he was not tried because of testimony that he helped prevent destruction at McElderry's. His doing this is not incompatible with being a leader; Benjamin Lynch, one of the convicted, reportedly said during the riot, "Gentlemen, we have gone far enough, if we go further we shall lose the sympathies of the people." Dyer, at any rate, was reported to have said, "I have got the party and can send them where I please," and to have bought drinks for the mob who worked destruction on the McElderry and Ellicott homes. A citizen of Baltimore much later identified "Red Jacket" as "Samuel M. . . , a cooper in Franklin street." This was Samuel Mass, a Jacksonian politician who had been president of the Maryland Executive Council the year before. Mass was arrested for leading a meeting, two days after the riot, of Tenth Ward Citizens who deplored the violence but also warned Reverdy Johnson that he would be deservedly driven out of Baltimore should he have the impudence to return.[61] Dyer and Mass were leaders of the plebian wing of the Jacksonians; when Roger B. Taney went to Annapolis to urge an indemnity for the victims of the riot, Baltimore's Democratic representatives pointedly avoided calling on him, causing Taney to lament that they, like Baltimore's Jacksonian editor, should countenance the

[59] *Globe*, Aug. 19, 1835.

[60] Witnesses identified Samuel Reed as a leader because he "acted like a madman" and Peter Harman as one because he wore a brass plate on his hat and a curtain ring around his neck. Baltimore *Gazette*, Dec. 28, 31, 1835.

[61] Dyer's name was that most frequently brought up in the trials; the testimony suggests he both directed the mob and modified its destructiveness at points. Dyer was born in Germany in 1807 and came with his parents to Baltimore in 1812. His father was the first president of Baltimore's Hebrew Congregation and one of the first beef packers in the United States. First identified in the *Baltimore Directory* of 1842 as a butcher, Leon Dyer was, because of his popularity, appointed acting mayor in the wake of Baltimore's Bread Riot of 1837. See Isidore Blum, *The Jews of Baltimore: An Historical Summary of Their Progress and Status from the Early Days to the Year 1910* (Baltimore, 1910), 9–10. Archibald Hawkins identified Mass as "Red Jacket" in perhaps the best of the historical accounts of the riot. He is the only historian to mention the Bossière affair, and his correctness about this encourages confidence that his identification of Mass may be right. *The Life and Times of the Honorable Elijah Stansbury* (Baltimore, 1874), 90–118.

political leadership of Leon Dyer and his sort.[62] The riot occurred because people were generally convinced of the exploitation by the bank's "partners" of the bank's creditors, but possibly the leaders and the most active rioters were lower-middle-class Jacksonians who found in the incident the perfect illustration of Jacksonian rhetoric about the people versus the monied interests, which they took considerably more to heart than did party leaders. When Henry Brown heard in the country that the people were rising up against the "monied aristocrats," he rushed to town, getting there in time to help sack at least John B. Morris's house. When an acquaintance chided Brown because Morris was "the poor man's friend," Brown said had he known that, he would not have hurt Morris's home, but went on railing against the "damned aristocrats."[63]

This political situation would explain how Moses Davis, a town drunk, presumably, from the joking newspaper references to him as a "very *spirited* man," got one-fourth of the vote for mayor, to replace Hunt, who resigned. Davis' opponent was the law-and-order candidate, Samuel Smith, who was endorsed by the town's entire power structure from both parties. It would also explain why the vote declined one-third from the previous election despite strenuous attempts to get out the electorate for Smith to salvage "Baltimore's fair reputation." Benjamin C. Howard, one of the city's Democratic congressmen standing for reelection, ostentatiously avoided voting for Smith, despite his friendship for and earlier support of the riot victims. And the political situation would explain the unusual degree of emotive sincerity one senses in this riot's inflammatory handbills.[64]

It is difficult to see much social purposiveness in Jacksonian riots. In Baltimore the riot resulted largely in reaction. The next legislature passed a law making local communities financially responsible for riot damage and an indemnity bill paying the victims of riot fully for their losses out of Baltimore's harbor funds. As the attorneys and leaders of the creditors—who desperately tried to prevent the riot—feared, the incident aided the exploiters by transforming the question of choosing between Johnson and Co. and the creditors to that of supporting Johnson and Co. or the mob. The victimization largely ensured the restored social position of Johnson, Glenn, E. T. Ellicott, and McElderry. None were elected to popular office, but all remained prominent and respected. Reverdy Johnson steered his election to the United States Senate as adroitly through the state legisla-

[62] Roger B. Taney to James Mason Campbell, Mar. 6, 1836, Benjamin C. Howard Papers, Maryland Historical Society. Taney, who had promised to protect the partners' reputation in return for their earlier support, swung enough Democratic votes to the Indemnity Bill to ensure its passage, partly by getting a statement of support for it from Jackson himself. Taney to David M. Perine, May 28, June 2, June 20, July 10, 1834, Perine Papers; Samuel Tyler, *Memoir of Roger B. Taney* (Baltimore, 1872), 244–45.

[63] Baltimore *Gazette*, Dec. 14, 1835. The case illustrated the willingness of American juries to neglect legalism. The jury, after several hours deliberation, requested to ask the leading witness one question: was Brown "*very* drunk?" The judge said that should have nothing to do with their decision, but added that if they had reasonable doubt of his guilt they should acquit him, which they immediately did.

[64] Baltimore *Gazette*, Sept. 9, 1835; Baltimore *Republican*, Sept. 9, 1835; Roger B. Taney to James Mason Campbell, Sept. 25, 1835, Howard Papers.

ture as he had his Indemnity Bill and became attorney-general of the United States under Zachary Taylor.[65] But even had the riot succeeded in ruining or driving out its victims, it would in no way have promoted the relief of those people who lost heavily through the long-continuing trusteeship. The Washington rioters were more successful. Beverly Snow never returned to his nation's capital, no one even considered indemnifying blacks for their losses, and the city council made gestures toward meeting the rioters' demands for more stringent restrictions on free Negroes. The moral is one that runs through Jacksonian riots. Mobs often succeeded in their immediate goals but were in the long run counterproductive when directed against groups or institutions that had some social power. Mormons, Catholics, and abolitionists were all injured by riots, but more fundamentally drew much of their strength from these persecutions. Riots generally succeeded only when directed against the socially defenseless, particularly blacks.[66]

The American Irish riots illustrate the problem in interpreting Jacksonian mobs as socially purposive. Certainly the Irish had much to be unhappy about, both before and after their coming to the United States. There was some prejudice against them, they had comparatively low-paying jobs, their housing was bad, and they had to send their children to schools tinged with Protestantism. And so Irish rioting could be seen as the just social response of an oppressed group. But as one looks more closely, these riots seem less against the injustices of the system than over traditional religious and clan rivalries and against groups less socially influential than they. Many of the so-called Irish labor riots on the canals, railroads, and aqueducts generally turn out to have been imported clan battles between groups of Irish Catholics from different areas of the old country.[67] In an instance where they attacked management, records suggest that they were angrier about the foreman's Presbyterianism than his economic exploitation.[68] It is significant that the Irish participated in riots much more often in New York and Philadelphia where they were quickly welcomed into the political system than they did in Boston where they

[65] Bernard C. Steiner, *The Life of Reverdy Johnson* (Baltimore, 1914). The creditors' attorneys urged the avoidance of violence so that their legal case would not be endangered, and one of them, William P. Preston, wrote a personal note to Mayor Hunt on August 9, 1835, urging strong action to prevent riot. William P. Preston Papers, Maryland Historical Society.

[66] There are two exceptions: the antirent riots of upstate New York encouraged a political solution to an outdated system of land tenure, and the mobs in some areas of the North did rescue a few blacks and help create sympathy for the slave's plight, especially after the Fugitive Slave Law of 1850.

[67] Especially the Chesapeake and Ohio Canal riots of June 1834 and August 1839; the riot on the Baltimore and Washington Railroad, June 1834; the riots on the Croton Water Works in New York, 1840–41; and the riot on the Erie Railroad near Port Jervis, New York, 1849. Sir George C. Lewis described tellingly how patterns of Irish rioting developed in response to English injustice, but came to be directed, largely per force, against the safer target of other groups of Irish. *On Local Disturbances in Ireland; and on the Irish Church Question* (London, 1836).

[68] The Washington and Baltimore Railroad Riot in November 1834; see *Niles' Register*, 47 (Dec. 20, 1834): 272.

were given no political jobs prior to the Civil War. The Philadelphia riot case is illuminating. Philadelphia's first important postrevolutionary riot occurred in 1825 when a serious brawl broke out between Irish Catholics and Protestants just after they disembarked from the ship that brought them from Ireland; six years later a group of Irish Catholics attacked a parade of Orangemen celebrating the Battle of the Boyne, and a general brawl ensued.[69] In 1829 the first of a series of eight Philadelphia riots against blacks and abolitionists occurred in which Irish names bulk large among those arrested, though they were obviously abetted by many home-grown rioters, especially in the antiabolition affrays. And the various antebellum railroad, weaver, nativist, fireboy, and antiprostitution riots seem to have had roots in the same ethnic animosities.[70]

Had the oppressed Irish risen over their social hardships against the power structure, Rudé's conclusions about the crowd in history might apply to Jacksonian America, where, instead, riots featured Irish Catholics fighting Irish Protestants, Corkonions attacking Fardowners, and Irishmen harrassing blacks and their supporters. Indeed favorite targets in some antiblack riots were Negro orphan asylums, homes for perhaps the most hapless of American citizens.[71] The sad truth about the Jacksonian riots was that, though the performers had real grievances and fears, action was generally taken only when there was large promise of safety: by groups in situations and places where they had fairly broad political and social influence and against individuals and groups less popular than they.[72]

69 David Paul Brown, *Speech Before the Mayor's Court of Philadelphia, September 17, 1825, on the Subject of Riot and Assault and Battery* (Philadelphia, 1858); *A Full and Accurate Report of the Trial for Riot Before the Mayor's Court of Philadelphia on the 13th of October, 1831, Arising out of a Prostestant Procession on the 12th of July in Which the Contending Parties Were Protestants and Roman Catholics* (Philadelphia, 1831).

70 The many nativist riots, commonly seen as part of a "Protestant crusade" against Catholicism, had roots in much more complicated ethnic, religious, and social animosities in urban Jacksonian America. An able exploration of these many strands is William Baughin, "Nativism in Cincinnati Before 1860" (master's thesis, University of Cincinnati, 1950).

71 The Philadelphia Abolitonist Riot, May 1838; the New York Draft Riot, July 1863. The orphanage attacks allowed release of social anger not only against that group the rioters were determined to keep as social inferiors, but also against their philanthropic social "betters," who endowed the institutions and whom it would have been dangerous to attack directly.

72 Jacksonian riots could be fitted to the schemas social scientists have worked out for explaining civil disturbances, but this owes perhaps more to the flexibility of various models than their explanatory usefulness. "Social disequilibrium," the "expectation gap," the "J-curve of rising and declining satisfactions," and "relative deprivation" are sufficiently vague to be discoverable wherever sought. Chalmers Johnson, *Revolutionary Change* (Boston, 1966), 59–87, 119–34; Ivo K. Feierabend, Rosalind L. Feierabend, and Betty A. Nesvold, "Social Change and Political Violence: Cross National Patterns," and James C. Davies, "The J-Curve of Rising and Declining Satisfactions as a Cause of Some Great Revolutions and a Contained Rebellion," both in Graham and Gurr, *History of Violence*, 632–730; Gurr, *Why Men Rebel*, 3–91, 317–59. Jacksonian riots clustered in periods of general prosperity, the mid-1830s, 1840s, and 1850s.

Jeremiah Hughes's analysis of both the source and social effects of Jacksonian rioting was well taken:

> A radical error in democratic ethics begins to develope itself. The people have been told so often that all power, government, and authority of right belong to them and that they in fact are the only sovereigns here, that it is not to be wondered at that they occasionally mistake the true limit of that sovereignty, and undertake to exercise despotic powers. Who dare control the *People, a Free People?* Don't they make the government itself, and can't they rule it as they please? Such to a great extent is the political education of the day. . . . Governments are instituted mainly for the protection of the weak from the power of the strong. But for this they would not be endured. The majority are always powerful—they require no protection. To restrain an undue exercise of power against the weak is one great motive for which government is instituted.[73]

Hughes's concern about the weak, about minorities, is very much to the point. Victims, more than rioters, were the oppressed, the unpopular, the unprotected.

The psychological effects of rioting are even harder to gauge than its social results. Mobs when unopposed clearly enjoyed themselves; two Baltimore rioters said that they got their $100 and $500 worth of enjoyment–presumably sums lost to the bank–out of their night's work. The amorphousness of bourgeois-democratic society and the constant Jacksonian stress on power belonging to the people made attractive the sense of group identity and invincibility that came from being part of what John Quincy Adams called "the mobility." A song recorded by a Campbellite minister and temperance lecturer who led the Hancock County anti-Mormon mob in Illinois caught some of the "togetherness" of the riotous crowd: "Hancock is a beautiful place/The Antis all are brothers./And when one has a pumpkin pie/He shares it with the others."[74] Democracy's mythic heroes stand outside of society; most of the people who idolize them are enmeshed in it and, if Tocqueville and others are right, have strong desires to merge entirely with the mass.[75] The psychological appeal of riot in democratic society is that the situation gives a sense of acting by a higher code, of pursuing justice and possessing power free from any structural restraint, and at the same time allowing a complete absorption in the mass so that the individual will and the social will appear to be one. To riot is to be Natty Bumppo in crowd, to be Randolph Scott en masse–and this is a kind of apotheosis for democratic man, fulfilling the official doctrine that power belongs to him and allowing

[73] *Niles' Register*, 66 (July 27, 1844): 344–45.

[74] John Quincy Adams, *Memoirs* (Philadelphia, 1876), 9: 252; Thomas Brockman to Andrew Johnston, Jan. 1, 1847, in the Mormon Collection, Chicago Historical Society.

[75] Tocqueville, *Democracy in America*, 2: 109–13, 334–39; Erich Fromm, *Escape from Freedom* (New York, 1965), 17–38, 157–230; Hannah Arendt, *The Origins of Totalitarianism* (New York, 1958), 305–39.

him to escape the real system that attempts to share influence by making everyone powerless.[76] The most famous rioter of the Jacksonian period was also the prime developer of the popular Western story.[77] The permanent value of such mental satisfactions is less certain. Psychologically as well as socially, perhaps, people who associated themselves with groups victimized gained most from riot, if their groups were not permanently oppressed by it.[78]

The problem of riot control in the Jacksonian period centered in a democratic sense of the limitations on the state's right to use strong physical force against the people. Five people died in Baltimore because the guard did get reluctant permission to fire, although many citizens felt that all trouble would have vanished if the guard had been properly armed in the first place and that fact had been made known. Total peace returned when Smith organized his heavily armed patrols, but by this time the use of force was supplemented by a revulsion of feeling against the mob, particularly when it was learned that a large list of additional victims had been designated.[79] On the first day after the Washington riot began, the militia was seemingly instructed to try to awe the mob but not to interfere very actively if assaults were confined to black property. When Jackson returned to the city his strategy became one of conciliating the rioters while keeping enough troops around to prevent serious damage. Andrew Shiner was obviously repeating gossip but described Jackson's method accurately.

[76] Hannah Arendt's distinction between power based on concerted popular acquiescence and violence based on instrumental force is pertinent here, although perhaps a more telling contrast is between power, the essence of which Bertrand de Jouvenal defines as the ability "to command and to be obeyed," and influence, which is the abilty to dictate action only through an ongoing process of convincing or manipulating others to agree with a particular policy. Arendt, *On Violence* (New York, 1970), 35–56; Jouvenal, *On Power: The Nature and History of Its Growth* (Boston, 1948), 96. Louis Hartz suggests the vacuousness of the Jacksonian stress on "the will of the people" because the idea promised a direct power that inevitably created distaste for the realities of the political system meant to embody it. *Economic Policy and Democratic Thought: Pennsylvania 1776–1860* (Cambridge, Mass., 1948), 23–33, 309–20.

[77] E. Z. C. Judson was convicted of instigating the Astor Place Riot of 1849 in New York and was indicted for his part in a St. Louis election riot of 1852. As "Ned Buntline," he also was the leading developer of the dime novel. Jay Monaghan, *The Great Rascal: The Life and Times of Ned Buntline* (New York, 1952).

[78] Helpful studies of the psychological sources and effects of violence are Hans Toch, *Violent Men: An Inquiry into the Psychology of Violence* (Chicago, 1969); Silvan S. Tomkins, "The Psychology of Commitment: The Constructive Role of Violence and Suffering for the Individual and for His Society," in Martin B. Duberman, ed., *The Anti-Slavery Vanguard: New Essays on the Abolitionist* (Princeton, 1965), 270–98.

[79] Joint Committee of the Maryland General Assembly on the Baltimore Riots, *The Report of and Testimony Taken Before the Joint Committee of the Senate and House of Delegates of Maryland* (Annapolis, 1836); Baltimore *American*, Aug. 12, 1835; "Junius" in the Baltimore *Republican*, Mar. 5, 1836.

> When this great excitement commenced the Hon. Major General Andrew Jackson that wher president . . . wher absent from the City and when it got in it height the general arrived home and after he arrived home he sent a message to those gentelmen Mechanics to know what was the matter with them and if they were anny thing he could do for them in an Hon. way to promote their happiness he would do it.

When they complained of Negro actions, Jackson assured them "by the eternal god in this city" he would personally see that the blacks were punished if the mechanics had any disclosures to make about illegal activities, but he made clear "by the eternal god the law must be preserved at the Risk of Hasards." Minor sporadic incidents occurred later, but in a couple of weeks Washington "was as quiet as a church and the laws wher all respected."[80]

Outside of Washington, the multileveled character of American government kept riot control largely a local problem to be coped with by local officials. Such people, even more than Jackson, were often understandably sympathetic to their fellow citizen-voters or at least hesitant to attack any large group of them. Hence there was much truth to the frequent assertion that a greater show of determination on the part of authorities would have proved effective in stopping trouble. Some observers considered even a real show of determination an inadequate response to threatened violence. Roger Taney complained that the Baltimore bank mob ought to have been met by a "firm and free" use of guns at once, and Wendell Phillips accused the Boston mayor of being derelict in his duty for not having "ten men shot and sent to deserved graves" in the Garrison mob—this in a riot where the mayor acted with vigor and personal courage and where the total estimated damage was fifteen dollars.[81] Even gross dereliction of duty was perhaps better than Phillips's emotive and moralistic approach, which could only feed the paranoiac self-righteousness rioters, actual and potential, possess. The heaviest loss of life tended to occur in two riotous situations: when authorities wholly acquiesced in a mob's destructive tendencies—as was the case with the Mormons in Missouri, with some groups of gentiles later in Mormon-controlled Utah, and in alleged abolitionist and slave conspiracies in the South; or when force was used to keep a mob from their ends. Elijah Lovejoy would not have been killed if he had let his press be removed from Alton as he had from St. Louis. No one died at the Ursuline Convent, which the mob burned unopposed; twenty were victims of the military when the mob was not allowed to fire a Philadelphia Catholic church. How weigh the five bodies in Baltimore against the property of the bank partners or that of men whose crime was answering a public

[80] Shiner, diary, 60–61 ff. At least some damage to black property occurred as late as mid-September, although the major Washington papers did not mention it. Baltimore *Gazette,* Sept. 15, 1835; *Niles' Register,* 49 (Sept. 19, 1835): 33.

[81] Frank Otto Gatell, "Roger B. Taney, the Bank of Maryland and a Whiff of Grapeshot," *Maryland Historical Magazine,* 59 (1964): 262–67; Theodore Lyman III, ed. *Papers Relating to the Garrison Mob* (Cambridge, Mass., 1870), 7.

call to aid in keeping the peace? How put Beverly Snow's small property and dignity in the balance with the lives that it might have cost to protect them? In some cases even human life may be less important than using force, if absolutely necessary, to allow unpopular faiths to be followed, unpopular people to be protected, unpopular ideas to be heard.

The clearest result of Jacksonian rioting was the development of professional police and fire companies in large cities.[82] In the wake of the Baltimore riots there was a strong recognition of the lack of organized civil authority to cope with such problems. The only "republican solution" seemed to be organization of volunteer peace-keeping forces because a professional "army" to ensure order among the people was certainly a mark of despotism. City guards were formed in each Baltimore ward, and gout-ridden Henry Thompson headed a corps of City Horse Guards, but such organizations, without the stimulus of any very urgent business, quickly waned. At the same time, Sir Robert Peel's organization of the London police suggested that a professional police force need not be despotic and pointed to the solution that Americans would accept in the 1840s and 1850s.[83] Riots, along with the increasing problem of crime, made clear in urban areas at least that the old voluntary principle could no longer handle social control among a people growing, and growing apart in economic status and ethnic diversity. American democracy, very reluctantly, came to accept that order and freedom required not only a legal system, but professionals specifically responsible for upholding it and forcing its dictates on recalcitrant fellow citizens. If Andrew Jackson was a political symbol for the mythic anarchic American ensuring the triumph of a higher code by his own strength and integrity in a world neatly divided between virtuous men and monstrous enemies, Abraham Lincoln came to represent the sadder side of the democratic psyche: the need to assert man's potential for freedom through accepting cruel responsibilities for using force in a world where the morality of all men was a mixed bag and where both sides prayed to the same God. Lincoln in his famous law-and-order speech of 1837 used recent riots to argue that only in unswerving respect for the law lay real protection from vicious disintegration and despotism. He and his nation in the Civil War proved their willingness to insist on their conception of law even if it had to be imposed by military force.[84] In his *Battle-Pieces*, Herman Melville, the

[82] Roger Lane, *Policing the City: Boston 1822–1885* (Cambridge, Mass., 1967), 26–38; James F. Richardson, *The New York Police, Colonial Times to 1901* (New York, 1970), 28–30; Sam Bass Warner, *The Private City: Philadelphia in Three Periods of Its Growth* (Philadelphia, 1968), 125–57; Andrew H. Neilly, "The Violent Volunteers: A History of the Volunteer Fire Department of Philadelphia, 1736–1831" (Ph.D. dissertation, University of Pennsylvania, 1960).

[83] Baltimore *Gazette*, Sept. 13, 19, 1835; Baltimore *American*, Aug. 27, Sept. 12, 1835; Thompson, diary, Sept.–Oct. 1835.

[84] Abraham Lincoln, "Address Before the Young Men's Lyceum of Springfield, January 27, 1838," in *Collected Works*, ed. Roy P. Basler (New Brunswick, 1953), 1: 110–12; Harry Jaffa, *The Crisis of the House Divided: An Interpretation of the Lincoln-Douglas Debates* (New York, 1959), 183–232.

American who had most developed the theme of the heroically destructive potential of self-reliant individualism, noted how the Civil War marked society's tacit acceptance of his grimmer vision of man's fate—especially in a poem commenting on New York City's Draft Riot of 1863 where for the first time a professional police force was used not to control but to conquer "the Atheist roar of riot":

> Hail to the low dull rumble, dull and dead,
> And ponderous drag that shakes the wall.
> Wise Draco comes, deep in the midnight roll
> Of black artillery; he comes, though late;
> In code corroborating Calvin's creed
> And cynic tyrannies of honest kings;
> He comes, nor parlies; and the Town, redeemed,
> Gives thanks devout; nor, being thankful, heeds
> The grimy slur on the Republic's faith implied,
> Which holds that Man is naturally good,
> And—more—is Nature's Roman, never to be scourged.[85]

Still unshaken in their democratic convictions, Americans admitted in their prosecution of the Civil War and their growing resistance to rioters that the nation was in practice willing to temper the democratic myth of social responsibility through freedom with some of Draco's stern legalism and Calvin's harsh estimate of man's character and destiny. With a willingness, if you will, to use law not only to release human energy but to check and control it.

The Jacksonian experience suggests that riot is not antithetical to, or abnormal in, a democracy but the result of very basic tendencies and tensions within it. Because of these the riot situation poses in stark form many of the deepest dilemmas a democracy faces. To react harshly is to threaten groups who act within its bounds and in accord with some of its basic precepts; to react tolerantly is inevitably to make the state an accomplice in whatever is done. Riot crystallizes the paradox of vital democracy that must live in the shadow of twin totalitarianisms—that of total submission of all to the state's power and that of the tyranny of favored groups or individuals because of the state's weakness. And to avoid the ascendancy of either totalitarianism requires that democratic man live uneasily and creatively with the dangerous proclivities, potential and sometimes realized, in both his legalistic and anarchic myths.

[85] Herman Melville, "The Housetop," in *The Battle-Pieces,* ed. Hennig Cohen (New York, 1963), 89–90. The change in attitude toward the power of the state paralleled other intellectual shifts, some of which are traced in George M. Frederickson, *The Inner Civil War: Northern Intellectuals and the Crisis of the Union* (New York, 1965), in R. Jackson Wilson, *In Quest of Community* (New York, 1968), and in Hurst, *Law and the Conditions of Freedom.*

2 Suggestions for Further Reading

For the Indian policy of the federal government in the early years of the new nation, see Reginald Horsman, *Expansion and American Indian Policy, 1783–1812* (Michigan State University Press, 1967), and F. P. Prucha, *American Indian Policy in the Formative Years** (Harvard University Press, 1962). A special study of Indians during the revolutionary era is Barbara Graymont, *The Iroquois in the American Revolution** (Syracuse University Press, 1972). Attempts at acculturation are described in Robert F. Berkhofer, Jr., *Salvation and the Savage: An Analysis of Protestant Missions and American Indian Response 1787–1862** (Atheneum, 1972).

The literature on Indian removal from the Southeast is voluminous. Good starting points are Dale Van Every's *Disinherited: The Lost Birthright of the American Indian** (Morrow, 1966), and the collection of documents edited by Louis Filler and Allan Guttman, *Removal of the Cherokee Nation: Manifest Destiny or National Dishonor** (Heath, 1962). Robert S. Cotterill discusses the life of the Indians before their dispossession in *The Southern Indians: The Story of the Civilized Tribes Before Removal* (University of Oklahoma Press, 1954); and Grant Foreman tells the sad tale of removal in *Indian Removal: The Emigration of the Five Civilized Tribes of Indians**(2d ed.; University of Oklahoma Press, 1953). Angie Debo takes a close look at two of the Five Civilized Tribes in *The Road to Disappearance: A History of the Creek Indians* (University of Oklahoma Press, 1941), and *The Rise and Fall of the Choctaw Republic** (University of Oklahoma Press, 1961). See also Michael Rogin, *Fathers and Children: Andrew Jackson and the Subjugation of the American Indian** (Knopf, 1975).

A magnificent collection of primary sources is gathered in Robert H. Bremner, *et al.* (eds.), *Children and Youth in America: A Documentary History** (2 vols.; Harvard University Press, 1970–71). Two surveys of juvenile delinquency are Anthony M. Platt, *The Child Savers: The Invention of Delinquency** (University of Chicago Press, 1969), Robert M. Mennel, *Thorns and Thistles: Juvenile Delinquents in the United States, 1825–1940* (University Press of New England, 1973), and Stephen L. Schlossman, *Love and the American Delinquent: The Theory and Practice of "Progressive" Juvenile Justice, 1825–1920* (University of Chicago Press, 1977). For the background of poverty see Raymond A. Mohl, *Poverty in New York, 1783–1825* (Oxford University Press, 1971). The development of a variety of institutions during this period is described in David J. Rothman, *The Discovery of*

* Available in paperback edition.

*the Asylum** (Little, Brown, 1971).

A number of studies of violence in American history have appeared in recent years, but most have been superficial and lacking in perspective. A rather good collection of essays, many of them prepared for the President's Commission on the Causes and Prevention of Violence, is Hugh Davis Graham and Ted Robert Gurr (eds.), *Violence in America: Historical and Comparative Perspectives** (2 vols.; U.S. Government Printing Office, 1969), also available in one-volume editions from New American Library and Bantam. A useful collection of primary sources is Richard Hofstadter and Michael Wallace (eds.), *American Violence: A Documentary History** (Knopf, 1970), which includes a long introductory essay by Hofstadter. Leonard L. Richards, "*Gentlemen of Property and Standing*": *Anti-Abolition Mobs in Jacksonian America** (Oxford University Press, 1971) surveys one aspect of violence in this period.

3

The Ante-Bellum North and South

Religious Conflict in Ante-Bellum Boston

OSCAR HANDLIN

Religious conflict in early American history involved not merely discrimination against the non-Christian Indians and Africans but also hostility among competing Christian sects. Puritan intolerance in New England and Anglican establishment in the Southern colonies worked against the unification of the several Christian denominations. Although the Bill of Rights established a legal basis for religious toleration—at least at the federal level—as early as 1789, religious discrimination has been a persistent problem in American society.

One of the most virulent outbreaks of religious prejudice in American history occurred in the 1840s and 1850s, when tens of thousands of Irish Catholic immigrants arrived on the Eastern seaboard. Fleeing the horrors of famine in Ireland, many came to America destitute and deeply antagonistic toward all things English, including the Protestant religion. There had been Irish immigrants to America before—those deported in the civil wars of the seventeenth century and the United Irishmen refugees from the attempted republican rebellion of 1798. But never before had the Irish come in such numbers, and never had America been so ill prepared to receive them.

Many German Catholics also emigrated to America in these years, but the majority of the Germans avoided religious conflict by moving to the West, where they formed homogeneous farming communities and settled in cities such as St. Louis and Milwaukee. The Irish, in contrast, tended to gather in the older cities and in the new factory towns of the East, where they competed with the established residents for unskilled and industrial labor, thus intensifying negative feelings toward them. The United States economy had just begun to recover from the depression of 1837, which had closed thousands of businesses and manufacturing plants and caused widespread unemployment. Now, suddenly, there was a great flood of cheap labor, creating the first real labor surplus in American history. Industrialists responded by cutting wages drastically in the mills and other Eastern manufacturing enterprises. The laboring classes tended to blame the Irish for the worsening economic conditions. Religious bigotry and nativism added to the discontent, and violence of major proportions erupted in several Eastern cities. In Philadelphia, for example, a request that Catholic children be allowed to use the Catholic version of the Bible in public schools and that they be excused from Protestant religious exercises led to riots in which houses and churches were burned and at least thirty people were killed and over a hundred wounded.

The following selection is reprinted from a chapter in **Boston's Immigrants,** a study of Irish immigrants to Boston by Oscar Handlin, of Harvard University. In it, Handlin examines the rise of nativism and anti-Catholicism in Boston toward the middle of the nineteenth century.

We still drive out of Society the Ishmaels and Esaus. This we do not so much from ill-will as want of thought, but thereby we lose the strength of these outcasts. So much water runs over the dam—wasted and wasting![1]

Consciousness of identity particularized groups; but mere pluralism evoked no conflict in Boston society. Those coherently welded by circumstances of origin, economic status, cultural variations, or color differences often moved in distinct orbits, but were part of a harmonious system. In some instances, native Bostonians adopted newcomers; in others, they adapted themselves to the existence of aliens in their community. But whatever friction arose out of the necessity for making adjustments produced no conflict, until the old social order and the values upon which it rested were endangered.

Thus, while prejudice against color and servile economic origin confined the Negroes to restricted residential areas, distinct churches, special jobs, separate schools, and undesirable places in theaters until the 1850s, the relationships between Negroes and other Bostonians were stable and

[1] Theodore Parker, *A Sermon of the Dangerous Classes in Society* . . . (Boston, 1847), 12.

"Religious Conflict in Ante-Bellum Boston." Reprinted by permission of the publishers. From Oscar Handlin, *Boston's Immigrants*, Cambridge, Mass.: The Belknap Press of Harvard University Press, pp. 178–206.

peaceful.[2] Social and legal discriminations still limited Negro privileges in the Park Street Church in 1830, and incited protests when Alcott included a Negro child in his infant school.[3] But the stigmata and penalties for being different were slowly vanishing. Those who urged equality for the South were perforce obliged to apply their convictions at home. An attempt in 1822 to restrict the immigration of Negro paupers failed and repeated petitions after 1839 finally secured the repeal of laws against intermarriage, thus legalizing a process already in existence.[4] In 1855 separate schools were abolished and colored children unconditionally admitted to the public schools, so that by 1866 some 150 Negroes attended the primary, 103 the grammar, and five the high schools of Boston—in all, a high percentage of the Negro children of the city.[5] The state actively defended and protected Negroes' rights, even establishing missions for that purpose in Charleston and New Orleans where Boston colored seamen were often seized as fugitive slaves.[6] Public pressure forced the Eastern and New Bedford Railroads to admit colored people to their cars in the forties; and former slaves began to move to the same streets as whites.[7] In 1863, they were permitted to fight in the Union Army when Governor Andrew, with the aid of Lewis Hayden, recruited the Fifty-fourth Massachusetts Regiment, which included 300 fugitive slaves. In the same year, the militia was opened to them, and a colored company in Ward Six received a grant from the city. Negro regiments were segregated, but many prominent Bostonians "taking life and honor in their hands cast in their lot with" them.[8] By 1865, the Negroes, though still a separate part of Boston society, participated in its advantages without conflict. And most Bostonians agreed that "the theory of a natural antagonism and in-

[2] Cf., e.g., the sober editorial on Negro problems in *Daily Evening Transcript*, September 28, 1830; cf. also Mary Caroline Crawford, *Romantic Days in Old Boston* . . . (Boston, 1910), 249; Helen T. Catterall, *Judicial Cases Concerning American Slavery and the Negro* . . . (Washington, 1936), IV, 524.

[3] Cf. E. S. Abdy, *Journal of a Residence and Tour in the United States* . . . (London, 1835), I, 133 ff.; Odell Shepard, *Journals of Bronson Alcott* (Boston, 1938), 110.

[4] Cf. [Theodore Lyman, Jr.], *Free Negroes and Mulattoes, House of Representatives, January 16, 1822 . . . Report* . . . (Boston, n.d.); Henry Wilson, *History of the Rise and Fall of the Slave Power in America* (Boston, 1872), I, 489–92.

[5] 316 between the ages of 10 and 15 ("Report of the School Committee, 1866," *Boston City Documents, 1866*, no. 137, p. 188). Cf. also *Boston Pilot*, September 15, October 6, 1855.

[6] Cf. the letters of Edward Everett to John P. Bigelow, dated July 23, 1839, September 30, 1839 (Bigelow Papers [MSS., H. C. L.], Box V, VI); Arthur B. Darling, *Political Changes in Massachusetts* . . . (New Haven, 1925), 320; Catterall, *op. cit.*, IV, 511, 524; Edward Channing, *History of the United States* (New York, 1925), VI, 93 ff.

[7] Cf. Wilson, *op. cit.*, I, 492–95; Lady Emmeline S. Wortley, *Travels in the United States* . . . (New York, 1851), 60; Edward Dicey, *Six Months in the Federal States* (London, 1863), II, 215.

[8] *Exercises at the Dedication of the Monument to Colonel Robert Gould Shaw . . . May 31, 1897* . . . (Boston, 1897), 10; Henry Greenleaf Pearson, *Life of John A. Andrew* . . . (Boston, 1904), II, 70 ff.; William S. Robinson, "*Warrington*" *Pen-Portraits* . . . (Boston, 1877), 107, 274, 406; A. B. Hart, *Commonwealth History of Massachusetts* . . . (New York, 1930), IV, 535; *Boston City Documents, 1863*, no. 100, pp. 11, 18.

superable prejudice on the part of the white man against the black is a pure fiction. Ignorant men are always full of prejudices and antagonisms; and color has nothing to do with it."[9]

Group consciousness based upon religious differences was likewise not conducive to conflict. The Puritan dislike of Catholics had subsided during the eighteenth century,[10] and had disappeared in the early nineteenth as a result of the good feelings produced by revolutionary collaboration with the French and the growth of the latitudinarian belief that "inside of Christianity reason was free."[11] Governor Hancock had early abolished Pope's Day, and the Constitution of 1780 had eliminated the legal restrictions against Catholics. Catholics established a church in the city in 1789 "without the smallest opposition, for persecution in Boston had wholly ceased," and "all violent prejudices against the good bishop of Rome and the Church . . . he governs" had vanished, along with hostility towards hierarchical institutions in general.[12] Bishop Carroll, visit-

9 Robinson, *op. cit.*, 298; cf. also Dicey, *op. cit.*, I, 70, 74; *Massachusetts Senate Documents, 1841*, no. 51; *Massachusetts House Documents, 1841*, no. 17.

10 Thus with few exceptions there was a "general absence of anti-Catholic references" in eighteenth-century textbooks, and the Dudleian lectures were founded to counteract "the rapid rise of liberalism" (Rev. Arthur J. Riley, *Catholicism in New England* . . . [Washington, 1936], 23, 31, 225, 307). The only exception was the hostility, primarily political, to Jesuit activities in Maine (*ibid.*, 6, 193 ff.; Channing, *op. cit.*, II, 131 ff., 531, 545 ff.). Puritan intolerance sprang from the desire to found a "bible commonwealth" and was therefore directed against Baptists, Quakers, and Arminians as well (cf. Channing, *op. cit.*, II, 68; Ray Allen Billington, *Protestant Crusade, 1800–1860, A Study of the Origins of American Nativism* [New York, 1938], 7, 15, 18; Riley, *op. cit.*, 45 ff., 217 ff.). When priests visited Boston under circumstances that did not endanger the "Standing Order" they "received a cordial welcome befitting the social amenities exchanged between educated persons" (Riley, *op. cit.*, 190, 184 ff., 206, 207).

11 Octavius B. Frothingham, *Boston Unitarianism, 1820–1850* . . . (New York, 1890), 23; Archibald H. Grimké, *Life of Charles Sumner* . . . (New York, 1892), 38. For the popularity of the French in Boston, cf. H. M. Jones, *America and French Culture* . . . (Chapel Hill, 1927), 126; for the effect of the Revolution, cf. John G. Shea, "Catholic Church in American History," *American Catholic Quarterly Review*, January, 1876, I, 155; Billington, *op. cit.*, 19.

Those who regard anti-Catholicism as inherent in the nature of Protestant society and define "the Protestant milieu" as "nothing else than opposition to Catholicism" (Riley, *op. cit.*, vii, 1; "Anti-Catholic Movements in the United States," *Catholic World*, XXII [1876], 810; Billington, *op. cit.*, 1) have been hard put to explain the tolerance of the early nineteenth century. The simplest escape has been to mark it a period of subsidence arising from absorption in other problems (cf. Billington, *op. cit.*, 32; Humphrey J. Desmond, *Know-Nothing Party* [Washington, 1904], 12), with the anti-Catholicism of the forties and fifties simply a recrudescence of forces always present, thus missing completely the significance of the special factors that produced it in those two decades.

12 Samuel Breck, "Catholic Recollections," *American Catholic Historical Researches*, XII (1895), 146, 148; E. Percival Merritt, "Sketches of the Three Earliest Roman Catholic Priests in Boston," *Publications of the Colonial Society of Massachusetts*, XXV, 218 ff.; William Wilson Manross, *Episcopal Church in the United States, 1800–1840, A Study in Church Life* (New York, 1938), 59; Samuel Eliot Morison, *History of the Constitution of Massachusetts* . . . (Boston, 1917), 24.

ing Boston in 1791, preached before the Governor, pronounced the blessing at the annual election of the Ancient and Honorables, and was amazed at the good treatment accorded him. Bishop Cheverus commanded the respect and affection of all Protestants.

Thereafter the government was no longer hostile. The City Council frequently gave Catholics special privileges to insure freedom of worship, closing the streets near Holy Cross Church to exclude the noise of passing trucks.[13] It never took advantage of the laws that permitted it to tax all residents for sectarian purposes; on the contrary, Boston Protestants often contributed to Catholic churches and institutions. After 1799 no tithes were collected, by 1820 religious tests were abolished, and in 1833 Church and State completely separated.[14] The anti-Catholic activities of the *New York Protestant* and of the New York Protestant Association in the early thirties had no counterpart in Boston where an attempt to found an anti-Catholic paper (*Anti-Jesuit*) in 1829 failed.[15] Accepted as loyal members of the community, Catholics could easily partake of its opportunities.[16] Their right to be different was consistently defended by natives who urged that the particular sect each person chose was a private matter.

> In individual instances where our friends and acquaintances join the Romish Church, there may be reason either to be glad of it or to grieve. If they join the Church . . . because they need its peculiar influence for their own good, if never having found peace in Christ elsewhere they do find it there, ought we not to rejoice in such a result? Why should we doubt that some minds are better fitted to find a personal union with God by the methods of the Catholic Church than by any other?[17]

There were of course differences between the sects, expressed in theological disputations. As early as 1791 Thayer offered to debate any

[13] Cf. Merritt, *loc. cit.*, 205–07; Billington, *op. cit.*, 20; Josiah Quincy, *Figures of the Past from the Leaves of Old Journals* (Boston, 1883), 311, 312; *Minutes of the Selectmen's Meetings, 1811 to 1817 . . .* (*Volume of Records Relating to the Early History of Boston*, XXXVIII), *Boston City Documents, 1908*, no. 60, p. 69; James Bernard Cullen, *Story of the Irish in Boston . . .* (Boston, 1890), 125; Leo F. Ruskowski, *French Emigré Priests in the United States . . .* (Washington, 1940), 85.

[14] Cf. Morison, *op. cit.*, 24, 32; *Boston Catholic Observer*, April 17, 1847; Rev. James Fitton, *Sketches of the Establishment of the Church in New England* (Boston, 1872), 141; Darling, *op. cit.*, 23; Hart, *op. cit.*, IV, 12.

[15] Cf. Billington, *op. cit.*, 53 ff., 76. The Boston Irish Protestant Association which Billington claimed was anti-Catholic (*ibid.*, 78, n. 48) specifically disavowed such activities (cf. the correspondence in *Boston Pilot*, June 25, July 2, 1842; also *Boston Catholic Observer*, August 2, 1848).

[16] Cf., e.g., *Jesuit or Catholic Sentinel*, July 23, 1831; Marcus Lee Hansen, *Immigrant in American History . . .* (Cambridge, 1940), 107.

[17] James Freeman Clarke, *The Church . . . as It Was, as It Is, as It Ought to Be, a Discourse at the . . . Chapel . . . Church of the Disciples . . . 1848* (Boston, 1848), 13; Arthur M. Schlesinger, Jr., *Orestes A. Brownson . . .* (Boston, 1939), 175.

Protestant in a "controversial lecture."[18] Beecher and Bishop Fenwick, assisted by Father O'Flaherty, engaged in a series of debates in 1830–34, the most prominent of the period. And the religious press and sermons occasionally attacked Catholicism, sometimes violently, in the spirit of all contemporary disputes, while Protestant denominations urged their ministers to resist the spread of "Popery."[19]

But the expression of theological differences did not imply intolerance. Thus the Congregationalists urged their ministers to labor "in the spirit of prayer and Christian love . . . ," and even the *Christian Alliance and Family Visitor*, founded "to promote the union of Christians against Popery," failed to print "a single article or paragraph of any description against . . . Catholics."[20] Arguments were aimed against Catholicism, not against Catholics, just as they were against Methodism, or by the Orthodox against Unitarianism and by "Christians" against transcendentalists.[21] When Beecher became too violent, the *Boston Courier* and the Boston Debating Society, both non-Catholic, denounced him. For though some preferred one sect to another, the predominant feeling among Bostonians of this period was that "wherever holiness reigns, whether in the Protestant or Catholic communion . . . wherever there is a pious heart . . . there is a member of the true church."[22] Indeed, such men as Channing cared little for the particular sect in which they ministered. Their "whole concern was with religion, not even with Christianity otherwise than as it was, in . . . [their] estimation, the highest form of religion. . . ."[23]

Those who recognized distinctions between the sects generally felt that more important were

> the grand facts of Christianity, which *Calvinists* and *Arminians*, *Trinitarians* and *Unitarians*, *Papists* and *Protestants*, *Churchmen* and *Dissenters* all equally believe. . . . We all equally hold that he came . . . to save us from sin and death, and to publish a covenant of grace, by which all sincere penitents and good men are assured of favour and complete happiness in his future everlasting kingdom.[24]

In that vein, Holmes' "Cheerful Parson" affirmed,

18 Cf. *Columbian Centinel* (Boston), January 26, 1791; *ibid.*, February 2, 1791; *American Catholic Historical Researches*, V (1888), 51.

19 Cf. Dissertation Copy, 347, 348; Billington, *op. cit.*, 43 ff., 69 ff., 79. For the religious press in general, cf. Frank Luther Mott, *History of American Magazines* . . . (Cambridge, 1938), II, 60.

20 Cf. the complaints on this score in *Boston Catholic Observer*, March 1, 1848; also Billington, *op. cit.*, 86, 177.

21 Cf., e.g., Darling, *op. cit.*, 29; Clarence Hotson, "Christian Critics and Mr. Emerson," *New England Quarterly*, March, 1938, XI, 29 ff.

22 R. C. Waterston, "*The Keys of the Kingdom of Heaven*," *a Sermon* . . . (Boston, 1844), 13; cf. also Frothingham, *op. cit.*, 48; *Jesuit or Catholic Sentinel*, December 29, 1830; *ibid.*, February 26, 1831.

23 Frothingham, *op. cit.*, 6.

24 Richard Price, *Sermons on the Christian Doctrine as Received by the Different Denominations of Christians* . . . (Boston, 1815), 8.

Not damning a man for a different opinion,
I'd mix with the Calvinist, Baptist, Arminian,
Greet each like a man, like a Christian and brother,
Preach love to our Maker, ourselves and each other.[25]

And even the more conservative Baptists granted that "the various erring sects which constitute the body of Antichrist, have among them those who are beloved of God. . . ." "Wherein we think others err, they claim our pity; wherein they are right, our affection and concurrence."[26] In this roseate scheme of salvation there was room even for Jews, and from Bunker Hill, a poet proclaimed:

Christian and Jew, they carry out one plan,
For though of different faith, each in heart a man.[27]

Government action reflected the community's attitude towards immigrants. They were still welcome. The state had no desire to exclude foreigners or to limit their civic rights; on the contrary, during this period it relaxed some surviving restrictions.[28] Since the care of aliens was charged to the Commonwealth, the problem of poor relief aroused less hostility within Boston than outside it.[29] Yet nowhere was pauperism transmuted into a pretext for discrimination against the Irish. Legislation aimed only at barring the dependent, the insane, and the unfit, and shifted to newcomers part of the cost of those who could not support themselves. The function of the municipal Superintendent of Alien Passengers, under the act of 1837, was merely to prevent the landing of persons incompetent to maintain themselves, unless a bond be given that no such individual become a public charge within ten years, and to collect the sum of two dollars each from all other alien passengers as a commutation for such a bond.[30] All the subsequent changes in the law only modified it to conform with a decision of the Supreme Court.[31] Attempts to extend these

25 Cf. M. A. DeWolfe Howe, *Holmes of the Breakfast Table . . .* (New York, 1939), 17.

26 *Minutes of the Boston Baptist Association . . . 1812* (Boston, n.d.), 13.

27 Cf. Morris A. Gutstein, *Aaron Lopez and Judah Touro . . .* (New York, 1939), 98.

28 Cf. Massachusetts Commissioners of Alien Passengers and Foreign Paupers, *Report . . . 1851* (Boston, 1852), 14; also Edith Abbott, *Historical Aspects of the Immigration Problem . . .* (Chicago, 1926), 622, 739 ff.; *Cork Examiner*, July 6, 1853; *Massachusetts House Documents, 1828–29,* no. 25; *ibid., 1829–30,* no. 8; *Massachusetts Senate Documents, 1852*, no. 11.

29 Cf. the source of petitions for repeal of the state pauper laws, *Massachusetts Senate Documents, 1847*, no. 109.

30 *Ordinances of the City of Boston Passed Since the Year 1834 . . .* (Boston, 1843), 3, 4; Hart, *op. cit.*, IV, 143 ff.; Edith Abbott, *Immigration, Select Documents . . .* (Chicago, 1924), 105 ff., 148.

31 Cf. Norris v. City of Boston (7 *Howard's U.S. Reports*, 283, XVII, 139 ff.); *Massachusetts Senate Documents, 1847*, no. 109; *ibid., 1848*, no. 46; Peleg W. Chandler, *Charter and Ordinances of the City of Boston Together with Acts of the Legislature Relating to the City . . .* (Boston, 1850), 25 ff.; *Charter and Ordinances of the City of Boston Together with the Acts of the Legislature . . .* (Boston, 1856), 34 ff.

restrictive provisions failed, partly because of the pressure of shipping firms which profited by the immigrant traffic, but primarily because successive administrations recognized that, "The evils of foreign pauperism we cannot avoid," and it is "wise to avail ourselves of the advantages of direct emigration which increases the business of the State."[32]

In the two decades after 1830, however, the differences so tolerantly accepted impinged ever more prominently upon the Bostonians' consciousness. The economic, physical, and intellectual development of the town accentuated the division between the Irish and the rest of the population and engendered fear of a foreign group whose appalling slums had already destroyed the beauty of a fine city and whose appalling ideas threatened the fondest conceptions of universal progress, of grand reform, and a regenerated mankind. The vague discomforts and the latent distrusts produced by the problems of these strangers festered in the unconscious mind of the community for many years. Though its overt manifestations were comparatively rare, the social uneasiness was none the less real.

Thus pauperism aroused some resentment among those who saw Massachusetts overwhelmed by a rising tax bill;[33] and indigent artisans continually complained that Irishmen displaced "the honest and respectable laborers of the State; and . . . from their manner of living . . . work for much less per day . . . being satisfied with food to support the animal existence alone . . . while the latter not only labor for the body but for the mind, the soul, and the State."[34] Above all, as the newcomers developed consciousness of group identity and sponsored institutions that were its concrete expression, they drove home upon other Bostonians a mounting awareness of their differences, and provoked complaints that

> instead of assimilating at once with the customs of the country of their adoption, our foreign population are too much in the habit of retaining their own national usages, of *associating too exclusively with each other*, and living in groups together. These practices serve no good purpose, and tend merely to alienate those among whom they have chosen to reside. *It would be the part of wisdom, to* ABANDON AT ONCE ALL USAGES AND ASSOCIATIONS WHICH MARK THEM AS FOREIGNERS, *and to become in feeling and custom, as well as in privileges and rights, citizens of the United States.*[35]

The inability of the native-born to understand the ideas of their new neighbors perpetuated this gap between them, rousing the vivid fear that

32 *Massachusetts Senate Documents, 1852*, no. 7, p. 7. For the influence of shipping firms, cf. *Massachusetts Senate Documents, 1847*, no. 109, p. 5; Boston Board of Trade, *Second Annual Report of the Government . . . 1856* (Boston, 1856), 3.

33 For evidence of this complaint, cf. *American Traveller* (Boston), August 5, 1834; *American*, October 21, 1837; Abbott, *Immigration*, 112 ff.; Edith Abbott, *Historical Aspects of the Immigration Problem . . .* (Chicago, 1926), 572 ff., 758 ff.; *Massachusetts House Documents, 1836*, no. 30, pp. 9 ff.

34 Cf. *Massachusetts Senate Documents, 1847*, no. 109, p. 4.

35 *American* (Boston), October 21, 1837.

the Irish were "a race that will never be infused into our own, but on the contrary will always remain distinct and hostile."[36]

That fear was the more pronounced because the Catholic Church in these years was a church militant, conscious of its mission in the United States, vigorous and active in proselytization and the search for converts. In the strategy of the hierarchy, and in their own minds, immigrants played a clear role in this process of redemption: they had been carried across the waters by a Divine Providence to present an irrefutable example of fortitude and faith to their unbelieving neighbors, to leaven the dull mass of Protestant America and ultimately to bring the United States into the ranks of Catholic powers.[37] No figure was more insistently, clearly, and admiringly drawn in immigrant literature than that of the humble Irishman in every walk of life who succeeded in converting his employer, friend, or patron.[38] Though Bostonians could not do without the Irish servant girl, distrust of her mounted steadily; natives began to regard her as a spy of the Pope who revealed their secrets regularly to priests at confession.[39] The growth of Catholicism in England warned them that a staunchly Protestant country might be subverted. Meanwhile, close at home, the mounting power of the Oxford movement in the Episcopal Church, reflected in the estrangement of Bishop Eastburn and the Church of the Advent (1844 ff.), and a growing list of widely publicized conversions lent reality to the warning of Beecher and Morse that Catholics plotted to assume control of the West.[40]

Before 1850, the potential friction inherent in these fears broke out only infrequently and sporadically. Incepted by irresponsible elements, these spontaneous brawls were always severely criticized by the community. Indeed, they were only occasionally directed against aliens, more often involving neighborhoods or fire companies. The rowdies singled out no special group. In 1814 West Enders rioted against Spanish sailors, in 1829 against Negroes and Irishmen, and in 1846 against some drunken Irishmen in Roxbury; but these were no more significant than the count-

[36] Mayor Lyman (*Inaugural Addresses of the Mayors of Boston . . .* [Boston, 1894], I, 195).

[37] Cf., e.g., *Boston Catholic Observer*, February 16, 1848; Thomas D'Arcy McGee, *History of the Irish Settlers in North America . . .* (Boston, 1852), 71; Billington, *op. cit.*, 291.

[38] Cf. e.g., Ellie in Agnes E. St. John, "Ellie Moore or the Pilgrim's Crown," *Boston Pilot*, June 30–September 1, 1860.

[39] Cf. James O'Connor, "Anti-Catholic Prejudice," *American Catholic Quarterly Review*, I (1876), 13.

[40] Cf. Billington, *op. cit.*, 118 ff., 263; William Wilson Manross, *History of the American Episcopal Church* (New York, 1935), 283 ff.; *Boston Catholic Observer*, July 24, 1847; S. F. B. Morse, *Foreign Conspiracy Against the United States* (s.l., n.d. 3, 26, 29, [186–]; S. F. B. Morse, *Imminent Dangers to the Free Institutions of the United States . . .* (New York, 1854), *passim;* Louis Dow Scisco, *Political Nativism in New York State* (New York, 1901), 21.

less feuds between North Enders and South Enders, or between truckmen and sailors, details of which enlivened many a police dossier.[41]

The Broad Street riot was exceptional only in size. On June 11, 1837, a collision between a volunteer fire company and an Irish funeral procession led to an outbreak, quelled after an hour or so by the militia. Caused by hotheaded, unruly firemen, proverbially a disruptive factor, it in no way reflected the feeling of the community. The firemen were immediately repudiated, and partly as a result of the affair, Mayor Lyman took the first steps towards replacing the volunteer system with a paid fire department.[42] A less permanent result was the establishment by the disbanded firemen of the *American*, the first anti-Catholic paper in Boston which for somewhat less than a year attacked alternately the Irish and the "*paid patriots*" who replaced them.[43]

Because it served for many years as an argument throughout the country in the propaganda for and against Catholics, the Charlestown Convent fire received a greater degree of notoriety than any other riot.[44] This disturbance grew primarily out of the failure of the school and the rural community in which it was located to adjust themselves to each other. To the laborers who lived nearby, the convent was a strange and unfamiliar institution, with which it was difficult to be neighborly or to follow the customary social forms. In addition, Catholicism meant Irishmen and for non-Irish laborers the convent was a symbol of the new competition they daily encountered. Rebecca Reed's lurid stories of life in the convent and the bickering of the Bishop and the Charlestown Selectman over a cemetery on Bunker Hill provoked a sense of irritation that came to a head with the appearance and disappearance of Elizabeth Harrison, a demented nun.[45] The refusal of the Mother Superior to admit the Charlestown Selectmen to investigate the purported existence of dungeons and torture chambers until the very day of the fire inflamed

[41] Cf. "Boston as It Appeared to a Foreigner at the Beginning of the Nineteenth Century," *Bostonian Society Publications*, Series I, IV, 117, 118; Joseph E. Chamberlin, *Boston Transcript* . . . (Boston, 1930), 37 ff.; *Minutes of the Selectmen's Meetings, 1811 to 1817* . . . (*Volume of Records* . . . , XXXVIII), *Boston City Documents, 1908*, no. 60, p. 113; *Boston Pilot*, September 12, 1846; Arthur Wellington Brayley, *Complete History of the Boston Fire Department* . . . (Boston, 1889), 185, 186; Edward H. Savage, *Police Records and Recollections* . . . (Boston, 1873), 65, 66, 110, 257.

[42] Chamberlin, *op. cit.*, 48 ff.; Brayley, *Complete History*, 197 ff.; State Street Trust Company, *Mayors of Boston* . . . (Boston, [1914]), 15.

[43] Cf. *American*, October 21, 1837, March 17, 1838.

[44] There are numerous short accounts of this affair; but the best, though differing in interpretation from that offered here, is in Billington, *op. cit.*, 68 ff.

[45] Billington, *op. cit.*, 71 ff.; Shea, *op. cit.*, III, 462, 463; Charles Greely Loring, *Report of the Committee Relating to the Destruction of the Ursuline Convent* . . . (Boston, 1834), 8. Miss Harrison's disappearance was probably not important. In 1830 a rumor spread by the *New England Herald* (Vol. I, no. 28) that "a young lady, an orphan, has lately been inveigled into the Ursuline Convent . . . after having been cajoled to transfer a large fortune to the Popish massmen" was ridiculed and had no repercussions (cf. *United States Catholic Intelligencer*, April 24, 1830).

the forty or fifty Charlestown truckmen and New Hampshire Scotch-Irish brickmakers who led the curious mob; and her threat that, unless they withdrew, she would call upon the Bishop for a defense contingent of 20,000 Irishmen precipitated the holocaust.[46]

After the initial excitement, every section of public opinion in Boston greeted the fire with horror and surprise. Bostonians had not disliked the school; many had actually sent their children there. There is no evidence that the residents of the city had any connection with the plot; not a voice was raised in its support. The press condemned the absence of adequate protection, and deplored the "high-handed outrage." Bostonians asserted that "The Catholics . . . are as . . . loyal citizens as their brethren of any other denomination." A mass meeting at Faneuil Hall expressed sympathy with the unfortunate victims of mob action and, resolving "to unite with our Catholic brethren in protecting their persons, their property, and their civil and religious rights," recommended a reward for the capture of the criminals and compensation to the convent, as did similar meetings under John Cotton in Ward Eight, under Everett at Charlestown, and under Story at Cambridge.[47] A reward of $500 offered by Governor Davis resulted in the arrest of thirteen men, the trial of eight, and the conviction of one. The life imprisonment sentence for the one of whose guilt there seemed to be no doubt was far more significant than failure to convict those who might have been innocent.[48]

The convent, reestablished in Roxbury, failed "because of lack of harmony among the Sisters."[49] But the legislature was petitioned for compensation repeatedly in the next twenty years. Despite persistent reluctance to grant public funds for religious purposes, $10,000 was voted in 1846, but rejected by the Ursulines.[50] The rise of Know-Nothing sentiments thwarted further overtures, while anti-Catholic activities of city rowdies and the circulation of *Six Months in a Convent* somewhat balanced expressions of sympathy. But these antagonisms were more marked outside than within the city. None of the anti-Catholic papers founded after the publication of that scurrilous book were published in Boston.[51]

Occasional manifestations of hostility in the next few years were restricted in scope. The Montgomery Guards, the first Irish military

[46] Billington, *op. cit.*, 81, n. 85; Benj. F. Butler, *Autobiography and Personal Reminiscences . . .* (Boston, 1892), 111; Darling, *op. cit.*, 165, n. 79.

[47] Cf. Billington, *op. cit.*, 69, 81–85, 86, 108; Loring, *op. cit.*, 2, 6, 16; *American Traveller*, August 15, 19, 1834; [H. Ware, Jr.], *An Account of the Conflagration of the Ursuline Convent . . . by a Friend of Religious Toleration* (Boston, 1834), 3; Chamberlin, *op. cit.*, 44 ff.; *Jesuit or Catholic Sentinel*, August 16, 1834; *ibid.*, August 23, 1834; Crawford, *Romantic Days*, 22.

[48] Cf. Ware, *op. cit.*, 10; *Jesuit or Catholic Sentinel*, August 23, 1834; Billington, *op. cit.*, 86, 87; Loring, *op. cit.*, 4.

[49] Robert H. Lord, "Organizer of the Church in New England," *Catholic Historical Review*, XXII (1936), 182.

[50] Cf. Billington, *op. cit.*, 89, 110, n. 27; *Documents Relating to the Ursuline Convent in Charlestown* (Boston, 1842), 21, 22, 31; "Anti-Catholic Movements in the United States," *Catholic World*, XXII (1876), 814; *Boston Pilot*, February 18, 1854.

[51] Cf. *Boston Pilot*, April 16, 1853; Billington, *op. cit.*, 92 ff.

company, were attacked in 1837 by the rank and file of the Boston City Guards who refused to parade with an Irish company to uphold "the broad principle . . . that *in all institutions springing from our own laws, we all mingle in the same undisguised mass, whether native or naturalized.*" Although the native militiamen complained that "the press . . . condemned our conduct with . . . openmouthed language of wholesale reprehension . . . ," the very next year the same newspapers severely criticized the Irish soldiers who were finally disbanded in 1839.[52] In 1844 the reaction to the school quarrels in New York, to the riots in Philadelphia, and to the defeat of the national Whig ticket by the Irish vote produced a short-lived nativist branch of the Whig Party. Although the American Republicans under T. A. Davis gained the mayoralty in 1845, it was only on the eighth ballot, in an election fought primarily on the issue of the local water supply.[53] Nativism declined steadily thereafter. An attempt to revive it in 1847 failed so disastrously, that the *Boston Catholic Observer* could triumphantly proclaim nativism dying.[54]

Nativist fears failed to develop more significantly because the Irish before 1845 presented no danger to the stability of the old society. They were in a distinct minority and, above all, were politically impotent. In 1843 the Irish claimed no more than 200 voters in all Suffolk County, and in 1839, no more than 500, while in 1845 less than one-sixth of the adult male foreigners in Boston were citizens.[55] Only a few had secured the right to vote, or took an interest in politics; their opinions were still a matter of private judgment, with no influence upon the policies of the community. The old inhabitants, as individuals, might look down upon their new neighbors as unabsorbable incubi, but the still powerful tradition of tolerance stifled their accumulated resentments. The dominant group took no step to limit social and political rights or privileges until the ideals of the newcomers threatened to replace those of the old society. At that moment the tradition of tolerance was breached and long repressed hostilities found highly inflammable expression.

The crisis came when, after a decade of efforts in that direction, the Irish acquired a position of political importance. After 1840 their press insisted upon the duty "to themselves as well as to their families" of naturalization and a role in the government. Politicians sponsored societies which aided the unknowing and stimulated the indifferent to become citizens, and professional agents drew up papers, filled out forms, and rapidly turned out new voters for the sake of fees and political power.[56] Between 1841 and 1845, the number of qualified voters increased by 50

[52] Cf. *American*, October 21, 1837; *Boston Pilot*, February 3, 17, 1838, October 12, 1839.

[53] Cf. State Street Trust Company, *Mayors of Boston*, 17; Darling, *op. cit.*, 327–29; William G. Bean, Party Transformation in Massachusetts . . . (MS. H. C. L.), 228 ff.

[54] *Boston Catholic Observer*, August 28, June 19, July 24, 1847; Bean, *op. cit.*, 232 ff.

[55] Cf. *Jesuit or Catholic Sentinel*, January 18, 1834; *Boston Pilot*, November 9, 1839; George H. Haynes, "Causes of Know-Nothing Success in Massachusetts," *American Historical Review*, III (1897), 74, n. 1.

[56] Cf. *Boston Pilot*, February 19, 1853; Dissertation Copy, 367.

percent, then remained stable until 1852, when it grew by almost 15 percent in two years, while in the five years after 1850, the number of naturalized voters increased from 1,549 to 4,564. In the same period, the number of native voters grew only 14 percent.[57] Perennial political organizations flourished with every campaign and further mobilized the Irish vote.[58]

The coherence and isolation of Irish ideas facilitated political organization. And Irish leaders, consciously or unconsciously, encouraged group solidarity and the maintenance of a virtual Irish party. Though the Irish vote was not yet used to serve corrupt personal interest,[59] both those who aspired to gain public office in America through the support of a large bloc of voters and those who hoped to return as liberators to the Emerald Isle directed their energies towards activizing their countrymen. These efforts were so widespread that one of the most far-sighted Irish leaders complained that Irish political influence was being "fatally misused" and warned that "keeping up an Irish party in America is a fatal mistake, and . . . I will seek to induce them rather to blend and fuse their interests with American parties, than cause jealousy and distrust by acting as an exclusive and independent faction . . . a man has no right to interfere in American politics unless he thinks as an American. . . ."[60] But such views were rare.

With the political mobilization of the Irish in Boston, tolerance finally disappeared. The possibilities of Irish domination were the more startling because the political situation in Massachusetts, 1845–55, permitted a coherent, independent group to exercise inordinate influence. The unity of the old parties was crumbling as dissatisfied elements demanded new policies to meet the problems of reform, particularly those posed by slavery.[61] Although all, including the most conservative Abbott Lawrence, agreed on the ultimate desirability of reform, they were divided as to the methods of attaining it. Within each political party a restless group contended that the forces of good must prevail immediately, even at the expense of failure in national politics. Their insistence upon immediate, unequivocal action destroyed the coherence of the old alignments and yielded to the unified Irish the balance of power. For four years the reformers found these foreigners square in their path, defeating their most valued measures. In the critical year of 1854 this opposition drove them into a violent xenophobic movement that embodied all the hatreds stored up in the previous two decades.

Rantoul and Morton had blasted the stability of the Democrats, but

[57] Cf. Josiah Curtis, *Report of the Joint Special Committee . . . 1855 . . .* (Boston, 1856), 11; "Report and Tabular Statement of the Censors," *Boston City Documents, 1850,* no. 42, p. 12; Billington, *op. cit.,* 325, 326.

[58] Cf., e.g., *Boston Pilot,* July 8, 1860.

[59] The only instance of devious Irish politics in this period came in the election of John C. Tucker to the legislature in 1860 (cf. E. P. Loring and C. T. Russell, Jr., *Reports of Controverted Elections . . . 1853 to 1885 . . .* [Boston, 1886], 89 ff.).

[60] Richard O'Gorman to W. S. O'Brien, May 24, 1849, W. S. O'Brien Papers and Letters, 1819–1854 (MSS., N. L. I.), XVIII, no. 2, p. 547.

[61] Cf. Darling, *op. cit.,* 312 ff.

the Whig party was the first torn asunder by the anti-slavery men. In the early forties, some members had already deserted to the Liberty party, but until 1846 most anti-slavery Whigs continued to believe in "reform within the Party." Even in that year the magic personality of Webster nullified the damage done by Southern aggressions and the turbulent Texas and Mexico questions, and held in rein such conscientious rebels as Stephen C. Phillips, Charles Allen, and Sumner. But the Whig nomination of a slaveholder to the presidency and the rejection of the Wilmot Proviso by their National Convention in 1848 opened an unbridgeable gap between the two factions, though the Whigs remained strong enough to win the gubernatorial election that year and again in 1849.[62]

A similar development among the Democrats led a few to support Van Buren, the Free-Soil nominee in 1848, but the party quickly united to profit from the more serious division of its rivals. In addition, hoping for a coalition, it offered the Whig dissidents an anti-slavery plank in 1849. But these overtures failed; Free-Soilers still preferred cooperation with the Whigs to alliance with the Democrats who, nationally, were the most prominent supporters of the South's peculiar institution. But while Webster squinted at the federal scene and dreamed of the White House, the Whigs would have no meddling with reform. Though controlling the legislature of 1849, they failed to pass a single Free-Soil measure. Finally, their support of the Fugitive Slave Law, and particularly Webster's role in its enactment, completed the cleavage and consolidated the Free-Soil party in Massachusetts.[63]

When the gubernatorial election of 1850 gave no candidate a majority, Democratic ambitions, after seven years of famine, approached fulfillment. The constitution provided for the choice of a governor by an absolute majority, in the absence of which the election was thrown into the legislature—a situation susceptible to a great deal of political maneuvering. In this election the Democratic state platform had endorsed the Free-Soil program, though without a formal coalition. A trade between the two parties, which together had a majority in the legislature that convened in January, 1851, was inevitable. The Free-Soilers, anxious to be heard in Washington, were impatient with the Whig demand that the designation of a senator wait eleven months for a new legislature, and threw their votes for a Democratic governor. In return, the Democrats supported a radical policy and handed the United States senatorship and the organization of the legislature to the Free-Soilers. Banks became speaker of the House, and Henry Wilson, president of the Senate; although the former was nominally a Democrat, both were actually Free-Soilers. The reformers got the better of the bargain, passing a series of radical measures,

62 Cf. Robinson, *op. cit.*, 28–38, 416, 513; Bean, *op. cit.*, 8–38; Darling, *op. cit.*, 245 ff., 317, 334, 290, n. 67, 326; Wilson, *op. cit.*, I, 545 ff., II, 145 ff.; George S. Merriam, *Life and Times of Samuel Bowles* (New York, 1885), I, 45 ff.; *Reunion of the Free-Soilers of 1848–1852 . . . June 28, 1888* (Cambridge, 1888), 15, 17; Hart, *op. cit.*, IV, 97; Grimké, *op. cit.*, 182 ff., 190 ff.

63 Bean, *op. cit.*, 17, 28, 35 ff., 53 ff.; Darling, *op. cit.*, 340, 349–54; Grimké, *op. cit.*, 205; Haynes, *loc. cit.*, 80; Wilson, *op. cit.*, II, 247 ff.

including a general incorporation law to break the power of monopolies, a law for more democratic control of Harvard College, a homestead and mechanics' lien law, and measures ensuring the secret ballot and plurality voting in national elections.[64]

The coalition held through the election of 1851. But though the Free-Soilers managed to push through the Maine Law over Governor Boutwell's veto, they were dissatisfied. They disliked the governor, who had obstructed many reform measures, and they distrusted their Democratic allies, who had bolted in considerable numbers on Sumner's election to the United States Senate and had contrived to defeat a personal liberty law, acts to liberalize divorce, to protect the property rights of women, and to extend the powers of juries. Whittier voiced the apprehension of the Free-Soilers when he wrote, after seeing the governor's first message, "It is . . . monstrous and insulting. May God forgive us for permitting his election."[65]

The Free-Soilers now recognized the need of a reform in government to gain complete control of the state—a reform impossible under the existing conditions of amending the constitution, which called for a two-thirds vote in the House of Representatives of two successive legislatures on each clause.[66] With parties divided as they were, a simple majority was difficult enough, two-thirds almost impossible, and two-thirds in two successive legislatures out of the question. One solution was to change the basis of representation to reduce the influence of the conservative elements opposing them in Boston. But an attempt to do so in 1851 failed, leaving the reformers no alternative but a complete revamping of the constitution by a convention.[67]

In 1851 the Free-Soilers forced through the legislature a resolution for a constitutional convention. But when the question was presented to the voters, Democratic support was weak. The Irish, theretofore consistently Democrats, failed to follow their representatives who had indorsed revision. In the election several thousand who had voted for coalition candidates turned against the constitutional convention.[68] Of

[64] Cf. Bean, *op. cit.*, 54, 57, 64–87; Wilson, *op. cit.*, II, 347 ff.; *Address to the People of Massachusetts* (s.l., n.d., [Boston, 1852]), 3, 6, 7, 10 ff.; Robinson, *op. cit.*, 47, 433; Hart, *op. cit.*, IV, 99, 475.

[65] Alfred S. Roe, "Governors of Massachusetts . . . ," *New England Magazine*, XXV (1902), 547; Bean, *op. cit.*, 90–92, 113–20; Robinson, *op. cit.*, 433; *Address*, 5 ff.; Grimké, *op. cit.*, 209.

[66] A simple majority sufficed in the Senate (Bean, *op. cit.*, 116; Morison, *op. cit.*, 38).

[67] Bean, *op. cit.*, 88, 89. Legislators from Boston were elected on a general ticket which usually denied representation to minorities and gave the whole delegation to the Whigs (cf. Morison, *op. cit.*, 41).

[68] The election of 1851:

	GOVERNOR			CONVENTION	
	State	Boston		State	Boston
Winthrop (W)	64,611	7,388	no	65,846	7,135
Boutwell (D)	43,992	3,632			
Palfrey (FS)	28,599	1,294	yes	60,972	3,813

(*Boston Semi-Weekly Advertiser*, November 12, 1851; Bean, *op. cit.*, 109, 111.) Cf. also Morison, *op. cit.*, 42.

these, more than 1,100 were in Boston, and they were predominantly Irish Democrats bolting the party.[69]

When the Democratic State Convention again supported coalition and revision the following year, the Irish, under J. W. James, the Repeal leader, finally seceded from the party. Though opposing the Democrats in the state election of 1852, they supported the national Democratic party, which had repudiated Rantoul and coalition and whose presidential candidate, Pierce, was most acceptable as a conservative. Following the advice of Brownson and the *Pilot*, the Boston Irish became national Democrats and state Whigs. As a result of the confusion, the coalition ticket lost, but the project for a convention won.[70]

Impressed with the opportunity the convention presented for strengthening the party and consolidating its position, the Free-Soilers made special exertions in the March election and gained control. Their imprint upon the constitution that resulted was unmistakable. Single-unit senatorial districts and plurality elections by secret ballots were proposed. To decrease the power of the executive, many appointive offices, including the Council, became elective; the judiciary was controlled by limiting the term of office and extending the powers of jurors; and the use of public funds for religious education was prohibited. While these measures would render government more responsive to the voice of the people, the proposed constitution was undemocratic in its most important provision. By changing the system of representation to favor country towns at the expense of large cities, bailiwicks of conservatism, the reformers unquestionably compromised their principles.[71]

With one important exception party lines held in the vote on the adoption of the constitution. The opposition of the few conscientious Free-Soilers who would not support the unfair system of representation was trivial compared with the force of conservative Irish Catholic opinion clamoring for defeat.[72] At the Democratic Convention which indorsed the constitution, James again led a seceding group of Boston Irishmen who formed a party of their own. Pressure for recruitment and organization of voters increased. In September the Calvert Naturalization Society in the South End joined the Ward Three Association of the North End. The *Pilot* repeatedly warned that "no Catholic . . . can possibly vote for this . . . Constitution without giving up rights for which he has been all along contending," and Brownson pointed out its revolutionary implications.[73]

69 Bean's claim that the Free-Soilers bolted (*op. cit.*, 111) is wholly illogical since they wanted the convention and the Irish did not (for the Free-Soilers' attitude on constitutional change, cf. Robinson, *op. cit.*, 401 ff.).

70 Cf. in general, Bean, *op. cit.*, 127 ff., 217–20. For the new attempt to revise the constitution, cf. *Massachusetts Senate Documents, 1852*, no. 36, pp. 6 ff.

71 Cf. J. B. Mann, *Life of Henry Wilson . . .* (Boston, 1872), 36 ff.; Hon. Charles Allen, *Speech . . . at Worcester, Nov. 5, 1853* (s.l., n.d.), 1–3; Bean, *op. cit.*, 147–66; Morison, *op. cit.*, 49–60; Henry F. Brownson, *Orestes A. Brownson's Middle Life . . .* (Detroit, 1899), II, 465, 466; Mann, *op. cit.*, 43.

72 For Free-Soil opposition, cf. Bean, *op. cit.*, 168, 177.

73 Cf. Brownson, *Brownson's Middle Life*, II, 455 ff.; Dissertation Copy, 377–78; Bean, *op. cit.*, 221.

In their campaign, the Irish joined the die-hard Whigs under Abbott Lawrence, who led "hundreds of honest men gulled by their sophistry" in opposing a constitution which seriously curtailed the influences of State Street in politics. Lawrence conferred with Bishop Fitzpatrick on the problem, and Whig newspapers appealed particularly to the Irish. Against this alliance the reformers' contention that the *Boston Pilot* was "trying to lead Irishmen into the jaws of a Boston aristocracy as remorseless as the one they had left Ireland to get rid of" counted little. The combination of Irish votes and cotton money in Boston defeated the constitution and elected a Whig ticket.[74]

In this crisis the reformers inveighed against the lords of the counting house and bemoaned the slowness of rank-and-file Whigs to recognize their true interests, but concluded that while the former could never be redeemed, and the latter would have to be educated, the main obstacle to reform was Catholic opposition. And by this time they had learned that differences with the Irish were too deep to be easily eradicated; they could only be fought. Butler, sensitive to every shift in popular opinion, realized that the "performance, which struck down the Constitution, invoked a bitterness among the people against the Catholic religion, such as had never before been, to any considerable degree, either felt or foreshadowed in the State of Massachusetts."[75]

Through the early months of 1854 a series of unconnected events heightened resentment against Catholics and evoked many antipathies developed since 1830. In December, 1853, Father Gavazzi, a rebellious priest, lectured in Boston on the reactionary role of the Church.[76] A few months later, the visit of the papal nuncio Bedini, who had been connected with the massacre of revolutionaries in Bologna, though not provoking the expected riot, did refresh memories of Irish opposition to liberalism.[77] Meanwhile, events at home confirmed that impression. Failure of the enforcement of the prohibition laws was laid at the door of the Irish, and the State Temperance Committee announced it would fight Catholicism as part of its struggle for human freedom.[78] The Burns case

[74] Robinson, *op. cit.*, 204; Bean, *op. cit.*, 162, 166, 174–79; Butler, *op. cit.*, 119. The analysis of the vote from which Morison concludes that "the wards where most of the Irish-born population then lived did not poll so heavy a negative vote as the fashionable residential districts" (*op. cit.*, 63) is not valid because the wards were gerrymandered in the redistricting of 1850 to split the Irish vote (cf. Dissertation Copy, 383). Even in 1854 votes against the Know-Nothings showed no special concentration in any area (cf. *Boston Atlas*, November 14, 1854). Bean has shown that votes to defeat the constitution came from Boston: the 5,915 negative balance of Suffolk County more than offset the 997 positive balance elsewhere in the state (*op. cit.*, 173).

[75] Butler, *op. cit.*, 120.

[76] Cf. *Boston Semi-Weekly Advertiser*, November 30, December 3, 1853; Billington, *op. cit.*, 301.

[77] *Boston Pilot*, October 8, 1853, February 11, 1854; Billington, *op. cit.*, 300–02; Desmond, *op. cit.*, 72; Shea, *op. cit.*, IV, 360 ff.

[78] *Massachusetts Life Boat*, September 19, 1854; cf. also *Address of the State Temperance Committee to the Citizens of Massachusetts on the Operation of the Anti-Liquor Law* (Boston, 1853), 2; Billington, *op. cit.*, 323.

clearly linked the immigrants to pro-slavery forces and man-hunters. The *Pilot* supported the rendition of the fugitive slave; and the selection of the Columbian Artillery and Sarsfield Guards to protect him against indignant mobs seeking his freedom incited an inflammatory handbill:

> AMERICANS TO THE RESCUE!
> AMERICANS! SONS OF THE REVOLUTION!!
> A body of seventy-five Irishmen, known as the
> "*Columbian Artillery*"
> have volunteered their services to shoot down the
> citizens of Boston! and are now under arms to defend
> Virginia in kidnapping a Citizen of Massachusetts!
> Americans! These Irishmen have called us
> "Cowards and Sons of Cowards"!
> Shall we submit to have our Citizens shot
> down by a set of Vagabond Irishmen?

that turned many reformers against the Irish.[79] Finally, their defense of the Kansas-Nebraska Act connected them with the slave power, and drew criticism from such respectable sources as the *Commonwealth*, the *Worcester Spy*, and Theodore Parker.[80]

Distrust of the Irish at once encouraged and was stimulated by attacks upon Catholics. Hatred and violence marched arm in arm, sustaining and strengthening each other. Early in 1853, the purported kidnapping of Hannah Corcoran, a Baptist convert, almost led to a riot. In the same year the city government entered into a long-drawn-out controversy with the Catholics over their right to build a church on the "Jail lands." In May, 1854, John S. Orr, the Angel Gabriel, led a mob that carried away a cross from the Catholic Church in Chelsea, and in July a church was blown up in Dorchester. *The Wide Awake: and the Spirit of Washington*, a vituperative sheet, appeared in October, 1854, to combat the "swarms of lazaroni from abroad"; and a venomous stream of anti-Papist literature reached Boston, particularly in the form of Frothingham's convent novels (1854).[81]

Meanwhile, as slavery absorbed the attention of Congress and the country, excited Free-Soilers found "every indication that the people are awakening from their unaccountable stupor on the . . . question."[82] The Kansas-Nebraska Bill infuriated even Everett and the conservative

79 Cf. *Boston Pilot*, June 3, 1854; *Irish-American*, September 23, 1854; Billington, *op. cit.*, 435, n. 81; Bean, *op. cit.*, 187, 239, 241.

80 Cf. Bean, *loc. cit.*, 239 ff.; Carl Wittke, *We Who Built America* . . . (New York, 1939), 168.

81 *Boston Pilot*, April 9, December 10, 1853, May 13, 1854, January 20, 1855; *Wide Awake: and the Spirit of Washington* (Boston), October 7, 1854; Billington, *op. cit.*, 305–13, 348 ff., 368; Bean, *op. cit.*, 207, 209; Shea, *op. cit.*, IV, 509; Charles W. Frothingham, *Six Hours in a Convent:—or—The Stolen Nuns!* . . . (Boston, 1855).

82 Albert G. Browne to Sumner, July 28, 1854, Sumner Correspondence (MSS., H. C. L.), XXV, no. 109.

Webster Whigs. Sumner's correspondents informed him that "all parties seem to be approaching that happy state of . . . dissolution, for which we have sighed so long."[83] A Freedom party tentatively formed in Boston, a "Republican" convention adopted a radical program, and a host of excited energies eagerly sought an outlet. Precisely where the immense anti-slavery impulse would be exerted was uncertain, however.[84]

But the Boston municipal elections of December, 1853, had already revealed the ultimate outlet. Only one month after their decisive defeat on the constitution, the reformers rallied to resist the reelection of Nathaniel Seaver, a Whig supported by the liquor interests. As the "Citizens Union party," they appealed to nativist feelings and drew 2,000 Whig votes, the entire Free-Soil vote, and 500 voters who had not troubled to go to the polls a month earlier.[85] These 500 voters came from a tremendous fund of non-voting citizens, many of them Whigs disgusted with their party's vacillation.[86] The lesson to the reformers was obvious and was confirmed by simultaneous elections in Charlestown and Roxbury:[87] the Irish stood in the way of reform; reform forces could best be augmented and galvanized on an anti-Irish basis; the dormant voters must be awakened by an anti-alien alarm.

By 1853 the Order of the Star-Spangled Banner, a nativist secret organization popularly known as the Know-Nothings, had emerged in New York State.[88] Early in 1854 it spread into Massachusetts, swiftly, though quietly and unobtrusively, drawing "into its lodges tens of thousand of . . . anti-Nebraska men, ripe for Republicanism. . . ."[89] These recruits, inwardly ashamed of adopting means incompatible with the principles they professed, wrapped themselves in mantles of secrecy which served as a "spiritual fist-law" for gaining ascendancy without the use of force, and pursued their "purposes with the same disregard of the purposes of the structure external to . . . [themselves] which in the case of the individual is called egoism."[90]

In July, Henry Wilson, already a member, began to harness Know-

[83] Seth Webb, Jr., July 14, 1854, *ibid.*, XXV, no. 72; also Bean, *op. cit.*, 188 ff.

[84] Cf. Amasa Walker to Sumner, Sumner Correspondence, July 2, 1854, XXV, no. 15; Bean, *op. cit.*, 193; Merriam, *op. cit.*, I, 122.

[85] Cf. *Boston Semi-Weekly Advertiser*, December 10, 1853.

BOSTON ELECTIONS, 1853

GOVERNOR	(Nov.)	MAYOR	(Dec.)
Whig	7,730	Whig	5,651
Free-Soil	1,403	Citizens Union	4,691
Coalition Democrat	2,455	Young Men's League	2,010
Hunker Democrat	821	Democrat	596
Total	12,409	Total	12,948

(*Boston Semi-Weekly Advertiser*, November 16, December 14, 1853.)

[86] Cf. Darling, *op. cit.*, 290.

[87] Cf. Bean, *op. cit.*, 246.

[88] Cf. Billington, *op. cit.*, 380; Bean, *op. cit.*, 226; Desmond, *op. cit.*, 66; Scisco, *op. cit.*, 63 ff., 71 ff.

[89] Pearson, *op. cit.*, I, 65.

[90] Cf. Georg Simmel, "Sociology of Secrecy and of Secret Societies," *American Journal of Sociology*, XI (1906), 446 ff., 489.

Nothingism to the anti-slavery cause, and Seth Webb, Jr., decided, "Know-Nothingism is to be an important, perhaps the controlling, element in our state election; it will probably take us out of the hands of the Whigs. Into whose hands it will put us, nobody can tell."[91] The Know-Nothings presented the clearest platform in the next election. Without the support of the intellectual fronts of reform—Adams, Phillips, and Sumner—who felt no ends justified nativist methods, they elected Henry J. Gardner, formerly president of the Boston Common Council, to the governorship by the unprecedented majority of 33,000, and gained complete control of the legislature in November. Until 1857, they ruled the state.[92]

Everywhere the success of the party rested upon thousands of new men drawn into politics by nativism.[93] The complexion of the new legislators reflected the ranks from which they rose. Among them were no politicians, and few lawyers. They were true representatives of those for whom they spoke. They included a few rascals and self-seekers; but by and large they were honest men, convinced that they were acting in the best interests of the community. Even the Democratic editor of the *Post* had to admit later that "the moral tone of the party was unquestioned. . . ."[94] Many did not even feel a personal antagonism to the Irish; J. V. C. Smith, an amateur sculptor, and Know-Nothing mayor in 1854, associated with them in business and executed a fine bust of Bishop Fitzpatrick.[95]

Although the Know-Nothings made numerous mistakes, their administration was progressive and fruitful. They relaid the basis for the school system, abolished imprisonment for debt, established the first insurance commission, took the first steps to eliminate danger from railroad

[91] Webb to Sumner, July 14, 1854, Sumner Correspondence, XXV, no. 72; cf. also Wilson to Sumner, July 2, 1854, *ibid.*, XXV, no. 12; Bean, *op. cit.*, 192; Harry J. Carman and R. H. Luthin, "Some Aspects of the Know-Nothing Movement Reconsidered," *South Atlantic Quarterly*, XXXIX (1940), 221.

[92] Roe, *loc. cit.*, 653; Haynes, *loc. cit.*, 68; Bean, *op. cit.*, 259 ff.; George H. Haynes, "Know-Nothing Legislature," *New England Magazine*, XVI (1897), 21, 22.

[93] Robinson, *op. cit.*, 219. In Boston, 1,101 voters who had not gone to the polls in 1853 cast their ballots for the Know-Nothings together with the whole coalition reform vote, and almost half the Whig vote.

GUBERNATORIAL VOTES IN BOSTON

	1853	1854
Whig	7,730	4,196
Know-Nothing	...	7,661
Free-Soil	1,403	401
Democrat	2,455	1,252
Hunker Democrat	821	...
	12,409	13,510

(*Boston Atlas*, November 14, 1854; *Boston Semi-Weekly Advertiser*, November 16, 1853.)

[94] Benjamin P. Shillaber, "Experiences During Many Years," *New England Magazine*, VIII (1893), 722; George H. Haynes, "Know-Nothing Legislature," *Annual Report of the American Historical Association . . . 1896* (Washington, 1897), I, 178 ff.; Roe, *loc. cit.*, 654.

[95] State Street Trust Company, *Mayors of Boston*, 23.

crossings, extended the power of juries, strengthened the temperance, homestead and women's rights laws, made vaccination compulsory, and assumed a firm anti-slavery position by passing a personal liberty law and petitioning for the removal of Judge Loring, who had presided at the fugitive slave cases. In general, they embodied in their legislation the program of the party of reform. By 1855, they had sent Wilson to the United States Senate, amended the constitution so that a plurality sufficed in the gubernatorial election, and introduced many other innovations vetoed by the more conservative governor.[96]

The party's anti-foreign accomplishments were quite insignificant. To begin with, they disclaimed any intention of excluding immigrants, but stressed the necessity of making them "be as we are."[97] The most prominent achievement was the disbanding of the Irish military companies which annoyed natives particularly because they carried off prizes at drills. They served no useful purpose and in 1853 the *Boston Pilot* had itself suggested their dissolution. A breach of military discipline provided the pretext for the abolition of the Bay State Artillery in September, followed early the next year by the elimination of the remaining companies. Foreigners on the police force and in state agencies were discharged, and a number of cruel deportations displayed an ugly animus against helpless aliens. Finally, the misdeeds of individual members, notably of the Hiss Nunnery Committee, were exploited by the opposition and did much to discredit the party and obscure its constructive achievements.[98]

Ostensibly the party had acquired power to restrict the influence of immigrants in politics. Yet, though it had absolute control of the government, it failed to pass a single measure to that effect. In 1854, a bill to exclude paupers was not considered until the end of the session, and then referred to committee where it died. A literacy amendment to the constitution was rejected, and an amendment requiring a twenty-one-year residence for citizenship, which passed, was defeated at the second vote by the next Know-Nothing legislature.[99] Once reform, the essential feature of Know-Nothingism in Massachusetts, was assured, the party

96 Cf. Billington, *op. cit.*, 425; Robinson, *op. cit.*, 62, 209, 210; Bean, *op. cit.*, 166, 268, 272–77, 284, 286–88; Merriam, *op. cit.*, I, 126, 132 ff., 164; Haynes, "Know-Nothing Legislature," *Annual Report of the American Historical Association . . . 1896,* I, 180–84; Bean, *loc. cit.*, 322.

97 Bean, *op. cit.*, 261.

98 Cf. Dissertation Copy, 389; Desmond, *op. cit.*, 77; *Boston Pilot,* May 13, 1854, April 7, May 12, 1855; Abbott, *Immigration,* 160, 161; Billington, *op. cit.*, 414 ff.; Bean, *op. cit.*, 291 ff.; Shea, *op. cit.*, IV, 510.

99 Cf. *Debates and Proceedings in the Massachusetts Legislature . . . 1856, Reported for the Boston Daily Advertiser* (Boston, 1856), 141, 343, 348; Bean, *loc. cit.*, 322; Billington, *op. cit.*, 413. Most of these measures were sponsored by the purely nativist branch of the party, which declined in importance after 1854 and left the reformers in complete control (cf. Bean, *op. cit.*, 248). To those overlooking the concrete accomplishments of the 1854 legislature, the Free-Soilers under Wilson seemed to have "captured" the Know-Nothing organization in 1855 (cf., e.g., Haynes, "Causes of Know-Nothing Success," *loc. cit.*, III, 81). In fact, true nativists like Morse had so little sympathy for Massachusetts Know-Nothingism that they charged it was "a Jesuitical ruse, gotten up for the purpose of creating a sympathy in favor of the church" (Morse, *Foreign Conspiracy*, 31).

leaders attempted to jettison the anti-Catholic program. But the intolerance they had evoked could not readily be dispelled. Its influence persisted long after the death of the party it had served.

The Know-Nothings dissolved over the question of slavery, for the national party drew its strength from incompatible sources. In Massachusetts it was anti-slavery; elsewhere in the North it was unionist; in Virginia and throughout the South, it was pro-slavery.[100] Lack of a unified program inevitably split the party. Despite their strategic position in Congress, they could unite on few measures. Finally, when the national convention adopted a pro-slavery plank in June, 1855, the Northerners under Henry Wilson bolted and the Massachusetts Council on August 7 adopted an uncompromising liberal position. At the same time a section of the party broke away and met at Worcester in June, called itself the Know-Somethings or American Freemen, and advocated an abolition platform and an end to secrecy.

The nomination of Fillmore, a pro-slavery man, in 1856, completed the break between the state and national parties and a *de facto* coalition with the rising Republican party spontaneously formed. The latter nominated no candidate to oppose Gardner for the governorship, and most Know-Nothings voted for Frémont.[101] Thereafter the Know-Nothings in the state were absorbed in the tremendous growth of the new party, and Banks led the remnants to the Republicans in 1857–58 on his election to the governorship.[102]

100 Cf. Bean, *loc. cit.*, 324 ff.; E. Merton Coulter, *William Brownlow . . .* (Chapel Hill, 1937), 124 ff.; Scisco, *op. cit.*, 137; Carman and Luthin, *loc. cit.*, 223.

101 Cf. Billington, *op. cit.*, 407 ff., 426; James Ford Rhodes, *History of the United States . . .* (New York, 1893), II, 89 ff.; Bean, *op. cit.*, 295–322, 339 ff.; Mann, *op. cit.*, 50; Scisco, *op. cit.*, 146 ff.; Wilson, *op. cit.*, II, 423 ff.; Merriam, *op. cit.*, I, 165, 173 ff.; cf. also Fred H. Harrington, "Frémont and the North Americans," *American Historical Review*, XLIV (1939), 842 ff.

VOTE IN BOSTON, 1856

PRESIDENTIAL		GUBERNATORIAL	
Frémont (R)	7,646	Gardner (KN)	7,513
Fillmore (KN)	4,320	Gordon (Fillmore KN)	7,511
Buchanan (D)	5,458	Bell (Whig)	1,449
	17,424	Beach (D)	5,392
			16,865

(*Boston Semi-Weekly Advertiser*, November 5, 1856.)

102 Cf. Fred H. Harrington, "Nathaniel Prentiss Banks . . . ," *New England Quarterly*, IX (1936), 645 ff. The "straight" American party nominated candidates in 1857 and 1858 but received a meager vote and then expired (Bean, *op. cit.*, 362–65). Gardner's personal popularity helped them in the former year but in the latter they received less than 2,000 votes.

VOTES FOR GOVERNOR IN BOSTON

	1857	1858
Republicans	4,224	6,298
Know-Nothings	4,130	1,899
Democrats	5,171	6,369
	13,525	14,566

(*Boston Semi-Weekly Advertiser*, November 4, 1857; *Boston Daily Courier*, November 3, 1858.)

Produced by the same reform impulse that fathered Know-Nothingism, the Republican party continued to express animosity towards the Irish, "their declared and uncompromising foe." The defeat of Frémont in 1856 was laid at the door of the Irish Catholics, and confirmed the party's hostility to them. In retaliation, it helped pass an amendment in 1857 making ability to read the state constitution in English and to write prerequisites to the right to vote; and in 1859, another, preventing foreigners from voting for two years after naturalization.[103]

Though the restrictive legislation affected all foreigners, the venom of intolerance was directed primarily against the Irish. Waning group consciousness among the non-Irish gave promise of quick acculturation, and similarities in economic condition, physical settlement, and intellectual outlook had left little room for disagreement. In fact, the Irish found all others united with the natives against them. A Negro was as reluctant to have an Irishman move into his street as any Yankee,[104] and though the Germans distrusted the Know-Nothings and resented the two-year amendment, liberal principles led them into the Republican party.[105]

Indirectly, the Know-Nothing movement revived Irish nationalism. In Boston, nationalist activities first assumed the guise of the Irish Emigrant Aid Society, whose innocuous title concealed a secret revolutionary club, ostensibly aimed at organizing a liberating invasion of Ireland. Though some hotheads spoke of chartering ships to transport an army of Irish-Americans across the Atlantic, most recognized the obvious futility of such efforts. By and large, they hoped to organize politically, to support anti-English parties in America, to prepare for the Anglo-American war that would free Ireland, and to mobilize support against Know-Nothingism.[106] That the last motive, presumably incidental, was in fact primary, was clear from the movement's exclusively American character: it had no counterpart in Ireland. While expanding rapidly throughout 1855, the organization had little ultimate success. The clergy opposed it, cautious prosecution of would-be liberators in Cincinnati checked its growth, and internal quarrels finally dissipated its strength.[107]

But failure did not end the quest for a fatherland. So long as the Irish were unaccepted in Boston, they looked back across the ocean. There was "always . . . some . . . machination to draw money from the pockets of the deluded lower order of Irish. . . ."[108] The Fenian

[103] Cf. Bean, *op. cit.*, 367–72; Bean, *loc. cit.*, 323; Charles Theo. Russell, *Disfranchisement of Paupers* . . . (Boston, 1878), 8; *Massachusetts House Documents, 1857*, no. 114; *ibid., 1859*, no. 34.

[104] Cf., e.g., the petition of the residents of Elm Street (Bean, *op. cit.*, 206).

[105] Cf. Ernest Bruncken, *German Political Refugees in the United States* . . . (s.l., 1904), 45 ff.

[106] Cf. the illuminating report of Consul Grattan to Crampton, Boston, November 23, 1855, British Embassy Archives, F.O. 115/160; also Rowcroft to Crampton, November 12, 1855, *ibid.*, F.O. 115/160.

[107] Cf. Grattan to Crampton, January 21, 1856, *ibid.*, F.O. 115/172; Grattan to Crampton, March 4, 1856, *ibid.*, F.O. 115/172; Abbott, *Historical Aspects*, 475, 476; *Citizen* (New York), August 25, 1855, February 9, 1856.

[108] Lousada to Russell, September 8, 1864, British Consular Correspondence, F.O. 5/973.

Brotherhood emerged after 1859 and despite ecclesiastical disapproval grew in secret until it held its first national convention in Chicago in 1863. Its "centres" in Boston were numerous and active.[109]

Moreover, the Irish persisted in their opposition to reform. With Brownson, they believed Know-Nothingism "an imported combination of Irish Orangism, German radicalism, French Socialism and Italian . . . hate" and regarded Republicanism as its pernicious successor.[110] After 1856 they consistently supported the conservative Democratic party, voting for Buchanan and Douglas.[111] Although the violent phase had passed, the bitterness of conflict and antagonism remained. Out of it had grown a confirmed definition of racial particularism: the Irish were a different group, Celtic by origin, as distinguished from the "true" Americans, who were Anglo-Saxon, of course.[112] Once aroused, hatred could not be turned off at the will of those who had provoked it. The *Springfield Republican* sanely pointed out that "the American party, starting upon a basis of truth . . . has gone on, until [it] . . . denies to an Irishman . . . any position but that of a nuisance. . . ."[113] Group conflict left a permanent scar that disfigured the complexion of Boston social life even after the malignant growth producing it had disappeared.

[109] Cf. Jeremiah O'Donovan-Rossa, *Rossa's Recollections* . . . (Mariner's Harbor, N.Y., 1898), 271, 272, 381; "Proceedings . . . ," British Consular Correspondence, F.O. 5/973; E. Wells to Lousada, *ibid.*, F.O. 5/973; *Boston Pilot,* November 21, 1863.

[110] Cf. Bean, *op. cit.*, 257.

[111] Cf. references to *Irish-American* and *Boston Pilot,* 1856–1860, Dissertation Copy, 397, ns. 301–03; *Boston Pilot,* November 3, 1860; *Boston Post,* November 7, 1860.

[112] Cf., e.g., "The Anglo-Saxon Race," *North American Review,* LXXIII (1851), 34 ff., 53.

[113] *Springfield Daily Republican,* July 10, 1857.

The Cult of True Womanhood: 1820-1860

BARBARA WELTER

The decades before the Civil War resounded with the cry of reform. Hardly any institution in American life escaped the scrutiny of some group determined to change it. There were campaigns for the abolition of slavery, for penal reform, for better care of the insane, for temperance, for communal living, for industrial socialism, and for many other schemes to improve the status quo. Not the least of these was a campaign for women's rights led by such impressive figures as Elizabeth Cady Stanton, Frances Wright, and the Grimke sisters.

As we saw earlier, women had always been a valuable commodity in colonial America. In seventeenth-century Virginia, wives were actually sold by the Virginia Company, which transported young women from England and exchanged them for one hundred and fifty pounds of good tobacco. Once obtained such a wife was kept hard at work according to her husband's needs.

As long as American society was primarily agricultural, there was a fairly clear-cut distinction between the functions of men and women. Most of the woman's time was taken up with housework and child-rearing. When she had time, she joined the men in the fields, where there was always plenty of labor for both sexes.

With urban society, however, came challenges to the traditional division of labor between the sexes. As industrialization proceeded and the income of factory workers dropped, it became necessary for some women to leave the home to take factory jobs alongside their husbands. Thus, instead of finding themselves with more free time as a result of increasing mechanization, they found themselves working at two full-time jobs—as factory operative and housewife. "Woman's work" of caring for the home had by this time acquired a taboo for most men, and a double standard of behavior that bore no relation to the actual circumstances of society or the differences between the sexes was fast taking root.

For the growing ranks of middle-class women, however, the Industrial Revolution brought an increase in leisure time. These women did not have to work outside the home, and the multiplication of labor-saving household devices, coupled with the availability of household servants as a result of recent immigration, freed them considerably for new interests and activities. It was this newly leisured class of women that produced most of the members of the ante-bellum women's rights movement. In fact, many of the leaders of this campaign were women who had become interested in the anti-slavery movement but found themselves excluded from active participation in it merely on the basis of their sex.

In the following study, Barbara Welter, of Hunter College, describes the ideal of "True Womanhood" that was exalted in the popular literature of the day—partly as a reaction against the rising ambitions of many middle-class women. This literature, which stressed the desirability of such "feminine" traits as submissiveness and domesticity, ran decidedly counter to the movement for women's rights. Apparently, the literature enjoyed a wider and more influential audience than did the feminists.

The nineteenth-century American man was a busy builder of bridges and railroads, at work long hours in a materialistic society. The religious values of his forebears were neglected in practice if not in intent, and he occasionally felt some guilt that he had turned this new land, this temple of the chosen people, into one vast countinghouse. But he could salve his conscience by reflecting that he had left behind a hostage, not only to fortune, but to all the values which he held so dear and treated so lightly. Woman, in the cult of True Womanhood[1] presented by the women's

[1] Authors who addressed themselves to the subject of women in the mid-nineteenth century used this phrase as frequently as writers on religion mentioned God. Neither group felt it necessary to define their favorite terms; they simply assumed—with some justification—that readers would intuitively understand exactly what they meant. Frequently what people of one era take for granted is most striking and revealing to the student from another. In a sense this analysis of the ideal woman of the mid-nineteenth century is an examination of what writers of that period actually meant when they used so confidently the vague phrase True Womanhood.

"The Cult of True Womanhood: 1820–1860," by Barbara Welter. From *American Quarterly*, XVIII (Summer 1966), 151–74.

magazines, gift annuals and religious literature of the nineteenth century, was the hostage in the home.[2] In a society where values changed frequently, where fortunes rose and fell with frightening rapidity, where social and economic mobility provided instability as well as hope, one thing at least remained the same—a true woman was a true woman, wherever she was found. If anyone, male or female, dared to tamper with the complex of virtues which made up True Womanhood, he was damned immediately as an enemy of God, of civilization, and of the Republic. It was a fearful obligation, a solemn responsibility, which the nineteenth-century American woman had—to uphold the pillars of the temple with her frail white hand.

The attributes of True Womanhood, by which a woman judged herself and was judged by her husband, her neighbors and society, could be divided into four cardinal virtues—piety, purity, submissiveness and domesticity. Put them all together and they spelled mother, daughter, sister, wife—woman. Without them, no matter whether there was fame, achievement or wealth, all was ashes. With them she was promised happiness and power.

Religion or piety was the core of woman's virtue, the source of her strength. Young men looking for a mate were cautioned to search first for piety, for if that were there, all else would follow.[3] Religion belonged to woman by divine right, a gift of God and nature. This "peculiar susceptibility" to religion was given her for a reason: "the vestal flame of piety, lighted up by Heaven in the breast of woman" would throw its beams into the naughty world of men.[4] So far would its candle power reach that the "Universe might be Enlightened, Improved, and Harmo-

[2] The conclusions reached in this article are based on a survey of almost all of the women's magazines published for more than three years during the period 1820–60 and a sampling of those published for less than three years; all the gift books cited in Ralph Thompson, *American Literary Annuals and Gift Books, 1825–1865* (New York, 1936), deposited in the Library of Congress, the New York Public Library, the New-York Historical Society, Columbia University Special Collections, Library of the City College of the University of New York, Pennsylvania Historical Society, Massachusetts Historical Society, Boston Public Library, Fruitlands Museum Library, the Smithsonian Institution and the Wisconsin Historical Society; hundreds of religious tracts and sermons in the American Unitarian Society and the Galatea Collection of the Boston Public Library; and the large collection of nineteenth-century cookbooks in the New York Public Library and the Academy of Medicine of New York. Corroborative evidence not cited in this article was found in women's diaries, memoirs, autobiographies and personal papers, as well as in all the novels by women which sold over 75,000 copies during this period, as cited in Frank Luther Mott, *Golden Multitudes: The Story of Best Sellers in the United States* (New York, 1947), and H. R. Brown, *The Sentimental Novel in America, 1789–1860* (Durham, N.C., 1940). This latter information also indicated the effect of the cult of True Womanhood on those most directly concerned.

[3] As in "The Bachelor's Dream," in *The Lady's Gift: Souvenir for All Seasons* (Nashua, N.H., 1849), p. 37.

[4] *The Young Ladies' Class Book: A Selection of Lessons for Reading in Prose and Verse*, ed. Ebenezer Bailey, Principal of Young Ladies' High School, Boston (Boston, 1831), p. 168.

nized by WOMAN!!"[5] She would be another, better Eve, working in cooperation with the Redeemer, bringing the world back "from its revolt and sin."[6] The world would be reclaimed for God through her suffering, for "God increased the cares and sorrows of woman, that she might be sooner constrained to accept the terms of salvation."[7] A popular poem by Mrs. Frances Osgood, "The Triumph of the Spiritual over the Sensual," expressed just this sentiment, woman's purifying passionless love bringing an erring man back to Christ.[8]

Dr. Charles Meigs, explaining to a graduating class of medical students why women were naturally religious, said that "hers is a pious mind. Her confiding nature leads her more readily than men to accept the proffered grace of the Gospel."[9] Caleb Atwater, Esq., writing in *The Ladies' Repository*, saw the hand of the Lord in female piety: "Religion is exactly what a woman needs, for it gives her that dignity that best suits her dependence."[10] And Mrs. John Sandford, who had no very high opinion of her sex, agreed thoroughly: "Religion is just what woman needs. Without it she is ever restless or unhappy. . . ."[11] Mrs. Sandford and the others did not speak only of that restlessness of the human heart, which St. Augustine notes, that can only find its peace in God. They spoke rather of religion as a kind of tranquilizer for the many undefined longings which swept even the most pious young girl, and about which it was better to pray than to think.

One reason religion was valued was that it did not take a woman away from her "proper sphere," her home. Unlike participation in other societies or movements, church work would not make her less domestic or submissive, less a True Woman. In religious vineyards, said the *Young Ladies' Literary and Missionary Report*, "you may labor without the apprehension of detracting from the charms of feminine delicacy." Mrs. S. L. Dagg, writing from her chapter of the Society in Tuscaloosa, Alabama, was equally reassuring: "As no sensible woman will suffer her intellectual pursuits to clash with her domestic duties" she should concentrate on religious work "which promotes these very duties."[12]

[5] A Lady of Philadelphia, *The World Enlightened, Improved, and Harmonized by* WOMAN!! A lecture, delivered in the City of New York, before the Young Ladies' Society for Mutual Improvement, on the following question, proposed by the society, with the offer of $100 for the best lecture that should be read before them on the subject proposed:—What is the power and influence of woman in moulding the manners, morals and habits of civil society? (Philadelphia, 1840), p. 1.

[6] *The Young Lady's Book: A Manual of Elegant Recreations, Exercises, and Pursuits* (Boston, 1830), p. 29.

[7] *Woman as She Was, Is, and Should Be* (New York, 1849), p. 206.

[8] "The Triumph of the Spiritual over the Sensual: An Allegory," in *Ladies' Companion: A Monthly Magazine Embracing Every Department of Literature, Embellished with Original Engravings and Music* (New York), XVII (1842), 67.

[9] *Lecture on Some of the Distinctive Characteristics of the Female*, delivered before the class of the Jefferson Medical College, Jan. 1847 (Philadelphia, 1847), p. 13.

[10] "Female Education," *Ladies' Repository and Gatherings of the West: A Monthly Periodical Devoted to Literature and Religion*, I (Cincinnati), 12.

[11] *Woman, in Her Social and Domestic Character* (Boston, 1842), pp. 41–42.

[12] *Second Annual Report of the Young Ladies' Literary and Missionary Association of the Philadelphia Collegiate Institution* (Philadelphia, 1840), pp. 20, 26.

The women's seminaries aimed at aiding women to be religious, as well as accomplished. Mt. Holyoke's catalogue promised to make female education "a handmaid to the Gospel and an efficient auxiliary in the great task of renovating the world."[13] The Young Ladies' Seminary at Bordentown, New Jersey, declared its most important function to be "the forming of a sound and virtuous character."[14] In Keene, New Hampshire, the Seminary tried to instill a "consistent and useful character" in its students, to enable them in this life to be "a good friend, wife and mother," but more important, to qualify them for "the enjoyment of Celestial Happiness in the life to come."[15] And Joseph M'D. Mathews, Principal of Oakland Female Seminary in Hillsborough, Ohio, believed that "female education should be preeminently religious."[16]

If religion was so vital to a woman, irreligion was almost too awful to contemplate. Women were warned not to let their literary or intellectual pursuits take them away from God. Sarah Josepha Hale spoke darkly of those who, like Margaret Fuller, threw away the "One True Book" for others, open to error. Mrs. Hale used the unfortunate Miss Fuller as fateful proof that "the greater the intellectual force, the greater and more fatal the errors into which women fall who wander from the Rock of Salvation, Christ the Saviour. . . ."[17]

One gentleman, writing on "Female Irreligion," reminded his readers that "man may make himself a brute, and does so very often, but can woman brutify herself to his level—the lowest level of human nature—without exerting special wonder?" Fanny Wright, because she was godless, "was no woman, mother though she be." A few years ago, he recalls, such women would have been whipped. In any case, "woman never looks lovelier than in her reverence for religion" and, conversely, "female irreligion is the most revolting feature in human character."[18]

Purity was as essential as piety to a young woman, its absence as unnatural and unfeminine. Without it she was, in fact, no woman at all, but a member of some lower order. A "fallen woman" was a "fallen angel," unworthy of the celestial company of her sex. To contemplate the loss of purity brought tears; to be guilty of such a crime, in the women's magazines at least, brought madness or death. Even the language of the flowers had bitter words for it: a dried white rose symbolized "Death Preferable to Loss of Innocence."[19] The marriage night was the single

13 *Mt. Holyoke Female Seminary: Female Education. Tendencies of the Principles Embraced, and the System Adopted in the Mt. Holyoke Female Seminary* (Boston, 1839), p. 3.

14 *Prospectus of the Young Ladies' Seminary at Bordentown, New Jersey* (Bordentown, 1836), p. 7.

15 *Catalogue of the Young Ladies' Seminary in Keene, New Hampshire* (n.p., 1832), p. 20.

16 "Report to the College of Teachers, Cincinnati, October, 1840" in *Ladies' Repository*, I (1841), 50.

17 *Woman's Record: or Sketches of All Distinguished Women from "The Beginning" Till A.D. 1850* (New York, 1853), pp. 665, 669.

18 "Female Irreligion," *Ladies' Companion*, XIII (May–Oct. 1840), 111.

19 *The Lady's Book of Flowers and Poetry*, ed. Lucy Hooper (New York, 1842), has a "Floral Dictionary" giving the symbolic meaning of floral tributes.

great event of a woman's life, when she bestowed her greatest treasure upon her husband, and from that time on was completely dependent upon him, an empty vessel,[20] without legal or emotional existence of her own.[21]

Therefore all True Women were urged, in the strongest possible terms, to maintain their virtue, although men, being by nature more sensual than they, would try to assault it. Thomas Branagan admitted in *The Excellency of the Female Character Vindicated* that his sex would sin and sin again, they could not help it, but woman, stronger and purer, must not give in and let man "take liberties incompatible with her delicacy." "If you do," Branagan addressed his gentle reader, "you will be left in silent sadness to bewail your credulity, imbecility, duplicity, and premature prostitution."[22]

Mrs. Eliza Farrar, in *The Young Lady's Friend*, gave practical logistics to avoid trouble: "Sit not with another in a place that is too narrow; read not out of the same book; let not your eagerness to see anything induce you to place your head close to another person's."[23]

If such good advice was ignored the consequences were terrible and inexorable. In *Girlhood and Womanhood: or, Sketches of My Schoolmates*, by Mrs. A. J. Graves (a kind of mid-nineteenth-century *The Group*), the bad ends of a boarding school class of girls are scrupulously recorded. The worst end of all is reserved for "Amelia Dorrington: The Lost One." Amelia died in the almshouse "the wretched victim of depravity and intemperance" and all because her mother had let her be "high-spirited not prudent." These girlish high spirits had been misinterpreted by a young man, with disastrous results. Amelia's "thoughtless levity" was "followed by a total loss of virtuous principle" and Mrs. Graves editorializes that "the coldest reserve is more admirable in a woman a man wishes to make his wife, than the least approach to undue familiarity."[24]

A popular and often reprinted story by Fanny Forester told the sad tale of "Lucy Dutton." Lucy "with the seal of innocence upon her heart, and a rose-leaf on her cheek" came out of her vine-covered cottage and ran into a city slicker. "And Lucy was beautiful and trusting, and thoughtless: and he was gay, selfish and profligate. Needs the story to be

[20] See, for example, Nathaniel Hawthorne, *The Blithedale Romance* (Boston, 1852), p. 71, in which Zenobia says: "How can she be happy, after discovering that fate has assigned her but one single event, which she must contrive to make the substance of her whole life? A man has his choice of innumerable events."

[21] Mary R. Beard, *Woman as Force in History* (New York, 1946), makes this point at some length. According to common law, a woman had no legal existence once she was married and therefore could not manage property, sue in court, etc. In the 1840s and 1850s laws were passed in several states to remedy this condition.

[22] *Excellency of the Female Character Vindicated: Being an Investigation Relative to the Cause and Effects on the Encroachments of Men upon the Rights of Women, and the Too Frequent Degradation and Consequent Misfortunes of the Fair Sex* (New York, 1807), pp. 277, 278.

[23] By a Lady (Eliza Ware Rotch Farrar), *The Young Lady's Friend* (Boston, 1837), p. 293.

[24] *Girlhood and Womanhood: or, Sketches of My Schoolmates* (Boston, 1844), p. 140.

told? . . . Nay, censor, Lucy was a child—consider how young, how very untaught—oh! her innocence was no match for the sophistry of a gay, city youth! Spring came and shame was stamped upon the cottage at the foot of the hill." The baby died; Lucy went mad at the funeral and finally died herself. "Poor, poor Lucy Dutton! The grave is a blessed couch and pillow to the wretched. Rest thee there, poor Lucy!"[25] The frequency with which derangement follows loss of virtue suggests the exquisite sensibility of woman, and the possibility that, in the women's magazines at least, her intellect was geared to her hymen, not her brain.

If, however, a woman managed to withstand man's assaults on her virtue, she demonstrated her superiority and her power over him. Eliza Farnham, trying to prove this female superiority, concluded smugly that "the purity of women is the everlasting barrier against which the tides of man's sensual nature surge."[26]

A story in *The Lady's Amaranth* illustrates this dominance. It is set, improbably, in Sicily, where two lovers, Bianca and Tebaldo, have been separated because her family insisted she marry a rich old man. By some strange circumstance the two are in a shipwreck and cast on a desert island, the only survivors. Even here, however, the rigid standards of True Womanhood prevail. Tebaldo unfortunately forgets himself slightly, so that Bianca must warn him: "We may not indeed gratify our fondness by caresses, but it is still something to bestow our kindest language, and looks and prayers, and all lawful and honest attentions on each other." Something, perhaps, but not enough, and Bianca must further remonstrate: "It is true that another man is my husband, but you are my guardian angel." When even that does not work she says in a voice of sweet reason, passive and proper to the end, that she wishes he wouldn't but "still, if you insist, I will become what you wish; but I beseech you to consider, ere that decision, that debasement which I must suffer in your esteem." This appeal to his own double standards holds the beast in him at bay. They are rescued, discover that the old husband is dead, and after "mourning a decent season" Bianca finally gives in, legally.[27]

Men could be counted on to be grateful when women thus saved them from themselves. William Alcott, guiding young men in their relations with the opposite sex, told them that "nothing is better calculated to preserve a young man from contamination of low pleasures and pursuits than frequent intercourse with the more refined and virtuous of the other sex." And he added, one assumes in equal innocence, that youths should "observe and learn to admire, that purity and ignorance of evil which is the characteristic of well-educated young ladies, and which, when we are near them, raises us above those sordid and sensual considerations which hold such sway over men in their intercourse with each other."[28]

[25] Emily Chubbuck, *Alderbook* (2nd. ed.; Boston, 1847), II, 121, 127.

[26] *Woman and Her Era* (New York, 1864), p. 95.

[27] "The Two Lovers of Sicily," *The Lady's Amaranth: A Journal of Tales, Essays, Excerpts—Historical and Biographical Sketches, Poetry and Literature in General* (Philadelphia), II (Jan. 1839), 17.

[28] *The Young Man's Guide* (Boston, 1833), pp. 229, 231.

The Rev. Jonathan F. Stearns was also impressed by female chastity in the face of male passion, and warned woman never to compromise the source of her power: "Let her lay aside delicacy, and her influence over our sex is gone."[29]

Women themselves accepted, with pride but suitable modesty, this priceless virtue. *The Ladies' Wreath*, in "Woman the Creature of God and the Manufacturer of Society," saw purity as her greatest gift and chief means of discharging her duty to save the world: "Purity is the highest beauty—the true pole-star which is to guide humanity aright in its long, varied, and perilous voyage."[30]

Sometimes, however, a woman did not see the dangers to her treasure. In that case, they must be pointed out to her, usually by a male. In the nineteenth century any form of social change was tantamount to an attack on woman's virtue, if only it was correctly understood. For example, dress reform seemed innocuous enough and the bloomers worn by the lady of that name and her followers were certainly modest attire. Such was the reasoning only of the ignorant. In another issue of *The Ladies' Wreath* a young lady is represented in dialogue with her "Professor." The girl expresses admiration for the bloomer costume—it gives freedom of motion, is healthful and attractive. The "Professor" sets her straight. Trousers, he explains, are "only one of the many manifestations of that wild spirit of socialism and agrarian radicalism which is at present so rife in our land." The young lady recants immediately: "If this dress has any connexion with Fourierism or socialism, or fanaticism in any shape whatever, I have no disposition to wear it at all . . . no true woman would so far compromise her delicacy as to espouse, however unwittingly, such a cause."[31]

America could boast that her daughters were particularly innocent. In a poem on "The American Girl" the author wrote proudly:

> Her eye of light is the diamond bright,
> Her innocence the pearl,
> And these are ever the bridal gems
> That are worn by the American girl.[32]

Lydia Maria Child, giving advice to mothers, aimed at preserving that spirit of innocence. She regretted that "want of confidence between mothers and daughters on delicate subjects" and suggested a woman tell her daughter a few facts when she reached the age of twelve to "set her

29 *Female Influence: and the True Christian Mode of Its Exercise; a Discourse Delivered in the First Presbyterian Church in Newburyport, July 30, 1837* (Newburyport, 1837), p. 18.

30 W. Tolles, "Woman the Creature of God and the Manufacturer of Society," *Ladies' Wreath* (New York), III (1852), 205.

31 Prof. William M. Heim, "The Bloomer Dress," *Ladies' Wreath*, III (1852), 247.

32 *The Young Lady's Offering: or Gems of Prose and Poetry* (Boston, 1853), p. 283. The American girl, whose innocence was often connected with ignorance, was the spiritual ancestress of the Henry James heroine. Daisy Miller, like Lucy Dutton, saw innocence lead to tragedy.

mind at rest." Then Mrs. Child confidently hoped that a young lady's "instinctive modesty" would "prevent her from dwelling on the information until she was called upon to use it."[33] In the same vein, a book of advice to the newly married was titled *Whisper to a Bride*.[34] As far as intimate information was concerned, there was no need to whisper, since the book contained none at all.

A masculine summary of this virtue was expressed in a poem, "Female Charms":

> I would have her as pure as the snow on the mount—
> As true as the smile that to infamy's given—
> As pure as the wave of the crystalline fount,
> Yet as warm in the heart as the sunlight of heaven.
> With a mind cultivated, not boastingly wise,
> I could gaze on such beauty, with exquisite bliss;
> With her heart on her lips and her soul in her eyes—
> What more could I wish in dear woman than this.[35]

Man might, in fact, ask no more than this in woman, but she was beginning to ask more of herself, and in the asking was threatening the third powerful and necessary virtue, submission. Purity, considered as a moral imperative, set up a dilemma which was hard to resolve. Woman must preserve her virtue until marriage and marriage was necessary for her happiness. Yet marriage was, literally, an end to innocence. She was told not to question this dilemma, but simply to accept it.

Submission was perhaps the most feminine virtue expected of women. Men were supposed to be religious, although they rarely had time for it, and supposed to be pure, although it came awfully hard to them, but men were the movers, the doers, the actors. Women were the passive, submissive responders. The order of dialogue was, of course, fixed in Heaven. Man was "woman's superior by God's appointment, if not in intellectual dowry, at least by official decree." Therefore, as Charles Elliott argued in *The Ladies' Repository*, she should submit to him "for the sake of good order at least."[36] In *The Ladies' Companion* a young wife was quoted approvingly as saying that she did not think woman should "feel and act for herself" because "when, next to God, her husband is not the tribunal to which her heart and intellect appeals—the golden bowl of affection is broken."[37] Women were warned that if they tampered with this quality they tampered with the order of the Universe.

The Young Lady's Book summarized the necessity of the passive vir-

[33] *The Mother's Book* (Boston, 1831), pp. 151, 152.

[34] Mrs. L. H. Sigourney, *Whisper to a Bride* (Hartford, 1851), in which Mrs. Sigourney's approach is summed up in this quotation: "Home! Blessed bride, thou art about to enter this sanctuary, and to become a priestess at its altar!," p. 44.

[35] S. R. R., "Female Charms," *Godey's Magazine and Lady's Book* (Philadelphia), XXXIII (1846), 52.

[36] Charles Elliott, "Arguing with Females," *Ladies' Repository*, I (1841), 25.

[37] *Ladies' Companion*, VIII (Jan. 1838), 147.

tues in its readers' lives: "It is, however, certain, that in whatever situation of life a woman is placed from her cradle to her grave, a spirit of obedience and submission, pliability of temper, and humility of mind, are required from her."[38]

Woman understood her position if she was the right kind of woman, a true woman. "She feels herself weak and timid. She needs a protector," declared George Burnap, in his lectures on *The Sphere and Duties of Woman*. "She is in a measure dependent. She asks for wisdom, constancy, firmness, perseverance, and she is willing to repay it all by the surrender of the full treasure of her affections. Woman despises in man every thing like herself except a tender heart. It is enough that she is effeminate and weak; she does not want another like herself."[39] Or put even more strongly by Mrs. Sandford: "A really sensible woman feels her dependence. She does what she can, but she is conscious of inferiority, and therefore grateful for support."[40]

Mrs. Sigourney, however, assured young ladies that although they were separate, they were equal. This difference of the sexes did not imply inferiority, for it was part of that same order of Nature established by Him "who bids the oak brave the fury of the tempest, and the alpine flower lean its cheek on the bosom of eternal snows."[41] Dr. Meigs had a different analogy to make the same point, contrasting the anatomy of the Apollo of the Belvedere (illustrating the male principle) with the Venus de Medici (illustrating the female principle). "Woman," said the physician, with a kind of clinical gallantry, "has a head almost too small for intellect but just big enough for love."[42]

This love itself was to be passive and responsive. "Love, in the heart of a woman," wrote Mrs. Farrar, "should partake largely of the nature of gratitude. She should love, because she is already loved by one deserving her regard."[43]

Woman was to work in silence, unseen, like Wordsworth's Lucy. Yet, "working like nature, in secret" her love goes forth to the world "to regulate its pulsation, and send forth from its heart, in pure and temperate flow, the life-giving current."[44] She was to work only for pure affection, without thought of money or ambition. A poem, "Woman and Fame," by Felicia Hemans, widely quoted in many of the gift books, concludes with a spirited renunciation of the gift of fame:

> Away! to me, a woman, bring
> Sweet flowers from affection's spring.[45]

[38] *The Young Lady's Book* (New York, 1830), American edition, p. 28. (This is a different book than the one of the same title and date of publication cited in note 6.)

[39] *Sphere and Duties of Woman* (5th ed.; Baltimore, 1854), p. 47.

[40] *Woman*, p. 15.

[41] *Letters to Young Ladies* (Hartford, 1835), p. 179.

[42] *Lecture*, p. 17.

[43] *The Young Lady's Friend*, p. 313.

[44] Maria J. McIntosh, *Woman in America: Her Work and Her Reward* (New York, 1850), p. 25.

[45] *Poems and a Memoir of the Life of Mrs. Felicia Hemans* (London, 1860), p. 16.

"True feminine genius," said Grace Greenwood (Sara Jane Clarke), "is ever timid, doubtful, and clingingly dependent; a perpetual childhood." And she advised literary ladies in an essay on "The Intellectual Woman"—"Don't trample on the flowers while longing for the stars."[46] A wife who submerged her own talents to work for her husband was extolled as an example of a true woman. In *Women of Worth: A Book for Girls*, Mrs. Ann Flaxman, an artist of promise herself, was praised because she "devoted herself to sustain her husband's genius and aid him in his arduous career."[47]

Caroline Gilman's advice to the bride aimed at establishing this proper order from the beginning of a marriage: "Oh, young and lovely bride, watch well the first moments when your will conflicts with his to whom God and society have given the control. Reverence his *wishes* even when you do not his *opinions*."[48]

Mrs. Gilman's perfect wife in *Recollections of a Southern Matron* realizes that "the three golden threads with which domestic happiness is woven" are "to repress a harsh answer, to confess a fault, and to stop (right or wrong) in the midst of self-defense, in gentle submission." Woman could do this, hard though it was, because in her heart she knew she was right and so could afford to be forgiving, even a trifle condescending. "Men are not unreasonable," averred Mrs. Gilman. "Their difficulties lie in not understanding the moral and physical nature of our sex. They often wound through ignorance, and are surprised at having offended." Wives were advised to do their best to reform men, but if they couldn't, to give up gracefully. "If any habit of his annoyed me, I spoke of it once or twice, calmly, then bore it quietly."[49]

A wife should occupy herself "only with domestic affairs—wait till your husband confides to you those of a high importance—and do not give your advice until he asks for it," advised *The Lady's Token*. At all times she should behave in a manner becoming a woman, who had "no arms other than gentleness." Thus "if he is abusive, never retort."[50] *A Young Lady's Guide to the Harmonious Development of a Christian Character* suggested that females should "become as little children" and "avoid a controversial spirit."[51] *The Mother's Assistant and Young Lady's Friend* listed "Always Conciliate" as its first commandment in "Rules for Conjugal and Domestic Happiness." Small wonder that these same rules ended with the succinct maxim: "Do not expect too much."[52]

[46] Letter "To an Unrecognized Poetess, June, 1846" (Sara Jane Clarke), *Greenwood Leaves* (2nd ed.; Boston, 1850), p. 311.

[47] "The Sculptor's Assistant: Ann Flaxman," in *Women of Worth: A Book for Girls* (New York, 1860), p. 263.

[48] Mrs. Clarissa Packard (Mrs. Caroline Howard Gilman), *Recollections of a Housekeeper* (New York, 1834), p. 122.

[49] *Recollections of a Southern Matron* (New York, 1838), pp. 256, 257.

[50] *The Lady's Token: or Gift of Friendship*, ed. Colesworth Pinckney (Nashua, N.H., 1848), p. 119.

[51] Harvey Newcomb, *Young Lady's Guide to the Harmonious Development of Christian Character* (Boston, 1846), p. 10.

[52] "Rules for Conjugal and Domestic Happiness," *Mother's Assistant and Young Lady's Friend* (Boston, III (April 1843), 115.

As mother, as well as wife, woman was required to submit to fortune. In *Letters to Mothers* Mrs. Sigourney sighed: "To bear the evils and sorrows which may be appointed us, with a patient mind, should be the continual effort of our sex. . . . It seems, indeed, to be expected of us; since the passive and enduring virtues are more immediately within our province." Of these trials "the hardest was to bear the loss of children with submission" but the indomitable Mrs. Sigourney found strength to murmur to the bereaved mother: "The Lord loveth a cheerful giver."[53] *The Ladies' Parlor Companion* agreed thoroughly in "A Submissive Mother," in which a mother who had already buried two children and was nursing a dying baby saw her sole remaining child "probably scalded to death. Handing over the infant to die in the arms of a friend, she bowed in sweet submission to the double stroke." But the child "through the goodness of God survived, and the mother learned to say 'Thy will be done.' "[54]

Woman then, in all her roles, accepted submission as her lot. It was a lot she had not chosen or deserved. As *Godey's* said, "The lesson of submission is forced upon woman." Without comment or criticism the writer affirms that "to suffer and to be silent under suffering seems the great command she has to obey."[55] George Burnap referred to a woman's life as "a series of suppressed emotions."[56] She was, as Emerson said, "more vulnerable, more infirm, more mortal than man."[57] The death of a beautiful woman, cherished in fiction, represented woman as the innocent victim, suffering without sin, too pure and good for this world but too weak and passive to resist its evil forces.[58] The best refuge for such a delicate creature was the warmth and safety of her home.

The true woman's place was unquestionably by her own fireside—as daughter, sister, but most of all as wife and mother. Therefore domesticity was among the virtues most prized by the women's magazines. "As society is constituted," wrote Mrs. S. E. Farley, in the "Domestic and Social Claims on Woman," "the true dignity and beauty of the female character seem to consist in a right understanding and faithful and cheerful performance of social and family duties."[59] Sacred Scripture reenforced social pressure: "St. Paul knew what was best for women when he

[53] *Letters to Mothers* (Hartford, 1838), p. 199. In the diaries and letters of women who lived during this period the death of a child seemed consistently to be the hardest thing for them to bear and to occasion more anguish and rebellion, as well as eventual submission, than any other event in their lives.

[54] "A Submissive Mother," *The Ladies' Parlor Companion: A Collection of Scattered Fragments and Literary Gems* (New York, 1852), p. 358.

[55] "Woman," *Godey's Lady's Book,* II (Aug. 1831), 110.

[56] *Sphere and Duties of Woman,* p. 172.

[57] Ralph Waldo Emerson, "Woman," *Complete Writings of Ralph Waldo Emerson* (New York, 1875), p. 1180.

[58] As in Donald Fraser, *The Mental Flower Garden* (New York, 1857). Perhaps the most famous exponent of this theory is Edgar Allan Poe, who affirms in "The Philosophy of Composition" that "the death of a beautiful woman is unquestionably the most poetical topic in the world. . . ."

[59] "Domestic and Social Claims on Woman," *Mother's Magazine,* VI (1846), 21.

advised them to be domestic," said Mrs. Sandford. "There is composure at home; there is something sedative in the duties which home involves. It affords security not only from the world, but from delusions and errors of every kind."[60]

From her home woman performed her great task of bringing men back to God. *The Young Ladies' Class Book* was sure that "the domestic fireside is the great guardian of society against the excesses of human passions."[61] *The Lady at Home* expressed its convictions in its very title and concluded that "even if we cannot reform the world in a moment, we can begin the work by reforming ourselves and our households–It is woman's mission. Let her not look away from our own little family circle for the means of producing moral and social reforms, but begin at home."[62]

Home was supposed to be a cheerful place, so that brothers, husbands and sons would not go elsewhere in search of a good time. Woman was expected to dispense comfort and cheer. In writing the biography of Margaret Mercer (every inch a true woman) her biographer (male) notes: "She never forgot that it is the peculiar province of woman to minister to the comfort, and promote the happiness, first, of those most nearly allied to her, and then of those, who by the Providence of God are placed in a state of dependence upon her."[63] Many other essays in the women's journals showed woman as comforter: "Woman, Man's Best Friend," "Woman, the Greatest Social Benefit," "Woman, a Being to Come Home To," "The Wife: Source of Comfort and the Spring of Joy."[64]

One of the most important functions of woman as comforter was her role as nurse. Her own health was probably, although regrettably, delicate.[65] Many homes had "little sufferers," those pale children who wasted

[60] *Woman*, p. 173.

[61] *The Young Ladies' Class Book*, p. 166.

[62] T. S. Arthur, *The Lady at Home: or, Leaves from the Every-Day Book of an American Woman* (Philadelphia, 1847), pp. 177, 178.

[63] Caspar Morris, *Margaret Mercer* (Boston, 1840), quoted in *Woman's Record*, p. 425.

[64] These particular titles come from: *The Young Ladies' Oasis: or Gems of Prose and Poetry*, ed. N. L. Ferguson (Lowell, 1851), pp. 14, 16; *The Genteel School Reader* (Philadelphia, 1849), p. 271; and *Magnolia*, I (1842), 4. A popular poem in book form, published in England, expressed very fully this concept of woman as comforter: Coventry Patmore, *The Angel in the Home* (Boston, 1856 and 1857). Patmore expressed his devotion to True Womanhood in such lines as:

> The gentle wife, who decks his board
> And makes his day to have no night,
> Whose wishes wait upon her Lord,
> Who finds her own in his delight. (p. 94)

[65] The women's magazines carried on a crusade against tight lacing and regretted, rather than encouraged, the prevalent ill health of the American woman. See, for example, *An American Mother, Hints and Sketches* (New York, 1839), pp. 28 ff., for an essay on the need for a healthy mind in a healthy body in order to better be a good example for children.

away to saintly deaths. And there were enough other illnesses of youth and age, major and minor, to give the nineteenth-century American woman nursing experience. The sickroom called for the exercise of her higher qualities of patience, mercy and gentleness as well as for her housewifely arts. She could thus fulfill her dual feminine function—beauty and usefulness.

The cookbooks of the period offer formulas for gout cordials, ointment for sore nipples, hiccough and cough remedies, opening pills and refreshing drinks for fever, along with recipes for pound cake, jumbles, stewed calf's head and currant wine.[66] *The Ladies' New Book of Cookery* believed that "food prepared by the kind hand of a wife, mother, sister, friend" tasted better and had a "restorative power which money cannot purchase."[67]

A chapter of *The Young Lady's Friend* was devoted to woman's privilege as "ministering spirit at the couch of the sick." Mrs. Farrar advised a soft voice, gentle and clean hands, and a cheerful smile. She also cautioned against an excess of female delicacy. That was all right for a young lady in the parlor, but not for bedside manners. Leeches, for example, were to be regarded as "a curious piece of mechanism . . . their ornamental stripes should recommend them even to the eye, and their valuable services to our feelings." And she went on calmly to discuss their use. Nor were women to shrink from medical terminology, since "if you cultivate right views of the wonderful structure of the body, you will be as willing to speak to a physician of the bowels as the brains of your patient."[68]

Nursing the sick, particularly sick males, not only made a woman feel useful and accomplished, but increased her influence. In a piece of heavy-handed humor in *Godey's* a man confessed that some women were only happy when their husbands were ailing that they might have the joy of nursing him to recovery, "thus gratifying their medical vanity and their love of power by making him more dependent upon them."[69] In a similar vein a husband sometimes suspected his wife "almost wishes me dead—for the pleasure of being utterly inconsolable."[70]

In the home women were not only the highest adornment of civilization, but they were supposed to keep busy at morally uplifting tasks.

[66] The best single collection of nineteenth-century cookbooks is in the Academy of Medicine of New York Library, although some of the most interesting cures were in handwritten cookbooks found among the papers of women who lived during the period.

[67] Sarah Josepha Hale, *The Ladies' New Book of Cookery: A Practical System for Private Families in Town and Country* (5th ed.; New York, 1852), p. 409. Similar evidence on the importance of nursing skills to every female is found in such books of advice as William A. Alcott, *The Young Housekeeper* (Boston, 1838), in which, along with a plea for apples and cold baths, Alcott says, "Every female should be trained to the angelic art of managing properly the sick," p. 47.

[68] *The Young Lady's Friend*, pp. 75–77, 79.

[69] "A Tender Wife," *Godey's*, II (July 1831), 28.

[70] "My Wife! A Whisper," *Godey's*, II (Oct. 1831), 231.

Fortunately most of housework, if looked at in true womanly fashion, could be regarded as uplifting. Mrs. Sigourney extolled its virtues: "The science of housekeeping affords exercise for the judgment and energy, ready recollection, and patient self-possession, that are the characteristics of a superior mind."[71] According to Mrs. Farrar, making beds was good exercise, the repetitiveness of routine tasks inculcated patience and perseverance, and proper management of the home was a surprisingly complex art: "There is more to be learned about pouring out tea and coffee, than most young ladies are willing to believe."[72] *Godey's* went so far as to suggest coyly, in "Learning vs. Housewifery," that the two were complementary, not opposed: chemistry could be utilized in cooking, geometry in dividing cloth, and phrenology in discovering talent in children.[73]

Women were to master every variety of needlework, for, as Mrs. Sigourney pointed out, "needle-work, in all its forms of use, elegance, and ornament, has ever been the appropriate occupation of woman."[74] Embroidery improved taste; knitting promoted serenity and economy.[75] Other forms of artsy-craftsy activity for her leisure moments included painting on glass or velvet, Poonah work, tussy-mussy frames for her own needlepoint or water colors, stands for hyacinths, hair bracelets or baskets of feathers.[76]

She was expected to have a special affinity for flowers. To the editors of *The Lady's Token*, "A Woman never appears more truly in her sphere, than when she divides her time between her domestic avocations and the culture of flowers."[77] She could write letters, an activity particularly feminine since it had to do with the outpourings of the heart,[78] or practice her drawingroom skills of singing and playing an instrument. She might even read.

Here she faced a bewildering array of advice. The female was dangerously addicted to novels, according to the literature of the period. She should avoid them, since they interfered with "serious piety." If she simply couldn't help herself and read them anyway, she should choose

[71] *Letters to Young Ladies*, p. 27. The greatest exponent of the mental and moral joys of housekeeping was the *Lady's Annual Register and Housewife's Memorandum Book* (Boston, 1838), which gave practical advice on ironing, hair curling, budgeting and marketing, and turning cuffs—all activities which contributed to the "beauty of usefulness" and "joy of accomplishment" which a woman desired (I, 23).

[72] *The Young Lady's Friend*, p. 230.

[73] "Learning vs. Housewifery," *Godey's*, X (Aug. 1839), 95.

[74] *Letters to Young Ladies*, p. 25. W. Thayer, *Life at the Fireside* (Boston, 1857), has an idyllic picture of the woman of the house mending her children's garments, the grandmother knitting and the little girl taking her first stitches, all in the light of the domestic hearth.

[75] "The Mirror's Advice," *Young Maiden's Mirror* (Boston, 1858), p. 263.

[76] Mrs. L. Maria Child, *The Girl's Own Book* (New York, 1833).

[77] *The Lady's Token*, p. 44.

[78] T. S. Arthur, *Advice to Young Ladies* (Boston, 1850), p. 45.

edifying ones from lists of morally acceptable authors. She should study history since it "showed the depravity of the human heart and the evil nature of sin." On the whole, "religious biography was best."[79]

The women's magazines themselves could be read without any loss of concern for the home. *Godey's* promised the husband that he would find his wife "no less assiduous for his reception, or less sincere in welcoming his return" as a result of reading their magazine.[80] *The Lily of the Valley* won its right to be admitted to the boudoir by confessing that it was "like its namesake humble and unostentatious, but it is yet pure, and, we trust, free from moral imperfections."[81]

No matter what later authorities claimed, the nineteenth century knew that girls *could* be ruined by a book. The seduction stories regard "exciting and dangerous books" as contributory causes of disaster. The man without honorable intentions always provides the innocent maiden with such books as a prelude to his assault on her virtue.[82] Books which attacked or seemed to attack woman's accepted place in society were regarded as equally dangerous. A reviewer of Harriet Martineau's *Society in America* wanted it kept out of the hands of American women. They were so susceptible to persuasion, with their "gentle yielding natures" that they might listen to "the bold ravings of the hard-featured of their own sex." The frightening result: "Such reading will unsettle them for their true station and pursuits, and they will throw the world back again into confusion."[83]

The debate over women's education posed the question of whether a "finished" education detracted from the practice of housewifely arts. Again it proved to be a case of semantics, for a true woman's education was never "finished" until she was instructed in the gentle science of homemaking.[84] Helen Irving, writing on "Literary Women," made it very clear that if women invoked the muse, it was as a genie of the household lamp. "If the necessities of her position require these duties at her hands, she will perform them nonetheless cheerfully, that she knows herself capable of higher things." The literary woman must conform to the same standards as any other woman: "That her home shall be made a loving place of rest and joy and comfort for those who are dear to her, will be the first wish of every true woman's heart."[85] Mrs. Ann Stephens told women who wrote to make sure they did not sacrifice one domestic duty.

79 R. C. Waterston, *Thoughts on Moral and Spiritual Culture* (Boston, 1842), p. 101. Newcomb's *Young Lady's Guide* also advised religious biography as the best reading for women (p. 111).

80 *Godey's*, I (1828), 1. (Repeated often in *Godey's* editorials.)

81 *The Lily of the Valley*, n. v. (1851), p. 2.

82 For example, "The Fatalist," *Godey's*, IV (Jan. 1834), 10, in which Somers Dudley has Catherine reading these dangerous books until life becomes "a bewildered dream. . . . O passion, what a shocking perverter of reason thou art!"

83 Review of *Society in America* (New York, 1837) in *American Quarterly Review* (Philadelphia), XXII (Sept. 1837), 38.

84 "A Finished Education," *Ladies' Museum* (Providence), I (1825), 42.

85 Helen Irving, "Literary Women," *Ladies' Wreath*, III (1850), 93.

"As for genius, make it a domestic plant. Let its roots strike deep in your house. . . ."[86]

The fear of "blue stockings" (the eighteenth-century male's term of derision for educated or literary women) need not persist for nineteenth-century American men. The magazines presented spurious dialogues in which bachelors were convinced of their fallacy in fearing educated wives. One such dialogue took place between a young man and his female cousin. Ernest deprecates learned ladies ("A *Woman* is far more lovable than a *philosopher*") but Alice refutes him with the beautiful example of their Aunt Barbara, who "although she *has* perpetrated the heinous crime of writing some half dozen folios" is still a model of "the spirit of feminine gentleness." His memory prodded, Ernest concedes that, by George, there was a woman: "When I last had a cold she not only made me a bottle of cough syrup, but when I complained of nothing new to read, set to work and wrote some twenty stanzas on consumption."[87]

The magazines were filled with domestic tragedies in which spoiled young girls learned that when there was a hungry man to feed French and china painting were not helpful. According to these stories many a marriage is jeopardized because the wife has not learned to keep house. Harriet Beecher Stowe wrote a sprightly piece of personal experience for *Godey's*, ridiculing her own bad housekeeping as a bride. She used the same theme in a story, "The Only Daughter," in which the pampered beauty learns the facts of domestic life from a rather difficult source, her mother-in-law. Mrs. Hamilton tells Caroline in the sweetest way possible to shape up in the kitchen, reserving her rebuke for her son: "You are her husband—her guide—her protector—now see what you can do," she admonishes him. "Give her credit for every effort: treat her faults with tenderness; encourage and praise whenever you can, and depend upon it, you will see another woman in her." He is properly masterful, she properly domestic, and in a few months Caroline is making lumpless gravy and keeping up with the darning. Domestic tranquility has been restored and the young wife moralizes: "Bring up a girl to feel that she has a responsible part to bear in promoting the happiness of the family, and you make a reflecting being of her at once, and remove that lightness and frivolity of character which makes her shrink from graver studies."[88] These stories end with the heroine drying her hands on her apron and vowing that *her* daughter will be properly educated, in piecrust as well as Poonah work.

The female seminaries were quick to defend themselves against any suspicion of interfering with the role which nature's God had assigned to women. They hoped to enlarge and deepen that role, but not to change its setting. At the Young Ladies' Seminary and Collegiate Institute in Monroe City, Michigan, the catalogue admitted few of its graduates would be likely "to fill the learned professions." Still, they were called to "other scenes of usefulness and honor." The average woman is to be "the

[86] "Women of Genius," *Ladies' Companion*, XI (1839), 89.

[87] "Intellect vs. Affection in Woman," *Godey's*, XVI (1846), 86.

[88] "The Only Daughter," *Godey's*, X (Mar. 1839), 122.

presiding genius of love" in the home, where she is to "give a correct and elevated literary taste to her children, and to assume that influential station that she ought to possess as the companion of an educated man."[89]

At Miss Pierce's famous school in Litchfield, the students were taught that they had "attained the perfection of their characters when they could combine their elegant accomplishments with a turn for solid domestic virtues."[90] Mt. Holyoke paid pious tribute to domestic skills: "Let a young lady despise this branch of the duties of woman, and she despises the appointments of her existence." God, nature and the Bible "enjoin these duties on the sex, and she cannot violate them with impunity." Thus warned, the young lady would have to seek knowledge of these duties elsewhere, since it was not in the curriculum at Mt. Holyoke. "We would not take this privilege from the mother."[91]

One reason for knowing her way around a kitchen was that America was "a land of precarious fortunes," as Lydia Maria Child pointed out in her book *The Frugal Housewife: Dedicated to Those Who Are Not Ashamed of Economy*. Mrs. Child's chapter "How to Endure Poverty" prescribed a combination of piety and knowledge—the kind of knowledge found in a true woman's education, "a thorough religious *useful* education."[92] The woman who had servants today might tomorrow, because of a depression or panic, be forced to do her own work. If that happened she knew how to act, for she was to be the same cheerful consoler of her husband in their cottage as in their mansion.

An essay by Washington Irving, much quoted in the gift annuals, discussed the value of a wife in case of business reverses: "I have observed that a married man falling into misfortune is more apt to achieve his situation in the world than a single one . . . it is beautifully ordained by Providence that woman, who is the ornament of man in his happier hours, should be his stay and solace when smitten with sudden calamity."[93]

A story titled simply but eloquently "The Wife" dealt with the quiet heroism of Ellen Graham during her husband's plunge from fortune to poverty. Ned Graham said of her: "Words are too poor to tell you what I owe to that noble woman. In our darkest seasons of adversity, she has been an angel of consolation—utterly forgetful of self and anxious only to comfort and sustain me." Of course she had a little help from "faithful Dinah who absolutely refused to leave her beloved mistress," but even so Ellen did no more than would be expected of any true woman.[94]

[89] *The Annual Catalogue of the Officers and Pupils of the Young Ladies' Seminary and Collegiate Institute* (Monroe City, 1855), pp. 18, 19.

[90] *Chronicles of a Pioneer School* from 1792 to 1833: Being the History of Miss Sarah Pierce and Her Litchfield School, Compiled by Emily Noyes Vanderpoel; ed. Elizabeth C. Barney Buel (Cambridge, 1903), p. 74.

[91] *Mt. Holyoke Female Seminary*, p. 13.

[92] *The Frugal Housewife* (New York, 1838), p. 111.

[93] "Female Influence," in *The Ladies' Pearl and Literary Gleaner: A Collection of Tales, Sketches, Essays, Anecdotes, and Historical Incidents* (Lowell), I (1841), 10.

[94] Mrs. S. T. Martyn, "The Wife," *Ladies' Wreath*, II (1848–49), 171.

Most of this advice was directed to woman as wife. Marriage was the proper state for the exercise of the domestic virtues. "True Love and a Happy Home," an essay in *The Young Ladies' Oasis,* might have been carved on every girl's hope chest.[95] But although marriage was best, it was not absolutely necessary. The women's magazines tried to remove the stigma from being an "Old Maid." They advised no marriage at all rather than an unhappy one contracted out of selfish motives.[96] Their stories showed maiden ladies as unselfish ministers to the sick, teachers of the young, or moral preceptors with their pens, beloved of the entire village. Usually the life of single blessedness resulted from the premature death of a fiancé, or was chosen through fidelity to some high mission. For example, in "Two Sisters," Mary devotes herself to Ellen and her abandoned children, giving up her own chance for marriage. "Her devotion to her sister's happiness has met its reward in the consciousness of having fulfilled a sacred duty."[97] Very rarely, a "woman of genius" was absolved from the necessity of marriage, being so extraordinary that she did not need the security or status of being a wife.[98] Most often, however, if girls

[95] *The Young Ladies' Oasis,* p. 26.

[96] "On Marriage," *Ladies' Repository,* I (1841), 133; "Old Maids," *Ladies' Literary Cabinet* (Newburyport), II (1822) (microfilm), 141; "Matrimony," *Godey's,* II (Sept. 1831), 174; and "Married or Single," *Peterson's Magazine* (Philadelphia), IX (1859), 36, all express the belief that while marriage is desirable for a woman it is not essential. This attempt to reclaim the status of the unmarried woman is an example of the kind of mild crusade which the women's magazines sometimes carried on. Other examples were their strictures against an overly genteel education and against the affectation and aggravation of ill health. In this sense the magazines were truly conservative, for they did not oppose all change but only that which did violence to some cherished tradition. The reforms they advocated would, if put into effect, make woman even more the perfect female, and enhance the ideal of True Womanhood.

[97] *Girlhood and Womanhood,* p. 100. Mrs. Graves tells the stories in the book in the person of an "Old Maid" and her conclusions are that "single life has its happiness too," for the single woman "can enjoy all the pleasures of maternity without its pains and trials" (p. 140). In another one of her books, *Woman in America* (New York, 1843), Mrs. Graves speaks out even more strongly in favor of "single blessedness" rather than "a loveless or unhappy marriage" (p. 130).

[98] A very unusual story is Lela Linwood, "A Chapter in the History of a Free Heart," *Ladies' Wreath,* III (1853), 349. The heroine, Grace Arland, is "sublime" and dwells "in perfect light while we others struggle yet with the shadows." She refuses marriage and her friends regret this but are told her heart "is rejoicing in its *freedom.*" The story ends with the plaintive refrain:

> But is it not a happy thing,
>   All fetterless and free,
> Like any wild bird, on the wing,
>   To carol merrily?

But even in this tale the unusual, almost unearthly rarity of Grace's genius is stressed; she is not offered as an example to more mortal beings.

proved "difficult," marriage and a family were regarded as a cure.[99] The "sedative quality" of a home could be counted on to subdue even the most restless spirits.

George Burnap saw marriage as "that sphere for which woman was originally intended, and to which she is so exactly fitted to adorn and bless, as the wife, the mistress of a home, the solace, the aid, and the counsellor of that ONE, for whose sake alone the world is of any consequence to her."[100] Samuel Miller preached a sermon on women:

> How interesting and important are the duties devolved on females as WIVES . . . the counsellor and friend of the husband; who makes it her daily study to lighten his cares, to soothe his sorrows, and to augment his joys; who, like a guardian angel, watches over his interests, warns him against dangers, comforts him under trials; and by her pious, assiduous, and attractive deportment, constantly endeavors to render him more virtuous, more useful, more honourable, and more happy.[101]

A woman's whole interest should be focused on her husband, paying him "those numberless attentions to which the French give the title of *petits soins* and which the woman who loves knows so well how to pay . . . she should consider nothing as trivial which could win a smile of approbation from him."[102]

Marriage was seen not only in terms of service but as an increase in authority for woman. Burnap concluded that marriage improves the female character "not only because it puts her under the best possible tuition, that of the affections, and affords scope to her active energies, but because it gives her higher aims, and a more dignified position."[103] *The Lady's Amaranth* saw it as a balance of power: "The man bears rule over his wife's person and conduct. She bears rule over his inclinations: he governs by law; she by persuasion. . . . The empire of the woman is an empire of softness . . . her commands are caresses, her menaces are tears."[104]

99 Horace Greeley even went so far as to apply this remedy to the "dissatisfactions" of Margaret Fuller. In his autobiography, *Recollections of a Busy Life* (New York, 1868), he says that "noble and great as she was, a good husband and two or three bouncing babies would have emancipated her from a deal of cant and nonsense" (p. 178).

100 *Sphere and Duties of Woman*, p. 64.

101 *A Sermon: Preached March 13, 1808, for the Benefit of the Society Instituted in the City of New-York, for the Relief of Poor Widows with Small Children* (New York, 1808), pp. 13, 14.

102 *Lady's Magazine and Museum: A Family Journal* (London), IV (Jan. 1831), 6. This magazine is included partly because its editorials proclaimed it "of interest to the English-speaking lady at home and abroad" and partly because it shows that the preoccupation with True Womanhood was by no means confined to the United States.

103 *Sphere and Duties of Woman*, p. 102.

104 "Matrimony," *Lady's Amaranth*, II (Dec. 1839), 271.

Woman should marry, but not for money. She should choose only the high road of true love and not truckle to the values of a materialistic society. A story, "Marrying for Money" (subtlety was not the strong point of the ladies' magazines), depicts Gertrude, the heroine, ruing the day she made her crass choice: "It is a terrible thing to live without love. . . . A woman who dares marry for aught but the purest affection, calls down the just judgments of heaven upon her head."[105]

The corollary to marriage, with or without true love, was motherhood, which added another dimension to her usefulness and her prestige. It also anchored her even more firmly to the home. "My Friend," wrote Mrs. Sigourney, "if in becoming a mother, you have reached the climax of your happiness, you have also taken a higher place in the scale of being . . . you have gained an increase of power."[106] The Rev. J. N. Danforth pleaded in *The Ladies' Casket*, "Oh, mother, acquit thyself well in thy humble sphere, for thou mayest affect the world."[107] A true woman naturally loved her children; to suggest otherwise was monstrous.[108]

America depended upon her mothers to raise up a whole generation of Christian statesmen who could say "all that I am I owe to my angel mother."[109] The mothers must do the inculcating of virtue since the fathers, alas, were too busy chasing the dollar. Or as *The Ladies' Companion* put it more effusively, the father "weary with the heat and burden of life's summer day, or trampling with unwilling foot the decaying leaves of life's autumn, has forgotten the sympathies of life's joyous springtime. . . . The acquisition of wealth, the advancement of his children in worldly honor—these are his self-imposed tasks." It was his wife who formed "the infant mind as yet untainted by contact with evil . . . like wax beneath the plastic hand of the mother."[110]

[105] Elizabeth Doten, "Marrying for Money," *The Lily of the Valley*, n. v. (1857), p. 112.

[106] *Letters to Mothers*, p. 9.

[107] "Maternal Relation," *Ladies' Casket* (New York, 1850?), p. 85. The importance of the mother's role was emphasized abroad as well as in America. *Godey's* recommended the book by the French author Aimée-Martin on the education of mothers to "be read five times," in the original if possible (XIII, Dec. 1842, 201). In this book the highest ideals of True Womanhood are upheld. For example: "Jeunes filles, jeunes épouses, tendres mères, c'est dans votre âme bien plus que dans les lois du législateur que reposent aujourd'hui l'avenir de l'Europe et les destinées du genre humain," L. Aimée-Martin, *De l'Education des mères de famille ou de la civilisation du genre humain par les femmes* (Bruxelles, 1857), II, 527.

[108] *Maternal Association of the Amity Baptist Church:* Annual Report (New York, 1847), p. 2: "Suffer the little children to come unto me and forbid them not, is and must ever be a sacred commandment to the Christian woman."

[109] For example, Daniel Webster, "The Influence of Woman," in *The Young Ladies' Reader* (Philadelphia, 1851), p. 310.

[110] Mrs. Emma C. Embury, "Female Education," *Ladies' Companion*, VIII (Jan. 1838), 18. Mrs. Embury stressed the fact that the American woman was not the "mere plaything of passion" but was in strict training to be "the mother of statesmen."

The Ladies' Wreath offered a fifty-dollar prize to the woman who submitted the most convincing essay on "How May an American Woman Best Show Her Patriotism." The winner was Miss Elizabeth Wetherell, who provided herself with a husband in her answer. The wife in the essay of course asked her husband's opinion. He tried a few jokes first—"Call her eldest son George Washington," "Don't speak French, speak American"—but then got down to telling her in sober prize-winning truth what women could do for their country. Voting was no asset, since that would result only in "a vast increase of confusion and expense without in the smallest degree affecting the result." Besides, continued this oracle, "looking down at their child," if "we were to go a step further and let the children vote, their first act would be to vote their mothers at home." There is no comment on this devastating male logic and he continues: "Most women would follow the lead of their fathers and husbands," and the few who would "fly off on a tangent from the circle of home influence would cancel each other out."

The wife responds dutifully: "I see all that. I never understood so well before." Encouraged by her quick womanly perception, the master of the house resolves the question—an American woman best shows her patriotism by staying at home, where she brings her influence to bear "upon the right side for the country's weal." That woman will instinctively choose the side of right he has no doubt. Besides her "natural refinement and closeness to God" she has the "blessed advantage of a quiet life," while man is exposed to conflict and evil. She stays home with "her Bible and a well-balanced mind" and raises her sons to be good Americans. The judges rejoiced in this conclusion and paid the prize money cheerfully, remarking "they deemed it cheap at the price."[111]

If any woman asked for greater scope for her gifts the magazines were sharply critical. Such women were tampering with society, undermining civilization. Mary Wollstonecraft, Frances Wright and Harriet Martineau were condemned in the strongest possible language—they were read out of the sex. "They are only semi-women, mental hermaphrodites." The Rev. Harrington knew the women of America could not possibly approve of such perversions and went to some wives and mothers to ask if they did want a "wider sphere of interest" as these nonwomen claimed. The answer was reassuring. " 'NO!' they cried simultaneously. 'Let the men take care of politics, *we will take care of the children!*' " Again female discontent resulted only from a lack of understanding: women were not subservient, they were rather "chosen vessels." Looked at in this light the conclusion was inescapable: "Noble, sublime is the task of the American mother."[112]

111 "How May an American Woman Best Show Her Patriotism?" *Ladies' Wreath*, III (1851), 313. Elizabeth Wetherell was the pen name of Susan Warner, author of *The Wide Wide World* and *Queechy*.

112 Henry F. Harrington, "Female Education," *Ladies' Companion*, IX (1838), 293, and "Influence of Woman—Past and Present," *Ladies' Companion*, XIII (1840), 245.

"Women's Rights" meant one thing to reformers, but quite another to the True Woman. She knew her rights,

> The right to love whom others scorn,
> The right to comfort and to mourn,
> The right to shed new joy on earth,
> The right to feel the soul's high worth,
>
> . . . . . .
>
> Such women's rights, and God will bless
> And crown their champions with success.[113]

The American woman had her choice—she could define her rights in the way of the women's magazines and insure them by the practice of the requisite virtues, or she could go outside the home, seeking other rewards than love. It was a decision on which, she was told, everything in her world depended. "Yours it is to determine," the Rev. Mr. Stearns solemnly warned from the pulpit, "whether the beautiful order of society . . . shall continue as it has been" or whether "society shall break up and become a chaos of disjointed and unsightly elements."[114] If she chose to listen to other voices than those of her proper mentors, sought other rooms than those of her home, she lost both her happiness and her power —"that almost magic power, which, in her proper sphere, she now wields over the destinies of the world."[115]

But even while the women's magazines and related literature encouraged this ideal of the perfect woman, forces were at work in the nineteenth century which impelled woman herself to change, to play a more creative role in society. The movements for social reform, westward migration, missionary activity, utopian communities, industrialism, the Civil War—all called forth responses from woman which differed from those she was trained to believe were hers by nature and divine decree. The very perfection of True Womanhood, moreover, carried within itself the seeds of its own destruction. For if woman was so very little less than the angels, she should surely take a more active part in running the world, especially since men were making such a hash of things.

Real women often felt they did not live up to the ideal of True Womanhood: some of them blamed themselves, some challenged the standard, some tried to keep the virtues and enlarge the scope of womanhood.[116] Somehow through this mixture of challenge and acceptance, of change and continuity, the True Woman evolved into the New Woman—a transformation as startling in its way as the abolition of slavery or the coming of the machine age. And yet the stereotype, the "mystique" if

113 Mrs. E. Little, "What Are the Rights of Women?" *Ladies' Wreath,* II (1848–49), 133.

114 *Female Influence,* p. 18.

115 *Ibid.,* p. 23.

116 Even the women reformers were prone to use domestic images, i.e. "sweep Uncle Sam's kitchen clean" and "tidy up our country's house."

you will, of what woman was and ought to be persisted, bringing guilt and confusion in the midst of opportunity.[117]

The women's magazines and related literature had feared this very dislocation of values and blurring of roles. By careful manipulation and interpretation they sought to convince woman that she had the best of both worlds—power and virtue—and that a stable order of society depended upon her maintaining her traditional place in it. To that end she was identified with everything that was beautiful and holy.

"Who Can Find a Valiant Woman?" was asked frequently from the pulpit and the editorial pages. There was only one place to look for her—at home. Clearly and confidently these authorities proclaimed the True Woman of the nineteenth century to be the Valiant Woman of the Bible, in whom the heart of her husband rejoiced and whose price was above rubies.

[117] The "Animus and Anima" of Jung amounts almost to a catalogue of the nineteenth-century masculine and female traits, and the female hysterics whom Freud saw had much of the same training as the nineteenth-century American woman. Betty Friedan, *The Feminine Mystique* (New York, 1963), challenges the whole concept of True Womanhood as it hampers the "fulfillment" of the twentieth-century woman.

Cultural Aspects of the Industrial Revolution: Lynn, Massachusetts, Shoemakers and Industrial Morality, 1826–1860

PAUL FALER

The Industrial Revolution did not come to nineteenth-century America without a struggle. Alexander Hamilton had won the struggle with Thomas Jefferson over the future direction of the nation's economy—manufacturing, not agrarianism. The demographic realities of the early nineteenth century, however, continued to be Jeffersonian in shape. In 1820, for example, only five percent of the people of the United States lived in towns of 8,000 or over.

Before industrial development on the British scale could come to America, three vital ingredients had to be supplied: labor, capital, and technology. All three were eventually to come in large measure from Great Britain. Labor was forced to migrate, for example, from Ireland during the famine of the 1840s; investment capital appeared from London; and technology (sometimes stolen) was adapted from British industries to the American scene. Thus the Industrial Revolution crossed the Atlantic, in steerage as well as in first class accommodations.

The expansive mood of the United States in the antebellum years was exhibited not only in the westward march of the national boundary. Manifest destiny also included the concept of domination of the Western Hemisphere, and the development of American manufacturing was an essential part of that scheme. Bold entrepreneurial innovations, favored by governmental tariff policies and protected by incorporation laws, expanded with the nation. The extension of navigable waterways and railroads, often at direct or indirect public expense, aided in this process.

The unstable nature of the economy in this period, however, led to many more business failures than successes. The panic of 1837, for example, caused thousands of banks and other businesses to close their doors. But as is often the case in matters of this sort, the most substantial and permanent loss was incurred by the working people. The panic came in the midst of the changeover in the organization of industry from small scale domestic manufacturing operations to the larger and more efficient factory system. The preindustrial artisan was in control of his own work, and, what was more important, his own time. He could choose when to work and how hard. The "manufacturers," who supplied the artisans with material and orders and then collected the finished products for marketing, regularly complained about the untrustworthiness of the workers and the inefficiency of the process. The reorganization of work brought about by the introduction of the factory required the artisan to work at a pace and at a task determined by the factory owner. Time became the disciplining factor in the work life. There was strong resistance to this change on the part of the workers, but repeated depressions in the economy put the artisans (now become factory hands) at the mercy of the manufacturers. No longer able to work on their own, the workers were dependent on the factories for even a meager livelihood.

In order to produce a stable, reliable, and inexpensive work force for the new factory system, certain traditional patterns in personal and social life among the working class had to be altered. In the selection that follows, Paul Faler, of the University of Massachusetts at Boston, describes the attempts of one industrial city to effect that change. The successful efforts of the leading citizens of Lynn, Massachusetts, in this endeavor, and divisions within the working class itself, seriously hindered the development of a self-conscious class of working people who might have been able to exert greater pressure for economic equality in the industrial system.

Industrialization is usually described in connection with machinery, factories, and workers; or, when considered as a part of labor history, changes in wages, hours, and working conditions. Undeniably, all are crucial aspects. But what of the social and cultural side? The industrial revolution, after all, was more than a series of economic changes in the means of production. It was revolutionary as well in its transformation of traditional society; scarcely any part of the old order escaped its impact. Its cultural dimension is more easily grasped if one keeps in mind an earlier but now seldom used definition of industry—the earnest and constant attention to work. This ethic spills over into the social life of those who took it up.

Paul Faler, "Cultural Aspects of the Industrial Revolution: Lynn, Massachusetts, Shoemakers and Industrial Morality, 1826–1860", *Labor History*, XV (Summer, 1974), 367–94. Reprinted by permission of *Labor History* and the author.

An earlier version of this paper was prepared for the meeting of the Organization of American Historians in Chicago on April 11–14, 1973.

The cultural aspects of life in Lynn, Massachusetts, is the subject of this study. For Lynn's inhabitants, most of them shoemakers and their families, industrialization meant inner discipline and a tightening up of the moral code through either the abolition or drastic alteration of those customs, traditions, and practices that interfered with productive labor. More than ever before, life became oriented toward work. The objective was an orderly society, a "minature likeness of a well-regulated republic," as one Lynn reformer described it. Citizens would be self-reliant, hard-working, and sober; obedient to their superiors; attentive to their labors; and self-disciplined in all their pursuits. A new morality based on the paramount importance of work was taking shape, an industrial morality that was the cultural expression of the industrial revolution.

Industrial morality was not, as some have suggested, a product of the factory alone. The application of the work ethic in Lynn began long before the 1860s, when machinery and factories first appeared. The shoemakers were handworkers then, not factory operatives. The work-place was the shop or manufactory, not the factory. A cultural apparatus of ideas and institutions outside the work place was chiefly responsible for inculcating the new values.

Industrial morality profoundly affected the lives of Lynn's shoe-makers, both within and outside the workplace. This paper will examine several areas of change: poverty and dependency, temperance, recreation, and education. It will also attempt to explain why the new code of morality became a source of discord among the shoemakers and shaped their response to the Industrial Revolution.

Efforts to strengthen the new morality formally began in 1826 with the founding of the Society for the Promotion of Industry, Frugality and Temperance. The Society's founders and officers were prominent town-folk, mostly shoe manufacturers and leather dealers, but with a handful of clergymen and lawyers among them as well. Of the ward officials of the Society, the shoe bosses easily made up the largest element. Leading members included Thomas Bowler, Republican town clerk; Micajah Pratt, Lynn's largest shoe manufacturer; Jonathan Buffum, shoe manu-facturer, hardware and paint dealer, and publisher of the *Lynn Record*, the community's largest paper from 1830 to 1840; Jonathan Bacheller, owner of a prosperous dry goods store and Lynn postmaster from 1808 to 1829; and two other leading shoe manufacturers, Isaiah Breed and Ebenezer Brown.[1] Among the ward representatives were several of Lynn's 700 shoemakers, 60 percent of the town's adult population, whose support would be crucial to the Society's success.

As the Society's name indicated, members sought to promote values that would foster industry and help Lynn prosper as a manufacturing center. Industry required self-discipline, emphasis upon productive labor, and condemnation of wasteful habits. Industry, frugality, and temper-

[1] *Lynn Mirror*, December 30, 1826; *Weekly Messenger*, December 15, 1832. For statement of purpose and constitution of the Society, see *Lynn Mirror*, December 23, 1826. A Lynn citizen later estimated that 143 people joined the new society. "Lynn Scrapbooks," XXIV, II. Scrapbooks in Lynn Public Library.

ance, if conscientiously followed, would result in savings that would bring material reward to the wage earner and well being to the community. Several officers of the Society, not unexpectedly, were also founders and directors of the Lynn Institution for Savings which opened its doors in 1826, the year that the Society itself was founded. Isaac Story, a native of Marblehead and brother of Supreme Court Justice Joseph Story, was cashier. The directors included Josiah Newhall, a shoe manufacturer; Isaac Bassett, a leather dealer and shoe boss; and Robert Trevett, Lynn's first lawyer.[2]

One group of prominent citizens was absent—the merchants of West Lynn, men engaged in mercantile activities rather than in manufacturing. Theirs was the section of Lynn that most nearly resembled the mercantile centers of the North Shore in which the libertine morality of the eighteenth century was most deeply entrenched. Differing social and political forms emanated from distinctive economies. Lynn was Republican, Methodist, anti-Masonic, Democratic, and Free Soil; Salem was Federalist, orthodox or Unitarian, and Whig. The temperance movement in particular was strongest in rising manufacturing and farming towns; weakest in port cities, such as Salem and Boston. After 1826, rum sellers in West Lynn would be an annoying impediment to that sobriety manufacturing interests desired.[3]

The Society for Industry, Frugality, and Temperance—having 143 members in 1826 and increasing to 450 in 1830—had close ties to Lynn's religious bodies. Its meetings were alternately held at the Methodist and Congregational churches. Each of the town's remaining half dozen or so denominations—Quakers, Baptists, Unitarians, chief among them—sent delegations, suggesting that industrial morality had taken hold among the Congregationalists and Quakers as well as among the evangelical Methodists and Baptists who are usually identified as the authors of the new morality. The churches became vehicles for inculcating the values of this new morality. Preachers pledged themselves to temperance or abstinence and expected their parishioners to do the same. Beginning in the 1840s, thousands of students from the newly formed Sunday Schools marched under the banner of the cold-water army in monster temperance parades. Some churches established special courts that tried cases of infidelity, drunkenness, or immoral conduct. Morality and religion have obvious, intimate, and familiar ties, but the link between industrial morality and religion on the one hand and the industrial revolution on the other has never been fully explored. A brief sketch of the religious revival in Lynn from 1790 to about 1840 suggests the nature of the connection.

Before 1790, organized religion exerted little influence over Lynn's shoemakers. The town had only two religious bodies—the orthodox Congregationalists and the Society of Friends. The former, by 1790, had dwindled to a dozen or so male members, though the congregation had many times that number. The Friends numbered perhaps thirty families.

[2] *Lynn Mirror*, January 20, 1827.

[3] For resistance from West Lynn, see *The Star*, August 20, 1836, October 1, 1836; *Lynn Bay State*, November 22, 1849.

The rejuvenation of piety began in 1790 with the appearance in Lynn of Jesse Lee, an itinerant Methodist preacher whom Methodist Bishop Francis Asbury dispatched from New York City to New England. Making his way across Connecticut to Boston, Lee everywhere met with failure. After nearly three months of preaching in Boston, he claimed only a dozen converts. But the same length of time in Lynn produced scores of believers. Some 108 converts organized the First Methodist Church, the first of its kind in New England,[4] and Lynn would be the Methodist stronghold in New England for a century. By 1850, for example, there were 2,000 members in eight churches served by eight pastors and six lay preachers. The revival broadened in the three decades after 1790. A Baptist church was founded in 1816, an Episcopal chapel in 1819, a Unitarian Congregation in 1826. Congregationalism's decrepit First Church, cleansed of dissenters by the withdrawal first of Methodists, then of Unitarians, suddenly expanded with dozens of new members.

This broadly based religious revival in Lynn seems to support Donald Mathews' observation that the formation of churches during the Second Great Awakening was "an organizing process that helped give meaning and direction to people suffering in various degrees from the social strains of a nation on the move into new political, economic and geographical areas."[5] Churches lent a sense of purpose and community to a people whose ties to established institutions had been loosened by a quickening of economic activity. But if this is true of the founding of religious institutions, what of their adoption of a stern code of morality that became a hallmark of Protestantism?

First, although suspicion about sins of the flesh has been characteristic of Christianity, its intensity has varied considerably from generation to generation. A rigid moral code, in other words, is not inherent in Protestantism. Methodism is a case in point. Although its founder, John Wesley, had frowned on liquor, America's Methodists did little in the eighteenth and early nineteenth centuries to reinforce his strictures. As late as 1812, the General Conference refused to censure those Methodist preachers who sold "spirituous or malt liquors." It permitted preachers to sell and consume alcohol, and allowed church members to distill, retail, and drink liquor.[6] But the church moved steadily toward temperance and then abstinence over the next two decades until, by the

[4] George Henry Martin, "The Unfolding of Religious Faith in Lynn," *The Register of the Lynn Historical Society*, XVI, 16 (1912), 60–65. A hostile critic of Methodism, Parsons Cooke of the Calvinist First Congregational Church, asserted that Methodism succeeded because "it took hold of the doctrines which lay in the minds of almost all men here, and wrought them with the steam, levers, and pulleys of a new engine." Parsons Cooke, *A Century of Puritanism and a Century of Its Opposites* (Boston, 1855), 258.

[5] Donald G. Mathews, "The Second Great Awakening as an Organizing Process, 1780–1830: An Hypothesis," *American Quarterly*, XXI (Spring 1969), 25–43.

[6] *The History of American Methodism*, I (New York, 1964), 257–58; Charles W. Ferguson, *Organizing to Beat the Devil: Methodism and the Making of America* (New York, 1971), 359.

1820s, Methodists were in the vanguard of the prohibition movement. Had a rigid morality inhered in Methodism, it seems obvious, there would not have been such early laxity.

Secondly, nearly all Protestant denominations took an increasingly hard line against alcohol after 1820. The Congregational church in eighteenth-century Massachusetts had amply demonstrated that heavy drinking and a degree of sexual profligacy could coexist with religion. Ordination ceremonies invariably included liquor for the celebrants, and anywhere from a third to a half of refreshment expenses went for alcoholic beverages.[7] When a congregational minister called on a parishioner, he was usually offered a glass of brandy. Congregationalists also seemed indifferent to the fornication that frequently accompanied the custom of bundling. Such practices would be unthinkable by the 1840s. Lynn's moral reformation, however, had secular, not religious, origins. They derived from the pressure for greater discipline and control demanded by a competitive market economy.

To locate the social conditions that spawned the movement for industrial morality, it is necessary to trace briefly the changes in Lynn's social economy.

Shoemaking is essentially a series of cutting and stitching operations. The eighteenth-century shoemaker or cordwainer fashioned shoes from leather and fabric, performing each operation with his own hands. America's colonial status along with the lower price of British shoes limited the market for those women's shoes made in Lynn. In 1750, only three shoemakers sold enough of their wares to warrant the assistance of journeymen. Most of the town's shoemakers were self-employed farmer-craftsmen. A limited domestic market thus limited production. But expulsion of the English from this market, recognition of a national economy with ratification of the Constitution, a tariff on shoes imported from abroad, and improvements in transportation combined to expand greatly the potential market for Lynn shoes. Several changes followed to expand production. First, Lynn's residents gradually abandoned farming and devoted their full attention to shoemaking. They worked at their craft under the roofs of specialized structures which started to appear in the 1780s. Consequently, while the population remained constant at 2,000, production nonetheless increased from 60,000 pairs in 1770 to 175,000 in 1785. And although the population doubled from 2,000 to 4,000 by 1810, shoe output increased five fold.[8] Second, women began to be employed.

[7] Robert Rantoul of Salem attended an ordination in 1785 at the First Parish of Beverly. One-third of the total expenses went for strong drink, "which I suppose was not an unusual proportion of the expenses on such occasions. Ordinations were scenes of conviviality to the people generally, who assembled from all the towns in the neighborhood. Fiddling, dancing and various other sports were common." "Mr. Rantoul's Establishment in Business – Intemperance and Pauperism," Essex Institute *Historical Collections,* V, no. 6 (December, 1863), 241–47.

[8] Alonzo Lewis and James R. Newhall, *History of Lynn, Essex County Massachusetts* . . . (Boston, 1865), 335, 371; James R. Newhall, *Centennial Memorial of Lynn, Essex County, Massachusetts* (Lynn, 1876), 75, 63; United States Census

To speed production, cordwainers began to call upon their wives and children for assistance in stitching together the upper portion of the shoe in preparation for bottoming or making—that is, attaching the upper to the soles. Women were soon employed on a massive scale, filling jobs that ordinarily might have given work to the men of Lynn. But trade and shipbuilding in the ports of Essex County had attracted male wage earners to seafaring occupations, leaving openings for women whose traditional skills in sewing garments could be applied to shoes. In the post-Revolutionary decades, then, increased production came about through a shift in the work force from agriculture to manufacturing, the employment of women, and an enlarged labor supply.

During this phase in the evolution of shoe making, the merchant was the dominant entrepreneurial figure. Access to a vast market and command of capital were the twin sources of his power. He supplied Lynn's shoemakers with materials, then sold the finished product to shoe dealers and shopkeepers. The Lynn shoemakers, who formerly worked their own stock and sold directly to the customer, became subcontractors to the merchant, taking their pay in the commodities he provided. If the shoemaker employed journeymen, the master paid them in kind. This system of production contained a serious defect that led to its collapse. Although the merchant had access to the market and owned the raw materials, he had no control over the productive process. Wasteful and inefficient use of materials and shoddy goods were the results. Lynn's largest shoe merchant in the 1780s and 90s, Ebenezer Breed, complained furiously about the shoes he received from inept craftsmen; "confounded fools," he called them.[9] As the merchant suffered severe reverses, there appeared another class of entrepreneur who would eventually become the "shoe manufacturers." Tough, austere, methodical, and ambitious, they would transform the shoe industry and, simultaneously, usher in a set of personal and social values that eventually became industrial morality.

Like the merchant, the manufacturer possessed property—land, a retail store—which he translated into capital in the form of raw materials. Sometimes he obtained credit from a larger capitalist. Unlike the merchant, however, the manufacturer took command of the productive process by establishing a central shop that housed the sophisticated putting-out system prevailing in Lynn from about 1820 to the introduction of machinery and factories in the 1860s. Depending on the size of his business, the manufacturer's central shop was a one- or two-story wooden frame building. Several vital functions took place here, each performed by the boss or under his close scrutiny. First, the cutting of stock with a minimum of waste. No longer would the shoemaker be allowed to misuse the employer's stock and keep for himself enough material ("cabbage") to make and sell a few shoes on the side. The boss himself or an

---

Reports for 1810, 1830, 1850 and 1860; Commonwealth of Massachusetts, Secretary of the Commonwealth, *Statistics of the Condition and Products of Certain Branches of Industry in Massachusetts*, 1837, 1845, 1855.

[9] For an account of Breed's career, see Newhall, *Centennial Memorial*, 59–61.

expert cutter would wield the knife. Secondly, the boss would personally inspect the finished product brought in by the binders and shoemakers. If dissatisfied, he would reprimand or fire the mechanic on the spot. Finally, the central shop was partly a commissary from which the boss dispensed commodities to workers in payment for their labor.[10]

The shoe manufacturers were numerically a large group. In 1832 there were about forty—with the largest bloc, nearly all Quakers, each employing several or more cutters and hundreds of binders and shoemakers. Each sold tens of thousands of pairs of shoes, mainly through their own outlets in the South and West. Smaller bosses did their own cutting, employed as few as two to four binders and jours (who attached the uppers to the soles, doing whatever fitting, stitching and trimming was needed to finish the product); and then they peddled a few hundred pairs directly to customers or merchants in Boston.

The bulk of Lynn's population was made up of shoemakers and binders. The binders, or stitchers, were mostly women, either the daughters and wives of the shoemakers, or unattached women in surrounding towns. Working in the home, they stitched together the pieces that formed the upper part of the sole and then returned the uppers either directly to the shoemakers or to the boss in the central shop. The shoemakers (cordwainers, jours, mechanics) were white males. They worked by the piece in the home or, more often, in a small shop (commonly called a ten-footer) together with several other shoemakers who made up the shop's crew. They owned their own kit of tools but depended on the boss for lasts and leather. Most of the shoemakers were native born, having grown up in Lynn or migrated to the town from the hard-pressed farming areas of eastern Massachusetts, southern Maine, or New Hampshire. The heavy influx of Irish immigrants tended to bypass Lynn in favor of the port cities and textile factory towns. They made up only 9 percent of the town's population in 1850 and 15 percent in 1860. By 1860, approximately 10 percent of Lynn's shoemakers were Irish. Of the 840 shoemakers in Lynn in 1832, 56 percent were born in town. By 1860, however, the natives accounted for only 25 percent, the majority now being immigrants from elsewhere in New England.[11]

Lynn's putting-out system lacked machinery and factories, but the town itself resembled an immense manufactory, a coordinated mechanism of interrelated parts—morocco leather dressers and dealers, manufacturers and cutters, binders and shoemakers—each performing a specialized task necessary for completion of the finished product.

[10] Blanche E. Hazard, *The Organization of the Boot and Shoe Industry in Massachusetts Before 1875* (Cambridge, 1921); "Lynn Scrapbooks," II, 15, 50–53; vol. 11, 23. John Philip Hall, "The Gentle Craft: A Narrative of Yankee Shoemakers" (Unpublished Ph.D. Thesis: Columbia University, 1953).

[11] Barbara M. Solomon, "The Growth of the Population in Essex County, 1850–1860," Essex Institute *Historical Collections,* LIXV (1959), 82–103. Samples of 100 shoemakers from *Lynn Directories* of 1832, 1851, and 1860. Place of birth from *Vital Records of Lynn, Massachusetts to the End of the Year 1849,* 2 vols (Salem, 1905, 1906).

The architects and directors of the putting-out system were the manufacturers. They were, to repeat, the first to adopt the values that made up the new industrial morality. Hardworking, self-reliant, resourceful and shrewd, they were a tough and hardy breed. Their qualities of character had been forged and tempered in the market place. The formula for business success and personal fulfillment was simple: it combined prudence, economy, and the self-disciplined renunciation of the pleasures of the flesh. Benjamin Franklin Newhall, for one, recalled that he kept close check of his accounts, met all obligations promptly, and as a result reaped both a material and spiritual reward. Success prompted in him a feeling of great elation, pride in achievement, and an inner tranquility that suggested divine approbation.[12] The Lynn entrepreneurs were not unique. A similar process was unfolding elsewhere as shrewd and ambitious young men responded to the opportunities provided by an expanding market place.

About this time, a few miles away, in Groton, young Amos Lawrence began his apprenticeship as a shopkeeper-merchant. He was determined to avoid the "miserable bog or slough" of failure that swallowed up the improvident and careless who had not learned to put "restraint upon their appetite." The pitfalls he identified were the habit and customs of a libertine morality that prevailed in much of eighteenth-century America. Drinking was one of the most insidious and deadly, and the first that Lawrence overcame:

> We five boys were in the habit, every forenoon, of making a drink compounded of rum, raisens, sugar, nutmeg, &, with biscuit,—all palatable to eat and drink. After being in the store four weeks, I found myself admonished by my appetite of the approach of the hour for indulgence. Thinking the habit might make trouble if allowed to grow stronger, without further apology to my seniors I declined partaking with them. . . . During that whole period [five years] I never drank a spoonful though I mixed gallons daily for my old master and his customers. I decided not to be a slave to tobacco in any form, though I loved the odor of it then, and even now have in my drawer a superior Havana cigar . . . but only to smell of.

From then on Lawrence lived by a stringent code of conduct, his life governed by habits of "industry, economy and sobriety." He learned the wisdom of placing "business before friends," of judging all things by their utility, of "putting down every cent you receive and every cent you spend," of being "accurate," of having "system" in one's affairs at all times, and of eating "the bread of industry and quietness." He learned, above all, that "patience and perseverance will overcome all obstacles." Here in the making was a wealthy and powerful capitalist and the em-

[12] Benjamin F. Newhall, "Sketches of Lynn," numbers 33 and 34, in scrapbook, Lynn Historical Society. For biographical sketch of Newhall, Lewis and Newhall, *History of Lynn*, 570–71.

bodiment of a new morality. A merchant indeed, but cut from a different fabric than that of an eighteenth-century predecessor such as John Hancock: if Hancock can be likened to fine silk, Lawrence was like wire mesh.[13]

John C. Warren, a Boston physician whose life spanned the period from 1778 to 1856, discerned the shift in values that began around 1800. In his early life, he said, "the general and pernicious habit of a morning draught of flip or other stimulant" prevailed. Men of all classes spent the morning drinking hot punch, porter, brandy and water, and eating bread and cheese while arguing and chatting about topics of the day. "It may readily be imagined," Warren recalled, "that a conversation under such circumstances was not likely to be brief, and that no small part of the morning was wasted in this relaxation." The reason for such indulgent customs was that "time was not very important to most men at that period." Consequently, he stated, "from the peace of '83 until near the beginning of the present century very little business was done in Boston. About half a dozen merchants were sufficient to carry on the greater part of the foreign trade; and the rest were condemned to small business, which did not fill up their vacant hours."[14] Quickening economic activity led some Americans to view old ways differently. Entrepreneurs like Amos Lawrence and the Lynn shoe manufacturers were among the first to recognize that the slack and leisurely practices of the old culture were incompatible with the opportunities, and dangers, presented by the new order. Worse, in business self-indulgence would mean certain failure.

Entering a competitive market place that was a continual trial of their shrewdness and steadfastness, the rising entrepreneurs carried with them a conviction of their own personal righteousness. They confidently attributed their success to strength of character, self-discipline, and the correctness of the moral code by which they lived. They also recognized an obligation to others: "to whom much is given, of him will much be required." Here was a prescription for social leadership that they exercised with zeal and skill. And in the case of Lynn, they also recognized that success depended not only on their own industry, frugality, and temperance but upon like values from those they employed. All were parts of a single social entity. The idle, drunk, and dissolute were a burden upon the industrious wage earners and, unless reformed, would drag all into a "miserable bog or slough." The manufacturers exhibited a mature class consciousness that equated society's interests with their own. Those who gathered in December 1826 to form Lynn's Society for the Promotion of Industry, Frugality, and Temperance intended nothing less than a moral reformation in the culture of an entire city.

Lynn's poor were among the first to attract the Society's attention. That indifference which characterized the eighteenth century view of paupers and poor relief quickly came to an end in the 1820s. No longer would reformers fatalistically accept the view that "the poor ye always

[13] William R. Lawrence, ed., *Extracts from the Diary and Correspondence of the Late Amos Lawrence* (Boston, 1855), 24 ff.

[14] Edward Warren, ed., *The Life of John Collins Warren*, I (Boston, 1860), 15–19.

have with you." They attacked the causes of poverty which they identified as idleness, intemperance, and lax self-discipline. In the case of idleness, they would "banish it from the world" with a mandatory work regimen. For inmates of the poor house, confinement would become "a punishment and a terror to the intemperate and idle," and would instill a "strong sense of fear accompanied by absolute humility and contrition."[15] Although reformers sometimes made a distinction between the worthy and unworthy poor, the distinction rapidly crumbled in their eagerness to deal with "willful" offenders.

Lynn's poor fell roughly into two groups: those who were completely dependent upon the town for food and shelter, and who resided at the Alms House which the community had built in 1819; and those who were partly dependent and who lived at home but received some support from the town. Aid to the first group was in-the-house relief; aid to the second was out-of-the-house relief. The reformers proposed measures that significantly affected each group.

The slack discipline that permitted Alms House residents to wander the streets and converse with ordinary townsfolk ended in 1828. The town meeting, at the Society's urging, established regular visiting hours; at all other times the inmates would be isolated from the outside world. To enforce its order, the town appropriated $100 to construct a ten foot wooden fence topped with iron spikes. "This is the beginning of our economy in the poor house establishment," the *Lynn Mirror* proclaimed.[16] Overseers of the Poor transferred male inmates from farm work to shoemaking with materials furnished by Isaiah Breed, himself an Overseer, shoe manufacturer, and owner of the store that supplied commodities to the indigent shoemakers.[17] In 1828, the town deprived the poor of liquor; $120 had been spent on alcoholic beverages for the poor in the previous year. Although rejecting the recommendation of one reformer who proposed a diet of bread and water for able-bodied males on relief, the Overseers did apply sound business principles, and effectively reduced Poor House maintenance costs to a minimum. All three Overseers responsible for implementing the new policy were Quakers, and two were officers in the Society for the Promotion of Industry, Frugality, and Temperance. Their control over poor relief gave them a splendid opportunity to put their reforms into practice. But without approval of the town meetings that elected them, the changes could not have been made.

Reformers also changed the method of dispensing goods to the poor living outside the Alms House, many of them unemployed shoemakers whom depression periodically reduced to want. Overseers in the past gave

[15] *Lynn Mirror*, May 5, May 19, 1827, February 9, 1828. The Movement in Lynn was similar to efforts elsewhere to understand the causes of deviancy and dependency. See David Rothman, *Discovery of the Asylum: Social Order and Disorder in the New Republic* (New York, 1971). It is not unfair to assert that the reformers whom Rothman studies would have preferred the entire society to run according to the principles and regimen of the asylum.

[16] *Lynn Mirror*, May 10, 1828.

[17] *Weekly Messenger*, March 9, 1833.

needy citizens orders or credits drawn on local stores, allowing the recipient free choice in selecting those items he most needed. But a special committee reported that the poor did not choose wisely. They might buy meat instead of fish, flour instead of Indian meal, coffee instead of potatoes. The town therefore abolished the order system and directed the Overseers to stock staple commodities at the Alms House, doling these out in the amount they deemed sufficient.[18] One reformer also wished to humiliate the poor by publicly posting their names. Lynn's physicians aided the movement to banish idleness by agreeing in 1828 not to attend any family whose head was poor and a drunkard.

Massachusetts also lent support to local proponents of industrial morality. In 1831 it repealed an 1815 law prohibiting the use of cadavers for medical purposes. Many people thought it horrifying and disgusting to have one's body or that of a loved one desecrated by dissection. But the new measure did grant medical schools the right to practice anatomy on deceased paupers whose bodies were not claimed within twenty-four hours. Consequently, this law met research needs and also, in light of widespread opposition, calmed the fears of respectable and self-reliant citizens.[19]

Action to bring about temperance was another outgrowth of the movement for industrial morality and was, in the eyes of its advocates, the most effective way of insuring diligence and frugality. Before temperance reform began in Lynn, shoemakers and other citizens drank heavily and often. There were grog shops in every part of town, and "it was not a rare sight to witness the apprentice, and even the school boy, laying his change on the counter, and receiving his evening dram." Every visitor was offered the decanter, the tumbler, and sugar bowl as a gesture of welcome. No storekeeper could survive if he did not sell liquor by the glass or mug, and occasionally treat his customers to a drink. No workingman would labor unless his employer provided a half pint of liquor per day as part of his wages.[20]

In the shoe shops of Lynn, many cordwainers drank their daily pint of "white eye" and there were some "who went the whole quart." At eleven and four each day, a boy went to the rum shop with a two-quart bottle for a supply of "black strap," a popular drink of rum sweetened with molasses. The shoemaker who made the best shoe treated his fellows to drinks; so did the one who made the worst. "Every birthday of each operative was a 'treat', every holiday was a regular 'blowout'—and every 'raising,' training, election of civil or military officers, and even the ordination was an occasion for the circulation of the pail of punch." The man who reached his "majority" laid in a supply of the choicest liquors for visiting well wishers. Shoemakers who went to the shore for an outing

18 *Lynn Mirror*, March 15, 1828.

19 *Essex Democrat* (Salem), March 18, 1831. Letter from a "Poor Man" protesting the law, *Lynn Mirror*, February 5, 1831.

20 "Lynn Scrapbooks," XXIII, 6. Nathan Chase, a Lynn shoe manufacturer, recalled that he hired carpenters in 1823 to construct his first central shop. They threatened to quit unless he provided a liquor ration. "Lynn Scrapbooks," XXIII, 7.

"would as soon think of sailing on dry land as of having a 'good time' without plenty of punch." Drinking was indulged in by all—ministers, doctors, and teachers as well as by clerks, artisans, and workingmen, by young and old, by male and female.[21] These drinking patterns were part of a preindustrial culture that did not stress self-denial, self-discipline, or the subordination of pleasure to productive labor.

The emerging code of industrial morality gave work paramount place in life. Whatever distracted from this duty of work became objectionable. Lebbeus Armstrong, an early temperance advocate in New York, reported that "the effect of intoxicants on labour efficiency was the strongest argument that could be presented in support of temperance."[22] Temperance must be viewed as an integral part of the larger process of social disciplining and not merely as a "symbolic crusade."[23] Its connection with other reforms is especially close in the early years, for drinking seemed conducive to every vice—poverty, debauchery, crime, idleness, brawling, civil disturbances—that frustrated the new order. As the Lynn town meeting expressed it in 1835, "the use of intoxicating liquors is the source of more disturbance, crime and misery than all other causes together.[24] Lynn's inhabitants apparently agreed with the Society for the Promotion of Industry, Frugality, and Temperance which had earlier, in 1832, deleted "industry" and "frugality" from its name on the grounds that temperance would insure these virtues.

In the vanguard of the temperance movement, Lynn was one of the first towns in Massachusetts to request prohibition on the sale of spirituous liquors.[25] An elderly minister from Brookline who had attended ninety-four ordinations reported that one such ceremony in Lynn in 1843 was the first at which liquor was absent and ladies were present.[26] To encourage temperance, reformers used both moral suasion and legal coercion, as well as methods that fell somewhere in between. Some shoe manufacturers employed no worker who drank. "You alone," one temperance advocate announced to bosses, "must take the bold, manly and decisive measure to make all your workmen temperate, industrious, punctual and faithful in their business."[27] Nathan and Isaiah Breed, two of the town's largest employers, also invested heavily in real estate. Owning much of central Lynn, they leased no land to anyone who permitted liquor on the premises. In their own businesses, they hired only tee-

[21] For descriptions of drinking customs in Lynn, see "Lynn Scrapbooks," XXIII, 6, 7, 27; XXIV 6, 11; *Lynn Mirror*, August 12, 1837; *Lynn News*, September 3, 1847; *Lynn Record*, July 24, 1839.

[22] Quoted in John Krout, *Origins of Prohibition* (New York, 1925), 79.

[23] Joseph Gusfield makes this argument in *Symbolic Crusade* (Urbana, 1963), especially 5–6.

[24] *Lynn Record*, May 28, 1835.

[25] *Lynn Record*, March 27, 1833, for report of town meeting.

[26] David N. Johnson. *Sketches of Lynn: The Changes of Fifty Years* (Lynn, 1880), 412–13. Robert Rantoul, "Mr. Rantoul's Establishment in Business—Intemperance and Pauperism," Essex Institute *Historical Collections*, V, no. 6 (December 1863), 246.

[27] *Lynn Mirror*, November 24, 1827.

totalers.[28] Militia captains, agreeing to dispense with ardent spirits, limited their men to cider and beer.[29] Some fire companies, made up primarily of shoemakers, inserted temperance clauses in their by-laws to ban spirits from their meeting houses. Some doctors renounced the use of liquor for medicinal purposes and adopted the cold-water theories of Vincenz Preisnitz (1790–1851), the German doctor who, for good health, prescribed cold baths and a diet that included copious amounts of cold water (20–25 glasses per day) and cold, unseasoned food. Young ladies were urged to rebuff courting young men who drank.[30]

The principal coercive agents here were the law and the police. Temperance reformers succeeded in converting the new moral values into a binding legal code enforced by Lynn's constables.[31] In the past, the main task of the police had been to canvass Lynn before the town meeting and read the warrant explaining the business agenda to each citizen. Chosen annually by the selectmen, the constables were not professionals. They received no regular pay, wore no uniforms, and carried no weapons. Their badge of office was a long staff ringed at the top with alternating bands of colored stripes. But their function and composition changed as they were called upon to enforce the new code of industrial morality. In the late 1840s, the traditional staff was cut into pieces to make billy clubs. At about the same time, some constables became permanent members of the force.[32] A survey of arrests in Lynn during the late 1850s shows that the majority were for the illegal sale of liquor, drunkenness, and disorderly conduct, and not for serious crimes against persons or property.[33]

Many shoemakers, adopting the new moral code, altered their forms of recreation and leisure. Perhaps the most popular holiday for the preindustrial mechanic was 'Lection Day, celebrated in Massachusetts for nearly two centuries before its abolition in 1831. The last Wednesday in May marked the election of representatives to the General Court. Festivities began on this day and continued until the following Monday, though "the entire week partook of the flavor of a holiday." Tame activities included visiting friends, gathering spring flowers, and eating 'Lection Cake, a special pastry made with molasses, wine, fruits and spices and covered with a sugar glaze. There were also athletic contests like jumping and wrestling, and games of chance—pitching coppers, throwing props, and card playing. But these were not the diversions that

[28] "Life and Times of Nathan Breed," *Daily Evening Item*, April 10, 1908.

[29] *Lynn Mirror*, May 17, 1838; *The Locomotive*, June 8, July 27, 1842.

[30] *Lynn Mirror*, July 26, 1828.

[31] There were periodic demands by groups of "citizens" for constables to crack down on liquor sellers. See *Lynn News*, December 16, 1853, March 3, 1857, for items on petition campaigns headed by Nathan and Isaiah Breed, two of Lynn's manufacturers.

[32] Henry Fenno, ed., *Our Police: The Official History of the Police Department of the City of Lynn* (Lynn, 1895). The police received pistols in 1878 during a strike of shoe workers. Also see "Lynn Scrapbooks," XXXVI, 14–15.

[33] For police report on illegal drinking and gambling, see *Lynn Pioneer*, April 15, 1847. Arrest statistics for 1850s are in annual reports of the city marshal.

alarmed the partisans of industrial morality. 'Lection Day was also a time of heavy drinking, gambling, and wild and bawdy dancing at roadhouse taverns. Young men from the Lynn-Salem area journeyed to public houses on the Danvers Road or to Putnam's Tavern on the Danvers Plain to consume an assortment of drinks—egg pop, beer punch, flip and toddy. Adults paused between drinks long enough to watch horse races on Danvers Plain.[34] In 1831, the year 'Lection Day was abolished, Alonzo Lewis, Lynn historian and poet, commemorated the holiday with a poem describing the manner in which it had been celebrated by townsfolk:

And is Election Day no more?
Good old 'Lection . . .
No more shall we go up
To see "Old Willis!"
He has hung up his fiddle
On the last peg.
The days of old 'Lection are over.
The glorious days of "Landee John!"
When "Gid" used to hustle coppers,
And the niggers play "paw-paw"
On Boston Common.
No more shall we eat 'Lection Cake,
Or drink muddy beer,
Misnomered "ale,"
At "Old Bly's."
The days of dancing "Suke" are done,
And fat "Bet" shall shake her jolly sides no more
To the merry winding about
Of linked sweetness, long drawn out,
From old "Pompey's fiddle!"
No more shall "the Governor"
Sit in his great arm-chair,
To encounter the stare
Of the idle mixed multitude,
"Black spirits and white,
Blue spirits and gray,"
Barefoot and booted,
Maudlin and merry.
Yes, 'Lection is done
With all its paraphernalia
Of cocked-up hats and fun. . . .[35]

[34] Robert Rantoul, "Mr. Rantoul's Connexion with Town and Parochial Affairs—His Views of Religion," Essex Institute *Historical Collections,* VI, no. 2 (April 1864), 84. "Lynn Scrapbooks," 1, p. 7.
[35] *Lynn Mirror,* May 28, 1831.

Although it is doubtful that a holiday celebrated for two centuries suddenly disappeared, traditionalists would hereafter make merry only under the ban of respectable opinion.

Lynn shoemakers, like New Englanders generally, were also citizen soldiers. In the years following the war of 1812, they converted militia training days into occasions for boisterous fun. They ordinarily assembled once or twice a year, presumably for marching, shooting, and mock warfare. The purpose of training day, then, was to prepare for fighting, but it became a rolicking fall festival, one additional manifestation of eighteenth-century libertine morality. Proponents of industrial morality were understandably hostile. "Scenes of riot and drunkenness" were "disgusting and harmful." "Men and boys in a brutal state of intoxication, and even large numbers of females were to be observed mixing with the motley crowd." Militiamen attracted a large crowd of camp followers who gathered around "the numerous shanties located about the muster field." The enterprising proprietors of these "shanties" dispensed "ardent spirits" which encouraged "tumults and riots." Training day also attracted "pickpockets, gamblers, drunkards, profane swearers, with many others of a similar stamp." Worst of all, the excitement of parades, cannon fire, and soldiers in uniform enticed "innocent children and youths" to the field. They were youngsters "whom curiosity brought together, but whom nothing but night send home more corrupted than they went." "More mischief is here done in one day, more vicious inclinations here take root, than home, or the pulpit, can eradicate in a year." Military commanders contributed to the disorder by treating their men to rum dispensed from large barrels hauled on wagons.[36]

The abolition of compulsory militia training aided the cause of morality, but the volunteer fire companies that replaced the militia also offended reformers. Each unit, which numbered sixty men, was made up primarily of the neighborhood's shoemakers who supplied the muscle to operate the hand-pumped apparatus.[37] The companies frequently engaged in competitive musters that tested their speed, strength, and accuracy. But the fire houses also became important social and political centers in which the enginemen met for discussions generally well-lubricated by liquor. Fire company musters in the 1840s attracted several thousand onlookers who, at the conclusion, joined the festivities that accompanied the collation, or banquet, and the firemen's ball. The muster was the nineteenth-century equivalent of modern spectator sport. An 1846 contest, for example, drew 2,000 spectators; another in 1848 attracted 2,500.[38] The temperance movement made inroads among the shoemaker-enginemen. Some units became temperate; others remained drinkers. Those converted provide another indication of success of industrial morality among shoemakers, altering their lives outside the shop.

[36] *Lynn Mirror*, July 1, 1826, October 6, October 27, 1827.

[37] Membership lists often were included with constitutions and by-laws of the units. All are in the manuscript collections of the Lynn Historical Society. Also see *Lynn Tattler*, February 19, 1849.

[38] Lynn Forum, September 15, 1846; *Lynn Tattler*, April 1848; *Lynn Pioneer*, March 2, April 12, 1848.

Informal and spontaneous expressions of a loose morality on the part of the shoemakers also changed. In 1828, Lynn adopted a series of by-laws to prohibit objectionable forms of social behavior. Placed under the ban was the use of profane, obscene, or insulting language; shooting dice in any street, land, or alley; making tumultuous noises, and being rude in either speech or gesture toward females.[39] Furthermore, no person would be permitted any longer to bathe or swim in the nude within 200 feet of a dwelling.

Beginning in the 1830s and 1840s, the shoemakers lost access to the common lands to which they had gone for picnics and outings. Nahant Peninsula, for generations a favorite of shoemakers who wished to fish, drink, and relax, became a resort for the wealthy, most of them from Boston. By the 1840s, one could find on this rugged and scenic site "the Boston Butterflies who fly up and down between Boston and Nahant during the summer, luxuriating on the money which they have cajoled out of the people." It became the place "where the Boston aristocracy airs itself every summer and braces up for the dissipation of the coming winter." Another portion of Lynn's open land fell into the hands of Richard S. Fay, a wealthy Boston capitalist who guarded "his grounds from the profane step of Lynn shoemakers by a pack of savage dogs."[40] Although traditional forms of leisure and recreation did not suddenly cease, the changes that accompanied the industrial revolution were altering the shoemaker's life both in and outside the workplace.

Lynn's schools, as might be expected, helped to inculcate the new values, becoming an important instrument in shaping good character. Indeed, the annual reports of its school officials often read like the proceedings of the Society for the Promotion of Industry, Frugality, and Temperance. No longer could children be ignored or allowed to be initiated into society through the public house or neighborhood gang. Bad habits or dangerous opinions, once formed, would be difficult to change. Schools were a strong antidote. They were "the very places for cultivating self-restraint, order, decency and a regard for all the proprieties of life." In addition to useful knowledge, educators would teach "morals and manners," particularly "sobriety, industry and frugality, chastity, moderation and temperance." They also had to foster "habits of application, respect to superiors, and obedience to law."[41] One such habit was punctuality, "a habit invaluable to individual credit, successful business, and general tranquility." The importance of "having a place, time and order for everything, and everything in its order, time and place" was the all-encompassing maxim to be taught.[42]

[39] *Lynn Directory*, 1832, 29–31, lists by-laws adopted in 1828.

[40] *Essex County Washingtonian*, September 12, 1844; *Lynn News*, December 17, 1847. For Nahant's conversion to a wealthy resort, see Alonzo Lewis and James R. Newhall, *History of Lynn*, 62–63. *Lynn Pioneer*, May 24, 1848.

[41] Commonwealth of Massachusetts, State Board of Education, "Report from Lynn," in *Eighteenth Annual Report of the Board of Education* (Boston, 1855), 128. For a broader view of changes in the schools, see Michael B. Katz, *The Irony of Early School Reform: Educational Innovation in Mid-Nineteenth Century Massachusetts* (Cambridge, 1968).

[42] Town of Lynn. School Committee, *Annual Report for 1847–1848* (Lynn, 1848),

Control over education shifted from the neighborhood prudential committee to the town school committee with enlargement of the administrative unit from the neighborhood to the town.[43] This administrative change led to the accession to office of Lynn's prominent and wealthy rather than the obscure and middling townsfolk. The school committee stripped the prudential committees of the power to hire and fire teachers, to set the curriculum, and to prescribe a code of student conduct. Consonant with an 1826 State law, the school committee required of teaching candidates "evidence of good moral character." Reformers at the State level supplied such candidates by opening several normal schools for the purpose of properly training teachers. Emphasis upon "moral character" occurred simultaneously with the assignment to women of the primary responsibility for child rearing and for the defense of a stern moral code. Partly for this reason perhaps, a shift from male to female teachers took place in the elementary schools.

Reformers often encountered indifference to their efforts to tighten school discipline. Truancy was a major problem. In 1838, one third of those enrolled in Massachusetts' public schools were absent during the winter months. In the summer, this figure increased to 40 percent. The situation was worse in Lynn. Of the 1,430 town children in 1830 between four and fourteen years of age, 1,130 were enrolled in the common schools. Average attendance was about 650.[44] If the minds of the young were to be shaped properly, a way was needed to compel enrollment and attendance. Beginning in 1851, Massachusetts passed the first compulsory attendance laws. In subsequent years truant officers tracked down the runaways.

Reformers also encountered the obstinate cultural legacy of the eighteenth century, an age that had been indifferent to self-discipline, obedience to authority, and self-imposed restraints on natural impulses, or that had encouraged their opposites. The clash between the new nineteenth-century morality and the earlier immorality produced conflict in the schools. In 1838, the State Board of Education reported that 150 or more schools were "broken up by the insubordination of the scholars."[45]

Compliance to rules of behavior that students had not acquired in the home was the goal of Lynn's reformers and the teachers they hired. Because the great majority of students under twelve were the sons and daughters of shoemakers, their behavior provides a glimpse of their

---

7. Also see statement by City Solicitor and former school committee member, J. C. Stickney, *Lynn News*, December 20, 1853.

43 For transfer of power see Commonwealth of Massachusetts, State Board of Education, *First Annual Report of the Board of Education* (Boston, 1838), 28–37; *Tenth Annual Report*, 148–52.

44 State Board of Education, *First Annual Report*, 37. "Lynn Town Records, 1822–1835," 373. MS in Lynn City Hall.

45 State Board of Education, *Seventh Annual Report of the Board of Education* (Boston, 1844), 66–67. The secretary happily reported in 1844 that "at the present time, the breaking up of schools, through a successful insurrection of the scholars, is an exceedingly rare event. This is most gratifying."

families and of their rearing. Many families apparently did not stress the dictum of "everything in its time, order, and place." The eighteenth century tended to ignore truancy and tardiness. Students who went off to the beach at Nahant or berrying in the woods were simply imitating their parents' behavior. The school committee recognized the source of such disobedience: "Right control at home will generally secure obedience at school. Its want is often the true cause of the child's ill conduct and punishment."[46] To gain student compliance to the new rigorous code, teachers and school officials employed both persuasion and coercion. They preferred a "kind and paternal discipline," but used the whip and stick when paternalism failed.

The beating of "refractory" students caused heated controversy in Lynn. Josiah Hand, for one, was flogged with a wooden stick two-feet long and half-an-inch thick for refusing to sweep the classroom. City and school officials at first defended such practices. They argued that the teacher was an agent of the parent and thus entitled to treat the child as the parent would. But some parents did not share the values advanced by the teacher or the school board. On several occasions angry parents whose children had been physically chastised invaded the classroom and either berated or beat the teacher.[47] School officials therefore altered their position. Once the child entered the classroom, they claimed, the authority of the parent ended. Too many parents, one critic charged, "were total strangers to all discipline, whether mental or moral."

Massachusetts school reformers also began to segregate the sexes in the public schools. Floor plans for "model" schools provided for separate playgrounds, entrances, stairways, and halls. Boys and girls would be together in the classroom, to be sure, but always under the watchful eye of an instructor of sound moral character.[48]

The clash within the schools between the loose morality of the past and the more rigorous industrial morality was part of a broader struggle, one which encompassed such issues as poor relief, drinking habits, forms of recreation, leisure activities, sexual practices, and work habits. Advocates of industrial morality made significant gains over two decades, but complete success eluded them. Many townsfolk, though vulnerable to hardship and poverty, struggled mightily to avoid becoming public charges. Yet the number of inmates in the Alms House increased and relief rolls grew—not proportionate to population growth, to be sure, but upward nonetheless. Some of Lynn's inhabitants renounced drink in favor of cold water, but others persisted in heavy and frequent tippling. The boisterous brawling and earthiness of the eighteenth century disappeared from many public places but continued in a moral underground, away from the scrutiny and censure of respectable opinion.

What of the overall affect of industrial morality on Lynn shoemakers

[46] Town of Lynn, School Committee, *Annual Report for 1847–1848*, 7.

[47] For flogging cases in schools, see *Lynn Bay State*, June 13, 1850, January 23, 1857; *Lynn News*, July 26, 1850, February 20, 27, 1852, December 20, 1853, February 3, May 5, 1857. Town of Lynn. School Committee, *Annual Report for 1847–48*, 5.

[48] State Board of Education, *Fifth Annual Report of the Board of Education* (Boston, 1842), 126; *Tenth Annual Report* (Boston, 1847), 253.

and, if Lynn is at all representative of other manufacturing towns, of workingmen elsewhere?

Certainly, the impact of poor relief reform was especially profound. Long before the appearance of factories, the shoemaker was dependent on wages for his livelihood. Norman Ware is misleading (in his *Industrial Worker, 1840–1860*) when he asserts that "in 1830 nearly all the shoemakers of Lynn had owned their homes with some land about them." "Almost every family kept a pig and many had their own cow." Tax records do not support this view. Scarcely 10 percent of Lynn's adult males owned a pig, fewer still owned a cow. Less than 50 percent of the entire adult male population owned any real property whatever. Most shoemakers owned nothing. Ware's description may have been accurate for the cordwainers of 1800, but it was not true of the shoemaker from 1830 to 1860.[49] As early as 1830 the shoemaker was vulnerable to the vicissitudes and insecurity of a competitive capitalist market economy.

Changes in poor relief produced a dread of dependency in the shoemakers, and a compulsive drive to do all that was humanly possible to avoid pauperism—precisely the objective sought by the Society for the Promotion of Industry, Frugality, and Temperance. The depression of 1837–44 severely tested the resourcefulness of Lynn's shoemakers. Many foraged the woods for fuel, dug dandelions and clams for food, bartered with neighboring farmers or fishermen—anything to avoid going to the Overseers of the Poor.

A dread of pauperism is expressed in a letter to the *Lynn Pioneer* in 1848: "No person can contemplate the idea of becoming a pauper, without a feeling of horror. It seems like becoming a criminal. Many would as soon go to prison, as to a poor-house, and others would sooner go to their graves than to either."[50] That death would be preferable to dependency is evident in the suicide note left by an aging shoe cutter, Joseph Dwyer:

> As I grow old, and my health fails, and I find myself less able to provide for myself and live as I want to, and not to be dependent on others, who have as much as they can do to provide for themselves (no doubt they would do what they could for me in an emergency, but I prefer to help myself, one way or another), I take the method you will find when it happens. I have enjoyed life as well as the most of men, but cannot bear the idea of being a helpless, dependent old man. I paid my way so far, and owe nothing. Goodbye to all.[51]

The State's new poor houses were more feared than the local almshouses. When inmates of the Lynn Alms House were transferred to the new institution in Tewksbury, many were "dragged out screaming."

[49] Norman Ware, *The Industrial Worker, 1840–1860* (Chicago, 1964), 39–40. Town of Lynn, "Assessments and Taxes," 1832, MS, Lynn City Hall.

[50] *Lynn Pioneer*, March 15, 1848.

[51] "Lynn Scrapbooks," XVII, 45.

Equating dependency with shame deepened the shoemakers' determination to fight for their rights. Upon being told by one manufacturer that poor workmen should not have children, a mechanic angrily asked: "What impudence! Who made them rulers over us." The specter of poverty and the horror of dying among paupers and criminals was greatest for mechanics, who could no longer be assured of acquiring a "competency" under the rigorous competitive system. The word itself has disappeared from our vocabulary, but the pre-industrial mechanic looked upon a "competency" as a reward to which every able-bodied, diligent mechanic was entitled. He believed that during his working life as a mechanic—the years from 16 to 50 or 55—he would be able to set aside enough money to support himself after retirement. The period from retirement to death was "a portion of time which was never intended for a season of labor."[52] But under the new system, the shoemaker would have to labor until the moment "the green sod is closed over him." Those shoemakers who were determined to acquire "an honest maintenance" and escape pauperism succeeded only by "unparalleled exertions," often laboring twelve to sixteen hours a day in the crowded, poorly ventilated little shop of seven by nine feet. Such exertions might produce an unintended result. Lynn health officials reported that the life expectancy of Massachusetts shoemakers was twenty years less than for farmers.[53] The work day for shoemakers became longer, the labor more arduous. By the 1840s, shoemakers commonly worked beyond dark, taxing their eyes by the dim light of candle or lamp, and earning an average of $5 per week.

To avoid the shame of becoming a public charge some shoemakers turned to collective self-help, often in an informal way. They frequently aided one another by giving sustenance to a jobless shoemaker or loaning out a small boat for fishing. In the small shop where each crew of journeymen worked, a jour possessing a special skill might perform that skill for his fellow wage earner so that the employer would not "cut him down" (reduce his wages) or give him "the sack." Shoemakers also formed six cooperative stores and affiliated with the New England Protective Union, a federation of several hundred cooperatives that covered much of the New England region. Manned by volunteer help and operating on a strictly cash basis, these stores enabled the shoemaker to obtain more goods for less money. New England workingmen and mechanics established the most extensive network of cooperative stores in the region's history.

The shame and odium attached to poverty also caused shoemakers to reject charity from manufacturer-philanthropists whom they viewed as "plundering drones" responsible for their plight. When Isaiah Breed, one of Lynn's largest manufacturers and most prominent apostles of reform, proposed a soup kitchen to provide some relief during the 1837–44

[52] *The Awl,* August 21, 1844.

[53] Lynn. *Annual Report of the Board of Health of Lynn,* 1850, City Document #7, 14. Average age at death for Massachusetts farmers was sixty-five; for shoemakers forty-three.

depression, the mechanics responded with angry ridicule. They wanted work at good wages, not charity from the hands of a "grinder" from "extortion hollow" who lived off them.[54] They reacted in a similar manner a decade later when depressions struck the shoe trade with ominous regularity.[55] Their reluctance to accept poor relief stemmed from a public policy and pervasive ethos that made self-reliance a virtue and dependency a humiliation.

In considering other aspects of industrial morality—temperance, forms of recreation, codes of personal behavior—three groups of shoemakers are discernible by their differing responses. That the mechanics, like Americans generally, divided along cultural lines is familiar enough. Less well known or understood is the relationship between industrial morality and class consciousness.

One group of shoemakers were traditionalists, the bane of the reform forces. They stubbornly clung to customs and habits inherited from the loose eighteenth-century morality. They patronized rum dealers, beer and cider shops, attended Jim Crow shows and circuses, and frequented the town's saloons. Within their fire companies they carried on the raucous activities that had been such an important part of 'Lection Day and militia training. Despite condemnation by the reformers, they still played props and cards, hustled coppers, and danced to the fiddle. Many traditionalists lived in Lynn's western portion, once the site of modest mercantile activity and of the loose morality which that form of economy had produced. In West Lynn stood Caleb Wiley's grog shop. Frequently charged with selling liquor, Wiley was often acquitted of such violations because of the helpful testimony of his shoemaker customers. These traditionalists were mostly Democrats, usually of the Hunker or orthodox variety rather than anti-Masonic or, later, Free Soil wing. Ideologically and socially they remained aloof from the efforts of other shoemakers to form producer cooperatives and thus create, in embryonic shape, an alternative to capitalism. A desire for higher wages united them with other shoemakers, but the traditionalist was unlikely to respond to radical plans for social reconstruction. And if one is to accept the innuendoes of their critics, the traditionalists were men of inferior skill in shoemaking. They made "cacks" and "slaps" exclusively rather than the finer welted walking shoe. Their lack of skill may in fact have produced a diminished self-esteem that made them more accepting of their lot, more limited in their demands, and less eager for social reconstruction than the skilled shoemaker. In any case, those who clung to a traditional code and resisted the new industrial morality did not mount an articulate, organized challenge to the economic power of the shoe manufacturers.

A second group of shoemakers were the loyalists, who combined the new morality with deference toward their employers. They were model workers: self-reliant, self-disciplined, sober—and unprotesting. They were among the rank and file of the moral reform movement. Some joined the Society for the Promotion of Industry, Frugality, and Temperance

[54] *The Awl*, March 1, 1845.
[55] *Lynn News*, November 24, 1857.

and in town meetings voted for statutes that would chastise the poor, reshape the schools, deny licenses to liquor dealers, punish drunkards, and ban circuses and Jim Crow shows. Their signatures were probably among the 2,000 affixed to the petitions circulated by manufacturers Isaiah and Nathan Breed calling upon Lynn officials rigorously to enforce temperance laws. They often provided the convicting testimony in court cases against liquor dealers. Many loyalists were bound by ties of kinship, religion, or neighborhood to those shoe employers prominent in the moral reform movement. One can identify dozens of journeymen who were the brothers, sons, or fathers of manufacturers; often they worked for their relatives as wage earners. If one were to assess the numerical strength of the loyalists solely on the basis of elections, they and their employers made up a bare majority of Lynn's population. Like the traditionalists, they remained aloof from the efforts of other shoemakers to build class institutions as alternatives to those dominated by entrepreneurs. And like the entrepreneurs, they attributed poverty to idleness and self-indulgence rather than to exploitation.

Rebel mechanics were the third group. Culturally, they were nearly indistinguishable from the loyalists: each practiced temperance and frugality, and respected the canons of propriety in dress, speech, and demeanor. But the rebel mechanic was a vigorous critic of both capitalist exploitation *and* drink, economic injustice *and* moral degradation. Where the loyalist shoemakers attributed the employers' wealth to hard work, self-reliance, and shrewdness, the rebel claimed it was a product of petty fraud and heartless extortion. And where the loyalist attributed poverty to drink, the rebel mechanic reversed the causal connection and attributed drink to poverty and despair. His role in Lynn prompts the suggestion that the connection between working-class radicalism and a code of morality that was later termed "middle class," is the reverse of what some interpreters have argued. The most vigorous opponents of capitalist exploitation were those wage earners who had accepted a code of morality which they shared with their employers but used in their own class interest.

The rebel mechanics were the catalytic force among the shoemakers. They organized the Journeymen Cordwainers Society, drafted the circulars and constitution, edited the newspapers, founded the producers and consumers cooperatives. Yet at the same time their social gatherings, the cordwainers' tea parties, were models of teetotal decorum. They valued learning and education as a means of protecting themselves from the gullibility and ignorance that aided their oppressors, but insisted that shoeworkers and not employers control the schools. They also founded a workingmen's library as an auxiliary to their trade society. The rebel shoeworker might speak at the Washingtonian Total Abstinence Society on Friday night and the cordwainers' society on Saturday. From their work in the temperance movement, they learned how to use outdoor public meetings to solicit support from other shoemakers. In sum, the rebel mechanic combined the currents of moral reform and an emerging working-class consciousness.

The rebel mechanic exhibited a strong sense of self-dignity, pride, and self-esteem which served to stiffen his resistance to conditions he viewed as degrading. His heightened sense of worth derived from an ideology formed from three sources—the labor theory of value, republicanism, and, to a lesser extent, Christianity. This ideology enabled the rebel mechanic both to interpret what was happening to him and to fashion a cooperative network of social relations, as an alternative to competitive capitalism. From 1830 to 1860, the skilled shoemaker was in social decline, largely owing to the intense competition among wage earners for the right to work and, it follows, the right to live. The rebel mechanic identified the source of his trouble as the exploitation of employers whose control of raw materials enabled them to take from the mechanic a portion of everything he produced, leaving a wage that barely supported him and his family. Here was the root cause of both economic and moral degradation and here, too, was the point at which the rebel mechanic parted company with the loyalist.

Resolving to resist his degradation, the rebel mechanic sought to embrace industrial morality and unite with others like himself in a joint effort of collective self-help. Self-imposition of a rigorous code of moral conduct was not a way to respectability but rather a means of preserving personal pride and obtaining a sense of power and self-confidence at a time when the worker always seemed subject to outside control. He was proclaiming his independence from those external forces that governed him—whether employer or liquor. Obedience to the commands of another was slavery in his eyes; so, too, was his surrender to temptations that came from within. Addiction to alcohol was one form of bondage. Sam Hayward of Boston, a mechanic and a temperance lecturer who was a favorite among Lynn's artisans, explained his own conversion: "I was a football when a drunkard, kicked around by everybody." Hayward became temperate during the 1837–44 depression when a Washingtonian approached him and asked, "Sam, don't you want to be a *man* again?"

The drunkard, furthermore, was useless to everyone—family, friends, and, most important, to himself. The mechanic interpreted drunkenness as an admission of despair and surrender, a sign that the victim had succumbed, leaving him without will or direction. But the rebel shoeworkers who organized the Cordwainers Society and the Good Samaritan Temperance Society neither condemned the drunkard nor withheld their support from him. "Never forsake a brother—if he fail once, twice, or even the third time, receive him again."[56] Renouncing coercion, they chose moral suasion and mutual support, and thereby were distinguished from their temperate employers who readily employed coercion against the traditionalists among the shoeworkers.

Cultural differences impeded but did not prevent concerted action by shoemakers for limited ends. The traditionalists were neither inert nor hidebound. And even the loyalists' patience had its limits. A series of severe depressions in the 1850s brought about an economic crisis that

[56] *Essex County Washingtonian,* March 30, 1843. For a brief account of the mechanics presence in the Washingtonian movement, see John Krout, *Origins of Prohibition,* 182–202.

united shoemakers in a common effort to protect their economic interests. The result was the great shoemakers strike of 1860, perhaps the largest strike in New England's history, involving nearly 20,000 binders and shoemakers in the region's most important industry.

But despite the impressive solidarity of the moment, cultural tensions would remain. The cultural side of the industrial revolution—the new attitudes toward dependency, sexuality, drink and self-discipline, and the new forms of education, pleasure, and recreation—became a source of discord among shoemakers, dividing them along cultural lines, restricting social contact, and circumscribing the formation of class consciousness.

The Quest for Certainty: Slave Spirituals

LAWRENCE W. LEVINE

After slavery was well established in the New World, attempts were made by the masters to weaken the remaining elements of African culture in the slave community. Members of the same tribal groups were often separated, use of African languages were forbidden, and blacks were discouraged from continuing their religious practices. Since most African religions were linked with specific land areas where the ancestors of the people were buried, these religions would not have traveled well in any case. Unlike blacks in the Caribbean and in Brazil, who were able to preserve certain aspects of African culture because of the enormous concentrations of slaves from the same African regions as well as continuous massive imports of slaves directly from Africa, blacks in the United States were increasingly cut off from their African past as successive generations of slaves born here participated in the acculturative process.

It does not necessarily follow, however, that American blacks were left with no cultural and intellectual resources with which to form a new culture. Nor does the fact that the slaves left few written records of their past imply that their inner lives suffered from lack of substance. Until recent years, historians, sociologists, and anthropologists have vehemently disagreed over the extent to which distinctive African cultural traits have carried over into the culture of American blacks and over the impact of African culture on the United States, especially the South. In addition, the prior emphasis of some historians on the passivity and childlike qualities often attributed to the slaves has given rise to an impassioned controversy over the slave personality. These and other debates centering on the experience of slavery have aroused a greater interest than ever before in exploring the cultural and intellectual lives of the slaves, and historians are now drawing on the substantial body of source material that was previously utilized almost exclusively by anthropologists and folklorists. Apart from the descriptions of slave life provided by white observers, both sympathetic and hostile, the slaves themselves left a mass of illuminating material, including several hundred narratives composed by fugitive slaves, the religious and secular slave songs (primarily spirituals and work songs), and a large body of folktales.

The spirituals, particularly, provide significant insights into the developing intellectual life of the American bondsmen. After the beginning of the Second Great Awakening at the turn of the nineteenth century, revivalist churches, chiefly Baptist and Methodist, began to seek actively the conversion of the slaves. In this they sometimes had the support of slaveowners who were genuinely concerned for the spiritual welfare of their slaves or who were convinced that Christianity would increase the slaves' passivity. Other, perhaps more perceptive masters recognized the revolutionary potential of a religion that proclaimed all men equal before God, and they prohibited their slaves from participating in religious services of any kind. During the nineteenth century, what has been called the "invisible church" grew up among the slaves, who were taking the ideas of Christianity but altering them in subtle ways to make them their own. It was this church that produced many of the spirituals and that inspired such rebels as Nat Turner, who drew his imagery of wrath and judgment from the Bible.

In his book on the oral tradition of American blacks, Lawrence Levine, of the University of California at Berkeley, has drawn on the vast array of available folk materials to produce a remarkable study of the Afro-American subculture. The selection from that work reprinted below deals with the role the spirituals played in creating a world view among the slaves that gave them confidence in the face of an otherwise apparently hostile universe.

It is significant that the most common form of slave music we know of is sacred song. I use the term "sacred" not in its present usage as something antithetical to the secular world; neither the slaves nor their African forebears ever drew modernity's clear line between the sacred and the secular. The uses to which spirituals were put are an unmistakable indication of this. They were not sung solely or even primarily in churches or praise houses but were used as rowing songs, field songs, work songs, and social songs. Seated in a long cypress bark canoe on the Altamaha River in Georgia in 1845, Sir Charles Lyell listened to the six slave rowers improvise songs complimenting their master's family and celebrating a black woman of the neighborhood by comparing her beauty to that of the red bird. "Occasionally they struck up a hymn, taught them by the Methodists, in which the most sacred subjects were handled with strange familiarity, and which, though nothing irreverent was meant, sounded oddly to our ears, and, when following a love ditty, almost profane."[1] Mary Dickson Arrowood recalled slave boatmen in the late 1850s singing the following spirituals which, characteristically, were as congenial to the work situation as to the praise house:

Breddren, don' git weary,
Breddren, don' git weary,
Breddren, don' git weary,
Fo' de work is most done.

De ship is in de harbor, harbor, harbor,
De ship is in de harbor,
To wait upon de Lord. . . .

'E got 'e ca'go raidy, raidy, raidy,
'E got 'e ca'go raidy,
Fo' to wait upon de Lord.[2]

On the Sea Islands during the Civil War, Lucy McKim heard the spiritual *Poor Rosy* sung in a wide variety of contexts and tempos:

> On the water, the oars dip "Poor Rosy" to an even andante; a stout boy and girl at the hominy-mill will make the same "Poor Rosy" fly, to keep up with the whirling stone; and in the evening, after the day's work is done, "Heab'n shall-a be my home" [the final line of each stanza] peals up slowly and mournfully from the distant quarters.[3]

For the slaves, then, songs of God and the mythic heroes of their religion were not confined to a specific time or place, but were appropriate to almost every situation. It is in this sense that I use the concept sacred—not to signify a rejection of the present world but to describe the process of incorporating within this world all the elements of the divine. The religious historian Mircea Eliade, whose definition of sacred has shaped my own, maintains that for people in traditional societies religion is a means of extending the world spatially upward so that communication with the other world becomes ritually possible, and extending it temporally backward so that the paradigmatic acts of the gods and mythical

[1] [Sir Charles] Lyell, [*A Second Visit to the United States of North America* (New York, 1849)], I, 244–45.

[2] Mary Dickson Arrowood and Thomas Hoffman Hamilton, "Nine Negro Spirituals, 1850–61," *JAF* [*Journal of American Folklore*], 41 (1928), 582, 584.

[3] Lucy McKim, *Dwight's Journal of Music,* 21 (1862), 255.

ancestors can be continually re-enacted and indefinitely recoverable. By creating sacred time and space, Man can perpetually live in the presence of his gods, can hold on to the certainty that within one's own lifetime "rebirth" is continually possible, and can impose order on the chaos of the universe. "Life," as Eliade puts it, "is lived on a twofold plane; it takes its course as human existence and, at the same time, shares in a trans-human life, that of the cosmos or the gods."[4]

Claude Lévi-Strauss, who found these same cosmological outlooks in South America and Asia, has eloquently expressed the difficulties modern Westerners have in relating to them. As a boy he lived with his grandfather, the rabbi of Versailles, in a house which was linked to the synagogue by a long inner corridor. To the young Lévi-Strauss that long passage was appropriately symbolic: "Even to set foot in that corridor was an awesome experience; it formed an impassable frontier between the profane world and that other world from which was lacking precisely that human warmth which was the indispensable condition to my recognizing it as sacred."[5] For men and women of traditional societies, such as those the slaves had originally come from, such corridors were absent. This is not to deny that the slaves were capable of making distinctions between this world and the next. Of course they were, and some of their songs do reflect a desire to release their hold upon the temporal present. "Why don't you give up de world?" they sang at times. "We must leave de world behind." Or, again:

> This world is not my home.
> This world is not my home.
> This world's a howling wilderness,
> This world is not my home.[6]

But for the most part when they looked upon the cosmos they saw Man, Nature, and God as a unity; distinct but inseparable aspects of a sacred whole.

This notion of sacredness gets at the essence of the spirituals, and through them at the essence of the slave's world view. Denied the possibility of achieving an adjustment to the external world of the antebellum South which involved meaningful forms of personal integration, attainment of status, and feelings of individual worth that all human beings crave and need, the slaves created a new world by transcending the nar-

[4] Mircea Eliade, *The Sacred and the Profane* (New York, 1961), Chaps. 2, 4, and *passim*. For the similarity of Eliade's concept to the world view of West Africa, see W. E. Abraham, *The Mind of Africa* (London, 1962), Chap. 2; R. S. Rattray, *Religion and Art in Ashanti* (Oxford, 1927); and John S. Mbiti, *African Religions and Philosophies* (Garden City, N.Y., 1969), especially Chap. 3.

[5] Claude Lévi-Strauss, *Triste Tropiques* (New York, 1964), 215.

[6] William Francis Allen, Charles Pickard Ware, and Lucy McKim Garrison, *Slave Songs of the United States* (1867; reprint ed., New York, 1951), 27–28; William E. Barton, *Old Plantation Hymns: A Collection of Hitherto Unpublished Melodies of the Slave and the Freedmen* (Boston, 1899), 9.

row confines of the one in which they were forced to live. They extended the boundaries of their restrictive universe backward until it fused with the world of the Old Testament, and upward until it became one with the world beyond. The spirituals are the record of a people who found the status, the harmony, the values, the order they needed to survive by internally creating an expanded universe, by literally willing themselves reborn. In this respect I agree with the anthropologist Paul Radin that

> The ante-bellum Negro was not converted to God. He converted God to himself. In the Christian God he found a fixed point and he needed a fixed point, for both within and outside of himself, he could see only vacillation and endless shifting. . . . There was no other safety for people faced on all sides by doubt and the threat of personal distintegration, by the thwarting of instincts and the annihilation of values.[7]

The spirituals are a testament not only to the perpetuation of significant elements of an older world view among the slaves but also to the continuation of a strong sense of community. Just as the process by which the spirituals were created allowed for simultaneous individual and communal creativity, so their very structure provided simultaneous outlets for individual and communal expression. The overriding antiphonal structure of the spirituals—the call and response pattern which Negroes brought with them from Africa and which was reinforced in America by the practice of lining out hymns—placed the individual in continual dialogue with his community, allowing him at one and the same time to preserve his voice as a distinct entity and to blend it with those of his fellows. Here again slave music confronts us with evidence which indicates that, however seriously the slave system may have diminished the central communality that had bound African societies together, it was never able to destroy it totally or to leave the individual atomized and psychically defenseless before his white masters. In fact, the form and structure of slave music presented the slave with a potential outlet for his individual feelings even while it continually drew him back into the communal presence and permitted him the comfort of basking in the warmth of the shared assumptions of those around him. Those shared assumptions can be further examined by an analysis of the content of slave songs.

The most persistent single image the slave songs contain is that of the chosen people. The vast majority of the spirituals identify the singers as "de people dat is born of God," "We are the people of God," "we are de people of de Lord," "I really do believe I'm a child of God," "I'm a child ob God, wid my soul sot free," "I'm born of God, I know I am."

[7] Paul Radin, "Status, Phantasy, and the Christian Dogma," in Fisk University, *God Struck Me Dead: Religious Conversion Experiences and Autobiographies of Negro Ex-Slaves,* A. P. Watson, Paul Radin, and Charles S. Johnson, eds. (Nashville, 1945, unpublished typescript).

Nor is there ever any doubt that "To the promised land I'm bound to go," "I walk de heavenly road," "Heav'n shall-a be my home," "I gwine to meet my Saviour," "I seek my Lord and I find Him," "I'll hear the trumpet sound / In that morning."[8]

The force of this image cannot be diminished by the observation that similar images were present in the religious singing of white evangelical churches during the first half of the nineteenth century. White Americans could be expected to sing of triumph and salvation, given their long-standing heritage of the idea of a chosen people which was reinforced in this era by the belief in inevitable progress and manifest destiny, the spread-eagle oratory, the bombastic folklore, and, paradoxically, the deep insecurities concomitant with the tasks of taming a continent and developing an identity. But for this same message to be expressed by Negro slaves who were told endlessly that they were members of the lowliest of races *is* significant. It offers an insight into the kinds of barriers the slaves had available to them against the internalization of the stereotyped images their masters held and attempted consciously and unconsciously to foist upon them.

Not only did slaves believe that they would be chosen by the Lord, there is evidence that many of them felt their owners would be denied salvation. On a trip through the South, Harriet Martineau recorded the instance of a mistress being told by one of her slaves, "You no holy. We be holy. You in no state of salvation."[9] "Slaves knew enough of the orthodox theology of the time to consign all bad slaveholders to hell," Frederick Douglass wrote in his autobiography.[10] Some went even further than this. "No white people went to Heaven," a correspondent in the *Southern Workman* noted in 1897, summing up the attitude of his fellow slaves before the Civil War and added, "Many believe the same until this day."[11] The fugitive slave Charles Ball insisted that his fellow slaves refused to picture Heaven as a place where whites and blacks lived in perfect equality and boundless affection. "The idea of a revolution in the conditions of the whites and the blacks, is the corner-stone of the religion of the latter," he maintained. "Heaven will be no heaven to him [the slave], if he is not to be avenged of his enemies."[12] One hundred years later a former slave bore witness to Ball's assertion: "This is one reason why I believe in a hell. I don't believe a just God is going to take no such man as that [her master] into His Kingdom."[13] Martha Harrison re-

[8] Lines like these could be quoted endlessly. For the specific ones cited, see [Thomas Wentworth] Higginson, *Army Life* [*in a Black Regiment* (1869; Beacon Press ed., Boston, 1962)], 206, 216–17; Allen *et al., Slave Songs*, 7, 13, 58, 77, 104; Thomas P. Fenner, *Religious Folk Songs of the Negro as Sung on the Plantations* (1874; revised ed., Hampton, Va., 1909), 10–11, 48; J. B. T. Marsh, *The Story of the Jubilee Singers: With Their Songs* (Boston, 1880), 136, 167, 178.

[9] Quoted in J. L. Dillard, *Black English* (New York, 1972), 103.

[10] [Frederick] Douglass, *Life and Times* [*of Frederick Douglass* (revised ed., 1892; Collier reprint ed., New York, 1962)], 41.

[11] *SW* [*Southern Workman*], 26 (1897), 210.

[12] Charles Ball, *Fifty Years in Chains* (1837; reprint ed., New York, 1970), 220–22.

[13] Fisk University, *God Struck Me Dead*, 215.

counted how her master, "Old Bufford," who beat her mother savagely for refusing to sleep with him, offered on his death bed to spend seven thousand dollars to pay his way out of hell, "but he couldn'ta got out of hell, the way he beat my mammy."[14] Another former slave recalled that when her mistress died the slaves filed into the house "just a hollering and crying and holding their hands over their eyes, just hollering for all they could. Soon as they got outside of the house they would say, 'Old God damn son-of-a-bitch, she gone on down to hell.' "[15] Mary Reynolds described the brutality of Solomon, the white overseer on the Louisiana plantation where she had been a slave, and concluded simply, "I know that Solomon is burning in hell today, and it pleasures me to know it."[16]

Whether or not these reactions were typical, it is clear that a great many slaves agreed with H. B. Holloway that "It's going to be an awful thing up yonder when they hold a judgment over the way that things was done down here."[17] The prospect pleased slaves enough to become part of their repertory of jokes. The fugitive slave Lewis Clarke recounted two anecdotes with which the slaves on his Kentucky plantation used to delight each other. The first described the final conversation between a dying master and his slave: "Good-by, Jack; I have a long journey to go; farewell." "Farewell, massa! pleasant journey: you soon be dere, massa—*all de way down hill.*" The second told of a slave's reaction to the news that he would be rewarded by being buried in the same vault with his master: "Well, massa, one way I am satisfied, and one way I am not. I like to have good coffin when I die [but] I fraid, massa, when the debbil come take you body, he make mistake, and get mine."[18]

The confinement of much of the slave's new world to dreams and fantasies does not free us from the historical obligation of examining its contours, weighing its implications for the development of the slave's psychic and emotional structure, and eschewing the kind of reasoning that has led one historian to imply that, since the slaves had no alternatives open to them, their fantasy life was "limited to catfish and watermelons."[19] Their spirituals indicate clearly that there *were* alternatives open to them—alternatives which they themselves fashioned out of the fusion of their African heritage and their new religion—and that their fantasy life was so rich and so important to them that it demands understanding if we are even to begin to comprehend their inner world.

The God the slaves sang of was neither remote nor abstract, but as intimate, personal, and immediate as the gods of Africa had been. "O when I talk I talk wid God," "Mass Jesus is my bosom friend," "I'm

[14] Fisk University, *Unwritten History* [*of Slavery*, O. S. Egypt, J. Masuoka, and C. S. Johnson, eds. (Nashville, 1945, unpublished typescript)], 118.

[15] *Ibid.*, 134, 136.

[16] B. A. Botkin, ed., *Lay My Burden Down: A Folk History of Slavery* (Chicago, 1945), 121.

[17] *Ibid.*, 18.

[18] *Narrative of Lewis Clarke*, in *Interesting Memoirs and Documents Relating to American Slavery* (London, 1846), 87, 91.

[19] Stanley Elkins, *Slavery* (Chicago, 1959), 136.

goin' to walk with [talk with, live with, see] King Jesus by myself, by myself," were refrains that echoed through the spirituals.

In de mornin' when I rise,
  Tell my Jesus huddy [howdy] oh,
I wash my hands in de mornin' glory,
  Tell my Jesus huddy oh.

Gwine to argue wid de Father and chatter wid de son,
The last trumpet shall sound, I'll be there.
Gwine talk 'bout de bright world dey des' come from.
The last trumpet shall sound, I'll be there.

Gwine to write to Massa Jesus,
To send some Valiant soldier
To turn back Pharaoh's army, Hallelu!

"Good news, member, good news member," the slaves sang jubilantly, "And I heard-e from Heav'n today."[20]

The images of these songs were carried over into slave religious experiences. In a small South Carolina town in the 1850s, a white visitor questioned a young slave about his recent conversion experience:

"An den I went to hebben."
"What!" said I.
"An' den I went to hebben."
"Stop, Julius. You mean you had a dream, and thought you went to heaven."
"No, Sah: an' den I went to hebben, and dere I see de Lord Jesus, *a sittin' behind de door an' a reading his Bible.*"

There was no question, the white interrogator concluded, of the slave's "unmistakable sincerity" or of the fact that his fellow slave parishioners believed him implicitly.[21] "We must see, feel and hear something," an ex-slave exclaimed, "for our God talks to his children."[22] During a slave service in New Orleans in January of 1851, Fredrika Bremer witnessed the conversion of a black woman who, transported by religious enthusiasm, lept up and down with outstretched arms crying out "Hallelujah! Hallelujah!" and then, falling prostrate on the floor, lapsed into rigid quiescence. Gradually she recovered consciousness: "she talked to herself in a low voice, and such a beautiful, blissful expression was portrayed in

[20] Allen *et al., Slave Songs,* 2, 7, 15, 97–98; Barton, *Old Plantation Hymns,* 19, 30; Marsh, *Jubilee Singers,* 132.
[21] "The Religious Life of the Negro Slave [Second Paper]," *Harper's New Monthly Magazine,* 27 (1863), 681.
[22] Fisk University, *God Struck Me Dead,* 61.

her countenance that I would willingly experience that which she then experienced, saw, or perceived. It was no ordinary, no earthly scene. Her countenance was, as it were, transfigured."[23]

In these states of transfiguration slave converts commonly saw and conversed with God or Christ: "I looked to the east and there was . . . God. He looked neither to the right nor to the left. I was afraid and fell on my face. . . . I heard a voice from God saying, 'My little one, be not afraid for lo! I am with you always.' " "I looked away to the east and saw Jesus. . . . I saw God sitting in a big arm-chair." "I first came to know of God when I was a little child. He started talking to me when I was no more than nine years old." "I seen Christ with His hair parted in the center." "I saw Him when he freed my soul from hell." "I saw in a vision a snow-white train once and it moved like lightning. Jesus was on board and He told me that He was the Conductor." "I saw the Lord in the east part of the world. . . . His hair was parted in the middle and he looked like he had been dipped in snow and he was talking to me."[24] For the slave, Heaven and Hell were not concepts but places which could well be experienced during one's lifetime; God and Christ and Satan were not symbols but personages with whom meetings or confrontations were quite possible.

The heroes of the Scriptures—"Sister Mary," "Brudder Jonah," "Brudder Moses," "Brudder Daniel"—were greeted with similar intimacy and immediacy. In the world of the spirituals, it was not the masters and mistresses but God and Jesus and the entire pantheon of Old Testament figures who set the standards, established the precedents, and defined the values; who, in short, constituted the "significant others." The world described by the slave songs was a black world in which no reference was ever made to any white contemporaries. The slave's positive reference group was composed entirely of his own peers: his mother, father, sister, brother, uncles, aunts, preacher, fellow "sinners" and "mourners" of whom he sang endlessly, to whom he sent messages via the dying, and with whom he was reunited joyfully in the next world.

The same sense of sacred time and space which shaped the slave's portraits of his gods and heroes also made his visions of the past and future immediate and compelling. Descriptions of the Crucifixion communicate a sense of the actual presence of the singers: "Dey pierced Him in the side . . . Dey nail Him to de cross . . . Dey rivet His feet . . . Dey hanged him high . . . Dey stretch Him wide. . . ."

> Oh sometimes it causes me to tremble,—tremble,—tremble.
> Were you there when they crucified my Lord?[25]

[23] [Fredrika] Bremer, *America of the Fifties,* [Adolph B. Benson, ed. (New York, 1924)], 277–79.

[24] Fisk University, *God Struck Me Dead,* 4, 20, 30, 96, 101, 102, 154.

[25] Fenner, *Religious Folk Songs,* 162; E. A. McIlhenny, *Befo' De War Spirituals* (Boston, 1933), 39.

In 1818 a group of white Quaker students observed a Negro camp meeting. They watched in fascination and bewilderment as the black worshippers moved slowly around and around in a circle chanting:

We're traveling to Immanuel's land,
Glory! Halle-lu-jah.

Occasionally the dancers paused to blow a tin horn. The meaning of the ceremony gradually dawned upon one of the white youths: he was watching "Joshua's chosen men marching around the walls of Jericho, blowing the rams' horns and shouting, until the walls fell."[26] The students were witnessing the slaves' "ring shout"—that counterclockwise, shuffling dance which frequently lasted long into the night. The shout often became a medium through which the ecstatic dancers were transformed into actual participants in historic actions: Joshua's army marching around the walls of Jericho, the children of Israel following Moses out of Egypt. The shout, as Sir Charles Lyell perceived in 1845, frequently served as a substitute for the secular dance. It was allowed even where dancing was proscribed—"Hit ain't railly dancin' 'less de feets is crossed," "dancin' ain't sinful iffen de foots ain't crossed," two participants explained—and constituted still one more compelling feature of black religion. "Those who have witnessed these shouts can never forget them," Abigail Christensen has written. "The fascination of the music and the swaying motion of the dance is so great that one can hardly refrain from joining the magic circle in response to the invitation of the enthusiastic clappers, 'Now, brudder!' 'Shout, sister!' 'Come, belieber!' 'Mauma Rosa kin shout!' 'Uncle Danyel!' 'Join, shouters!' "[27]

The thin line between time dimensions is nowhere better illustrated than in the slave's visions of the future, which were, of course, a direct negation of his present. Among the most striking spirituals are those which pile detail upon detail in describing the Day of Judgment: "You'll see de world on fire . . . see de element a meltin', . . . see the stars a fallin' . . . see the moon a bleedin' . . . see the forked lightning, . . . Hear the rumblin' thunder . . . see the righteous marching, . . . see my Jesus coming . . . ," and the world to come where "Dere's no sun to burn you . . . no hard trials . . . no whips a crackin' . . . no stormy weather . . . no tribulation . . . no evil-doers . . . All is gladness in de

26 [Don] Yoder, *Pennsylvania Spirituals* [Lancaster, Pa., 1961)], 54–55.

27 There are numerous descriptions of the ring shout in the WPA [Works Progress Administration] Slave Narratives. Contemporary white descriptions include Lyell, *Second Visit*, I, 269–70; Bremer, *America of the Fifties*, 119; [John D.] Long, *Pictures of Slavery* [*in Church and State* (1857; reprint ed., New York, 1969)], 383; H. G. Spaulding, "Under the Palmetto," *Continental Monthly*, 4 (1863), 196–200; Abigail M. Holmes Christensen, "Spirituals and 'Shouts' of Southern Negroes," *JAF*, 7 (1894), 154–55; *The Nation*, May 30, 1867, 432–33. The Library of Congress recorded a superb example of the shout in 1934 which may be heard on its record, AAFS L3, *Afro-American Spirituals, Work Songs, and Ballads.*

Kingdom."[28] This vividness was matched by the slave's certainty that he would partake of the triumph of judgment and the joys of the new world:

> Dere's room enough, room enough, room enough in de heaven, my Lord
> Room enough, room enough, I can't stay behind.[29]

Continually, the slaves sang of reaching out beyond the world that confined them, of seeing Jesus "in de wilderness," of praying "in de lonesome valley," of breathing in the freedom of the mountain peaks:

> Did yo' ever
> Stan' on mountun
> Wash yo' han's
> In a cloud?[30]

Continually, they held out the possibility of imminent rebirth: "I look at de worl' an' de worl' look new, . . . I look at my hands an' they look so too . . . I looked at my feet, my feet was too."[31]

These possibilities, these certainties were not surprising. The religious revivals which swept large numbers of slaves into the Christian fold in the late eighteenth and early nineteenth centuries were increasingly based upon notions of individual, volitional conversion and, in the words of one southern minister, "a free salvation to all men thro' the blood of the Lamb." They were based on a practical and implied, if not invariably theological or overt, Arminianism: God would save all who believed in Him; Salvation was there for all to take hold of if they would. This doctrine more and more came to characterize the revivals of the Presbyterians and Baptists as well as those of the more openly Arminian Methodists.[32] The effects of this message upon the slaves who were exposed to and converted by it are illustrated graphically in the spirituals which were the products of these revivals and which continued to spread the evangelical word long after the revivals had passed into history. "What kind o' shoes is dem-a you wear? . . . Dat you can walk upon de air?" slaves asked in one of their spirituals, and answered by emphasizing the element of choice: "Dem shoes I wear am de gospel shoes; . . . An' you can wear

[28] Fenner, *Religious Folk Songs,* 8, 63–65; Marsh, *Jubilee Singers,* 240–41; Higginson, *Army Life,* 205; Allen *et al., Slave Songs,* 46, 53; Natalie Curtis Burlin, *Negro Folk-Songs* (New York, 1918–19), I, 37–42.

[29] Allen *et al., Slave Songs,* 6.

[30] *Ibid.,* 5; Burlin, *Negro Folk-Songs,* II, 8–9; Fenner, *Religious Folk Songs,* 12.

[31] Allen *et al., Slave Songs,* 75; Fenner, *Religious Folk Songs,* 127; Barton, *Old Plantation Hymns,* 26. The deep internalization of many of these spirituals is illustrated in the slaves' conversion experiences in which such lines as those above were incorporated verbatim into the slaves' own accounts of their conversions. See Fisk University, *God Struck Me Dead,* 24, 54, 87.

[32] [John] Boles, *The Great Revival,* [*1787–1805* (Lexington, Ky., 1972)], Chap. 9; Charles Johnson, *The Frontier Camp Meeting* [(Dallas, 1955)], Chap. 9; William G. McLoughlin, Jr., *Modern Revivalism* (New York, 1959), Chaps. 1–2.

dem ef-a you choose." "You got a right, I got a right," they sang, "We all got a right to de tree ob life."[33]

The religious music of the slaves is almost devoid of feelings of depravity or unworthiness, but is rather, as I have tried to show, pervaded by a sense of change, transcendence, ultimate justice, and personal worth. The spirituals have been referred to as "sorrow songs," and in some respects they were. The slaves sang of "rollin' thro' an unfriendly world," of being "a-trouble in de mind," of living in a world which was a "howling wilderness," "a hell to me," of feeling like a "motherless child," "a po' little orphan chile in de worl'," a "home-e-less child," of fearing that "Trouble will bury me down."[34]

But these feelings were rarely pervasive or permanent; almost always they were overshadowed by a triumphant note of affirmation. Even so despairing a wail as *Nobody Knows The Trouble I've Had* could suddenly have its mood transformed by lines like: "One morning I was a-walking down, . . . Saw some berries a-hanging down, . . . I pick de berry and I suck de juice, . . . Just as sweet as de honey in de comb." Similarly, amid the deep sorrow of *Sometimes I Feel Like a Motherless Chile*, sudden release could come with the lines: "Sometimes I feel like / A eagle in de air. . . . Spread my wings an' / Fly, fly, fly."[35] Slaves spent little time singing of the horrors of hell or damnation. Their songs of the Devil pictured a harsh but almost semicomic figure (often, one suspects, a surrogate for the white man), over whom they triumphed with reassuring regularity:

The Devil's mad and I'm glad,
He lost the soul he thought he had.[36]

Ole Satan toss a ball at me.
O me no weary yet . . .

Him tink de ball would hit my soul.
O me no weary yet . . .

De ball for hell and I for heaven.
O me no weary yet . . .[37]

Ole Satan thought he had a mighty aim;
He missed my soul and caught my sins.
Cry Amen, cry Amen, cry Amen to God!

[33] Fenner, *Religious Folk Songs*, 10; Theodore F. Seward, *Jubilee Songs* (New York, 1872), 48; Emily Hallowell, *Calhoun Plantation Songs* (Boston, 1901), 40.

[34] Allen *et al.*, *Slave Songs*, 30–31, 55, 94; Barton, *Old Plantation Hymns*, 9, 17–18, 24; Marsh, *Jubilee Singers*, 133, 167.

[35] Allen *et al.*, *Slave Songs*, 55; Mary Allen Grissom, *The Negro Sings a New Heaven* (Chapel Hill, 1930), 73.

[36] Allen *et al.*, *Slave Songs*, 107–08.

[37] *Ibid.*, 12.

He took my sins upon his back;
Went muttering and grumbling down to hell.
Cry Amen, cry Amen, cry Amen to God!

Ole Satan's church is here below.
Up to God's free church I hope to go.
Cry Amen, cry Amen, cry Amen to God![38]

For all their inevitable sadness, slave songs were characterized more by a feeling of confidence than of despair. There was confidence that contemporary power relationships were not immutable: "Did not old Pharaoh get lost, get lost, get lost, . . . get lost in the Red Sea?"; confidence in the possibilities of instantaneous change: "Jesus make de dumb to speak. . . . Jesus make de cripple walk. . . . Jesus give de blind his sight. . . . Jesus do most anything"; confidence in the rewards of persistence: "Keep a' inching along like a poor inchworm, / Jesus will come by'nd bye"; confidence that nothing could stand in the way of the justice they would receive: "You kin hender me here, but you can't do it dah," "O no man, no man, no man can hinder me"; confidence in the prospects of the future: "We'll walk de golden streets / Of de New Jerusalem." Religion, the slaves sang, "is good for anything, . . . Religion make you happy, . . . Religion gib me patience . . . O member, get Religion . . . Religion is so sweet."[39]

The slaves often pursued the "sweetness" of their religion in the face of many obstacles. Becky Ilsey, who was sixteen when she was emancipated, recalled many years later:

> 'Fo' de war when we'd have a meetin' at night, wuz mos' always 'way in de woods or de bushes some whar so de white folks couldn't hear, an' when dey'd sing a spiritual an' de spirit 'gin to shout some de elders would go 'mongst de folks an' put dey han' over dey mouf an' some times put a clof in dey mouf an' say: "Spirit don talk so loud or de patterol break us up." You know dey had white patterols what went 'roun' at night to see de niggers didn't cut up no devilment, an' den de meetin' would break up an' some would go to one house an' some to er nudder an' dey would groan er w'ile, den go home.[40]

Elizabeth Ross Hite testified that although she and her fellow slaves on a Louisiana plantation were Catholics, "lots didn't like that 'ligion."

[38] [Harriet Brent] Jacobs, *Incidents in the Life of a Slave Girl* [(1861; reprint ed., New York, 1973)], 73.

[39] Marsh, *Jubilee Singers,* 179, 186; Allen *et al., Slave Songs,* 10–11, 13, 93; Barton, *Old Plantation Hymns,* 30.

[40] McIlhenny, *Befo' De War Spirituals,* 31.

> We used to hide behind some bricks and hold church ourselves. You see, the Catholic preachers from France wouldn't let us shout, and the Lawd done said you gotta shout if you want to be saved. That's in the Bible.
>
> Sometimes we held church all night long, 'til way in the mornin'. We burned some grease in a can for the preacher to see the Bible by. . . .
>
> See, our master didn't like us to have much 'ligion, said it made us lag in our work. He jest wanted us to be Catholicses on Sundays and go to mass and not study 'bout nothin' like that on week days. He didn't want us shoutin' and moanin' all day 'long, but you gotta shout and you gotta moan if you wants to be saved.[41]

Slaves broke the proscription against unsupervised or unauthorized meetings by holding their services in secret, well-hidden areas, usually referred to as "hush-harbors." Amanda McCray testified that on her Florida plantation there was a praying ground where "the grass never had a chance ter grow fer the troubled knees that kept it crushed down," and Andrew Moss remembered that on the Georgia plantation where he grew up all the slaves had their private prayer grounds: "My Mammy's was a ole twisted thick-rooted muscadine bush. She'd go in dar and pray for deliverance of de slaves."[42] Even here the slaves were often discovered by the white patrols. "Den dey would rush in an' start whippin' an' beatin' de slaves unmerciful," West Turner of Virginia reported. ". . . an' do you know some o' dem devils was mean an' sinful 'nough to say, 'If I ketch you here servin' God, I'll beat you. You ain't got no time to serve God. We bought you to serve us.' "[43] Slaves found many ways to continue to speak with their gods. Patsy Larkin recalled that on her plantation the slaves would steal away into the cane thickets and pray in a prostrate position with their faces close to the ground so that no sound would escape. Kalvin Woods, a slave preacher, described how slave women would take old quilts and rags and soak them before hanging them up in the shape of a small room, "and the slaves who were interested about it would huddle up behind these quilts to do their praying, preaching and singing. These wet rags were used to keep the sound of their voices from penetrating the air." On a Louisiana plantation the slaves would gather in the woods at night, form a circle on their knees, and pray over a vessel of water to drown the sound.[44] The most commonly used method, in which the slaves had great confidence, was simply to turn a large pot upside down. "All the noise would go into that kettle,"

41 *Gumbo Ya-Ya: A Collection of Louisiana Folk Tales,* compiled by Lyle Saxon, Edward Dreyer, and Robert Tallant from materials gathered by workers of the WPA, Louisiana Writers' Project (Boston, 1945), 242.

42 WPA Slave Narratives, interviews with Amanda McCray (Fla.) and Andrew Moss (Tenn.).

43 WPA, [The] *Negro in Virginia* [(New York, 1940)], 110, 146.

44 John B. Cade, "Out of the Mouths of Ex-Slaves," *JNH* [*Journal of Negro History*], 20 (1935), 330–31.

an ex-slave explained. "They could shout and sing all they wanted to and the noise wouldn't go outside."[45]

Religious services were not confined to formal meetings, open or secret, but were often informal and spontaneous. One former slave remembered how religious enthusiasm could begin simply with a group of slaves sitting in front of their cabins after supper on a summer evening. Someone might start humming an old hymn; the humming would spread from house to house and would be transformed into song. "It wouldn't be long before some of them got happy and started to shouting. Many of them got converted at just such meetings."[46] Wherever the slaves practiced their religion—in formal church settings, in their own praise houses, in camp meetings, in their secret hush-harbors—it was characterized by physical and spiritual enthusiasm and involvement. A white visitor observing a slave religious gathering on a Georgia plantation noted that they sang "with all their souls and with all their bodies in unison; for their bodies rocked, their heads nodded, their feet stamped, their knees shook, their elbows and their hands beat time to the tune and the words which they sang with evident delight. One must see these people singing if one is rightly to understand their life."[47] Attempting to explain why the slaves shouted, an old slave preacher testified, "There is a joy on the inside and it wells up so strong that we can't keep still. It is fire in the bones. Any time that fire touches a man, he will jump."[48]

The slaves were no more passive receptors of sermons than they were of hymns and spirituals; they became participants in both forms of worship. Attending a slave service in New Orleans in the 1850s, Frederick Olmsted carefully recorded a single passage of the black preacher's sermon which was punctuated every few sentences with cries from the parishioners of "yes, glory!" "that's it, hit him again! hit him again! oh, glory! hi! hi! glory!" "glory, glory, glory,!" "Glory!—oh, yes! yes!—sweet Lord! sweet Lord!" "yes, sir! oh, Lord, yes!" "yes! yes!" "oh! Lord! help us!" "Ha! ha! HA!" "Glory to the Lord!" The responses were not confined to ejaculations of this kind, "but shouts, and groans, terrific shrieks, and indescribable expressions of ecstacy—of pleasure or agony—and even stamping, jumping, and clapping of hands, were added. The tumult often resembled that of an excited political meeting."[49] For many slaves shouting was both a compelling personal need and a religious requirement. A well-known joke told of a master who was so embarrassed by the uproar his slave made every Sunday at church that he promised

[45] Descriptions of the turned-down pot can be found in all the testimony of ex-slaves. See, for instance, Fisk University, *Unwritten History*, 35, 44, 53, 98, 173, 193, 222, 300; Fisk University, *God Struck Me Dead*, 147, 156; WPA Slave Narratives, interviews with Oliver Bell (Ala.), Henry Bobbitt (N.C.), Mary Gladdy (Ga.), Anne Matthews (Tenn.), Charles Hinton (Ark.).

[46] Fisk University, *God Struck Me Dead*, 171–72.

[47] Bremer, *America of the Fifties*, 150.

[48] Fisk University, *God Struck Me Dead*, 153.

[49] [Frederick Law] Olmsted, [*A Journey in the*] *Back Country* [(New York, 1863)], 187–96.

him a new pair of boots if he would stop making so much noise. The slave agreed to try, and at the next meeting he did his best to keep quiet so that he might win his prize, but the "spirit" proved too great a force to contain. "Glory to God!" he finally cried out. "Boots or no boots, glory to God!"[50]

The slaves clearly craved the affirmation and promise of their religion. It would be a mistake, however, to see this urge as exclusively other-worldly. When Thomas Wentworth Higginson observed that the spirituals exhibited "nothing but patience for this life—nothing but triumph in the next," he, and later observers who elaborated upon this judgment, were indulging in hyperbole. Although Jesus was ubiquitous in the spirituals, it was not invariably the Jesus of the New Testament of whom the slaves sang, but frequently a Jesus transformed into an Old Testament warrior whose victories were temporal as well as spiritual: "Mass Jesus" who engaged in personal combat with the Devil; "King Jesus" seated on a milk-white horse with sword and shield in hand. "Ride on, King Jesus," "Ride on, conquering King," "The God I serve is a man of war," the slaves sang.[51] This transformation of Jesus is symptomatic of the slaves' selectivity in choosing those parts of the Bible which were to serve as the basis of their religious consciousness. Howard Thurman, a Negro minister who as a boy had the duty of reading the Bible to his grandmother, was perplexed by her refusal to allow him to read from the Epistles of Paul.

> When at length I asked the reason, she told me that during the days of slavery, the minister (white) on the plantation was always preaching from the Pauline letters—"Slaves, be obedient to your masters," etc. "I vowed to myself," she said, "that if freedom ever came and I learned to read, I would never read that part of the Bible!"[52]

This experience and reaction were typical. Slaves simply refused to be uncritical recipients of a religion defined and controlled by white intermediaries and interpreters. No matter how respectfully and attentively they might listen to the white preachers, no matter how well they might sing the traditional hymns, it was their own preachers and their own songs that stirred them the most. Observing his black soldiers at religious services, Colonel Higginson wrote: "they sang reluctantly, even on Sunday, the long and short metres of the hymn-books, always gladly yielding to the more potent excitement of their own 'spirituals.'"[53] In Alabama, Ella Storrs Christian noted in her diary: "When Baptist Negroes attended the church of their masters, or when their mistress sang with them, they used

[50] WPA, *Negro in Virginia,* 108.

[51] Allen *et al., Slave Songs,* 10–11, 40, 51; Marsh, *Jubilee Singers,* 168, 203; Burlin, *Negro Folk-Songs,* II, 8–9.

[52] Howard Thurman, *Deep River* (New York, 1945), 16–17.

[53] Higginson, *Army Life,* 221.

hymn books, but in their own meetings they often made up their own words and tunes. They said their songs had 'more religion than those in the books.' "[54] "Dat ole white preachin' wasn't nothin'," Nancy Williams observed. "Ole white preachers used to talk wid dey tongues widdout sayin' nothin' but Jesus told us slaves to talk wid our hearts." "White folks can't pray right to de black man's God," Henrietta Perry agreed. "Cain't nobody do it for you. You got to call on God yourself when de spirit tell you."[55]

Of course there were many white preachers who were able to reach the slaves they preached to and who affected them in important ways. But even the most talented and devoted among them faced certain grave obstacles resulting from the tension between their desire to spread the Gospel and their need to use Christianity as a form of social control. In his autobiographical *Sketches from Slave Life*, published in 1855, the black minister Peter Randolph wrote that when he was a slave in Prince George County, Virginia, he and his fellow slaves had the rather uninspiring choice of listening to the white Reverend G. Harrison who taught them: "Servants obey your masters. Do not *steal* or *lie*, for this is very wrong. Such conduct is sinning against the Holy Ghost, *and is base ingratitude to your kind masters, who feed, clothe and protect you*," or the white Reverend James L. Goltney who warned: "It is the devil who tells you to try and be free."[56] The Reverend A. F. Dickson, whose Charleston congregation included over four hundred blacks and whose published sermons served as a model for other whites ministering to the slaves, reduced the Judeo-Christian ethic to a triad stressing humility, patience, and fear of sin.[57] The Reverend Charles C. Jones, who devoted so much of his life to propagating the Gospel among slaves, illustrated exactly what it was that limited his influence with them in the *Catechism* he published in 1844:

> Q. What command has God given to Servants, concerning obedience to their Masters?
>
> A. "Servants obey in all things your Masters . . . fearing God."
>
> Q. How are they to try to please their Masters?
>
> A. "With good will, doing service as unto the Lord and not unto men." . . .
>
> Q. But suppose the Master is hard to please, and threatens and punishes more than he ought, what is the Slave to do?
>
> A. Do his best to please him.

[54] Quoted in Dena J. Epstein, "Slave Music in the United States Before 1860: A Survey of Sources," *Music Library Association Notes*, 20 (1963), 205.

[55] WPA, *Negro in Virginia*, 108–09.

[56] Peter Randolph, *From Slave Cabin to the Pulpit: The Autobiography of Rev. Peter Randolph* (Boston, 1893), 196–97, 200–01. Pages 145–220 of this volume contain Randolph's earlier autobiography.

[57] A. F. Dickson, *Plantation Sermons, or Plain and Familiar Discourses for the Instruction of the Unlearned* (Philadelphia, 1856).

> Q. When the Slave suffers *wrongfully*, at the hands of his Master, and to please God, takes it patiently, will God reward him for it?
>
> A. Yes.
>
> Q. Is it right for the Slave *to run away*, or is it right to harbour a runaway?
>
> A. No. . . .
>
> Q. Will Servants have to account to God for the manner in which they serve their Masters on earth?
>
> A. Yes.[58]

In a catechistic exchange between a Methodist minister and a slave in Alabama, the message was even less subtle:

> Q. What did God make you for?
>
> A. To make a crop.[59]

This attempt to reduce Christianity to an ethic of pure submission was rejected and resented by the slaves. After listening to the white minister counsel obedience to whites, an old black worshipper in the African Church in Richmond declared: "He be d—–d! God am not sich a fool!"[60] Slaves generally suffered these sermons in silence, but there were exceptions. Victoria McMullen reported that her grandmother in Arkansas was punished for not going to church on the Sabbath but still she refused, insisting: "No, I don't want to hear that same old sermon: 'Stay out of your missus' and master's henhouse. Don't steal your missus' and master's chickens. Stay out of your missus' and master's smokehouse. Don't steal your missus' and master's hams.' I don't steal nothing. Don't need to tell me not to."[61] In the midst of a white minister's sermon, Uncle Silas, an elderly slave in Virginia, cried out: "Is us slaves gonna be free in Heaven?" The preacher looked up in surprise and anger, paused a moment, and then continued his sermon, but the old man persisted: "Is God gonna free us slaves when we git to Heaven?" A slave who was present described the rest of the encounter:

> Old white preacher pult out his handkerchief an' wiped de sweat fum his face. "Jesus says come unto Me ye who are free fum sin an' I will give you salvation." "Gonna give us freedom 'long wid salvation?" ask Uncle Silas. "De Lawd gives an' de Lawd takes away, and he dat is widdout sin is gonna have life everlasin',"

[58] Ralph Thomas Parkinson, *The Religious Instruction of Slaves, 1820–1860* (unpublished M.A. thesis, University of North Carolina, 1948), 81; C. C. Jones, [*The*] *Religious Instruction* [*of the Negroes in the United States* (1842; reprint ed., New York, 1969)], 198–201.

[59] Donald Matthews, *Slavery and Methodism* (Princeton, 1965), 87.

[60] James Redpath, *The Roving Editor: or, Talks with Slaves in the Southern States* (1859; reprint ed., New York, 1968), 19.

[61] Botkin, ed., *Lay My Burden Down*, 25–26.

> preached de preacher. Den he went ahead preachin', fast-like, widdout payin' no 'tention to Uncle Silas.[62]

The dilemma that white ministers faced was simple to grasp but not to resolve: the doctrine they were attempting to inculcate could easily subvert the institution of slavery—and both they and the slaves realized it. Thus tensions and contradictions were inevitable. William Meade, Episcopal Bishop of Virginia, could teach slaves in one sermon that "what faults you are guilty of towards your masters and mistresses are faults done against God Himself . . . I tell you that your masters and mistresses are God's overseers, and that, if you are faulty towards them, God Himself will punish you severely for it in the next world," while in another sermon he assured the slaves that "God is no respector of persons" and specifically applied the case of the rich man who went to Hell while the beggar at his gate went to Heaven to the life of the black slave.[63] The Methodist minister John Dixon Long, who preached in Maryland from 1839 to 1856, was continually disturbed by the "elementary and abstract preaching" he was forced to engage in and the "adulterated Gospel" he was forced to embrace because of slavery. "When you want to denounce sin," he wrote, "you must go to Adam and Eve, and to the Jews in the wilderness. You must be careful, however, when slaves are present, how you talk about Pharaoh making slaves of the Hebrews, and refusing to let the people leave Egypt. At any rate, you must make no direct application of the subject." During one of his sermons on the conduct of Cain toward Abel, a slave asked him if he thought it was right for one brother to sell another. Long was at first confused and finally could do no better than to counsel: "Colored friends, it is best for you not to discuss such questions here." "What preachers in the South," he complained, "can say with Paul that they have not shunned to declare the whole counsel of God?"[64] During a debate in the South Carolina legislature over a bill (ultimately passed in 1834) prohibiting slaves from learning to read and write, Whitemarsh B. Seabrook put it more succinctly: anyone who wanted slaves to read the *entire* Bible was fit for a "room in the Lunatic Asylum."[65]

Until such recent studies as Eugene Genovese's,[66] the important role of the Negro preacher in slavery was largely ignored by scholars, though the historical record is clear enough. In 1790 John Leland of Virginia noted that in their religious services the slaves "seem in general to put more confidence in their own colour, than they do in whites; when they

[62] WPA, *Negro in Virginia*, 109.

[63] Frederick Law Olmsted, *A Journey in the Seaboard Slave States* (1856; reprint ed., New York, 1969), 118–19; Parkinson, *Religious Instruction of Slaves*, 78.

[64] Long, *Pictures of Slavery*, 227–29, 269–70.

[65] William W. Freehling, *Prelude to Civil War: The Nullification Controversy in South Carolina* (New York, 1966), 335.

[66] Eugene D. Genovese, *Roll, Jordan, Roll: The World the Slaves Made* (New York, 1974), 255–79; Henry Mitchell, *Black Preaching* (Philadelphia, 1970), Chap. 3; Charles V. Hamilton, *The Black Preacher in America* (New York, 1972), Chap. 2.

attempt to preach, they seldom fail of being very zealous; their language is broken, but they understand each other, and the whites may gain their ideas."[67] Traveling in Alabama some fifty years later, Sir Charles Lyell observed, "the negroes like a preacher of their own race."[68] Touring the slave states of the eastern seaboard, Frederick Olmsted noted that black preachers were common: "On almost every large plantation, and in every neighborhood of small ones, there is one man who has come to be considered the head or pastor of the local church. The office among the negroes, as among all other people, confers a certain importance and power."[69] Henry Ravenel of South Carolina wrote that the slaves on his plantation "had local preachers of their own who conducted their services in the absence of the other [the white preacher]. This colored preacher was always one of great influence. . . ."[70] Amanda McCray, who had been a slave in Florida, recalled that the slave minister on her plantation was not obliged to engage in hard labor, went about the plantation "all dressed up" in a frock coat and store bought shoes, and was held in awe by the other slaves.[71] Northern whites who went South to work with the freedmen during and directly after the Civil War often commented upon the "great power which the chief elders of their churches possess over the rest of the negroes." Referring to an old slave preacher, a federal official in Alexandria, Virginia, exclaimed, "this old negro has more influence over the blacks, and does more good among them, than all the missionaries and chaplains who have been sent here."[72] "Mostly we had white preachers," Anthony Dawson of North Carolina remembered, "but when we had a black preacher that was heaven."[73]

Given the precariousness and delicacy of their position, it is not surprising that black preachers often repeated the message of their white counterparts. "We had some nigger preachers," an ex-slave in Tennessee recalled, "but they would say, 'Obey your mistress and marster.' They didn't know nothing else to say."[74] Frank Roberson described a typical service on the plantation where he was a slave. First the white minister rose and preached variations on the theme "Obey your master"; then his black colleague, Parson Tom, would get up and repeat everything that the white preacher had said, "because he was afraid to say anything different."[75] Nevertheless, the evidence indicates that the behavior of black preachers would vary radically with altered circumstances. William Parker, a Methodist minister in Virginia, told Helen Ludlow shortly after

67 Quoted in Herbert S. Klein, "Anglicanism, Catholicism, and the Negro Slave," in Anne Lane, ed., *The Debate Over Slavery* (Urbana, Ill., 1971), 179–80.

68 Lyell, *Second Visit*, II, 72.

69 Olmsted, *Seaboard*, 450.

70 [Henry William] Ravenal, ["Recollections of Southern Plantation Life"], *Yale Review*, 25 (1936), 766.

71 WPA Slave Narratives (Fla.).

72 Spaulding, *Continental Monthly*, 4 (1863), 195–97.

73 [Norman R.] Yetman, ed., *Life Under the "Peculiar Institution"* [New York, 1970)], 95.

74 Fisk University, *Unwritten History*, 259–60.

75 Cade, *JNH*, 20 (1935), 329.

the Civil War that in the 1820s he had been made a preacher when the white parson on his plantation discovered he could read. His duties consisted of assisting in the singing, leading the prayer meetings, and preaching when his white superior was absent, which was often. "You know de cullered people was obleege to hab white ministers in slavery times. He use' to come down onst in a while and preach up 'Sarvants, obey your marssas,' an' den I'd preach de gospil in between times 'cep' when he was to hear me; den I'd hab to take his tex'."[76] Parker's distinction between the "Gospel" and the message generally promulgated by the whites was commonly held among the slaves who knew the Scriptures had more to teach them than obedience. Anderson Edwards, a black preacher in Texas, was forced to preach what his master told him to: "he say tell them niggers iffen they obeys the master they goes to Heaven; but I knowed there's something better for them, but daren't tell them 'cept on the sly. That I done lots. I tells 'em iffen they keep praying, the Lord will set 'em free."[77]

Occasionally it was possible for a slave minister to disagree openly with his white colleague and to insist upon his own interpretation of the Scriptures. In 1847 an observer at a slave service in New Orleans wrote that as soon as the white minister had finished his sermon the black minister rose and corrected him:

> My brudder call your 'tention to de fact dat God did temp Abra'am; and den he go on to tell you 'bout Abra'am's temptation. Now I don't like dat word "temp-tation." "God can not be tempted wid evil; neither temptest he any man." Suppose we read that word temp *try*. Ah, my brudder (turning to the white preacher), why you no say *try?*—"After dese things God did *try* Abra'am." He try his people *now*. Who hasn't trials and triberlations from God? But I don't like dat word *temp*. I—*tell-you* (to the congregation) *God—don't—temp—any-body!*

Several years later this same white observer lived in a South Carolina courthouse town and found that week after week the slaves, tired from a hard day's work, would sleep through the white sermon at the Saturday evening services. "But let the congregation be surprised by the unexpected visit of some colored preacher, or let the exercises consist wholly of prayer, exhortation, and singing, and the fervor, vivacity, and life of the meeting would continue for the hour without diminishing." "None can move the negro," he concluded, "but a negro."[78]

There was great exaggeration in the last remark, of course. White preachers often moved the slaves, especially at the camp meetings. But it is true that slaves preferred black preachers who, all things considered,

[76] Mrs. M. F. Armstrong and Helen W. Ludlow, *Hampton and Its Students* (New York, 1874), 102.

[77] Botkin, ed., *Lay My Burden Down*, 26.

[78] "The Religious Life of the Negro Slave," *Harper's New Monthly Magazine*, 27 (1863), 482–83, 677.

were in a better position to understand the kind of message the slaves wanted to hear, as in this sermon delivered by a Negro Baptist minister named Bentley to a congregation of Georgia slaves in 1851:

> I remember on one occasion, when the President of the United States came to Georgia and to our town of Savannah. I remember what an ado the people made, and how they went out in big carriages to meet him. The clouds of dust were terrible, and the great cannon pealed forth one salute after another. Then the president came in a grand, beautiful carriage and drove to the best house in the whole town, and that was Mrs. Scarborough's! And when he came there he seated himself in the window. But a cord was drawn around the house to keep us negroes and other poor folks from coming too near. We had to stand outside and only get a sight of the president as he sat at the window. But the great gentlemen and the rich folks went freely up the steps and in through the door and shook hands with him. Now, did Christ come in this way? Did He come only to the rich? Did He shake hands only with them? No! Blessed be the Lord! He came to the poor! He came to us, and for our sakes, my brothers and sisters!

It is not surprising that the same slaves who would sit silently through sermons admonishing them to treat their masters and mistresses as they would treat the Lord, greeted Bentley's offering with several minutes of laughter, tears, stamping feet, and cries of "yes, yes! Amen! He came to us! Blessed be His name! Amen! Hallelujah!"[79]

Like other forms of Christianity, that preached to the slaves contained elements of what Karl Mannheim has identified as *ideology* and *utopia*.[80] The former, conducive to order and stability, and the latter, conducive to transcending and shattering the existing order, were so intermeshed that it is difficult to separate them into totally antithetical forms of slave religion. The teachings of white sermons and songs contained the seeds not merely of submission and docility but of egalitarianism and fundamental change, while those of black sermons and songs certainly can be seen as fostering the promulgation of stability as well as of discontent and the urge toward a different order of things. In spite of this important overlap, distinctions can be made: the religion the masters attempted to inculcate was laced with an emphasis upon morality, obedience, and right conduct as defined by the master class, while that which filled the sermons of black preachers and the songs of black folk was characterized by the apocalyptic visions and heroic exploits of the Scriptures. This was particularly true of slave spirituals, which were informed not by the Epistles of Paul but by the history of the Hebrew Children.

Judging from the songs of his black soldiers, Colonel Higginson concluded that their Bible was constructed primarily from the books of

[79] Bremer, *America of the Fifties*, 132–33.
[80] Karl Mannheim, *Ideology and Utopia* (New York, 1936).

Moses in the Old Testament and of Revelations in the New: "all that lay between, even the life of Jesus, they hardly cared to read or to hear." "Their memories," he noted at another point, "are a vast bewildered chaos of Jewish history and biography; and most of the great events of the past, down to the period of the American Revolution, they instinctively attribute to Moses."[81] Many of those northerners who came to the South to "uplift" the freedmen were deeply disturbed at the Old Testament emphasis of their religion. H. G. Spaulding complained that the ex-slaves needed to be introduced to "the light and warmth of the Gospel," and reported that a Union army officer told him: "Those people had enough of the Old Testament thrown at their heads under slavery. Now give them the glorious utterances and practical teachings of the Great Master."[82] Shortly after his arrival in Alabama in 1865, a northern army chaplain wrote of the slaves, "Moses is their *ideal* of all that is high, and noble, and perfect, in man," while Christ was regarded "not so much in the light of a *spiritual* Deliverer, as that of a second Moses."[83]

The essence of slave religion cannot be fully grasped without understanding this Old Testament bias. It is important that Daniel and David and Joshua and Jonah and Moses and Noah, all of whom fill the lines of the spirituals, were delivered in *this* world and delivered in ways which struck the imagination of the slaves. Over and over their songs dwelt upon the spectacle of the Red Sea opening to allow the Hebrew slaves past before inundating the mighty armies of the Pharaoh. They lingered delightedly upon the image of little David humbling the great Goliath with a stone–a pretechnological victory which postbellum Negroes were to expand upon in their songs of John Henry. They retold in endless variation the stories of the blind and humbled Samson bringing down the mansions of his conquerors; of the ridiculed Noah patiently building the ark which would deliver him from the doom of a mocking world; of the timid Jonah attaining freedom from his confinement through faith. The similarity of these tales to the situation of the slaves was too clear for them not to see it; too clear for us to believe that the songs had no worldly content for blacks in bondage. "O my Lord delivered Daniel," the slaves observed, and responded logically: "O why not deliver me, too?"

He delivered Daniel from de lion's den,
  Jonah from de belly ob de whale,
And de Hebrew children from de fiery furnace,
  And why not every man?[84]

[81] Higginson, *Army Life*, 27, 205.

[82] [H. G.] Spaulding, ["Under the Palmetto"], *Continental Monthly*, 4 (1863), 195–96.

[83] Quoted in Peter Kolchin, *First Freedom: The Responses of Alabama's Blacks to Emancipation and Reconstruction* (Westport, Conn., 1972), 118.

[84] Allen *et al.*, *Slave Songs*, 94; Fenner, *Religious Folk Songs*, 21; Marsh, *Jubilee Singers*, 134–35; McIlhenny, *Befo' De War Spirituals*, 248–49; *SW*, 41 (1912), 241.

In another spiritual the slaves rehearsed the triumphs of the Hebrew Children in verse after verse, concluding each with the comforting thought: "And the God dat lived in Moses' [Dan'el's, David's] time is jus' de same today." The "mighty rocky road" that "I must travel," another of the slaves' songs insisted, is "De rough, rocky road what Moses done travel."[85]

These songs state as clearly as anything can the manner in which the sacred world of the slaves was able to fuse the precedents of the past, the conditions of the present, and the promise of the future into one connected reality. In this respect there was always a latent and symbolic element of protest in the slave's religious songs which frequently became overt and explicit. Frederick Douglass asserted that for him and many of his fellow slaves the song, "O Canaan, sweet Canaan, / I am bound for the land of Canaan," symbolized "something more than a hope of reaching heaven. We meant to reach the *North*, and the North was our Canaan," and he wrote that the lines of another spiritual, "Run to Jesus, shun the danger, / I don't expect to stay much longer here," had a double meaning which first suggested to him the thought of escaping from slavery.[86] Similarly, when the black troops in Higginson's regiment sang:

We'll soon be free,
We'll soon be free,
We'll soon be free,
  When de Lord will call us home.

a young drummer boy explained to him, "Dey tink *de Lord* mean for say *de Yankees*."[87] These veiled meanings by no means invariably eluded the whites. At the outbreak of the Civil War slaves in Georgetown, South Carolina, were jailed for singing this song, and Joseph Farley, who had been a slave in Virginia and Kentucky, testified that white patrols would often visit the slaves' religious services and stop them if they said or sang anything considered offensive: "One time when they were singing, 'Ride on King Jesus, No man can hinder Thee,' the padderollers told them to stop or they would show him whether they could be hindered or not."[88]

There is no reason to doubt that slaves may have used their songs as a means of secret communication. An ex-slave told Lydia Parrish that when he and his fellow slaves "suspicioned" that one of their number was telling tales to the driver, they would sing lines like the following while working in the field:

O Judyas he wuz a 'ceitful man
  He went an' betray a mos' innocen' man.

85 Hallowell, *Calhoun Plantation Songs*, 30; Yetman, ed., *Life Under the "Peculiar Institution*," 112.
86 Douglass, *Life and Times*, 159–60.
87 Higginson, *Army Life*, 217.
88 *Ibid.;* Fisk University, *Unwritten History*, 124–25.

Fo' thirty pieces a silver dat it wuz done
He went in de woods an' 'e self he hung.[89]

As many writers have argued and as some former slaves have testified, such spirituals as the commonly heard "Steal away, steal away, steal away to Jesus!" could be used as explicit calls to secret meetings. Miles Mark Fisher was correct in seeing the slaves' songs as being filled with innuendo and hidden meaning. But it is not necessary to invest the spirituals with a secular function only at the price of divesting them of their religious content, as Fisher has done.[90] While we may make such clear-cut distinctions, I have tried to show that the slaves did not. For them religion never constituted a simple escape from this world, because their conception of the world was more expansive than modern man's.

Nowhere is this better illustrated than during the Civil War itself. While the war gave rise to such new spirituals as "Before I'd be a slave / I'd be buried in my grave, / And go home to my Lord and be saved!" or the popular *Many Thousand Go,* with its jubilant rejection of all the facets of slave life—"No more peck o'corn for me, . . . No more driver's lash for me, . . . No more pint o'salt for me, . . . No more hundred lash for me, . . . No more mistress' call for me"[91]—the important thing was not that large numbers of slaves now could create new songs which openly expressed their views of slavery; that was to be expected. More significant was the ease with which their old songs fit their new situation. With so much of their inspiration drawn from the events of the Old Testament and the Book of Revelation, the slaves had long sung of wars, of battles, of the Army of the Lord, of Soldiers of the Cross, of trumpets summoning the faithful, of vanquishing the hosts of evil. These songs especially were, as Higginson put it, "available for camp purposes with very little strain upon their symbolism." "We'll cross de mighty river," his troops sang while marching or rowing,

We'll cross de danger water, . . .
O Pharaoh's army drownded!
My army cross over.

"O blow your trumpet, Gabriel," they sang,

Blow your trumpet louder,
And I want dat trumpet to blow me home
To my new Jerusalem.

89 [Lydia] Parrish, *Slave Songs [of the Georgia Sea Islands* (1942; reprint ed., Hatboro, Pa., 1965)], 247.

90 "Actually, not one spiritual in its primary form reflected interest in anything other than a full life here and now" [(Miles Mark] Fisher, *Negro Slave Songs in the United States,* New York, 1963, 137).

91 Barton, *Old Plantation Hymns,* 25; Allen *et al., Slave Songs,* 48; James McKim, *Dwight's Journal of Music,* 21 (1862), 149.

But they also found their less overtly militant songs quite as appropriate to warfare. Their most popular and effective marching song was:

Jesus call you. Go in de wilderness,
  Go in de wilderness, go in de wilderness,
Jesus call you. Go in de wilderness
  To wait upon de Lord.[92]

Black Union soldiers found it no more incongruous to accompany their fight for freedom with the sacred songs of their bondage than they had found it inappropriate as slaves to sing their spirituals while picking cotton or shucking corn. Their religious songs, like their religion itself, was of this world as well as the next.

Slave songs present us with abundant evidence that in the structure of their music and dance, in the uses to which music was put, in the survival of the oral tradition, in the retention of such practices as spirit possession which often accompanied the creation of spirituals, and in the ways in which the slaves expressed their new religion, important elements of their shared African heritage remained alive not just as quaint cultural vestiges but as vitally creative elements of slave culture. This could never have happened if slavery had so completely closed in around the slave, so totally penetrated his personality structure as to reduce him to a kind of *tabula rasa* upon which the white man could write what he chose.

Slave songs provide us with the beginnings of a very different kind of hypothesis: that the preliterate, premodern Africans, with their sacred world view, were so imperfectly acculturated into the secular American society into which they were thrust, were so completely denied access to the ideology and dreams which formed the core of the consciousness of other Americans, that they were forced to fall back upon the only cultural frames of reference that made any sense to them and gave them any feeling of security. I use the word "forced" advisedly. Even if the slaves had had the opportunity to enter fully into the life of the larger society, they might still have chosen to retain and perpetuate certain elements of their African heritage. But the point is that they really had no choice. True acculturation was denied to most slaves. The alternatives were either to remain in a state of cultural limbo, divested of the old cultural patterns but not allowed to adopt those of their new homeland—which in the long run is no alternative at all—or to cling to as many as possible of the old ways of thinking and acting. The slaves' oral tradition, their music, and their religious outlook served this latter function and constituted a cultural refuge at least potentially capable of protecting their personalities from some of the worst ravages of the slave system.

The argument of Professors Tannenbaum and Elkins that the Protestant churches in the United States did not act as a buffer between the slave and his master is persuasive enough, but it betrays a modern pre-

[92] Higginson, *Army Life*, 201–02, 211–12.

occupation with purely institutional arrangements.[93] Religion is more than an institution, and because Protestant churches failed to protect the slave's inner being from the incursions of the slave system, it does not follow that the spiritual message of Protestantism failed as well. Certainly the slaves themselves perceived the distinction. Referring to the white patrols which frequently and brutally interfered with the religious services of the slaves on his plantation, West Turner exclaimed: "Dey law us out of church, but dey couldn't law 'way Christ."[94] Slave songs are a testament to the way in which Christianity provided slaves with the precedents, heroes, and future promise that allowed them to transcend the purely temporal bonds of the Peculiar Institution.

Historians have frequently failed to perceive the full importance of this because they have not taken the slave's religiosity seriously enough. A people cannot create a music as forceful and striking as slave music out of a mere uninternalized anodyne. Those who have argued that Negroes did not oppose slavery in any meaningful way are writing from a modern, political context. What they really mean is that the slaves found no *political* means to oppose slavery. But slaves, to borrow Professor Hobsbawm's term, were prepolitical beings in a prepolitical situation.[95] Within their frame of reference there were other—and from the point of view of personality development, not necessarily less effective—means of escape and opposition. If mid-twentieth-century historians have difficulty perceiving the sacred universe created by slaves as a serious alternative to the societal system created by southern slaveholders, the problem may be the historians' and not the slaves'.

Above all, the study of slave songs forces the historian to move out of his own culture, in which music plays a peripheral role, and offers him the opportunity to understand the ways in which black slaves were able to perpetuate much of the centrality and functional importance that music had for their African ancestors. In the concluding lines of his perceptive study of primitive song, C. M. Bowra has written:

> Primitive song is indispensable to those who practice it. . . . they cannot do without song, which both formulates and answers their nagging questions, enables them to pursue action with zest and confidence, brings them into touch with gods and spirits, and makes them feel less strange in the natural world. . . . it gives to them a solid centre in what otherwise would be almost chaos, and a continuity in their being, which would too easily dissolve before the calls of the implacable present. . . . through its words men, who might otherwise give in to the malice of circumstances, find their old powers revived or new powers stirring in them, and through these life itself is sustained and renewed and fulfilled.[96]

[93] Elkins, *Slavery,* Chap. 2; Frank Tannenbaum, *Slave and Citizen* (New York, 1946).

[94] WPA, *Negro in Virginia,* 110, 146.

[95] E. J. Hobsbawm, *Primitive Rebels* (New York, 1959), Chap. I.

[96] C. M. Bowra, *Primitive Song* (London, 1962), 285–86.

This, I think, sums up concisely the function of song for the slave. Without a general understanding of that function, without a specific understanding of the content and meaning of slave song, there can be no full comprehension of the effects of slavery upon the slave or the meaning of the society from which slaves emerged at emancipation.

3 Suggestions for Further Reading

An excellent introduction to the experiments in social reform that swept America in the first half of the nineteenth century is Alice Felt Tyler, *Freedom's Ferment: Phases of American Social History from the Colonial Period to the Outbreak of the Civil War** (University of Minnesota Press, 1944). A growing awareness of poverty in ante-bellum America is described in the first part of R. H. Bremmer's *From the Depths: The Discovery of Poverty in the United States** (New York University Press, 1956).

General introductions to the history of immigration in the United States are M. A. Jones, *American Immigration** (University of Chicago Press, 1960) and Leonard Dinnerstein and David M. Reimers, *Ethnic Americans: A History of Immigration and Assimilation** (Harper and Row, 1975). On ante-bellum immigration in particular, the standard work is Marcus L. Hansen, *The Atlantic Migration, 1607–1860** (Harvard University Press, 1940). John Cogley has provided us with an introduction to the Roman Catholic Church in the United States in his *Catholic America** (Dial, 1973). See also Jay P. Dolan, *The Immigrant Church: New York's Irish and German Catholics, 1815–1865* (Johns Hopkins Press, 1975). The conflict between established settlers and Irish immigrants in Boston is discussed in Barbara Miller Solomon, *Ancestors and Immigrants** (Harvard University Press, 1956). Ray A. Billington, in *The Protestant Crusade, 1800–1860** (Macmillan, 1938), deals more generally with religious conflict in the first half of the nineteenth century. The story of the Irish community in the United States is told by Carl Wittke in *The Irish in America** (Louisiana State University Press, 1956), while Terry Coleman's *Going to America** (Pantheon, 1972) describes, among other things, the Irish migration in the years 1846–1855. John Higham's *Strangers in the Land: Patterns of American Nativism, 1860–1925** (Rutgers University Press, 1955) provides useful insights into nativist sentiment during the ante-bellum years, although it is primarily concerned with a later period.

On nineteenth-century feminism there is useful information in the relevant portions of several general studies of American women. See, for example, Andrew Sinclair, *The Emancipation of the American Woman** (Harper & Row, 1965), first published under the title *The Better Half;* Eleanor Flexner, *Century of Struggle: The Women's Rights Movement in the United States** (Harvard University Press, 1959); and Robert E. Riegel, *American Feminists** (University of Kansas Press, 1963). A useful collection of documents is Aileen S. Kraditor (ed.), *Up from the Pedestal:*

* Available in paperback edition.

*Selected Writings in the History of American Feminism** (Quadrangle, 1968). Hannah Josephson examines the plight of women textile workers in *The Golden Threads: New England's Mill Girls and Magnates* (Duell, Sloan and Pearce, 1949). Impressive biographies of leading feminists in the ante-bellum period are Gerda Lerner, *The Grimke Sisters from South Carolina: Rebels Against Slavery** (Houghton Mifflin, 1967), and *Created Equal: A Biography of Elizabeth Cady Stanton* (Day, 1940) and *Susan B. Anthony: Rebel, Crusader, Humanitarian* (Beacon, 1959), both by Alma Lutz. A study related to the role of women in American society is Bernard Wishy, *The Child and the Republic: The Dawn of Modern American Child Nurture** (University of Pennsylvania Press, 1967). On the origins of the feminist movement see Miriam Gurko, *The Ladies of Seneca Falls: The Birth of the Women's Rights Movement** (Schocken Books, 1976). Two valuable new studies of this period are Nancy F. Cott, *The Bonds of Womanhood: "Woman's Sphere" in New England, 1780–1835* (Yale University Press, 1977) and Susan P. Conrad, *Perish the Thought: Intellectual Women in Romantic America, 1830–1860* (Oxford University Press, 1976).

Norman Ware's *The Industrial Worker, 1840–1860** (Houghton Mifflin, 1924) is still the standard work on the subject. For a fuller treatment of the situation in Lynn see the prize-winning Alan Dawley, *Class and Community: The Industrial Revolution in Lynn* (Harvard University Press, 1976). The title essay in Herbert G. Gutman's *Work, Culture and Society in Industrializing America** (Knopf, 1976) contains important material on time-work discipline and the resistance to the factory system.

A number of good books have appeared on slavery in the United States. Some of these are noted in the suggestions for further reading at the close of Section 1 (see pp. 000–00). Excellent recent books on the life of the slaves is John W. Blassingame, *The Slave Community: Plantation Life in the Antebellum South** (Oxford University Press, 1972); Eugene Genovese, *Roll, Jordan, Roll: The World the Slaves Made** (Pantheon Books, 1974); and Herbert G. Gutman, *The Black Family in Slavery and Freedom, 1750–1925* (Pantheon Books, 1976). Of particular interest here are works pertaining to the slaves' formulations of their own experience—the folktales, songs, and narratives that make up the distinctive oral tradition of black America. A brief presentation of the variety of primary source materials available to historians is William F. Cheek (ed.), *Black Resistance Before the Civil War** (Glencoe, 1970). Spirituals are collected in James Weldon Johnson and J. Rosamond Johnson (eds.), *The Books of American Negro Spirituals** (Viking, 1925, 1926). See also Harold Courlander, *Negro Folk Music U.S.A.** (Columbia University Press, 1963). On the relationship between African and New World religion, see Melville J. Herskovits, *The Myth of the Negro Past** (Harper

& Row, 1941). Folktales are collected in Langston Hughes and Arna Bontemps (eds.), *The Book of Negro Folklore** (Dodd, Mead, 1958); Richard Dorson (ed.), *American Negro Folktales** (Fawcett, 1967); and J. Mason Brewer (ed.), *American Negro Folklore** (Quadrangle, 1968). For analyses of black folklore see Alan Dundes (ed.), *Mother Wit from the Laughing Barrel: Readings in the Interpretation of Afro-American Folklore** (Prentice-Hall, 1973). Charles H. Nichols has surveyed and analyzed narratives composed by fugitive slaves in *Many Thousands Gone: The Ex-Slaves' Account of Their Bondage and Freedom** (Brill, 1963). Perhaps the most important of these narratives is the *Narrative of the Life of Frederick Douglass, an American Slave, Written by Himself** (Anti-Slavery Office, 1845). Readily available collections of narratives by former slaves are Gilbert Osofsky (ed.), *Puttin' On Ole Massa: The Slave Narratives of Henry Bibb, William Wells Brown, and Solomon Northup** (Harper & Row, 1969), and Arna Bontemps (ed.), *Great Slave Narratives** (Beacon, 1969), which presents the narratives of Olaudah Equiano, W. C. Pennington, and William and Ellen Craft. B. A. Botkin (ed.), *Lay My Burden Down: A Folk History of Slavery** (University of Chicago Press, 1945), and Norman R. Yetman (ed.), *Life Under the Peculiar Institution: Selections from the Slave Narrative Collection** (Holt, Rinehart and Winston, 1970), are samplings of narratives collected from former slaves under the auspices of the Federal Writers' Project in the 1930's. George P. Rawick describes slave life using the above collection as source material in *From Sundown to Sunup: The Making of the Black Community** (Greenwood, 1972). Three novels that expertly explore slave attitudes are Arna Bontemps' *Black Thunder** (Macmillan, 1936), the story of Gabriel's rebellion in 1800; Harold Courlander's *The African** (Crown, 1967), the tale of an African boy who is captured and sold into slavery in the Caribbean and the United States South; and Alex Haley's *Roots: The Story of an American Family* (Doubleday, 1976).

4 Westward Expansion

Legacy of Hate: The Conquest of the Southwest

RODOLFO ACUÑA

By the middle of the nineteenth century, three nonwhite ethnic minorities had become inhabitants of the United States against their will—Afro-Americans, American Indians, and Mexican-Americans. The last of these groups has traditionally received the least attention by historians. Their story and place in American history has been seen as less dramatic and less consequential than that of either blacks or Indians. But they are here. And in rather large numbers. While Chicanos—as Mexican-Americans have recently begun calling themselves—make up less than three percent of the total American population, they contribute over ten percent of the population in the Southwest. And in many areas of the United States from Texas to California, they are a majority in small towns and rural counties.

From the beginning they have been discriminated against on several counts: they are not considered white, they are of mixed (Spanish-Indian) ancestry, and they are predominantly Roman Catholic in religion. Any one of these characteristics would have led them to be victimized by the dominant ideology of Anglo-Saxon expansionists. The attitude of many Americans was expressed by a famous Texas gunman who, when asked how many notches he had in his gun, replied: "Thirty-seven—not counting Mexicans."

As the theory of manifest destiny and the rigorous drive for national expansion thrust the United States government westward, it was clear that the American leadership was not concerned with "counting Mexicans." Once the conquest was complete, however, and the vast and potentially rich Southwestern area was a part of the United States, there were the Mexicans, now residents on American soil, with many of them claiming hereditary property rights to land granted their families and communities by the Spanish and Mexican governments. These property rights were not recognized by the laws of the United States or by the individual states that the Mexican-Americans found themselves subject to, and much of the political activity of Chicanos in recent years—particularly the **Alianza** movement in New Mexico—has called for a restoration of those rights or for reparations of some kind.

The existence of large numbers of these "alien" peoples in the territories of New Mexico and Arizona delayed statehood for those areas for decades even after they had qualified constitutionally for admission to the Union. As the editor of **Harper's Weekly** wrote in 1876 after the Senate had passed a statehood bill: "New Mexico is virtually an ignorant foreign community under the influence of the Roman Church, and neither for the advantage of the Union nor for its own benefit can such an addition to the family of American States be urged."

In the selection reprinted below, Chicano historian Rodolfo Acuna, of the University of California at Northridge, describes the conquest of Northern Mexico by the United States in the second quarter of the nineteenth century. He properly points out the role of slavery and racism in this struggle and indicates the way recent historians have sought to justify the conquest in terms that indicate the continuing legacy of the racial and nationalistic attitudes of the nineteenth century.

The tragedy of the Mexican cession is that most Anglo-Americans have failed to recognize that the United States committed an act of violence against the Mexican people when it took Mexico's northwestern territory. The violence was not limited to the taking of the land; Mexico's territory was invaded, her people murdered, her land raped, and her possessions plundered. The memory of this destruction generated a distrust and dislike that is still vivid in the minds of many Mexicans, for the violence of the United States left deep scars. And for Chicanos–the Mexicans remaining within the boundaries of the new United States territories–the aggression was even more insidious, for the outcome of the Texas and Mexican-American wars made them a conquered people. The Anglo-Americans were the conquerors, and they evinced all of the arrogance of military victors.

The conquerors imposed upon the vanquished their version of what had happened in the wars. They created myths about the invasions and events that triggered them, especially in relation to the Texas War of 1836. Anglo-Americans in Texas were portrayed as freedom-loving settlers forced to rebel against the tyranny of Mexico. The most popular of the myths was that of the Alamo, which, in effect, became a justification to keep Mexicans in their place. According to Anglo-Americans, the Alamo was a symbolic confrontation between good and evil; the treacherous Mexicans succeeded in taking the fort only because they outnumbered the patriots and "fought dirty." This myth, with its ringing plea to "Remember the Alamo!" colored Anglo attitudes toward Mexicans, for it served to stereotype the Mexican eternally as the enemy and the Texas patriots as the stalwarts of freedom and democracy.

Such myths, as well as the Anglo-Americans' biased versions of Mexican-American history, helped to justify the inferior status to which the Chicano has been relegated—that of a conquered people. After the conquest, the original inhabitants found themselves continually denigrated by the Anglo-American victors. The fundamental issue that the wars were imperialistic and unjust was forgotten, and historians clothed the Anglo invasions of Mexican territory with the mantle of legitimacy. In the process, the violence and the aggression have been forgotten, and thus the myth that the United States is a peace-loving nation dedicated to democracy is perpetuated.[1]

THE CLASH OF TWO CULTURES

An integral part of the Anglo rationalizations for the conquest has been a tendency either to ignore or distort the events that led up to the initial clash in 1836. To Anglo-Americans, the Texas War was the result of a tyrannical or, at best, an incompetent Mexican government that was antithetical to the ideals of democracy and justice. Even today, such relatively unbiased sources as Cecil Robinson play down the expansionistic, land-hungry characteristics of the Texas settlers, and they write glowingly of the democratic civiliation they represented:

> The Americans who came into Texas . . . brought with them a deeply rooted democratic tradition. Herein lay the basis of another conflict, which was essentially cultural in its nature. The American colonist and the native Mexican soon discovered that the same words could have vastly different meanings, depending on the traditions and conditional attitudes of those who spoke them. *Democracy*, *justice*, and *Christianity*, thought at first to be ideals held in common, became rallying cries of a revolution because of the different interpretations put upon them by the American colonists and their Mexican rulers in Texas.[2]

The Anglo-American settlement in Texas began as early as 1819 when the United States acquired Florida from Spain. The Transcontinental Treaty with Spain drew the boundary of the United States in

[1] Robert A. Divine, ed., *American Foreign Policy* (New York: The World Publishing Company, 1966), pp. 11–18.

[2] Cecil Robinson, "Flag of Illusion," *The American West*, 5, no. 3 (May 1968): 15.

such a way that it excluded Texas. By the time the treaty was ratified in February 1821, Texas was part of Coahuila, a state in the independent Republic of Mexico. Meanwhile, Anglo-Americans made forays into Texas similar to those they had made into Florida. In 1819, James Long led an abortive invasion of the province with the aim of creating the "Republic of Texas." Long, like many Anglos, believed that Texas belonged to the United States and that "Congress had no right or power to sell, exchange, or relinquish an 'American possession.' "[3]

For a time Anglo filibustering [insurrectionist or revolutionary activity in a foreign country] activity in Texas was dormant, and Mexican authorities offered free land to groups of settlers. Moses Austin was given permission to establish a settlement in Texas, and although he died shortly afterwards, his son, Stephen, carried out his plan. In December 1821, Stephen founded the settlement of San Felipe de Austin. Soon Anglos were settling in Texas in great numbers; by 1830 there were about 20,000 settlers, along with about 2000 slaves.

Although settlers were supposed to abide by the conditions established by the Mexican government–that all immigrants must be Catholics and that they must take an oath of allegiance to Mexico–Anglo-Americans circumvented these laws. Moreover, they became resentful when Mexico tried to enforce the rules they had promised to obey. Mexico became increasingly alarmed at the continuing flood of immigrants, most of whom retained their Protestant religion.[4]

It was soon apparent that the Anglo-Texans had no intention of obeying Mexican law, for they believed that Mexico was incapable of putting into effect any form of democracy. Many settlers, among them Hayden Edwards, considered Mexicans to be the intruders of the Texas territory; these Anglos encroached upon lands belonging to native Mexicans. In Edwards' case, his grant conflicted with claims of Mexicans, Indians, as well as Anglo-American settlers. When he arbitrarily attempted to evict settlers from the land before a decision could be reached, Mexican authorities nullified his settlement contract and ordered him out of the territory. He and his followers seized the town of Nacogdoches, and on December 21, 1826, they proclaimed that they had established the Republic of Fredonia. Mexican officials, who were supported by some settlers (such as Stephen Austin), suffocated the Edwards revolt; however, the Anglo-American attitude was a portent of what was to follow. Many U.S. newspapers played up the rebellion as "200 Men Against a Nation!" and described Edwards and his followers as "apostles of democracy crushed by an alien civilization."[5]

It was at this time that U.S. President John Quincy Adams offered to buy Texas from Mexico for the sum of $1 million. Mexican authorities, however, were convinced that the United States had aided and abetted

[3] T. R. Fehrenbach, *Lone Star: A History of Texas and the Texans* (New York: The Macmillan Company, 1968), p. 128.

[4] Walter Prescott Webb, *The Texas Rangers: A Century of Frontier Defense* (Austin: University of Texas Press, 1965), pp. 21–22.

[5] Fehrenbach, pp. 163–64.

the Fredonia war, and they refused. Mexico tried to consolidate its control over Texas, but the number of Anglo-American settlers and the vastness of the territory made it an almost impossible task.[6]

Anglo-Americans in Texas were already creating a privileged caste, which depended in great part on the economic advantage given to them by their slaves. When, like most progressive nations, Mexico abolished slavery on September 15, 1829, by order of President Vicente Guerrero, Texans evaded the law by "freeing" their slaves and then signing them to lifelong contracts as indentured servants.[7] Despite this circumvention of the law, Anglos saw abolition as an invasion of their personal liberties. The tension, already rife, was compounded when Mexico decreed in 1830 that further Anglo-American immigration to Texas was to be cut off.[8] Anglos were outraged at the restrictions. Ill feelings between Mexicans and Anglos were aggravated further during the presidency of Andrew Jackson. Like Adams, Jackson attempted to negotiate with Mexico for the purchase of Texas, but he was willing to pay as much as $5 million. Mexico, already xenophobic as a result of the huge numbers of Anglo settlers, their economic dominance of the region, and their refusal to submit to Mexican laws, resisted the diplomatic pressure and moved more soldiers into the state of Coahuila, of which Texas was a part. Even before the Mexican reinforcements crossed into Texas, polarization between Mexicans and Anglo-Texans was pronounced, and the Anglos viewed the move as a Mexican invasion.

Anglo historians have repeatedly interpreted the events following this action as examples of the oppressive and arbitrary nature of the Mexican government, as contrasted to the democratic-oriented aims of the Texas settlers. When Texans defied the collection of customs and were incensed over Mexican attempts to end smuggling, United States citizens were sympathetic. It was obvious that the "war party" that rioted at Anáhuac in December 1831 had popular support. One of the leaders of the war party, Sam Houston, "was a known protégé of Andrew Jackson, now president of the United States. . . . Houston's motivation was to bring Texas eventually into the United States."[9]

In various ways the Anglos, who had been granted permission by the Mexican government to settle in Texas, worked to undermine the authority of their host. Anglo-Americans became more unwilling to display even a façade of respect for Mexican laws, and in the summer of 1832, a group of them attacked a Mexican garrison and were routed. In that same year, Colonel Juan Almonte made a goodwill tour of Texas and submitted a secret report on conditions in that province. The report recommended many concessions to the *Tejanos,* but it also urged that "the province be well stocked with Mexican troops."[10] The Texas his-

[6] Eugene C. Barker, *Mexico and Texas, 1821–1835* (New York: Russell & Russell, Inc., 1965), p. 52.

[7] Barker, pp. 74–80.

[8] Barker, pp. 80–82.

[9] Fehrenbach, p. 182.

[10] Fehrenbach, p. 180.

torian Fehrenbach criticized the Mexican actions: "It was virtually impossible for even a Mexican of goodwill to comprehend the fact that Anglo-Americans were capable of regulating themselves."[11] He continued:

> For this reason, the moves now made by the colonists were misunderstood by both Mexican liberals and conservatives alike. On their own initiative, the settlers of the *ayuntamiento* (city council) of San Felipe called a convention to meet on October 1, 1832. Sixteen Anglo-Texas districts responded.[12]

At this convention the Anglos drafted resolutions directed to the Mexican government and to the state of Coahuila. In essence, they called for more autonomy for Texas. Fehrenbach, like other U.S. historians, erroneously painted the picture of an oppressive Mexican government that was unsympathetic to the "colonists' just demands":

> Each of those resolutions was emphatically preceded by professions of loyalty to the *Mexican Confederation and the Constitution.* These were wholly sincere. But what the Texans were asking for was cultural pluralism, under Mexican sovereignty, and pluralism was not only foreign to the Hispanic nature but, in the light of the phobia against the United States that suffused most Mexicans, impossible to be weighed on merits. In fact, the very assemblies, so peaceful and so natural to the English-speaking experience and tradition, were entirely extra-legal under Mexican law. In Mexico, no initiative, except riot and insurrection, ever began with the people. Both liberals and conservatives, in office, ruled by decree. In this light, every Mexican official in Texas and in Mexico could only view the convention as some sort of enormous plot, aimed at the foundations of the nation.[13]

Fehrenbach and other Anglo-American historians failed to realize the existence of cultural pluralism in Mexico, where even Anglo-Americans were allowed to retain their culture. In truth, it was the Anglo who considered cultural pluralism alien to his nature. The events that followed bore out the Mexican's concern over the increasing Anglo-American independence in Texas.

A second convention was held in January 1833. Fehrenbach alleges that the Anglo-Americans acted in the traditional Anglo-American manner by drafting a constitution and presenting it to the central government, but he charges that the Mexicans looked upon it as a *pronunciamento*—a call to arms. He further states that Mexican historians viewed it as "a well-conceived plot to separate Texas from Mexico," which he admits "cannot entirely be denied," since prominent Anglo-Americans,

[11] Fehrenbach, p. 180.
[12] Fehrenbach, p. 180.
[13] Fehrenbach, p. 181.

among them Sam Houston, agitated for independence.[14] The delegates appointed Austin to submit the grievances and resolutions to Mexico City.

Austin left for Mexico City to press the demands of the Anglo-Americans in Texas. His priorities were to get the Mexican authorities to lift their restrictions on Anglo-American immigration and to grant Texas separate statehood. The slave issue also burned in his mind. Austin was anything but conciliatory, writing to a friend from Mexico City, "If our application is refused . . . I shall be in favor of organizing *without it.* I see no other way of saving the country from total anarchy and ruin. I am totally done with conciliatory measures and, for the future, shall be uncompromising as to Texas."[15]

On October 2, 1833, he wrote a letter to the *ayuntamiento* at San Antonio encouraging it to declare Texas a separate state. He later excused his action, explaining that he had done so "in a moment of irritation and impatience"; nevertheless, his actions were not those of a moderate. The contents of the note fell into the hands of the Mexican authorities, who had begun to question Austin's good faith. Subsequently, they imprisoned him, and much of what Austin had accomplished in the way of compromise was undone. Contributing to the general distrust were the actions of U.S. Minister to Mexico Anthony Butler, whose crude attempts to bribe Mexican officials to sell Texas infuriated Mexicans. He offered one official $200,000 to play ball.[16] Matters grew worse when, in May 1834, Antonio López de Santa Anna seized the presidency.

López de Santa Anna is an enigma in Mexican history. From his rise to power at Tampico in 1829 to his fall in 1855, he remained a disruptive influence in Mexican politics. During this period there was a struggle for control of the country between the conservatives, who represented the landed interests of the nation (along with the church and military), and the liberals, who wanted Mexico to become a modern state, controlled by the merchants of the nation. Santa Anna manipulated both factions, switching from one party to another in order to seize power. He greatly added to the disunity of the times, weakening Mexico and making it easy prey to the ambitions of the United States. Moreover, Santa Anna's perfidy has given United States historians a scapegoat in assigning responsibility for the wars. Many historians point out that there were secessionist movements in several of the Mexican states as the result of Santa Anna's abolition of federalism; however, these same historians fail to point out that the United States went through a similar phase in its quest to forge a nation.

Whatever Santa Anna's role, the Texas revolt had already been planned, with men such as William Barret Travis, F. M. Johnson, and Sam Houston active in agitating for separation from Mexico. For that

[14] Fehrenbach, p. 181.

[15] Nathaniel W. Stephenson, *Texas and the Mexican War: A Chronicle of the Winning of the Southwest* (New York: United States Publishing Company, 1921), p. 51.

[16] Stephenson, p. 52: on Austin's letter, also see Barker, p. 128.

matter, the majority of Anglo-Americans were unwilling to submit to the Mexican government.

The war party in Texas was strong. In the autumn of 1834, Henry Smith published a pamphlet entitled *Security for Texas*. He advocated open defiance of the Mexican authority. The political situation became more polarized, and Mexican troops assembled in Coahuila. Intrigue dominated the Texas scene. Not only were there many individuals advocating independence, but Anglo land companies had agents, both in Washington, D.C., and in Texas, lobbying for a change. Prominent among these companies was the Galveston Bay and Texas Land Company of New York, which was in collusion with Anthony Butler, the U.S. Minister to Mexico.[17]

On July 13, 1835, a general amnesty released Austin from prison. While on his way to Texas, he wrote a letter from New Orleans to a cousin expressing the view that Texas should be Americanized even though it was still a state of Mexico, and indicating that it should one day come under the American flag. In this letter he called for a massive immigration of Anglo-Americans, "*each man with his rifle*," whom he hoped would come "passports or no passports, *anyhow*." He continued: "For fourteen years I have had a hard time of it, but nothing shall daunt my courage or abate my . . . object . . . to *Americanize* Texas."[18]

Fehrenbach defended Austin's letter and admonished Mexican historians for their condemnation of the Texas leader:

> The call for a massive and illegal entry of armed Americans was not so much a plot to join Texas to the United States as it was Austin seeking, from the most logical source, all the help he could get—just as Israelis, beset by Arabs, called upon Jewry all over the world. Neither Texas in the 19th century, nor Israel more than a century later, had any doubt of their right to defend themselves. What was at stake was more than mere boundaries.[19]

THE TEXAS REVOLT

It would be simplistic to blame Austin and all the Anglo-Texan settlers for the conflict. Austin was, indeed, better than most; he belonged to the peace party, which at first opposed a confrontation with the Mexicans. Ultimately, however, this faction joined the "hawks." Eugene C. Barker, a Texas historian, states that the immediate cause of the war was "the overthrow of the nominal republic and the substitution of centralized oligarchy," which allegedly would have placed the Texans more strictly under the control of Mexico.[20] Barker, however, admits

[17] Stephenson, p. 52.
[18] Fehrenbach, p. 188.
[19] Fehrenbach, p. 189.
[20] Barker, p. 146.

that "Earnest patriots like Benjamin Lundy, William Ellery Channing, and John Quincy Adams saw in the Texas revolution a disgraceful affair promoted by sordid slaveholders and land speculators. Even to the critical ear of the modern historian their arguments sound plausible."[21] However, he denies that the slave issue had anything to do with the revolt and says that the land question retarded rather than accelerated the hostilities.

Barker draws a parallel between the Texas revolt and the American Revolution, stating: "In each, the general cause of revolt was the same—a sudden effort to extend imperial authority at the expense of local privilege."[22] In fact, in both instances the central governments were attempting to enforce existing laws that conflicted with the illegal activities of some very articulate men. Barker further attempts to justify the Anglo-Texans' actions by observing: "At the close of summer in 1835 the Texans saw themselves in danger of becoming the alien subjects of a people to whom they deliberately believed themselves morally, intellectually, and politically superior. The racial feeling, indeed, underlay and colored Texan-Mexican relations from the establishment of the first Anglo-American colony in 1821."[23] Therefore, the conflict, according to Barker, was inevitable and, consequently, justified.

It is difficult to pin the Texan apologists down. They admit that racism played a leading role in the causes for revolt; that smugglers were upset with Mexico's enforcement of her import laws; that Texans were upset about emancipation laws; and that an increasing number of the new arrivals from the United States actively agitated for independence. But despite these admissions, historians like Barker refuse to assign guilt to their countrymen. Instead, Barker writes: "Had there been no atmosphere of racial distrust enveloping the relations of Mexico and the colonists, a crisis might not have followed. Mexico might not have thought it necessary to insist so drastically on unequivocal submission, or the colonists might not have believed so firmly that submission would endanger their liberty."[24] Barker is simply justifying Anglo-American racism and, in the process, is spreading around the guilt by speculating about what might have been.

In any case, the antipathies of the Texans escalated into a full-scale rebellion. Austin gave the call to arms on September 19, 1835, stating, "War is our only recourse. There is no other remedy."[25] It was symbolically significant that he changed his name back from Estévan to Stephen.[26]

Too many historians have portrayed Mexico's attempt to suffocate the insurrection as an invasion and the Texas victory that followed as a victory of a small band of patriots against the "Huns" from the south. Dr. Félix D. Almaraz, a member of the history department of the Uni-

[21] Barker, p. 147.
[22] Barker, p. 148.
[23] Barker, pp. 148–49.
[24] Barker, p. 162.
[25] Fehrenbach, p. 189.
[26] Fehrenbach, p. 189.

versity of Texas at Austin, underscores this, writing: "All too often, Texan specialists have interpreted the war as the defeat of a culturally inferior people by a culturally superior class of Anglo frontiersmen. . . ."[27]

In reality, the Anglo-Americans enjoyed very real advantages. As mentioned, they had a sizeable population; they were "defending" terrain with which they were familiar; and although most of the 5000-or-so Mexicans living in the territory did not join them, the Anglos themselves were united. In contrast, the Mexican nation was divided, and the centers of power were thousands of miles away from Texas. From the interior of Mexico, Santa Anna led an army of about 6000 conscripts, many of whom had been forced into the army and were then marched hundreds of miles over hot, arid desert land. In addition, many were Mayan and did not speak Spanish. In February 1836, the majority arrived in San Antonio, Texas, sick and ill-prepared to fight. Although the Mexican army outnumbered the Anglo contingent, the latter were much better armed and enjoyed the position of being the defenders. (Until World War I, this was a decided advantage during wartime.) Santa Anna, on the other hand, had overextended his supply lines and was many miles from his base of power.

The 187 men who were defending San Antonio refused to surrender to Santa Anna's forces and took refuge in a former mission, the Alamo. In the ten days of fighting that followed, the Texans inflicted heavy casualties on the Mexican forces, but eventually the Mexicans' sheer superiority in numbers won out. Much has been written about Mexican cruelty in relation to the Alamo affair and about the heroics of the doomed men. The result, as mentioned early in this chapter, was the creation of the Alamo myth. Within the broad framework of what actually happened—187 Texans barricading themselves in the Alamo in defiance of Santa Anna's force and the eventual triumph of the Mexicans—there has been much distortion. Walter Lord, in an article entitled "Myths and Realities of the Alamo," sets much of the record straight.[28] Since the myth has provided Anglo-Americans with a major justification for their historical and psychological subjugation of the Chicano, the story of the Alamo demands a brief retelling.

Texas mythology portrays the Alamo heroes as freedom-loving defenders of their homes; they were supposedly all good Texans. Actually, two-thirds of the defenders were recent arrivals from the United States, and only a half dozen had been in Texas for more than six years.[29] Moreover, the character of the defenders is questionable. A work that is admittedly biased, but that nevertheless casts considerable light on the Alamo and its defenders, is Rafael Trujillo Herrera's *Olvídate de El*

[27] Félix D. Almaraz, "The Historical Heritage of the Mexican American in 19th-Century Texas," *The Role of the Mexican American in the History of the Southwest* (Edinburg, Tex.: Inter-American Institute, Pan American College, 1969), pp. 20–21.

[28] Walter Lord, "Myths and Realities of the Alamo," *The American West,* 5, no. 3 (May 1968).

[29] Lord, p. 20.

Alamo.[30] Trujillo advances the thesis that the United States was an aggressor nation and that it should rename itself the United States of Anglo-America. The use of "America" to him symbolizes the ambitions of Anglo-Americans to conquer the whole of the Western Hemisphere. According to Trujillo, the men in the Alamo were adventurers and not virtuous idealists as they frequently are portrayed by Texas historians. Trujillo reveals that William Barret Travis was a murderer; he killed a man who had made advances to his wife. Rather than confess, Travis allowed a slave to be tried and convicted for his crime, and he fled to Texas, abandoning his wife and two children. James Bowie was an infamous brawler who had made a fortune running slaves and had wandered into Texas searching for lost mines and more money. And then there was the fading Davey Crockett, a legend in his own time, who fought for the sake of fighting. Many others in the Alamo were men who had come to Texas for riches and glory; a minority were men who had responded to Austin's call to arms. These defenders were not the sort of men who could be classified as peaceful settlers fighting for their homes.

The folklore of the Alamo goes beyond the legendary names of the defenders. According to Walter Lord, it is riddled with dramatic half-truths that have been accepted as history.[31] The defenders at the Alamo are portrayed as selfless heroes who sacrificed their lives to buy more time for their comrades-in-arms. As the story is told, William Barret Travis told his men that they were doomed; he drew a line in the sand with his sword, saying that all who crossed it would elect to remain and fight to the last. Supposedly all the men there valiantly stepped across the line, with a man in a cot begging to be carried across it. This hopelessness and bravery of the defenders has been dramaticized in many Hollywood movies.

The facts are that the Alamo had little strategic value, the men fully expected help, and the Alamo was the best fortified fort west of the Mississippi. While the defenders only numbered about 180, they had twenty-one cannons to the Mexican's eight or ten. The Anglo-Americans were expert marksmen and had rifles with a range of 200 yards; in contrast, the Mexicans were poorly equipped, inadequately trained, and were armed with smooth-bore muskets with a range of only 70 yards. In addition, the walls of the Alamo were thick, concealing the defenders, while the latter had clear shots. In short, ill-prepared, ill-equipped, and ill-fed Mexicans attacked well-armed and professional soldiers.[32] Lastly, from all reliable sources, it is doubtful whether Travis ever drew a line in the sand. The San Antonio survivors, females and noncombatants, did not tell the story until many years later, when the tale had become well circulated and the myth was a legend. In addition, there was a man who escaped, Louis Rose.[33]

[30] Rafael Trujillo Herrera, *Olvídate de El Alamo* (Mexico, D.F.: La Prensa, 1965).
[31] Lord, p. 18.
[32] Santa Anna had not committed all of his soldiers to the Alamo. The majority were assigned to other commands.
[33] Lord, p. 22.

Probably the most widely circulated story was that of the alleged heroism and last stand of the aging Davey Crockett who, when the end came, fell "fighting like a tiger," killing Mexicans with his bare hands. This is a myth; seven of the defenders surrendered, and Crockett was among them. They were executed.[34]

The importance of these myths about the Alamo is that they falsely build up the valor of the Anglo-Texans at the expense of the Mexicans, who have been portrayed as treacherous, ruthless killers. This stereotyping conditioned Anglo attitudes about the Mexicans, and it served as a rationalization for later aggression against Mexico and the Anglo's mistreatment of Chicanos. It is also significant that the Spanish-surnamed "defenders" within the Alamo conspicuously have been omitted from the roll call of Texas heroes.

As stated previously, the Alamo had no strategic military value. It represented a battle where two fools engaged in a useless conflict. Travis's stand delayed Santa Anna's timetable by only four days, as the Mexicans took San Antonio on March 6, 1836. At first, the stand at the Alamo did not even have propaganda value. Afterwards, Houston's army dwindled, with many volunteers rushing home to help their families flee from the advancing Mexican army. Moreover, most Anglo-Texans were not proud of the Alamo and realized they had been badly beaten.[35] It did, nevertheless, eventually result in massive aid from the United States in the form of volunteers, arms, and money. The cry of "Remember the Alamo" became a call to arms for Anglo-Americans in both Texas and the United States.[36]

After the Alamo and the defeat of another garrison at Goliad, southeast of San Antonio, Santa Anna was in full control. He ran Sam Houston out of the territory northwest of the San Jacinto River and then camped an army of about 1100 men near San Jacinto. There, he skirmished with Houston on April 20, 1836, but did not follow up his advantage. Predicting that Houston would attack on April 22, Santa Anna and his men settled down and rested for the anticipated battle. The Texans, however, attacked during the *siesta* hour on April 21. Santa Anna had made an incredible blunder. He knew that Houston had an army of 1000, yet he was lax in his precautionary defenses. The surprise attack caught him totally off guard. Shouts of "Remember the Alamo! Remember Goliad!" filled the air.

Many historians have dwelt upon the violence and cruelty of the Mexicans in Texas, especially in relation to the victory at Goliad. It is true that Santa Anna gave no quarter in his encounters with the Texans, but the issue of Anglo-American violence usually has been evaded. The battle at San Jacinto was literally a slaughter of the Mexican forces. Few prisoners were taken. Instead, those who surrendered "were clubbed and stabbed, some on their knees. The slaughter . . . became methodical: the Texan riflemen knelt and poured a steady fire into the packed, jostling

[34] Lord, p. 24.
[35] Lord, p. 25.
[36] Lord, p. 25.

ranks. . . ."[37] They shot the "Meskins" down as they fled. The final count showed 630 Mexicans dead versus 2 Texans.

The battle of San Jacinto generated considerable pride among Anglo-Americans in Texas and the United States. However, the widow Peggy McCormick, on whose property the battle was fought, was more candid about the feelings of her race toward Mexicans. She "objected strenuously that the hundreds of unburied Mexicans ruined the value of her property." She called Houston shortly after the battle and requested that he remove "them stinking Mexicans." Houston replied: "Madam, your land will be famed in history as the classic spot upon which the glorious victory of San Jacinto was gained!" The lady replied: "To the devil with your glorious victory! . . . Take off your stinking Mexicans."[38]

Houston's successful surprise attack ended the war. He captured Santa Anna, who had no choice but to sign the territory away. In October, Houston was elected president of the Republic of Texas.

The Texas victory prepared the way for the Mexican-American War. It whipped up emotions against Mexicans and fed the growing nationalism of the young Anglo-American nation. It is true that the United States had not officially taken sides, but men, money, and supplies had poured in to aid fellow Anglo-Americans. Of course, not all Anglo-Americans approved of the war, but as it proceeded many sided with the Anglos in Texas. An awareness of the struggle of fellow Anglo-Americans increased. The battle of the Alamo swung many of the fence sitters behind the Anglo-*Tejanos*. The deaths of Bowie, Crockett, and Travis seemed to justify whatever happened to the Mexicans, much the same as the death of Custer would later seem to justify the slaughter of the red man. More important was the hatred generated by the war. The Mexican was pictured as cruel, treacherous, tyrannical, and as an enemy who could not be trusted. These stereotypes lingered long after the war and can still be detected in Anglo attitudes toward the Chicano. The Texas War left a legacy of hate and determined the status of the Mexicans left behind as that of a conquered people.

THE MEXICAN-AMERICAN WAR

The war with Mexico typifies the expansionistic fervor of the United States during the nineteenth century. Inexorably, it seemed, the nation moved its boundaries westward, often by provoking its neighbors into war. In the mid-1840s, Mexico was the target. Anglo-Americans could not resist expansion into territory that seemed so lucrative—in this case, the unused land of the Mexican-held Southwest.

Although the United States was not a nation of overwhelming size or wealth, it was a dangerous country with which to share a border; it

[37] Fehrenbach, p. 232.

[38] Marilyn McAdams Sibley, *Travelers in Texas, 1761–1860* (Austin: University of Texas Press, 1967), pp. 108–09.

was arrogant in foreign affairs, partially because its citizens believed in their inherent cultural and racial superiority. Mexico, on the other hand, was considered to be a nation with a future greater than that of the United States. However, it was plagued with financial problems, internal ethnic conflicts, and poor leadership. The general anarchy within the nation conspired against its cohesive development.[39]

The Texas War, which Harriet Martineau called "the most high-handed theft of modern times," was only the prelude. Carl Degler, in *Out of Our Past*, has summed up the realities:

> [It] had not ended in a clear-cut victory for the Texans because Mexico refused to acknowledge the independence of the newly declared Republic even though the Mexican government was powerless to exercise control over its erstwhile subjects. This, however, did not prevent the Texans from negotiating annexation to the United States. In 1845, as inclusion of Texas in the United States came closer to reality, Mexico agreed to full recognition of the Republic of Texas on the condition that annexation to the United States would not take place. In the light of history, Mexico had good reason to fear that annexation was merely a prelude to further encroachments upon Mexican territory. Neither the United States nor the Texans, however, permitted the Mexican concern to impede annexation. When Texas was incorporated into the American Union, the stage was set for war between the United States and Mexico.[40]

By 1844, the pull of "Manifest Destiny" in relation to Texas took precedence over any considerations of Mexico's legal right to the Southwest. James K. Polk, who strongly advocated the annexation of Texas and expansionism in general, won the presidency by only a small margin, but his election was interpreted as a mandate for national expansion. Outgoing President Tyler decided to act and called upon Congress to annex Texas by joint resolution; the measure was passed a few days before the inauguration of Polk, who accepted the arrangement. In December 1845, Texas became a state.

Mexico promptly broke off diplomatic relations with the United States, and Polk ordered General Zachary Taylor into Texas to protect the border. The location of the border, however, was dubious. Texas contended it was at the Rio Grande, but based on historical precedent, Mexico claimed it was 150 miles further north, at the Nueces River.[41]

[39] Charles A. Hale, *Mexican Liberalism in the Age of Mora, 1821–1853* (New Haven, Conn.: Yale University Press, 1968), pp. 11–12, 16.

[40] Carl N. Degler, *Out of Our Past: The Forces That Shaped Modern America*, rev. ed. (New York: Harper & Row, Publishers, Inc., 1970), p. 107.

[41] José María Roa Barcena, *Recuerdos De La Invasión Norte Americana (1846–1848)*, ed. I. Antonio Castro Leal (México: Editorial Porrua, S. A., 1947), pp. 25–27. This author reviews historical precedent.

Taylor took his forces across the Nueces into the disputed territory, but refrained for a time from proceeding to the Rio Grande.

Meanwhile, in November 1845, Polk sent John Slidell on a secret mission to Mexico to negotiate for the disputed area. The presence of Anglo-American troops between the Nueces and the Rio Grande and the annexation of Texas seemed to make an absurdity of negotiations, and the Mexicans refused to see Polk's minister. Moreover, Slidell insisted on being received on terms offered by the United States, which was full acceptance of his credentials instead of the ad hoc status offered by Mexican authorities.[42] Slidell returned to Washington in March 1846, convinced that Mexico would have to be "chastised" before it would negotiate. By March 28, Taylor had advanced to the Rio Grande with an army 4000 strong.

Polk, incensed at Mexico's refusal to meet with Slidell on his terms and at General Mairano Paredes' reaffirmation of his country's claims to all of Texas, had already decided to fight. When Mexican forces crossed the Rio Grande and attacked Taylor's contingent, a move that Polk undoubtedly expected, the president had his excuse. He prepared his war message, and on May 13, 1846, Congress declared war and authorized the recruitment and supplying of 50,000 troops.

As Polk saw it, "Mexico has . . . shed American blood upon the American soil."[43] In other words, the United States was justified in its actions; the country was provoked into war.

Years later, Ulysses S. Grant said that he believed Polk wanted and planned for war to be provoked, and that the annexation of Texas was, in fact, an act of aggression. He added: "I had a horror of the Mexican War . . . only I had not moral courage enough to resign. . . . I considered my supreme duty was to my flag."[44]

From the beginning, the outcome of the war was never in doubt. The poorly equipped and poorly led Mexican army stood little chance against the thrust of expansion-minded Anglos. But even before war had been declared, Anglo-Americans, and Polk in particular, were sure of success. Polk's plan for the war consisted of three stages: (1) Mexicans would be cleared out of Texas; (2) Anglos would occupy California and New Mexico; and (3) U.S. forces would march to Mexico City to force the beaten government to make peace on Polk's terms. And that was the way the campaign basically went. In the end, at a relatively small cost in

[42] Albert C. Ramsey, ed. and trans., *The Other Side or Notes for the History of the War Between Mexico and the United States* (reprint ed., New York: Burt Franklin, 1970), pp. 28–29; and Ramón Alcaraz *et al., Apuntes Para La Historice Del La Guerra Entra Mexico y Los Estados Unidos* (Mexico: Tipografía De Manuel Payno, Hijo, 1848), pp. 27–28.

[43] J. D. Richardson, *A Compilation of the Messages and Papers of the Presidents,* 10 vols. (Washington, D.C., 1905), 4: 428–42, quoted in Arvin Rappaport, ed., *The War with Mexico: Why Did It Happen?* (New York: Rand McNally & Company, 1964), p. 16.

[44] Grady McWhiney and Sue McWhiney, eds., *To Mexico with Taylor and Scott, 1845–1847* (Waltham, Mass: Praisdell Publishing Co., 1969), p. 3.

men and money, the war netted the United States huge territorial gains: all of the Pacific coast from below San Diego to the Forty-ninth Parallel, and the whole area between the coast and the Continental Divide.

THE RATIONALE FOR CONQUEST

Glenn W. Price, author of *Origins of the War with Mexico: The Polk-Stockton Intrigue,* stated: "Americans have found it rather more difficult than other peoples to deal rationally with their wars. We have thought of ourselves as unique, and of this society as specially planned and created to avoid the errors of all other nations."[45]

Many Anglo-American historians still attempt to ignore the Mexican-American War by simply stating that it was a "bad war," which took place during the United States' era of Manifest Destiny. This is as dangerous as German historians dismissing World War II by saying that it occurred during Germany's era of *lebensraum.* In fact, the very discussion of Manifest Destiny has distracted historians from the central issue of planned Anglo-American aggression.

Historians write that Manifest Destiny had its roots in Puritan ideas, which continue to influence Anglo-American thought to this day. The doctrine of Manifest Destiny was based in concept on that of predestination, which was part of the Calvinist doctrine: God destined you to go either to heaven or to hell. This belief in predestination was based in great measure on the doctrine of the "chosen people," of the Old Testament. The Puritans believed they were the chosen people of the New World. This belief carried over to the Anglo-American conviction that God had made them custodians of democracy and that they had a mission to spread its principles. As the young nation expanded west, survived its infancy in spite of the War of 1812, and enjoyed both commercial and industrial success, its sense of destiny heightened. The Monroe Doctrine of the 1820s told the world that the Americas were no longer open for colonialization or conquest; however, it did not say anything about that limitation applying to the United States. Many citizens were beginning to believe that God had destined them to own and occupy all of the land from ocean to ocean and pole to pole. This mission was to spread the principles of democracy and Christianity to the unfortunates of the hemisphere. In the 1830s and 1840s, Mexico became the victim of this early-day Anglo-American version of *lebensraum.*

Further obscuring the issue of planned Anglo-American aggression is what Professor Price exposes as the rhetoric of peace, which the United States has traditionally used to justify its aggressions. The Mexican-American War is a study in the use of this rhetoric.

Consider, for example, Polk's war message of May 11, 1846, in which he gave his reasons for going to war:

[45] Glen W. Price, *Origins of the War with Mexico: The Polk-Stockton Intrigue* (Austin: University of Texas Press, 1967), p. 7.

> The strong desire to establish peace with Mexico on liberal and honorable terms, and the readiness of this Government to regulate and adjust our boundary and other causes of difference with that power on such fair and equitable principles as would lead to permanent relations of the most friendly nature, induced me in September last to seek reopening of diplomatic relations between the two countries.[46]

He went on to state that the United States had made every effort not to inflame Mexicans, but that the Mexican government had refused to receive an Anglo-American minister. Polk then reviewed the events leading to the war and concluded: "As war exists, and, notwithstanding all our efforts to avoid it, exists by the act of Mexico herself, we are called upon every consideration of duty and patriotism to vindicate with decision the honor, the rights, and the interests of our country."[47]

This rhetoric—that it was the duty of the United States to go to war to maintain the peace and uphold its honor—is reminiscent of most U.S. involvements. The need to justify the United States' actions is evident in histories that offer different theories as to why the United States stole Mexico's territory. In 1920 Justin F. Smith received a Pulitzer prize in Anglo-American history for a work that blamed the war on Mexico. What is amazing is that Smith allegedly examined more than 100,000 manuscripts, 120,000 books and pamphlets, and 200 or more periodicals to come to this conclusion. It is fair to speculate that he was rewarded for relieving the Anglo-American conscience. This two-volume "study," entitled *The War with Mexico*, used analyses such as the following to support its thesis:

> At the beginning of her independent existence, our people felt earnestly and enthusiastically anxious to maintain cordial relations with our sister republic, and many crossed the line of absurd sentimentality in the cause. Friction was inevitable, however. The Americans were direct, positive, brusque, angular and pushing; and they would not understand their neighbors on the south. The Mexicans were equally unable to fathom our goodwill, sincerity, patriotism, resoluteness and courage; and certain features of their character and national condition made it far from easy to get on with them.[48]

This attitude of righteousness on the part of government officials and historians toward their aggressions spills over to the relationships between the majority society and minority groups. Anglo-Americans believe that the war was advantageous to the Southwest and to the Mexicans who

[46] Rappaport, p. 16.
[47] Rappaport, p. 16.
[48] Justin H. Smith, *The War With Mexico*, vol. 2 (Gloucester, Mass.: Peter Smith Publisher, 1963), p. 310.

remained or later migrated there. They now had the benefits of democracy and were liberated from their tyrannical past. In other words, Mexicans should be grateful to the Anglo-Americans. If Mexicans and the Anglo-Americans clash, the rationale runs, naturally it is because the Mexican cannot understand or appreciate the merits of a free society, which must be defended against the ingrates. Therefore, domestic war, or repression, is justified by the same kind of rhetoric that justifies international aggression.

Fortunately, revisionist historians challenged the propagandists. Ramón Eduardo Ruíz has swept away the smoke screen created by many of his predecessors. In *The Mexican War: Was It Manifest Destiny?* he writes:

> No war waged by the United States has won more striking victories than the Mexican War of 1846–1848. After an unbroken string of military triumphs from Buena Vista to Chapultepec and the operation of their first foreign capital, Americans added the sprawling territories of New Mexico and California to their domain. The United States had also fulfilled its Manifest Destiny, that belief of American expansionists that Providence had willed them a moral mission to occupy all adjacent lands. No American can deny that war had proved profitable.[49]

Ruíz further points out that there is little interest in the United States in what has been labeled the Mexican War, reinforcing the tendency of Anglo-Americans to forget unpleasant memories. Ruíz contrasts the bland Anglo-American reaction to the war with that of the Mexican: "The war is one of the tragedies of history. Unlike the Americans who have relegated the conflict to the past, Mexicans have not forgotten. Mexico emerged from the war bereft of half of its territory, a beaten, discouraged, and divided people."[50] Ruíz's work reviews the different theories behind the war, demonstrating the attempts of scholars to justify the war.

Recent works by other authors indict the United States for having "manufactured the war." Price's bold revisionist monograph, mentioned earlier, clearly shows Mexico as the victim of a conspiracy to force it into war in order to steal its territory. The work centers around the activities of Commodore Robert F. Stockton, who went to Texas before it was annexed to the United States, and who encouraged republican leaders of that state to attack Mexico in order to draw the latter into a war. Stockton assured them that the United States would back Texas when it was invaded; in turn, California and the Southwest would be annexed to the United States. In this scheme Stockton, a very wealthy man, used his own money, and he received the active encouragement of President James Polk, a man who rhetorically spoke of peace.

[49] Ramón Eduardo Ruíz, ed., *The Mexican War: Was It Manifest Destiny?* (New York: Holt, Rinehart and Winston, Inc., 1963), p. 1.

[50] Ruíz, p. 1.

THE MYTH OF A NONVIOLENT NATION

Most works on the Mexican-American War have dwelt on the causes and results of the war, sometimes dealing with war strategy. It is necessary, however, to go beyond this point, since the war has left very real scars, and since Anglo-American actions in Mexico are remembered as vividly as some Southerners remember Sherman's march to the sea. Surely the Mexicans' attitude toward Anglo-Americans has been influenced by the war just as the United States' easy victory conditioned Anglo-American behavior toward Mexicans. Fortunately, many Anglo-Americans condemned this aggression and flatly accused their fellows of being insolent, land hungry, and of having manufactured the war. Abiel Abbott Livermore in *The War with Mexico Reviewed*[51] accused his country, writing:

> Again, the pride of race has swollen to still greater insolence the pride of country, always quite active enough for the due observance of the claims of universal brotherhood. The Anglo-Saxons have been apparently persuaded to think themselves the chosen people, anointed race of the Lord, commissioned to drive out the heathen, and plant their religion and institutions in every Canaan they could subjugate.[52]

Livermore's work, published in 1850, was awarded the American Peace Society prize for "the best Review of the Mexican War and the principles of Christianity, and an enlightened statesmanship." As the cause of the war, he wrote: "Our treatment both of the red man and the black man has habituated us to feel our power and forget right."[53] He further observed: "The passion for land, also, is a leading characteristic of the American people. . . . The god Terminus is an unknown deity in America. Like the hunger of the pauper boy of fiction, the cry had been, 'more, more, give us more.' "[54]

Through Livermore, a perspective unfolds that is not included in most books on the war. Otis A. Singletary's *The Mexican War*, like others of this mold, merely narrates the battles and their outcomes. Livermore builds an excellent case upon which to convict the United States of war crimes if the standards set by the Nuremburg trials after World War II had been followed: he describes an active policy of conquest and plunder.

[51] Some historians question the validity of Livermore's work because he was an abolitionist who allegedly set out to prove that the war was a slaveholders' crusade. However, history is the process of selection, and I find Livermore's book enlightening and in many ways more honest than the works of Justin Smith, who tailors the facts to fit his conclusions.

[52] Abiel Abbott Livermore, *The War With Mexico Reviewed* (Boston, Mass.: American Peace Society, 1850), p. 8.

[53] Livermore, p. 11.

[54] Livermore, p. 12.

There is ample evidence that the United States provoked the war. We have already quoted General Grant's impressions. The war itself was even more insidious. Zachary Taylor's artillery leveled the Mexican city of Matamoros, killing hundreds of innocent civilians with *la bomba* (the bomb). Many Mexicans jumped into the Rio Grande, relieved of their pain by a watery grave.[55] The occupation that followed was even more terrorizing. Taylor's regular army was allegedly kept in control, but the volunteers presented another matter.

> The regulars regarded the volunteers, of whom about two thousand had reached Matamoros by the end of May, with impatience and contempt. . . . They robbed Mexicans of their cattle and corn, stole their fences for firewood, got drunk, and killed several inoffensive inhabitants of the town in the streets.[56]

There were numerous eyewitnesses to these incidents. For example, on July 25, 1846, Grant wrote to Julia Dent:

> Since we have been in Matamoros a great many murders have been committed, and what is strange there seemes [sic] to be very week [sic] means made use of to prevent frequent repetitions. Some of the volunteers and about all the Texans seem to think it perfectly right to impose on the people of a conquered City to any extent, and even to murder them where the act can be covered by dark. And how much they seem to enjoy acts of violence too! I would not pretend to guess the number of murders that have been committed upon the persons of poor Mexicans and our soldiers, since we have been here, but the number would startle you.[57]

Meanwhile, correspondents reported acts of useless and wanton destruction.[58]

Taylor knew about the atrocities, but as Grant observed, little was done to restrain the men. In a letter to his superiors, Taylor admitted that "There is scarcely a form of crime that has not been reported to me as committed by them."[59] Taylor requested that they send no further troops from the state of Texas to him. These marauding acts were not limited to Taylor's men. The cannons from U.S. naval ships destroyed much of the civilian sector of Vera Cruz, leveling a hospital, churches, and homes. The bomb did not discriminate as to age or sex. Anglo-American troops repeated their performance in almost every city they invaded; first it was put to the test of fire and then plundered. The

[55] T. B. Thorpe, *Our Army on the Rio Grande;* quoted in Livermore, p. 126.

[56] Alfred Hoyt Bill, *Rehearsal for Conflict* (New York: Alfred A. Knopf, Inc., 1947), p. 122.

[57] John Y. Simon, *The Papers of Ulysses S. Grant,* vol. 1 (London, England, and Amsterdam, Holland: Feffer & Simons, Inc., 1967), p. 102.

[58] Livermore, p. 140.

[59] Quoted in Livermore, pp. 148–49.

gringo volunteers had little respect for anything, desecrating churches and abusing priests and nuns.

During these campaigns, military executions were common. Captured soldiers and civilians were executed, usually hanged, for cooperating with the guerillas. An interesting sidelight is that many Irish immigrants, as well as some other Anglos, deserted to the Mexican side, forming the San Patricio Corps. They went over to the Mexicans "due to the inborn distaste of the masses for war, to bad treatment, and to poor subsistence."[60] Many of the Irish were also Catholics, and they resented the treatment of Catholic priests and nuns by the invading Protestants. It is estimated that as many as 260 Anglo-Americans fought with the Mexicans at Churubusco in 1847. "Some eighty appear to have been captured. . . . A number were found not guilty of deserting and were released. About fifteen, who had deserted before the declaration of war, were merely branded with a "D," and fifty of those taken at Churubusco were executed."[61] Others received two hundred lashes and were forced to dig graves for their executed comrades.[62]

We do not have to go to Mexican sources to chronicle the reign of terror spread by the Yankee troops. Memoirs, diaries, and news articles written by Anglo-Americans document it. Here, we shall concentrate on Samuel E. Chamberlain's *My Confessions*. He was only 17 when he enlisted in the army to fight the "greasers." Most of his "confessions" deal with the invasion of Mexico and the atrocities of the Anglos, especially the Texas Rangers. The author creates a mood, reflecting the racism of the invaders. At the Mexican city of Parras, he wrote: "We found the patrol had been guilty of many outrages. . . . They had ridden into the church of San José during Mass, the place crowded with kneeling women and children, and with oaths and ribald jest had arrested soldiers who had permission to be present."[63]

On another occasion, he described a massacre by volunteers, mostly from Yell's Cavalry, at a cave:

> On reaching the place we found a "greaser" shot and *scalped*, but still breathing; the poor fellow held in his hands a Rosary and a medal of the "Virgin of Guadalupe," only his feeble motions kept the fierce harpies from falling on him while yet alive. A Sabre thrust was given him in mercy, and on we went at a run. Soon shouts and curses, cries of women and children reached our ears, coming apparently from a cave at the end of the ravine. Climbing over rocks we reached the entrance, and as soon as we could see in the comparative darkness a horrid sight was before us. The cave was full of our volunteers yelling like fiends, while on the rocky floor lay over twenty Mexicans, dead and dying in pools of blood.

[60] Smith, vol. 1, p. 550, fn. 6.

[61] Smith, vol. 2, p. 385, fn. 18.

[62] Livermore, p. 160.

[63] Samuel E. Chamberlain, *My Confessions* (New York: Harper & Brothers, 1956), p. 75.

> Women and children were clinging to the knees of the murderers shrieking for mercy.[64]

Chamberlain continued:

> Most of the butchered Mexicans had been scalped; only three men were found unharmed. A rough crucifix was fastened to a rock, and some irreverent wretch had crowned the image with a bloody scalp. A sickening smell filled the place. The surviving women and children sent up loud screams on seeing us, thinking we had returned to finish the work!

Chamberlain concluded: "No one was punished for this outrage."[65]

Near Satillo, Chamberlain reported the actions of Texas Rangers. His descriptions are graphic. A drunken Anglo "entered the church and tore down a large wooden figure of our Saviour, and making his lariat fast around its neck, he mounted his horse and galloped up and down the *plazuela*, dragging the image behind him. The venerable white-haired Priest, in attempting to rescue it, was thrown down and trampled under the feet of the Ranger's horse."[66] The Mexicans were enraged and attacked the Texan; meanwhile, the Rangers had returned: "As they charged into the square, they saw their miserable comrade hanging to the cross, his skin hanging in strips, surrounded by crowds of Mexicans. With yells of horror, the Rangers charged on the mass with Bowie Knife and revolver, sparing neither age or sex in their terrible fury."[67]

Chamberlain is explicit in his contempt for the Rangers: "General Taylor not only collected the money [from the Mexican people][68] assessed by force of arms, but he let loose on the country packs of human bloodhounds called Texas Rangers."[69] He goes on to describe the Rangers' brutality at the Rancho de San Francisco on the Camargo road near Agua Fria:

> The place was surrounded, the doors forced in, and all the males capable of bearing arms were dragged out, tied to a post and shot! . . . Thirty-six Mexicans were shot at this place, a half hour given for the horrified survivors, women and children, to remove their little household goods, then the torch was applied to the houses, and by the light of the conflagration the ferocious *Tejanos* rode off to fresh scenes of blood.[70]

[64] Chamberlain, p. 87.
[65] Chamberlain, p. 88.
[66] Chamberlain, p. 174.
[67] Chamberlain, p. 174.
[68] According to Chamberlain, Taylor collected over $1 million from the inhabitants of Nuevo Veon and Tamaulipas.
[69] Chamberlain, p. 176.
[70] Chamberlain, p. 177.

These wanton acts of cruelty, witnessed by one man, are augmented by the reports of other chroniclers, adding to the evidence that the United States, through the deeds of its soldiers, left a legacy of hate in Mexico.

The omission of war atrocities in Anglo-American histories has led too many Anglo-Americans to view the conflict as a glamorous war, where Mexicans were beaten in a fair fight and were lucky to have lost only their land. This indifference on the part of Anglos has rubbed salt in the Mexicans' wounds and has kept alive old hatreds. It has perpetuated the reality for Chicanos that they are a conquered people: the Mexicans and the Indians are the only peoples in the United States who were forced to become part of that country after the occupation of their lands by Anglo-American troops.

THE TREATY OF GUADALUPE HIDALGO

By late August 1847, the war was almost at an end, with General Winfield Scott defeating Santa Anna in a hard-fought battle at Churubusco. It placed the Anglo-Americans at the gates of Mexico City. Santa Anna made overtures for an armistice, and for two weeks negotiations were conducted. However, Santa Anna reorganized his defenses during this period, and, in turn, the Anglo-Americans renewed their relentless attacks. On September 13, 1847, Scott drove into the city. Although the Mexicans fought valiantly for their capital, the battle left 4000 of their men dead with another 3000 taken prisoner. On September 13, before the occupation of Mexico began, the *Niños Heroes* (the Boy Heros) fought off the conquerors and leapt to their deaths rather than surrender. These teenage cadets were Francisco Márquez, Agustín Melgar, Juan Escutia, Fernando Montes Oca, Vicente Suárez, and Juan de la Barrera. They became "a symbol and image of this unrighteous war."[71]

Although the Mexicans were beaten, fighting continued. The presidency devolved to the presiding justice of the Supreme Court, Manuel de la Peña y Peña. He knew that Mexico had lost and that it was his duty to salvage as much as possible. Pressure mounted, for the United States was in control of much of present-day Mexico.

Nicholas Trist, sent to Mexico to act as peace commissioner, had been unable to start negotiations until January 1848. Trist arrived in Vera Cruz on May 6, 1847, where he had a "vigorous but temporary tiff with Scott." Negotiations were conducted through the British legation, but were delayed by Trist's illness. This delay compromised a speedy settlement, and after the fall of Mexico City, Secretary of State James Buchanan wanted to revise Trist's instructions. He ordered Trist to break off negotiations and come home.[72] Polk apparently had begun to consider

[71] Alfonso Zabre, *Guide to the History of Mexico: A Modern Interpretation* (Austin, Tex.: The Pemberton Press, 1969), p. 300.

[72] Dexter Perkins and Glyndon G. Van Deusen, *The American Democracy: Its Rise to Power* (New York: The Macmillan Company, 1964), p. 237.

demanding more territory from Mexico and paying less for it. Trist, however, with the support of Winfield Scott, decided to ignore Polk's order, and he proceeded to negotiate on the original terms. Mexico, badly beaten, her government in a state of turmoil, had no choice but to agree to the Anglo-American's proposals.

On February 2, 1848, the Mexicans agreed to the Treaty of Guadalupe Hidalgo, in which Mexico accepted the Rio Grande as the Texas border and ceded the Southwest (which incorporates the present-day states of Arizona, California, New Mexico, Utah, Nevada, and parts of Colorado) to the United States in return for $15 million.

Polk was furious about the treaty; he considered Trist "contemptibly base" for having ignored his orders. Yet he had no choice but to submit the treaty to the Senate. With the exception of article X, the Senate ratified the treaty on March 10, 1848, by a vote of 28 to 14. To insist on more territory would have meant more fighting, and both Polk and the Senate realized that the war was already beginning to be unpopular in many sections. The treaty was sent to the Mexican Congress for its ratification; although the Congress had difficulty forming a quorum, the agreement was ratified on May 19 by a 52 to 35 vote.[73] Hostilities between the two nations were now officially ended. Trist, however, was branded as a "scoundrel," because Polk was disappointed in the settlement. There was considerable support and fervor in the United States for the acquisition of all Mexico.[74]

Contrary to popular belief, Mexico did not abandon its citizens who lived within the bounds of the new U.S. territory. The Mexican negotiators were concerned about the Mexicans left behind, and they expressed great reservations about these people being forced to "merge or blend" into Anglo-American culture. They protested the exclusion of provisions that protected the Mexican citizens' rights, land titles, and religion.[75] They wanted to know the Mexican's status, and they wanted to protect his rights by treaty.

The provisions that specifically refer to the Mexican and his rights are found in articles VIII and IX and the omitted article X. Taken in the context of the reluctance of Mexican officials to abandon their people to a nation that had virtually no respect for Mexicans, it is easier to understand why Chicanos are so angry about violations to their cultural identity.

Under the Treaty of Guadalupe Hidalgo, the Mexican left behind had one year to choose whether to return to the interior of Mexico or to remain in "occupied Mexico." About 2000 elected to leave; however, most remained in what they considered *their* territory. This situation was very similar to that of other conquered people, for the legality of the forced seizure is still an issue.

[73] Robert Selph Henry, *The Story of the Mexican War* (New York: Frederick Ungar Publishing Co., 1950), p. 390.

[74] See John D. P. Fuller, *The Movement for the Acquisition of All Mexico* (New York: Da Capo Press, 1969).

[75] Letter from Commissioner Trist to Secretary Buchanan, Mexico, 25 January 1848, Senate Executive Documents, no. 52, p. 283.

Article IX of the treaty guaranteed Mexicans "the enjoyment of all the rights of citizens of the United States according to the principles of the Constitution; and in the meantime shall be maintained and protected in the free enjoyment of their liberty and property, and secured in the free exercise of their religion without restriction."[76] This article and the United States' adherence to it have long been debated by scholars. Most sources admit that the Anglo-Americans have respected the Chicano's religion; on the other hand, Chicanos and well-known scholars contend that the rights of cultural integrity and rights of citizenship have been constantly violated. Lynn I. Perrigo in *The American Southwest* summarizes the guarantees of articles VIII and IX, writing: "In other words, besides the right and duties of American citizenship, they [the Mexicans] would have some special privileges derived from their previous customs in language, law, and religion."[77]

In spite of these guarantees, Chicanos have been subjected to cultural genocide, as well as to violations of their rights. *A Documentary History of the Mexican Americans*, published in 1971, states:

> As the only minority, apart from the Indians, ever acquired by conquest, the Mexican Americans have been subjected to economic, social, and political discrimination, as well as a great deal of violence at the hands of their Anglo conquerors. During the period from 1865 to 1920, there were more lynchings of Mexican Americans in the Southwest. But the worst violence has been the unrelenting discrimination against the cultural heritage—the language and customs—of the Mexican Americans, coupled with the economic exploitation of the entire group. Property rights were guaranteed, but not protected, by either the federal or state governments. Equal protection under law has consistently been a mockery in the Mexican-American communities.[78]

Just as controversial is the explicit protection of property. Although most analyses do not consider the omitted article X, this article had comprehensive guarantees protecting "all prior and pending titles to property of every description."[79] When this provision was deleted by the U.S. Senate, Mexican officials protested. Anglo-American emissaries reassured them by drafting a Statement of Protocol on May 26, 1848, which read:

> The American government by suppressing the Xth article of the Treaty of Guadalupe Hidalgo did not in any way intend to annul the grants of lands made by Mexico in the ceded territories. These grants . . . preserve the legal value which they may possess,

[76] Wayne Moquin *et al.*, eds., *A Documentary History of the Mexican American* (New York: Frederick A. Praeger, Publishers, 1971), p. 185.

[77] Lynn I. Perrigo, *The American Southwest* (New York: Holt, Rinehart and Winston, Inc., 1971), p. 176.

[78] Moquin, p. 181.

[79] Perrigo, p. 176.

> and the grantees may cause their legitimate (titles) to be acknowledged before the American tribunals.
>
> Conformable to the law of the United States, legitimate titles to every description of property, personal and real, existing in the ceded territories, are those which were legitimate titles under the Mexican law of California and New Mexico up to the 13th of May, 1846, and in Texas up to the 2nd of March, 1836.[80]

It is doubtful, considering the Mexican opposition to the treaty, whether the Mexican Congress would have ratified the treaty without this clarification. The vote was close. The Statement of Protocol was reinforced by articles VIII and XI, which guaranteed Mexicans rights of property and protection under the law. In addition, court decisions have generally interpreted the treaty as protecting land titles and water rights. Nevertheless, the fact remains that property was seized and individual rights were violated—largely through political manipulation.

It is one thing to make a treaty and another to live up to it. The United States has had a singularly poor record in complying with its treaty obligations, and as subsequent chapters will show, nearly every one of the obligations discussed above was violated, confirming the prophecy of Mexican diplomat Manuel Cresencio Rejón who, at the time the treaty was signed, commented:

> Our race, our unfortunate people will have to wander in search of hospitality in a strange land, only to be ejected later. Descendants of the Indians that we are, the North Americans hate us, their spokesmen depreciate us, even if they recognize the justice of our cause, and they consider us unworthy to form with them one nation and one society, they clearly manifest that their future expansion begins with the territory that they take from us and pushing [sic] aside our citizens who inhabit the land.[81]

CONCLUSION

Manuel Cresencio Rejón affirms the legacy left behind by Anglo conquest and violence. Mexicans were the victims of unjust aggressions and transgressions against them and their nation. Mingled with feelings of Anglo-American racial and cultural superiority, the violence created a legacy of hate on both sides that has continued to the present. The image of the *Tejano* has become that of the obnoxious, rude oppressor

[80] *Compilation of Treaties on Force* (Washington, D.C.: U.S. Government Printing Office, 1899), p. 402; quoted in Perrigo, p. 176.

[81] Antonio de la Peña y Reyes, *Algunos Documentos Sobre el Tratado de Guadalupe-Hidalgo* (Mexico, D.F.: Sec de Rel Ext, 1930), p. 159; quoted in Richard Gonzáles, "Commentary on the Treaty of Guadalupe Hidalgo," in Feliciano Rivera, *A Mexican American Source Book* (Menlo Park, Calif.: Educational Consulting Associates, 1970), p. 185.

throughout Latin America, whereas most Anglo-Americans considered Chicanos as foreigners with inferior rights. As a result of the Texas War and the Anglo-American aggressions of 1845–1848, the occupation of Chicano territory began, and colonization started to take form. The attitude of the Anglo, during the period of subjugation following the wars, is reflected in the conclusions of the noted Texan historian and past-president of the American Historical Association, Walter Prescott Webb:

> A homogenous European society adaptable to new conditions was necessary. This Spain did not have to offer in Arizona, New Mexico, and Texas. Its frontier, as it advanced, depended more and more on an Indian population. . . . This mixture of races meant in time that common soldiers in the Spanish service came largely from pueblo or sedentary Indian stock, whose blood, when compared to that of the plain Indians, was as ditch water. It took more than a little mixture of Spanish blood and mantle of Spanish service to make valiant soldiers of the timid pueblo Indians.[82]

A new era had begun, and according to the Anglo-American, it had a homogenous and racially superior people to lead it. The conquest laid the framework of the colony and justified the economic and political privilege established by the conquerors. Most Anglo-Americans, historians and laymen alike, are inflicted with a historical amnesia as to how they acquired it and how they maintained control over the conquered land and people.

[82] Walter Prescott Webb, *The Great Plains* (New York: Grosset & Dunlap, Inc., 1931), pp. 125–26.

The Frontier Tradition: An Invitation to Violence

JOE B. FRANTZ

No part of American history is more celebrated in myth and popular culture than the Old West. For many people the world over, the cowboy or Western gunman of the second half of the nineteenth century is the quintessential American. Self-assured, self-reliant, quick to avenge a wrong or protect someone's honor, the cowboy/gunman operated out of a code of justice that required sudden, usually fatal, retaliation to assure a modicum of order in the otherwise lawless West. Or so the movies and Western pulp novels would have us believe. The truth, on the other hand, is not quite that noble.

Lawless the West was, but not that lawless. In 1860, approximately one-third of the United States was still in territorial status. But within a generation most of this unorganized portion of the country had been accepted into statehood. During that period a major effort was made in the West to establish an effective system of law enforcement. The difficulty of that task can be seen clearly when one realizes that today there are still portions of the United States in which effective law enforcement is largely absent. Also then, as now, it was sometimes difficult to determine precisely which side the law enforcement officials were on.

The noble gunman of legend was more often than not someone who killed for self-aggrandizement of one sort or another. Most of the violence of the Old West, however, was not generated by lone gunmen but by organized groups of settlers who were struggling for ascendency in the rapidly changing frontier areas.

A major factor in the struggle for law and order in the newly organized states and territories of the West was the vigilante band. These "respectable" citizens adjudicated not wisely but too well. Their victims rarely had recourse to due process or legal defense of any kind, even where such procedures were well established. Too often the victims of the vigilantes were members of groups whose presence on the high plains was judged undesirable and whose elimination was considered appropriate.

In the essay that follows, Joe B. Frantz, of the University of Texas, takes pains to debunk the frontier tradition. Historians such as Frederick Jackson Turner, who argued that the frontier was the place where the American was made, have glossed over the egregious violence in order to celebrate the individualism supposedly fostered there. While Frantz is within the Turner tradition in expressing pride in American individualism, he looks upon the violence plain and sees there an expression of an ugly streak in the American character that has not yet been eradicated but must be brought under control before the United States can develop a truly modern and humane society.

On September 26, 1872, three mounted men rode up to the gate of the Kansas City fair, which was enjoying a huge crowd of perhaps 10,000 people. The bandits shot at the ticket seller, hit a small girl in the leg, and made off for the woods with something less than a thousand dollars. It was highhanded, and it endangered the lives of a whole host of holiday-minded people for comparatively little reward.

What makes the robbery and the violence notable is not the crime itself but the way it was reported in the Kansas City *Times* by one John N. Edwards. In his front-page story he branded the robbery "so diabolically daring and so utterly in contempt of fear that we are bound to admire it and revere its perpetrators."

Two days later the outlaws were being compared by the *Times* with the knights of King Arthur's Round Table:

> It was as though three bandits had come to us from storied Odenwald, with the halo of medieval chivalry upon their garments and shown us how the things were done that poets sing of. Nowhere else in the United States or in the civilized world, probably, could this thing have been done.[1]

Quite likely this deed was perpetrated by the James brothers: Jesse and Frank, and a confederate. The details really do not matter. What pertains is the attitude of the innocent toward the uncertainly identified guilty. The act had been perpetrated by violent, lawless men. If the *Times* is any indication, a respectable section of the people approved of

[1] William A. Settle Jr., *Jesse James Was His Name* (Columbia, Mo.: University of Missouri Press, 1966), pp. 44 ff.

"The Frontier Tradition: An Invitation to Violence" by Joe B. Frantz is reprinted from *Violence in America: Historical and Comparative Perspectives*, A Report Submitted to the National Commission on the Causes and Prevention of Violence, edited by Hugh Davis Graham and Ted Robert Gurr. Published by Bantam Books, Inc., 1969.

their action. No one, of course, thought to ask the little girl with the shattered leg how she felt about such courage. Nearly seventeen months later, Edwards was quoted in the St. Louis *Dispatch* as preferring the Western highwayman to the Eastern, for "he has more qualities that attract admiration and win respect. . . . This come from a locality . . . which breeds strong, hardy men—men who risk much, who have friends in high places, and who go riding over the land, taking all chances that come in the way." The purpose here is not to belabor one resonably anonymous newspaperman of nearly a century ago, but merely to point up a fact—and a problem—of the American frontier.

The frontier placed a premium on independent action and individual reliance. The whole history of the American frontier is a narrative of taking what was there to be taken. The timid never gathered the riches, the polite nearly never. The men who first carved the wilderness into land claims and town lots were the men who moved in the face of dangers, gathering as they progressed. The emphasis naturally came to be placed on gathering and not on procedures. Great tales of gigantic attainments abound in this frontier story; equally adventurous tales of creative plundering mark the march from Jamestown to the Pacific. It was a period peopled by giants, towers of audacity with insatiable appetites. The heroes are not the men of moderate attitudes, not the town planners and commercial builders, not the farmers nor the ministers nor the teachers. The heroes of the period, handed along to us with all the luster of a golden baton, are the mighty runners from Mt. Olympus who ran without looking back, without concern about social values or anywhere they might be going except onward.

We revere these heroes because they were men of vast imagination and daring. We also have inherited their blindness and their excesses.

Just by being here, the frontier promised the spice of danger. And danger, to paraphrase Samuel Johnson, carries its own dignity. Danger therefore was the negotiable coin of the American frontier, and the man who captured his share of danger was a man of riches, beholden only to himself.

To live with danger means to be dependent to a considerable degree on one's own resources, and those resources in turn must be many and varied. Courage and self-reliance, while not exclusive with the frontiersman, take on an enlarged dimension because so many instances of their use can be recalled. Whereas the town neighbor or the corporate manager may need a type of moral courage that exceeds the physical in its wear and tear on the human soul, such downtown courage is hardly recountable and seldom even identifiable. But when the frontiersman has faced down an adversary, he usually has a fixed moment in his life when he can regale an audience or when others can recall admiringly his dauntlessness. Even a foolhardy adventure brings applause. To the human actor no reward is more desirable.

The fact that back East, which meant from ten miles behind the cutting edge of civilization all the way to the more sophisticated capitals of Europe, men were daily facing monumental problems of planning, and sometimes even of surviving, meant nothing to the frontiersman. Nothing in the frontiersman's way of life gave him any sympathy for the man who made his decisions on paper or in the vacuum of an office or stall. Decision was made on the spot, face to face. The questions were simple; the solutions, equally simple. Today that heritage of the frontier continues in more remote areas. The subtleties of law and order escape the isolated mountain man, for instance, whether he be in Wyoming or in eastern Kentucky. If a man does wrong, you chastise him. Chastisement can take any form that you think is necessary to hold him in line. One of the acceptable forms is murder, which means that lesser violence visited upon the offending person is even more acceptable. Such behavior has the advantage of being swift and certain, without the agony of deciding what is comparatively just and without the expense of trials and jails and sociologists and welfare workers.

Of course, one reason that this simplistic attitude toward settlement of problems prevailed on the frontier was a physical one of lack of jails. Where do you put a man when you possibly have no place to put yourself? To be neat and economical, you must put him away. This may mean tying him to a tree and leaving him to starve or be stung to death; if he has been real mean, you might like to wrap him in rawhide and then let the sun shrink the rawhide slowly around him until he is gradually strangled. Or you might find it more economical to find a convenient tree with a branch a sufficient height off the ground. The scarcity of jails then, either nonexistent or inadequate, often left the frontiersman with little choice, insofar as he was concerned, except to hang, lynch, or ignore the offender.[2]

What do you do with a man whose crime may not really warrant execution? Either you execute him anyway, stifling your doubts, or you let him go. If you let him go, as happened frequently, then you may have set a killer at large to roam. In Arkansas in the generation during which Judge Isaac C. Parker ran his notorious Federal court, more than 13,000 cases were docketed, of which 9,500 were either convicted by jury trial or entered pleas of guilty. During a 25-year period at Fort Smith, 344 persons were tried for offenses punishable by death, 174 were convicted, and 168 were sentenced to hang. Actually 88 of these were hanged, and six others died either in prison or while attempting to escape.

By current standards the hangings themselves would have been invitations to violence. One contemporary of the judge tells of the hanging of John Childers, a halfblood Cherokee Indian charged with killing a peddler for his horse. A thunderstorm had come up, and a bolt of lightning struck nearby just as the death trap was sprung. "A moment later the ghastly work was done, the cloud had vanished and all that was mortal of John Childers hung limp and quivering," the reporter writes. "The entire proceeding, the grim service of the law . . . filled the spectators with awe."

[2] William Ransom Hogan, *The Texas Republic* (Norman: University of Oklahoma Press, 1946), pp. 261 ff., relates several accounts of decisions engendered in early Texas by a lack of prison facilities.

Standing next to Judge Parker in local fame was George Maledon, a smallish Bavarian celebrated as "the prince of hangmen" for having executed more than 60 criminals and shooting two to death during 22 years prior to 1894. Twice he executed six men at one time and on three other occasions he hanged five together. People discussed his record with all the enthusiastic calm of a present-day discussion of Willie Mays' possibilities for overtaking the home-run record of Babe Ruth. As for Maledon, when he was once asked by a lady whether he had qualms of conscience, he replied in his soft way, "No, I have never hanged a man who came back to have the job done over." This same reporter describes Judge Parker as "gentle, kind, familiar and easily approached."[3]

The truth is, the lawman was as closely associated with violence as the outlaw. The greatest gunfighters frequently played both sides of the law, shooting equally well. Bill Hickok comes down as a great lawman in Kansas. He also shared a good many of the qualities of a mad dog. Hickok first came to public notoriety near Rock Creek, Nebraska, where from behind a curtain in the Russell, Majors, and Waddell station he put a single rifle bullet through the heart of one David McCanles, who had come with a hired hand and his twelve-year-old son to protest nonpayment of a debt. Hickok was acquitted on a plea of self-defense. For this dubious bit of law tending, Hickok became a national hero, although it took a half-dozen years for his notoriety to become nationwide. He filled in that time by doing creditable work for the Union Army, and pursuing a postwar career as a gambler in Missouri and Kansas. This stretch of social service was punctuated by a town square gun duel which left Hickok standing and his adversary forever departed.

In his long hair and deerskin suit, Hickok could have joined any police confrontation in Chicago or Berkeley a century later. Nonetheless he became a deputy U.S. marshal out of Fort Riley, and helped rescue thirty-four men besieged by redskins fifty miles south of Denver. With this background he was elected sheriff of Ellis County, Kans., in August 1869. He killed only two men, which is not meant as an apologia, for he was credited with many more. His fame as a stanchion of the law brought him to Abilene as city marshal in the spring of 1871. Whereas his [predecessor], the revered Tom Smith, had operated from the mayor's office, Hickok utilized the Alamo Saloon, where he could fill in his time playing poker and drinking the whiskey for which he also had a storied appetite. He ran a tight, two-fisted town, especially aimed at keeping undisciplined Texas cowboys in hand. When six months later he killed Phil Coe, as well as (by mistake) his own policeman, he was soon sent packing by the town. Naturally enough, he left this life as the result of a shot in the back while playing poker in a Black Hills gambling joint.[4] This violent man

[3] Frank L. Van Eaton, *Hell on the Border* (Fort Smith, Ark.: Hell on the Border Publishing Co., 1953), pp. 32 ff., 72. Glenn Shirley, whose *Law West of Fort Smith* (New York: Henry Holt & Co., 1957) is the best book on Judge Parker, puts the figure at 160 men sentenced to die and 79 hanged, p. ix.

[4] Kent Ladd Steckmesser, *The Western History in History Legend* (Norman: University of Oklahoma Press, 1965), pp. 106 ff.

is the hero who is supposed to have quelled violence on the frontier and to have brought the blessings of organized law and order to our Western civilization. But he was ever ready to kill, on either side of the law.

One writer, detailing the lives of the bad men of the West, has put together an appendix consisting of the bad men and another one of the peace officers. Among the bad men he lists are Judge Roy Bean, who dispensed the "Law West of the Pecos."[5] Hickok is also listed with the bad men. Ben Thompson shot up Kansas and almost crossed with Hickok, and wound up as a city marshal of Austin, Texas. Bill Longley was a deputy sheriff and one of the more notorious killers in the business. Doc Holliday was a lawman in both Kansas and Arizona under Wyatt Earp. And Arizona remains split to this day whether Earp belongs with the bad men or the good. Certainly the frontier story is replete with men of peace who were equally men of violence.

Undoubtedly a lot of the violence spawned on the frontier emanated from the restlessness engendered by successive wars. The American Revolution, the War of 1812, the Mexican War, and the Civil War all disgorged some men who had tasted action and could not return to the discipline of the settled world. Consequently they stayed on the frontier, where their training and penchant for direct action held some value. Undoubtedly this was more true of the survivors of Civil War action than of any of the other major wars. The men who fought in the Western areas of the Civil War, both North and South, enjoyed more than a little activity as guerrillas. But what does a guerrilla do when he has no more excuse for hit-and-run tactics? Either he settles down on a Missouri farm or he continues to hit and run against targets of his own devising. The most notorious of such men would have to be the James brothers, though their company is entirely too large. The Jameses could rob and kill almost with impunity if they selected their targets well. Since the James boys had been on the Southern side, they were cheered by their Southern fellows, embittered by the outcome of the war, who felt a bit of reflected glory in the harassment of the cold-blooded Yankees. Reputedly, Ben Thompson tried to get John Wesley Hardin to kill Wild Bill Hickok because Hickok shot only Southern boys. For once Hardin, the most prolific killer of them all, turned down an opportunity to notch his gun again. Had he shot the Yankee Hickok, he might have become a true Southern hero instead of just another killer—well, not just another killer—who needed to be put away. All across the West the antagonisms of the late conflict continued, and were justified really in the name of the war. It did not matter that you killed, so much as whom you killed.

Running parallel with this tendency for a strong individual to range himself actively on one side or the other of the law is the tendency throughout history of men and groups to take the law into their own hands, sometimes with reasonably lofty motives. As John Walton Caughey has written, "to gang up and discipline an alleged wrongdoer is an ancient

[5] George D. Hendricks, *The Bad Man of The West* (San Antonio: The Naylor Co., 1941), p. 272.

and deep-seated impulse."[6] Whether such impulses run counter to a belief in the orderly pursuit of government is not debatable here. The fact is that throughout history societies, both frontier and long fixed, have moved through phases of private settlement of what should be public disputes. The operation of the Ku Klux Klan in a settled South with its centuries-old civilization is a case in point. Vigilantism is a disease or a manifestation of a society that feels a portion of its people are out of joint and must be put back in place whether the niceties of legal procedure are observed or not. That the end justifies the means is the authorizing cliché.

Not unmixed with vigilantism is frequently a fair share of racism, which has its own curious history on the American frontier. In some ways the frontier was the freest of places, in which a man was judged on the quality of his work and his possession of such abstractions as honesty, bravery, and shrewdness. The Chinese merchant, the Negro cowboy, the Indian rider—all were admired because of what they could do within the frontier community and not because of their pigmentation. On the other hand, the only good Indian was a dead Indian, "shines" could seldom rise above the worker level, and "coolies" were something to take potshots at without fear of retribution, either civic or conscience. Just as lynching a Negro in parts of the South was no crime, so shooting an Indian or beating an Oriental or a Mexican was equally acceptable. Like all societies, the frontier had its built-in contradictions.

In Kansas cowtowns, shooting Texas cowboys was a defensible act per se; popular agreement in that area was that although there might here and there be a decent cowboy, nonetheless most cowboys were sinister characters who were likely to ruin your daughter or your town. In other words, cowboys and Texans were in the same class as snakes—the garter snake can be a friendly reptile in your garden, but stomp him anyway in case he grows into a dangerous rattler.

But then, cowboys, whether Texan or Montanan, had a notoriously brazen unconcern toward nesters and grangers as Wyoming's Johnson County war will attest. How could the cattleman believe in legal law enforcement if, as one stockman put it, no jury of "Methodist, Grangers and Anti-Stock" would convict the most blatant cattle thief? A. S. Mercer, who felt that cattlemen were a menace to his Wyoming, nonetheless concluded that "as a matter of fact, less stealing and less lawlessness [occur] on the plains of the West than in any other part of the world."[7] Backing himself, Mercer quotes the Federal census report of 1890, which points out that the Northeastern states, "which are supposed to be most civilized," had 1,600 criminals to the million people while Wyoming ran 25 percent less, or 1,200 to the million. However, the real cattleman dislike was for the sheepherder, who was lower than a nester,

[6] John Walton Caughey, *Their Majesties the Mob* (Chicago: University of Chicago Press, 1960), p. vii.

[7] A. S. Mercer, *The Banditti of the Plains* (San Francisco: The Grabhorn Press, 1935), pp. 6–7.

rustler, or even a cowboy who had married a squaw. As one Scotsman who emigrated opined, when he brought his flock down from the hills in Scotland, people would exclaim, "here comes the noble shepherd and his flock." Out west, however, they said "here comes that damned sheepherder and his bunch of woolies!"[8]

Certainly the cowboy treatment of the sheepman showed something less than the normal extension of dignity due a fellowman. Cattlemen tried intimidation, and if that failed, they tried violence. If mere violence were not enough, next came murder, either for the sheepman or his flocks. As public sympathy was generally with the cattlemen, the sheepman had no recourse at law if his herder were killed or his sheep driven off the range. As a general rule, as in most vigilante situations, the cowboy always tried to outnumber his sheepherding adversary by five or ten to one, preferably all on horseback to the one herder on foot.

Nowhere was the sense of vigilante violence more noticeable than in the cattleman-sheepman feud. It was vigilantism, for the cowman looked on the sheepman's mere presence as immoral and illegal, an intrusion on his frontier life as he knew it. Along the upper reaches of Wyoming's Green River, for instance, a masked group, organized by the cattlemen, attacked four sheep camps simultaneously. The group blindfolded the herders, tied them to trees, and spent the remainder of the night clubbing to death 8,000 head of sheep. From wholesale dispatch of sheep to wholesale dispatch of men is really but a short, sanguine jump.

The Graham-Tewksbury quarrel furnishes another example. The Grahams and the Tewksburys had hated each other in Texas, and when both families moved to Arizona, the hatred moved in the wagons with them. Originally both Grahams and Tewksburys ran cattle, but in Arizona the Tewksburys turned to sheep after awhile. The usual charges of range violation, and the natural animosity for Tewksburys by Grahams, and vice versa, led to occasional potshotting that was looked upon by all but the participants as good clean fun.

Open conflict erupted when eight cowboys rode into the Tonto Basin of central Arizona, not really suspecting danger. But the Tewksbury brothers with five cronies were holed up in the basin, and in ten seconds three cowboys were dead and two others wounded. Within a month, the cowboys had besieged the Tewksbury ranch headquarters, killing John Tewksbury. Retaliation followed retaliation. Within five years, all peaceable ranchers had been driven from the country, and twenty-six cattlemen and six sheepmen had been killed. None of this was considered murder, but simply an intermittent pitched battle to see who would prevail. And not at all incidentally, the Graham-Tewksbury feud provided the plot of one of Zane Grey's most widely accepted eye-popping novels, *To The Last Man*, read by youth and adult, western housewife and New York dentist alike.

The coming of barbed wire into the cattle country led to another

[8] Quoted in Charles Wayland Towne and Edward Norris Wentworth, *Shepherds' Empire* (Norman: University of Oklahoma Press, 1943), p. 256.

outburst of vigilantism. Violence alone was insufficient against barbed wire because it was an inanimate object that did not directly pit man against man. Like the men it fenced in and fenced out, barbed wire was savage, unrefined, cruel, and hard. And in a sense, like the men whose ranges it controlled, it helped make the Great Plains finally fit for settlement.

As fence-cutting skirmishes broke out from Texas all the way north to Montana, people were killed, property destroyed, business crippled, and otherwise peaceful citizens alienated from one another. Men cut fences because their cattle were thirsty and their tanks were enclosed, or because they desired the good grass now out of bounds, or because the large ranching syndicates had fenced in whole counties. The XIT Ranch in Texas enclosed within wire grasslands approximately the size of the State of Connecticut. To fence in the XIT required 6,000 miles of single-strand wire. The Spur Ranch, also in Texas, erected a drift fence in 1884–85 that strung out for fifty-seven miles, while an old Two Circle Bar cowboy told of seeing ten wagonloads of barbed wire in the middle 1880s in transit from Colorado City, Texas, to the Matador Ranch. Again, men gunned down fence builders, violated enclosed land, and otherwise took the law into their own hands in resisting the coming of a new order. But legality eventually prevailed, and many men who had fought the new orderliness came to embrace it.

In effect, vigilantism was nothing more than lynching. Despite the fact that the South has been internationally damned for its lynching proclivities, it must share some of the tradition with other parts of the world, most notably with the frontier. Nowhere was lynch justice more swift, certain, or flourishing than on the frontier. Human life simply was not as valuable on the frontier as property. Taking a human life was almost as casual as our killing 50,000 people a year now by automobile murder. The fact that Colt's revolver and the repeating rifle were present and the courtroom was frequently absent undoubtedly aided such an attitude. Mitigating or extenuating circumstances for the transgressor were virtually unknown. Either he done it or he didn't.

Granville Stuart, the leading Montana vigilante, tells the story of a Billy Downs who was suspected of selling whiskey to Indians, stealing horses, and killing cattle. One July 4 the vigilantes ordered Downs and another man, an unsavory character known as California Ed, from Downs' house. Both men pleaded guilty to stealing horses from Indians, which was hardly a crime, but denied ever stealing from white men. On the other hand investigation showed their pen with twenty-six horses with white men's brands, none of the brands their own. A fresh bale of hides bore the brand of the Fergus Stock Co. The two men were carried out to a nearby grove and hanged.[9]

Cattle Kate, otherwise known as Ella Watson and mentioned in Owen

[9] Granville Stuart, *Forty Years on The Frontier* (Cleveland: The Arthur H. Clark Co., 1925), vol. 11, p. 206.

Wister's *The Virginian,* and her companion Jim Averill were accused of branding mavericks. In the summer of 1889 they swung from a pine.[10]

In Las Vegas, New Mexico, the following warning was posted in 1880:

> To murderers, confidence men, thieves:
>
> The citizens of Las Vegas are tired of robbery, murder, and other crimes that have made this town a byword in every civilized community. They have resolved to put a stop to crime even if in obtaining that end they have to forget the law, and resort to a speedier justice than it will afford. All such characters are, therefore, notified that they must either leave this town or conform themselves to the requirement of law, or they will be summarily dealt with. The flow of blood MUST and SHALL be stopped in this community, and good citizens of both the old and new towns have determined to stop it if they have to HANG by the strong arm of FORCE every violator of law in this country.
>
> Vigilantes[11]

Not too far away, in Socorro, New Mexico, the vigilantes hanged a Mexican monte dealer because they were incensed at his two employers, despite the fact that those employers were paying the vigilantes $12 a day to keep their monte tables open.[12]

In effect, the Western frontier developed too swiftly for the courts of justice to keep up with the progression of people. Therefore the six-gun or rope seemed superior to judicial procedure. In 1877, for instance, Texas alone had 5,000 men on its wanted list.[13] And Theodore Roosevelt pointed out, "the fact of such scoundrels being able to ply their trade with impunity for any length of time can only be understood if the absolute wildness of our land is taken into account." Roosevelt tells how in 1888 "notorious bullies and murderers have been taken out and hung, while the bands of horse thieves have been regularly hunted down and destroyed in pitched fights by parties of armed cowboys."[14] Small wonder that foppish Bat Masterson was once fined $8 for shooting a citizen through the lung. After all, the man had deserved it.

In Denver, according to one visitor from England, "murder is a comparatively slight offense," a sign of being fashionable.

[10] Charles A. Guernsey, *Wyoming Cowboy Days* (New York: G. P. Putnam's Sons, 1936), p. 91.

[11] Miguel Antonio Otero, *My Life on The Frontier 1864–1882* (New York: The Press of the Pioneers, 1935), pp. 205–06.

[12] Jim McIntire, *Early Days in Texas; A Trip to Hell and Heaven* (Kansas City, Mo.: McIntire Publishing Co., 1902), pp. 142–43.

[13] Carl Coke Rister, "Outlaws and Vigilantes of the Southern Plains, 1865–1885," *Mississippi Valley Historical Review,* XIX (1932–1933), pp. 537, 544–45.

[14] "Sheriff's Work on a Ranch," *Century Magazine,* XXXVI, No. 1 (May-Oct., 1888), p. 40. "Ranch Life in the Far West," *Century Magazine,* XXXV, No. 4 (Feb. 1888), p. 505.

> Until two or three years ago, assassination—incidental not deliberate assassination—was a crime of every day . . . . Unless a ruffian is known to have killed half-a-dozen people, and to have got, as it were, murder on the brain, he is almost safe from trouble in these western plains. A notorious murderer lived near Central City; it was known that he had shot six or seven men; but no one thought of interfering with him on account of his crimes . . . .[15]

The truth is that vigilantism, or "group action in lieu of regular justice," as Caughey calls it, reflects the thinking of a substantial body of local sentiment. The community sits in judgment. It condones because it believes. However, a vital difference exists between vigilantism of the frontier and the vigilantism of the latter twentieth century. The pioneer was beyond the reach of regular justice; he had to fill the vacuum. Sometimes he filled it with grave concern for the decencies of human relations. More often he moved in a state of emotion, even as modern society would like to have done following the deaths of the two Kennedys, when the identities of the assassins were suspected.

In his penetrating study of vigilantism, Caughey points out the John Snyder-James Reed dispute arising out of the frustrations of the Donner party in 1846. A month behind schedule, nerves frayed, the members of the Donner party were at each other's throats. When Snyder whipped Reed's team, Reed naturally objected. So Snyder brought his heavy whip down on Reed. To quote Caughey, "Reed drew his knife, Mrs. Reed rushed in between the two men and was struck by the whip, and then Reed, half-blinded in his own blood, plunged the knife into his antagonist. Immediately he was contrite as a man could be; he took the boards from his wagon to make the rude coffin in which Snyder was buried."

What to do? The party was well beyond the reach of U.S. law, in the upper remoteness of Mexican territory, and totally out of touch with any legal jurisdiction. The members held a trial of some sort, Reed pled defense of his wife, and the evidence indicated unpremeditated and justifiable homicide. But his companions saw the action in another light, did not like to hang or shoot Reed, and so banished him empty-handed from the train. Undoubtedly it would have been a slow death sentence, except that his daughter slipped him a gun and ammunition in the night and he made it to California safely, later to participate in the rescue of what was left of that unfortunate party.

Caughey also mentions a rare acquittal. In this instance, in the Green River country of Wyoming, a man named Williams shot and killed a teamster who had repeatedly threatened his life. Williams offered to stand trial, but the group was not disposed to try him, believing that he had acted in self-defense. But when another man, apparently without provocation, killed one of his mates, a volunteer posse went after the malefactor, could not locate him, and brought Williams back to the Green River

[15] William Hepworth Dixon, *New American*, pp. 139–141, quoted in Carl Coke Rister, *Southern Plainsmen* (Norman: University of Oklahoma Press, 1938), pp. 192–93.

ferry to stand trial. Since it was the 4th of July, a festive crowd was on hand, court was convened, Williams challenged its jurisdiction, and an argument ensued which led to a riotous melee. The fact that it was the Fourth of July and that some of the Spirit of Independence was liquid undoubtedly contributed to the scuffle. The trial was not resumed, Williams felt that his presence was "wholly irrelevant" to the current circumstances, and he withdrew. The court was never adjourned, for it didn't seem necessary.

Far to the south, at the same time in Arizona, two young Arkansans quarreled, fought, and were pulled apart, whereupon one of them whipped out a knife and killed his assailant. The company promptly chose a judge and jury, found the knife-wielder guilty, and the next morning had the whole company vote on the verdict. A firing squad was chosen by lot, six men were given rifles with blank loads, and six had powder and ball. When they buried the man, they posted a brief statement over the grave of what had happened. As Caughey concludes:

> Months out of the trail, the emigrants certainly were beyond the reach of regular courts. There even was question what government had jurisdiction. If society was to do anything about crime on the trail, it would have to be through improvised group action. In their minds the forty-niners asserted this same justification—that they had left regular justice a couple of thousand miles behind and that it had to be the vigilante response or none at all. Other parts of the frontier could also assert that they were remote or cut off from established courts.[16]

The difficulty with frontier vigilantism is that it has no stopping place. Men accustomed to taking law into their hands continue to take law into their hands even after regular judicial processes are constituted. They continue to take the law into their hands right into these days of the 1960s. They do not approve of a man or a situation, and they cannot wait for the regular processes to assist their realizations. They might not know a frontier if they saw one, and they certainly are not aware of the extension of the frontier spirit down to themselves. But they do know that they must get rid of the offending member or section of civilization. So they burn down a ghetto, they loot and pillage, they bury three civil rights workers beneath a dam, or they shoot a man in a caravan in Dallas or on a motel balcony in Memphis. True, to them the law and the other civilized processes may be available, but like the frontiersman they cannot wait. But whereas some frontiersmen had an excuse, these people merely operate in a spirit which does violence even to the memory of the frontier.

So much of vigilantism of the frontier had no place at all in a legally constituted society. The vigilantes of San Francisco in the 1850s were operating after legal redress had been properly constituted. The Mexican,

[16] Caughey, *Their Majesties the Mob*, pp. 6–9.

Juanita, "a very comely, quiet, gentle creature apparently, [who] behaved herself with a great deal of propriety," was visited in Downieville on the night of July 4, 1851, by a Joseph Cannon. When he literally fell through the door, Juanita sprang out of bed and stabbed the drunken intruder. She was seized, the cry went out that she had stabbed a popular citizen, a court was formed in the Downieville plaza, and a jury of twelve men was selected from the crowd that gathered.

> Towards night they found the woman guilty and sentenced her to be hung at sundown . . . they gave her half an hour to get ready to die. She was finally taken down to the bridge, about four feet high from the bridge, and a rope put up over the crossbeam, with a noose attached to the end of it . . . this woman walked up the ladder, unsupported, and stood on the scantling, under the rope, with the hungriest, craziest, wildest mob standing around that ever I saw anywhere.
>
> The woman adjusted the rope around her own neck, pulling out her braid of hair, and at the firing of a pistol, two men with hatchets, at each end, cut the rope which held the scantling, and down everything went, woman and all. The mob then turned upon Dr. Aiken, who was still a resident of that city, because he had tried to defend the woman; and they drove the gambler with whom the woman was living out of town, and also some other friends of the woman, showing from first to last the utter irresponsibility of mobs.
>
> The hanging of the woman was murder. No jury in the world, on any principle of self-defense or protection of life and property, would ever have convicted the woman . . . there was considerable ill feeling toward Mexican gamblers and women generally, and there was no other way but to hang her. During the trial of the woman, ropes had to be brought into requisition to keep the mob back; they would once in a while make a rush for her, and the conductors of the prosecution would have to appeal to them, calling on them to remember their wives, mothers and daughters, to give this woman a fair trial; and in that way they were kept quiet until this woman was executed.[17]

The execution of Sheriff Henry Plummer in Montana ranks equally as a miscarriage of justice. Montana was sufficiently settled, as was Downieville, for men to have recourse to law. They did not choose to follow the slow process of judicial weighing of evidence but preferred to move with frontier dispatch. Undoubtedly Henry Plummer, sheriff at Lewiston, was the principal in a gang of road agents. Undoubtedly Plummer's agent had a hundred murders in their archives. How many assaults and robberies they had committed is impossible to determine. Certainly the vigilantes

[17] David P. Barstow, Statement 1878, from the H. H. Bancroft Collection, University of California, Berkeley, quoted in Caughey, pp. 47–50.

had provocation for forming. Certainly too the vigilantes had reason to believe that Plummer et al. were guilty beyond reasonable doubt. "Every good citizen in Alder Gulch" joined the vigilante organization, fearing that the Plummer gang might take alarm and disperse, not to be rounded up again.

Accordingly, four Virginia City vigilantes arrived at Bannack to order the immediate execution of Plummer and his confederates. Shortly Bannack had a branch organization of the Virginia City vigilantes. Off the Bannack vigilantes went, finding one of the confederates in a cabin and the other at a gaming table in a saloon. Plummer was found "at his cabin, in the act of washing his face . . . he was marched to a point, where . . . he joined Stinson and Ray, and thence the three were conducted under a formidable escort to the gallows." Plummer himself had erected the gallows the previous season.

> Terrible must have been its appearance as it loomed up in the bright starlight, the only object visible to the gaze of the guilty men, on that long waste of ghastly snow. A negro boy came up to the gallows with rope before the arrival of the cavalcade. All the way, Ray and Stinson filled the air with curses. Plummer, on the contrary, first begged for his life, and, finding that unavailing, resorted to argument . . . .
>
> "It is useless," said one of the Vigilantes, "for you to beg for your life; that affair is settled, and cannot be altered. You are to be hanged. You cannot feel harder about it than I do; but I cannot help it if I would."
>
> Plummer asked for time to pray. "Certainly," replied the Vigilante, "but say your prayers up there," at the same time pointing to the crossbeam of the gallows-frame.

Regardless of whether they deserved to die, and the evidence indicates that they did, the three men had been executed without trial. They had been executed because the vigilantes of Virginia City had sent word to Bannack to seize them and execute them. To Montanans the presence of judicial procedures was not pertinent.[18]

Some excuse might be made for Montana being a truly crude frontier. Texas cannot hide behind such a claim. An independent republic in 1836, a State in 1845, by a comparison with the remainder of the western frontier it enjoyed a relatively sophisticated political society. And yet in the 1850s in Brownsville the Abbe' Domenech witnessed still another example of vigilante action. During a fandango a half-drunk North American killed a Mexican by stabbing him in the abdomen. As he fled for the sanctuary of Mexico across the river, the American was captured. On the next morning a trumpet summoned the people to pronounce sentence. A future sheriff took over, and without commentary called for "those who

[18] Nathaniel Pitt Langford, *Vigilante Days and Ways* (Boston, 1890), vol. II, pp. 162–69, quoted in Caughey, pp. 80–85.

vote for his death step this way. Let the rest remain as they are." It was as casual as a New England town meeting voting an ordinance. The crowd shouted and to a man moved forward.

The action had been so precipitate that the gallows wasn't even ready, but a post was found outside a church. The future sheriff, inexperienced at this sort of thing, did not make a good gallows, so that the culprit was constrained to say to him, "Let me do it. You don't know your business." The prisoner seized the rope, tied the knot, and put it around his neck. After a short speech regarding the evilness of drunkenness, "which made a deep impression on the crowd," he hung from the post outside the church. Texas was a formal State in the United States of America, Brownsville was an old city that had gone through the war with Mexico, Texas had almost all the judicial procedures it has today, and the mob hanged a man for murder, even though the Mexican he had wounded did not actually die until the day after the hanging. A few years later a visitor to Texas was to observe: "in this lawless region men were seldom convicted of homicide, and never punished . . . if you want distinction in this country, kill somebody!"[19]

Kansas, of course, had been reasonably civilized since the latter 1850s. Perhaps some sympathy could be extracted for its problems with Texas cowhands, suddenly released from discipline like sailors in a foreign liberty port, but what do you do about a situation like the following?

The year is 1884. Caldwell, Kansas, is undergoing a "moral spasm." Mayor Albert M. Colson and the council stand "for pure and simple good order." The town has a strong Women's Christian Temperance Union. Through the winter and spring of 1885 the movement for prohibition of liquor gathers strength, including the support of a Quaker-run newspaper, the Caldwell *Free Press.* Shortly after two whisky peddlers were arrested, the house of the *Free Press* editor burned to the ground. Then in November, 1885, the county attorney caused the arrest of a "blind tiger" operator. As he was being marched to the railroad depot, an armed mob besieged the two men escorting him in the baggage room of the train station. The new mayor, George Reilly, intervened and locked the prisoner in the city jail. But the mob reformed and turned the prisoner loose. The sheriff then arrested eighteen Caldwellites.

Threats followed, one on top of the other. Finally on December 8, at one o'clock in the morning, a group of men posing as law officers awakened one of the whisky peddlers and marched him off into the night. His body was found at dawn, "dangling stiffly from a crossbeam in the pelting sleet that prefaced the winter's first snow. A note protruding from one pocket—addressed 'To House Burners' and signed 'Vigilance Committee' "—advised the other peddler as well as six other whisky sellers to feel themselves warned. The mistress of the hanged man said she recognized two members of the lynching party, but when she was brought into court, she refused to confirm the identification, apparently having been threatened by the forces of law and order. As a grandson of the

[19] Albert D. Richardson, *Beyond The Mississippi,* p. 226, quoted in Rister, *Southern Plainsmen,* pp. 190–91.

editor said years later, "Sentiment by the abiding element began to get so strong that someone had to be hung." The town leaders of Caldwell itself formed a 130-strong Law and Order League. Although some more deliberate citizens condemned such voluntary association, an assembly of perhaps 400 Caldwellites at the local opera house not only endorsed the Law and Order League's aim of enforcement of all laws in the statute books, but collected a private reward to help them in their work. These latter developments are a long generation removed from the frontier, but not from the frontier tradition.[20]

Forming a vigilance committee in Kansas carried no sinister implications within a community. Thus the editor of Topeka *Commonwealth* wrote routinely in the summer of 1875: "A vigilance committee has been organized at Dodge City, and it would not be surprising if some of the telegraph poles were found ornamented some of these days."[21]

Actually the idea of the vigilance committee goes back to puritan forefathers, whether it is their pointing out witches at Salem or their branding an "A" on a young girl's flesh. Back in 1830 in Illinois a mining rush wrapped around the unexciting metal of lead, ran the town of Galena, Illinois, into the usual welter of saloons, gambling halls, and disregard for law and order. Local citizens formed a vigilance committee. In effect the good moral people who violated the rights of the Mormons at Nauvoo were a self-constituted vigilance group. Iowa, never prominently associated with violence, had its own lead and land rush in the 1840s, and again the law-respecting farmers formed vigilance committees to rid Dubuque of its raffish lead-mining element and Keokuk of its "coarse and ferocious water men."

When in 1862 a gold strike along the Colorado River followed on the heels of a strike on the lower Gila, Tucson became a community cluttered with cut-throats. The moral people felt that these outlaws must surely have been spawned by the vigilance committees in San Francisco, who in ridding their town of a worthless element had sent it instead packing into the future Territory of Arizona.

Undoubtedly the most effective of the vigilance committees, insofar as numbers of hanged victims is concerned, belongs to the Black Hills of South Dakota during the middle and latter 1870s. Deadwood was wide open, which meant that it was wide open for riffraff and equally wide open for vigilantes. It was just a case of who could take over.

The truth is, every frontier State went through its period of lawlessness and its corresponding period of mobocracy designed to bring the lawless element under control. Further, the reformers did not cease imposing their personal ideas of reform with the coming of judicial processes. The truth is also that a century later, with or without our frontier background as justification, groups of citizens still make charges outside the law, and some even insist on enforcing those charges. A proper frontier tradition is great and effective, a true heritage for a people who must

[20] Robert R. Dykstra, *The Cattle Towns* (New York: Alfred A. Knopf, 1968), pp. 285–92.

[21] Rister, *Southern Plainsmen*, pp. 196–97.

have heroes to point directions. But a frontier heritage misstated and misapplied is a disservice to the true cause of heritage and a negation of the freedom for which many frontiersmen gave their lives.

Invariably we return to a continuing, fundamental problem of race hatred. Nowadays it is dramatized as between black and white. Once it was between red and white. The hatred may not have been endemic, but the incursions of the white men on the Indian land drove the red man again and again to desperate, savage, and invariably futile war. The missionary loved the red man, from the days of the Spaniard clustered around the Texas and California missions down to the Quakers preaching brotherly love during the Indian massacres of President Grant's days. The fur trader also found the Indian a friend, and particularly found great comfort in the Indian woman. The Indian accepted both occupational groups.

But the one man who could neither assimilate the Indian nor be accepted by his red brother was the farmer. As the farmer moved westward, cutting back the forests, muddying up the streams, and beating back the game, the Indian's enmity toward him grew deadly. As for the frontiersmen, the Indian ranked somewhere below the dog. Certainly the Indian was well below the Negro slave, for the latter had function and utility. How do you handle an element for which there is no positive use? You exterminate it, especially if in your eyes it has murderous propensities. And so the inevitable, as virtually all the world knows, happened. The conflict between the two races, in the words of Ralph Gabriel, "like a forest fire, burned its way westward across the continent."[22] The noble savage was not noble at all in the sight of his adversary but a beast who bashed babies' heads up against trees and tore skin bit by bit from women's bodies. Each atrocity on either side evoked an equal retaliation. The list is long and painful, and no credit to either side.

From the standpoint of twentieth century society, however, the white-Indian conflict for 300 years has important implications. For one thing, during the periodic lapses into peace which the young American nation enjoyed, these vacations from war did not by any means allow only for dull consolidation of the nation's politics and economics; instead they offered prime time for violent internal action. Almost always an Indian war was going on somewhere. On some wing of the frontier the white man was being menaced by the Indian, or he was menacing the Indian. He was running the Indian out of the woods, he was running him off the grasslands, he was running him across the desert and over the mountains to the west. With an insatiable earth hunger he was destroying the Indians' hunting grounds, until eventually he destroyed the game itself. This is not to discount those sincere Americans who had an interest in Indian culture and a desire for the two races to live side by side, but merely to point out that if any young man, full of the rising sap of the springtime of life, wanted to flex his muscles and pick a fight, he could find some Indian to fight against. The fact that the frontier also attracted the rootless and the drifters, and that these were often desperate men,

[22] Ralph Henry Gabriel, *The Lure of The Frontier; A Story of Race Conflict* (New Haven: Yale University Press, 1929), pp. 4–6.

added to the conflict and the inability to maintain peaceful Indian relations.

A mere listing of the battles with Indians would cover hundreds of pages in six-point type. Take the Pequot War, King Philip's War, the French and Indian War, the Natchez War, the Fox War, Pontiac's Rebellion, Lord Dunmore's War, the problems of George Rogers Clark and at a later day William Henry Harrison, the Creek War, the Blackhawk War (which enlisted the attention of young frontiersman Abraham Lincoln), the Seminole War, all the raids by the Comanches and Apaches and Kiowas against the Texans and all the raids by the Texans against the Comanches, the Apaches, and the Kiowas, the Cheyenne-Arapaho War, the Sioux War, the Washita War, the Red River War, and the Ghost Dance Wars—these go on and on, seemingly without end. Where do you want to fight? When do you want to fight?

And if you get home from a war or a skirmish, you have instant hero status if you have halfway behaved yourself. There is a premium on killing Indians, a premium whose dividends continue through life. Men who came in after the end of Indian wars falsely delegated themselves as Indian fighters as they grew older and no one could prove them wrong. Often, criminal acts against other white men could be forgiven because a man had distinguished himself in combat against the Indians. Thus the retreating Indians constituted a kind of omnipresent safety valve for those people who liked to dance with danger, vitalize themselves with violence, and renew themselves with revenge.

Actually, although the only good Indian might be a dead one, there were two types of Indian. There were the peaceful ones, like California's 150,000 "Digger" Indians, a tranquil people who lived off the product of the land. There were also the warrior Indians, like the Sioux and the Apache. The white frontiersman generally looked on both with suspicion and distaste. California's miners murdered the Diggers as though they were endangered by them. On the other hand, murdering the warrior Indian was often a question of killing before you got killed, which simplified the problem. Skilled horsemen, these Indians, largely from the Great Plains, hit and ran with tactics that would have brought admiration from such mounted generals as Phil Sheridan, Jeb Stuart, or Erwin Rommel. Theirs was lightning warfare, and at full run they could loose twenty arrows while their longer-shooting foes were trying to reload. The wars themselves are reasonably straightforward, and could perhaps be condoned as inexorable conflicts. But the individual atrocities have no justification, even though at the time the perpetrators were often saluted as heroes. This latter statement holds true for both sides.

Nowhere has a lust for blood been more deeply etched than in the infamous Sand Creek massacre. Shortly after sundown on November 28, 1864, Col. J. M. Chivington and his men left Fort Lyon, Colorado, to surround the followers of Chief Black Kettle. At dawn Chivington's militia charged through the camp of 500 peaceful Indians, despite Black Kettle's raising an American and then a white flag. Not just warriors were killed. Women and children were dragged out, shot, knifed, scalped, clubbed, mutilated, their brains knocked out, bosoms ripped open. Four hundred and fifty Indians in varying stages of insensate slaughter lay about the campground. There is no defense whatsoever for the action. It was bloodier than Chicago or Detroit or Harlem ever thought of being. Chivington and his cohorts were widely hailed as heroes by many of their fellow Americans.

Perfidy was not all on one side. During the summer of 1866, troops working on the Powder River road were constantly harassed by Indian attack. In a complete, efficient, and economical performance the Sioux killed every straggler, raided every wagon train bringing in supplies, and attacked every wood-cutting party. Finally in December, when a wood train was assaulted, Capt. W. J. Fetterman led a party to its relief. The Indians ambushed him, and left all eighty-two members of his party to rot on the field of battle. What Sitting Bull's detachment did to reckless and feckless Colonel George A. Custer at the Little Big Horn is known to everyone who ever looked at the Old Anheuser-Busch calendar or a Remington painting. Two hundred and sixty-five men were completely wiped out by 2,500 Sioux.[23]

Finally in the 1880s Geronimo, a "thin-lipped, square-cut, hard-eyed, savagely cruel hater of all white men" began his personal last frontier. In one six-month period, Geronimo's raiders officially killed eighty-five soldiers, settlers, and reservation Indians in American territory, plus an uncounted number below the Mexican border. A superb strategist, Geronimo lost only six warriors during this period. Official United States decided that such activity could not be tolerated and sent twenty-five detachments under Gen. Nelson A. Miles after the ragged Apache. Desperate, Geronimo turned to needless terror, killing, among others, between 500 and 600 Sonorans during his campaign to escape capture. But time and space ran out on him, and he was caught and put aside.[24]

Of course, the classic account of racial arrogance, or disdain, belongs to Judge Roy Bean, who ranks with Billy the Kid as the most overrated, overblown character along the entire frontier. When a man was hauled before him for murdering a Chinese laborer along the Southern Pacific tracks building beyond the Pecos, Judge Bean freed the accused man, asserting that nowhere in his law book could he find a rule against killing a Chinese.

Sometimes it was not racial arrogance at all, but a simple antagonism to people with different outlooks. Thus Joseph Smith, Brigham Young, and other Mormons ran into the inflammatory and adamant opposition of local people, whether they lived in northeastern Ohio, Missouri, Illinois, or Utah. The Gentiles, believing presumably in all the Christian precepts, including love thy neighbor, did not love anyone whose faith was so far from theirs. It was difficult enough for a Campbellite on the frontier to accept a Baptist or one of John Knox's followers; Catholic and Jews were barely tolerable; the Mormon, a latecomer to the world of organized

[23] Ray Allen Billington, *Westward Expansion* (New York: The Macmillan Co., 1960), pp. 653–72.

[24] Joe B. Franz and Julian E. Choate Jr., *The American Cowboy* (Norman: University of Oklahoma Press, 1955), pp. 127–38.

religion, was downright intolerable. His position was made less tenable by the fact that he tended to prosper, which induced Gentile grumbling that Mormons must be in league with the devil. And then one night at Carthage, Missouri, a properly organized area, a mob broke into the jail where Joseph Smith and his brother had been lodged for protection, and slaughtered the two Mormon leaders. Back east across the river, angry Gentiles served notice that the Mormons could leave or else.

Harassed even after they established their cooperative society in the midst of the individualistic West, the Mormons felt threatened as their first decade in the Territory of Utah came to a close. The result was another verse in that old chapter on retaliation. In September 1857, 140 emigrants were passing through southern Utah on their way to California. Although most were sincere, pious farmers intent on a new life in California, there were a few hotspurs among the group. On September 7 the caravan was attacked by Indians, with seven white men killed. To relieve the ensuing siege, one Missourian in the party slipped out to seek assistance. A fanatical Mormon, perhaps mistaking his intention, killed him.

Fearful that his murder would bring Federal retaliation, the Mormon's neighbors hastened to cover the evidence. Accordingly, they sent word to the train that the Indians had been pacified and that the party could proceed across the territory. As the emigrants filed out of their siege site, they were shot down one by one. Altogether 120 persons were murdered, with seventeen children only being spared. The years since have brought an understanding of the tensions under which the Mormons perpetrated this massacre at Mountain Meadows, but for purposes here the fact remains that feared violence was anticipated by preemptory violence.

The war with Mexico undoubtedly has some roots in racial arrogance on both sides. In fact, the whole severance of Texas from Mexico was brought about by men from the United States lately come to that vast area, and impatient with Mexican law and administration. Because the Mexicans felt that the Anglos represented a materialistic and restless culture, they were equally intolerant of their Anglo neighbors. To them, explaining the loss of Texas in the Texan revolution was no problem. After all, Texas had won only one battle during the entire altercation; it just happened to be the last one at San Jacinto. Mexico's army was experienced, and one Mexican soldier was certainly worth an indeterminate number of *yanqui* soldiers any day. War feeling in Mexico was as high and as bloodthirsty as it was in the States.

The ensuing overwhelming defeat of the Mexican forces and the wholesale dissection of Mexican territory into the giant maw of the North Americans only exacerbated distrust between the two nations. For the next forty years Mexicans raided north of the Rio Grande. The Texans called them bandits. In pursuit of the Mexicans, Texans ranged south of the Rio Grande, where the Mexicans called them bandits. Both sides were right, and both were equally wrong. Again, as with the Indians, the killing of one race by another was perfectly justified back home. The Texas Rangers, a law enforcement group, raided Mexicans along with

Indians as natural enemies, and seldom gave any Mexican, whether a national of the United States or of Mexico, the benefit of the doubt.

Nor did the Rangers respect boundaries. In the best frontier tradition they pursued the enemy to his ultimate lair. There is the famous instance—famous at least to Texans—of Capt. L. H. McNelly, a 130-pound consumptive who was a living definition of deathless courage, chasing onto the Mexican side of the Rio Grande in the face of an overwhelming number of enemies, all pledged to his swift undoing. From the American bank of the river a sergeant in the U.S. Army sent Captain McNelly a note that the Secretary of War was ordering him back on the American side lest an international incident be provoked. McNelly's reply was terse and understandable, and must have caused some feeling when it was relayed to Washington. Simply and explicitly he told the Secretary of War to go to hell, this was his fight.

If during this essay it seems as if the frontier heritage is predominantly negative and directed toward violence, such a conclusion is misleading. The purpose here has been to examine a facet of the frontier heritage, that surface which not only condoned but actually encouraged the idea and practice of violence but which undoubtedly plays a role in shaping twentieth-century American attitudes. The examination could go into as much detail as the danger[;] the frontier heritage established the idea of the individual's arming himself. This activity is almost unique with the United States frontier. Instead of a central armory to which men could go to gather their arms, each man bore his own. He thus had it always at the ready. When danger arose, he could get together with another man, and another and another, until an armed mob was on its way. It might be a mob in the best posse sense, or it might be an extra-legal group which felt that its private preserves and attitudes were threatened. But it was always a mob.

The prevalence of arms over the fireplace of every frontier cabin or stacked by the sod-house door endures in the defense which groups like the National Rifle Association membership carry on today against attempts to register arms and control the sale of guns and ammunition. A man had to have a gun, not solely for game to feed his family but because he had to be ready to defend. This heritage continues. As of this writing, it still prevails in most parts of the Nation. Almost no other country permits such widespread individual ownership, but the United States through its frontier experience has historical justification. In pioneer days a frontier boy came of age when his father presented him his own gun as surely as a town boy came of age by putting on long pants or his sister became a woman by putting up her hair. In many areas of the United States in A.D. 1969 a boy still becomes a man, usually on his birthday or at Christmas, when his father gives him a gun. A generally accepted age is twelve, although it may come even a half-dozen years sooner. The gun may be nothing more than a target weapon, but the boy is shown how to use it and how to take care of it, and he is a gun owner and user, probably for the next sixty years of his expected life on this earth. Whether he shoots sparrows out of the eaves of the house, quail and deer in season, or his fellowman with or without provocation remains for his personal history to unfold. The fact is that in his gun ownership he is following a tradition that goes back to John Smith and Jamestown and has persisted ever since.

And yet, as every schoolboy knows, the frontier has given us other traits which also mark us and often improve us. The frontier made us materialistic, because we needed things to survive. The frontier, by the very act of its being there for the taking and taming, gave us an optimistic belief in progress which again has marked the nation for greatness. The frontier fostered individualism as in no other region of the world. It gave us mobility; a man could move up and down the social, economic, and political scale without regard to what he had been before. The frontiersman could remold institutions to make them work. The frontiersman did not necessarily believe in individual freedom, except for himself, for he turned to his constituted government for every kind of help, particularly economic. The frontier also made him physically mobile long before the mechanics of transportation made such mobility easy. The frontier made him generous, even prodigal and extravagant, particularly where national resources were concerned. The frontier undoubtedly made the American nationalistic.

Thus we see a blending of a man's qualities that is both good and bad. If the good could somehow be retained, while those qualities which have outlived their usefulness could be eschewed or dismissed forever, the human material which constitutes this nation could develop in the direction of an improved society. To argue which facets of the frontier experience have outlived their utility can be argued interminably, but certainly the wistful look backwards which Americans, informed and uninformed, cast toward the violence associated with the frontier has no place in a nation whose frontier has worn away. The time for everyone, from scenario writers to political breast beaters to economic and social individualists, to proclaim the virtues of the frontiersman and his reliance on simple solutions and direct action does not befit a nation whose problems are corporate, community, and complex.

Work Camp and Chinatown

GUNTHER BARTH

Too often the study of immigration in American history deals only with the Atlantic migration, overlooking the fact that there were several waves of immigration from East Asia. The first major wave was a large-scale migration from the Pearl River Delta area of China into California and the West during the gold rush, beginning in 1848. The second was an influx of Japanese settlers on the West Coast around the turn of the twentieth century.

Toward the middle of the nineteenth century, political unrest in China displaced many peasants and urban poor. Many of the latter migrated to Latin America and the American tropics under a system of contract labor that was much like indentured servitude. There they sometimes replaced African slaves, whose numbers were dwindling because of the abolition or suppression of the Atlantic slave trade. These Oriental laborers were called "coolies," which in China meant merely unskilled laborers but which in the Western Hemisphere soon acquired the connotation of bound, or involuntary, laborers. In this sense of the word, very few of the Chinese immigrants to the United States were technically coolies, although they were under the strict control of those Chinese organizations who had arranged for their passage, most notoriously, the Six Companies. Most of these immigrants had belonged to the free peasantry in China and thus had roots in the same class that produced the Irish and German immigrants of the period.

If it was difficult for white European immigrants to find a place in the relatively stable Eastern society at mid-century, it was even more difficult for East Asians to move into the highly fluid, rapidly changing, rambunctious society of California. Next to the blacks, the Chinese were the immigrant group most different from the dominant whites. Their physical appearance was distinctive, and they tended to preserve their own language, religion, customs, and culture. Over half of these immigrants were married men who had left their families in China and who found it necessary to work hard and live extremely frugally in order to send money home, to visit their families in China, or to return to China permanently. All these factors tended to set the Chinese apart from white America, though by 1852 the Chinese in California alone numbered 25,000 and made up 10 percent of the state's total population.

Although the Chinese were at first fairly well received because of a desperate shortage of unskilled labor in California, they found themselves less and less welcome as more white laborers became available. They soon came to dominate the restaurant and laundry businesses in San Francisco and in the northern part of the state. Furthermore, they demonstrated an ability to take over apparently worthless mining claims and make them pay by working harder and longer than the white miners. This phenomenon produced so much hostility in the mining camps that the Chinese were frequently barred from owning or working claims. The willingness of the Celestials (as they were often called) to work long hours at low pay, which had originally worked in their favor, came to be seen by white migrants from the East and the South as unfair competition.

As early as 1852 attempts were made to bar the Chinese from admission to the West Coast. Anti-Chinese sentiment culminated in the passage of the Chinese Exclusion Act of 1882. Although this law was intended to halt immigration for only a ten-year period, it virtually put a stop to Chinese migration to the United States. Ironically, it had the effect of opening the West Coast to Japanese immigration, which was stimulated by the need to fill various jobs in the expanding economy that would earlier have been filled by the Chinese.

In his book on the Chinese in the United States in the middle of the nineteenth century, Gunther Barth, of the University of California at Berkeley, has included a chapter on the working and recreational life of the sojourners. That chapter is reprinted below. One can see there the isolation of the Chinese workers and understand clearly the necessity for the development of the Chinatowns which provided the illusion of community and a taste of the familiar for those so far from home.

An invisible control system based on district loyalty, filial piety, and fear circumscribed the realm of Chinese California and re-enforced the basic allegiances of traders and miners in isolated mountain camps. These sentiments formed a stronger and more effective confine than the bricks and mortar of the walls of the visible world, or the chains of daily drudgery that bound the indentured emigrants. Consequently, the Chinese quarters of the cities needed merely to symbolize the presence of control without duplicating the whole system. They permitted a release for emotions checked by restraint and oppression, and provided a brief retreat from work in an alien environment into a world resembling home.

Long before large numbers of Chinese withdrew from California's countryside in the 1870s and crowded into settlements in urban centers, Chinatowns acquired a vital role as safety valves of the control system.[1] In these quarters, islands of freedom and license within the reach of the lowliest bordered on centers of authority and oppression. In a crude mixture of order and chaos, the headquarters of district companies and tongs neighbored the theaters and gambling halls. The Chinatowns fleetingly admitted indentured emigrants to a life of affluence. Visions of that leisure once had stimulated the sojourners' dreams of success and had prompted them to leave home and risk years of certain hardship in a strange country in the struggle for an uncertain fortune. The Chinese quarter liberated the indentured emigrants briefly from the shackles of work which debt bondage placed on their shoulders. For hours the excitement of a gambling table or the air of abundance pervading one of the great public festivals elevated them above their lowly status. These brighter interludes added color and brought relief from the gray monotony and strict discipline of an austere world of work.

Descriptions of San Francisco's Chinese quarters in official reports and newspaper accounts of the 1850s and 1860s furnish more useful information than the political, sociological, and missionary polemics, or the fantastic tales of succeeding decades.[2] The Chinatown of popular fancy, if it ever existed at all, flourished between 1882 and 1906. Some of the later belletristic sources also give a broader perspective of the extraordinary life in Chinatown.[3]

The 1850s and 1860s labeled the Chinese quarters in San Francisco

[1] A few accounts, such as Arnold Genthe and Will Irwin, *Pictures of* [San Francisco's] *Old Chinatown* (New York, 1908), and Edgar M. Kahn, "Chinatown and the Cable Cars," *Cable Car Days in San Francisco* (Stanford, [1940]), 77–84, in passing touch on this function of Chinatown.

[2] [Alfred Trumble], *The 'Heathen Chinee' at Home and Abroad. Who He Is; What He Looks Like; How He Works and Lives; His Virtues, Vices and Crimes. A Complete Panorama of the Chinese in America. By an Old Californian* (New York, [1882]), and Walter J. Raymond, *Horrors of the Mongolian Settlement, San Francisco, Cal. An Enslaved and Degraded Race of Paupers, Opium Eaters and Leepers* (Boston, [1886?]), combine several aspects.

[3] William Purviance Fenn, *Ah Sin and His Brethren in American Literature* (Peking, [1933]), and John Burt Foster, "China and the Chinese in American Literature, 1850–1950," unpub. diss. University of Illinois, 1952, looked into the literary merits of the writings on Chinatown. Chester B. Fernald, *The Cat and the Cherub and Other Stories* (New York, 1896), and William Norr, *Stories of Chinatown. Sketches from Life in the Chinese Colony of Mott, Pell and Doyers Streets* (New York, [1892]), proved to be helpful.

variously. Little Canton and Little China were two of the appellations in use. However, the name "China Town" appeared as early as 1853 in newspaper reports.[4] Sacramento Street, where Chinese had first located canvas houses in 1849 between Kearny and Dupont Streets, was called by the sojourners T'ang Yen Gai, *t'ang-jen chieh*—the Street of the Men of T'ang, Chinese (Cantonese) Street.[5] The early Chinese occupied scattered localities in San Francisco which were yet a far cry from the later strictly confined area of Chinatown, roughly encircled by California, Stockton, Broadway, and Kearny Streets, and depicted in the "Official Map of Chinatown in San Francisco" published under the supervision of the Special Committee of the Board of Supervisors in July, 1885.[6] In these pages the term Chinatown has been applied indiscriminately to all Chinese settlements in the United States, without regard for *the* Chinatown. Chinese quarters in urban areas, isolated fishing villages, or stores in distant mining camps, irrespective of size or location, all harbored the world of freedom, license, and escape which sanctioned their existence.

In mountain villages and mining towns Chinese stores were the focus of life. As soon as several Chinese moved into a settlement, one of them sent to Marysville, Sacramento, Stockton, or some other supply center for the groceries and other wares needed by the colony.[7] These he sold to his comrades without at first discontinuing his regular work. If the colony increased in numbers, he rented a small store and formed a trading company with the assistance of friends, clan association, or district company. Often, a Chinese physician began to dispense medicines from a supply of drugs ranged along one side of the store, and an itinerant barber made it a place of call. In a short time, an auspicious name, goods from San Francisco, and news from the Pearl River Delta made the store the resort of all Chinese in the vicinity.[8]

In time the aspiring merchant hired a cook who at first was available only for banquets but later ran a small restaurant in an annex. Another

[4] *Alta,* November 21, 1853, October 15, 1857, February 8 (quoting Oroville *Record*), 18, 1858, February 17, 1859; *Herald*, April 12, July 10, 1852, January 17, June 23, 1853; William H. Goetzmann, *Army Exploration in the American West, 1803–1863* (New Haven, 1959), 401. Foster, "China and the Chinese in American Literature, 1850–1950," p. 141, dates the application of the name Chinatown "only after 1860."

[5] William J. Hoy, "Chinatown Devises Its Own Street Names," *California Folklore Quarterly* (Berkeley), 2:72 (April 1943); Hoy, (trans.), "Gold Mountain, Big City, Chinese Map," *California Historical Society Quarterly*, 27:256–58 (September 1948).

[6] "San Francisco As It Is. Chinese Population," *Herald,* April 12, 1852; *Herald,* December 8, 1853, August 22, 1854, June 12, 1857; *Alta,* October 30, 1851, April 25, November 15, 1853, February 15, September 2, 3, 4, 1854, October 15, 1857, May 7, 23, 1858. Willard B. Farwell, *The Chinese at Home and Abroad* (San Francisco, 1885), also has the map, originally part of the Appendix of the San Francisco *Municipal Reports for 1884–85*.

[7] Loomis to Lowrie, December 10, 1860, April 17, 1862, CPBFM.

[8] J. D[ouglas]. Borthwick, *Three Years in California* (Edinburgh, 1857), 266–67, describes briefly the interior of a store.

room housed a couch for opium smokers or a table for gamblers; once a slave girl found her way into the store, another island of freedom and license sprang into existence.[9] On the mining frontier old timers remembered hearing at dusk the call "mei hanna [probably *mo k'un na*]," and took it as a signal for all Chinese who wanted to gamble.[10] Their hunch, essentially correct, did slight injustice to the precise meaning of the invitation, "Not yet to bed." Frequently sojourners from isolated settlements, craving greater diversions than the country store offered, visited larger Chinatowns. In September California farmers came from far and near to Sacramento for the state fair, in October Chinese from the countryside flocked to the capital for their religious festivals.[11] Hardly any of the pictorial advertisements of early California stage lines failed to depict a couple of Chinese traveling on top of the coach.[12] Entire mining companies left their tents, huts, and claims with the beginning of the rainy season to winter in Chinatown.

San Francisco's Chinatown was similar to those of other California settlements.[13] Its Chinese population in the 1850s and 1860s was hardly larger than that of some of the half-forgotten mining towns, where no traces of Chinese life have been preserved save the remnants of a general store, the skeleton of a gambling hall, a dilapidated joss house, or simply the words China or Chinese which were among the most popular of California place names derived from nationalities.[14]

Few indentured emigrants ever shook off the shackles of work for periods longer than a New Year's celebration, a day in the theater, or a night at the fan-tan table. With the explosion of the last firecracker, an actor's closing line, and the loss of the last copper cash, the pressure of the control system brought the sojourners back to their life of service.

[9] *Herald*, August 8, 1853, quoting the Mokelumne *Calaveras Chronicle*, about Chinese gambling and women at Mokelumne Hill.

[10] Fern Coble Trull, "The History of the Chinese in Idaho from 1864 to 1910," unpub. diss., University of Oregon, 1946, p. 30.

[11] Demas Barnes, *From the Atlantic to the Pacific, Overland. A Series of Letters, Describing a Trip from New York, via Chicago, Atchison, the Great Plains, Denver, the Rocky Mountains, Central City, Colorado, Dakota, Pike's Peak, Laramie Park, Bridger's Pass, Salt Lake City, Utah, Nevada, Austin, Washoe, Virginia City, the Sierras and California to San Francisco, Thence Home, by Acapulco, and the Isthmus of Panama* (New York, 1866), 93–95; Hoffmann, *Californien, Nevada und Mexico*, 282–83.

[12] For examples see Harry T. Peters, *California on Stone* (Garden City, New York, 1935), plates 44, 108.

[13] In 1860 Chinese California numbered 34,919 inhabitants. They concentrated in the following counties: El Dorado (4,762), Calaveras (3,657), San Francisco (2,719), Amador (2,568), Placer (2,392), Sierra (2,208), Butte (2,177), Nevada (2,147). "The Indians and Chinese in California," *Alta*, January 13, 1863; Sandmeyer, *Anti-Chinese Movement in California*, 19; Rose Hum Lee, "The Decline of Chinatowns in the United States," *American Journal of Sociology* (Chicago), 54:424 (March 1949).

[14] Erwin Gudde (comp.), *California Place Names; The Origin and Etymology of Current Geographical Names* (2nd rev. ed., Berkeley, 1960), 59.

For a few hours, the atmosphere of Chinatown had alleviated their homesickness. Their dreams of freedom, dignity, and grandeur released by the visit, vanished rapidly in the ordinary air of Chinese California. Incessant toil and drudgery, rigid regimentation, and strict supervision again filled their ordinary world of labor and debt bondage. Less colorful and exotic than Chinatown, this world of labor has never been adequately depicted, although it harbored the majority of Chinese sojourners and formed the setting which gave Chinatown meaning and value.

Mining and railroad construction work absorbed the masses of indentured emigrants. In both occupations large groups of laborers could be easily employed, regimented, and controlled. In mining companies and construction gangs agents of the merchant-creditors applied Chinese California's invisible controls to the world of work. The indentured emigrants' constant drudgery sustained debt bondage in Chinese California. In the 1850s and 1860s the Chinese drifted also into other pursuits. They found employment as fishermen, freighters, wood choppers, washermen, gardeners, farm hands, and cooks. The world of control also dominated these occupations, although they attracted far fewer laborers than mining and railroad construction.[15]

The life of service in early Chinese California centered around mining. Various sources frequently registered the number of Chinese miners during the 1850s and 1860s. The Sacramento *Daily Union* estimated on October 10, 1855, that 20,000 out of 36,557 Chinese on the Pacific Coast mined in the California gold region. Thirty thousand out of 48,391 Chinese worked the mines in 1862, according to the calculations of Chinese merchants in San Francisco.[16] By 1873 the Chinese formed the largest single ethnic or national group of of miners, Americans included.[17] However, contemporary writers and chroniclers failed almost completely to record the habits of the Chinese miners. The world of regimented

[15] Loomis to Lowrie, March 5, 1864, CPBFM; *Alta*, September 20, October 1, 1849, May 11, 1850, March 31, 1851, March 1, August 28, October 1, 18, 1852, March 24, 28, April 25, May 20, September 28, 1853, February 2, March 25, 1854, August 26, September 16, 1856, October 15, 1857, May 30, July 17, 23, August 13, 1858, June 16, October 29, November 2, 3, December 13, 1859, February 9, 26, May 24, July 7, October 20, 1860, January 14, 28, March 1, 5, 16, 17, 19, April 16, August 22, 1861, March 12, May 7, October 17, November 14, 1862, May 5, July 28, December 9, 1864, March 2, June 6, 1865, January 14, April 1, 5, July 26, September 16, 1866, May 12, June 9, September 29, 1867, May 9, 1868; *Herald*, April 12, August 29, 1852, May 16, 23, 1853, January 11, 1854, October 27, 1855, July 2, 18, 24, August 13, 1858, June 6, 1859, May 12, June 16, 1860; [Augustus W. Loomis], "How Our Chinamen Are Employed," *Overland Monthly*, 2:231–240 (March 1869). For data on Orientals in specific industries turn to Ping Chiu, *Chinese Labor in California, 1850–1880; An Economic Study* (Madison, 1963).

[16] "Report of the Joint Select Committee Relative to the Chinese Population of the State of California," Appendix B, Brooks, *Appendix to the Opening Statement*, 73.

[17] John S. Hittell, *The Resources of California, Comprising the Society, Climate, Salubrity, Scenery, Commerce and Industry of the State* (6th rev. ed., San Francisco, 1874), 40–41; Rodman W. Paul, *California Gold, The Beginning of Mining in the Far West* (Cambridge, 1947), 320.

drudgery in the mountain camps has to be pieced together from incidental remarks of travelers, the reminiscences of pioneers, newspaper accounts, and scenes preserved in lithographs and on letter sheets.

Missionary reports and news items depict the arrival of Chinese newcomers at San Francisco, their lodging in company houses, and their subsequent dispatch to the mining region. These accounts form the border stones of the mosaic delineating the life of service in California.[18] The Chinese on landing in San Francisco usually remained there but a few days. They "then proceeded by the steamers to Sacramento, Stockton, Marysville, and other points on the Sacramento and San Joaquin Rivers."[19] In these supply centers and in other outfitting posts agents directed the companies of indentured emigrants into the Mother Lode Country, distributing the miners into camps between Mariposa in the South and Downieville in the North. The "portly Chinese Agent, Si Mong, one of our merchant princes," stated the Stockton *Republican* in describing a supervisor, "is a stout important looking personage, apparently about thirty-five years of age." He is "quite wealthy and dressed in the most approved American fashion . . . , has dispensed with his tail appendage, . . . and has taken unto himself a Mexican lady for a wife, . . . by whom he has one or two children."[20]

The Chinese miner in the foothills of the Sierra retained his blue cotton blouse and his "broad trowsers, his wooden shoes," and "his broad brimmed hat." He wore "his hair close cropped before with a long jet black queue hanging down behind."[21] His concession to Western civilization consisted of working in American-made boots that were always too

18 Speer to Lowrie, December 18, 1852, Loomis to Lowrie, March 1, 9, June 25, September 19, 1860, April 17, 1862, June 29, 1863, CPBFM; *Alta*, May 2, 18, July 29, 1851, February 26, March 28, May 2, 5, June 8, 1852, May 14, October 14, 1854, May 6, 1857, June 8, August 3, 1860, October 17, 1861; *Herald*, May 17, August 20, December 29, 1851, April 11, 1852, March 2, 1853, July 2, 6, 1857, May 10, 1859; *Daily Evening News*, February 16, 1854; Robert Glass Cleland, ed., *Apron Full of Gold; Letters of Mary Jane Megquier from San Francisco, 1849–1856* (San Marino, 1949), 58.

19 Speer, *Humble Plea*, 18; *Alta*, June 15, 1853, June 16, 1855 (quoting Georgetown *News*), May 24, July 31 (Stockton *Argus*), 1857, February 18, September 23, 1860; *Herald*, April 21, 1852 (Sacramento *Union*), October 28, November 24, 1854; John Russell Bartlett, *Personal Narrative of Explorations and Incidents in Texas, New Mexico, California, Sonora, and Chihuahua; Connected with the United States and Mexican Boundary Commission, During the Years 1850, '51, '52, and '53*, 2 vols. (New York, 1854), II, 12; "Mining Life in California," *Harper's Weekly*, 1:632 (October 3, 1857).

20 *Herald*, June 5, 1858 (quoting Stockton *Republican*). For a brief description of the Sacramento agency see Speer to Lowrie, December 18, 1852; for Placerville, Marks to Solis-Cohen, January 13, 1854, Solis-Cohen, "A California Pioneer; The Letters of Bernhard Marks to Jacob Solis-Cohen (1853–1857)." *Publications of the American Jewish Historical Society*, 44:22–23 (September 1954).

21 Edward Eberstadt, ed. *Way Sketches; Containing Incidents of Travel Across the Plains, From St. Joseph to California in 1850, With Letters Describing Life and Conditions in the Gold Region By Lorenzo Sawyer, Later Chief Justice of the Supreme Court of California* (New York, 1926), 124.

large for him. As some observers speculated, he probably delighted in gaining a maximum return from his purchase money. The isolation in which he and his countrymen labored in strictly controlled companies strengthened their adherence to their customary way of life. While "traveling in a desolate mountain region" in 1868, Charles Loring Brace "was much impressed by the sad, lonely form of a Chinaman, walking pensively toward a solitary grave, and scattering little papers as he went, . . . his prayers to the spirit of his ancestors and to the departed."[22]

On the banks of the rivers and in ravines, a correspondent of the San Francisco *Herald* found companies of twenty or thirty Chinese "inhabiting close cabins, so small that one . . . would not be of sufficient size to allow a couple of Americans to breathe in it. Chinamen, stools, tables, cooking utensils, bunks, etc., all huddled up together in indiscriminate confusion, and enwreathed with dense smoke, present a spectacle which is . . . suggestive of anything but health and comfort."[23] The Chinese miners enjoyed little ease. If not crowded into abandoned cabins they dwelt in tents and brush huts. In groups of a hundred they banded together in short-lived villages which studded the Mother Lode or occupied camps deserted by white miners. Rice, dried fish, and tea formed the staples of their diet. Pork and chicken represented the luxuries in the life of service in Chinese California.[24]

Ordinarily the Chinese worked only placers with rockers, long toms, and river dams in companies of ten to thirty men who were supervised by bosses.[25] Occasionally the reports of the United States Commissioner noted Chinese hired for quartz operations or employed in several quartz mills "for certain inferior purposes, such as dumping cars, surface excavation, etc."[26] At times the superstitions of the workers prevented the bosses from engaging their companies in types of mining which disturbed the multitude of gods inhabiting mountains, meadows, and rivers. Apart from this limitation, drawings and photos show headmen and crews in any place where other miners left the Chinese undisturbed.[27] The head-

[22] Charles Loring Brace, *The New West: Or, California in 1867–1868* (New York, 1869), 227.

[23] *Herald*, November 28, 1857.

[24] *Alta*, August 24, 1858 (quoting Mariposa *Gazette*), describes such a Chinese village in the vicinity of Coulterville, Mariposa County. Additional details appear in "Chinese Coulterville Burned Down," *Alta*, July 22, 1859 (Mariposa *Star*), which reports the complete destruction of the village by fire. Rebuilt, fire destroyed Chinese Coulterville again on August 8, 1862; *Alta*, August 22, 1862. Borthwick, *Three Years in California*, 143; Marryat, *Mountains*, 295–96.

[25] "Chinamen in Rich Diggings," *Alta*, October 9, 1858 (quoting Sacramento *Union*), depicts the operation of a successful Chinese company on the junction of the North and Middle forks of the American River.

[26] Rossiter W. Raymond, *Statistics of the Mines and Mining in the States and Territories West of the Rocky Mountains* (Washington, 1872), 4. This report was also published as *House Ex. Doc. 10*, 42 Cong., 1 Sess.

[27] For pictures of Chinese miners and camps see "A Series of Interesting Sketches and Scenes in California," *Gleason's Pictorial Drawing Room Companion* (Boston), 3:277 (October 30, 1852); Borthwick, *Three Years in California*, facing 264; "The

men bought the claims and directed the reworking of the deserted diggings, the "scratching," as American miners labeled the desolate placers. "Long files of Chinamen alone break the monotony of the landscape as they scrape and wash the sands in the nearly dry beds of the torrents," Ludovic de Beauvoir observed on his tour through the Sierra Nevada.[28]

The Chinese quickly took to the rocker method of placer mining, Charles Peters noted, and "a line of sluice boxes appeared to be especially adapted to their use." They introduced the Chinese water wheel and the bailing bucket, attached to ropes and manipulated by two men, to clear holes of water. Given a choice, the Orientals continued to use their familiar tools in their own way.[29] Their working methods endeared the Chinese miners to the numerous water companies which found in them faithful customers.

Among the miners "were Chinamen of the better class," J. Douglas Borthwick noted, "who no doubt directed the work, and paid the common men very poor wages—poor at least in California."[30] Charles Peters recorded several colorful episodes in the life of Ah Sam, a Chinese boss, who in 1856 "had a large company of coolies working on Auburn Ravine," near Ophir in Placer County. For twenty-five dollars Ah Sam acquired a log cabin from six Americans who had mined the ground and dissolved their partnership. Some of his men, under his personal supervision, washed three thousand dollars out of the dirt floor of the cabin, thus justifying his speculation that the American miners' practice of clearing their gold dust nightly in a blower before the fire had left the floor covered with particles of gold. However, Ah Sam never admitted to more than three hundred dollars profit. That, he felt, was all he had

---

Cradle and the Manner of Using It," in "Mining for Gold in California," *Hutchings' Magazine*, 2:5 (July 1857); J. Ross Browne, "Washoe Revisited [Third Paper]," *Harper's Monthly* (New York), 31:160 (July 1865); [Charles Peters], *The Autobiography of Charles Peters, In 1915 the Oldest Pioneer Living in California Who Mined in 'The Days of Old, The Days of Gold, The Days of '49'. Also Historical Happenings, Interesting Incidents and Illustrations of The Old Mining Towns in The Good Luck Era, The Placer Mining Days of the '50s* (Sacramento, [1915]), 142; Carl I. Wheat, ed. "'California's Bantam Cock,' The Journals of Charles E. DeLong, 1854–1863," *California Historical Society Quarterly*, 9: facing 348 (December 1930); Peters, *California on Stone*, plates 22, 28; Newell D. Chamberlain, *The Call of Gold; True Tales on the Gold Road to Yosemite* ([Mariposa, 1936]), facing 26; Mae Hélène Bacon Boggs, (comp.), *My Playhouse Was A Concord Coach; An Anthology of Newspaper Clippings and Documents Relating to Those Who Made California History During the Years 1822–1888* ([Oakland, 1942]), 119.

28 Agnes and Helen Stephenson, (trans.), *Pekin, Jeddo, and San Francisco. The Conclusion of a Voyage Round the World. By the Marquis* [Ludovic] *de Beauvoir* (London, 1872), 252.

29 *Autobiography of Charles Peters*, 141–42; James W. Bartlett, "Annotations to Cox's Annals of Trinity County," Isaac Cox, *The Annals of Trinity County* (Eugene, Oregon, 1940), 210; Robert F. G. Spier, "Tool Acculturation Among 19th-Century California Chinese," *Ethnohistory* (Bloomington), 5:111 (Spring 1958).

30 Borthwick, *Three Years in California*, 263.

realized with his scheme, since he subtracted from his gain the twenty-seven hundred dollars that two of his men had cheated him out of. These two members of his company, while Ah Sam was busily looking after the cabin floor, discovered, unknown to him, a nugget worth a little less than three thousand dollars as they were shoveling dirt into his sluice box line a short distance from the cabin. They concealed their find, left at night, and sold the nugget in San Francisco.[31]

The ordinary life of Chinese miners with its regimentation and supervision by headmen precluded such escapades. Extreme cases depicting disciplinary measures were most likely to find their way into the newspapers. At Drytown in Amador County a Chinese miner who had stolen four hundred dollars received twenty-five lashes and lost his queue. When he was returned to his mining company his countrymen whipped him again, cut off his left ear, marched him to San Francisco, and shot him by the road.[32] However, the long chain of uneventful days, filled with drudgery and toil, was more typical of the life of Chinese miners.

The working discipline of the mining companies, enforced by constant supervision, accounted for the mass of conflicting reports about the miners' diligence. At times the authors of these accounts marveled at the laborers' incessant toil, "burrowing like ants in the depths" of river beds and ravines; at other times they criticized the miners' lengthy siestas and gay nights. Now and then the workers openly fought the bosses' discipline because there was " 'too muchee workee and too little payee.' "[33] Outside the reach of the headmen's control the Orientals quickly adjusted the rate of their drudgery to their own standards of industry. Cut off from an alien environment by customs and habits, with the bosses controlling contacts with the settlements, the miners eagerly relied on such diversions as the company of their comrades or the nearby Chinese store provided after the working hours.[34]

31 *Autobiography of Charles Peters*, 143–45. "A Chinaman in Luck," *Herald*, March 24, 1856, records the discovery of a hidden purse in an abandoned cabin by a Chinese miner. See also C. B. Glancock, *A Golden Highway; Scenes of History's Greatest Gold Rush Yesterday and Today* (Indianapolis, [1934]), 122.

32 *Herald*, June 6, 1853.

33 Eduard Vischer, "A Trip to the Mining Regions in the Spring of 1859. 'Californischer Staats-Kalender' in the Leap Year A. D. 1860," *California Historical Society Quarterly*, 11:230 (September 1932); Brace, *New West*, 218.

34 The general picture of Chinese miners is chiefly based on: *Alta*, May 2, 18, July 29, 1851, May 2, 5, 14, 15, June 26, 1852, February 16, June 15, October 12, 13, December 29, 1853, March 4 (quoting Jackson *Sentinel*), 14 (Nevada *Journal*), 29 (Mokelumne *Calaveras Chronicle*), July 6, August 23 (Marysville *Express*), September 11 (Grass Valley *Telegraph*), 1854, May 21 (Mokelumne *Calaveras Chronicle*), June 11 (Sacramento *Union*), June 16, October 26 (Nevada *Democrat*), 1855, October 13, 1856 (Shasta *Republican*), May 19 (Auburn *Press*), July 13 (Auburn *Placer Herald*), 21 (Mariposa *Gazette*), 23 (Mariposa *Democrat*), August 8, October 8, December 2 (Marysville *Express*), 1857, February 1, 13 (Hornitas *Democrat*), 15, March 1 (Sacramento *Bee*), 14 (Placerville *Index*), August 5, 24, October 9, November 11 (Shasta *Courier*), December 5, 6, 1858, January 19 (Auburn *Placer Herald*), 31 (Sonora *Democrat*), February 16 (Coloma

Companies of docile Chinese laborers slowly but surely found their way into the "great army laying siege to Nature in her strongest citadel," the construction crews of the Central Pacific building the Western section of the Transcontinental Railroad.[35] Smaller projects prepared the way for and accompanied the ultimate employment of ten thousand Chinese in the completion of the Pacific Railway.[36] In the late 1850s one hundred and fifty of the five hundred hands working on the San Francisco and Marysville Railroad were Chinese, "employed by a Chinese subcontractor."[37] Other early California railroads, such as the Sacramento and Vallejo Railroad, also used Chinese in grading and track-laying. In 1869 one thousand "obedient Chinese toiled like ants from morning to night" on the construction of the Virginia and Truckee Railroad in the

---

Times), May 21, October 9 (Sacramento *Standard*), 1859, September 23, December 8 (Mariposa *Gazette*), 1860, April 3 (Sacramento *Union*), August 10 (Stockton *Independent*), October 8 (Mariposa *Gazette*), 1861, March 12, 1862, January 13, May 3 (North San Juan *Hydraulic Press*), 1863, July 26, August 6, 1866, November 10, 1867, June 17, 1869; *Herald*, October 27 (Mokelumne *Calaveras Chronicle*), December 29, 1851, March 6, April 25, May 9 (Sacramento *Union*), 10 (Mokelumne *Calaveras Chronicle*), 12 (Marysville *Express*), June 9 (Sacramento *State Journal*), November 26, 1852, March 18, May 24, June 6 ,8, 9, July 4, November 9, 26, December 8, 1853, March 27, 1854, July 31 (Butte *Record*), August 6 (Mokelumne *Calaveras Chronicle*), November 12, 1855, March 24 (Auburn *Press*), April 21 (Mariposa *Gazette*, Jackson *Ledger*), May 4, 11, 1856, March 15, 23 (Mariposa *Gazette*), June 12, November 10 (Shasta *Courier*), 1858, March 16, April 2, 1861; Carr, *Pioneer Days*, 69–70; William Shaw, *Golden Dreams and Waking Realities; Being the Adventures of a Gold-Seeker in California and the Pacific Islands* (London, 1851), 50, 56, 64, 65–66, 81–82, 86, 94–95, 122; Franklin Langworthy, *Scenery of the Plains, Mountains and Mines: A Diary Kept upon the Overland Route to California, By Way of the Great Salt Lake: Travels in the Cities, Mines, and Agricultural Districts–Embracing the Return by the Pacific Ocean and Central America, In the Years 1850, '51, '52 and '53* (Ogdensburg, New York, 1855), 184; Marryat, *Mountains*, 295–97; Speer, *Humble Plea*, 19–26; "Mining for Gold in California," *Hutchings' Magazine*, 2:5 (July 1857); "Mining Life in California," *Harper's Weekly*, 1:632–33 (October 3, 1857); Borthwick, *Three Years in California*, 51, 55, 143–45, 262–67, 319; Holbrook, "Chinadom in California. In Two Papers.–Paper the Second," *Hutchings' Magazine*, 4:173 (October 1859); Horace Greeley, *An Overland Journey, from New York to San Francisco, in the Summer of 1859* (New York, 1860), 288–89; Francis P. Farquhar, ed. *Up and Down California in 1860–1864. The Journal of William H. Brewer, Professor of Agriculture in the Sheffield Scientific School from 1864 to 1903* (Berkeley, 1949), 330, 481; Browne, "Washoe Revisited," *Harper's Monthly*, 31:159–61 (July 1865); Bowles, *Our New West*, 400; Conwell, *Why and How*, 126–27; de Beauvoir, *San Francisco*, 250–53.

35 Albert D. Richardson, *Beyond the Mississippi: From the Great River to the Great Ocean. Life and Adventure on the Prairies, Mountains, and Pacific Coast, 1857–1867* (Hartford, 1867), 462.

36 *Senate Rept. 689*, 44 Cong., 2 Sess., 667, 723; "How Our Chinamen Are Employed," *Overland*, II (March 1869), 232.

37 "Monthly Record of Current Events," *Hutchings' Magazine*, 4:238 (November 1859).

Washoe and Comstock mines of Nevada, "spurred on continually by urgent supervisors."[38]

The steady demand for laborers on the Central Pacific Railroad attracted increasing numbers of Chinese. Between 1863 and 1868 many left the mines, and a large portion of them ended up in the construction force. In the mid-1860s Chinese merchants and American firms at San Francisco, such as Koopmanschap & Co. and Sisson, Wallace, & Co., also began to supply groups of laborers directly from China.[39] Agents of the Central Pacific recruited men in the mountain districts of the Pearl River Delta. They paid for outfit and passage, and received in return from each Chinese a promissory note for $75 in United States gold coin, secured by endorsement of family and friends. The contract provided for regular installments, to complete repayment of the debt within seven months from the time the newcomers commenced labor on the railroad.[40] These shipments tripled the figures of Chinese arriving at the San Francisco Custom House in 1868 and 1869 as compared with the four preceding years. Soon the "rugged mountains . . . swarmed with Celestials, shoveling, wheeling, carting, drilling and blasting rocks and earth."[41]

The use of indentured emigrants and contract laborers on the Pacific section of the Transcontinental Railway provided ammunition for the political warfare following the completion of the road. However, the hearings of congressional investigation committees, the arguments of lawyers, and the explanations of company executives and engineers throw little light on the daily drudgeries of the construction crews. The amassed material leaves the impression that politicians, financeers, lawyers, accountants, and engineers alone built the road.[42] The San Francisco earthquake and fire of 1906 destroyed all existing records of the Southern Pacific Company, including those of the Central Pacific Company. Later attempts to restore the files met with little success.[43] There are incidental remarks of travelers, the information in early railroad guides, and the jottings of itinerant newspaper editors, but these sources fall short of the observations of Hemmann Hoffmann, a Swiss student, who worked as Chinese overseer on the Central Pacific near Dutch Flat in Placer County in 1864 and 1865 and whose notes furnish the outline for the following sketch of the life and work of the Chinese construction companies.[44]

38 Eliot Lord, *Comstock Mining and Miners. A Reprint of the 1883 Edition* (Berkeley, 1959), 253, 355.

39 *Senate Rept. 689*, 44 Cong., 2 Sess., 724.

40 *Alta*, June 24, 1869, contains a statement by a foreman of the Central Pacific about the contract of Chinese laborers.

41 "Chinese Arrivals at San Francisco Custom House," Coolidge, *Chinese Immigration*, 498; Richardson, *Beyond the Mississippi*, 462.

42 [F. S. Hickman, publisher], *The Pacific Rail Road, Congressional Proceedings in the Thirty-seventh, Thirty-eighth, and Forty-first Congresses* (West Chester, Pennsylvania, 1875); *Senate Ex. Doc. 51*, 50 Cong., 1 Sess.

43 Robert Hancocks, Assistant Editor, Bureau of News, Southern Pacific Company, to G. Barth, September 2, 1959; Irene Authier Keeffe, Director, Union Pacific Historical Museum, to G. Barth, September 17, 1959.

44 Hoffmann, *Californien, Nevada und Mexico*, 210–25. See also Effie Mona Mack,

Along the projected line of work between Dutch Flat and the Nevada boundary, numerous small huts crowded the camps of Chinese workers. The laborers slept and ate on simple wooden cots. Chinese bosses, working with the overseers, effectively kept discipline in the companies. The extra workers in the compounds enabled the headmen to live up to their contracts and to report a complete company of toilers for work every morning. The extras substituted for those workers who on the previous evening had succumbed to the attractions of Chinese stores in the nearby settlements, but who would doubtless show up again for work in a few days. The replacements also filled the gaps left by comrades unable to shake off the effects of a dissolute night. The headmen received wages for the number of men which they regularly reported, and divided the money among all members of their gang. Groups of twelve to twenty men formed a mess and kept a cook who obtained his provisions from the nearest Chinese merchant. At times the kitchen of the white workers furnished meat for the Chinese rice bowls.

During the long working day of grading and track-laying, the sheer number of Chinese workers compensated for the delay caused by the running conversation which accompanied the laborers' drudgery. The multitude of his comrades enabled the individual worker to interrupt his toil frequently for a sip of tea or the forbidden taste of a small pipe of tobacco. At the mercy of his bosses and headmen, disciplined on the job and in the camp, the worker took every opportunity to minimize the effect of the control. Whenever the slightest obstacle interrupted the routine curious laborers crowded together for a brief dispute over the event.

The masses of laborers on the Pacific Railroad appeared to occasional observers as well regimented gangs and smoothly running working machines. Chinese formed part of the celebrated construction crew which on April 28, 1869, laid ten miles of track in a single day. To one of the editors of the *Alta*, the Chinese railroad workers often seemed "in these dreary solitudes . . . the presiding genius." Regimentation and discipline, however, vanished completely when basic differences between district companies broke into the open. The final days of the construction of the Pacific Railroad brought not only the track-laying feast but also the "Grand Chinese Battle in the Salt Lake Valley" between members of the Sze Yap Company and the Yeong Wo Company.[45]

Annual festivals, celebrated with public spectacles and tradition-honored ceremonies, provided a regular outlet from the rigid controls of the

---

Nevada, A History of the State from the Earliest Times through the Civil War (Glendale, California, 1936), 374–75; Wesley S. Griswold, *A Work of Giants; Building the First Transcontinental Railroad* (New York, [1962]), 108–25; and Robert West Howard, *The Great Iron Trail; The Story of the First Trans-Continental Railroad* (New York, [1962]), 224–36.

45 *Alta*, April 25, 30, May 1, 8, 12, 1869; J. N. Bowman, "Driving the Last Spike at Promontory, 1869," *California Historical Society Quarterly*, 36:265–66 (September 1957).

work camp.[46] The atmosphere of the gambling halls, theaters, and other centers of entertainment and diversion quickly released the indentured emigrants from the confines of constant toil and loneliness and gave them a substitute for the missing home. Since the ordinary life of Chinese workers resembled a succession of days of reckoning, their religious festivals furnished a string of holidays. Like their system of control or their methods of work, most of their temporary escapes followed forms familiar from the homeland. Scenes of freedom and license gained significance from the work and drudgery which filled the ordinary days of the sojourners.

The observance of the traditional holidays interrupted the routine. During these celebrations, employers of Chinese mining companies in Mariposa County informed the United States Commissioner of Mining Statistics, the laborers "leave the mines *en masse*, and cannot be induced to work, for sometimes a week altogether."[47] These festivities momentarily linked the world of Chinese sojourners in California with the familiar scenes of the Pearl River Delta. The impressive ceremonies which formed part of the popular cycle of the three festivals of the living and the three festivals of the dead, though Californian in their setting, gave even on-lookers the illusion of glimpsing life in villages and towns along the course of the Chu Kiang.[48] Of these six traditional holidays the Dragon-boat festival never took deep roots in Chinese California, while New Year's from the beginning occupied a dominant position as the greatest and gayest occasion of the year.

The first recorded Chinese New Year celebration in the United States on February 1, 1851, only incidentally served the needs of Chinese California. Primarily it enhanced the status of a single individual. Norman Assing entertained as his guests "a number of policemen . . . , many ladies and 'China Boys.'" Within two years, however, the celebration lost its private character and assumed the traits of a "grand holiday . . . , with the moving multitude of Celestials rigged out in their finest toggery."[49] Step by step distinctive features of the holiday emerged until the festival became a California ritual at the beginning of the 1860s.

The blaze and the noise of firecrackers signaled the beginning of the New Year's Festival. For as many as six days the din of the squibs filled the air, except during "quiet hours" established in negotiations between the chief of police and the headmen of the district companies. Gay workers who crowded the roofs of the brick stores with hundreds of packages of explosives at their side, abandoned yearlong restraints and pitched ignited bombs into the crowded alleys. Huge strings of firecrackers, suspended from the balconies of restaurants, temples, and company houses, emitted noise and fumes over the multitude of Chinese dressed in new blue cot-

[46] Densmore, *Chinese in California*, 64–66, lists the main festivals of the Chinese in San Francisco.

[47] Raymond, *Statistics of Mines and Mining*, 4.

[48] *Alta*, October 30, 1853, February 17, 1855, February 16, May 7, 1858, January 23, 1860, February 18, 1863; *Herald*, April 4, 1852.

[49] *Alta*, February 3, 1851, February 8, 1853.

ton suits. "The Chinese throughout the State have been celebrating their New Year's Day with an energy which does them credit," the *Alta* observed in 1858. "The number of firecrackers burned and the quantity of noise and smoke let loose are beyond calculation," the paper marveled.[50]

The narrow streets presented the appearance of a small-scale bombardment. A pall of smoke covered the freshly cleaned quarter. The aristocracy of Chinatown donned their "costly fur and silk robes," with "black satin pants fitting tightly at the ankles," and "snow-white stockings and heavy sandals, lined or covered with silk or satin," and made their rounds of New Year's calls. Tables laden with the choicest fruits and conserves greeted these special guests. The multitudes flocked into the brilliantly lighted temples, the festively decorated theater, or the cook shops "where swarms were feasting in the highest apparent bliss." In this pandemonium, filled with the explosions of firecrackers, the din of gongs, the music of countless orchestras, and the elated ejaculations of a thousand voices, the mass of Chinese forgot the grey monotony of their work-filled days.[51]

In the spring the Ch'ing-ming, one of the three festivals of the dead, provided an outlet for pent-up emotions. In early Chinese California, the district companies, clan associations, or groups of men on this day visited the tombs of their members and friends to sweep the graves clean. In the course of two decades this "Chinese Feast of the Dead" developed an elaborate ritual. Covering a period of three or four days, the festival centered around a ceremony in the open brick enclosure, or temple, of San Francisco's Lone Mountain Cemetery.[52]

Nearly every party of Chinese visitors announced its arrival with a fusillade of firecrackers before they arranged around each grave roast pigs, oranges, bananas, pieces of fresh sugar cane, and tiny porcelain cups filled with brandy. After the worshippers had burned baskets of varicolored papers and conducted other rites, they collected the offerings again. Exchanging congratulations and laughs with their living friends, each group of visitors traveled back to a sumptuous banquet in Chinatown, the rich merchants in the courtliest hacks, followed by an "express wagon loaded with common laborers . . . while a third would be filled

[50] *Alta*, February 14, 1858.

[51] *Alta*, February 8, 1853, January 29, 30, 1854, February 8, 17, 1855, January 25, 26, 1857, February 14, 16, 1858, February 2, 4, 1859, January 21, 22, 23, 31, 1862, February 18, 19, 1863, January 14, February 6, 9, 1864, January 2, 26, 27, 28, 1865, January 1, February 12, 14, 15, 1866, February 3, 1867, February 9, 10, 1869; *Herald*, February 15, 20, 1855, February 5, 6, 1856, January 25, 26, 1857, February 13, 14, 1858, February 3, 5, 1859, January 23, 1860, February 11, 12, 1861, January 29, 31, 1862; Huggins, (comp.), *Continuation of the Annals of San Francisco*, 36. For additional descriptions of the New Year's festivities see Farquhar, ed. *Journal of William H. Brewer*, 243, 360–70; Hoffmann, *Californien, Nevada und Mexico*, 316; Rusling, *Across America*, 311–12; J. W. Ames, "Day in Chinatown," *Lippincott's Magazine* (Philadelphia) 16:496–97 (October 1875); Mary Cone, *Two Years in California* (Chicago, 1876), 188–90.

[52] "Chinese Temple at Lone Mountain," *Alta*, January 10, 1864. See also *Alta*, November 25, 1863.

with women of the public class only." In the fall, the Feast of Souls and the Midautumn or Moon Festival marked similar ceremonies.[53]

In addition to these and other fixed holidays, Chinese California relied on a multitude of festivities to disrupt temporarily the monotony and restraint of work-filled days. "Where the purse will admit," Augustus W. Loomis observed in 1868, "but few legitimate occasions for feasting are allowed to pass unimproved."[54] The headman's recovery from a dangerous illness, the safe arrival of travelers, or the opening of a temple occasioned elaborate pageants. Universal gaiety and jollity surrounded weddings as well as funerals. The pompous entombment of wealthy Chinese, formally bewailed by groups of official mourners, Buddhist priests, and honored with an impressive procession, or conducted in American style with a richly trimmed mahogany coffin, first class hearse, and thirty carriages of attendants, contrasted with the feasting and mirth which followed. During fashionable nuptial ceremonies, such as the marriage between Cum Chum of the house of Lun Wo & Co. and Ah Too, or the wedding of Tom Quan of the firm of Hong Yuen & Co. to Lai Nyne, banquets, musical performances, and fireworks for one day excited Chinatown. Smaller weddings bridged the interludes between the great affairs.[55]

The pageants of holidays and ceremonies relied for staging on the available settings. They centered around temples, but included restaurants, theaters, gambling houses, opium dens, and brothels in the less ceremonious yet more popular pursuits of the holidays. In the summer of 1853 the Sze Yap Company constructed the first joss house in San Francisco. It dominated all other temples in Chinese California until the Ning Yeong Company opened a larger temple in August 1864, on Dupont Alley, on a lot in the center of the block formed by Pacific, Dupont, Broadway, and Kearny Streets, paying $4,000 for the lot, $12,000 for the construction, and the enormous sum of $16,000 for furniture and decoration. These two temples maintained their leading position among the eight joss houses existing in 1875 and the thirteen located on the Official Map of Chinatown

[53] *Herald,* April 3, 4, 5, 12, 1852, October 11, 1853, April 3, 4, 21, 1856, April 19, 1858 (quoting Butte *Record*), April 5, 1860 ("The Chinese Festival Tsing Ming," from Sacramento *Standard*), April 5, October 12, 1861; *Alta,* April 4, 5, September 30, October 22, 1852, April 11, October 11, 1853, February 25, 1854, October 20, 1855, April 27, 1856, March 28, 1861, April 6, 1862, August 23, 1866, April 4, 1868; Caroline C. Leighton, "Chinese Feast of the Dead," *Life at Puget Sound with Sketches of Travel in Washington Territory, British Columbia, Oregon and California, 1865–1881* (Boston, 1884), 215–17.

[54] [Augustus W. Loomis], "The Old East in the New West," *Overland Monthly,* 1:363 (October 1868).

[55] *Alta,* July 27, August 21, 1851, March 28, 1852, February 25, 1854, November 14, 1855, December 10, 1856, October 10, 1857, February 18, 19, 21, April 23, June 9, 1858, May 9, June 19, July 9, August 24, 1859, January 9, June 7, August 5, 16, December 2, 17, 1860, March 28, 1861, June 22, October 6, 24, 1862, February 19, June 3, October 28, 1863, February 28, November 2, 1864, September 14, 1866, April 5, 8, 27, May 26, November 4, 1867; *Herald,* April 8, November 15, 16, 1855, December 20, 22, 1857, February 20, June 26, 1858, April 25, 1859, March 28, 1861; Huggins, (comp.), *Continuation of the Annals of San Francisco,* 80.

in 1885. The California Supreme Court preserved the public character of the Buddhist rites in the spring of 1859. The justices decided in their review of John Eldridge *v.* See Yup Company that the court had no power to determine whether " 'this or that form of religious or superstitious worship—unaccompanied by acts prohibited by law—is against public policy or morals.' "[56]

Tucked away in ordinary dingy business blocks of Chinatown, the joss houses suggested only to the Chinese sojourners the splendor and magnificence of the Honam Temple or other edifices in the Pearl River Delta.[57] Several flights of narrow stairs led up to the chambers of the enthroned deities located in the top stories of the buildings to guard the idols against thieves and to insure that nothing used by human hands came above the gods. The first "Chinese church," the Sze Yap's temple, was designed by the San Francisco architect Lewis R. Townsend. Except for the "great" Chinese architect who allegedly supervised the construction of John Parrott's Granite Block in 1852, there is no record of any significant activity by oriental designers in early Chinese California.[58]

The sojourners adapted existing American structures to their cultural needs by adding elaborate balconies, paper or bronze lanterns, richly colored inscriptions, and rows of porcelain pots. Similarly, they substituted their own colorful names for the official designations of Chinatown's thoroughfares.[59] A crude brick building with a tin roof formed the joss house in Fiddletown, Amador County, an ugly adobe box constructed in the Spanish-Mexican manner housed the temple at Dutch Flat, Placer County. Wooden frame structures or log buildings served in other settlements, such as San Andreas in Calaveras County or Weaverville in Trinity County. Only the elaborate interior decoration fostered the illusion of ornate Chinese temples.[60]

56 *Alta,* July 10, 15, 16, 1853, April 5, 1856, May 11, June 19, 1859, January 24, August 16, 1860, January 28, 1861, August 23, 1864, January 27, 1865, August 17, 1867; Eldridge *v.* See Yup Company, 17 Cal. 45; Williams, "City of the Golden Gate," *Scribner's Monthly,* 10:285 (July 1875); Lloyd, *Lights and Shades in San Francisco,* 272–75.

57 Loomis to Lowrie, November 18, 1859, CPBFM.

58 *Alta,* July 10, 15, 16, 1853; Harold Kirker, "Eldorado Gothic, Gold Rush Architects and Architecture," *California Historical Society Quarterly,* 38:33–34 (March 1959). Lewis R. Townsend is listed in the San Francisco *City Directory,* 1854, 134, as architect and in the *Directory,* 1858, 271, as architect and civil engineer; he is briefly mentioned in Harold Kirker, *California's Architectural Frontier; Style and Tradition in the Nineteenth Century* (San Marino, 1960), 76, 215.

59 "The Chinese Quarter," *Herald,* July 25, 1853; "Chinese Houses on Jackson Street," *Herald,* January 7, 1858; Benjamin, *Three Years in America,* I, 281; Hoy, "Chinatown Devises Its Own Street Names," *California Folklore Quarterly,* 2: 71–75 (April 1943).

60 *Alta,* April 5, 1856, July 24, 1860, August 23, 1864, January 27, 1865; *Herald,* April 21, 1856; Holbrook, "Chinadom in California. In Two Papers—Paper the First," *Hutchings' Magazine,* IV (September, 1859), 131–32; Todd, *Sunset Land,* 275–77; Robert von Schlagintweit, *Californien, Land und Leute* (Köln, 1871), 332–34; Cone, *Two Years in California,* 191–95; Densmore, *Chinese in California,* 61–62; Theodor Kirchhoff, *Californische Kulturbilder* (Kassel, 1886), 99–100.

Restaurants and theaters furnished the extraordinary life of Chinese California with other focal points during the hours when the religious ceremonies turned into feast days. Every restaurant, from the lowliest soup kitchen to the famous cafés of the rich and the dissolute, held its banquets. Musicians and entertainers, in ravishing, dainty garments, lent excitement to a life void of ordinary diversions. To the accompaniment of brass gong, moon guitar, Tartar fiddle, drums, and cymbals they sang operatic ballads, frequently celebrating the past glory of ancient dynasties. At the stage in which food meant less to the guests than liquor and games, the feasters drank and played and played and drank, and their expressions showed a fierceness usually hidden beneath the mask of placid docility that they assumed under regimentation.[61]

On holidays festive multitudes thronged boxes, pit, and balcony of Chinatown's theaters. Following the actors' lines, the singing, the jugglers' feats, and the music of the orchestra, visitors lost themselves in an illusionary world which their imagination built despite the contrast between the barren stage and the actors' dazzling finery. Long historical dramas seemed as endless as the audience's craving for the extension of the illusion. In such plays as "The Return of Sit Ping Quai [Hsieh P'ing-kuei]" the Chinese sojourners suffered for days the warrior's anguish, endured his hardships, basked in his fame, and finally found their way home with the hero to his virtuous wife.

The familiarity of the onlookers with the content of romances, dramas, and ballads, told and retold by storytellers, facilitated the process. The participants in the eagerly solicited world of fancy squatted on crowded benches in a plain hall. On stage Sit Ping Quai balanced on one table protected by a mighty and impassable torrent from the pursuing Princess Liufa three feet away on another. The spectators' freed imagination, however, conveniently dissolved the reality of their world which lacked similar ready escapes from a daily routine of hardship and oppression.[62]

[61] *Alta*, October 4, 25, 1849, January 11, September 18, 1850, May 15, 1862; *Herald*, September 30, 1858, May 2, 1860; E[lisha]. S[mith]. Capron, *History of California, From Its Discovery to the Present Time; Comprising Also a Full Description of Its Climate, Surface, Soil, Rivers, Towns, Beasts, Birds, Fishes, State of Its Society, Agriculture, Commerce, Mines, Mining, etc. With a Journal of the Voyage from New York to San Francisco, and Back, via Panama* (Boston, 1854), 154–56; C. J. W. R., "A Dinner with the Chinese," *Hutchings' Magazine*, 1:512–13 (May 1857); Ames, "Day in Chinatown," *Lippincott's Magazine*, 16:497–500 (October 1875); "A Chinese Reception," *Harper's Weekly*, 21:466 (June 9, 1877); F. Taylor, *Between the Gates* (Chicago, 1878), 107–10; Densmore, *Chinese in California*, 47–48; William Henry Bishop, *Old Mexico and Her Lost Provinces; A Journey in Mexico, Southern California, and Arizona by Way of Cuba* (New York, 1883), 338; Daniel Knower, *The Adventures of a Forty-Niner. An Historic Description of California, with Events and Ideas of San Francisco and its People in those Early Days* (Albany, 1894), 49, 81; Genthe and Irwin, *Pictures of Old Chinatown*, 26–32.

[62] *Alta*, October 6, 7, 18, 20, December 20, 25, 1852, April 1, September 2, December 19, 1853, December 14, 1856, May 11, August 12, 15, 1857, February 23, 1859, January 6, May 10, 11, 12, 14, 15, 16, 17, 1860, February 17, 1865, November 21,

Year in, year out, regardless of the occasion, Chinatown provided respite from daily drudgeries. Since the set of holidays barely furnished a legitimate excuse for the enjoyment of these escapes, their pursuit lay outside of the accepted cycles of diversion. The visit to a gambling hall, a brothel, or an opium den added precious hours of freedom to the life of indentured emigrants who lacked the means for these entertainments in their homeland. In Chinese California they saw themselves momentarily admitted to that life of leisure which in part had motivated them to leave their native village in search for a fortune overseas. The dreams of an opium smoker or the dissipations waiting in a house of prostitution ranked second in attraction to the fascination which a gambling table radiated.[63] Here, desperate daring could change the course of a gambler's life with one single stroke of luck.

Games of chance particularly attracted the men who existed at the point of no return. Hunting for escapes from their daily hardships, they readily took solace in a set of simple games which combined a maximum of thrill with a constant chance of sudden gain. With the fate of gamesters continually hanging upon a breath, they fatalistically accepted an adverse verdict of chance. Accustomed to attribute almost every phenomenon of nature to the intervention of supernatural powers, the sojourners hardly questioned the outcome of a gambling game in which chance played a slightly greater role than it appeared to in the daily course of their lives. Only a short step separated divination from gambling, and the circulation of a handbook for calculating the prices of chances and

---

1867, January 28, June 18, September 20, 1868; *Herald,* August 16, October 6, 8, 10, 17, 18, 19, 20, 21, 22, 23, 24, December 22, 1852, March 10, 27, 31, April 1, November 27, 1853, April 26, 1858, May 11, August 11, 1860; "The Royal Theatre, A Popular Performance," in "Character Sketches in San Francisco: An Evening in the Chinese Quarter," *Frank Leslie's Illustrated Newspaper* (New York), 46:422 (August 24, 1878); Densmore, "Chinese Theatres," *Chinese in California,* 54–58; George Augustus Sala, "The Drama in China Town," *America Revisited: From the Bay of New York to the Gulf of Mexico, and From Lake Michigan to the Pacific,* 2 volumes (3rd ed., London, 1883), II, 238–52; MacMinn, "Celestial Entertainments," *Theater of the Golden Era in California,* 493–508; Lois Rodecape, "Celestial Drama in the Golden Hills; The Chinese Theatre in California, 1849–1869," *California Historical Society Quarterly,* 23:97–116 (June 1944), Alice Henson Ernst, "The Chinese Theatre," *Trouping in Oregon Country; A History of Frontier Theatre* (Portland, [1961]), 96–102.

63 Loomis to Lowrie, November 18, 1859, CPBFM; *Herald,* December 22, 1852, July 15, 1853, September 22, December 29, 1854, April 14, July 28, August 17, 1855, March 22, 26, 27, October 31, November 1, 1857, January 16, November 28, 1858; *Alta,* September 18, 1853, September 22, 1854, August 28, 1863, January 11, 1864, February 15, 1866; Bowles, *Our New West,* 406; Williams, "City of the Golden Gate," *Scribner's Monthly,* 10:283–84 (July 1875); Ames, "Day in Chinatown," *Lippincott's Magazine,* 16:500 (October 1875); Vogel, *Vom Indischen Ocean bis zum Goldlande,* 421; "Elysium of the Opium Smoker," in "Character Sketches in San Francisco: An Evening in the Chinese Quarter," *Leslie's Illustrated,* 46:422 (August 24, 1878); Taylor, *Between the Gates,* 115–16; Densmore, *Chinese in California,* 99–101; Iza Duffus Hardy, "In China Town," *Belgravia* (London), 43:218–19 (December 1880).

the prizes for the literary lottery called "White Pigeon Ticket" suggested an application of the art.[64]

Lithographs, letter sheets, and broadsides depict scenes in Chinese gambling houses in early California. Reminiscences, travelogues, news accounts, and official reports add color to these contours.[65] Great numbers of silent spectators motionlessly observed the gamblers' moves. The voice of a richly dressed singer, the music of an accompanying orchestra, and a view of the exciting scenes compensated these onlookers for their lack of Chinese copper cash to participate in a round of fan-tan, the most popular game.[66] The tension produced by various games served one end: they furnished a sudden escape from confines and anxieties. Between two quickened heartbeats gambling offered an abrupt breath of the diluted air of freedom.

The type of game was unimportant. If somebody took the fan-tan counters away or destroyed the pie-gow [*p'ai-chiu*] blocks, the sojourners would bet on the number of seeds in an uncut orange. While merchants

[64] Stewart Culin, "Popular Literature of the Chinese Laborers in the United States," *Oriental Studies, A Selection of Papers Read Before the Oriental Club of Philadelphia, 1888–1894* (Boston, 1894), 54–55.

[65] Speer to Lowrie, December 18, 1852, CPBFM; *Alta,* November 12, 1852, May 18, 1855, March 2, September 2, 4, 5, 11, 12, 1857, November 13, 17, December 17, 18, 22, 1858, October 2, 1860; *Herald,* October 29, 1852, March 21, July 23, 25, 1853, February 11, 22, June 30, 1854, March 30, 1856, September 6, 12, December 12, 1857, December 3, 16, 17, 1858, February 25, March 13, November 2, 1859, September 29, October 2, 1860; California State Senate, *Chinese Immigration 1876,* 44, 47, 60, 89, 100, 110, 116, 124, 152; *Senate Rept. 689,* 44 Cong., 2 Sess., 10, 151, 191. 192, 196, 222, 224, 240, 309, 829; California State Senate, *Chinese Immigration 1878,* 109, 112, 125, 165, 175, 187, 189, 217; Capron, *History of California,* 150–51; Soulé, *Annals,* 382–83; Balduin Möllhausen, *Wanderungen durch die Prairien und Wüsten des westlichen Nordamerika vom Mississippi nach den Küsten der Südsee im Gefolge der von der Regierung der Vereinigten Staaten unter Lieutenant* [Amiel Weeks] *Whipple ausgesandten Expedition* (2nd ed., Leipzig, 1860), 461–62; Todd, *Sunset Land,* 277–80; Charles Nordhoff, *California* (New York, 1872), 87–89; Albert S. Evans, *À la California. Sketches of Life in the Golden State* (San Francisco, 1873), 287–90; Rusling, *Across America,* 310–11; Densmore, *Chinese in California,* 97–98; Chamberlain, *Call of Gold,* 145. For scenes in Chinese gambling houses see Peters, *California on Stone,* 57, 62, 69, 121, plates 22, 61; Soulé, *Annals,* 383 (also reproduced in Henry Evans, *Curious Lore of San Francisco's Chinatown* (San Francisco, 1955), 7); Sala, *America Revisited,* II, 272; Bishop, *Old Mexico and Her Lost Provinces,* 339; Wheat, ed. "Journals of Charles E. DeLong," *California Historical Society Quarterly,* 9:facing 348 (December 1930); Boggs, (comp.), *Anthology of Newspaper Clippings and Documents,* 119.

[66] For a description of the games among the Chinese in the United States see Stewart Culin, *The Gambling Games of the Chinese in America. Fán t'án: the Game of Repeatedly Spreading Out. And Pák kòp piú or, the Game of White Pigeon Ticket* (Philadelphia, 1891), and "Chinese Games [in America] with Dice and Dominoes," *Report of the U.S. National Museum, under the Direction of the Smithsonian Institution, For the Year Ending June 30, 1893* (Washington, 1895), 491–537, based on a preliminary study, *Chinese Games with Dice—Read Before the Oriental Club of Philadelphia, March 14, 1889* (Philadelphia, 1889).

and professional gamblers grew steadily richer from the profits which these means of escape in Chinatown produced, the picture of the losing indentured emigrant appeared again and again. Having paid off his debts and saved for years to return to his family in China, on the eve of his departure the free man might drop into a gambling house, lose his savings in one night, and turn back, with great surface indifference, to begin a life of service again.

In the scheme of control and work Chinatown ensured the drudgery of mining company and railroad construction crews. With major commodities and supplies under their management, the merchant-creditors profited from the sojourners' very existence at a time when the debtors' labor furnished a constant return on the initial investment in indentured emigrants. The mass of lowly workers earned just enough to keep alive their hopes and guarantee their acquiescence to the system, but not enough to free themselves from it. Chinatown also gave these workers in an alien environment the illusion of home.

Chinatown and work camp fulfilled an essential role in Chinese California. However, their significance went beyond the confines of the regimented world in which the small realm of diversion provided only the background for the large domain of work. Chinatown and work camp also furnished the major contacts with the alien world that encompassed Chinese California. The vast variety of reactions to the newcomers crystallized around these vital institutions. Chinatown and work camp provoked incidents of strife and stimulated humanitarian attempts at acculturation as the Americans became aware of the sojourners in their midst.

The Birth and Death of the Plains Indians

PETER FARB

After the appearance of the white man in the Western Hemisphere, different Indian groups went through various cultural changes as they struggled to preserve their identity and their lands. Perhaps the most impressive product of the Indians' adaptations to the white presence on the American continent was the elaborate culture that evolved among the nomadic tribes of the Great Plains once they acquired the white man's animal—the horse.

When the Indians of Latin America first saw the conquistadors astride the horses they had brought from Spain to the Western world, they thought the two were a single animal (a mistake that may also account for the mythical centaur). The Indians soon learned, however, that man and horse were separate creatures and that the latter could be domesticated to great advantage. The Spaniards introduced horses in Mexico in the sixteenth century, and herds of the animals spread northward over the plains. Late in the seventeenth century, North American Indians began to breed Spanish horses. When white settlers reached the Great Plains over a century later, they met the first mounted Indians ever to be seen—the prototypes of the fierce, proud Indians encountered today in Western movies.

By the time of their first real contacts with whites, the Indians were well on their way to developing a complex culture that centered on the horse and the buffalo, the great native of the plains on which they relied for food, shelter, and clothing. The horse had literally transformed their lives by dramatically increasing their mobility and giving them greater effectiveness in waging war and in hunting the all-important buffalo. By the time of the Civil War, more than two-thirds of the Indians that remained in the United States belonged to the Great Plains civilization.

In his book **Man's Rise to Civilization as Shown by the Indians of North America from Primeval Times to the Coming of the Industrial State,** Peter Farb, an anthropologist previously on the staff of the

New York Museum of Natural History, examines the life and history of the American Indians and traces their cultural evolution. Although many scholars have quarreled with Farb's perspectives and have accused him of oversimplifying cultural and historical elements to accommodate his theory, the book stands as a valuable and beautifully written introduction to the varieties of American Indian life. The following selection, taken from this book, is a chapter in which Farb discusses the impact of the horse on the various Indian cultures that coalesced into the Plains group.

The tragic end of the Plains Indian culture at the close of the nineteenth century was marked by the massacre of Indians at Wounded Knee, South Dakota. Wovoka, the last of the great Indian messiahs, had dreamed of a resurgence of the declining Indian culture, but the greater powers of the United States government held sway.

THE GREAT AMERICAN EPIC

To many people, the typical Indian was the Plains Indian, a painted brave in full regalia, trailing a war bonnet, astride a horse which he rode bareback, sweeping down upon a wagon train, in glorious technicolor. In actual fact, the picturesque culture of the Plains Indian was artificial, not aboriginal, and it did not last very long. The amalgam known as the Plains culture was not fully accomplished until the early 1800's—and like the spring grass of the high plains, it withered quickly.

This culture emerged almost inconspicuously in the middle of the eighteenth century as its catalytic agent, the horse, spread northward from Spanish settlements in New Mexico. Within only a few generations, the horse was found throughout the central heartland of the continent, and Indians from all directions spilled onto the plains. They originally spoke many different languages and had various customs, but they all found in the horse a new tool to kill greater numbers of bison than they had ever believed possible. They became inconceivably rich in material goods, far beyond their wildest dreams, and like a dream it all faded. By about 1850, the Plains culture was already on the wane as the "manifest destiny" of a vigorous United States to push westward shoved them aside. The fate of the Plains Indians had been sealed with the arrival of the first miners and the first prairie schooner. The battles of extermination between Plains

Indians and United States cavalry represent America's own great epic—its *Iliad*, its *Aeneid*, its Norse saga—but this epic was no more true than any other.

Despite the surrounded forts, the saving of the last bullet for oneself, the occasional acts of heroism, and the frequent acts of bestiality on both sides—despite this picture portrayed in the Great American Epic, there was remarkably little formal combat. Deaths and hardship there were in plenty as the Plains Indians met their catastrophic end, but most deaths were due to starvation, exposure, disease, brutality, and alcoholism, and not to bullets. In all the actual battles between White soldiers and Indian braves, only several thousand deaths on both sides were due to bullets and arrows. The wars of the plains were not epics but mopping-up operations. In the process, the millions of bison very nearly vanished without leaving any survivors, the plains were turned into a dust bowl, and the once-proud Indian horsemen were broken in body and spirit.

The famed Plains Indian culture did not exist in all its glory when Coronado first explored the plains. Lured on by tales of rich lands, where kings were supposed to be lulled to sleep by the chimes of golden bells, Coronado eventually reached Kansas in 1541. Here the Spaniards saw the beast they had been hearing so much about: the remarkable "cow," actually a bison, as large as a Spanish bull, but with an enormous mane and small curved horns. They also met some impoverished Indians who lived in conical tipis "built like pavilions," according to the chronicler of the expedition. He was particularly impressed by the way the bison seemed to provide most of the materials needed by the Indians:

> With the skins they build their houses; with the skins they clothe and show themselves; from the skins they make ropes and also obtain wool. With the sinews they make threads, with which they sew their clothes and also their tents. From the bones they shape awls. The dung they use for firewood, since there is no other fuel in that land. The bladders they use as jugs and drinking containers.[1]

Hunting bison on foot was not productive, and it certainly could not support large numbers of Indians. Such hunting was practiced largely by the wretched nomads who moved around in small groups and who lived off the occasional weakened bison they could kill or those they could stampede over bluffs. Most of the aboriginal cultures on the plains and prairies were based on the cultivation of maize, beans, and squash. Agriculture had spread westward from the eastern Woodlands, and it followed the fingerlike extensions of rivers throughout the arid Dakotas, Texas, and virtually to the foothills of the Rockies. Hunting bison, for these people, was only incidental to the primary subsistence based on agriculture. They went on a hunt about once a year to supplement their vegetable diet and to obtain hides, sinew, bone, and other raw materials.

Once the horse arrived on the plains, that way of life changed. The

[1] This quote and subsequent ones from the Coronado expedition are from *Eyes of Discovery* by John Bakeless, New York: Dover, 1961, pp. 92–93.

nomadic bison hunters became ascendant over the farmers, who either were driven off their lands or abandoned agriculture to become bison hunters themselves. Indians had never seen the horse until the Spaniards brought it to the New World, for sometime during the great glacial melt it had become extinct in North America. The Indians obtained the first horses after the Spaniards settled New Mexico in 1598. (Contrary to previous belief, the Indians captured no horses from de Soto, Coronado, or other early explorers, for these horses either died or were taken home again.) The Spaniards prohibited the sale of horses to Indians, but the revolt of the Pueblo Indians between 1680 and 1692 threw some of the animals on the Indian markets of North America. The Spaniards restocked their herds, which proliferated, but they were unable to prevent further horse stealing by Indians. Horses were bartered–or stolen–from Indian group to group. Soon a whole new Indian profession of horse merchant grew up, and the animals–as well as the knowledge of how to break and train them–spread northward from New Mexico. In addition, some Spanish horses had gone wild and roamed the plains in herds. The Spaniards called them *mesteños* ("wild"), from which the English word "mustangs" is derived.

By the first half of the eighteenth century, enterprising Indian merchants had already sold the horse to Indians as far north as the Northern Shoshone of Wyoming and taught them its management. The Shoshone slowly built up their herds and learned to ride as if they had been born to the saddle. No longer did they have to remain impoverished and secretive inhabitants of the Rocky Mountains, at the mercy of more powerful Indian groups. They swooped down the eastern flanks of the mountains and onto the high plains, where they found a bonanza in bison and a way to even the score with their traditional persecutors, the Blackfoot. From all over, other Indian groups converged on the plains and quickly adapted themselves to an economy based on the bison. The lands of the agriculturists were usurped, and the plains became a maelstrom of varied and often conflicting cultures.

A LIVING EXPERIMENT IN CULTURE CHANGE

The stolen, bartered, bought, or captured horse was a new cultural element in the heartland of North America, and it changed the entire way of life there.[2] The whole of the plains, from Alberta to Texas, became peopled by groups of great diversity who had come from all directions and often from great distances. There were Athabaskans from the north (Kiowa-Apache), Algonkians (Cree, Cheyenne, Blackfoot) and Siouans (Mandan, Crow, Dakota) from the east, Uto-Aztecans (Comanche, Ute) from the west, Caddoans (Pawnee, Arikara) from the south. The plains

[2] An excellent summary of the effect of the horse on many Indian cultures is [F. G.] Roe [*The Indian and the Horse*, Norman: University of Oklahoma Press, 1955]. See also [J. C.] Ewers ["The Horse in Blackfoot Indian Culture," *Bureau of American Ethnology Bulletin*, 1955].

became a melting pot for more than thirty different peoples, belonging to at least five language stocks. It has given anthropologists a living laboratory of culture change. Culture change is the way in which a group alters because of new circumstances, or the way it borrows traits from other cultures and fits them into the configurations of its own.

By about 1800 the gross differences in culture among all these peoples had disappeared; the Sun Dance ceremony, for example, was eventually observed by virtually every tribe. Of course differences apparent to the trained eye of the anthropologist still existed; yet it is remarkable that a people from the eastern forests and another from the Great Basin of the West, two thousand miles away, should within only a few generations have become so nearly identical. Even more remarkable, this homogeneity was achieved with great speed, was not imposed on unwilling people by a more powerful group, and was done in the absence of a common tongue—save for "sign language," the lingua franca of the Plains tribes.

The Plains Cree demonstrate how a people originally distant from the plains in both culture and geography eventually could become so typical of it. The Cree were first recorded in the *Jesuit Relations* of 1640, but at that time they had nothing to do with the plains at all. They inhabited the forests between Hudson Bay and Lake Superior, and they were roving hunters and gatherers of wild rice. Their culture was typical of the Northern Algonkian bands, and after the Hudson's Bay Company was founded they turned to trapping. The demand by Whites for more beaver pelts led them to push westward; because they had obtained guns from White traders, they were able to dispossess the previous inhabitants. By about the middle of the eighteenth century, some of the Cree had already penetrated to the west of Lake Winnipeg. Their culture had changed considerably. It was now parasitic on the White trader for weapons, clothing, and cooking utensils—and sometimes even food, because the Cree spent his time trapping rather than hunting. Then the Cree living farthest west discovered the resource of the bison. Historical records reveal that as early as 1772 they had developed primitive ways of hunting bison, although they still did not possess the horse. Within only a generation, though, the Plains Cree had emerged—a typical equestrian Plains tribe, very different in customs and outlook from the Cree that still inhabited the forests, although both groups continued to speak the same language.

And all this was due to the horse. No longer were just stray or stampeded bison taken, but the herds were pursued on swift horses and the choicest animals killed. No longer was the whole animal utilized for raw materials, which had so impressed the chronicler of the Coronado expedition, but the Indians could now afford the luxury of waste. They stocked the tipi with supplies for the future: meat dried in the sun (jerkee), or else pounded and mixed with fat and berries to become pemmican. Even though most of the Plains Indians never saw a White close up until their swift decline, his influence was felt profoundly as his goods and trade articles flowed westward across the plains by barter from one tribe to another. Tipis almost twenty-five feet in diameter were filled to overflowing with new-found riches. An economic revolution, for which the Indians' traditions had not prepared them, took place. The women no longer toiled in the fields—for gardening was not as profitable as hunting, nor could it be practiced in the presence of nomadic horsemen —and they stopped making pottery because brass kettles were obtained from Whites. Permanent villages disappeared, and with them went the elaborate customs and crafts, rules for marriage and residence.

After the Indians discovered the effectiveness of rifles, an armaments race began on the plains. Just as Indians earlier had realized the value of horses, and those lacking them were driven to obtain them by any means, the acquisition of rifles upset the entire balance of power. As soon as one tribe acquired firepower, the competition for others to obtain equal armaments became fierce. Not only the rifles had to be acquired, but there was also a continuing need for powder and for lead. The Indians were driven to take ever greater chances in raids to steal horses which they might barter for guns and ammunition. For a period of nearly fifty years, the plains became an arena of turmoil in which the status quo changed from year to year, as successive groups became supreme in supplies of horses or guns, or in the powerful allies they could muster.

THE MAKE-BELIEVE INDIANS

The Plains Indians in their heyday were a study in hyperbole, and as make-believe as the set for a western movie. They sprang from greatly differing traditions, from farmers and from hunters and from collectors of wild plants. Each contributed something of its own that created almost overnight a flamboyant culture whose vigor was for a time unequaled. In this world of hyperbole, many traditions that existed in non–Plains Indian societies became wildly exaggerated. Other Indians also possessed clubs and associations, but none were so extravagant in ritual and insignia as the Plains warrior societies. Indians elsewhere also believed in the reality of visions, but none so relentlessly pursued the vision quest and were so caught up in the emotional excesses of religion as the Plains tribes. Other Indians tortured captives, but none evoked pain so exquisitely in their own bodies.

A special kind of social organization developed on the plains that is known as the composite tribe. Wherever the composite tribe is found, it always signifies a breakdown in culture with a subsequent readaptation. Sometimes the breakdown is due to population loss through migration or increased warfare, as occurred to the Pueblo Indians around the Rio Grande River of New Mexico. Sometimes it is due to the disturbance of the resource base through economic exploitation by outsiders, as has been characteristic of primitive African societies. Occasionally, as happened on the North American plains, it is due to the loss of old culture traits and the borrowing of new ones. Whatever the cause, composite tribes usually arise after an alien culture appears; and almost everywhere Whites have penetrated around the world their presence has resulted in the formation of the composite tribe.

A distinguishing characteristic of the composite tribe is that descent reckoning is unspecific: It can be through either the father's or the mother's line, or both. Marital residence rules also are unspecific, and the newly married couple lives with whichever relatives expediency suggests. The composite tribe of the Plains Indians was much more a collection of bands than were the Zuni or the Iroquois lineal tribes. During most of the year the bison lived scattered in small herds, but during the late summer rutting season they came together in huge herds that blackened the plains. The Indians responded with a parallel social cycle. Most of the year a number of Plains Indian families lived together as a band, uniting only at the time of the summer encampment with other bands for tribal ceremonies and a communal hunt. Furthermore, band membership tended to change, and many Plains Indians belonged to several bands during their lifetimes. One cause of the changing membership within bands was the constant feuding, which often became so oppressive that the only way to preserve any peace at all was by fragmentation of the original band. The Plains Indians appear to have been no more complex in their social organization than the Eskimo and the Great Basin Shoshone bands, but that is not really true. They became functioning tribes at least during their summer encampments, and they managed to maintain that identity the rest of the year, even though they broke up into small bands.

The primary way in which identity was achieved was not through clans but through nonkinship sodalities. The word "sodality" is derived from the Latin *sodalis*, which means "comrade" or "associate," and in a modern society it is equivalent to fraternities and sororities, political parties, service clubs like the Rotary or the Lions, and religious organizations. It is an association that binds people together around a single interest. It may be the burial association of the Irish-American immigrants in the last century, credit associations in medieval Europe, even the crop-watching societies in Chinese villages. When the Plains tribes united in the summer, they were crosscut by a bewildering variety of sodalities with ceremonial, social, and military functions. There were dance societies and feasting societies, and even societies based on a common supernatural experience. Some societies were only for women, like the craft guilds of the Cheyenne. Others were open to both men and women, like the tobacco societies of the Crow, which revolved around the raising of special kinds of tobacco for ceremonial use.

The Cheyenne, as just one example, had six military societies that somewhat resembled the dueling societies of German students. A youth was permitted to join any one of them if he could demonstrate his courage, but he usually chose to go into the one his father belonged to. These societies served not only as the tribe's military force but as its police as well. And each of the six had a particular area of responsibility, such as protecting the movement of the encampment from one place to another, or enforcing the rules against individual hunting that might scare away the bison. Only the bravest of the brave warriors could belong to the elite military society known as the Contraries. Somewhat like the Zuni Mudheads, they were privileged clowns. They did the opposite of everything:

They said *no* when they meant *yes;* went away when called and came near when told to go away; called left *right;* and sat shivering on the hottest day.

A special development in the warrior societies was found among the Mandan, Hidatsa, Arapaho, and Blackfoot, which had a hierarchy of societies. The societies were arranged in order of the age of their members, and as the members grew older they moved up a step. In this way a warrior society existed for every male from the youngest to the oldest, with the exception of the effeminate male known as a berdache. No scorn was attached to his position; he was regarded with pity and with a degree of sacred awe for being the victim of a condition that was not of his own doing. Even the berdache found his place in Plains Indian society. He permanently adopted woman's clothing and woman's role; he became skilled in the female tasks of beadwork or skin-tanning, and he was eligible to join the women's societies.

The richness and diversity of the Plains sodalities is explained by the lack of lineal residential groups. The need for non-kin sodalities was so great on the plains because they filled the social void caused by the absence of clans. Had these non-kin sodalities failed to develop, with their complexity of rules and regulations that often seem so ridiculous to us today, the tribes would have been reduced to mere collections of bands. The sodalities brought unity to one of the most diverse collections of people on earth.

COUPS AND SCALPING

Almost all the sodalities had religious aspects, and almost all were concerned with war in one way or another. The various cultures had engaged in warfare even before they migrated onto the plains and obtained horses, but with the emergence of the Plains Indian culture during the nineteenth century, warfare became as ritualized as medieval knighthood. Only during the very twilight of the Plains culture did large battles take place that pitted Indian against Indian or Indian against the United States Army, with each group seeking to exterminate the other. Previous to that, tactics consisted of forays and raids by small war parties; the conflicts were brief and usually indecisive.

The Plains Indians fought not to win territory or to enslave other tribes, but for a variety of different reasons. One was the capture of horses, which had a high economic value. Another reason . . . was that external strife served to unify the tribe internally. A tribe, especially one as fragile as the composite tribe unified only by non-kin sodalities, needed a common enemy as a rationale for its existence. A third reason was that war was regarded as a game in which the players might win status. In this game, exploits were graded according to the dangers involved. The exploit itself was known as the *coup,* from the French trapper's word for "blow," because originally it signified that the brave had struck the enemy's body with a special stick that was often striped like a barber pole. Later, "counting coups" referred to the recital by the brave of all his war deeds; as he immodestly proclaimed each one he gave a blow against a pole with his ax. These recitals went on endlessly. Each time a young man accumulated a new honor, he used it as an excuse to recount his old exploits. If he lied about his exploits, though, or even shaded the truth a bit, he was challenged immediately by someone who had been along on the same war party.

Each Plains tribe had its own ranking for coups. Among the Blackfoot, stealing an enemy's weapons was looked upon as the highest exploit. Among some other tribes, the bravest deed was to touch an enemy without hurting him. The least important exploit usually was killing an enemy, but even that deed was ranked according to the way it was done and the weapons that were used. The whole business of counting coups often became extremely involved. Among the Cheyenne, for example, coups could be counted by several warriors on a single enemy, but the coups were ranked in the strict order in which the enemy was touched by the participants; it was immaterial who actually killed or wounded him. Like a sort of heraldry, these deeds were recorded in picture writing on tipis and on bison robes. They gave the warrior the right to hold public office. Among many tribes, each coup earned an eagle's feather, and the achieving of many coups accounts for the elaborate headdresses of some of the Plains war leaders.

Scalps taken from dead or wounded enemies sometimes served as trophies, but they were insignificant when compared with counting coups. Many Plains tribes did not take scalps at all until the period of their swift decline, which began in the middle of the last century. Most people believe that all Indians took scalps, and that scalp-hunting was exclusively a New World custom. Neither idea is true. Herodotus, the ancient Greek historian, mentioned the taking of scalps by the Scythians, for example. In South America scalp-taking as a custom was practically unknown; in North America it *may* have existed before the arrival of Whites, but only in a few areas in the eastern Woodlands. Many historians still question whether scalp-taking was an aboriginal Indian practice or rather one learned quite early from the White settlers.

Whatever its exact origins, there is no doubt that scalp-taking quickly spread over all of North America, except in the Eskimo areas; nor is there any doubt that its spread was due to the barbarity of White men rather than to the barbarity of Red men. White settlers early offered to pay bounties on dead Indians, and scalps were actual proof of the deed. Governor Kieft of New Netherland is usually credited with originating the idea of paying for Indian scalps, as they were more convenient to handle than whole heads, and they offered the same proof that an Indian had been killed. By liberal payments for scalps, the Dutch virtually cleared southern New York and New Jersey of Indians before the English supplanted them.[3] By 1703 the colony of Massachusetts was paying the equivalent of about $60 for every Indian scalp. In the mid-eighteenth

[3] [W. T.] Hagan [*American Indians,* Chicago: University of Chicago Press, 1961], p. 15, is the source for the origin of scalping.

century, Pennsylvania fixed the bounty for a male Indian scalp at $134; a female's was worth only $50. Some White entrepreneurs simply hatcheted any old Indians that still survived in their towns. The French also used scalp-taking as an instrument of geopolitics. In the competition over the Canadian fur trade, they offered the Micmac Indians a bounty for every scalp they took from the Beothuk of Newfoundland. By 1827 an expedition to Newfoundland failed to find a single survivor of this once numerous and proud people.[4]

Among the Plains tribes, apparently only the Dakota and the Cree placed any value on scalps; both tribes were late immigrants to the Plains from the East, where they probably learned the practice from Whites. Nor was there as much torturing of captives by Plains tribes as was once believed. The tradition of the White settler's saving his last bullet for himself to avoid a horrible death was a needless precaution. Unlike the Indians of the eastern Woodlands, the Plains Indians killed swiftly. They looked upon the White custom of hanging, for example, as cruel and barbaric.

CAUSES OF WARFARE

The Great American Epic has traditionally regarded the Plains Indians as the most "warlike" on the continent. Indeed, history does confirm that the heartland of the continent was an arena for continual strife. Yet, stating that a Blackfoot, for example, was "warlike" reveals nothing. The entire Blackfoot tribe did not habitually engage in war because individual members possessed "warlike" personalities. Individual men go to war for individual reasons: for social prestige, for economic rewards and for booty, because of religious convictions—even to escape from frustrations at home. Entire societies, though, do not go to war for such personal reasons. The fact is that the individual Blackfoot was warlike simply because his whole cultural system obliged him to be that way.

All the various theories as to why groups of people go to war fall into four general categories. The first states that it is the very physical nature of man to be pugnacious and aggressive. Such a view of man holds that a warlike urge is biologically inherent in him. This is an old theory, and it keeps popping up from time to time in new presentations, most recently in Konrad Lorenz' *On Aggression* (1966). But there is no evidence in the physical makeup of man to suggest that he has been fashioned as a warlike animal. Man, in truth, is a puny creation, lacking fangs, claws, thick skin, speed, or other adaptations for combat. The whole idea of the innate belligerency of man is laid to rest by evidence that warfare is virtually absent among the most primitive of men, those whose "true" biological nature might appear to be closest to the surface. The Great

[4] The extinction of the Beothuk is described in [F. W.] Hodge ["Handbook of American Indians North of Mexico," *Bureau of American Ethnology Bulletin*, 1906 (reprinted New York: Pageant Books, 1960)], p. 142.

Basin Shoshone, for example, never waged war, nor did most other very simple societies before the arrival of Whites.

The second explanation is an affront to logic: Men are warlike because they are warlike. Such an explanation is ridiculous, but even so noted an anthropologist as Ralph Linton wrote that the Plains Indians would not have been so interested in war if "they had not been warlike."[5] Similar statements exist in Ruth Benedict's *Patterns of Culture*. Obviously, such logic is akin to explaining obesity in middle-aged males by saying that many middle-aged males are obese.

The third explanation is a psychological one, and it probably boasts the most adherents–which is understandable, for these people can bolster their case by surveys, personality tests, statistical analyses, and other impressive tools of modern scholarship. Even before the widespread use of such tests and surveys, Freud, in an exchange of correspondence with Einstein in 1932 about the causes of war, agreed that "there is an instinct for hatred and destruction . . . which goes halfway to meet the efforts of the warmongers."[6] All of these psychological studies, though, can explain only the motivations behind why *individuals* go to war. The real point is that although individuals slug each other in a barroom brawl or drop napalm from airplanes over Vietnam, individuals do not go to war. Only societies do that.

That leaves the fourth explanation, which states simply that the causes for war are to be found within the cultures of the contending groups. This explanation avoids confusing the issue with related problems, such as individual motivations or the kinds of warfare practiced. The Plains Indians confirm this cultural explanation. For one thing, the composite tribes of the Plains Indians could not have survived without external enemies, real or imagined, against whom their warrior associations could unite. For another, the Plains culture was artificial, brought into being by the reverberations sent across the continent by the arrival of the Whites. The Whites upset delicate adjustments the Indians had made to each other over very long periods of time. As just one example, the French encouraged warfare between the Ojibway and surrounding groups; the Ojibway spread westward and displaced Siouan tribes, which migrated westward and southward to the plains; there the Sioux displaced Hidatsa and Mandan, who in turn stirred up the Cheyenne and others. The whole unreal situation was very much like a series of balls caroming off one another and resulting in new rebounds.

Most important, once all these groups were on the plains and had altered their cultures by acquiring horses and guns, their whole make-believe world had to be kept in motion or it would collapse. Horses had to be stolen so they could be bartered for more guns to aid in the stealing of more horses. Many White traders encouraged the strife to capitalize on it by selling guns, liquor, and kitchenware. The herds of bison, once

[5] *The Study of Man* by Ralph Linton, New York: Appleton-Century, 1936, p. 463.

[6] Freud's letter on the causes of war is in *Character and Culture*, Vol. 9 in *The Collected Papers of Sigmund Freud*, New York: Collier Books, 1963, p. 141.

thought limitless, dwindled, and as they did there was additional cause for strife over hunting territories. In any event, there were good cultural—that is, social, political, economic, and technological—reasons why the Plains Indians were warlike. They were that way not because of their biology or their psychology, but because their new White-induced culture demanded it.[7]

THE NEW RICH

Among the Mandan, Hidatsa, Arapaho, and Blackfoot, a member of a war society purchased his way up the ladder of age-grades until he arrived at the topmost grade and was thereupon entitled to wear the famous feathered bonnet. At each step, he selected a seller from the next older brotherhood, and then purchased his rights. A buyer was free to select any seller he wanted, but he usually chose someone from his father's family. Often, as part of the payment, the purchaser had to relinquish his wife to the seller for a time; if the purchaser was unmarried, he had to borrow a wife from a relative. The whole business of joining an age-grade brotherhood was accompanied by an elaborate etiquette that was also somewhat sophomoric and not unlike the mock seriousness of today's Masonic initiation.

Membership in other kinds of societies was also often purchased, and in fact many things were for sale among the Plains tribes: sacred objects, religious songs, and even the description of a particularly good vision. The right to paint a particular design on the face during a religious ceremony might cost as much as a horse. Permission just to look inside someone's sacred bundle of fetishes and feathers was often worth the equivalent of a hundred dollars. A Crow is known to have paid two horses to his sponsor to get himself invited into a tobacco society, and the candidate's family contributed an additional twenty-three horses. A prudent Blackfoot was well advised to put his money into a sacred bundle, an investment that paid him continued dividends. The investment was as safe as today's government bond is; and it was readily negotiable at a price usually higher than the purchase price. By permitting the bundle to be used in rituals, its owner received fees that were like dividends. As the Plains tribes became richer, the price of sacred bundles continued to rise, much as the price of a stock-exchange seat goes up during prosperous times.

[7] Two excellent papers on Plains warfare are by [W. W.] Newcomb ["A Re-examination of the Causes of Plains Warfare," *American Anthropologist*, 1950, pp. 317–29; and "Toward an Understanding of War," in G. L. Dole and R. L. Carneiro, eds., *Essays in the Science of Culture in Honor of Leslie A. White*, New York: Thomas Y. Crowell, 1960, pp. 317–36]. See also [B.] Mishkin ["Rank and Warfare Among Plains Indians," *American Ethnological Society Monograph*, 1940] for the importance of economic factors. Various theories of primitive warfare in general can be found in [H. H.] Turney-High [*Primitive Warfare: Its Practices and Concepts,* Columbia: University of South Carolina Press, 1949].

Until they became horsemen, almost none of these tribes had ever known wealth. The Comanche, for example, had been an impoverished Shoshonean people from the Great Basin before the nineteenth century. Most of the other tribes only a few decades before had been marginal hunters, all of whose possessions could be dragged along by a single dog. But the Plains tribes learned the laws of the marketplace rapidly, both from each other and from the White trader. The accumulation of wealth became important, but it was not incorporated into the societies in any meaningful way. Perhaps it would have been in time, and the Plains tribes might have served economic theorists as the very models of the steps by which societies become capitalistic.

Anthropologists can do no more than guess what might have happened to the concept of wealth had the Plains culture endured for another century, or even for a few more decades. Some indication is given by tribes such as the Kiowa, who learned how to use wealth to create more wealth. A Kiowa warrior was forced by custom to give away some of his wealth, but he also learned to hoard it, not only for himself but also to keep it in his family through inheritance. Classes based on wealth arose in what had once been an egalitarian society. The wealthiest classes could afford to give their sons certain benefits. They equipped them with the best horses and guns and sent them down the road to military glory at an early age. And when the son of a wealthy Kiowa achieved an exploit, everyone heard about it, for the wealthy controlled the channels of publicity through their ability to give gifts. Such publicity paid further economic benefits: The scion of a wealthy Kiowa, with his well-publicized exploits, could increase his wealth even more because he easily obtained followers for a raiding party.

Not knowing what to do with the new-found wealth that crammed their tipis, the Plains Indians regarded it as materially unimportant, but valued it as a status symbol. It became another way to count coups, to get one up on a neighbor. And since the primary way to acquire wealth was to steal horses from someone else, wealth became a validation of bravery. The warrior also could be sure that no one forgot his prowess by the constant reminder of gifts. Gift-giving emphasized that the giver was brave enough to go out and steal more wealth anytime he felt like it.

The sudden wealth achieved by the mass slaughter of bison changed customs in other ways also. It took only a moment for a man on horseback to kill a bison with a bullet, but it still remained a long and arduous task for his wife to dress the hide for sale to the White trader. As a result, a shortage of women arose and a premium was placed on them to the extent that eventually "bride price" was paid. Men always needed the hands of extra women to dress the skins, and the parents of a healthy girl could negotiate her marriage from a position of strength. At the same time, polygyny, which probably had existed in some tribes to a limited extent, became widespread, for a good hunter needed as many wives as he could afford. There are even instances known of berdaches being taken on as second wives, not for any sexual variety they might offer, but merely because they performed women's tasks.

VISION QUESTS

Most North American Indians greatly respected visions, but few immersed themselves so deeply in them as did the Plains tribes. Sometimes a spirit might come of its own accord in a vision, just to befriend a mortal, but usually the Plains Indian had to go in active pursuit of his vision. He did this by isolating himself, fasting and thirsting, and practicing self-torture, at the same time imploring the spirits to take pity on his suffering. The youth gashed his arms and legs, and among the Crow it was the custom to cut off a joint from a finger of the left hand. Cheyenne vision-seekers thrust skewers of wood under pinches of skin in the breast; these skewers were attached to ropes, which in turn were tied to a pole. All day the youth leaned his full weight away from the pole, pulling and tugging at his own flesh while he implored the spirits to give him a vision.

Mortification of the flesh has always held a fascination for religious fanatics everywhere, for it is the most obvious way that this too, too human flesh can break its link with the world of men and approach the threshold of the gods. Among those who have groped toward deities in this way are the Jewish Essenes around the Dead Sea, the many ascetic orders of Christian monks, the Whirling Dervishes of Islam, and the hermits of Buddhism.

The spirit might at last take pity on the Plains Indian youth—actually it was dehydration, pain, and delirium taking their effects—and give him supernatural guidance. A successful vision supported the youth for the rest of his life. He always had a guardian spirit on whom he could call for help and guidance, although from time to time he had to repeat the self-torture to renew his familiarity with the spirit. During his vision, the youth usually learned what items—such as feathers, a stone pipe, a piece of skin, maize kernels—he should collect for a sacred medicine bundle and put in a small pouch. A particularly lucky youth might also receive his own songs, which when sung served as a call to supernatural aid; that they sounded like gibberish to everyone else only reinforced the belief that he had received a unique vision. A few youths failed to receive any visions at all, even though they tried repeatedly. Those who could not obtain a vision on their own could sometimes purchase one, as well as a replica of the successful visionary's sacred medicine bundle.

What is remarkable about such visions is that they were not invariably experienced, since the entire Plains culture worked toward producing them. Every Plains youth grew up believing firmly in the reality of the vision, so no resistance to the idea had to be overcome. Secondly, the youth worked himself into an intense emotional state by starvation, thirst, self-torture, exposure to the sun, and isolation—all of which are known to produce hallucinations. Thirdly, the shape in which the vision came to him was predetermined by the structure of the myths and visions he had heard about since childhood. Finally, in retelling his vision, he unconsciously reconstructed it and filled in gaps, adapting it to the norms of behavior of his culture—much as we do in reporting an incoherent dream, no matter how sincerely we believe we are not distorting it.

Plains Indian visions were clearly recognized as differing from person to person and from tribe to tribe. Some of the individual differences were biological and psychological. An Indian with an auditory personality might hear loud calls of birds or gibberish songs, whereas a visual type would be apt to see a horse with strange markings. Probably some individual fears and anxieties went into the vision. Despite the Plains warrior's attitude of fearlessness, a common vision was the sudden transformation of rocks and trees into enemies; but the youth was made invulnerable to their arrows by his guardian spirit. Often the vision involved the visit of some animal. An eagle might fly by, the flapping of its wings sounding like crashes of thunder; and bison, elk, bears, and hawks appeared quite often among the nobler beasts. Among the Pawnee (who, alone of the Plains tribes, had worked out an orderly system of religious beliefs, including a supreme being), the stars and other heavenly bodies entered quite freely into visions.

The desire for a vision existed among most of the Indians of North America, and it seems to have developed in two different directions. Among some Indians, it led directly to shamanism, for shamans were believed to be recipients of particularly intense visions and to have the power to summon up new visions at will. The other line of development led to visions of more limited power that had to be sought after. In this second category, there was a great range of variation, from the Plains youth, who suffered ordeals, to the Great Basin Shoshone, who passively waited for the spirit to find him.

Before the contrasting attitudes of the Plains tribes and the Great Basin Shoshone can be explained, the vision must first be recognized for what it is: a resort to supernatural aid in a dangerous undertaking, in which individual skill alone is not enough to guarantee success. The Plains culture provided numerous such dangerous undertakings, such as riding among a herd of stampeding bison or stealthily entering an enemy camp. For the Plains warrior, the rewards of such undertakings were certainly great enough to compensate for the few days of self-torture and fasting required to obtain a guardian spirit. The arid country of the Great Basin Shoshone, however, provided no such rewards. There the land yielded a bare minimum, and the rewards went not to the man who showed courage and daring, but to the one who simply exerted industry in collecting seeds or grasshoppers. Any yearning for visions that existed among the Great Basin Shoshone was not for protection in the dangers of the hunt or in warfare, but for the cure of snake bites or sickness.[8]

The various responses of different cultures toward visions partly explains why some Indians took enthusiastically to the White man's alcohol and others did not. The use of firewater was particularly intense among the Plains, as well as among the nearby forest Indians, who were the ancestors of many Plains Indians. Alcohol was promptly recognized by the Plains Indians as a short-cut method of producing derangement of the senses and hallucinations. In primeval North America the Plains tribes had

[8] For a discussion of the vision quest in several cultures, see [R.] Underhill ["Ceremonial Patterns in the Greater Southwest," *American Ethnological Society Memoir*, 1948].

been remarkably free from the use of hallucinogenic plants such as peyote and mushrooms. The Plains vision-seekers were not even fortunate enough to have *Datura* or Jimsonweed, for its original range in the West was probably in only portions of the Southwest and southern California. Nor had the Plains tribes learned that tobacco, which they smoked in a few ritual puffs, could be swallowed to produce considerable discomfort and emotional upset, the way many Central and South American Indians used it.

Only when the Plains culture was disintegrating rapidly after about 1850 did a hallucinogenic cactus known as peyote take hold. Peyote is native to northern Mexico, but it spread like a grass fire from tribe to tribe as far north as the Canadian plains. Although peyote is used elsewhere in North America to a limited extent, it was most widely and promptly accepted by the Plains tribes. Peyote afforded a way to seek visions; it also provided an escape from the humiliation of the complete defeat by Whites in the latter part of the last century.

THE END OF A CULTURE

After the Civil War, a tide of White settlers streamed westward, and they sealed the fate of the Plains tribes. Treaty after treaty was broken by Whites as the Indian lands were crisscrossed by easterners covetous of acreage and precious metals. At first the Whites tried to restrict the Plains Indians to valueless territories, but that policy soon changed to a war of extermination. Said General William Tecumseh Sherman in 1867: "The more I see of these Indians, the more convinced I am that they all have to be killed or be maintained as a species of paupers." To help clear the Indians from the plains, the Whites struck at their food base, the bison. They themselves not only destroyed the animals, but they also contrived to get the Indians to collaborate with them by offering to buy vast quantities of such delicacies as bison tongue.

Tensions between the Whites and the Plains Indians increased during the 1870's. On July 5, 1876, newspapers reporting celebrations of the young nation's Centennial reported also the news of a humiliating defeat. The elite Seventh Cavalry, a tough outfit of 260 men, which was organized specifically for killing Plains Indians—and led by Lieutenant Colonel Custer—had been annihilated on June 25 by a combined force of Sioux and Cheyenne in the battle of Little Bighorn. But for Sitting Bull and Crazy Horse, the victory over Custer had been empty, and only marked the beginning of the end for the Plains Indians. From that time on troops pursued them mercilessly from waterhole to waterhole; their women and children were slaughtered before their eyes, their encampments and their riches burned. The glory and the poetry had gone out of the Plains Indians. Mighty chiefs emerged from hiding as miserable fugitives, hungry and without bullets for their guns. The survivors, like so many cattle, were herded onto reservations, where rough handling, cheap whiskey, starvation, exposure, and disease severely depleted their numbers.

The very end of the Plains culture can be dated exactly. In 1890 the surviving Plains Indians enthusiastically listened to a native messiah who foretold the return of dead Indians and the magical disappearance of the Whites. Alarmed, the United States government sent out cavalry to suppress this Ghost Dance, as it was called. While being placed under arrest, Sitting Bull was accidentally killed; and some three hundred Sioux, mostly women and children waiting to surrender at Wounded Knee Creek, South Dakota, were massacred by trigger-happy troops. Wounded Knee marked the end of any hopes the Plains Indians still cherished. The Ghost Dance had proven as make-believe as the rest of their improbable culture.

4 Suggestions for Further Reading

Several books deal in general fashion with the westward movement of settlers in North America. The standard work is Ray A. Billington, *Westward Expansion* (rev. ed.; Macmillan, 1967), but more relevant here is his *The Far Western Frontier, 1830–1860** (Harper & Row, 1956). See also *The New Country: A Social History of the American Frontier, 1776–1890** (Oxford University Press, 1974) by Richard A. Bartlett. The basic studies of the doctrine of Manifest Destiny are A. K. Weinberg, *Manifest Destiny** (Johns Hopkins Press, 1935), and Frederick Merk, *Manifest Destiny and Mission in American History: A Reinterpretation** (Knopf, 1963).

The standard survey of Mexican American history is Carey McWilliams, *North from Mexico: The Spanish-Speaking People of the United States** (Lippincott, 1949). See also Matthew S. Meier and Feliciano Rivera, *The Chicanos: A History of Mexican Americans** (Hill and Wang, 1972). Regional history is stressed in Ernesto Galarza, Herman Gallegos, and Julian Samora, *Mexican Americans in the Southwest** (McNally and Loftin, 1969).

Aggression in the Old West is evaluated in W. Eugene Hollon, *Frontier Violence: Another Look** (Oxford University Press, 1974). An ambitious study covering primarily the early period is Richard Slotkin, *Regeneration Through Violence: The Mythology of the American Frontier, 1600–1860** (Wesleyan University Press, 1973). Vigilantism is explored comparatively in *Vigilante Politics* (University of Pennsylvania Press, 1976), edited by H. Ron Rosenbaum and Peter C. Sederberg. The classic Western novel exploring these themes is Walter Van Tilburg Clark, *The Ox Bow Incident** (Random House, 1940).

The Chinese immigration to the West Coast of the United States has received very little attention from historians. Virtually the only works on the subject are Mary Coolidge, *Chinese Immigration* (Henry Holt, 1909), which was written with the hope of reopening immigration after it was brought to a halt by the Chinese Exclusion Act of 1882, and Gunther Barth, *Bitter Strength: A History of the Chinese in the United States, 1850–1870* (Harvard University Press, 1964). A recent study of the reception met by Chinese immigrants in America is Stuart C. Miller, *The Unwelcome Immigrant: The American Image of the Chinese, 1785–1882** (University of California Press, 1969). The conflict between the Chinese immigrants and Americans is described in Alexander Saxton, *The Indispensable Enemy: Labor and the Anti-Chinese Move-*

* Available in paperback edition.

*ment in California** (University of California Press, 1971), and Elmer Sandmeyer, *The Anti-Chinese Movement in California** (University of Illinois Press, 1939). In *The Challenge of the American Dream: The Chinese in the United States** (Wadsworth, 1971), Francis L. K. Hsu provides a general introduction to the entire Chinese experience here. For an account of some of the problems that the Chinese faced in the United States, see Herbert Asbury, *The Barbary Coast: An Informal History of the San Francisco Underworld** (Knopf, 1933) and Victor Nee and Brett de Bar Nee, *Longtime Californ': A Documentary History of an American Chinatown** (Pantheon Books, 1973).

Two basic anthropological studies of the Plains Indians are E. A. Hoebel, *The Cheyennes: Indians of the Great Plains** (Holt, Rinehart and Winston, 1960), and R. H. Lowie, *Indians of the Plains** (McGraw-Hill, 1954). For the impact of the horse on Indian culture, see F. G. Roe, *The Indian and the Horse* (University of Oklahoma Press, 1955). Mari Sandoz movingly recounts the breakup of the Plains Indian culture in *Cheyenne Autumn** (Hastings House, 1953). The defeat of the Sioux is described in Robert Utley, *Last Days of the Sioux Nation** (Yale University Press, 1963). United States Government policy is described in M. Thomas Bailey, *Reconstruction in Indian Territory: A Story of Avarice, Discrimination, and Opportunism* (Kennikat Press, 1972). Thomas Berger's novel *Little Big Man** (Dial, 1964) presents an authentic picture of elements of Plains Indian culture.

Illustration Credits *(Continued from page ii)*

8: Culver Pictures, Inc.
9: The Bettmann Archive, Inc.
108–9: Ernst Haas/Magnum Photos.
190–91: The Bettmann Archive, Inc.
298–99: Brown Brothers.

8
B 9
C 0
D 1
E 2
F 3
G 4
H 5
I 6
J 7